Discovering Computers
Fundamentals
Fifth Edition

Discovering Computers

Fundamentals
Fifth Edition

Gary B. Shelly

Misty E. Vermaat

Contributing Authors

Jeffrey J. Quasney

Susan L. Sebok

Jeffrey J. Webb

Steven M. Freund

Shelly Cashman Series®
An imprint of Course Technology, Cengage Learning

COURSE TECHNOLOGY
CENGAGE Learning·

Australia • Brazil • Japan • Korea • Mexico • Singapore • Spain • United Kingdom • United States

COURSE TECHNOLOGY
CENGAGE Learning™

Discovering Computers: Fundamentals, Fifth Edition
Gary B. Shelly
Misty E. Vermaat

Executive Editor: Alexandra Arnold

Senior Product Manager: Reed Curry

Associate Product Manager: Klenda Martinez

Editorial Assistant: Jon Farnham

Marketing Director: Tristen Kendall

Marketing Coordinator: Julie Schuster

Print Buyer: Julio Esperas

Content Project Manager: Matthew Hutchinson

Consultant: Joel Sadagursky

Researcher: F. William Vermaat

Development Editor: Lyn Markowicz

Proofreader: Nancy Lamm

Final Reader: Pam Baxter

Management Services: Pre-Press PMG

Interior Designer: Pre-Press PMG

Art Director: Bruce Bond

Cover and Text Design: Joel Sadagursky

Cover Photos: Jon Chomitz

Illustrator: Pre-Press PMG

Compositor: Pre-Press PMG

Printer: RRD Menasha

For product information and technology assistance, contact us at
Cengage Learning Academic Resource Center, 1-800-423-0563

For permission to use material from this text or product,
submit all requests online at **cengage.com/permissions**
Further permissions questions can be emailed to
permissionrequest@cengage.com

ISBN-10: 1-4239-2702-8

ISBN-13: 978-1-4239-2702-0

Course Technology
25 Thomson Place
Boston, MA 02210
USA

Cengage Learning is a leading provider of customized learning solutions with office locations around the globe, including Singapore, the United Kingdom, Australia, Mexico, Brazil and Japan. Locate your local office at:
international.cengage.com/region

Cengage Learning products are represented in Canada by Nelson Education, Ltd.

For your lifelong learning solutions, visit **course.cengage.com**

Printed in the United States of America
1 2 3 4 5 6 7 14 13 12 11 10 09 08

Discovering Computers
Fundamentals
Fifth Edition

Contents

Special Feature
MAKING USE OF THE WEB

CHAPTER 3
Application Software

CHAPTER 4
The Components of the System Unit

CHAPTER 5
Input and Output 165

CHAPTER 10

Computer Security, Ethics, and Privacy 361

Special Feature
DIGITAL ENTERTAINMENT 397

CHAPTER 11

Information System Development and Programming Languages 405

CHAPTER 12

Enterprise Computing 451

Discover Computers
and make concepts real with . . .

Online Companion

Use the Online Companion at scsite.com/dcf5e to bring unparalleled currency to the learning experience. Access additional information about important topics and make use of online learning games, practice tests, and additional reinforcement. Gain access to this dynamic site through CoursePort, Course Technology's login page.

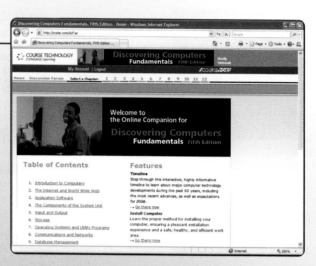

Learn How To

Apply the concepts presented in the chapter to every day life with these hands-on activities. See the Learn How To activities in action with visual demonstrations on the Online Companion.

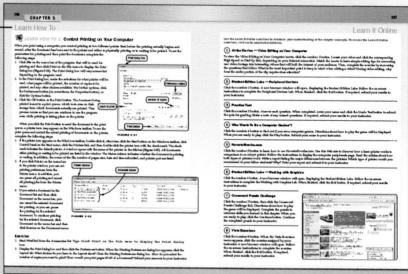

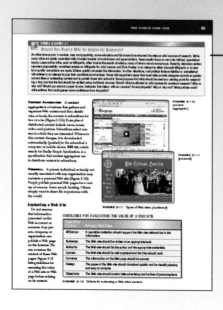

Ethics and Issues

Ethics and Issues boxes raise controversial, computer-related topics of the day, challenging readers to closely consider general concerns of computers in society.

practical, hands-on elements.

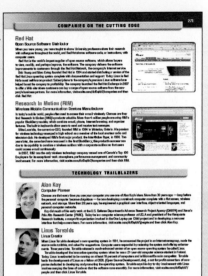

Companies on the Cutting Edge

Everyone who interacts with computers should be aware of the key computer-related companies. Each chapter profiles two of these key companies.

Technology Trailblazers

The Technology Trailblazers section in each chapter offers a glimpse into the life and times of the more famous leaders of the computer industry.

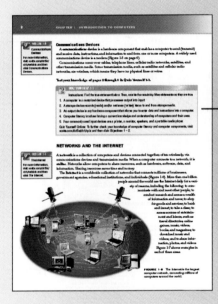

Quiz Yourself

Three Quiz Yourself boxes per chapter help ensure retention by reinforcing sections of the chapter material, rather than waiting for the end of the chapter to test. Use Appendix A for a quick check of the answers, and access additional Quiz Yourself quizzes on the Online Companion for interactivity and easy use.

Career Corner

Each chapter ends with a Career Corner feature that introduces a computer career opportunity relating to a topic covered in the chapter.

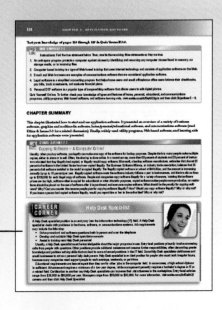

Discover Computers
and make concepts real with . . .

Web Link

Obtain current information
and a different perspective
about key terms and
concepts by visiting the
Web addresses in the Web
Links found in the margins
throughout the book.

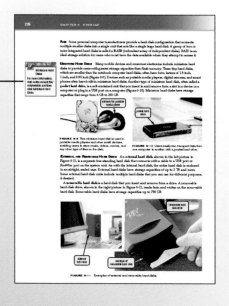

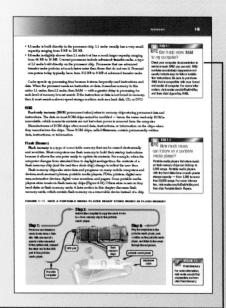

Looking Ahead

The Looking Ahead boxes offer a
glimpse of the latest advances in
computer technology that will be
available, usually within five years.

FAQ

FAQ (frequently asked questions)
boxes offer common questions and
answers about subjects related to
the topic at hand.

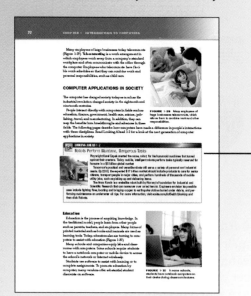

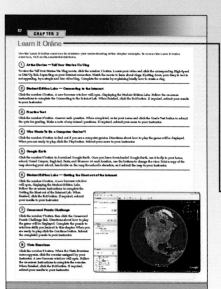

Learn It Online

The Learn It Online exercises, which
include brand new online videos,
practice tests, interactive labs, learning
games, and Web-based activities, offer
a wealth of online reinforcement.

interactive Web elements.

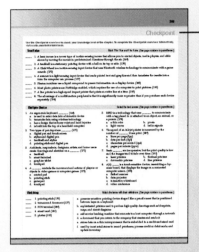

Checkpoint
Use these multiple choice, true/false, matching, short answer, and working together exercises to reinforce understanding of the topics presented in the chapter.

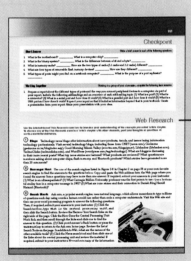

Web Research
Each Web Research exercise requires follow-up research on the Web, and suggests writing a short article or presenting the findings of the research to the class.

Chapter Review
Use the Chapter Review before taking an examination to ensure familiarity with the computer concepts presented. This section includes each objective, followed by a one- or two-paragraph summary.

Key Terms
Before taking a test, use the Key Terms page as a checklist of terms to know. Visit a Key Terms page on the Online Companion and click any term for additional information.

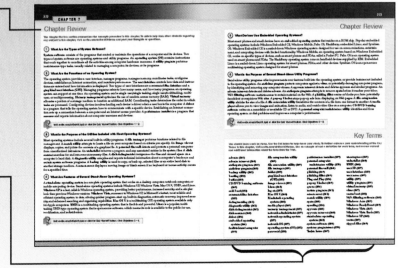

Discover Computers
and make concepts real with . . .

Chapter Objectives and Table of Contents

Before reading the chapter, carefully read through the Objectives and Contents to discover knowledge that will be gleaned from chapter.

Initial Chapter Figure

Carefully study the first figure in each chapter because it provides an easy-to-follow overview of the major purpose of the chapter.

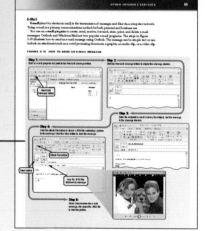

Step Figures

Each chapter includes numerous step figures that present the more complex computer concepts using a step-by-step pedagogy.

pedagogical elements.

Glossary/Index

The Glossary/Index at the back of the book not only provides page references, it also offers definitions for all the key terms included in the text and boxed features.

Special Features

Five special features following Chapters 1, 2, 5, 7, and 10 encompass topics from the history of computers, to what's hot on the Web, to a buyer's guide, to the latest in new technology.

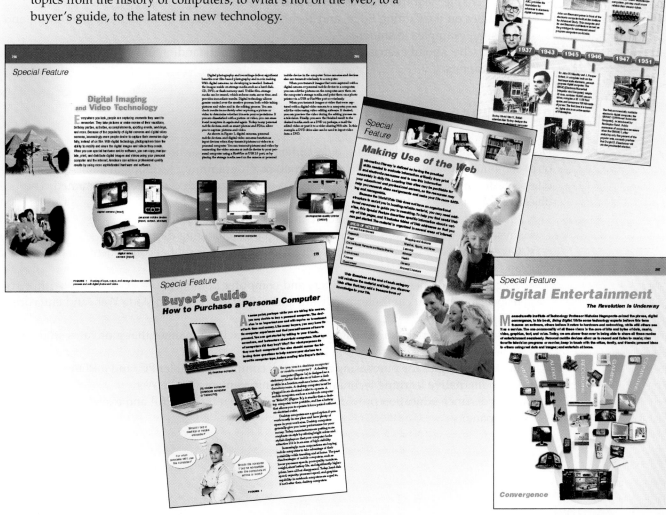

Preface

The Shelly Cashman Series® offers the finest textbooks in computer education. This book is our answer to the many requests we have received from instructors and students for a textbook that provides a succinct, yet thorough, introduction to computers.

In *Discovering Computers: Fundamentals, Fifth Edition*, you will find an educationally sound, highly visual, and easy-to-follow pedagogy that presents a complete, yet to the point, treatment of introductory computer subjects. Students will finish the course with a solid understanding of computers, how to use computers, and how to access information on the World Wide Web.

NEW TO THIS EDITION

Discovering Computers: Fundamentals, Fifth Edition includes exciting new features, certain to engage and challenge students, making learning with *Discovering Computers: Fundamentals, Fifth Edition* an enriched experience. These new features include:

- Comprehensive updates for currency, including coverage of new hardware and software, digital communications, social networking and other societal issues, career opportunities, and industry trends.
- Brand new CNET At the Movies videos highlight current events of interest to students in the world of technology, bringing relevance to the concepts course.
- Brand new Blogging exercise on the Web Research page engages students and brings relevance to the concepts course.
- Revised chapter features such as Ethics and Issues, Looking Ahead, FAQ, Web Links, Companies on the Cutting Edge, and Technology Trailblazers include the most relevant and interesting examples to students.
- Updated Checkpoint exercises reinforce students' understanding of key concepts presented in the chapters.

OBJECTIVES OF THIS TEXTBOOK

Discovering Computers: Fundamentals, Fifth Edition is intended for use as a stand-alone textbook or in combination with an applications, Internet, or programming textbook in a one-quarter or one-semester introductory computer course. No experience with computers is assumed. The objectives of this book are to:

- Provide a concise, yet comprehensive introduction to computers
- Present the most-up-to-date technology in an ever-changing discipline
- Give students an understanding of why computers are essential components in business and society
- Teach the fundamentals of computers and computer nomenclature, particularly with respect to personal computer hardware and software, the World Wide Web, and enterprise computing
- Present the material in a visually appealing and exciting manner that motivates students to learn
- Present strategies for purchasing a notebook computer, a Tablet PC, and a PDA
- Offer alternative learning techniques and reinforcement via the Web
- Offer distance-education providers a textbook with a meaningful and exercise-rich Online Companion

DISTINGUISHING FEATURES

To date, more than six million students have learned about computers using a *Discovering Computers* textbook. With the additional World Wide Web integration and interactivity, streaming up-to-date audio and video, extraordinary step-by-step visual drawings and photographs, unparalleled currency, and the Shelly and Cashman touch, this book will make your computer concepts course exciting and dynamic. Distinguishing features of this book include:

A Proven Pedagogy

Careful explanations of complex concepts, educationally-sound elements, and reinforcement highlight this proven method of presentation.

Essential Computer Concepts Coverage

This book offers the same breadth of topics as our well-known *Discovering Computers 2009: Complete*, but the depth of coverage focuses on the basic knowledge required to be computer literate in today's digital world.

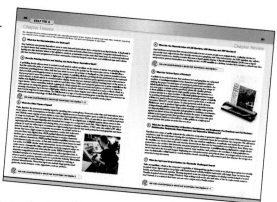

A Visually Appealing Book that Maintains Student Interest

The latest technology, pictures, drawings, and text are combined artfully to produce a visually appealing and easy-to-understand book. Many of the figures include a step-by-step presentation (see page 141), which simplifies the more complex computer concepts. Pictures and drawings reflect the latest trends in computer technology.

Latest Technologies and Terms

The technologies and terms your students see in this book are those they will encounter when they start using computers. Only the latest application software packages are shown throughout the book.

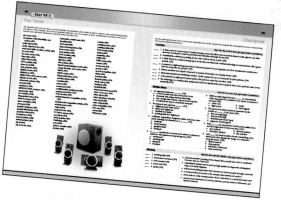

World Wide Web Enhanced

This book uses the World Wide Web as a major supplement. The purpose of integrating the World Wide Web into the book is to (1) offer students additional information and currency on important topics; (2) use its interactive capabilities to offer creative reinforcement and online quizzes; (3) make available alternative learning techniques with Web-based learning games, practice tests, and interactive labs; (4) underscore the relevance of the World Wide Web as a basic information tool that can be used in all facets of society; (5) introduce students to doing research on the Web; and (6) offer instructors the opportunity to organize and administer their traditional campus-based or distance-education-based courses on the Web using the Blackboard platform. This textbook, however, does not depend on Web access to be used successfully. The Web access adds to the already complete treatment of topics within the book.

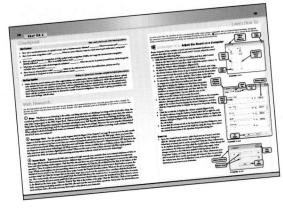

Extensive End-of-Chapter Materials

A notable strength of this book is the extensive student activities at the end of each chapter. Well-structured student activities can make the difference between students merely participating in a class and students retaining the information they learn. The activities in this book include: Chapter Review, Key Terms, Checkpoint, Web Research, Learn How To, and Learn It Online.

ORGANIZATION OF THIS TEXTBOOK

Discovering Computers: Fundamentals, Fifth Edition provides a thorough, but succinct, introduction to computers. The material is divided into twelve chapters, five special features, and a glossary/index.

Chapter 1 – Introduction to Computers   In Chapter 1, students are introduced to basic computer concepts, such as what a computer is, how it works, and what makes it a powerful tool.

Special Feature – Timeline: Milestones in Computer History   In this special feature, students learn about the major computer technology developments during the past 72 years.

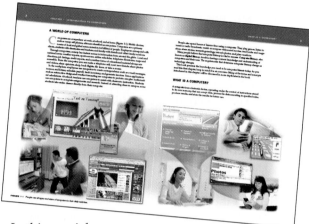

Chapter 2 – The Internet and World Wide Web   In Chapter 2, students learn about the Internet, World Wide Web, browsers, e-mail, FTP, and instant messaging.

Special Feature – Making Use of the Web   In this special feature, more than 150 popular up-to-date Web sites are listed and described. Now includes a section on Online Social Networks and Media Sharing. Basic searching techniques are also introduced.

Chapter 3 – Application Software   In Chapter 3, students are introduced to a variety of business software, graphics and multimedia software, home/personal/educational software, and communications software.

Chapter 4 – The Components of the System Unit   In Chapter 4, students are introduced to the components of the system unit; how memory stores data, instructions, and information; and how the system unit executes an instruction.

Chapter 5 – Input and Output   Chapter 5 describes the various methods of input and output, and commonly used input and output devices.

Special Feature – Digital Imaging and Video Technology   In this special feature, students are introduced to using a personal computer, digital camera, and digital video camera to manipulate and distribute photographs and video.

Chapter 6 – Storage   In Chapter 6, students learn about various storage media and storage devices.

Chapter 7 – Operating Systems and Utility Programs   In Chapter 7, students learn about a variety of stand-alone operating systems, network operating systems, and embedded operating systems.

Special Feature – Buyer's Guide: How to Purchase a Personal Computer   In this special feature, students are introduced to purchasing a desktop computer, notebook computer, and Tablet PC.

Chapter 8 – Communications and Networks   Chapter 8 provides students with an overview of communications technology and applications.

Chapter 9 – Database Management   Chapter 9 presents students with the advantages of organizing data in a database and describes various types of data.

Chapter 10 – Computer Security, Ethics, and Privacy   In Chapter 10, students learn about computer and Internet risks, ethical issues surrounding information accuracy, intellectual property rights, codes of conduct, information privacy, and computer-related health issues.

Special Feature: Digital Entertainment   In this special feature, students are introduced to the personal computer as a digital entertainment device.

Chapter 11 – Information System Development and Programming Languages   In Chapter 11, students are introduced to the system development cycle and guidelines for system development. This chapter also presents the program development cycle, program design methods, and popular programming languages.

Chapter 12 – Enterprise Computing   In Chapter 12, students learn about the special computing requirements used in an enterprise-sized organization.

Appendix A – Quiz Yourself Answers   Appendix A provides the answers for the Quiz Yourself questions in the text.

Glossary/Index – The Glossary/Index includes a definition and page references for every key term presented in the book.

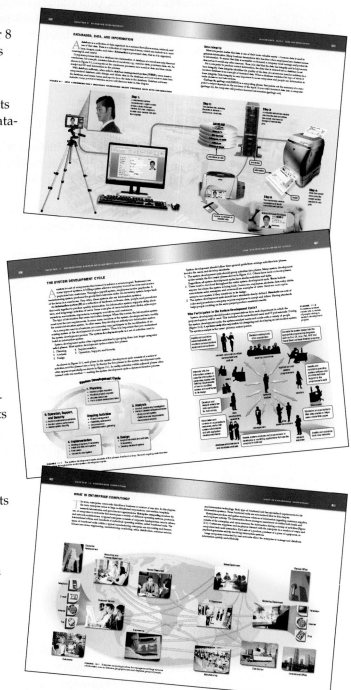

SHELLY CASHMAN SERIES INSTRUCTOR RESOURCES

The Shelly Cashman Series is dedicated to providing you with all of the tools you need to make your class a success. The contents of the Instructor Resources and Course Presenter discs (1-4239-2703-6) are described below. Information on all supplementary materials is available through your Course Technology representative or by calling one of the following telephone numbers: Colleges, Universities, Continuing Education Departments, Post-Secondary Vocational Schools, and Career Colleges, Business, Industry, Government, Trade, Retailer, Wholesaler, Library, and Resellers, 1-800-648-7450; K-12 Schools, Secondary Vocational Schools, Adult Education, and School Districts, 1-800-824-5179; Canada, 1-800-268-2222.

Instructor Resources
The Instructor Resources includes both teaching and testing aids.

Instructor's Manual   The Instructor's Manual is made up of Microsoft Word files, which include lecture notes that summarize the sections of the chapters, figures and boxed elements found in the chapters, teacher tips, classroom activities, and lab activities.

Syllabus   Sample syllabus, which can be customized easily to a course, is included. The syllabus covers policies, class and lab assignments and exams, and procedural information.

Figure Files   Illustrations for every figure in the textbook are available in electronic form. Figures are provided both with and without callouts. Use this ancillary to present a slide show in lecture or to print transparencies for use in lecture with an overhead projector. If you have a personal computer and LCD device, this ancillary can be an effective tool for presenting lectures.

Solutions to Exercises   Solutions are included for all end-of-chapter exercises.

Test Bank & Test Engine   The ExamView test bank includes 112 questions for every chapter (40 multiple-choice, 5 modified multiple-choice, 25 true/false, 5 modified true/false, 20 completion, 10 matching, 3 essays and 2 cases with 2 case-based questions each). The test bank also includes page number references, and when appropriate, figure references. The test bank comes with a copy of the test engine, ExamView, the ultimate tool for your objective-based testing needs.

Printed Test Bank   A Rich Text Format (.rtf) version of the test bank you can print also is included.

Data Files for Students   All the files that are required by students to complete the exercises are included. You can distribute the files on the Instructor Resources disc to your students over a network, or you can have them follow the instructions on the inside back cover of this book to obtain the Data Files for Students.

Course Presenter
Course Presenter is a one-click-per-slide presentation system on disc that provides PowerPoint slides for every subject in each chapter. Use this presentation system to give interesting, well-organized, and knowledge-based lectures. Several brand new computer-related video clips are available for optional presentation. Course Presenter provides consistent coverage for multiple lecturers.

Student Edition Labs

Our Web-based interactive labs help students master hundreds of computer concepts, including input and output devices, file management and desktop applications, computer ethics, virus protection, and much more. Featuring up-to-the-minute content, eye-popping graphics, and rich animation, the highly interactive Student Edition Labs offer students an alternative way to learn through dynamic observation, step-by-step practice, and challenging review questions. Access the free Student Edition Labs from the *Discovering Computers: Fundamentals, Fifth Edition* Online Companion at scsite.com/dcf5e or see the Student Edition Lab exercises on the Learn It Online pages at the end of each chapter. Also available on CD at an additional cost.

Online Content

Blackboard is the leading distance learning solution provider and class-management platform today. Course Technology has partnered with Blackboard to bring you premium online content. Instructors: Content for use with *Discovering Computers: Fundamentals, Fifth Edition* is available in a Blackboard Course Cartridge and includes topic reviews, case projects, review questions, test banks, practice tests, custom syllabus, and more. Thomson Course Technology also has solutions for several other learning management systems. Please visit http://www.course.com today to see what's available for this title.

Blackboard

SAM 2007

Add more flexibility to your course with SAM.

SAM (Skills Assessment Manager) helps you energize your training assignments by allowing students to train and test on important computer skills in an active, hands-on environment. By adding SAM to your curriculum, you can:

- Reinforce your students' knowledge of key skills with hands-on application exercises.
- Allow your students to "learn by listening" with rich audio in their computer labs.
- Build computer concepts exams from a test bank of more than 50,000 objective-based questions.
- Schedule your students' assignments with powerful administrative tools.
- Track student exam grades and training progress using helpful reports by class or by student.

SAM features assessment, training, and project-grading solutions for skills in both Microsoft Office 2003 and Office 2007. Let SAM save you time in grading, while students get hands-on practice on valuable real-world skills.

CourseCasts — Learning on the Go. Always available. . . always relevant.

Want to keep up with the latest technology trends relevant to you? Visit our site to find a library of podcasts, CourseCasts, featuring a "CourseCast of the Week", and download them to your mp3 player at http://coursecasts.course.com

Our fast-paced world is driven by technology. You know because you're an active participant —always on the go, always keeping up with technological trends, and always learning new ways to embrace technology to power your life.

Ken Baldauf, a faculty member of the Florida State University Computer Science Department, is responsible for teaching technology classes to thousands of FSU students each year. He knows what you know; he knows what you want to learn. He's also an expert in the latest technology and will sort through and aggregate the most pertinent news and information so you can spend your time enjoying technology, rather than trying to figure it out.

Visit us at http://coursecasts.course.com to learn on the go!

About Our Covers

Learning styles of students have changed, but the
Shelly Cashman Series' dedication to their success has
remained steadfast for over 30 years. We are committed
to continually updating our approach and content to
reflect the way today's students learn and experience new
technology.

This focus on the user is reflected in our bold cover
design, which features photographs of real students
using the Shelly Cashman Series in their courses. Each
book features a different user, reflecting the many ages,
experiences, and backgrounds of all of the students
learning with our books. When you use the Shelly
Cashman Series, you can be assured that you are learning
computer skills using the most effective courseware
available.

We would like to thank the administration and faculty
at the participating schools for their help in making
our vision a reality. Most of all, we'd like to thank the
wonderful students from all over the world who learn
from our texts and appear on our covers.

CHAPTER 1

Introduction to Computers

OBJECTIVES

After completing this chapter, you will be able to:

1. Recognize the importance of computer literacy
2. Identify the components of a computer
3. Discuss the uses of the Internet and World Wide Web
4. Identify the categories of software
5. Describe the categories of computers
6. Identify the types of computer users
7. Discuss various computer applications in society

CONTENTS

A WORLD OF COMPUTERS

Computers are everywhere: at work, at school, and at home (Figure 1-1). Mobile devices, such as many cell phones, often are classified as computers. Computers are a primary means of local and global communication for billions of people. Employees correspond with clients, students with classmates and teachers, and family with friends and other family members.

Through computers, society has instant access to information from around the globe. Local and national news, weather reports, sports scores, airline schedules, telephone directories, maps and directions, job listings, credit reports, and countless forms of educational material always are accessible. From the computer, you can make a telephone call, meet new friends, share photos and videos, share opinions, shop, book flights, file taxes, or take a course.

In the workplace, employees use computers to create correspondence such as e-mail messages, memos, and letters; calculate payroll; track inventory; and generate invoices. Some applications such as automotive design and weather forecasting use computers to perform complex mathematical calculations. At school, teachers use computers to assist with classroom instruction. Students use computers to complete assignments and research. Instead of attending class on campus, some students take entire classes directly from their computer.

FIGURE 1-1 People use all types and sizes of computers in their daily activities.

People also spend hours of leisure time using a computer. They play games, listen to music or radio broadcasts, watch or compose videos and movies, read books and magazines, share stories, research genealogy, retouch photos, and plan vacations.

Many people believe that computer literacy is vital to success. **Computer literacy**, also known as **digital literacy**, involves having a current knowledge and understanding of computers and their uses. The requirements that determine computer literacy change as technology changes.

This book presents the knowledge you need to be computer literate today. As you read this first chapter, keep in mind it is an overview. Many of the terms and concepts introduced in this chapter will be discussed in more depth later in the book.

WHAT IS A COMPUTER?

A **computer** is an electronic device, operating under the control of instructions stored in its own memory, that can accept data, process the data according to specified rules, produce results, and store the results for future use.

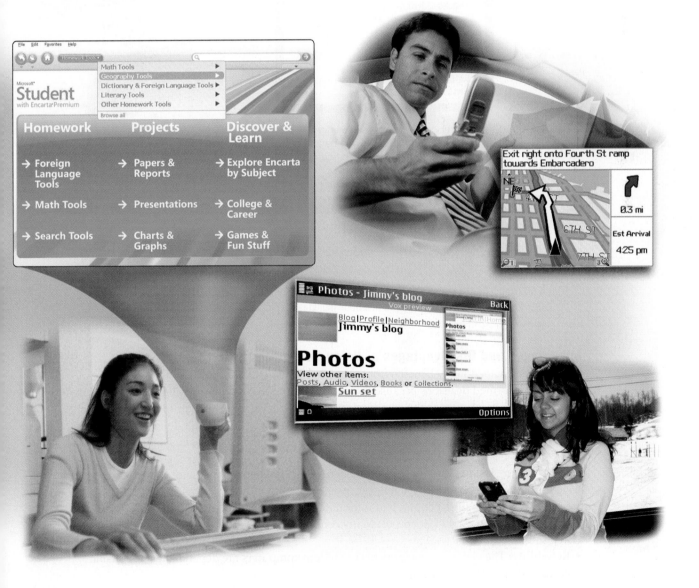

Data and Information

Computers process data into information. **Data** is a collection of unprocessed items, which can include text, numbers, images, audio, and video. **Information** conveys meaning and is useful to people.

As shown in Figure 1-2, for example, computers process several data items to print information in the form of a grade report.

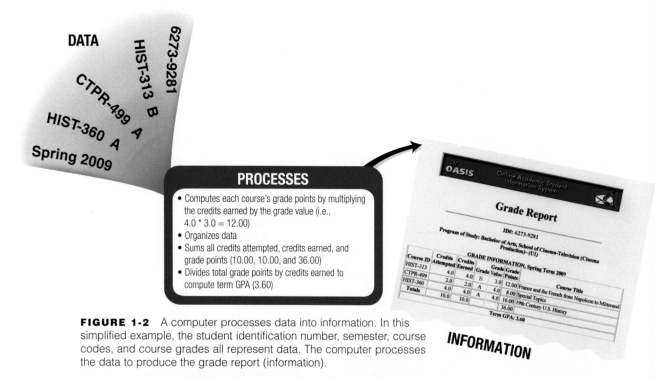

FIGURE 1-2   A computer processes data into information. In this simplified example, the student identification number, semester, course codes, and course grades all represent data. The computer processes the data to produce the grade report (information).

FAQ 1-1

Is data a singular or plural word?

The word data is plural for datum. With respect to computers, however, it is accepted and common practice to use the word data in both the singular and plural context. For more information, visit scsite.com/dcf5e/ch1/faq and then click Data.

An **FAQ** (frequently asked question) helps you find answers to commonly asked questions. Web sites often post an FAQ section, and each chapter in this book includes FAQ boxes related to topics in the text.

Advantages and Disadvantages of Using Computers

Society has reaped many benefits from using computers. Both business and home users can make well-informed decisions because they have instant access to information from anywhere in the world. A **user** is anyone who communicates with a computer or utilizes the information it generates. Students, another type of user, have more tools to assist them in the learning process. Read Looking Ahead 1-1 for a look at the next generation of benefits from using computers.

ADVANTAGES OF USING COMPUTERS   The benefits of computers are possible because computers have the advantages of speed, reliability, consistency, storage, and communications.

- **Speed:** When data, instructions, and information flow along electronic circuits in a computer, they travel at incredibly fast speeds. Many computers process billions or trillions of operations in a single second.
- **Reliability:** The electronic components in modern computers are dependable and reliable because they rarely break or fail.

- **Consistency:** Given the same input and processes, a computer will produce the same results — consistently. Computers generate error-free results, provided the input is correct and the instructions work.
- **Storage:** Computers store enormous amounts of data and make this data available for processing anytime it is needed.
- **Communications:** Most computers today can communicate with other computers, often wirelessly. Computers allow users to communicate with one another.

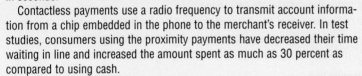

LOOKING AHEAD 1-1

Paying by Cell Phone

Fumbling for spare change at a vending machine or swiping your credit card at the checkout lane may be eliminated with upcoming contactless, or proximity, payments using a cell phone. By waving your phone in front of a merchant's wireless receiver, your credit or debit transactions can be completed in seconds.

Contactless payments use a radio frequency to transmit account information from a chip embedded in the phone to the merchant's receiver. In test studies, consumers using the proximity payments have decreased their time waiting in line and increased the amount spent as much as 30 percent as compared to using cash.

Security issues have been addressed in the test systems. For example, the transaction would be initiated only when entering a password or PIN (personal identification number) on the phone. Also, the cell phone must touch or pass within a few inches of the receiver in order to complete the wireless payment.

For more information, visit scsite.com/dcf5e/ch1/looking and then click Cell Phone Payments.

DISADVANTAGES OF USING COMPUTERS Some disadvantages of computers relate to the violation of privacy, public safety, the impact on the labor force, health risks, and the impact on the environment.

- **Violation of Privacy:** In many instances, where personal and confidential records were not protected properly, individuals have found their privacy violated and identities stolen.
- **Public Safety:** Adults, teens, and children around the world are using computers to share publicly their photos, videos, journals, music, and other personal information. Some of these unsuspecting, innocent computer users have fallen victim to crimes committed by dangerous strangers.
- **Impact on Labor Force:** Although computers have improved productivity and created an entire industry with hundreds of thousands of new jobs, the skills of millions of employees have been replaced by computers. Thus, it is crucial that workers keep their education up-to-date. A separate impact on the labor force is that some companies are outsourcing jobs to foreign countries instead of keeping their homeland labor force employed.
- **Health Risks:** Prolonged or improper computer use can lead to health injuries or disorders. Computer users can protect themselves from health risks through proper workplace design, good posture while at the computer, and appropriately spaced work breaks. Another health risk, called computer addiction, occurs when someone becomes obsessed with using the computer.
- **Impact on Environment:** Computer manufacturing processes and computer waste are depleting natural resources and polluting the environment. Strategies that can help protect the environment include recycling, regulating manufacturing processes, extending the life of computers, and immediately donating replaced computers.

Information Processing Cycle

Computers process data (input) into information (output). A computer often holds data, information, and instructions in storage for future use. Instructions are the steps that tell the computer how to perform a particular task. Some people refer to the series of input, process, output, and storage activities as the **information processing cycle**. Recently, communications also has become an essential element of the information processing cycle.

THE COMPONENTS OF A COMPUTER

A computer contains many electric, electronic, and mechanical components known as **hardware**. These components include input devices, output devices, a system unit, storage devices, and communications devices. Figure 1-3 shows some common computer hardware components.

Input Devices

An **input device** is any hardware component that allows you to enter data and instructions into a computer. Six widely used input devices are the keyboard, mouse, microphone, scanner, digital camera, and Web cam (Figure 1-3).

A computer keyboard contains keys you press to enter data into the computer. A mouse is a small handheld device. With the mouse, you control movement of a small symbol on the screen, called the pointer, and you make selections from the screen.

A microphone allows a user to speak into the computer. A scanner converts printed material (such as text and pictures) into a form the computer can use.

With a digital camera, you take pictures and then transfer the photographed images to the computer or printer instead of storing the images on traditional film. A Web cam is a digital video camera that allows users to create a movie or take still pictures electronically.

WEB LINK 1-1

Input Devices

For more information, visit scsite.com/dcf5e/ch1/weblink and then click Input Devices.

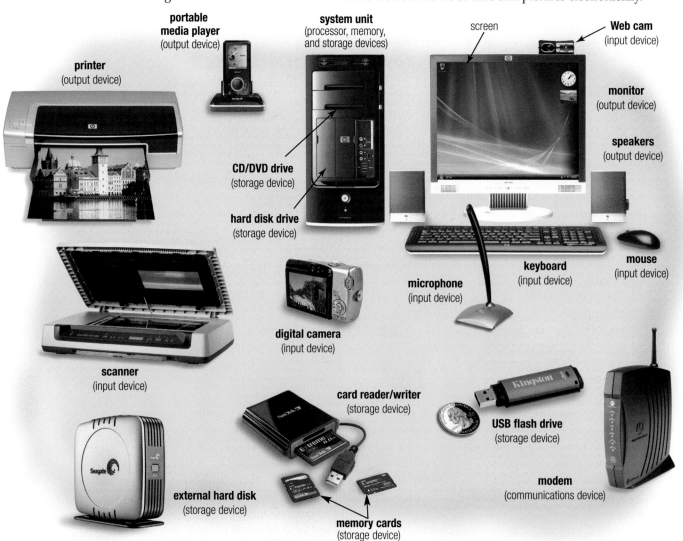

portable media player (output device)

system unit (processor, memory, and storage devices)

screen

Web cam (input device)

printer (output device)

monitor (output device)

speakers (output device)

CD/DVD drive (storage device)

hard disk drive (storage device)

keyboard (input device)

mouse (input device)

microphone (input device)

digital camera (input device)

scanner (input device)

card reader/writer (storage device)

USB flash drive (storage device)

modem (communications device)

external hard disk (storage device)

memory cards (storage device)

FIGURE 1-3   Common computer hardware components include the keyboard, mouse, microphone, scanner, digital camera, Web cam, printer, monitor, speakers, portable media player, system unit, hard disk drive, external hard disk, USB flash drive, card reader/writer, memory cards, and modem.

Output Devices

An **output device** is any hardware component that conveys information to one or more people. Four commonly used output devices are a printer, a monitor, speakers, and a portable media player (Figure 1-3).

A printer produces text and graphics on a physical medium such as paper. A monitor displays text, graphics, and videos on a screen. Speakers allow you to hear music, voice, and other audio (sounds). You can transfer audio, video, and digital images from a computer to a portable media player, and then listen to the audio, watch the video, or view the images on the media player.

WEB LINK 1-2

Output Devices

For more information, visit scsite.com/dcf5e/ch1/weblink and then click Output Devices.

System Unit

The **system unit** is a case that contains electronic components of the computer that are used to process data (Figure 1-3). The circuitry of the system unit usually is part of or is connected to a circuit board called the motherboard.

Two main components on the motherboard are the processor and memory. The **processor**, also called the **central processing unit** (**CPU**), is the electronic component that interprets and carries out the basic instructions that operate the computer. **Memory** consists of electronic components that store instructions waiting to be executed and data needed by those instructions. Most memory keeps data and instructions temporarily, which means its contents are erased when the computer is shut off.

Storage Devices

Storage holds data, instructions, and information for future use. For example, computers can store hundreds or millions of customer names and addresses. Storage holds these items permanently.

A computer keeps data, instructions, and information on **storage media**. Examples of storage media are USB flash drives, hard disks, CDs, DVDs, and memory cards. A **storage device** records (writes) and/or retrieves (reads) items to and from storage media. Storage devices often function as a source of input because they transfer items from storage to memory.

A USB flash drive is a portable storage device that is small and lightweight enough to be transported on a keychain or in a pocket (Figure 1-3). The average USB flash drive can hold about 2 billion characters.

A hard disk provides much greater storage capacity than a USB flash drive. The average hard disk can hold more than 320 billion characters. Hard disks are enclosed in an airtight, sealed case. Although some are portable, most are housed inside the system unit (Figure 1-4). Portable hard disks are either external or removable. An external hard disk is a separate, free-standing unit, whereas you insert and remove a removable hard disk from the computer or a device connected to the computer.

A compact disc is a flat, round, portable metal disc with plastic coating. One type of compact disc is a CD, which can hold from 650 million to 1 billion characters. You can access a CD using most CD and DVD drives (Figure 1-5). Another type of compact disc is a DVD, which has enough storage capacity to store two full-length movies or 17 billion characters. To access a DVD, you need a DVD drive.

Some portable devices, such as digital cameras, use memory cards as the storage media. You can use a card reader/writer (Figure 1-3) to transfer stored items, such as digital photos, from the memory card to a computer or printer.

FIGURE 1-4 Most hard disks are housed inside the system unit.

FIGURE 1-5 To access a CD or DVD, you need a CD or DVD drive.

Communications Devices

A **communications device** is a hardware component that enables a computer to send (transmit) and receive data, instructions, and information to and from one or more computers. A widely used communications device is a modem (Figure 1-3 on page 6).

Communications occur over cables, telephone lines, cellular radio networks, satellites, and other transmission media. Some transmission media, such as satellites and cellular radio networks, are wireless, which means they have no physical lines or wires.

Test your knowledge of pages 2 through 8 in Quiz Yourself 1-1.

 QUIZ YOURSELF 1-1

Instructions: Find the true statement below. Then, rewrite the remaining false statements so they are true.

1. A computer is a motorized device that processes output into input.

2. A storage device records (reads) and/or retrieves (writes) items to and from storage media.

3. An output device is any hardware component that allows you to enter data and instructions into a computer.

4. Computer literacy involves having a current knowledge and understanding of computers and their uses.

5. Four commonly used input devices are a printer, a monitor, speakers, and a portable media player.

Quiz Yourself Online: To further check your knowledge of computer literacy and computer components, visit scsite.com/dcf5e/ch1/quiz and then click Objectives 1 – 2.

NETWORKS AND THE INTERNET

A **network** is a collection of computers and devices connected together, often wirelessly, via communications devices and transmission media. When a computer connects to a network, it is **online**. Networks allow computers to share resources, such as hardware, software, data, and information. Sharing resources saves time and money.

The **Internet** is a worldwide collection of networks that connects millions of businesses, government agencies, educational institutions, and individuals (Figure 1-6). More than one billion people around the world use the Internet daily for a variety of reasons, including the following: to communicate with and meet other people; to conduct research and access a wealth of information and news; to shop for goods and services; to bank and invest; to take a class; to access sources of entertainment and leisure, such as travel directories, online games, music, videos, books, and magazines; to download music and videos; and to share information, photos, and videos. Figure 1-7 shows examples in each of these areas.

FIGURE 1-6 The Internet is the largest computer network, connecting millions of computers around the world.

FIGURE 1-7 Users access the Internet for a variety of reasons.

FAQ 1-2

What Web sites do users visit on the Internet?

A recent survey found that users visit various types of Web sites, as shown in the chart below. For more information, visit scsite.com/dcf5e/ch1/faq and then click Web Sites.

Web Site Usage

Percentage of Internet Users

60
50
40
30
20
10
0

Travel · Entertainment · Buying · Auctions · Banking

Source: Stanford University

People connect to the Internet to exchange information with others around the world. E-mail allows you to send messages to other users. With instant messaging, you can have a live conversation with another connected user. In a chat room, you can communicate with multiple users at the same time — much like a group discussion. You also can use the Internet to make a telephone call.

Businesses, called access providers, offer access to the Internet free or for a fee. By subscribing to an access provider, you can use your computer and a modem to connect to the many services of the Internet.

The **Web**, short for World Wide Web, is one of the more popular services on the Internet. The Web contains billions of documents called Web pages. A **Web page** can contain text, graphics, audio, and video. The eight screens shown in Figure 1-7 on the previous page are examples of Web pages.

Web pages often have built-in connections, or links, to other documents, graphics, other Web pages, or Web sites. A Web site is a collection of related Web pages. Some Web sites allow users to access music and videos that can be downloaded, or transferred to storage media in a computer or portable media player, and then listen to the music through speakers, headphones, or earphones, or view the videos on a display device.

Anyone can create a Web page and then make it available, or publish it, on the Internet for others to see. Millions of people worldwide join online communities, each called a **social networking Web site**, that encourage

WEB LINK 1-5

Sharing Videos

For more information, visit scsite.com/dcf5e/ch1/weblink and then click Sharing Videos.

members to share their interests, ideas, stories, photos, music, and videos with other registered users. Hundreds of thousands of people today also use blogs to publish their thoughts on the Web. A **blog** is an informal Web site consisting of time-stamped articles in a diary or journal format, usually listed in reverse chronological order. Podcasts are a popular way people verbally share information on the Web. A **podcast** is recorded audio stored on a Web site that can be downloaded to a computer or a portable media player such as an iPod.

COMPUTER SOFTWARE

Software, also called a **program**, is a series of instructions that tells the computer what to do and how to do it. You interact with a program through its user interface. Software today often has a graphical user interface. With a **graphical user interface** (**GUI** pronounced gooey), you interact with the software using text, graphics, and visual images such as icons (Figure 1-8). An icon is a miniature image that represents a program, an instruction, or some other object. You can use the mouse to select icons that perform operations such as starting a program.

The two categories of software are system software and application software.

System Software

System software consists of the programs that control or maintain the operations of the computer and its devices. System software serves as the interface between the user, the application software, and the computer's hardware. Two types of system software are the operating system and utility programs.

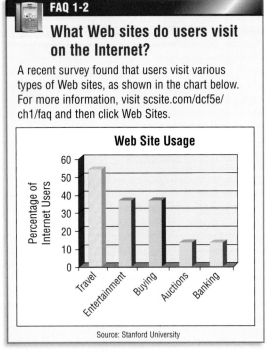

FIGURE 1-8 The graphical user interface of Windows Vista, Microsoft's latest operating system.

OPERATING SYSTEM An **operating system** is a set of programs that coordinates all the activities among computer hardware devices. It provides a means for users to communicate with the computer and other software. Many of today's computers use Windows Vista (Figure 1-8) or Windows XP, two of Microsoft's operating systems, or Mac OS X, Apple's operating system.

When a user starts a computer, portions of the operating system load into memory from the computer's hard disk. It remains in memory while the computer is on.

UTILITY PROGRAM A **utility program** allows a user to perform maintenance-type tasks usually related to managing a computer, its devices, or its programs. For example, you can use a utility program to transfer digital photos to a CD or DVD. Most operating systems include several utility programs for managing disk drives, printers, and other devices and media. You also can buy utility programs that allow you to perform additional computer management functions.

WEB LINK 1-6

Windows Vista

For more information, visit scsite.com/dcf5e/ch1/weblink and then click Windows Vista.

Application Software

Application software consists of programs designed to make users more productive and/or assist them with personal tasks. A widely used type of application software related to communications is a Web browser, which allows users with an Internet connection to access and view Web pages. Other popular application software includes word processing software, spreadsheet software, database software, and presentation graphics software.

Many other types of application software exist that enable users to perform a variety of tasks. These include personal information management, note taking, project management, accounting, document management, computer-aided design, desktop publishing, paint/image editing, audio and video editing, multimedia authoring, Web page authoring, personal finance, legal, tax preparation, home design/landscaping, travel and mapping, education, reference, and entertainment (e.g., games or simulations). As shown in Figure 1-9, you often purchase application software from a store that sells computer products. Read Ethics & Issues 1-1 for a related discussion.

FIGURE 1-9 Stores that sell computer products have shelves stocked with software for sale.

ETHICS & ISSUES 1-1

What Can Be Done to Combat Computer Addiction?

The notion that a person can become addicted to computer use has existed since the 1970s. Today, the extensive list of activities that people engage in with computers provides an ever growing list of reasons why some become computer addicted. While experts disagree on the specific definition of computer addiction, they generally agree that a person is computer addicted when obsessive use of a computer negatively impacts health, personal life, and professional life. The media reports extreme examples of computer addiction with growing frequency. One man died after playing a computer game for 86 hours while foregoing food and sleep. Another died after spending almost a week using a computer. Such incidents are rare, but experts consider the problem to be widespread, especially among children. China classifies more than 2.6 million people under the age of 18 as computer addicts. Sometimes mistakenly, parents feel that computer use is a healthier alternative to television or video games and, therefore, permit excessive computer use. For adults, computer addiction often leads to less time spent with family and has proven to be as potent a cause for divorce as gambling or substance abuse. What steps should parents and society take to combat computer addiction? Why? How can software providers help to alleviate the problem? Should certain software include built-in timers to disable the software after a certain number of hours, and then not enable it again until a set number of hours has elapsed? Why or why not? Do you believe that those identified as computer addicts should receive health insurance benefits for counseling services? Why or why not?

Installing and Running Programs

The instructions in a program are stored on storage media such as a hard disk or compact disc. When purchasing software from a computer store, you typically receive a box that includes a CD(s) or DVD(s) that contains the program. If you purchase software from a Web site on the Internet, you download the program; that is, the program is transferred from the Web site to the hard disk in your computer.

Installing is the process of setting up software to work with the computer, printer, and other hardware components. When you buy a computer, it usually has some software preinstalled on its hard disk. This enables you to use the computer the first time you turn it on. To begin installing additional software from a CD or DVD, insert the program disc in a CD or DVD drive. When you download a purchased program, the Web site typically provides instructions for how to install the software on your hard disk.

Once software is installed, you can run it. When you instruct the computer to **run** an installed program, the computer loads it, which means the program is copied from storage to memory. Once in memory, the computer can carry out, or **execute**, the instructions in the program so that you can use the program. Figure 1-10 illustrates the steps that occur when a user installs and runs a program that assists students with homework.

FIGURE 1-10   INSTALLING AND RUNNING A COMPUTER PROGRAM

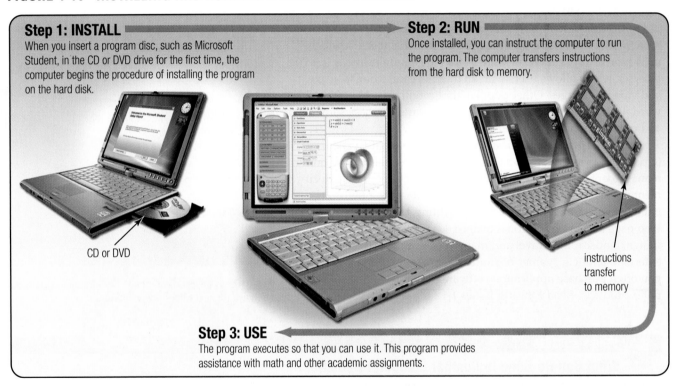

Step 1: INSTALL
When you insert a program disc, such as Microsoft Student, in the CD or DVD drive for the first time, the computer begins the procedure of installing the program on the hard disk.

CD or DVD

Step 2: RUN
Once installed, you can instruct the computer to run the program. The computer transfers instructions from the hard disk to memory.

instructions transfer to memory

Step 3: USE
The program executes so that you can use it. This program provides assistance with math and other academic assignments.

Software Development

A **programmer**, sometimes called a **developer**, is someone who develops software or writes the instructions that direct the computer to process data into information. Complex programs can require thousands to millions of instructions.

Programmers use a programming language or program development tool to create computer programs. Popular programming languages include C++, Visual C#, Visual Basic, JavaScript, and Java. Figure 1-11 shows part of a program.

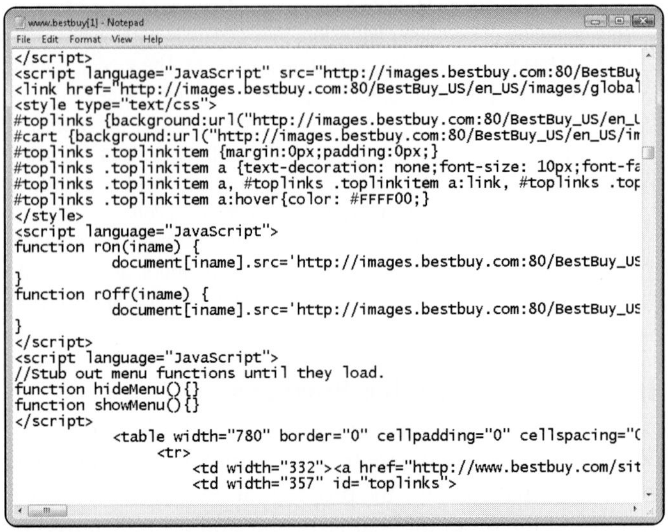

FIGURE 1-11 Some of the instructions in a program.

Test your knowledge of pages 8 through 12 in Quiz Yourself 1-2.

CATEGORIES OF COMPUTERS

Industry experts typically classify computers in seven categories: personal computers, mobile computers and mobile devices, game consoles, servers, mainframes, supercomputers, and embedded computers. A computer's size, speed, processing power, and price determine the category it best fits. Due to rapidly changing technology, however, the distinction among categories is not always clear-cut.

Figure 1-12 summarizes the seven categories of computers. The following pages discuss computers and devices that fall in each category.

CATEGORIES OF COMPUTERS

Category	Physical Size	Number of Simultaneously Connected Users	General Price Range
Personal computers (desktop)	Fits on a desk	Usually one (can be more if networked)	Several hundred to several thousand dollars
Mobile computers and mobile devices	Fits on your lap or in your hand	Usually one	Less than a hundred dollars to several thousand dollars
Game consoles	Small box or handheld device	One to several	Several hundred dollars or less
Servers	Small cabinet	Two to thousands	Several hundred to a million dollars
Mainframes	Partial room to a full room of equipment	Hundreds to thousands	$300,000 to several million dollars
Supercomputers	Full room of equipment	Hundreds to thousands	$500,000 to several billion dollars
Embedded computers	Miniature	Usually one	Embedded in the price of the product

FIGURE 1-12   This table summarizes some of the differences among the categories of computers.

PERSONAL COMPUTERS

WEB LINK 1-7

Personal Computers

For more information, visit scsite.com/dcf5e/ch1/weblink and then click Personal Computers.

A **personal computer** is a computer that can perform all of its input, processing, output, and storage activities by itself. A personal computer contains a processor, memory, and one or more input, output, and storage devices. They also often contain a communications device.

Two popular styles of personal computers are the PC (Figure 1-13) and the Apple (Figure 1-14). These two types of computers use different operating systems. PC and PC-compatible computers usually use a Windows operating system. Apple computers usually use a Macintosh operating system (Mac OS X). The term, PC-compatible, refers to any personal computer based on the original IBM personal computer design. Companies such as Dell and Toshiba sell PC-compatible computers.

Two types of personal computers are desktop computers and notebook computers.

FIGURE 1-13 The PC and PC-compatible computers usually use a Windows operating system.

FIGURE 1-14 Apple computers, such as the iMac, usually use a Macintosh operating system.

Desktop Computers

A **desktop computer** is designed so that the system unit, input devices, output devices, and any other devices fit entirely on or under a desk or table. In some models, the monitor sits on top of the system unit, which is placed on the desk. The more popular style of system unit is the tall and narrow tower, which can sit on the floor vertically.

MOBILE COMPUTERS AND MOBILE DEVICES

A **mobile computer** is a personal computer you can carry from place to place. Similarly, a **mobile device** is a computing device small enough to hold in your hand. The most popular type of mobile computer is the notebook computer.

Notebook Computers

A **notebook computer**, also called a **laptop computer**, is a portable, personal computer designed to fit on your lap. Notebook computers are thin and lightweight, yet can be as powerful as the average desktop computer. Notebook computers usually are more expensive than desktop computers with equal capabilities.

On a typical notebook computer, the keyboard is on top of the system unit, and the display attaches to the system unit with hinges (Figure 1-15). These computers weigh on average from 2.5 to more than 10 pounds (depending on configuration), which allows users easily to transport the computers from place to place. Most notebook computers can operate on batteries or a power supply or both.

display

keyboard

hinge

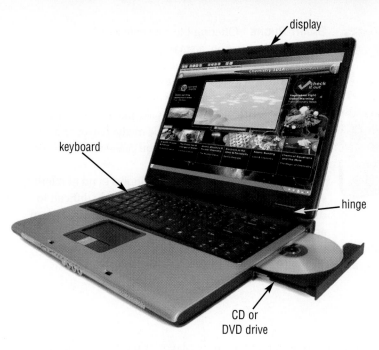

CD or
DVD drive

FIGURE 1-15   On a typical notebook computer, the keyboard is on top
of the system unit, and the display attaches to the system unit with hinges.

TABLET PC   Resembling a letter-sized slate, the **Tablet PC** is a special type
of notebook computer that allows you to write or draw on the screen using a digital pen (Figure 1-16). For users who prefer typing instead of handwriting, you can
attach a keyboard to Tablet PCs that do not include one already. Tablet PCs are useful
especially for taking notes in locations where the standard notebook computer is not
practical. Tablet PCs are used widely in the medical and legal communities.

digital pen

FIGURE 1-16   A Tablet PC
combines the features of a
traditional notebook computer
with the simplicity of pencil
and paper.

Mobile Devices

Mobile devices, which are small enough to carry in a pocket, usually store programs
and data permanently on memory inside the system unit or on small storage media
such as memory cards. You often can connect a mobile device to a personal computer
to exchange information. Some mobile devices are **Internet-enabled**, meaning they can
connect to the Internet wirelessly.

Three popular types of mobile devices are handheld computers, PDAs, and smart
phones.

HANDHELD COMPUTER   A **handheld computer**, sometimes referred to as **Ultra-Mobile
PC (UMPC)**, is a computer small enough to fit in one hand. Because of their reduced
size, the screens on handheld computers are small. Industry-specific handheld computers serve mobile employees, such as parcel delivery people, whose jobs require them
to move from place to place.

PDA   A **PDA** (personal digital assistant) provides personal organizer functions such
as a calendar, an appointment book, an address book, a calculator, and a notepad
(Figure 1-17). Most PDAs also offer a variety of other application software such as
word processing, spreadsheet, personal finance, and games.

Many PDAs are Internet-enabled so that users can check e-mail and access the Web.
Some also provide camera and phone capabilities and can function as a portable
media player.

The primary input device of a PDA is the **stylus**, which looks like a small ballpoint pen,
but uses pressure instead of ink to write and draw.

stylus

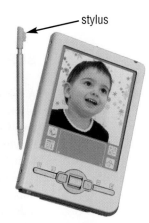

FIGURE 1-17   Some PDAs also
function as a portable media player.

FIGURE 1-18 Smart phones, such as the iPhone shown in this figure, allow you to display maps, access the Web, listen to music, check e-mail, and share photos and videos.

SMART PHONE   Offering the convenience of one-handed operation, a **smart phone** is an Internet-enabled phone that usually also provides PDA capabilities. In addition to basic phone capabilities, a smart phone allows you to send and receive e-mail messages and access the Web — usually for an additional fee. Many models also function as a portable media player and include built-in cameras so that you can share photos or videos (Figure 1-18).

As smart phones and PDAs continue a trend of offering similar functions, it is becoming increasingly difficult to differentiate between the two devices. This trend, known as convergence, has led manufacturers to refer to PDAs and smart phones simply as **handhelds**. Some factors that affect a consumer's purchasing decision include the device's size, screen size, and capabilities of available software.

GAME CONSOLES

A **game console** is a mobile computing device designed for single-player or multiplayer video games (Figure 1-19). Standard game consoles use a handheld controller(s) as an input device(s); a television screen as an output device; and hard disks, CDs, DVDs, and/or memory cards for storage. The compact size and light weight of game consoles make them easy to use at home, in the car, in a hotel, or any location that has an electrical outlet. Three popular models are Microsoft's Xbox 360, Nintendo's Wii, and Sony's PlayStation 3.

A handheld game console is small enough to fit in one hand. With the handheld game console, the controls, screen, and speakers are built into the device. Some models use cartridges to store games; others use a miniature type of CD or DVD. Many handheld game consoles can communicate wirelessly with other similar consoles for multiplayer gaming. Two popular models are Nintendo DS Lite and Sony's PlayStation Portable (PSP).

In addition to gaming, many console models allow users to listen to music, watch movies, and connect to the Internet.

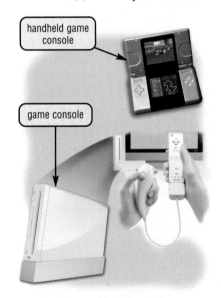

handheld game console

game console

FIGURE 1-19 Game consoles provide hours of video game entertainment.

SERVERS

A **server** controls access to the hardware, software, and other resources on a network and provides a centralized storage area for programs, data, and information (Figure 1-20). Servers support from two to several thousand connected computers at the same time.

People use personal computers or terminals to access data, information, and programs on a server. A terminal is a device with a monitor, keyboard, and memory.

FIGURE 1-20 A server controls access to resources on a network.

MAINFRAMES

A **mainframe** is a large, expensive, powerful computer that can handle hundreds or thousands of connected users simultaneously (Figure 1-21). Mainframes store huge amounts of data, instructions, and information. Most major corporations use mainframes for business activities. With mainframes, large businesses are able to bill millions of customers, prepare payroll for thousands of employees, and manage thousands of items in inventory. One study reported that mainframes process more than 83 percent of transactions around the world.

Servers and other mainframes can access data and information from a mainframe. People also can access programs on the mainframe using terminals or personal computers.

SUPERCOMPUTERS

A **supercomputer** is the fastest, most powerful computer — and the most expensive (Figure 1-22). The fastest supercomputers are capable of processing more than 135 trillion instructions in a single second.

Applications requiring complex, sophisticated mathematical calculations use supercomputers. Large-scale simulations and applications in medicine, aerospace, automotive design, online banking, weather forecasting, nuclear energy research, and petroleum exploration use a supercomputer.

FIGURE 1-21 Mainframe computers can handle thousands of connected computers and process millions of instructions per second.

FIGURE 1-22 This supercomputer simulates various environmental occurrences such as global climate changes, pollution, and earthquakes.

EMBEDDED COMPUTERS

An **embedded computer** is a special-purpose computer that functions as a component in a larger product. A variety of everyday products contain embedded computers:
- Consumer electronics
- Home automation devices
- Automobiles
- Process controllers and robotics
- Computer devices and office machines

Because embedded computers are components in larger products, they usually are small and have limited hardware. Embedded computers perform various functions, depending on the requirements of the product in which they reside. Embedded computers in printers, for example, monitor the amount of paper in the tray, check the ink or toner level, signal if a paper jam has occurred, and so on. Figure 1-23 shows some of the many embedded computers in cars.

Adaptive cruise control systems detect if cars in front of you are too close and, if necessary, adjust the vehicle's throttle, may apply brakes, and/or sound an alarm.

Advanced airbag systems have crash-severity sensors that determine the appropriate level to inflate the airbag, reducing the chance of airbag injury in low-speed accidents.

Tire pressure monitoring systems send warning signals if tire pressure is insufficient.

Cars equipped with wireless communications capabilities, called telematics, include such features as navigation systems and Internet access.

Drive-by-wire systems sense pressure on the gas pedal and communicate electronically to the engine how much and how fast to accelerate.

FIGURE 1-23 Some of the embedded computers designed to improve your safety, security, and performance in today's automobiles.

EXAMPLES OF COMPUTER USAGE

Every day, people around the world rely on different types of computers for a variety of applications. To illustrate the range of uses for computers, this section takes you on a visual and narrative tour of five categories of users: a home user, a small office/home office (SOHO) user, a mobile user, a power user, and a large business user.

Home User

In an increasing number of homes, the computer is a basic necessity. Each family member, or **home user**, spends time on the computer for different reasons. These include budgeting and personal financial management, Web access, communications, and entertainment (Figure 1-24).

On the Internet, home users access a huge amount of information, conduct research, take college classes, pay bills, manage investments, shop, listen to the radio, watch movies, read books, play games, file taxes, book airline reservations, and make telephone calls. They also communicate with others around the world through e-mail, blogs, instant messaging, and chat rooms. Home users share ideas, interests, photos, music, and videos on social networking Web sites, or online social networks.

Many home users have a portable media player, so that they can listen to downloaded music and/or podcasts at a later time through earphones attached to the player. They also usually have one or more game consoles to play video games.

Today's homes typically have one or more desktop computers. Some home users network multiple desktop computers throughout the house, often wirelessly. These small networks allow family members to share an Internet connection and a printer.

Home users have a variety of software. They type letters, homework assignments, and other documents with word processing software. Personal finance software helps the home user with personal finances, investments, and family budgets. Other software assists with preparing taxes, keeping a household inventory, setting up maintenance schedules, and protecting computers against threats and unauthorized intrusions (read Ethics & Issues 1-2 for a related discussion).

FAQ 1-3

Can I watch a DVD on my computer?

Yes, in most cases. Simply insert the DVD in the computer's DVD drive. Within a few seconds, you should see the DVD begin to play on your computer's screen. If the DVD does not play, it is possible you need to run a program that starts the DVD. For more information, visit scsite.com/dcf5e/ch1/faq and then click DVDs.

Reference software, such as encyclopedias, medical dictionaries, or a road atlas, provides valuable information for everyone in the family. With entertainment software, the home user can play games, compose music, research genealogy, or create greeting cards. Educational software helps adults learn to speak a foreign language and youngsters to read, write, count, and spell.

FIGURE 1-24a (personal financial management)

FIGURE 1-24b
(Web access)

FIGURE 1-24c
(communications)

FIGURE 1-24d (entertainment)

FIGURE 1-24 The home user spends time on a computer for a variety of reasons.

ETHICS & ISSUES 1-2

What Should Be Done about Identity Theft?

Using e-mail and other techniques on the Internet, scam artists are employing a technique known as phishing to try to steal your personal information, such as credit card numbers, banking information, and passwords. For example, an e-mail message may appear to be a request from your credit card company to verify your Social Security number and online banking password. Instead, the information you submit ends up in the hands of the scammer, who then uses the information for a variety of unethical and illegal acts. Sadly, the result often is identity theft. You can help to deter identity theft in several ways: 1) shred your financial documents before discarding them, 2) do not click links in unsolicited e-mail messages, and 3) enroll in a credit monitoring service. Consumer advocates often blame credit card companies and credit bureaus for lax security standards. Meanwhile, the companies blame consumers for being too gullible and forthcoming with private information. Both sides blame the government for poor privacy laws and light punishments for identity thieves. But while the arguments go on, law enforcement agencies bear the brunt of the problem by spending hundreds of millions of dollars responding to complaints and finding and processing the criminals. Who should be responsible for protecting the public from Internet identity theft? Why? Should laws be changed to stop it, or should consumers change behavior? What is an appropriate punishment for identity thieves? Given the international nature of the Internet, how can foreign identity thieves be handled?

Small Office/Home Office User

Computers assist small business and home office users in managing their resources effectively. A **small office/home office (SOHO)** includes any company with fewer than 50 employees, as well as the self-employed who work from home. Small offices include local law practices, accounting firms, travel agencies, and florists. SOHO users typically use a desktop computer. Many also use smart phones.

SOHO users access the Internet — often wirelessly — to look up information such as addresses (Figure 1-25a), directions, postal codes, flights, and package shipping rates or to make telephone calls.

FIGURE 1-25a   (Web access)

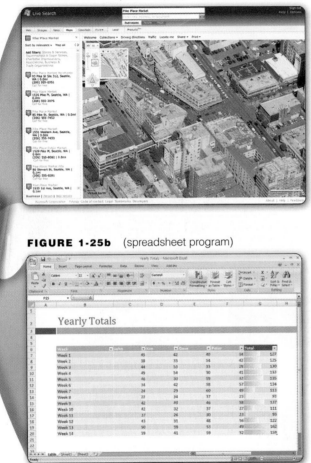

FIGURE 1-25b   (spreadsheet program)

FIGURE 1-25   People with a home office and employees in small offices typically use a personal computer.

Nearly all SOHO users communicate through e-mail. Many have entered the e-commerce arena and conduct business on the Web. Their Web sites advertise products and services and may provide a means for taking orders.

To save money on hardware and software, small offices often network their computers. For example, the small office connects one printer to a network for all employees to share.

SOHO users often have basic business software such as word processing and spreadsheet software to assist with document preparation and finances (Figure 1-25b). They are likely to use other industry-specific types of software. A candy shop, for example, will have software that allows for taking orders and payments, updating inventory, and paying vendors.

Mobile User

Today, businesses and schools are expanding to serve people across the country and around the world. Thus, increasingly more employees and students are **mobile users**, who work on a computer while away from a main office, home office, or school (Figure 1-26). Some examples of mobile users are sales representatives, real estate agents, insurance agents, meter readers, package delivery people, journalists, and students.

notebook computer

Tablet PC

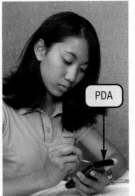

PDA

smart phone

FIGURE 1-26   Mobile users have notebook computers, Tablet PCs, PDAs, and smart phones so that they can work, do homework, send messages, or connect to the Internet while away from a wired connection.

Mobile users often have a notebook computer, Tablet PC, smart phone, or other mobile device. With these computers and devices, the mobile user can connect to other computers on a network or the Internet, often wirelessly accessing services such as e-mail and the Web. Mobile users can transfer information between their mobile devices and another computer.

The mobile user works with basic business software such as word processing and spreadsheet software. With presentation graphics software, the mobile user can create and deliver presentations to a large audience by connecting a mobile computer or device to a video projector that displays the presentation on a full screen.

Power User

Another category of user, called a **power user**, requires the capabilities of a powerful desktop computer, called a workstation. Examples of power users include engineers, scientists, architects, desktop publishers, and graphic artists (Figure 1-27). Power users typically work with multimedia, combining text, graphics, audio, and video into one application. These users need computers with extremely fast processors because of the nature of their work.

The power user's workstation contains industry-specific software. For example, engineers and architects use software to draft and design floor plans, mechanical assemblies, or vehicles. A desktop publisher uses software to prepare marketing literature. A graphic artist uses software to create sophisticated drawings. This software usually is expensive because of its specialized design.

Power users exist in all types of businesses. Some also work at home. Their computers typically have network connections and Internet access.

FIGURE 1-27 This graphic artist uses a powerful computer to create a drawing.

Large Business User

A large business has hundreds or thousands of employees or customers that work in or do business with offices across a region, the country, or the world. Each employee or customer who uses a computer in the large business is a **large business user** (Figure 1-28).

Many large companies use the words, **enterprise computing**, to refer to the huge network of computers that meets their diverse computing needs. The network facilitates communications among employees at all locations. Users access the network through desktop computers, mobile computers, and mobile devices.

Large businesses use computers and the computer network to process high volumes of transactions in a single day. Although they may differ in size and in the products or services offered, all generally use computers for basic business activities. For example, they bill millions of customers or prepare payroll for thousands of employees. Some large businesses use blogs to open communications among employees and/or customers.

Large businesses typically have e-commerce Web sites, allowing customers and vendors to conduct business online. The Web site showcases products, services, and other company information. Customers, vendors, and other interested parties can access this information on the Web.

The marketing department in a large business uses desktop publishing software to prepare marketing literature. The accounting department uses software for accounts receivable, accounts payable, billing, general ledger, and payroll activities.

Large business users work with word processing, spreadsheet, database, and presentation graphics software. They also may use calendar programs to post their schedules on the network. And, they might use smart phones or other mobile devices to maintain contact information. E-mail programs and Web browsers enable communications among employees, vendors, and customers.

FIGURE 1-28 A large business can have hundreds or thousands of users in offices across a region, the country, or the world.

Many employees of large businesses today telecommute (Figure 1-29). **Telecommuting** is a work arrangement in which employees work away from a company's standard workplace and often communicate with the office through the computer. Employees who telecommute have flexible work schedules so that they can combine work and personal responsibilities, such as child care.

COMPUTER APPLICATIONS IN SOCIETY

The computer has changed society today as much as the industrial revolution changed society in the eighteenth and nineteenth centuries.

People interact directly with computers in fields such as education, finance, government, health care, science, publishing, travel, and manufacturing. In addition, they can reap the benefits from breakthroughs and advances in these fields. The following pages describe how computers have made a difference in people's interactions with these disciplines. Read Looking Ahead 1-2 for a look at the next generation of computer applications in society.

FIGURE 1-29 Many employees of large businesses telecommute, which allows them to combine work and other responsibilities.

LOOKING AHEAD 1-2

Robots Perform Mundane, Dangerous Tasks

Playwright Karel Capek created the name, robot, for his humanoid machines that turned against their creators. Today, mobile, intelligent robots perform tasks typically reserved for humans in a $5 billion global market.

Tomorrow's practical and versatile robots will serve a variety of personal and industrial needs. By 2010, the expected $17 billion market should include products to care for senior citizens, transport people in major cities, and perform hundreds of thousands of mobile utility jobs, such as picking up and delivering items.

The Anna Konda is a snakelike robot built by Norway's Foundation for Industrial and Scientific Research that can maneuver over varied terrain. Engineers envision its possible uses include fighting fires, locating and bringing oxygen to earthquake victims buried under debris, and performing maintenance on underwater oil rigs. For more information, visit scsite.com/dcf5e/ch1/looking and then click Robots.

Education

Education is the process of acquiring knowledge. In the traditional model, people learn from other people such as parents, teachers, and employers. Many forms of printed material such as books and manuals are used as learning tools. Today, educators also are turning to computers to assist with education (Figure 1-30).

Many schools and companies equip labs and classrooms with computers. Some schools require students to have a notebook computer or mobile device to access the school's network or Internet wirelessly.

Students use software to assist with learning or to complete assignments. To promote education by computer, many vendors offer substantial student discounts on software.

FIGURE 1-30 In some schools, students have notebook computers on their desks during classroom lectures.

Sometimes, the delivery of education occurs at one place while the learning occurs at other locations. For example, students can take a class on the Web. More than 70 percent of colleges offer some type of distance learning classes. A few even offer entire degrees online.

Finance

Many people and companies use computers to help manage their finances. Some use finance software to balance checkbooks, pay bills, track personal income and expenses, manage investments, and evaluate financial plans. This software usually includes a variety of online services. For example, computer users can track investments and do online banking (Figure 1-31). With **online banking**, users access account balances, pay bills, and copy monthly transactions from the bank's computer right into their computers.

Investors often use **online investing** to buy and sell stocks and bonds — without using a broker. With online investing, the transaction fee for each trade usually is much less than when trading through a broker.

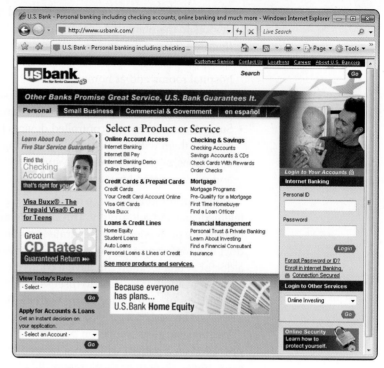

FIGURE 1-31 Many financial institutions' Web sites offer online banking.

Government

A government provides society with direction by making and administering policies. To provide citizens with up-to-date information, most government offices have Web sites. People access government Web sites to file taxes, apply for permits and licenses, pay parking tickets, buy stamps, report crimes, apply for financial aid, and renew vehicle registrations and driver's licenses.

Employees of government agencies use computers as part of their daily routine. Military and other agency officials use the U.S. Department of Homeland Security's network of information about domestic security threats to help protect our nation. Law enforcement officers have online access to the FBI's National Crime Information Center (NCIC) through in-vehicle computers, fingerprint readers, and mobile devices (Figure 1-32). The NCIC contains more than 52 million missing persons and criminal records, including names, fingerprints, parole/probation records, mug shots, and other information.

FIGURE 1-32 Law enforcement officials have in-vehicle computers and mobile devices to access emergency, missing person, and criminal records in computer networks in local, state, and federal agencies.

Health Care

Nearly every area of health care uses computers. Whether you are visiting a family doctor for a regular checkup, having lab work or an outpatient test, or being rushed in for emergency surgery, the medical staff around you will be using computers for various purposes:
- Doctors use the Web and medical software to assist with researching and diagnosing health conditions.
- Doctors use e-mail to correspond with patients.
- Pharmacists use computers to file insurance claims.
- Robots can deliver medication to nurse stations in hospitals.
- Computers and computerized devices assist doctors, nurses, and technicians with medical tests.

- Hospitals and doctors use computers and mobile devices to maintain and access patient records (Figure 1-33).
- Computers monitor patients' vital signs in hospital rooms and at home.
- Surgeons implant computerized devices, such as pacemakers, that allow patients to live longer.
- Surgeons use computer-controlled devices to provide them with greater precision during operations, such as for laser eye surgery and robot-assisted heart surgery.

Two forms of long-distance health care are telemedicine and telesurgery. Through **telemedicine**, health-care professionals in separate locations conduct live conferences on the computer. For example, a doctor at one location can have a conference with a doctor at another location to discuss a bone X-ray. Live images of each doctor, along with the X-ray, are displayed on each doctor's computer.

With **telesurgery**, a surgeon performs an operation on a patient who is not located in the same physical room as the surgeon. Telesurgery enables surgeons to direct robots to perform an operation via computers connected to a high-speed network.

FIGURE 1-33 Doctors, nurses, technicians, and other medical staff use computers and mobile devices to access patient records.

Science

All branches of science, from biology to astronomy to meteorology, use computers to assist them with collecting, analyzing, and modeling data. Scientists also use the Internet to communicate with colleagues around the world.

Breakthroughs in surgery, medicine, and treatments often result from scientists' use of computers. Tiny computers now imitate functions of the central nervous system, retina of the eye, and cochlea of the ear. A cochlear implant allows a deaf person to listen. Electrodes implanted in the brain stop tremors associated with Parkinson's disease. Cameras small enough to swallow — sometimes called a camera pill — take pictures inside your body to detect polyps, cancer, and other abnormalities (Figure 1-34).

FIGURE 1-34   HOW A CAMERA PILL WORKS

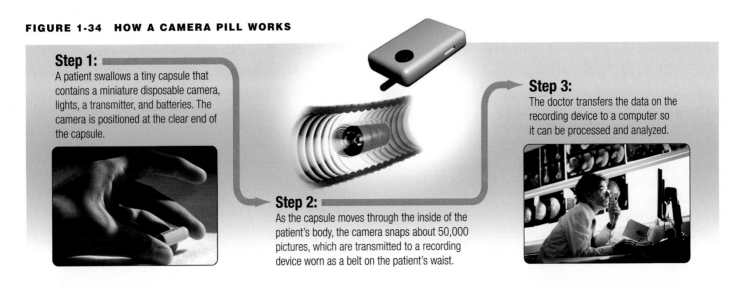

Step 1:
A patient swallows a tiny capsule that contains a miniature disposable camera, lights, a transmitter, and batteries. The camera is positioned at the clear end of the capsule.

Step 2:
As the capsule moves through the inside of the patient's body, the camera snaps about 50,000 pictures, which are transmitted to a recording device worn as a belt on the patient's waist.

Step 3:
The doctor transfers the data on the recording device to a computer so it can be processed and analyzed.

Publishing

Publishing is the process of making works available to the public. These works include books, magazines, newspapers, music, film, and video. Special software assists graphic designers in developing pages that include text, graphics, and photos; artists in composing and enhancing songs; filmmakers in creating and editing film; and journalists and mobile users in capturing and modifying video clips.

Many publishers make their works available online (Figure 1-35). Some Web sites allow you to copy the work, such as a book or music, to your desktop computer, handheld computer, smart phone, or other mobile device.

Travel

Many vehicles manufactured today include some type of onboard navigation system. Some mobile users prefer to carry specialized handheld navigation devices (Figure 1-36).

In preparing for a trip, you may need to reserve a car, hotel, or flight. Many Web sites offer these services to the public. For example, you can order airline tickets on the Web. If you plan to drive somewhere and are unsure of the road to take to your destination, you can print directions and a map from the Web.

Manufacturing

Computer-aided manufacturing (CAM) refers to the use of computers to assist with manufacturing processes such as fabrication and assembly. Often, robots carry out processes in a CAM environment. CAM is used by a variety of industries, including oil drilling, power generation, food production, and automobile manufacturing. Automobile plants, for example, have an entire line of industrial robots that assemble a car (Figure 1-37).

FIGURE 1-35 Many magazine and newspaper publishers make the content of their publications available online.

FIGURE 1-36
This handheld navigation device gives users turn-by-turn voice-prompted directions to a destination.

FIGURE 1-37 Automotive factories use industrial robots to weld car bodies.

Test your knowledge of pages 13 through 25 in Quiz Yourself 1-3.

QUIZ YOURSELF 1-3

Instructions: Find the true statement below. Then, rewrite the remaining false statements so they are true.

1. A desktop computer is a portable, personal computer designed to fit on your lap.

2. A personal computer contains a processor, memory, and one or more input, output, and storage devices.

3. Each large business user spends time on the computer for different reasons that include budgeting and personal financial management, Web access, communications, and entertainment.

4. A home user requires the capabilities of a workstation or other powerful computer.

5. Mainframes are the fastest, most powerful computers — and the most expensive.

6. With embedded computers, users access account balances, pay bills, and copy monthly transactions from the bank's computer right into their personal computers.

Quiz Yourself Online: To further check your knowledge of categories of computers, computer users, and computer applications in society, visit scsite.com/dcf5e/ch1/quiz and then click Objectives 5 – 7.

CHAPTER SUMMARY

Chapter 1 introduced you to basic computer concepts. You learned about the components of a computer. Next, the chapter discussed networks, the Internet, and computer software. The many different categories of computers, computer users, and computer applications in society also were presented.

This chapter is an overview. Many of the terms and concepts introduced will be discussed further in later chapters. For a history of hardware and software developments, read the Timeline that follows this chapter.

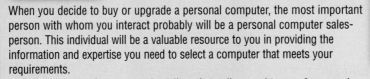

CAREER CORNER   Personal Computer Salesperson

When you decide to buy or upgrade a personal computer, the most important person with whom you interact probably will be a personal computer salesperson. This individual will be a valuable resource to you in providing the information and expertise you need to select a computer that meets your requirements.

Computer manufacturers and retailers that sell several types of personal computers need competent salespeople. A **personal computer salesperson** must be computer literate and have a specific knowledge of the computers he or she sells. The salesperson also must have a working knowledge of computer peripherals (printers, scanners, cameras, etc.). In addition, a successful salesperson has a friendly, outgoing personality that helps customers feel comfortable. Through open-ended questions, the salesperson can determine a customer's needs and level of experience. With this information, the salesperson can choose the best computer for the customer and explain the features of the computer in language the customer will understand. Most computer salespeople also can recommend a qualified installer for your computer or qualified service technician.

Computer salespeople typically have at least a high school diploma. Before reaching the sales floor, however, salespeople usually complete extensive company training programs. These programs often consist of self-directed, self-paced Web-training classes. Most salespeople also participate in training updates, often on a monthly basis.

Personal computer salespeople generally earn a guaranteed amount plus a commission for each sale. A computer salesperson can earn about $45,000 a year. Top salespeople can be among a company's more highly compensated employees, earning in excess of $90,000 including commissions. For more information, visit scsite.com/dcf5e/ch1/careers and then click Personal Computer Salesperson.

Dell
Direct Business Computer Manufacturer

As a leading manufacturer of personal computers, Dell prides itself on its direct approach to computer sales. The company hosts one of the world's largest volume e-commerce Web sites where customers can configure and price computers and electronic components, order computers, and track their orders online.

Founded by Michael Dell in 1984, the company sells more computers globally than any computer company, placing it 34th on the FORTUNE 500.

Dell partnered with Ask.com in 2007 to develop energy-efficient servers for the search engine company. Ask.com became Dell's first corporate participant in the "Plant a Tree for Me" program, which helps protect the environment by planting thousands of trees to offset carbon emissions associated with the electricity generated to power computer equipment. For more information, visit scsite.com/dcf5e/ch1/companies and then click Dell.

Apple Computer
Introducing Innovative Technologies

Millions of computer users in more than 120 countries loyally use Apple Computer's hardware and software with a passion usually reserved for sports teams and musical groups.

Steven Jobs and Stephen Wozniak founded Apple in 1976 when they marketed the Apple I, a circuit board they had developed in Jobs's garage. In 1977, Apple Computer incorporated and introduced the Apple II, the first mass-marketed personal computer. Apple introduced the Macintosh product line in 1984, which featured a graphical user interface.

Under Jobs's direction as CEO, Apple introduced award-winning desktop and notebook computers, the OS X operating system, iWork, iLife, and professional applications. The iPod is the world's most popular portable media player, and the iTunes Music Store is the number one online music store. Apple entered the smart phone market in 2007 with its iPhone. For more information, visit scsite.com/dcf5e/ch1/companies and then click Apple Computer.

TECHNOLOGY TRAILBLAZERS

Bill Gates
Microsoft's Founder

Bill Gates, the founder of Microsoft Corporation, suggests that college students should learn how to learn by getting the best education they can. Because he is considered by many as the most powerful person in the computing industry, it might be wise to listen to him.

Gates learned to program computers when he was 13. Early in his career, he developed the BASIC programming language for the MITS Altair, one of the first microcomputers. He founded Microsoft in 1975 with Paul Allen, and five years later, they provided the first operating system, called MS-DOS, for the IBM PC. Today, Microsoft's Windows and Office products dominate the software market.

In July 2008, Gates relinquished his day-to-day role in the company. He continues as chairman and advisor while devoting more time to his philanthropic efforts. For more information, visit scsite.com/dcf5e/ch1/people and then click Bill Gates.

Anne Mulcahy
Xerox CEO

Color printing and consulting services are the two areas where the Xerox Corporation can make a difference, according to Anne Mulcahy, the company's CEO and chairman of the board. She should know the nature of the business, having started her career with the Stamford, Connecticut-based corporation more than 30 years ago as a field sales representative.

One of Mulcahy's first decisions after landing the top job in 2001 was eliminating the corporation's tagline, "The Document Company." She believes the company's name, standing solo, speaks for itself in the printing, copying, and services worlds. Her ethical and values-based leadership decisions to revamp the company have revolved around Xerox's roots of innovation and customer care. She is a member of the boards of directors of Target Corporation, Citigroup, and Catalyst, a not-for-profit organization supporting women in business. For more information, visit scsite.com/dcf5e/ch1/people and then click Anne Mulcahy.

Chapter Review

The Chapter Review section summarizes the concepts presented in this chapter. To obtain help from other students regarding any subject in this chapter, visit scsite.com/dcf5e/ch1/forum and post your thoughts or questions.

1 Why Is Computer Literacy Important?

Computer literacy, also called **digital literacy**, involves having current knowledge and understanding of computers and their uses. As computers become an increasingly important part of daily living, many people believe that computer literacy is vital to success.

2 What Are the Components of a Computer?

A **computer** is an electronic device, operating under the control of instructions stored in its own memory, that can accept data, process the data according to specified rules, produce results, and store the results for future use. The electric, electronic, and mechanical components of a computer, or **hardware**, include input devices, output devices, a system unit, storage devices, and communications devices. An **input device** allows you to enter data or instructions into a computer. An **output device** conveys information to one or more people. The **system unit** is a case that contains the electronic components of a computer that are used to process data. A **storage device** records and/or retrieves items to and from storage media. A **communications device** enables a computer to send and receive data, instructions, and information to and from one or more computers.

 Visit scsite.com/dcf5e/ch1/quiz or click the Quiz Yourself button. Click Objectives 1 – 2.

3 How Are the Internet and World Wide Web Used?

The **Internet** is a worldwide collection of networks that connects millions of businesses, government agencies, educational institutions, and individuals. People use the Internet to communicate with and meet other people; conduct research and access information and news; shop for goods and services; bank and invest; take classes; for entertainment and leisure; download music and videos; and share information, photos, and videos. The **Web**, short for World Wide Web, contains billions of documents called Web pages.

4 What Are the Categories of Software?

Software, also called a **program**, is a series of instructions that tells the computer what to do and how to do it. The two categories of software are system software and application software. **System software** consists of the programs that control or maintain the operations of a computer and its devices. Two types of system software are the **operating system**, which coordinates activities among computer hardware devices, and **utility programs**, which perform maintenance-type tasks usually related to managing a computer, its devices, or its programs. **Application software** consists of programs designed to make users more productive and/or assist them with personal tasks. Popular application software includes Web browser, word processing software, spreadsheet software, database software, and presentation graphics software.

 Visit scsite.com/dcf5e/ch1/quiz or click the Quiz Yourself button. Click Objectives 3 – 4.

5 What Are the Categories of Computers?

Industry experts typically classify computers into seven categories: personal computers, mobile computers and mobile devices, game consoles, servers, mainframes, supercomputers, and embedded computers. A **personal computer** is a computer that can perform all of its input, processing, output, and storage activities by itself. A **mobile computer** is a personal computer that you can carry from place to place, and a **mobile device** is a computing device small enough to hold in your hand. A **game console** is a mobile computing device designed for single-player or multiplayer video games. A **server** controls access to the hardware, software, and other resources on a network and provides a centralized storage area for programs, data, and information. A **mainframe** is a large, expensive, powerful computer that can handle hundreds or thousands of connected users simultaneously and can store huge amounts of data, instructions, and information. A **supercomputer** is the fastest, most powerful, and most expensive computer and is used for applications requiring complex, sophisticated mathematical calculations. An **embedded computer** is a special-purpose computer that functions as a component in a larger product.

Chapter Review

6 What Are the Types of Computer Users?

Computer users can be separated into five categories: home user, small office/home office user, mobile user, power user, and large business user. A **home user** is a family member who uses a computer for a variety of reasons, such as budgeting and personal financial management, Web access, communications, and entertainment. A **small office/home office (SOHO)** includes any company with fewer than 50 employees or a self-employed individual who works from home and uses basic business software and sometimes industry-specific software. **Mobile users** are employees and students who work on a computer while away from a main office, home office, or school. A **power user** can exist in all types of businesses and uses powerful computers to work with industry-specific software. A **large business user** works in or interacts with a company with many employees and uses a computer and computer network that processes high volumes of transactions in a single day.

7 What Computer Applications Are Used in Society?

You may interact directly with computers in fields such as education, finance, government, health care, science, publishing, travel, and manufacturing. In education, students use computers and software to assist with learning or take distance learning classes. In finance, people use computers for **online banking** to access information and **online investing** to buy and sell stocks and bonds. Government offices have Web sites to provide citizens with up-to-date information, and government employees use computers as part of their daily routines. In health care, computers are used to maintain patient records, assist doctors with medical tests and research, file insurance claims, provide greater precision during operations, and as implants. All branches of science use computers to assist with collecting, analyzing, and modeling data and to communicate with scientists around the world. Publishers use computers to assist in developing pages and make their works available online. Many vehicles use some type of online navigation system to help people travel more quickly and safely. Manufacturers use **computer-aided manufacturing (CAM)** to assist with manufacturing processes.

Visit scsite.com/dcf5e/ch1/quiz or click the Quiz Yourself button. Click Objectives 5 – 7.

Key Terms

You should know the Key Terms. Use the list below to help focus your study. To further enhance your understanding of the Key Terms in this chapter, visit scsite.com/dcf5e/ch1/terms. See an example of and a definition for each term, and access current and additional information about the term from the Web.

application software (11)	handheld computer (15)	notebook computer (14)	smart phone (16)
blog (10)	handhelds (16)	online (8)	social networking Web site (10)
central processing unit (CPU) (7)	hardware (6)	online banking (23)	software (10)
communications device (8)	home user (18)	online investing (23)	storage device (7)
computer (3)	information (4)	operating system (11)	storage media (7)
computer literacy (3)	information processing cycle (5)	output device (7)	stylus (15)
computer-aided manufacturing (CAM) (25)	input device (6)	PDA (15)	supercomputer (17)
data (4)	installing (12)	personal computer (14)	system software (10)
desktop computer (14)	Internet (8)	personal computer salesperson (26)	system unit (7)
developer (12)	Internet-enabled (15)	podcast (10)	Tablet PC (15)
digital literacy (3)	laptop computer (14)	power user (21)	telecommuting (22)
embedded computer (17)	large business user (21)	processor (7)	telemedicine (24)
enterprise computing (21)	mainframe (17)	program (10)	telesurgery (24)
execute (12)	memory (7)	programmer (12)	Ultra-Mobile PC (UMPC) (15)
FAQ (4)	mobile computer (14)	run (12)	user (4)
game console (16)	mobile device (14)	server (16)	utility program (11)
graphical user interface (GUI) (10)	mobile users (20)	small office/home office (SOHO) (20)	Web (10)
	network (8)		Web page (10)

Checkpoint

Use the Checkpoint exercises to check your knowledge level of the chapter. To complete the Checkpoint exercises interactively, visit scsite.com/dcf5e/ch1/check.

True/False

Mark T for True and F for False. (See page numbers in parentheses.)

_____ 1. Most people do not believe that computer literacy is vital to success. (3)

_____ 2. A computer contains many electric, electronic, and mechanical components known as hardware. (6)

_____ 3. The circuitry of the system unit usually is part of or is connected to a circuit board called the server. (7)

_____ 4. A network is a collection of computers and devices connected together, often wirelessly, via communications devices and transmission media. (8)

_____ 5. Web pages rarely have built-in connections, or links, to other documents, graphics, other Web pages, or Web sites. (10)

_____ 6. With a graphical user interface, you interact with the software using text, graphics, and visual images such as icons. (10)

_____ 7. System software serves as the interface between the user, the application software, and the computer's hardware. (10)

_____ 8. Because embedded computers are components in larger products, they usually are large and include extensive hardware. (18)

_____ 9. Large businesses typically have e-commerce Web sites, allowing customers and vendors to conduct business online. (21)

_____ 10. Employees who telecommute have flexible work schedules so that they can combine work and personal responsibilities, such as child care. (22)

Multiple Choice

Select the best answer. (See page numbers in parentheses.)

1. Computer literacy, also known as digital literacy, involves having a current knowledge and understanding of _____. (3)
   a. computer programming
   b. computers and their uses
   c. computer repair
   d. all of the above

2. _____ is/are a collection of unprocessed items, which can include text, numbers, images, audio, and video. (4)
   a. Information
   b. Instructions
   c. Programs
   d. Data

3. Millions of people worldwide join online communities, each called _____ , that encourage members to share their interests, ideas, stories, photos, music, and videos with other registered users. (10)
   a. a podcast
   b. enterprise computing
   c. a social networking Web site
   d. a blog

4. _____ consists of the programs that control or maintain the operations of the computer and its devices. (10)
   a. System software
   b. A communications device
   c. A graphical user interface (GUI)
   d. Application software

5. Two types of _____ are desktop computers and notebook computers. (14)
   a. servers
   b. supercomputers
   c. mainframe computers
   d. personal computers

6. Three popular types of _____ are handheld computers, PDAs, and smart phones. (15)
   a. mobile devices
   b. notebook computers
   c. desktop computers
   d. tower computers

7. _____ refers to the huge network of computers that meets a large company's diverse computing needs. (21)
   a. Enterprise computing
   b. Embedded computing
   c. Telecommuting
   d. Application software

8. When using _____ , users access account balances, pay bills, and copy monthly transactions from a bank's computer right into their computers. (23)
   a. e-commerce
   b. online banking
   c. personal finance software
   d. accounting software

Matching

Match the terms with their definitions. (See page numbers in parentheses.)

_____ 1. information processing cycle (5)

_____ 2. processor (7)

_____ 3. storage device (7)

_____ 4. operating system (11)

_____ 5. handheld computer (15)

a. fastest, most powerful computer — and the most expensive

b. a computer small enough to fit in one hand

c. records (writes) and/or retrieves (reads) items to and from storage media

d. series of input, process, output, and storage activities

e. electronic component that interprets and carries out the basic instructions for a computer

f. set of programs that coordinates all the activities among computer hardware devices

Checkpoint

Short Answer

Write a brief answer to each of the following questions.

1. What does it mean to be computer literate? _____ What is a computer? _____
2. How is an input device different from an output device? _____ What are commonly used input and output devices? _____
3. What are five common storage devices? _____ How are they different? _____
4. How is hardware different from software? _____ What are two types of system software and how are they used? _____
5. How do computers benefit individuals' health care? _____ How does telesurgery differ from telemedicine? _____

Working Together

Working in a group of your classmates, complete the following team exercise.

1. Computers are everywhere. Watching television, driving a car, using a charge card, ordering fast food, and the more obvious activity of typing a term paper on a personal computer, all involve interaction with computers. For one day, have each member of your team make a list of every computer he or she encounters (be careful not to limit yourselves just to the computers you see). Meet with the members of your team and combine your lists. Consider how each computer is used. How were the tasks the computers perform done before computers? Create a group presentation and share your findings with the class.

Web Research

Use the Internet-based Web Research exercises to broaden your understanding of the concepts presented in this chapter. To discuss any of the Web Research exercises in this chapter with other students, post your thoughts or questions at scsite.com/dcf5e/ch1/forum.

(1) Blogs   Blogs profiling the music industry discuss new technologies, legal issues, podcasts, and business news. Visit the CNET blog (blogs.cnet.com) and then locate the Digital Noise: Music & Tech feature. Read at least three stories and associated comments and then summarize these stories. On what topics do the bloggers commenting on these stories agree and disagree? Then visit the iLounge (ilounge.com) Web site and read reviews of at least three new products for the iPod. Would you purchase any of the products discussed? What podcasts are available to download? Which earphones and speakers received favorable reviews?

(2) Scavenger Hunt   Use one of the search engines listed in Figure 2-8 in Chapter 2 on page 58 or your own favorite search engine to find the answers to the following questions. Copy and paste the Web address from the Web page where you found the answer. Some questions may have more than one answer. If required, submit your answers to your instructor. (1) Who designed the icons for the original Macintosh computer? (2) Two National Science Foundation (NSF) programs were established in 1997 to interconnect 50 university and scientific computing sites. What colleges host these two sites? What were the locations of the five original NSF-financed supercomputer centers? (3) What is the name of the first spreadsheet program? (4) Which programming language developed by the U.S. Department of Defense was named to honor a famous woman mathematician?

(3) Search Sleuth   Visit the Google Web site (google.com) and then click the About Google link at the bottom of the page. Using your word processing program, answer the following questions and then, if required, submit your answers to your instructor. (1) Below Our Company, click Jobs at Google. What job opportunities are available for students? (2) Click your browser's Back button or press the BACKSPACE key to return to the About Google page. Below the Our Products heading, click the Google Labs link. Describe three of the prototypes being developed. (3) Click your browser's Back button to return to the Google home page. In the Google Search text box, type blog and click the Google Search button. Approximately how many hits resulted? Do any definitions appear? If so, list the definitions. How much time did it take to complete the search? (4) In the Google Search text box, type video blog and click the Search button. Compare this to your earlier search. Are there more or fewer hits? How much time did it take to complete the second search? (5) Click one of the resulting video blog links and review the information. Write a 50-word summary. Using the information contained within the Web site, do you think you have sufficient knowledge to create a blog?

Learn How To

Use the Learn How To activities to learn fundamental skills when using a computer and accompanying technology. Complete the exercises and submit them to your instructor. Premium Activity: The icon indicates you can see a visual demonstration of the associated Learn How To activity by visiting scsite.com/dcf5e/ch1/howto.

LEARN HOW TO 1: Start and Close a Program

A program accomplishes tasks on a computer. You can start any program by using the Start button.

Complete these steps to start the Web browser program called Internet Explorer:
1. Click the Start button ( ) at the left of the Windows taskbar on the bottom of the screen to display the Start menu.
2. Click All Programs on the Start menu to display the All Programs list (Figure 1-38).
3. Click the program name, Internet Explorer, in the All Programs list to open the Internet Explorer browser window (Figure 1-39).

An item in the All Programs list might have an open folder icon next to it. When this occurs, click the item and another list will appear. Click the program name in this list to start the program. Some program names might appear on the Start menu itself. If so, click any of these names to start the corresponding program.

Below the line on the left side of the Start menu, Windows displays the names of the programs recently opened on the computer. You can start any of these programs by clicking the name of the program.

To close a program, click the Close button ( ) in the upper-right corner of the window. If you have created but not saved a document, Windows will ask if you want to save the document. If you do not want to save it, click the No button in the displayed dialog box. If you want to save it, refer to Learn How To number 1 in Chapter 3 on page 130.

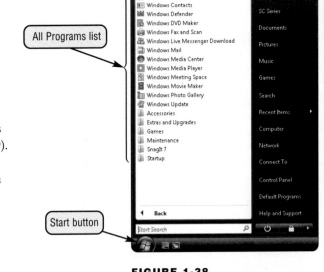

FIGURE 1-38

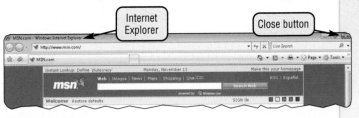

FIGURE 1-39

Exercise

1. Using the Start button, start the program named WordPad found in the Accessories list in the All Programs list. WordPad is a word processing program. Type the following: To start a program, click the program name in the All Programs list and then type your name. Click the Print button ( ) on the toolbar. Submit the printout to your instructor.
2. Close the WordPad program. If you are asked if you want to save changes to the document, click the No button. Start the WordPad program again, type some new text, and then close the WordPad program. When the dialog box is displayed, click the Cancel button. What happened? Now, close the WordPad window without saving the document. Submit your answer to your instructor.
3. Using the Start button, start the e-mail program on the computer. What is the name of the e-mail program? In the program window, what menu names are displayed on the menu bar at the top of the window? Close the e-mail program. Submit your answers to your instructor.

LEARN HOW TO 2: Create and Use Your Own Blog

A blog can contain any information you wish to place in it. Originally, blogs consisted of Web addresses, so that an individual or group with a specific interest could direct others to useful places on the Web. Today, blogs contain addresses, thoughts, diaries, and anything else a person or group wants to share.

Once you have created a blog, you can update it. A variety of services available on the Web can help you create and maintain your blog. One widely used service is called Blogger. To create a blog using Blogger, complete the following steps:

1. Start your Web browser, type www.blogger.com in the Address bar, and then press the ENTER key to display the Blogger home page (Figure 1-40).
2. Click the CREATE YOUR BLOG NOW arrow on the Blogger home page.
3. Enter the data required on the 'Create an account' page. Your user name and password will allow you to change and manage your blog. Your Display name is the name that will be shown on the blog as the author of the material on the blog. Many people use their own names, but others use pseudonyms as their "pen names" so that they are not readily identifiable.
4. Click the Continue arrow and then enter your Blog title and Blog address. These are the names and addresses everyone will use to view your blog.
5. Click the Continue arrow to display the 'Choose a template' screen.
6. Choose a template for your blog and then click the Continue arrow.
7. Your blog will be created for you. When you see the 'Your blog has been created' screen, click the Start posting arrow.
8. From the screen that is displayed, you can post items for your blog, specify settings, change the template, and view your blog.
9. When you have posted all your information, click the Sign out button at the top right of the screen. You will be logged out.
10. To edit your blog and add or change information on it, visit the Blogger home page and sign in by entering your user name and password. You will be able to post to your blog.
11. Others can view your blog by entering its address in the browser's Address bar and then pressing the ENTER key.

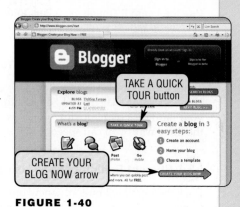

FIGURE 1-40

Exercise

1. Start your Web browser and visit www.blogger.com. Click the TAKE A QUICK TOUR button and go through all the screens that explain about a blog. What did you learn that you did not know? What type of blog do you find most compelling — a group or an individual blog? Why? Submit your answers to your instructor.
2. Optional: Create your own blog. Carefully name it and begin your posts at this time. What is your blog name and address? What is its primary purpose? Is it an individual or group blog? Write a paragraph containing the answers to these questions and any other information you feel is pertinent. Submit this paragraph to your instructor.

 LEARN HOW TO 3: Use the Discovering Computers Fundamentals 5e Online Companion (scsite.com/dcf5e)

The Discovering Computers Fundamentals 5e Online Companion provides a variety of activities and exercises. To use the site, you first must register and establish a user name and password. Perform the following steps to register:
1. Start the Web browser.
2. Type scsite.com/dcf5e in the Address bar of the Web browser. Press the ENTER key.
3. When the registration page is displayed, click the New User Registration link.
4. Follow the on-screen instructions to complete registration.

When you first type a Web address to display a page from the dcf5e site, you must enter your user name and password to gain access to the site. When you are finished using the site, close the browser so that no one else can visit the site with your user name and password.

Exercise

1. Start the Web browser on your computer.
2. Type scsite.com/dcf5e/ch1/howto in the Address bar of the browser and then press the ENTER key.
3. If the registration page is displayed and you have not yet registered, complete the steps above. If you are registered, enter your user name and password, and then click the Enter button.
4. Navigate to the Chapter 1 home page.
5. Visit each of the Exercises Web pages.
6. Click the browser's Close button to close the program.
7. Write a report that describes the use of each of the Exercises pages you visited. Which page do you think will prove the most valuable to you when using the book and the Web site? Why? Which will be the least useful? Why? Submit your report to your instructor.

Learn It Online

Use the Learn It Online exercises to reinforce your understanding of the chapter concepts. To access the Learn It Online exercises, visit scsite.com/dcf5e/ch1/learn.

① At the Movies — Speed Up Your Hard Drive (aka Hard Disk)

To view the Speed Up Your Hard Drive movie, click the number 1 button. Locate your video and click the corresponding High-Speed or Dial-Up link, depending on your Internet connection. Watch the movie to learn how to optimize the speed of your hard disk by removing unnecessary files. Then, complete the exercise by answering the questions that follow: What are the three ways you can speed up your computer? Why is it beneficial to do this periodically?

② Student Edition Labs — Using Input Devices

Click the number 2 button. A new browser window will open, displaying the Student Edition Labs. Follow the on-screen instructions to complete the Using Input Devices Lab. When finished, click the Exit button. If required, submit your results to your instructor.

③ Practice Test

Click the number 3 button. Answer each question. When completed, enter your name and click the Grade Test button to submit the quiz for grading. Make a note of any missed questions. If required, submit your score to your instructor.

④ Who Wants To Be a Computer Genius^2?

Click the number 4 button to find out if you are a computer genius. Directions about how to play the game will be displayed. When you are ready to play, click the Play button. Submit your score to your instructor.

⑤ Google Maps

Click the number 5 button to learn how to locate businesses in your area, view a location's surroudings via satellite, and find directions from one location to another. Print a copy of the Google Maps page and then step through the exercise. If required, submit your results to your instructor.

⑥ Student Edition Labs — Using Windows

Click the number 6 button. A new browser window will open, displaying the Student Edition Labs. Follow the on-screen instructions to complete the Using Windows Lab. When finished, click the Exit button. If required, submit your results to your instructor.

⑦ Crossword Puzzle Challenge

Click the number 7 button, and then click the Crossword Puzzle Challenge link. Directions about how to play the game will be displayed. Complete the puzzle to reinforce skills you learned in this chapter. When you are ready to play, click the Continue button. Submit the completed puzzle to your instructor.

⑧ Vista Exercises

Click the number 8 button. When the Vista Exercises menu appears, click the exercise assigned by your instructor. A new browser window will open. Follow the on-screen instructions to complete the exercise. When finished, click the Exit button. If required, submit your results to your instructor.

Timeline

MILESTONES IN COMPUTER HISTORY

Dr. John V. Atanasoff and Clifford Berry design and build the first electronic digital computer. Their machine, the Atanasoff-Berry-Computer, or ABC, provides the foundation for advances in electronic digital computers.

John von Neumann poses in front of the electronic computer built at the Institute for Advanced Study. This computer and its von Neumann architecture served as the prototype for subsequent stored program computers worldwide.

William Shockley, John Bardeen, and Walter Brattain invent the transfer resistance device, eventually called the transistor. The transistor would revolutionize computers, proving much more reliable than vacuum tubes.

1937   **1943**   **1945**   **1946**   **1947**   **1951**

Dr. John W. Mauchly and J. Presper Eckert, Jr. complete work on the first large-scale electronic, general-purpose digital computer. The ENIAC (Electronic Numerical Integrator And Computer) weighs 30 tons, contains 18,000 vacuum tubes, occupies a 30 × 50 foot space, and consumes 160 kilowatts of power. The first time it is turned on, lights dim in an entire section of Philadelphia.

The first commercially available electronic digital computer, the UNIVAC I (UNIVersal Automatic Computer), is introduced by Remington Rand. Public awareness of computers increases when the UNIVAC I, after analyzing only five percent of the popular vote, correctly predicts that Dwight D. Eisenhower will win the presidential election.

During World War II, British scientist Alan Turing designs the Colossus, an electronic computer created for the military to break German codes. The computer's existence is kept secret until the 1970s.

Dr. Grace Hopper considers the concept of reusable software in her paper, "The Education of a Computer." The paper describes how to program a computer with symbolic notation instead of the detailed machine language that had been used.

The IBM 305 RAMAC system is the first to use magnetic disk for external storage. The system provides storage capacity similar to magnetic tape that previously was used, but offers the advantage of semi-random access capability.

More than 200 programming languages have been created.

IBM introduces two smaller, desk-sized computers: the IBM 1401 for business and the IBM 1620 for scientists. The IBM 1620 initially is called the CADET, but IBM drops the name when campus wags claim it is an acronym for, Can't Add, Doesn't Even Try.

Fortran (FORmula TRANslation), an efficient, easy-to-use programming language, is introduced by John Backus.

1952　1953　1957　1958　1959　1960

The IBM model 650 is one of the first widely used computers. Originally planning to produce only 50 machines, the system is so successful that eventually IBM manufactures more than 1,000. With the IBM 700 series of machines, the company will dominate the mainframe market for the next decade.

Core memory, developed in the early 1950s, provides much larger storage capacity than vacuum tube memory.

Jack Kilby of Texas Instruments invents the integrated circuit, which lays the foundation for high-speed computers and large-capacity memories. Computers built with transistors mark the beginning of the second generation of computer hardware.

COBOL, a high-level business application language, is developed by a committee headed by Dr. Grace Hopper. COBOL uses English-like phrases and runs on most business computers, making it one of the more widely used programming languages.

IBM

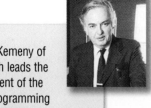

Dr. John Kemeny of Dartmouth leads the development of the BASIC programming language. BASIC will be used widely on personal computers.

Computer Science Corporation becomes the first software company listed on the New York Stock Exchange.

CSC STOCK PRICE
NYSE/COMPOSITE
Corrected Data for Dividends

DATE	PRICE	HIGH	LO
1/02/68	2.83	2.97	2
1/03/68	2.60	2.81	2
1/04/68	2.	2	
1/05/68		4	
1/08/68			
1/09/68	5	2.60	
1/10/68		2	
		.51	
		2.51	13.500
		2.48	23.400
		2.49	7.800

CSC

Under pressure from the industry, IBM announces that some of its software will be priced separately from the computer hardware. This unbundling allows software firms to emerge in the industry.

Digital Equipment Corporation (DEC) introduces the first minicomputer, the PDP-8. The machine is used extensively as an interface for time-sharing systems.

In a letter to the editor titled, "GO TO Statements Considered Harmful," Dr. Edsger Dijsktra introduces the concept of structured programming, developing standards for constructing computer programs.

ARPANET

The ARPANET network, a predecessor of the Internet, is established.

1964   1965   1968   1969   1970

The number of computers has grown to 18,000. Third-generation computers, with their controlling circuitry stored on chips, are introduced. The IBM System/360 computer is the first family of compatible machines, merging science and business lines.

Alan Shugart at IBM demonstrates the first regular use of an 8-inch floppy (magnetic storage) disk.

Fourth-generation computers, built with chips that use LSI (large-scale integration) arrive. While the chips used in 1965 contained as many as 1,000 circuits, the LSI chip contains as many as 15,000.

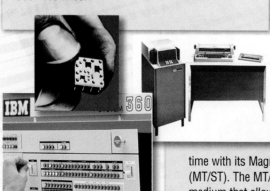

IBM introduces the term word processing for the first time with its Magnetic Tape/Selectric Typewriter (MT/ST). The MT/ST was the first reusable storage medium that allowed typed material to be edited without having to retype the document.

MITS, Inc. advertises one of the first microcomputers, the Altair. Named for the destination in an episode of *Star Trek*, the Altair is sold in kits for less than $400. Although initially it has no keyboard, no monitor, no permanent memory, and no software, 4,000 orders are taken within the first three months.

VisiCalc, a spreadsheet program written by Bob Frankston and Dan Bricklin, is introduced. Originally written to run on Apple II computers, VisiCalc will be seen as the most important reason for the acceptance of personal computers in the business world.

The IBM PC is introduced, signaling IBM's entrance into the personal computer marketplace. The IBM PC quickly garners the largest share of the personal computer market and becomes the personal computer of choice in business.

tors of ViSiCalc

Ethernet, the first local area network (LAN), is developed at Xerox PARC (Palo Alto Research Center) by Robert Metcalf. The LAN allows computers to communicate and share software, data, and peripherals. Initially designed to link minicomputers, Ethernet will be extended to personal computers.

The first public online information services, CompuServe and the Source, are founded.

1971 1975 1976 1979 1980 1981

Dr. Ted Hoff of Intel Corporation develops a microprocessor, or microprogrammable computer chip, the Intel 4004.

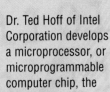

IBM offers Microsoft Corporation cofounder, Bill Gates, the opportunity to develop the operating system for the soon-to-be announced IBM personal computer. With the development of MS-DOS, Microsoft achieves tremendous growth and success.

The first computer virus, Elk Cloner, is spread via Apple II floppy disks, which contained the operating system. A short rhyme would appear on the screen when the user pressed Reset after the 50th boot of an infected disk.

Steve Jobs and Steve Wozniak build the first Apple computer. A subsequent version, the Apple II, is an immediate success. Adopted by elementary schools, high schools, and colleges, for many students, the Apple II is their first contact with the world of computers.

Alan Shugart presents the Winchester hard drive, revolutionizing storage for personal computers.

3,275,000 personal computers are sold, almost 3,000,000 more than in 1981.

Apple introduces the Macintosh computer, which incorporates a unique, easy-to-learn, graphical user interface.

Compaq, Inc. is founded to develop and market IBM-compatible PCs.

Hewlett-Packard announces the first LaserJet printer for personal computers.

Microsoft

Microsoft has public stock offering and raises approximately $61 million. Within 20 years, Microsoft's stock is worth nearly $350 billion or 5,735 times the amount raised in the initial public stock offering.

Hayes introduces the 300 bps smart modem. The modem is an immediate success.

1982   **1983**   **1984**   **1986**   **1988**

Instead of choosing a person for its annual award, *TIME* magazine names the computer Machine of the Year for 1982, acknowledging the impact of computers on society.

Lotus Development Corporation is founded. Its spreadsheet software, Lotus 1-2-3, which combines spreadsheet, graphics, and database programs in one package, becomes the best-selling program for IBM personal computers.

Microsoft surpasses Lotus Development Corporation to become the world's top software vendor.

World Wide Web Consortium releases standards that describe a framework for linking documents on different computers.

Several companies introduce computers using the Pentium processor from Intel. The Pentium chip is the successor to the Intel 486 processor. It contains 3.1 million transistors and is capable of performing 112,000,000 instructions per second.

While working at CERN, Switzerland, Tim Berners-Lee invents an Internet-based hypermedia enterprise for information sharing. Berners-Lee will call this innovation the World Wide Web.

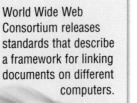

Microsoft releases Microsoft Office 3 Professional, the first version of Microsoft Office.

1989   1991   1992   1993

The Intel 486 becomes the world's first 1,000,000 transistor microprocessor. It crams 1.2 million transistors on a .4" x .6" sliver of silicon and executes 15,000,000 instructions per second — four times as fast as its predecessor, the 80386 chip.

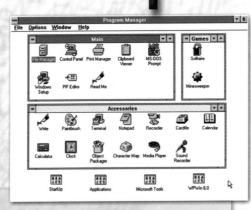

Microsoft releases Windows 3.1, the latest version of its Windows operating system. Windows 3.1 offers improvements such as TrueType fonts, multimedia capability, and object linking and embedding (OLE). In two months, 3,000,000 copies of Windows 3.1 are sold.

The White House launches its Web site, which includes an interactive citizens' handbook and White House history and tours.

U.S. Robotics introduces the PalmPilot, a low-cost, user-friendly personal digital assistant (PDA).

Sun Microsystems launches Java, an object-oriented programming language that allows users to write one application for a variety of computer platforms.

Microsoft releases Windows NT 4.0, an operating system for client-server networks.

Jim Clark and Marc Andreessen found Netscape and launch Netscape Navigator 1.0, a browser for the World Wide Web.

1994   1995   1996   1997

Linus Torvalds creates the Linux kernel, a UNIX-like operating system that he releases free across the Internet for further enhancement by other programmers.

Microsoft releases Windows 95, a major upgrade to its Windows operating system. Windows 95 consists of more than 10,000,000 lines of computer instructions developed by 300 person-years of effort.

Intel introduces the Pentium II processor with 7.5 million transistors. The new processor, which incorporates MMX technology, processes video, audio, and graphics data more efficiently and supports applications such as movie editing, gaming, and more.

Microsoft releases Internet Explorer 4.0 and seizes a key place in the Internet arena. This new Web browser is greeted with tremendous customer demand.

Microsoft introduces Office 2000, its premier productivity suite, offering new tools for users to create content and save it directly to a Web site without any file conversion or special steps.

Apple Computer introduces the iMac, the next version of its popular Macintosh computer. The iMac abandons such conventional features as a floppy disk drive but wins customers with its futuristic design, see-through case, and easy setup.

Open source software, such as the Linux operating system and the Apache Web server created by unpaid volunteers, begin to gain wide acceptance among computer users.

1998

1999

E-commerce, or electronic commerce, booms. Companies such as Dell, E*TRADE, and Amazon.com spur online shopping, allowing buyers to obtain a variety of goods and services.

Governments and businesses frantically work to make their computers Y2K (Year 2000) compliant, spending more than $500 billion worldwide. Y2K noncompliant computers cannot distinguish whether 01/01/00 refers to 1900 or 2000, and thus may operate using a wrong date. This Y2K bug can affect any application that relies on computer chips, such as ATMs, airplanes, energy companies, and the telephone system.

Microsoft ships Windows 98, an upgrade to Windows 95. Windows 98 offers improved Internet access, better system performance, and support for a new generation of hardware and software.

Shawn Fanning, 19, and his company, Napster, turn the music industry upside down by developing software that allows computer users to swap music files with one another without going through a centralized file server. The Recording Industry of America, on behalf of five media companies, sues Napster for copyright infringement and wins.

Microsoft releases major operating system updates with Windows XP for the desktop and servers. Windows XP is significantly more reliable than previous versions, features a 32-bit computing architecture, and offers a new look and feel. Pocket PC 2002 offers the handheld computer user a familiar Windows interface and consistent functionality.

Microsoft ships Windows 2000 and Windows Me. Windows 2000 offers improved behind-the-scenes security and reliability.

Intel unveils its Pentium 4 chip with clock speeds starting at 1.4 GHz. The Pentium 4 includes 42 million transistors.

2000

2001

E-commerce achieves mainstream acceptance. Annual e-commerce sales exceed $100 billion, and Internet advertising expenditures reach more than $5 billion.

Telemedicine uses satellite technology and video conferencing to broadcast consultations and to perform distant surgeries. Robots are used for complex and precise tasks. Computer-aided surgery uses virtual reality to assist with training and planning procedures.

Microsoft introduces Office XP, the next version of the world's leading suite of productivity software. Features include speech and hand-writing recognition, smart tags, and task panes.

Dot-com companies (Internet based) go out of business at a record pace — nearly one per day — as financial investors withhold funding due to the companies' unprofitability.

After several years of negligible sales, the Tablet PC is reintroduced as the next-generation mobile PC. The lightweight device, the size of a three-ring notebook, is ideal for people on the go.

Digital video cameras, DVD writers, easy-to-use video editing software, and improvements in storage capabilities allow the average computer user to create Hollywood-like videos with introductions, conclusions, scenes rearranged, music, and voice-over.

Wireless computers and devices, such as keyboards, mouse devices, home networks, and wireless Internet access points become commonplace. Latest operating systems include support for both the Wi-Fi (wireless fidelity) and Bluetooth standards. Wireless capabilities are standard on many personal mobile devices.

2002

2003

Microsoft launches its .NET strategy, which is a new environment for developing and running software applications featuring ease of development of Web-based services.

Microsoft ships Office 2003, the latest version of its flagship Office suite. More than 400 million people in 175 nations and 70 languages are using a version of Office.

Intel ships its revamped Pentium 4 chip with the 0.13 micron processor and Hyper-Threading (HT) Technology, operating at speeds of 3.06 GHz. This new development eventually will enable processors with a billion transistors to operate at 20 GHz.

DVD writers begin to replace CD writers (CD-RW). DVDs can store up to eight times as much data as CDs. Uses include storing home movies, music, photos, and backups.

In an attempt to maintain their current business model of selling songs, the Recording Industry Association of America (RIAA) files more than 250 lawsuits against individual computer users who offer copyrighted music over peer-to-peer networks.

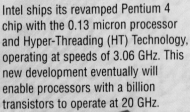

Companies such as RealNetworks, Microsoft, Sony, and Wal-Mart stake out turf in the online music store business started by Apple Computer. In the previous year, Apple's iTunes Music Store Web site sold nearly 20 million songs for 99 cents each.

USB flash drives become a cost-effective way to transport data and information from one computer to another.

Video-Pod

Apple releases the latest version of its popular pocket-sized iPod portable media player. First it played songs, then photos, then podcasts, and now, in addition, up to 150 hours of music videos and TV shows on a 2.5" color display.

Flat-panel LCD monitors overtake bulky CRT monitors as the popular choice of computer users. Flat-panel LCD monitors offer several advantages including physical size, weight, true display size, better power consumption, and no radiation emission.

Major retailers begin requiring suppliers to include radio frequency identification (RFID) tags or microchips with antennas, which can be as small as 1/3 of a millimeter across, in the goods they sell. RFIDs eventually may eliminate long checkout lines.

Microsoft introduces Visual Studio 2005. The product includes Visual Basic, Visual C#, Visual J#, Visual C++, and SQL Server. Microsoft also releases a Visual Studio 2005 Express Edition for hobbyists, students, and nonprofessionals.

Spam, spyware, phishing, pharming, spim, and spit take center stage, along with viruses, as major nuisances to the 801 million computer users worldwide.

Spyware
Spam Pharming
Phishing
Spim Spit

2004   2005

106 million, or 53 percent, of the 200 million online population in America accesses the Internet via speedy broadband.

Linux, the open source operating system, makes major inroads into the server market as a viable alternative to Microsoft Windows, Sun's Solaris, and the UNIX operating systems.

The smart phone overtakes the PDA as the personal mobile device of choice. A smart phone offers the user a cell phone, full personal information management and e-mail functionality, a Web browser, instant message capabilities, and even the ability to listen to music, watch and record video, play games, and take pictures.

Microsoft unveils Windows XP Media Center Edition 2005. This operating system allows users to access the routine capabilities of a Windows XP-based PC while focusing on delivering media content such as music, digital photos, movies, and television.

Blogging
Podcasting

Blogging and podcasting become mainstream methods for distributing information via the Web.

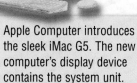

Linux

Apple Computer introduces the sleek iMac G5. The new computer's display device contains the system unit.

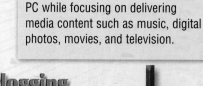

Microsoft releases the Xbox 360, its latest game console. Features include the capability to play music, display photos, and network with computers and other Xbox games.

Sony launches its PlayStation 3. New features include a Blu-ray Disc player, high-definition capabilities, and always-on online connectivity. Sony hopes to continue its advantage over Microsoft. Since the release of Microsoft's Xbox 360 in 2005, Sony's PS2 has outsold the Xbox 360 by nearly a 2-to-1 margin. Nintendo releases the Wii, featuring the wireless Wii Remote that allows users to control the game using physical gestures as well as traditional button presses through the use of motion-sensing technology.

Microsoft and Mozilla release new versions of their respective Web browsers. Microsoft's Internet Explorer 7 and Mozilla's Firefox 2 offer easier browsing through the use of tabs and allow search capabilities directly from the toolbar. They also offer enhanced security features to protect from phishing and to help defend against malware.

San Francisco and Philadelphia are among municipalities across the United States deploying low-cost, high-speed, broadband wireless connectivity to all points within their jurisdiction. Citizens access the Internet at broadband speeds using wireless desktop computers, notebook computers, or mobile devices to connect to Wi-Fi access points.

myspace.com
a place for friends™

Web 2.0, a term coined in 2004, becomes a household term with the popularity of social networking Web sites such as MySpace, Facebook, and YouTube. MySpace reaches 80 million registered users, most between the ages of 18 and 40. Facebook surpasses 13 million registered users and becomes the number one photo sharing site on the Web. YouTube becomes the most popular video sharing Web site with people watching and sharing more than 70 million videos a day.

2006

Google

Google, founded in 1998, is the most used search engine, capturing 54 percent of the market over Yahoo! and MSN. It is estimated that Google receives approximately 1 billion search requests per day.

Intel introduces its Core 2 Duo processor family. Boasting record-breaking performance while using less power, the family consists of five desktop computer processors and five mobile computer processors. The desktop processor includes 291 million transistors, yet uses 40 percent less power than the Pentium processor.

IBM produces the fastest supercomputer called Blue Gene/L. It can perform approximately 28 trillion calculations in the time it takes you to blink your eye, or about one-tenth of a second. They also start a project called the World Community Grid that links nearly 100,000 personal computers worldwide. Computer owners volunteer the use of their computers when the computers otherwise would be sitting idle. The Blue Gene/L primarily is used to explore hydrodynamics, quantum chemistry, molecular dynamics, climate modeling, and financial modeling, while the World Community Grid will be used, among other projects, to maintain an up-to-date HIV/AIDS database as the virus evolves into drug-resistant forms.

Apple begins selling Macintosh computers with Intel microprocessors.

In response to Apple's popular iPod, Microsoft unveils the Zune. Among its features is a 30 GB portable media player; the Zune Marketplace music service; wireless technology; a built-in FM tuner; and a bright, 3″ screen.

Intel introduces Core 2 Quad, a four-core processor made for dual-processor servers and desktop computers. The larger number of cores allows for more energy-efficient performance and optimizes battery performance in notebook computers.

As the popularity of YouTube has grown, so have video blogs, or vlogs. Vlogs allow users to video their message instead of entering text via a regular blog. The growth in the popularity of vlogs can be attributed to several factors, including the use of video portable media players. Podcasting also has increased in popularity for the same reasons. A podcast is distinguished from other digital audio formats by its capability to be downloaded automatically.

Apple introduces the iPhone and sells 270,000 phones in the first two days. iPhone uses iTouch technology that allows you to make a call simply by tapping a name or number in your address book. It also stores and plays music like an iPod. Apple sells its one billionth song on iTunes.

Apple releases its Mac OS X version 10.5 "Leopard" operating system, available in a desktop version and server version. The system includes a significantly revised desktop, with a semitransparent menu bar and an updated search tool that incorporates the same visual navigation interface as iTunes. Other features include an auto-mated backup utility and the capability to perform searches across multiple computers.

VoIP (Voice over Internet Protocol) providers expand usage to include Wi-Fi phones. The phones enable high-quality service through a Wireless-G network and high-speed Internet connection.

2007

Half of the world's population uses cell phones. More and more people are using a cell phone in lieu of a landline in their home. Although some studies predict that 37 percent of Americans will use their cell phone as their sole telephone, a major concern is their use for 911 calls. Only 58 percent of U.S. emergency dispatch centers have the technology to track cell phone calls.

Blu-ray and HD DVD increase in popularity. While a Blu-ray Disc (BD) can hold more data than an HD DVD disc, the HD DVD players are much less expensive and still have enough capacity to hold a high-definition movie. A Blu-ray Disc can store about 9 hours of high-definition (HD) video on a 50 GB disc and about 23 hours of standard-definition (SD) video. HD DVD capacity is limited to a maximum of 45 GB.

Microsoft releases the latest version of its flagship Office suite. New features include the most significant update to the user interface in more than a decade, including the introduction of the Ribbon, which replaces the toolbars in most of the programs, and the capability to save documents in XML and PDF formats.

Microsoft ships the latest version of its widely used operating system, Windows Vista. Windows Vista focuses on greatly improving security, deployment, manageability, and performance. Vista offers a Basic interface and the Aero interface, which offers several graphic features including transparent windows. Internet Explorer 7 is included with Windows Vista.

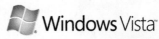

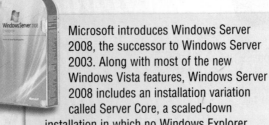

Microsoft introduces Windows Server 2008, the successor to Windows Server 2003. Along with most of the new Windows Vista features, Windows Server 2008 includes an installation variation called Server Core, a scaled-down installation in which no Windows Explorer shell is installed and all configuration and maintenance is accomplished entirely through command-line interface windows.

Bill Gates announces his retirement from Microsoft. He will continue as chairman and advisor on key development projects. Gates plans to devote more time to the Bill & Melinda Gates Foundation and its work on global health and education.

The Versatile Multilayer Disc (HD VMD) is introduced and is intended to compete with HD DVD and Blu-ray Disc. The HD VMD has a capacity of 30 GB per side. Players are available for as low as $150, and some have USB ports for connection to external storage devices.

Online social networks continue to grow in popularity, with MySpace and Facebook being the most widely used. Combined social networking Web sites total almost 1 billion users, with MySpace and Facebook alone boasting more than 360 million users. YouTube continues to gain users. In 2008, presidential candidates use the popular video sharing Web site as an outlet for promoting their candidacies. The number of blogs has grown to more than 100 million.

2008

In February 2009, federal law will require that all full-power television stations broadcast only in digital format. Analog television owners will be required to purchase a converter box to view over-the-air digital programming. Between January 2008 and March 2009, all U.S. households can request up to two coupons, worth $40 each, to be used toward the purchase of digital-to-analog converter boxes. Analog televisions connected to a paid provider such as cable or satellite television service will not need an additional converter box.

Nintendo Wii becomes a leader in game consoles and is being used in revolutionary ways, such as training surgeons. Studies show that surgeons who play the video game for 3 hours a week make 37 percent fewer mistakes on laparoscopic surgery and perform the surgery 27 percent faster.

WiMAX goes live! The advantage of this technology is the capability to access video, music, voice, and video calls wherever and whenever desired. Average download speeds are between 2 Mbps and 4 Mbps. By year's end, Sprint anticipates 100 million users on its network.

Notebook computer sales continue to rise, overtaking desktop computers. Advances in technology and decreasing notebook computer prices have businesses as well as individuals rapidly replacing desktop computers with more mobile notebook computers.

CHAPTER 2

The Internet and World Wide Web

OBJECTIVES

After completing this chapter, you will be able to:

1. **Explain how to access and connect to the Internet**
2. **Explain how to view pages and search for information on the Web**
3. **Describe the types of Web sites**
4. **Identify the steps required for Web publishing**
5. **Describe the types of e-commerce**
6. **Explain how e-mail, mailing lists, instant messaging, chat rooms, VoIP, FTP, and newsgroups and message boards work**
7. **Identify the rules of netiquette**

CONTENTS

THE INTERNET

One of the major reasons business, home, and other users purchase computers is for Internet access. The **Internet**, also called the **Net**, is a worldwide collection of networks that links millions of businesses, government agencies, educational institutions, and individuals. The Internet is a widely used research tool, providing society with access to global information and instant communications.

Today, more than one billion users around the world access a variety of services on the Internet, some of which are shown in Figure 2-1. The World Wide Web and e-mail are two of the more widely used Internet services. Other services include chat rooms, instant messaging, and VoIP (Voice over Internet Protocol). This chapter discusses each of these Internet services.

The Internet has its roots in a networking project started by an agency of the U.S. Department of Defense. The goal was to build a network that (1) allowed scientists at different locations to share information and work together on military and scientific projects and (2) could function even if part of the network were disabled or destroyed by a disaster such as a nuclear attack. That network, called ARPANET, became functional in September 1969, linking scientific and academic researchers across the United States.

The original network consisted of four main computers, one each located at the University of California at Los Angeles, the University of California at Santa Barbara, the Stanford Research Institute, and the University of Utah. Each computer served as a host on the network. A **host** or **server** is any computer that provides services and connections to other computers on a network. By 1984, the network had more than 1,000 individual computers linked as hosts. Today, more than 500 million hosts connect to this network, which became known as the Internet.

FIGURE 2-1a (Web — conduct research, read a blog, share videos)

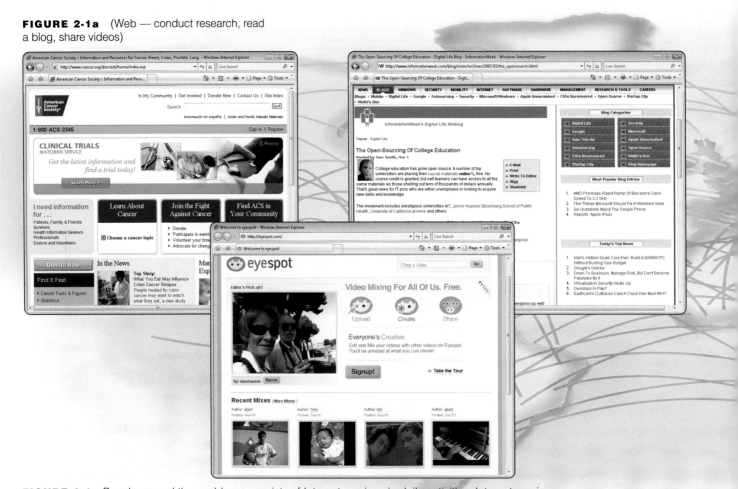

FIGURE 2-1 People around the world use a variety of Internet services in daily activities. Internet services allow users to access the Web for activities such as conducting research, reading blogs, or sharing videos; sending e-mail messages; or conversing with others using chat rooms, instant messaging, or VoIP.

The Internet consists of many local, regional, national, and international networks. Both public and private organizations own networks on the Internet. These networks, along with telephone companies, cable and satellite companies, and the government, all contribute toward the internal structure of the Internet.

Each organization on the Internet is responsible only for maintaining its own network. No single person, company, institution, or government agency controls or owns the Internet. The **World Wide Web Consortium** (**W3C**), however, oversees research and sets standards and guidelines for many areas of the Internet. Nearly 400 organizations from around the world are members of the W3C.

WEB LINK 2-1

W3C

For more information, visit scsite.com/dcf5e/ch2/weblink and then click W3C.

HOW THE INTERNET WORKS

Data sent over the Internet travels via networks and communications media owned and operated by many companies. The following sections present various ways to connect to these networks on the Internet.

Connecting to the Internet

Employees and students often connect to the Internet through a business or school network. Some homes and small businesses use dial-up access to connect to the Internet. **Dial-up access** takes place when the modem in your computer uses a standard telephone line to connect to the Internet. A dial-up connection, however, is slow-speed technology.

FIGURE 2-1b (e-mail)

FIGURE 2-1c (chat room)

FIGURE 2-1d (instant messaging)

FIGURE 2-1e (VoIP)

Many home and small business users opt for higher-speed Internet connections. **DSL** (digital subscriber line) is a technology that provides high-speed Internet connections using regular telephone lines. A **cable modem** allows access to high-speed Internet services through the cable television network. **Fiber to the Premises** (**FTTP**) uses fiber-optic cable to provide high-speed Internet access to home and business users. **Fixed wireless** high-speed Internet connections use a dish-shaped antenna on your house or business to communicate with a tower location via radio signals. A **Wi-Fi** (wireless fidelity) network uses radio signals to provide Internet connections to wireless computers and devices. A **wireless modem** allows access to the Internet through a cellular network. A **satellite modem** communicates with a satellite dish to provide high-speed Internet connections via satellite.

In most cases, higher-speed connections are always on, that is, connected to the Internet the entire time the computer is running. With dial-up access, by contrast, you must establish the connection to the Internet.

Mobile users access the Internet using a variety of technologies. Most hotels and airports provide Internet connections. Wireless Internet access technologies, such as through Wi-Fi networks, allow mobile users to connect easily to the Internet with notebook computers, Tablet PCs, smart phones, and other personal mobile devices while away from a telephone, cable, or other wired connection. Home users often set up a Wi-Fi network. Many public locations, such as airports, hotels, schools, and coffee shops, are **hot spots** that provide Wi-Fi Internet connections to users with mobile computers or devices.

FAQ 2-1

Is free Wi-Fi becoming more popular?

Free Wi-Fi is growing in popularity. In addition to being able to access free Wi-Fi in public locations such as fast food restaurants and coffee shops, some cities also are offering Wi-Fi free-of-charge to residents and guests. For this reason, residents of these cities no longer need to pay for Internet access. For more information, visit scsite.com/dcf5e/ch2/faq and then click Free Wi-Fi.

Access Providers

An **access provider** is a business that provides individuals and companies access to the Internet free or for a fee. For example, some Wi-Fi networks provide free access while others charge a per use fee. Other access providers often charge a fixed amount for an Internet connection, usually about $5 to $22 per month for dial-up access and $13 to $200 for higher-speed access.

Users access the Internet through ISPs, online service providers, and wireless Internet service providers. An **ISP** (**Internet service provider**) is a regional or national access provider. A regional ISP usually provides Internet access to a specific geographic area. A national ISP is a business that provides Internet access in cities and towns nationwide. National ISPs usually offer more services and have a larger technical support staff than regional ISPs. Examples of national ISPs are AT&T Worldnet Service and EarthLink.

In addition to providing Internet access, an **online service provider** (OSP) also has many members-only features. These features include special content and services such as news, weather, legal information, financial data, hardware and software guides, games, travel guides, e-mail, photo communities, online calendars, and instant messaging. The fees for using an OSP sometimes are slightly higher than fees for an ISP. The two more popular OSPs are AOL (America Online) and MSN (Microsoft Network). AOL also provides free access to its services to any user with a high-speed Internet connection.

A **wireless Internet service provider** (**WISP**) is a company that provides wireless Internet access to computers and mobile devices, such as smart phones and PDAs, with built-in wireless capability (such as Wi-Fi) or to computers using wireless modems or wireless access devices. Wireless modems usually are in the form of a card that inserts in a slot in a computer or mobile device. Examples of wireless Internet service providers include AT&T, Boingo Wireless, Sprint Broadband Direct, T-Mobile, and Verizon Wireless.

WEB LINK 2-2

Wireless Modems

For more information, visit scsite.com/dcf5e/ch2/weblink and then click Wireless Modems.

How Data Travels the Internet

Computers connected to the Internet work together to transfer data and information around the world. Several main transmission media carry the heaviest amount of traffic on the Internet. These major carriers of network traffic are known collectively as the **Internet backbone**.

In the United States, the transmission media that make up the Internet backbone exchange data at several different major cities across the country. That is, they transfer data from one network to another until it reaches its final destination (Figure 2-2).

FIGURE 2-2   HOW A HOME USER'S DATA MIGHT TRAVEL THE INTERNET USING A CABLE MODEM CONNECTION

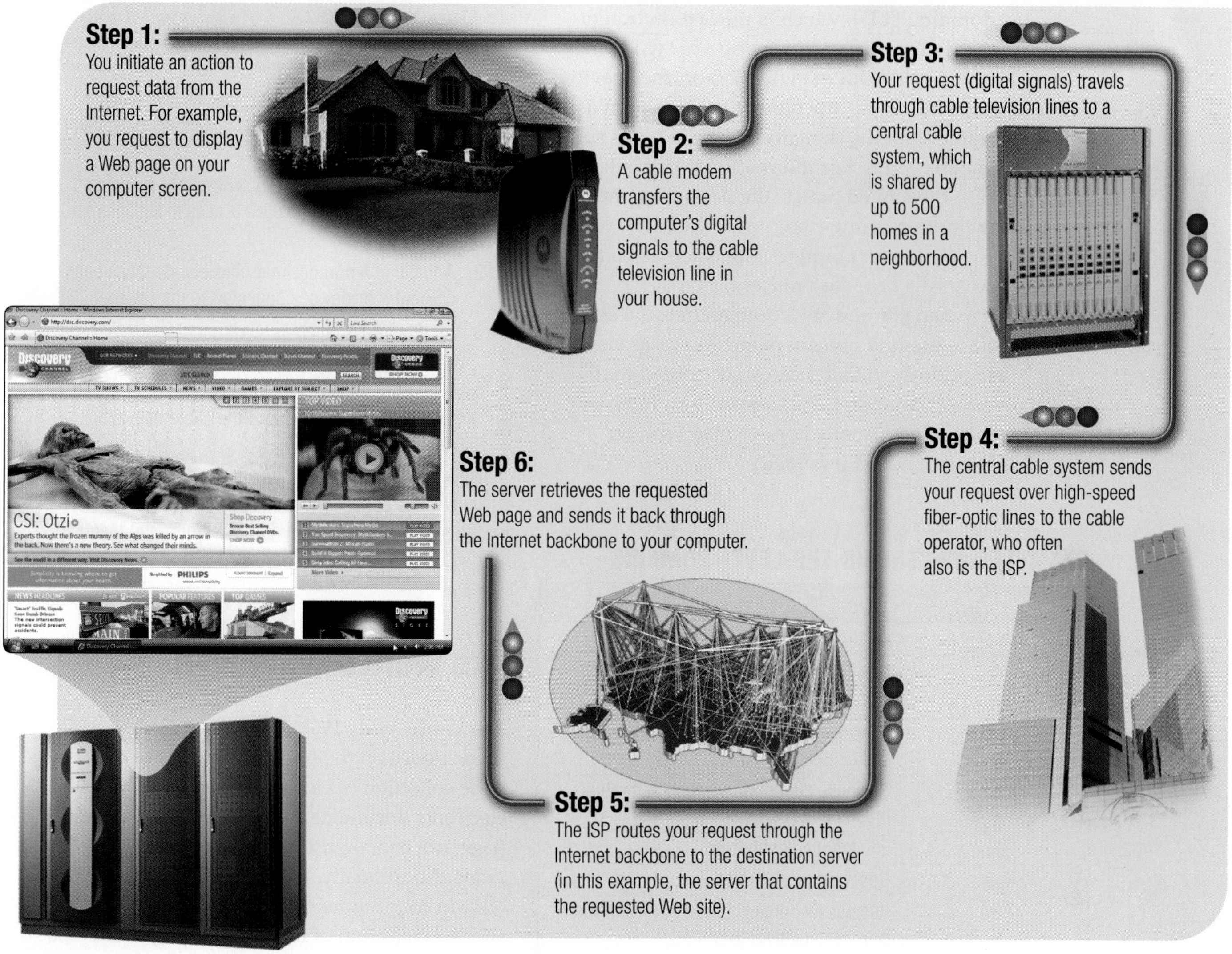

Step 1:
You initiate an action to request data from the Internet. For example, you request to display a Web page on your computer screen.

Step 2:
A cable modem transfers the computer's digital signals to the cable television line in your house.

Step 3:
Your request (digital signals) travels through cable television lines to a central cable system, which is shared by up to 500 homes in a neighborhood.

Step 4:
The central cable system sends your request over high-speed fiber-optic lines to the cable operator, who often also is the ISP.

Step 6:
The server retrieves the requested Web page and sends it back through the Internet backbone to your computer.

Step 5:
The ISP routes your request through the Internet backbone to the destination server (in this example, the server that contains the requested Web site).

Internet Addresses

The Internet relies on an addressing system much like the postal service to send data to a computer at a specific destination. An **IP address**, short for Internet Protocol address, is a number that uniquely identifies each computer or device connected to the Internet. The IP address usually consists of four groups of numbers, each separated by a period. In general, the first portion of each IP address identifies the network and the last portion identifies the specific computer.

These all-numeric IP addresses are difficult to remember and use. Thus, the Internet supports the use of a text name that represents one or more IP addresses. A **domain name** is the text version of an IP address. Figure 2-3 shows an IP address and its associated domain name. As with an IP address, the components of a domain name are separated by periods.

The text in the domain name up to the first period identifies the type of Internet server. The www in Figure 2-3, for example, indicates a Web server. The Internet server portion of a domain name often is not required.

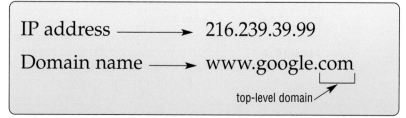

IP address ⟶ 216.239.39.99

Domain name ⟶ www.google.com

top-level domain

FIGURE 2-3   The IP address and domain name for the Google Web site.

Every domain name contains a **top-level domain (TLD)**, which is the last section of the domain name. A generic TLD (gTLD), such as the com in Figure 2-3 on the previous page, identifies the type of organization associated with the domain. Figure 2-4 lists some generic TLDs. For international Web sites outside the United States, the domain name also includes a country code TLD (ccTLD), which is a two-letter country code, such as au for Australia or fr for France.

When you specify a domain name, a server translates the domain name into its associated IP address so that data can be routed to the correct computer. This server is an Internet server that usually is associated with an Internet access provider.

EXAMPLES OF GENERIC TOP-LEVEL DOMAINS

Generic TLD	Intended Purpose
aero	Aviation community members
biz	Businesses of all sizes
cat	Catalan cultural community
com	Commercial organizations, businesses, and companies
coop	Business cooperatives such as credit unions and rural electric co-ops
edu	Educational institutions
gov	Government agencies
info	Businesses, organizations, or individuals providing general information
jobs	Employment or human resource businesses
mil	Military organizations
mobi	Delivery and management of mobile Internet services
museum	Accredited museums
name	Individuals or families
net	Network provider
org	Nonprofit organizations
pro	Certified professionals such as doctors, lawyers, and accountants
tel	Internet communications
travel	Travel industry

FIGURE 2-4 In addition to the generic TLDs listed in this table, proposals for newer TLDs continually are evaluated.

Test your knowledge of pages 50 through 54 in Quiz Yourself 2-1.

QUIZ YOURSELF 2-1

Instructions: Find the true statement below. Then, rewrite the remaining false statements so they are true.

1. An access provider is a business that provides individuals and companies access to the Internet free or for a fee.
2. A WISP is a number that uniquely identifies each computer or device connected to the Internet.
3. An IP address, such as www.google.com, is the text version of a domain name.
4. A satellite modem allows access to high-speed Internet services through the cable television network.

Quiz Yourself Online: To further check your knowledge of accessing and connecting to the Internet, visit scsite.com/dcf5e/ch2/quiz and then click Objective 1.

THE WORLD WIDE WEB

The **World Wide Web (WWW)**, or **Web**, a widely used service on the Internet, consists of a worldwide collection of electronic documents. Each electronic document on the Web, called a **Web page**, can contain text, graphics, audio, and video. Additionally, Web pages usually have built-in connections to other documents. A **Web site** is a collection of related Web pages and associated items, such as documents and pictures, stored on a Web server. A **Web server** is a computer that delivers requested Web pages to your computer. Some industry experts use the term **Web 2.0** to refer to Web sites that allow users to modify Web site content, provide a means for users to share personal information (such as social networking Web sites), and have application software built into the site for visitors to use (such as e-mail and word processing programs).

Browsing the Web

A **Web browser**, or **browser**, is application software that allows users to access and view Web pages. To browse the Web, you need a computer that is connected to the Internet and that has a Web browser. The more widely used Web browsers for personal computers are Internet Explorer, Firefox, Opera, and Safari.

With an Internet connection established, you start a Web browser. The browser retrieves and displays a starting Web page, sometimes called the browser's home page. Figure 2-5 shows how a Web browser displays a home page.

The more common usage of the term, **home page**, refers to the first page that a Web site displays. Similar to a book cover or a table of contents for a Web site, the home page provides information about the Web site's purpose and content. Often it provides connections to other documents, Web pages, or Web sites, which can be downloaded to a computer or mobile device. **Downloading** is the process of a computer receiving information, such as a Web page, from a server on the Internet.

FIGURE 2-5 HOW A WEB BROWSER DISPLAYS A HOME PAGE

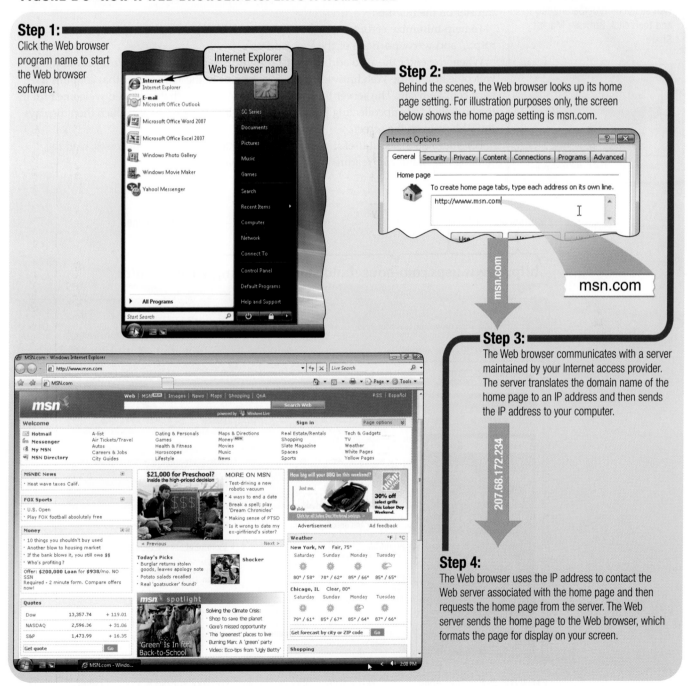

Step 1:
Click the Web browser program name to start the Web browser software.

Step 2:
Behind the scenes, the Web browser looks up its home page setting. For illustration purposes only, the screen below shows the home page setting is msn.com.

Step 3:
The Web browser communicates with a server maintained by your Internet access provider. The server translates the domain name of the home page to an IP address and then sends the IP address to your computer.

Step 4:
The Web browser uses the IP address to contact the Web server associated with the home page and then requests the home page from the server. The Web server sends the home page to the Web browser, which formats the page for display on your screen.

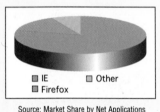
Web Addresses

A Web page has a unique address, which is called a **URL** (Uniform Resource Locator) or **Web address**. For example, the home page for the United States Postal Service Web site has a Web address of http://www.usps.com. A Web browser retrieves a Web page using its Web address.

If you know the Web address of a Web page, you can type it in the Address bar at the top of the browser window. If you type http://www.usps.com/household/stampcollecting/welcome.htm as the Web address in the Address bar and then press the ENTER key, the browser downloads and displays the Web page shown in Figure 2-6.

A Web address consists of a protocol, domain name, and sometimes the path to a specific Web page or location on a Web page. Many Web page addresses begin with http://. The http, which stands for Hypertext Transfer Protocol, is a set of rules that defines how pages transfer on the Internet.

To help minimize errors, many browsers and Web sites do not require you enter the http:// and www portions of the Web address.

When you enter the Web address, http://www.usps.com/household/stampcollecting/welcome.htm in the Web browser, it sends a request to the Web server that contains the usps.com Web site. The server then retrieves the Web page that is named welcome.htm in the household/stampcollecting path and delivers it to your browser, which then displays the Web page on the screen.

For information about useful Web sites and their associated Web addresses, read the Making Use of the Web feature that follows this chapter.

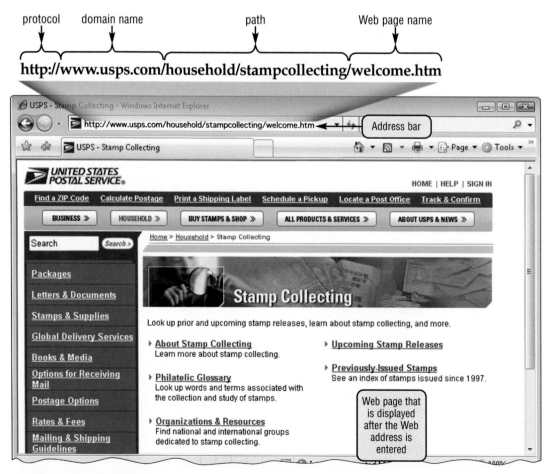

FIGURE 2-6   After entering the Web address http://www.usps.com/household/stampcollecting/welcome.htm in the Address bar, this Web page at the United States Postal Service Web site is displayed.

Navigating Web Pages

Most Web pages contain links. A **link**, short for **hyperlink**, is a built-in connection to another related Web page or part of a Web page. Links allow you to obtain information in a nonlinear way. That is, instead of accessing topics in a specified order, you move directly to a topic of interest.

Branching from one related topic to another in a nonlinear fashion is what makes links so powerful. Some people use the phrase, **surfing the Web**, to refer to the activity of using links to explore the Web.

On the Web, a link can be text or an image. Text links may be underlined and/or displayed in a color different from other text on the Web page. Pointing to, or positioning the pointer on, a link on the screen typically changes the shape of the pointer to a small hand with a pointing index finger. Pointing to a link also sometimes causes the link to change in appearance. The Web page shown in Figure 2-7 contains a variety of link types, with the pointer on one of the links.

Each link on a Web page corresponds to a Web address or document. To activate a link, you **click** it, that is, point to the link and then press the left mouse button. Clicking a link causes the Web page or document associated with the link to be displayed on the screen. The linked object might be on the same Web page, a different Web page at the same Web site, or a separate Web page at a different Web site in another city or country. Many current Web browsers support **tabbed browsing**, where the top of the browser displays a tab (similar to a file folder tab) for each Web page you open. To move from one open Web page to another, you click the tab in the Web browser. Read Looking Ahead 2-1 for a look at the next generation of Web surfing.

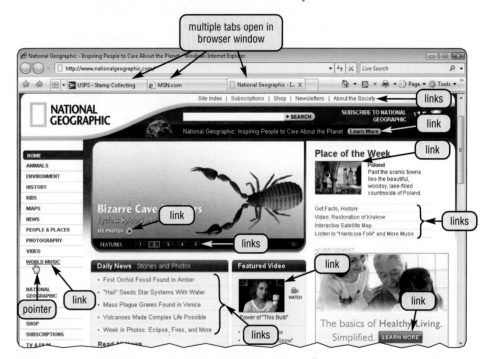

FIGURE 2-7 This browser window has several open tabs. The current tab shows a Web page that has various types of links: text that is underlined, text in a different color, and images.

LOOKING AHEAD 2-1

Internet Speeds into the Future

High-quality video conferencing and video-streaming technologies are among the new opportunities the Internet2 will bring to students, educators, and researchers across the globe.

The not-for-profit Internet2 project connects more than 206 educational and 60 research institutions via a high-speed private network. When used solely as a research tool, Internet2 applications process massive amounts of data, such as linking observatories atop Hawaii's tallest mountains and video conferences from 20 remote sites across the world.

By 2020, the Internet2 will allow Web surfers to access more than 250 million Web sites at speeds perhaps 10,000 times faster than today's Internet. Schools have used the Internet2 for interactive video conferences linking authors with readers, music composers with conductors, and operating room doctors with medical students. For more information, visit scsite.com/dcf5e/ch2/looking and then click Internet2.

Searching for Information on the Web

The Web is a global resource of information. A primary use of the Web is to conduct research by searching for specific information, including text, graphics, audio, and video. The first step in successful searching is to identify the main idea or concept in the topic about which you are seeking information. Determine any synonyms, alternate spellings, or variant word forms for the topic. Then, use a search tool to locate the information.

Two types of search tools are search engines and subject directories. A **search engine** is a program that finds Web sites, Web pages, images, videos, news, and other information related to a specific topic. A **subject directory** classifies Web pages in an organized set of categories or groups, such as sports or shopping, and related subcategories.

Some Web sites offer the functionality of both a search engine and a subject directory. Google and Yahoo!, for example, are widely used search engines that also provide a subject directory. To use Google or Yahoo!, you enter the Web address (google.com or yahoo.com) in the Address bar in a browser window. The table in Figure 2-8 lists the Web addresses of several popular general-purpose search engines and subject directories.

WIDELY USED SEARCH TOOLS

Search Tool	Web Address	Search Engine	Subject Directory
A9	a9.com	X	
AlltheWeb	alltheweb.com	X	
AltaVista	altavista.com	X	
AOL Search	search.aol.com	X	
Ask	ask.com	X	
Dogpile	dogpile.com	X	
Excite	excite.com	X	X
Gigablast	gigablast.com	X	X
Google	google.com	X	X
Live Search	live.com	X	
LookSmart	looksmart.com	X	X
Lycos	lycos.com	X	
MSN	msn.com	X	X
Netscape Search	search.netscape.com	X	
Open Directory Project	dmoz.org	X	X
WebCrawler	webcrawler.com	X	
Yahoo!	yahoo.com	X	X

FIGURE 2-8 Many search engines and subject directories allow searching about any topic on the Web.

SEARCH ENGINES A search engine is particularly helpful in locating Web pages about certain topics or in locating specific Web pages, images, videos, news, and other information for which you do not know the exact Web address. Some search engines look through Web pages for all types of information. Others can restrict their searches to a specific type of information, such as images, videos, audio, news, maps, people or businesses, and blogs.

Search engines require that you enter a word or phrase, called **search text**, that describe the item you want to find. Figure 2-9 shows how to use the Google search engine to search for the phrase, Michigan golf courses. The results shown in Step 3 include more than two million links to Web pages, called hits, that reference Michigan golf courses. Each hit in the list has a link that, when clicked, displays an associated Web site or Web page. Most search engines sequence the hits based on how close the words in the search text are to one another in the titles and descriptions of the hits. Thus, the first few links probably contain more relevant information.

If you enter a phrase with spaces between the words in the search text, most search engines display results (hits) that include all of the words. Techniques you can use to improve your searches include the following:

- Use specific nouns and put the most important terms first in the search text.
- Use the asterisk (*) to substitute characters in words. For example, retriev* returns retrieves, retrieval, retriever, and any other variation.
- Use quotation marks to create phrases so the search engine finds the exact sequence of words.
- List all possible spellings, for example, email, e-mail.
- Before using a search engine, read its Help information.
- If the search is unsuccessful with one search engine, try another.

FIGURE 2-9   HOW TO USE A SEARCH ENGINE

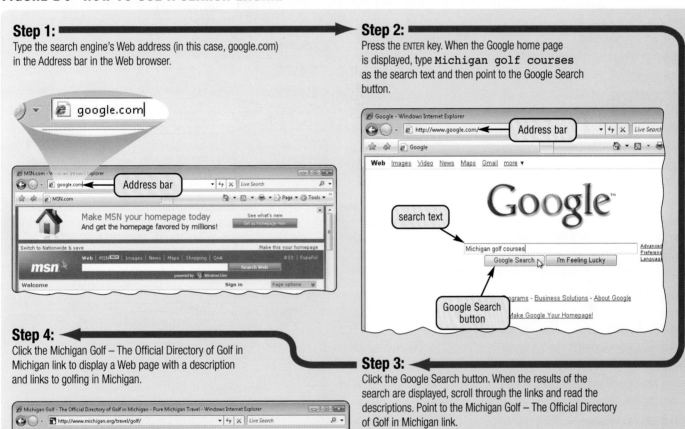

Step 1:
Type the search engine's Web address (in this case, google.com) in the Address bar in the Web browser.

Step 2:
Press the ENTER key. When the Google home page is displayed, type Michigan golf courses as the search text and then point to the Google Search button.

Step 4:
Click the Michigan Golf – The Official Directory of Golf in Michigan link to display a Web page with a description and links to golfing in Michigan.

Step 3:
Click the Google Search button. When the results of the search are displayed, scroll through the links and read the descriptions. Point to the Michigan Golf – The Official Directory of Golf in Michigan link.

SUBJECT DIRECTORIES   A subject directory provides categorized lists of links arranged by subject. Using this search tool, you can locate a particular topic by clicking links through different levels, moving from the general to the specific. Figure 2-10 shows how to use Yahoo!'s subject directory to search for house plans Web sites.

FIGURE 2-10   HOW TO USE A SUBJECT DIRECTORY

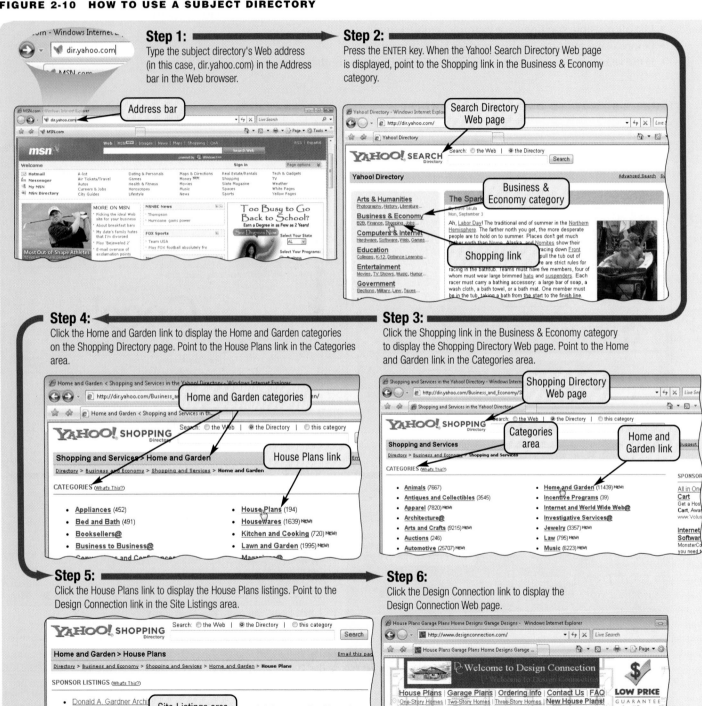

Step 1:
Type the subject directory's Web address (in this case, dir.yahoo.com) in the Address bar in the Web browser.

Step 2:
Press the ENTER key. When the Yahoo! Search Directory Web page is displayed, point to the Shopping link in the Business & Economy category.

Step 4:
Click the Home and Garden link to display the Home and Garden categories on the Shopping Directory page. Point to the House Plans link in the Categories area.

Step 3:
Click the Shopping link in the Business & Economy category to display the Shopping Directory Web page. Point to the Home and Garden link in the Categories area.

Step 5:
Click the House Plans link to display the House Plans listings. Point to the Design Connection link in the Site Listings area.

Step 6:
Click the Design Connection link to display the Design Connection Web page.

Types of Web Sites

Twelve types of Web sites are portal, news, informational, business/marketing, educational, entertainment, advocacy, blog, wiki, online social network, content aggregator, and personal. Many Web sites fall into more than one of these categories.

PORTAL A **portal** is a Web site that offers a variety of Internet services from a single, convenient location (Figure 2-11a). Most portals offer the following free services: search engine and/or subject directory; news; sports and weather; Web publishing; reference tools such as yellow pages, stock quotes, and maps; shopping; and e-mail and other forms of online communications. Popular portals include AltaVista, AOL, Excite, GO.com, iGoogle, LookSmart, Lycos, MSN, Netscape, and Yahoo!.

FIGURE 2-11a
(portal)

NEWS A news Web site contains newsworthy material including stories and articles relating to current events, life, money, sports, and the weather (Figure 2-11b). Newspapers and television and radio stations are some of the media that maintain news Web sites.

FIGURE 2-11b
(news)

INFORMATIONAL An informational Web site contains factual information (Figure 2-11c). Many United States government agencies have informational Web sites providing information such as census data, tax codes, and the congressional budget. Other organizations provide information such as public transportation schedules and published research findings.

FIGURE 2-11c
(informational)

BUSINESS/MARKETING A business/marketing Web site contains content that promotes or sells products or services (Figure 2-11d). Nearly every business has a business/marketing Web site. Many companies also allow you to purchase their products or services online.

FIGURE 2-11d
(business/
marketing)

EDUCATIONAL An educational Web site offers exciting, challenging avenues for formal and informal teaching and learning (Figure 2-11e). For a more structured learning experience, companies provide online training to employees; and colleges offer online classes and degrees. Instructors often use the Web to enhance classroom teaching by publishing course materials, grades, and other pertinent class information.

FIGURE 2-11e
(educational)

FIGURE 2-11 Types of Web sites. *(continued on next page)*

FIGURE 2-11f
(entertainment)

FIGURE 2-11g
(advocacy)

FIGURE 2-11h
(blog)

FIGURE 2-11i
(wiki)

FIGURE 2-11j
(online social network)

FIGURE 2-11   Types of Web sites. *(continued)*

ENTERTAINMENT   An entertainment Web site offers an interactive and engaging environment (Figure 2-11f). Popular entertainment Web sites offer music, videos, sports, games, ongoing Web episodes, sweepstakes, chats, and more.

ADVOCACY   An advocacy Web site contains content that describes a cause, opinion, or idea (Figure 2-11g). These Web sites usually present views of a particular group or association.

BLOG   A **blog**, short for Weblog, is an informal Web site consisting of time-stamped articles, or posts, in a diary or journal format, usually listed in reverse chronological order (Figure 2-11h). A blog that contains video clips is called a **video blog** or **vlog.** The term **blogosphere** refers to the worldwide collection of blogs, and the **vlogosphere** refers to all vlogs worldwide. Blogs reflect the interests, opinions, and personalities of the author and sometimes site visitors. Blogs have become an important means of worldwide communications.

WIKI   A **wiki** is a collaborative Web site that allows users to create, add to, modify, or delete the Web site content via their Web browser. Most wikis are open to modification by the general public. Wikis usually collect recent edits on a Web page so that someone can review them for accuracy. The difference between a wiki and a blog is that users cannot modify original posts made by the blogger. A popular wiki is Wikipedia, a free Web encyclopedia (Figure 2-11i). Read Ethics & Issues 2-1 for a related discussion.

ONLINE SOCIAL NETWORKS   An **online social network**, also called a **social networking Web site**, is a Web site that encourages members in its online community to share their interests, ideas, stories, photos, music, and videos with other registered users (Figure 2-11j). Popular social networking Web sites include Facebook and MySpace, which alone has more than 28 million visitors each day. A **media sharing Web site** is a specific type of online social network that enables members to share media such as photos, music, and videos. Flickr, Fotki, and Webshots are popular photo sharing communities; Eyespot, Google Video, and YouTube are popular video sharing communities.

Should You Trust a Wiki for Academic Research?

As wikis have grown in number, size, and popularity, some educators and librarians have shunned the sites as valid sources of research. While many wikis are tightly controlled with a limited number of contributors and expert editors, these usually focus on narrowly-defined, specialized topics. Large online wikis, such as Wikipedia, often involve thousands of editors, many of whom remain anonymous. Recently, television station reporters purposefully vandalized entries on Wikipedia for John Lennon and Elvis Presley in an attempt to either discredit Wikipedia or to test how quickly corrections are made. Editors quickly corrected the information. In other situations, rival political factions falsified or embellished wiki entries in an attempt to give their candidate an advantage. Some wiki supporters argue that most wikis provide adequate controls to quickly correct false or misleading content and to punish those who submit it. Some propose that wikis should be used as a starting point for researching a fact, but that the fact should be verified using traditional sources. Should wikis be allowed as valid sources for academic research? Why or why not? Would you submit a paper to your instructor that cites a wiki as a source? An encyclopedia? Why or why not? What policies could wikis enforce that could garner more confidence from the public?

CONTENT AGGREGATOR   A **content aggregator** is a business that gathers and organizes Web content and then distributes, or feeds, the content to subscribers for free or a fee (Figure 2-11k). Examples of distributed content include news, music, video, and pictures. Subscribers select content in which they are interested. Whenever this content changes, it is downloaded automatically (pushed) to the subscriber's computer or mobile device. **RSS 2.0**, which stands for Really Simple Syndication, is a specification that content aggregators use to distribute content to subscribers.

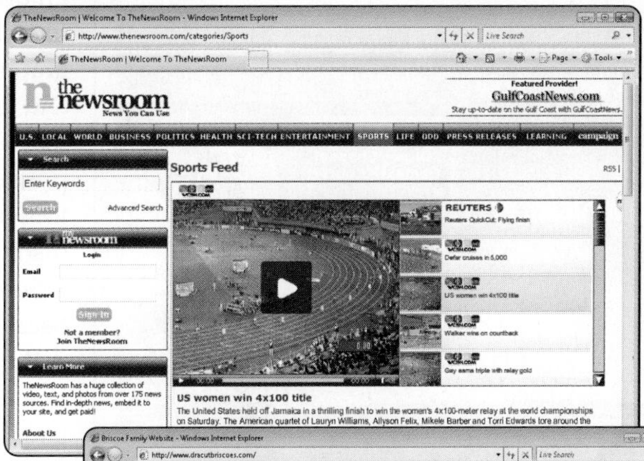

FIGURE 2-11k (content aggregator)

FIGURE 2-11l (personal)

PERSONAL   A private individual or family not usually associated with any organization may maintain a personal Web site (Figure 2-11l). People publish personal Web pages for a variety of reasons. Some are job hunting. Others simply want to share life experiences with the world.

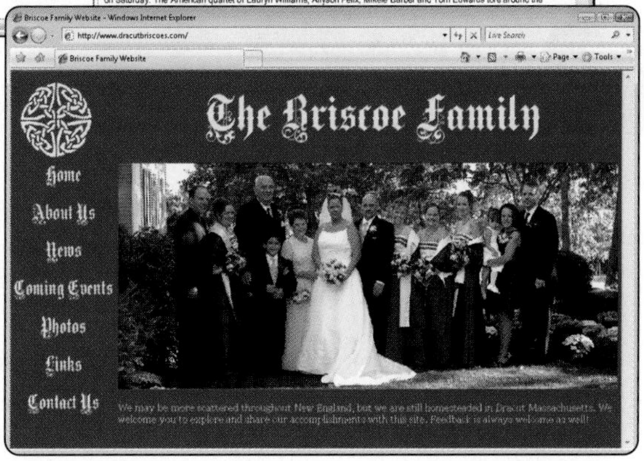

FIGURE 2-11   Types of Web sites. *(continued)*

Evaluating a Web Site

Do not assume that information presented on the Web is correct or accurate. Any person, company, or organization can publish a Web page on the Internet. No one oversees the content of these Web pages. Figure 2-12 lists guidelines for assessing the value of a Web site or Web page before relying on its content.

GUIDELINES FOR EVALUATING THE VALUE OF A WEB SITE

Evaluation Criteria	Reliable Web Sites
Affiliation	A reputable institution should support the Web site without bias in the information.
Audience	The Web site should be written at an appropriate level.
Authority	The Web site should list the author and the appropriate credentials.
Content	The Web site should be well organized and the links should work.
Currency	The information on the Web page should be current.
Design	The pages at the Web site should download quickly and be visually pleasing and easy to navigate.
Objectivity	The Web site should contain little advertising and be free of preconceptions.

FIGURE 2-12   Criteria for evaluating a Web site's content.

Multimedia on the Web

Most Web pages include more than just formatted text and links. The more exciting Web pages use multimedia. **Multimedia** refers to any application that combines text with graphics, animation, audio, video, and/or virtual reality. The sections that follow discuss how the Web uses these multimedia elements.

GRAPHICS   A **graphic**, or graphical image, is a digital representation of nontext information such as a drawing, chart, or photo. Many Web pages use colorful graphical designs and images to convey messages (Figure 2-13).

FIGURE 2-13   This Web page uses colorful graphical designs and images to convey its messages.

Of the graphics formats that exist on the Web, the two more common are JPEG and GIF formats. JPEG (pronounced JAY-peg) is a format that compresses graphics to reduce their file size, which means the file takes up less storage space. The goal with JPEG graphics is to reach a balance between image quality and file size. Digital photos often use the JPEG format. GIF (pronounced jiff) graphics also use compression techniques to reduce file sizes. The GIF format works best for images that have only a few distinct colors, such as company logos.

Some Web sites use thumbnails on their pages because graphics can be time-consuming to display. A **thumbnail** is a small version of a larger graphic. You usually can click a thumbnail to display a larger image.

ANIMATION   Many Web pages use **animation**, which is the appearance of motion created by displaying a series of still images in sequence. Animation can make Web pages more visually interesting or draw attention to important information or links.

AUDIO   On the Web, you can listen to audio clips and live audio. **Audio** includes music, speech, or any other sound. Simple applications on the Web consist of individual audio files available for download to a computer or device. Once downloaded, you can play (listen to) the contents of these files. Audio files are compressed to reduce their file sizes. For example, the **MP3** format reduces an audio file to about one-tenth its original size, while preserving much of the original quality of the sound.

Some music publishers have Web sites that allow users to download sample tracks free to persuade them to buy the entire CD. Other Web sites allow a user to purchase and download an entire CD (Figure 2-14). It is legal to download copyrighted music only if the song's copyright holder has granted permission for users to download and play the song. Copyright issues led to the development of **digital rights management** (DRM), a strategy designed to prevent illegal distribution of music and other digital content.

To listen to an audio file on your computer, you need special software called a **player**. Most current operating systems contain a player. Popular players include iTunes, RealPlayer, and Windows Media Player.

Some applications on the Web use streaming audio. **Streaming** is the process of transferring data in a continuous and even flow. Streaming allows users to access and use a file while it is transmitting. For example, streaming audio enables you to listen to music as it downloads to your computer.

Podcasting is another popular method of distributing audio. A **podcast** is recorded audio, usually an MP3 file, stored on a Web site that can be downloaded to a computer or a portable media player such as an iPod. Examples of podcasts include music, radio shows, news stories, classroom lectures, political messages, and television commentaries. Podcasters register their podcasts with content aggregators. Subscribers select podcast feeds they want to be downloaded automatically whenever they connect.

FIGURE 2-14 HOW TO PURCHASE AND DOWNLOAD MUSIC

Step 1:
Display the music Web site on the screen. Search for, select, and pay for the music you want to purchase from the music Web site.

Step 2:
Download the music from the Web site's server to your computer's hard disk.

Step 3a:
Listen to the music from your computer's hard disk.

Step 3b: Download music from your computer's hard disk to a portable media player. Listen to the music through earphones attached to the portable media player.

VIDEO On the Web, you can view video clips or watch live video. **Video** consists of full-motion images that are played back at various speeds. Most video also has accompanying audio. You can use the Internet to watch live and prerecorded coverage of your favorite television programs or enjoy a live performance of your favorite vocalist. You can upload, share, or view video clips at a video sharing Web site such as YouTube. Educators, politicians, and businesses are using video blogs and video podcasts to engage students, voters, and consumers.

Video files often are compressed because they are quite large in size. These clips also are quite short in length, usually less than 10 minutes, because they can take a long time to download. The Moving Pictures Experts Group (MPEG) defines a popular video compression standard, a widely used one called MPEG-4 or **MP4.** As with streaming audio, streaming video allows you to view longer or live video images as they download to your computer.

VIRTUAL REALITY **Virtual reality** (VR) is the use of computers to simulate a real or imagined environment that appears as a three-dimensional (3-D) space. VR involves the display of 3-D images that users explore and manipulate interactively. A VR Web site, for example, might show a room with furniture. Users walk through such a VR room by moving an input device forward, backward, or to the side.

WEB LINK 2-3

YouTube
For more information, visit scsite.com/dcf5e/ch2/weblink and then click YouTube.

PLUG-INS Most Web browsers have the capability of displaying basic multimedia elements on a Web page. Sometimes, a browser might need an additional program, called a plug-in. A **plug-in**, or **add-on**, is a program that extends the capability of a browser. You can download many plug-ins at no cost from various Web sites (Figure 2-15).

POPULAR PLUG-IN APPLICATIONS

Plug-In	Description	Web Address
Acrobat Reader	View, navigate, and print Portable Document Format (PDF) files — documents formatted to look just as they look in print	adobe.com
Flash Player	View dazzling graphics and animation, hear outstanding sound and music, display Web pages across an entire screen	adobe.com
Java	Enable Web browser to run programs written in Java, which add interactivity to Web pages	java.sun.com
QuickTime	View animation, music, audio, video, and VR panoramas and objects directly in a Web page	apple.com
RealPlayer	Listen to live and on-demand near-CD-quality audio and newscast-quality video; stream audio and video content for faster viewing; play MP3 files; create music CDs	real.com
Shockwave Player	Experience dynamic interactive multimedia, 3-D graphics, and streaming audio	adobe.com
Windows Media Player	Listen to live and on-demand audio, play or edit WMA and MP3 files, burn CDs, and watch DVD movies	microsoft.com

FIGURE 2-15 Most plug-ins can be downloaded free from the Web.

Web Publishing

Before the World Wide Web, the means to share opinions and ideas with others easily and inexpensively was limited to the media, classroom, work, or social environments. Today, businesses and individuals convey information to millions of people by creating their own Web pages.

Web publishing is the development and maintenance of Web pages. To develop a Web page, you do not have to be a computer programmer. For the small business or home user, Web publishing is fairly easy as long as you have the proper tools.

The five major steps to Web publishing are as follows:

1. Plan a Web site
2. Analyze and design a Web site
3. Create a Web site
4. Deploy a Web site
5. Maintain a Web site

Figure 2-16 illustrates these steps with respect to a personal Web site.

FIGURE 2-16   HOW TO PUBLISH YOUR RESUME ON THE WEB

Step 1:
Plan a Web site.
Think about issues that could affect the design of the Web site.

Step 2:
Analyze and design a Web site. Design the layout of the elements of the Web site.

Step 3:
Create a Web site. Use word processing software or Web page authoring software to create the Web site.

Step 4:
Deploy a Web site. Save the Web site on a Web server.

Step 5:
Maintain a Web site.
Visit your Web site regularly to be sure it is working and current.

E-Commerce

E-commerce, short for electronic commerce, is a business transaction that occurs over an electronic network such as the Internet. Anyone with access to a computer, an Internet connection, and a means to pay for purchased goods or services can participate in e-commerce.

Three types of e-commerce are business-to-consumer, consumer-to-consumer, and business-to-business. Business-to-consumer (B2C) e-commerce consists of the sale of goods and services to the general public. For example, Dell has a B2C Web site. Instead of visiting a computer store to purchase a computer, customers can order one directly from the Dell Web site.

A customer (consumer) visits an online business through an **electronic storefront**, which contains product descriptions, images, and a shopping cart (Figure 2-17). The **shopping cart** allows the customer to collect purchases. When ready to complete the sale, the customer enters personal data and the method of payment, preferably through a secure Internet connection.

Instead of purchasing from a business, consumers can purchase from each other. For example, with an **online auction**, users bid on an item being sold by someone else. The highest bidder at the end of the bidding period purchases the item. Consumer-to-consumer (C2C) e-commerce occurs when one consumer sells directly to another, such as in an online auction. eBay is one of the more popular online auction Web sites.

Most e-commerce, though, actually takes place between businesses, which is called business-to-business (B2B) e-commerce. Many businesses provide goods and services to other businesses, such as online advertising, recruiting, credit, sales, market research, technical support, and training.

As an alternative to entering credit card, bank account, or other financial information online, some shopping and auction Web sites allow consumers to use an online payment service such as PayPal or Google Checkout. To use an online payment service, you create an account that is linked to your credit card or funds at a financial institution. When you make a purchase, you use your online payment service account, which transfers money for you without revealing your financial information.

WEB LINK 2-4

PayPal

For more information, visit scsite.com/dcf5e/ch2/weblink and then click PayPal.

FIGURE 2-17   E-commerce activities include shopping for goods.

Test your knowledge of pages 54 through 68 in Quiz Yourself 2-2.

QUIZ YOURSELF 2-2

Instructions: Find the true statement below. Then, rewrite the remaining false statements so they are true.

1. A blog is a Web site that uses a regularly updated journal format to reflect the interests, opinions, and personalities of the author and sometimes site visitors.

2. A Web browser classifies Web pages in an organized set of categories and related subcategories.

3. Business-to-consumer e-commerce occurs when one consumer sells directly to another, such as in an online auction.

4. The more widely used search engines for personal computers are Internet Explorer, Firefox, Opera, and Safari.

5. To develop a Web page, you have to be a computer programmer.

Quiz Yourself Online: To further check your knowledge of Web browsers, searching, types of Web sites, Web publishing, and e-commerce, visit scsite.com/dcf5e/ch2/quiz and then click Objectives 2 – 5.

OTHER INTERNET SERVICES

The Web is only one of the many services on the Internet. The Web and other Internet services have changed the way we communicate. We can send e-mail messages to the president, have a discussion with experts about the stock market, chat with someone in another country about genealogy, and talk about homework assignments with classmates via instant messages. Many times, these communications take place completely in writing — without the parties ever meeting each other.

At home, work, and school, people use computers and Internet-enabled mobile devices so that they always have instant access to e-mail, mailing lists, instant messaging, chat rooms, VoIP (Voice over IP), FTP (File Transfer Protocol), and newsgroups and message boards. The following pages discuss each of these Internet services.

E-Mail

E-mail (short for electronic mail) is the transmission of messages and files via a computer network. Today, e-mail is a primary communications method for both personal and business use.

You use an **e-mail program** to create, send, receive, forward, store, print, and delete e-mail messages. Outlook and Windows Mail are two popular e-mail programs. The steps in Figure 2-18 illustrate how to send an e-mail message using Outlook. The message can be simple text or can include an attachment such as a word processing document, a graphic, an audio clip, or a video clip.

FIGURE 2-18   HOW TO SEND AN E-MAIL MESSAGE

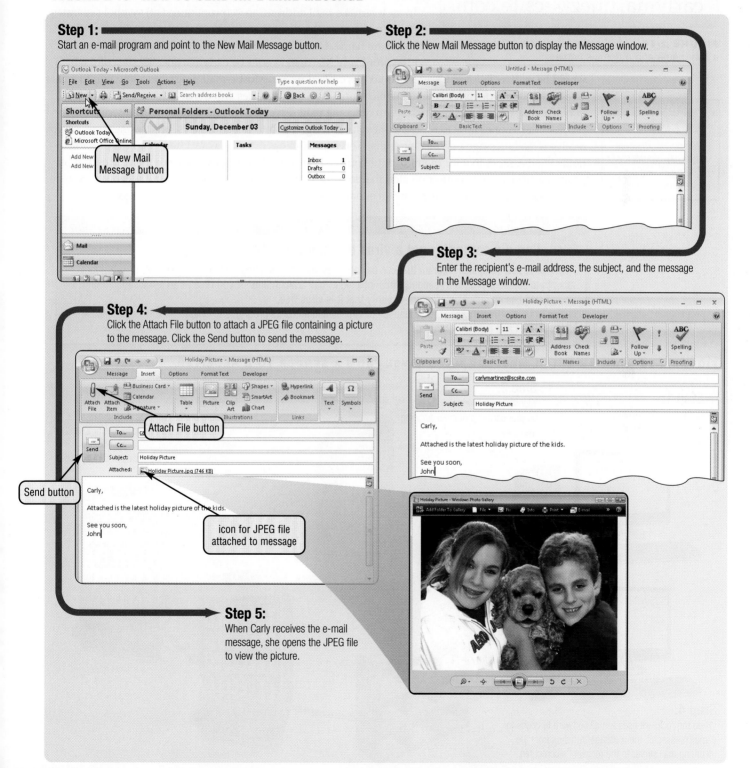

Step 1:
Start an e-mail program and point to the New Mail Message button.

Step 2:
Click the New Mail Message button to display the Message window.

Step 3:
Enter the recipient's e-mail address, the subject, and the message in the Message window.

Step 4:
Click the Attach File button to attach a JPEG file containing a picture to the message. Click the Send button to send the message.

Step 5:
When Carly receives the e-mail message, she opens the JPEG file to view the picture.

Internet access providers typically supply an e-mail program as a standard part of their Internet access services. To use these Web-based e-mail programs, you connect to the Web site and set up an e-mail account, which typically includes an e-mail address and a password.

Just as you address a letter when using the postal system, you must address an e-mail message with the e-mail address of your intended recipient. Likewise, when someone sends you a message, he or she must have your e-mail address. An **e-mail address** is a combination of a user name and a domain name that identifies a user so that he or she can receive Internet e-mail (Figure 2-19). A **user name** is a unique combination of characters, such as letters of the alphabet and/or numbers, that identifies a specific user.

carlymartinez@scsite.com

FIGURE 2-19 An e-mail address is a combination of a user name and a domain name.

In an Internet e-mail address, an @ (pronounced at) symbol separates the user name from the domain name. Your service provider supplies the domain name. Using the example in Figure 2-19, a possible e-mail address for Carly Martinez would be carlymartinez@scsite.com, which would be read as follows: Carly Martinez at s c site dot com. Most e-mail programs allow you to create an **address book**, or contacts folder, which contains a list of names and e-mail addresses.

When you send an e-mail message, an outgoing mail server that is operated by your Internet access provider determines how to route the message through the Internet and then sends the message. As you receive e-mail messages, an incoming mail server — also operated by your Internet access provider — holds the messages in your mailbox until you use your e-mail program to retrieve them. Most e-mail programs have a mail notification alert that informs you via a message and/or sound when you receive new mail. Figure 2-20 illustrates how an e-mail message may travel from a sender to a receiver.

FAQ 2-3

Can my computer get a virus through e-mail?

Yes. A virus is a computer program that can damage files and the operating system. One way that virus authors attempt to spread a virus is by sending virus-infected e-mail attachments. If you receive an e-mail attachment, you should use an antivirus program to verify that it is virus free.

For more information, read the section about viruses and antivirus programs in Chapter 7, and visit scsite.com/ dcf5e/ch2/faq and then click Viruses.

FIGURE 2-20   **HOW AN E-MAIL MESSAGE MAY TRAVEL FROM A SENDER TO A RECEIVER**

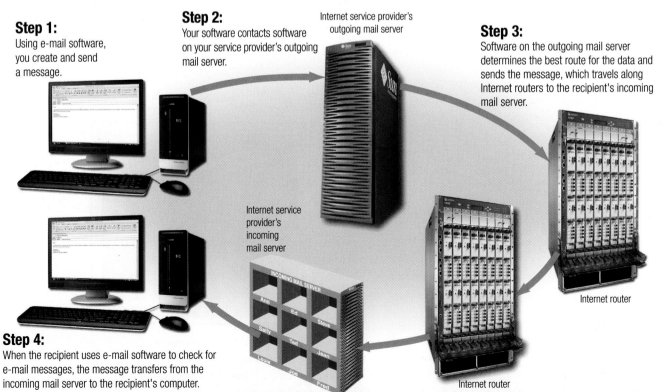

Step 1:
Using e-mail software, you create and send a message.

Step 2:
Your software contacts software on your service provider's outgoing mail server.

Internet service provider's outgoing mail server

Step 3:
Software on the outgoing mail server determines the best route for the data and sends the message, which travels along Internet routers to the recipient's incoming mail server.

Internet service provider's incoming mail server

Internet router

Step 4:
When the recipient uses e-mail software to check for e-mail messages, the message transfers from the incoming mail server to the recipient's computer.

Internet router

Mailing Lists

A **mailing list** is a group of e-mail names and addresses given a single name. When a message is sent to a mailing list, every person on the list receives a copy of the message in his or her mailbox. To add your e-mail name and address to a mailing list, you subscribe to it. To remove your name, you **unsubscribe** from the mailing list.

Thousands of mailing lists exist about a variety of topics in areas of entertainment, business, computers, society, culture, health, recreation, and education. To locate a mailing list dealing with a particular topic, you can search for the search text, mailing list, in a search engine.

WEB LINK 2-6

Mailing Lists

For more information, visit scsite.com/dcf5e/ch2/weblink and then click Mailing Lists.

Instant Messaging

Instant messaging (IM) is a real-time Internet communications service that notifies you when one or more people are online and then allows you to exchange messages or files or join a private chat room with them (Figure 2-21). Some IM services support voice and video conversations. For IM to work, both parties must be online at the same time. Also, the receiver of a message must be willing to accept messages.

To use IM, you may have to install instant messenger software on the computer or device, such as a smart phone, you plan to use. Some operating systems, such as Windows Vista, include an instant messenger. No standards currently exist for IM. To ensure successful communications, all individuals on the contact list need to use the same or a compatible instant messenger.

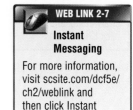

WEB LINK 2-7

Instant Messaging

For more information, visit scsite.com/dcf5e/ch2/weblink and then click Instant Messaging.

FIGURE 2-21   AN EXAMPLE OF INSTANT MESSAGING

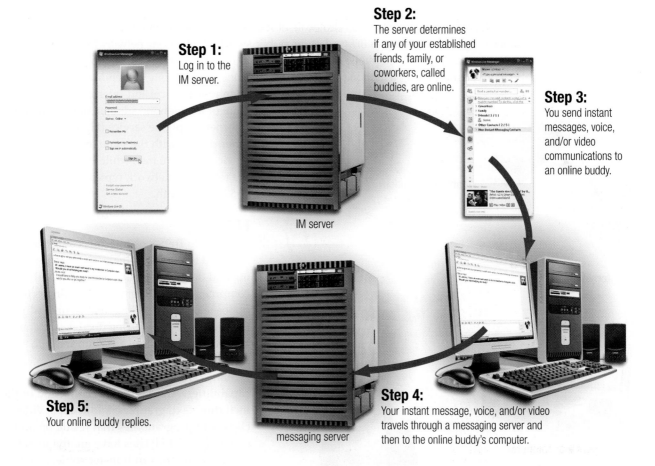

Step 1:
Log in to the IM server.

Step 2:
The server determines if any of your established friends, family, or coworkers, called buddies, are online.

Step 3:
You send instant messages, voice, and/or video communications to an online buddy.

IM server

Step 4:
Your instant message, voice, and/or video travels through a messaging server and then to the online buddy's computer.

Step 5:
Your online buddy replies.

messaging server

Chat Rooms

A **chat** is a real-time typed conversation that takes place on a computer. **Real time** means that you and the people with whom you are conversing are online at the same time. A **chat room** is a location on an Internet server that permits users to chat with each other. Anyone in the chat room can participate in the conversation, which usually is specific to a particular topic.

As you type on your keyboard, a line of characters and symbols is displayed on the computer screen. Others connected to the same chat room server also see what you type (Figure 2-22). Some chat rooms support voice chats and video chats, in which people hear or see each other as they chat.

To start a chat session, you connect to a chat server through a program called a chat client. Today's browsers usually include a chat client. If yours does not, you can download a chat client from the Web. Once you have installed a chat client, you can create or join a conversation on the chat server to which you are connected.

FIGURE 2-22   As you type, the words and symbols you enter are displayed on the computer screens of other people in the same chat room.

VoIP

VoIP (Voice over IP, or Internet Protocol), also called Internet telephony, enables users to speak to other users over the Internet (instead of the public switched telephone network).

To place an Internet telephone call, you need a high-speed Internet connection (e.g., via cable or DSL modem); Internet telephone service; a microphone or telephone, depending on the Internet telephone service; and Internet telephone software or a telephone adapter, depending on the Internet telephone service (Figure 2-23). Calls to other parties with the same Internet telephone service often are free, while calls that connect to the telephone network typically cost about $15 to $25 per month.

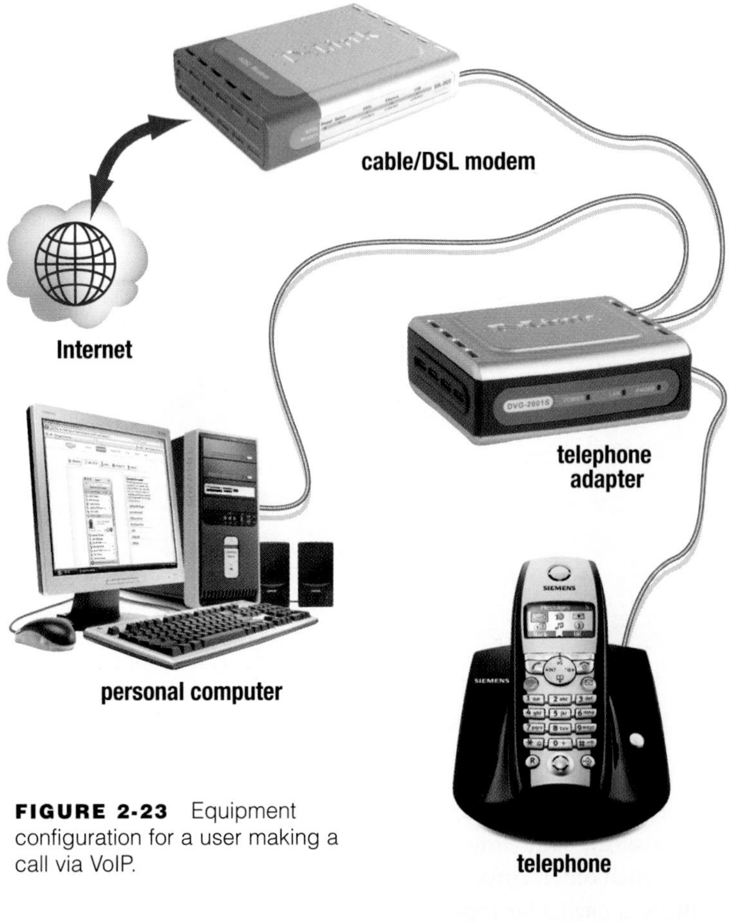

cable/DSL modem

Internet

telephone adapter

personal computer

FTP

FTP (File Transfer Protocol) is an Internet standard that permits the process of file uploading and downloading (transferring) with other computers on the Internet. Uploading is the opposite of downloading; that is, **uploading** is the process of transferring documents, graphics, and other objects from your computer to a server on the Internet.

Many operating systems include FTP capabilities. An FTP site is a collection of files including text, graphics, audio clips, video clips, and program files that reside on an FTP server. Many FTP sites have anonymous FTP, whereby anyone can transfer some, if not all, available files. Some FTP sites restrict file transfers to those who have authorized accounts (user names and passwords) on the FTP server.

FIGURE 2-23   Equipment configuration for a user making a call via VoIP.

telephone

Newsgroups and Message Boards

A **newsgroup** is an online area in which users have written discussions about a particular subject (Figure 2-24). To participate in a discussion, a user sends a message to the newsgroup, and other users in the newsgroup read and reply to the message. Some major newsgroup topic areas include news, recreation, society, business, science, and computers.

Some newsgroups require you to enter a user name and password to participate in the discussion. For example, a newsgroup for students taking a college course may require a user name and password to access the newsgroup. This ensures that only students in the course participate in the discussion. To participate in a newsgroup, typically you use a program called a newsreader.

A popular Web-based type of discussion group that does not require a newsreader is a **message board**. Many Web sites use message boards instead of newsgroups because they are easier to use.

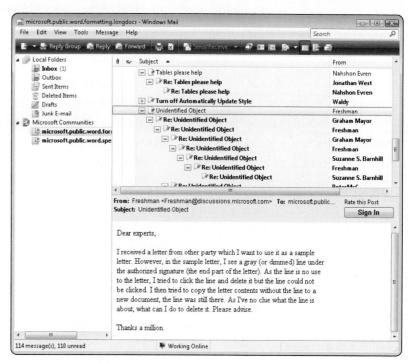

FIGURE 2-24 Users in a newsgroup read and reply to other users' messages.

NETIQUETTE

Netiquette, which is short for Internet etiquette, is the code of acceptable behaviors users should follow while on the Internet; that is, it is the conduct expected of individuals while online. Netiquette includes rules for all aspects of the Internet, including the World Wide Web, e-mail, instant messaging, chat rooms, FTP, and newsgroups and message boards. Figure 2-25 outlines some of the rules of netiquette.

NETIQUETTE

Golden Rule: Treat others as you would like them to treat you.

1. In e-mail, chat rooms, and newsgroups:
   - Keep messages brief. Use proper grammar, spelling, and punctuation.
   - Be careful when using sarcasm and humor, as it might be misinterpreted.
   - Be polite. Avoid offensive language.
   - Read the message before you send it.
   - Use meaningful subject lines.
   - Avoid sending or posting flames, which are abusive or insulting messages. Do not participate in flame wars, which are exchanges of flames.
   - Avoid sending spam, which is the Internet's version of junk mail. Spam is an unsolicited e-mail message or newsgroup posting sent to many recipients or newsgroups at once.
   - Do not use all capital letters, which is the equivalent of SHOUTING!

   - Use **emoticons** to express emotion. Popular emoticons include

:) Smile	:\ Undecided	:l Indifference
:(Frown	:o Surprised	

   - Use abbreviations and acronyms for phrases:

BTW	by the way
IMHO	in my humble opinion
FYI	for your information
TTFN	ta ta for now
FWIW	for what it's worth
TYVM	thank you very much

   - Clearly identify a spoiler, which is a message that reveals a solution to a game or ending to a movie or program.

2. Read the FAQ (frequently asked questions), if one exists. Many newsgroups and Web pages have an FAQ.
3. Do not assume material is accurate or up-to-date. Be forgiving of other's mistakes.
4. Never read someone's private e-mail.

FIGURE 2-25 Some of the rules of netiquette.

Test your knowledge of pages 68 through 73 in Quiz Yourself 2-3.

QUIZ YOURSELF 2-3

Instructions: Find the true statement below. Then, rewrite the remaining false statements so they are true.

1. A chat room is a location on an Internet server that permits users to chat with each other.
2. An e-mail address is a combination of a user name and an e-mail program that identifies a user so that he or she can receive Internet e-mail.
3. FTP uses the Internet (instead of the public switched telephone network) to connect a calling party to one or more called parties.
4. Netiquette is the code of unacceptable behaviors while on the Internet.
5. VoIP enables users to subscribe to other users over the Internet.

Quiz Yourself Online: To further check your knowledge of e-mail, mailing lists, instant messaging, chat rooms, VoIP, FTP, newgroups and message boards, and netiquette, visit scsite.com/dcf5e/ch2/quiz and then click Objectives 6 – 7.

CHAPTER SUMMARY

This chapter presented the history and structure of the Internet. It discussed the World Wide Web at length, including topics such as browsing, navigating, searching, Web publishing, and e-commerce (read Ethics & Issues 2-2 for a related discussion). It also introduced other services available on the Internet, such as e-mail, instant messaging, chat rooms, VoIP, FTP, and newsgroups and message boards. Finally, the chapter listed rules of netiquette.

ETHICS & ISSUES 2-2

Should Companies Be Able to Track Your Online Habits?

When you visit a Web site that includes an advertisement, someone probably is recording the fact that you visited that Web site and viewed the advertisement with your browser. Over time, companies that specialize in tracking who views which online advertisements can amass an enormous amount of information about your online Web surfing habits. This collection of information is considered to be part of your online profile. One company claims that through the use of advertisements on Web pages, it can track well over one billion Web page views per day. Through tracking the Web sites a user visits, the products they buy, and the articles they read, a company may attempt to profile the visitor's beliefs, associations, and habits. Although a user may think he or she is anonymous while navigating the Web, the company can attempt through various means to link the user's true identity with the user's online profile. The company can sell online profiles, with or without the user's true identity, to other advertisers or organizations. Should organizations be allowed to track your Web surfing habits? Why or why not? Should organizations be allowed to associate your real identity with your online identity and profit from the information? Should companies give you the option of not being tracked? What are the benefits and dangers of online tracking?

CAREER CORNER   **Web Developer**

If you are looking for a job working with the latest Internet technology, then Web developer could be the career for you. A **Web developer** analyzes, designs, develops, implements, and supports Web applications and functionality. Specialized programming skills required include HTML, JavaScript, Java, Perl, C++, and VBScript. Developers also need multimedia knowledge, including Photoshop, Flash, and Dreamweaver. Developers must be aware of emerging technologies, such as Web 2.0 and know how they can be used to enhance a Web presence. Web 2.0 developers must be able to build event-driven environments, such as RSS feeds.

A Web developer must be able to appreciate a client's needs, recognize the technologies involved to meet those needs, and explain those technologies to the client. For example, if the client is a large corporation seeking to set up an online store, a Web developer must understand e-commerce and be able to explain requirements, probable costs, and possible outcomes in a way the client can understand.

Educational requirements vary from company to company and can range from a high school education to a four-year degree. Many companies place heavy emphasis on certifications. Two of the more popular certifications are available through the International Webmasters Association (IWA) and the World Organization of Webmasters (WOW). A wide salary range exists — from $41,000 to $80,000 — depending on educational background and location. For more information, visit scsite.com/dcf5e/ch2/careers and then click Web Developer.

Google
Popular Search Engine

The founders of Google, the leading Internet search engine, state that their mission is to organize the world's information. Every day, their Web site handles hundreds of millions of queries for information. In seconds, it can locate specific phrases and terms on four billion Web pages by using more than 10,000 connected computers.

Sergey Brin and Larry Page launched Google in 1998 in a friend's garage. The name is derived from "googol," which is the name of the number 1 followed by 100 zeros. Google announced in 2007 the launch of its universal search system, which blends information from a variety of separate sources, including video, news, books, images, and maps, with Web sites to produce a single set of results. For more information, visit scsite.com/dcf5e/ch2/companies and then click Google.

Yahoo!
Popular Web Portal

Yahoo!, the first navigational portal to the Web, began as a hobby for Jerry Yang and David Filo when they were doctoral candidates in electrical engineering at Stanford University. They started creating and organizing lists of their favorite Web sites in 1994. The following year, they shared their creation, named Yahoo!, with fellow students and then released their product to the Internet community.

Yahoo! is an acronym for Yet Another Hierarchical Officious Oracle. What makes Yahoo! unique is that staff members build the directory by assuming the role of a typical Web researcher. As part of Yahoo! Elections 2008, the company cosponsored the first online-only presidential debates for the Democratic and Republican candidates. The two debates allowed voters to question the candidates directly, participate in the debate in real time, and determine which candidate gave the best performance. For more information, visit scsite.com/dcf5e/ch2/companies and then click Yahoo!.

TECHNOLOGY TRAILBLAZERS

Tim Berners-Lee
Creator of the World Wide Web

The World Wide Web (WWW) has become one of the more widely used Internet services, and its roots are based on Tim Berners-Lee's work. Berners-Lee is credited with creating the first Web server, browser, and Web addresses.

He developed his ideas in 1989 while working at CERN, the European Particle Physics Laboratory in Geneva, Switzerland, and based his work on a program he had written for his own use to track random associations. Today, he works quietly in academia as director of the World Wide Web Consortium (W3C) at the Massachusetts Institute of Technology.

Queen Elizabeth II bestowed the Order of Merit upon the British-born Lee in 2007. Limited to 24 living members, this award recognizes distinguished service in science, art, literature, and the armed forces, as well as the promotion of culture. For more information, visit scsite.com/dcf5e/ch2/people and then click Tim Berners-Lee.

Meg Whitman
eBay President and CEO

Meg Whitman joined eBay in 1998 and has been instrumental in helping the company become the world's largest online marketplace. Before that time, she was an executive for the Keds Division of the Stride Rite Corporation and general manager of Hasbro Inc.'s Preschool Division. She then served as president and CEO of Florists Transworld Delivery (FTD).

She credits her success to listening to the loyal eBay community, and she occasionally answers their e-mail messages personally. She holds degrees in economics from Princeton University and management from the Harvard Business School.

eBay fields hundreds of millions of searches daily for products. In 2007, Whitman broadened eBay's platform by offering auctions to Chinese mobile customers and by acquiring ticket reseller StubHub for $310 million. For more information, visit scsite.com/dcf5e/ch2/people and then click Meg Whitman.

CHAPTER 2

Chapter Review

The Chapter Review section summarizes the concepts presented in this chapter. To obtain help from other students regarding any subject in this chapter, visit scsite.com/dcf5e/ch2/forum and post your thoughts or questions.

(1) How Can You Access and Connect to the Internet?

The **Internet** is a worldwide collection of networks that links millions of businesses, government agencies, educational institutions, and individuals. Employees and students often connect to the Internet through a business or school network. Some home and small businesses connect to the Internet with **dial-up access**, which uses a modem in the computer and a standard telephone line. Many home and small business users opt for higher-speed connections. **DSL** provides high-speed Internet connections using regular copper telephone lines. A **cable modem** allows access to high-speed Internet services through the cable television network. **Fiber to the Premises (FTTP)** uses fiber-optic cable to provide high-speed Internet access. **Fixed wireless** high-speed Internet connections use a dish-shaped antenna to communicate via radio signals. **Wi-Fi** uses radio signals to provide Internet connections to wireless computers and devices. A **wireless modem** accesses the Internet through a cellular network. A **satellite modem** communicates with a satellite dish to provide high-speed Internet connections. An **access provider** is a business that provides access to the Internet free or for a fee. An **ISP (Internet service provider)** is a regional or national access provider. An **online service provider** (OSP) provides Internet access in addition to members-only features. A **wireless Internet service provider** (WISP) provides wireless Internet access to computers and mobile devices with built-in wireless capability (such as Wi-Fi) or to computers using wireless access devices.

 Visit scsite.com/dcf5e/ch2/quiz or click the Quiz Yourself button. Click Objective 1.

(2) How Can You View a Web Page and Search for Information on the Web?

A **Web browser**, or **browser**, is application software that allows users to access and view Web pages. When you type a **Web address** in the Address bar of a browser window, a computer called a **Web server** delivers the requested Web page to your computer. Most Web pages contain links. A **link** is a built-in connection that, when clicked, displays a related Web page or part of a Web page. Two search tools are search engines and subject directories. A **search engine** finds Web sites, Web pages, images, videos, news, and other information related to a specific topic. Search engines require **search text** that describes the item you want to find. A **subject directory** classifies Web pages in an organized set of categories or groups.

(3) What Are the Types of Web Sites?

A **portal** is a Web site that offers a variety of Internet services from a single location. A news Web site contains newsworthy material. An informational Web site contains factual information. A business/marketing Web site promotes or sells products or services. An educational Web site offers avenues for teaching and learning. An entertainment Web site offers an interactive and engaging environment. An advocacy Web site describes a cause, opinion, or idea. A **blog** is an informal Web site consisting of time-stamped articles, or posts, in a diary or journal format, usually listed in reverse chronological order. A **wiki** is a collaborative Web site that allows users to create, add to, modify, or delete the Web site content via their Web browser. An **online social network**, or **social networking Web site**, encourages members to share their interests, ideas, stories, photos, music, and videos with other registered users. A **content aggregator** is a business that gathers and organizes Web content and then distributes, or feeds, the content to subscribers for free or a fee. A personal Web site is maintained by a private individual or family.

(4) What Are the Steps Required for Web Publishing?

Web publishing is the development and maintenance of Web pages. The five major steps to Web publishing are: (1) plan a Web site, (2) analyze and design a Web site, (3) create a Web site, (4) deploy a Web site, and (5) maintain a Web site.

(5) What Are the Types of E-Commerce?

E-commerce, short for electronic commerce, is a business transaction that occurs over an electronic network such as the Internet. Business-to-consumer (B2C) e-commerce consists of the sale of goods and services to the general public. Consumer-to-consumer (C2C) e-commerce occurs when one consumer sells directly to another, such as an **online auction**. Business-to-business (B2B) e-commerce takes place between businesses that exchange goods and services.

 Visit scsite.com/dcf5e/ch2/quiz or click the Quiz Yourself button. Click Objectives 2 – 5.

Chapter Review

 6 **How Do E-Mail, Mailing Lists, Instant Messaging, Chat Rooms, VoIP, FTP, and Newsgroups and Message Boards Work?**

E-mail (short for electronic mail) is the transmission of messages and files via a computer network. A **mailing list** is a group of e-mail names and addresses given a single name, so that everyone on the list receives a message sent to the list. **Instant messaging** (**IM**) is a real-time Internet communications service that notifies you when one or more people are online. A **chat room** is a location on an Internet server that permits users to **chat**, or conduct real-time typed conversations. **VoIP** (Voice over IP, or Internet Protocol) enables users to speak to other users over the Internet instead of the public switched telephone network. **FTP** (File Transfer Protocol) is an Internet standard that permits file **uploading** and **downloading** with other computers on the Internet. A **newsgroup** is an online area in which users have written discussions about a particular subject. A **message board** is a popular Web-based type of discussion group that is easier to use than a newsgroup.

7 **What Are the Rules of Netiquette?**

Netiquette, which is short for Internet etiquette, is the code of acceptable behaviors users should follow while on the Internet. Keep messages short. Be polite. Use **emoticons**. Read the FAQ if one exists. Do not assume material is accurate or up-to-date, and never read someone's private e-mail.

 Visit scsite.com/dcf5e/ch2/quiz or click the Quiz Yourself button. Click Objectives 6 – 7.

Key Terms

You should know the Key Terms. Use the list below to help focus your study. To further enhance your understanding of the Key Terms in this chapter, visit scsite.com/dcf5e/ch2/terms. See an example of and a definition for each term, and access current and additional information about the term from the Web.

access provider (52)	Fiber to the Premises (FTTP) (52)	online auction (68)	user name (70)
add-on (66)	fixed wireless (52)	online service provider (52)	video (65)
address book (70)	FTP (72)	online social network (62)	video blog (62)
animation (64)	graphic (64)	player (64)	virtual reality (VR) (65)
audio (64)	home page (55)	plug-in (66)	vlog (62)
blog (62)	host (50)	podcast (64)	vlogosphere (62)
blogosphere (62)	hot spots (52)	portal (61)	VoIP (72)
browser (54)	hyperlink (57)	real time (71)	Web (54)
cable modem (52)	instant messaging (IM) (71)	RSS 2.0 (63)	Web 2.0 (54)
chat (71)	Internet (50)	satellite modem (52)	Web address (56)
chat room (71)	Internet backbone (52)	search engine (58)	Web browser (54)
click (57)	IP address (53)	search text (58)	Web developer (74)
content aggregator (63)	ISP (Internet service provider) (52)	server (50)	Web page (54)
dial-up access (51)		shopping cart (68)	Web publishing (66)
digital rights management (64)	link (57)	social networking Web site (62)	Web server (54)
domain name (53)	mailing list (71)	streaming (64)	Web site (54)
downloading (55)	media sharing Web site (62)	subject directory (58)	Wi-Fi (52)
DSL (52)	message board (73)	surfing the Web (57)	wiki (62)
e-commerce (67)	MP3 (64)	tabbed browsing (57)	wireless Internet service provider (WISP) (52)
electronic storefront (68)	MP4 (65)	thumbnail (64)	wireless modem (52)
e-mail (69)	multimedia (64)	top-level domain (TLD) (54)	World Wide Web (WWW) (54)
e-mail address (70)	Net (50)	unsubscribe (71)	World Wide Web Consortium (W3C) (51)
e-mail program (69)	netiquette (73)	uploading (72)	
emoticons (73)	newsgroup (73)	URL (56)	

Checkpoint

Use the Checkpoint exercises to check your knowledge level of the chapter. To complete the Checkpoint exercises interactively, visit scsite.com/dcf5e/ch2/check.

True/False

Mark T for True and F for False. (See page numbers in parentheses.)

_____ 1. A host or server is any computer that provides services and connections to other computers on a network. (50)

_____ 2. DSL is a technology that provides high-speed Internet connections over the cable television network. (52)

_____ 3. A domain name is the numeric version of an IP address. (53)

_____ 4. A Web 2.0 Web site may include application software built into the site for visitors to use. (54)

_____ 5. Tabbed browsing refers to the practice of Web sites keeping tabs on their visitors. (57)

_____ 6. A search engine is a program that finds Web sites, Web pages, images, videos, news, and other information related to a specific topic. (58)

_____ 7. A social networking Web site encourages members in its online community to share their interests, ideas, stories, photos, music, and videos with other registered users. (62)

_____ 8. Streaming disallows users from accessing and using a file while it is transmitting. (64)

_____ 9. A plug-in, or add-on, is a program that extends the capability of a browser. (66)

_____ 10. VoIP enables users to speak to other users over the Internet (instead of the public switched telephone network). (72)

Multiple Choice

Select the best answer. (See page numbers in parentheses.)

1. Although it is slow-speed technology, some homes and small businesses use _____ to connect to the Internet. (51)
   a. a satellite modem
   b. a cable modem
   c. DSL
   d. dial-up access

2. A _____ allows access to the Internet through a cellular network. (52)
   a. cable modem
   b. wireless modem
   c. satellite modem
   d. hot spot

3. _____ is the process of a computer receiving information, such as a Web page, from a server on the Internet. (55)
   a. Uploading
   b. Downloading
   c. Social networking
   d. Blogging

4. A _____ is a specific type of online social network that enables members to share photos, music, and videos. (62)
   a. blog
   b. wiki
   c. podcast
   d. media sharing Web site

5. A _____ is recorded audio stored on a Web site that can be downloaded to a computer or a portable media player. (64)
   a. podcast   b. wiki
   c. blog   d. portal

6. _____ is a strategy designed to prevent illegal distribution of music and other digital content. (64)
   a. A threaded discussion
   b. VoIP
   c. Digital rights management
   d. Podcasting

7. In _____ e-commerce, customers purchase from other consumers. (68)
   a. consumer-to-business
   b. business-to-business
   c. consumer-to-consumer
   d. business-to-consumer

8. The _____ standard permits uploading and downloading of files on the Internet. (72)
   a. message board
   b. newsgroup
   c. FTP
   d. mailing list

Matching

Match the terms with their definitions. (See page numbers in parentheses.)

_____ 1. hot spots (52)

_____ 2. video blog (62)

_____ 3. MP3 (64)

_____ 4. e-mail address (70)

_____ 5. emoticon (73)

a. used to express emotions in e-mail, chat rooms, and newsgroups

b. provide public Wi-Fi Internet connections to users with mobile computers or devices

c. combination of a user name and a domain name that identifies an Internet user

d. a blog that contains video clips

e. built-in connection to a related Web page or part of a Web page

f. format that reduces an audio file to about one-tenth its original size

Checkpoint

Short Answer — Write a brief answer to each of the following questions.

1. Describe three different types of modems. _____ What is Fiber to the Premises (FTTP)? _____
2. How is a Web page different from a Web site? _____ How can you use a Web address to display a Web page? _____
3. What are the differences between blogs, wikis, and podcasts? _____ When might you use each? _____
4. What is one specification used by content aggregators to distribute content? _____ How might you evaluate the accuracy of a Web site? _____
5. How do you interact with a mailing list? _____ When might you use a newsgroup? _____

Working Together — Working in a group of your classmates, complete the following team exercises.

1. This chapter lists 12 types of Web sites: portal, news, informational, business/marketing, educational, entertainment, advocacy, blog, wiki, online social network, content aggregator, and personal. Working as a team, use the Internet to find at least two examples of each type of Web site. For each Web site, identify the Web address, the multimedia elements used, the purpose of the Web site, and the type of Web site. Explain why you classified each site as you did. Then, keeping in mind the purpose of each Web site, rank the sites in terms of their effectiveness. Share your findings in a report and/or a presentation with the class.

Web Research

Use the Internet-based Web Research exercises to broaden your understanding of the concepts presented in this chapter. To discuss any of the Web Research exercises in this chapter with other students, post your thoughts or questions at scsite.com/dcf5e/ch2/forum.

① Blogs Many of the best blogs in the blogosphere have received awards for their content and design. For example, loyal blogging fans nominate and vote for their favorite blogs by visiting the Blogger's Choice Awards Web site (bloggerschoiceawards.com). Visit this Web site, click the Best Blog Design, Best Blog About Blogging, and Best Education Blog links, and view some of the blogs receiving the largest number of votes. Then visit other award sites, including the Interactive Media Awards (interactivemediaawards.com), Bloggies (bloggies.com), Best of Blogs (thebestofblogs.com), and Weblog Awards (weblogawards.org). What blogs, if any, received multiple awards on the different Web sites? Who casts the votes? What criteria are used to judge these blogs?

② Scavenger Hunt Use one of the search engines listed in Figure 2-8 in Chapter 2 on page 58 or your own favorite search engine to find the answers to the following questions. Copy and paste the Web address from the Web page where you found the answer. Some questions may have more than one answer. If required, submit your answers to your instructor. (1) The World Wide Web Consortium (W3C) sets Internet standards. What is the purpose of the W3C's Markup Validation Service? (2) What cable company was established in 1858 to carry instantaneous communications across the ocean that eventually would be used for Internet communications? (3) What was eBay's original name, and what was the first item offered for auction? (4) How many Web pages is Google currently searching?

③ Search Sleuth The Internet has provided the opportunity to access encyclopedias online. One of the more comprehensive encyclopedia research sites is Encyclopedia.com. Visit this Web site and then use your word processing program to answer the following questions. Then, if required, submit your answers to your instructor. (1) What is Today's Featured Topic on the site's home page? (2) Click the letter, B, in the Browse by alphabet section and then click the Blo-Bon link. Scroll down to the first blog entry and then click this link. What is the definition of a blog? What are the titles of three related articles? (3) Type "MP3" as the keyword in the Search text box and then press the ENTER key or click the Research button. How many articles discussing MP3 are found on the Encyclopedia.com Web site? (4) Type "netiquette" as the keyword in the Search text box and then press the ENTER key or click the Research button. Click one of the personal computer links, review the material, and, if required, submit to your instructor a 50-word summary of the information you read.

Learn How To

Use the Learn How To activities to learn fundamental skills when using a computer and accompanying technology. Complete the exercises and submit them to your instructor. Premium Activity: The icon indicates you can see a visual demonstration of the associated Learn How To activity by visiting scsite.com/dcf5e/ch2/howto.

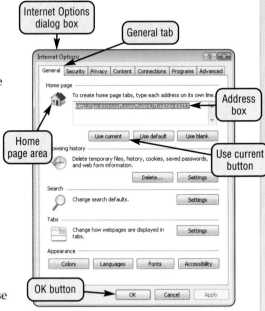

FIGURE 2-26

LEARN HOW TO 1: Change a Web Browser's Home Page

When you start a Web browser, a Web page is displayed. You can change the page that appears when you start a Web browser or when you click the Home button on the browser toolbar by completing the following steps:

1. With the browser running, navigate to the Web page you would like to make your Home page.
2. Click the Tools button arrow and then click Internet Options to display the Internet Options dialog box shown in Figure 2-26.
3. Click the Use current button.
4. Click the OK button in the Internet Options dialog box.

When you start the browser or click the Home button on the browser toolbar, the selected Web page will be displayed.

Exercise

1. Start your Web browser. Write down the address of the browser's current home page. Then, change the browser's home page to www.cnn.com. Close the browser.
2. Start your Web browser. What is the lead story on cnn.com? Use links on the page to view several stories. Which story do you find most interesting? Click the Home button on the browser toolbar. What happened? Submit these answers to your instructor.
3. Change the browser's home page to your school's home page. Click the Home button on the browser toolbar. Click the Calendar or Events link, and then locate two campus events of which you were unaware. Report these two campus events to your instructor.
4. Change the browser's home page back to the address you wrote down in Step 1.

LEARN HOW TO 2: Search the Web for Driving Directions, Addresses, and Telephone Numbers

In addition to searching the Web for information using search engines such as Google and Yahoo!, some Web sites are designed specifically to search for other information such as driving directions, addresses, and telephone numbers.

Search for Driving Directions

1. Start your Web browser, type www.mapquest.com in the Address bar, and then press the ENTER key to display the MapQuest home page. If necessary, scroll down to display the Directions box.
2. Type the starting address (or intersection), city, state, and ZIP code (if you know it) in the appropriate text boxes in the Starting Location area of the Directions box.
3. Type the ending address (or intersection), city, state, and ZIP code (if you know it) in the appropriate text boxes in the Ending Location area of the Directions box.
4. Click the Get Directions button to display the driving directions.

Search for the Address and Telephone Number of a Business

1. If necessary, start your Web browser. Type www.infospace.com in the Address bar, and then press the ENTER key to display the InfoSpace home page.
2. Click the Find a Business by Name option button.
3. Type the name of the business in the Name of Business text box, type the City where the business is located (if you know it), and then select the State from the State* drop-down list.
4. Click the SEARCH button to display the search results.
5. Click the phone link on the Web page with the search result(s) to display the telephone number.
6. Close your Web browser.

Exercise

1. If necessary, start Internet Explorer by clicking the Start button, and then click Internet Explorer on the Start menu. Type www.mapquest.com in the Address bar, and then press the ENTER key. Search for driving directions between your address and the address of a friend or family member. How many miles are between the two addresses? How long would it take you to drive from your address to the other address? Write a paragraph explaining whether you would or would not use MapQuest to retrieve driving directions. Submit this paragraph to your instructor.

2. Think about a company for which you would like to work. In your Web browser, display the InfoSpace Web page (www.infospace.com) and then search for the address and telephone number of this company. If InfoSpace does not display the desired information, what other Web sites might you be able to use to search for the address and telephone number for a company?

 LEARN HOW TO 3: Bid and Buy a Product from eBay

Online auctions have grown to be a favorite shopping space for many people. A leading online auction Web site is eBay. To submit a bid for an item on eBay, complete the following steps:

1. Type www.ebay.com in the Address bar of your browser. Press the ENTER key to display the eBay home page (Figure 2-27).
2. You must be registered to bid on eBay. If you are registered, click the Sign in link, enter your eBay User ID and Password, and then click the Sign In Securely button. If not, click the register link and follow the instructions.
3. Pick an item you find interesting and on which you might bid.
4. Enter your item in the search text box and then click the Search button.
5. Scroll through the page to see the available items.
6. To bid on an item, click the item's description and then click the Place Bid button. The eBay Web site contains reminders that when you bid on an item, you are entering into a contract to purchase the item if you are the successful bidder. Bidding on eBay is serious business.
7. Enter the amount of your bid. Click the Continue button.
8. You will confirm your bid and receive notification about your bid.
9. You will be notified by e-mail if you won the bid. If so, you will arrange with the seller for payment and shipment.

FIGURE 2-27

Exercise

1. Start your browser and display the eBay home page.
2. In the search text box, enter the name of an upcoming sporting event you would like to attend followed by the word, tickets. For example, enter Super Bowl tickets as the entry. Click the Search button.
3. Did you find available tickets? Were there more tickets available than you expected, or fewer? Are the bid prices reasonable or ridiculous? How many bids were made for all the tickets? How much time is left to bid? What items did you find you were not expecting? Submit answers to these questions to your instructor.
4. Enter an item of your choice in the search text box. If you feel so inclined, bid on an item. Do you think this manner of buying goods is valuable? Why? Will you visit eBay again? Why? Submit answers to these questions to your instructor.

Learn It Online

Use the Learn It Online exercises to reinforce your understanding of the chapter concepts. To access the Learn It Online exercises, visit scsite.com/dcf5e/ch2/learn.

(1) At the Movies — Tell Your Stories Via Vlog

To view the Tell Your Stories Via Vlog movie, click the number 1 button. Locate your video and click the corresponding High-Speed or Dial-Up link, depending on your Internet connection. Watch the movie to learn about vlogs. If jotting down your diary in text is not appealing, try a simple and free video blog. Complete the exercise by explaining briefly how to create a vlog.

(2) Student Edition Labs — Connecting to the Internet

Click the number 2 button. A new browser window will open, displaying the Student Edition Labs. Follow the on-screen instructions to complete the Connecting to the Internet Lab. When finished, click the Exit button. If required, submit your results to your instructor.

(3) Practice Test

Click the number 3 button. Answer each question. When completed, enter your name and click the Grade Test button to submit the quiz for grading. Make a note of any missed questions. If required, submit your score to your instructor.

(4) Who Wants To Be a Computer Genius^2?

Click the number 4 button to find out if you are a computer genius. Directions about how to play the game will be displayed. When you are ready to play, click the Play button. Submit your score to your instructor.

(5) Google Earth

Click the number 5 button to download Google Earth. Once you have downloaded Google Earth, use it to fly to your home, school, Grand Canyon, Baghdad, Paris, and Moscow. At each location, use the buttons to change the view. Print a copy of the map showing your school, handwrite on the map the school's elevation, and submit the map to your instructor.

(6) Student Edition Labs — Getting the Most out of the Internet

Click the number 6 button. A new browser window will open, displaying the Student Edition Labs. Follow the on-screen instructions to complete the Getting the Most out of the Internet Lab. When finished, click the Exit button. If required, submit your results to your instructor.

(7) Crossword Puzzle Challenge

Click the number 7 button then click the Crossword Puzzle Challenge link. Directions about how to play the game will be displayed. Complete the puzzle to reinforce skills you learned in this chapter. When you are ready to play, click the Continue button. Submit the completed puzzle to your instructor.

(8) Vista Exercises

Click the number 8 button. When the Vista Exercises menu appears, click the exercise assigned by your instructor. A new browser window will open. Follow the on-screen instructions to complete the exercise. When finished, click the Exit button. If required, submit your results to your instructor.

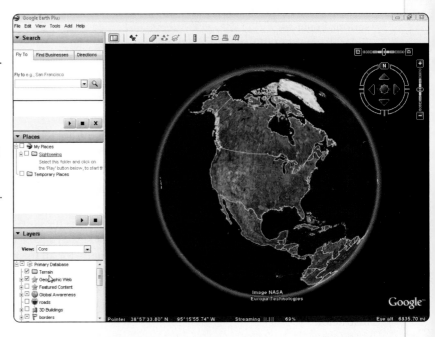

Making Use of the Web

Information literacy is defined as having the practical skills needed to evaluate information critically from print and electronic resources and to use this information accurately in daily life. Locating Web sites may be profitable for your educational and professional careers, as the resources may help you research class assignments and make your life more fulfilling and manageable.

Because the World Wide Web does not have an organizational structure to assist you in locating reliable material, you may need additional resources to guide you in searching. To help you find useful Web sites, this Special Feature describes specific information about a variety of Web pages, and it includes tables of Web addresses so that you can get started. The material is organized in several areas of interest.

AREAS OF INTEREST	
Fun and Entertainment	Shopping and Auctions
Research	Weather, Sports, and News
Blogs	Learning
Online Social Networks and Media Sharing	Science
Travel	Health
Environment	Careers
Finance	Arts and Literature
Government	

Web Exercises at the end of each category will reinforce the material and help you discover Web sites that may add a treasure trove of knowledge to your life.

Fun and Entertainment
THAT'S ENTERTAINMENT

Rock 'n' Roll on the Web

Consumers place great significance on buying entertainment products for fun and recreation. Nearly 10 percent of the United States's economy is spent on attending concerts and buying DVDs, CDs, reading materials, sporting goods, and toys.

Many Web sites supplement our cravings for fun and entertainment. For example, you can see and hear the musicians inducted into the Rock and Roll Hall of Fame and Museum (Figure 1). If you need an update on your favorite reality-based television program or a preview of an upcoming movie, E! Online and Entertainment Tonight provide the latest features on television and movie stars. The Internet Movie Database contains credits and reviews of more than 849,000 titles.

Watch the surfers riding the waves in Washington and romp with pandas at the San Diego Zoo. Web cams can display live video on Web pages, taking armchair travelers across the world for views of natural attractions, historical monuments, colleges, and cities. Many Web sites featuring Web cams are listed in the table in Figure 2.

FUN AND ENTERTAINMENT WEB SITES

Web Cams	Web Address
AfriCam Virtual Game Reserve	africam.com
Camvista Global	camvista.com
Discovery Kids — Live Cams	kids.discovery.com/cams/cams.html
EarthCam — Webcam Network	earthcam.com
NOAA ESRL Global Monitoring Division — South Pole Live Camera	cmdl.noaa.gov/obop/spo/livecamera.html
Panda Cam San Diego Zoo	sandiegozoo.org
WebCam Central	camcentral.com
Westport, Washington Surfcam	westportlodging.com/westport_web_cams.html
Wild Birds Unlimited Bird FeederCam	wbu.com/feedercam_home.htm
WorldLIVE	worldlive.cz/en/webcams

Entertainment	Web Address
AMG All Music Guide	allmusic.com
E! Online	eonline.com
Entertainment Weekly's EW	ew.com/ew
The Internet Movie Database (IMDb)	imdb.com
Old Time Radio (OTR) — Radio Days: A Soundbite History	otr.com
Orisinal: Morning Sunshine	ferryhalim.com/orisinal
Rock and Roll Hall of Fame and Museum	rockhall.com
World Radio Network (WRN)	wrn.org
Yahoo! Entertainment	entertainment.tv.yahoo.com

For more information about fun and entertainment Web sites, visit scsite.com/dcf5e/ch2/web.

FIGURE 1 Visitors exploring the Rock and Roll Hall of Fame and Museum Web site will find history, exhibitions, programs, and the names and particulars of the latest inductees.

FIGURE 2 When you visit Web sites offering fun and entertainment resources, you can be both amused and informed.

FUN AND ENTERTAINMENT WEB EXERCISES

1 Visit the WorldLIVE site listed in Figure 2. View two of the Web cams closest to your hometown, and describe the scenes. Then, visit the Discovery Kids — Live Cams Web site and view one of the animal cams in the Live Cams. What do you observe? Visit another Web site listed in Figure 2 and describe the view. What are the benefits of having Web cams at these locations throughout the world?

2 What are your favorite movies? Use The Internet Movie Database Web site listed in Figure 2 to search for information about two of these films, and write a brief description of the biographies of the major stars and director for each movie. Then, visit one of the entertainment Web sites and describe three of the featured stories. At the Rock and Roll Hall of Fame and Museum Web site, view the information about Elvis and one of your favorite musicians. Write a paragraph describing the information available about these rock stars.

Research
SEARCH AND YE SHALL FIND

Information on the Web

A recent Web Usability survey conducted by the Nielsen Norman Group found that 88 percent of people who connect to the Internet use a search engine as their first online action. Search engines require users to type words and phrases that characterize the information being sought. Yahoo! (Figure 3), Google, and AltaVista are some of the more popular search engines. The key to effective searching on the Web is composing search queries that narrow the search results and place the most relevant Web sites at the top of the results list.

Keep up with the latest developments by viewing online dictionaries and encyclopedias that add to their collections of computer and product terms on a regular basis. Shopping for a new computer can be a daunting experience, but many online guides can help you select the components that best fit your needs and budget. If you are not confident in your ability to solve a problem alone, turn to online technical support. Web sites often provide streaming how-to video lessons, tutorials, and real-time chats with experienced technicians. Hardware and software reviews, price comparisons, shareware, technical questions and answers, and breaking technology news are found on comprehensive portals. Figure 4 lists popular research Web sites.

RESEARCH WEB SITES

Research	Web Address
A9	a9.com
AlltheWeb	alltheweb.com
AltaVista	altavista.com
Ask.com	ask.com
CNET	cnet.com
eHow	ehow.com
Google	google.com
HotBot	hotbot.com
Librarians' Internet Index	lii.org
PC911	pcnineoneone.com
Switchboard	switchboard.com
Techbargains	techbargains.com
Webopedia	webopedia.com
Windows Live Search	live.com
ZDNet	zdnet.com

For more information about research Web sites, visit scsite.com/dcf5e/ch2/web.

FIGURE 3 The Yahoo! News Web site provides the latest technology news along with business, sports, entertainment, and health features.

FIGURE 4 Web users can find information by using research Web sites.

RESEARCH WEB EXERCISES

1 Use two of the search engines listed in Figure 4 to find three Web sites that review the latest cell phones from Motorola and Samsung. Make a table listing the search engines, Web site names, and the phones' model numbers, suggested retail price, and features.

2 Visit the Webopedia Web site. Search this site for five terms. Create a table with two columns: one for the cyberterm and one for the Web definition. Then, create a second table listing five recently added or updated words and their definitions on this Web site. Next, visit the Techbargains Web site to choose the components you would buy if you were building a customized desktop computer and notebook computer. Create a table for both computers, listing the computer manufacturer, processor model name or number and manufacturer, clock speed, RAM, cache, number of expansion slots, and number of bays.

Blogs
EXPRESS YOURSELF

Blogosphere Growing Swiftly

Internet users are feeling the need to publish their views, and they are finding Weblogs, or blogs for short, the ideal vehicle. The blogosphere began as an easy way for individuals to express their opinions on the Web. Today, this communication vehicle has become a powerful tool, for individuals, groups, and corporations are using blogs to promote their ideas and advertise their products. It is not necessary to have a background in Web design to be able to post to a blog.

Bloggers generally update their Web sites frequently to reflect their views. Their posts range from a paragraph to an entire essay and often contain links to other Web sites. The more popular blogs discuss politics, lifestyles, and technology.

Individuals easily may set up a blog free or for a fee, using Web sites such as Blogger (Figure 5), Cooeey, and TypePad. In addition, online social networks may have a built-in blogging feature. Be cautious of the information you post on your blog, especially if it is accessible to everyone online.

Corporate blogs, such as The GM FastLane Blog, discuss all aspects of the company's products, whereas all-encompassing blogs, such as the Metafilter Community Weblog and others in Figure 6, are designed to keep general readers entertained and informed.

Blogs are affecting the manner in which people communicate, and some experts predict they will one day become our primary method of sharing information.

BLOGS WEB SITES

Blog	Web Address
A List Apart	alistapart.com
Blog.com	blog.com
Blog Flux	topsites.blogflux.com
Blogger	blogger.com
Bloglines	bloglines.com
Blogstream	blogstream.com
Boing Boing: A Directory of Wonderful Things	boingboing.net
Cooeey	cooeey.com
Davenetics * Politics + Media + Musings	davenetics.com
Geek News Central	geeknewscentral.com
GM FastLane Blog	fastlane.gmblogs.com
kottke.org: home of fine hypertext products	kottke.org
MetaFilter Community Weblog	metafilter.com
Scripting News	scripting.com
TypePad	typepad.com
For more information about blogs Web sites, visit scsite.com/ dcf5e/ch2/web.	

FIGURE 5 Google's Blogger Web publishing service hosts thousands of blogs ranging from business to personal interests.

FIGURE 6 These blogs offer information about technology, news, politics, and entertainment.

BLOGS WEB EXERCISES

1. Visit three of the blog Web sites listed in Figure 6. Make a table listing the blog name, its purpose, the author, its audience, and advertisers, if any, who sponsor the blog. Then, write a paragraph that describes the information you found on each of these blogs.

2. Many Internet users read the technology blogs to keep abreast of the latest developments. Visit the Geek News Central and Scripting News blogs listed in Figure 6 and write a paragraph describing the top story in each blog. Read the posted comments, if any. Then, write another paragraph describing two other stories found on these blogs that cover material you have discussed in this course. Write a third paragraph discussing which one is more interesting to you. Would you add reading blogs to your list of Internet activities? Why or why not?

Online Social Networks and Media Sharing
CHECK OUT MY NEW PHOTOS

Online Social Networks and Media Sharing Web Sites More Popular than Ever

Do you ever wonder what your friends are doing? What about your friends' friends? The popularity of online social networks has increased dramatically in recent years. Online social networks, such as those listed in Figure 7, allow you to create a personalized profile that others are able to view online. These profiles may include information about you such as your hometown, your age, your hobbies, and pictures. You also may create links to your friends' pages, post messages for individual friends, or bulletins for all of your friends to see. Online social networks are great places not only to keep in touch with your friends, but to reconnect with old friends and meet new friends!

If you would like to post pictures and videos and do not require the full functionality of an online social network, you might consider a media sharing Web site, which is a type of online social network. Media sharing Web sites such as YouTube (Figure 8) and Phanfare allow you to post media, including photos and videos, for others to view, print, and/or download. Media sharing Web sites, which may be free or charge a fee, provide a quick, efficient way to share photos of your last vacation or videos of your family reunion.

ONLINE SOCIAL NETWORKS AND MEDIA SHARING

Online Social Networks	Web Address
AIM Pages Social Network	aimpages.com
Club Penguin	clubpenguin.com
Facebook	facebook.com
MySpace — a place for friends	myspace.com
Media Sharing	**Web Address**
flickr	flickr.com
MyPhotoAlbum	myphotoalbum.com
Phanfare	phanfare.com
Picasa Web Albums	picasa.com
Shutterfly * Shutterfly Studio	shutterfly.com
Twango	twango.com
Yahoo! Video	video.yahoo.com
YouTube	youtube.com

For more information about online social networks and media sharing Web sites, visit scsite.com/dcf5e/ch2/web.

FIGURE 7 Online social networks and media sharing Web sites are popular ways to keep in touch with friends, meet new people, and share media.

FIGURE 8 The YouTube Web site features videos about current events, hobbies, musicians, and political issues.

ONLINE SOCIAL NETWORKS AND MEDIA SHARING WEB EXERCISES

1 Many individuals now use online social networks. Visit two online social networks listed in Figure 7. (If you are attempting to access an online social network from your classroom and are unable to do so, your school may have restricted use of social networking Web sites.) Compare and contrast these two sites by performing the following actions and recording your findings. First, create a profile on each of these sites. If you find a Web site that charges a fee to sign up, choose another Web site. How easy is the sign-up process? Does either Web site ask for any personal information you are uncomfortable sharing? If so, what information? Once you sign up, make a list of five of your closest friends, and search for their profiles on each of these two sites. What site contains more of your friends? Browse each site and make a list of its features. In your opinion, what site is better? Explain why.

2 Media sharing Web sites make it extremely easy to share photos and videos with friends, family, and colleagues. Before choosing an online media sharing Web site to use, you should do some research. Visit two media sharing Web sites in Figure 7. Is there a fee to post media to these Web sites? If so, how much? Are these Web sites supported by advertisements? Locate the instructions for posting media to these Web sites. Are the instructions straightforward? Do these Web sites impose a limit on the number and/or size of media files you can post? Summarize your responses to these questions in two or three paragraphs.

Travel
GET PACKING!

Explore the World without Leaving Home

When you are ready to arrange your next travel adventure or just want to explore destination possibilities, the Internet provides ample resources to set your plans in motion.

To discover exactly where your destination is on this planet, cartography Web sites, including MapQuest and Maps.com, allow you to pinpoint your destination. View your exact destination using satellite imagery with Google Maps (Figure 9) and Live Search Maps.

Some good starting places are general travel Web sites such as Expedia Travel, Cheap Tickets, and Travelocity. Many airline Web sites allow you to reserve hotel rooms and rental cars while booking a flight. These all-encompassing Web sites, including those in Figure 10, have tools to help you find the lowest prices and details on flights, car rentals, cruises, and hotels.

TRAVEL WEB SITES

General Travel	Web Address
CheapTickets	cheaptickets.com
Expedia Travel	expedia.com
Kayak	kayak.com
Sidestep	sidestep.com
Travelocity	travelocity.com
Cartography	**Web Address**
Google Maps	maps.google.com
Live Search Maps	local.live.com
MapQuest	mapquest.com
Maps.com	maps.com
Travel and City Guides	**Web Address**
Frommer's Travel Guides	frommers.com
Greatest Cities	greatestcities.com
U.S.-Parks US National Parks and Monuments Travel Guide	us-parks.com
Virtual Tourist	virtualtourist.com
For more information about travel Web sites, visit scsite.com/dcf5e/ch2/web.	

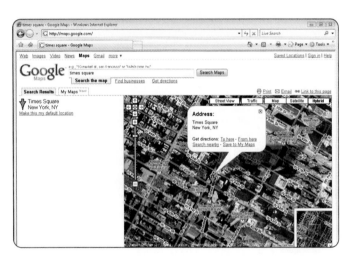

FIGURE 9 Google Maps provides location information and satellite imagery for many regions on this planet.

FIGURE 10 These travel resources Web sites offer travel information to exciting destinations throughout the world.

TRAVEL WEB EXERCISES

1 Visit one of the cartography Web sites listed in Figure 10 and obtain the directions from your campus to one of these destinations: the White House in Washington, D.C.; Elvis's home in Memphis, Tennessee; Walt Disney World in Orlando, Florida; or the Grand Old Opry in Nashville, Tennessee. How many miles is it to your destination? What is the estimated driving time? Use the Google Maps Web site to obtain an overhead image of this destination. Then, visit one of the general travel Web sites listed in the table and plan a flight from the nearest major airport to one of the four destinations for the week after finals and a return trip one week later. What airline, flight numbers, and departure and arrival times did you select?

2 Visit one of the travel and city guides Web sites listed in Figure 10, and choose a destination for a getaway this coming weekend. Write a one-page paper giving details about this location, such as popular hotels and lodging, expected weather, population, local colleges and universities, parks and recreation, ancient and modern history, and tours. Include a map or satellite photograph of this place. Why did you select this destination? How would you travel there and back? What is the breakdown of expected costs for this weekend, including travel expenditures, meals, lodging, and tickets to events and activities? What Web addresses did you use to complete this exercise?

Environment
THE FUTURE OF THE PLANET

Making a Difference for Earth

From the rain forests of Africa to the marine life in the Pacific Ocean, the fragile ecosystem is under extreme stress. Many environmental groups have developed Web sites, including those listed in Figure 11, in attempts to educate worldwide populations and to increase resource conservation. The New American Dream Web site (Figure 12) contains information for people who would like to help safeguard the environment.

On an international scale, the Environmental Sites on the Internet Web page developed by the Royal Institute of Technology in Stockholm, Sweden, has been rated as one of the better ecological Web sites. Its comprehensive listing of environmental concerns range from aquatic ecology to wetlands.

The U.S. federal government has a number of Web sites devoted to specific environmental concerns. For example, the U.S. Environmental Protection Agency (EPA) provides pollution data, including ozone levels and air pollutants, for specific areas. Its AirData Web site displays air pollution emissions and monitoring data from the entire United States and is the world's most extensive collection of air pollution data.

ENVIRONMENT WEB SITES

Name	Web Address
Central African Regional Program for the Environment (CARPE)	carpe.umd.edu
Earthjustice	earthjustice.org
EarthTrends: Environmental Information	earthtrends.wri.org
Environmental Defense	edf.org
Environmental Sites on the Internet	www.ima.kth.se/im/envsite/envsite.htm
EPA AirData — Access to Air Pollution Data	epa.gov/air/data
Global Warming	globalwarming.org
GreenNet	gn.apc.org
New American Dream	newdream.org
University of Wisconsin — Milwaukee Environmental Health and Safety Resources	uwm.edu/Dept/EHSRM/EHSLINKS
USGS Acid rain data and reports	bqs.usgs.gov/acidrain
World-Wide Web Virtual Library: Botany/Plant Biology	ou.edu/cas/botany-micro/www-vl/

For more information about environment Web sites, visit scsite.com/dcf5e/ch2/web.

FIGURE 11 Environment Web sites provide vast resources for ecological data and action groups.

FIGURE 12 A visit to the New American Dream Web site provides information about supporting the environment.

ENVIRONMENT WEB EXERCISES

1 The New American Dream Web site encourages consumers to reduce the amount of junk mail sent to their homes. Using the table in Figure 11, visit the Web site and write a paragraph stating how many trees are leveled each year to provide paper for these mailings, how many garbage trucks are needed to haul this waste, and other statistics. Read the letters that you can use to eliminate your name from bulk mail lists. To whom would you mail these letters? How long does it take to stop these unsolicited letters?

2 Visit the EPA AirData Web site. What is the highest ozone level recorded in your state this past year? Where are the nearest air pollution monitoring Web sites, and what are their levels? Where are the nearest sources of air pollution? Read two reports about two different topics, such as acid rain and air quality, and summarize their findings. Include information about who sponsored the research, who conducted the studies, when the data was collected, and the impact of this pollution on the atmosphere, water, forests, and human health. Whom would you contact for further information regarding the data and studies?

Finance
MONEY MATTERS

Cashing In on Financial Advice

You can manage your money with advice from financial Web sites that offer online banking, tax help, personal finance, and small business and commercial services.

If you do not have a personal banker or a financial planner, consider a Web adviser to guide your investment decisions. The Yahoo! Finance Web site (Figure 13) provides financial news and investment information.

If you are ready to ride the ups and downs of the NASDAQ and the Dow, an abundance of Web sites listed in Figure 14, including Reuters and Morningstar, can help you pick companies that fit your interests and financial needs.

Claiming to be the fastest, easiest tax publication on the planet, the Internal Revenue Service Web site contains procedures for filing tax appeals and contains IRS forms, publications, and legal regulations.

FIGURE 13 Yahoo! Finance Web site contains features information related to financing a college education.

FINANCE WEB SITES

Advice and Education	Web Address
Bankrate	bankrate.com
LendingTree	lendingtree.com
Loan.com	loan.com
The Motley Fool	fool.com
MSN Money	moneycentral.msn.com
Wells Fargo	wellsfargo.com
Yahoo! Finance	finance.yahoo.com
Stock Market	**Web Address**
AIG VALIC	valic.com
E*TRADE Financial	us.etrade.com
Financial Engines	financialengines.com
Merrill Lynch Direct	mldirect.ml.com
Morningstar	morningstar.com
Reuters	reuters.com/investing
Vanguard	vanguard.com
Taxes	**Web Address**
H&R Block	hrblock.com
Internal Revenue Service	irs.gov
Jackson Hewitt	jacksonhewitt.com
Liberty Tax Service	libertytax.com

For more information about finance Web sites, visit scsite.com/dcf5e/ch2/web.

FIGURE 14 Financial resources Web sites offer general information, stock market analyses, and tax advice, as well as guidance and money-saving tips.

FINANCE WEB EXERCISES

1 Visit three advice and education Web sites listed in Figure 14 and read their top business world reports. Write a paragraph about each, summarizing these stories. Which stocks or mutual funds do these Web sites predict as being sound investments today? What are the current market indexes for the DJIA (Dow Jones Industrial Average), S&P 500, and NASDAQ, and how do these figures compare with the previous day's numbers?

2 Using two of the stock market Web sites listed in Figure 14, search for information about Microsoft, Adobe Systems, and one other software vendor. Write a paragraph about each of these stocks describing the revenues, net incomes, total assets for the previous year, current stock price per share, highest and lowest prices of each stock during the past year, and other relevant investment information.

Government
STAMP OF APPROVAL

Making a Federal Case for Useful Information

When it is time to buy stamps to mail your correspondence, you no longer need to wait in long lines at your local post office. The U.S. Postal Service has authorized several corporations to sell stamps online.

You can recognize U.S. Government Web sites on the Internet by their .gov top-level domain abbreviation. For example, The Library of Congress Web site is loc.gov. Government and military Web sites offer a wide range of information. The Time Service Department Web site will provide you with the correct time. If you are looking for a federal document, FedWorld (Figure 15) lists thousands of documents distributed by the government on its Web site. For access to the names of your congressional representatives, visit the extensive Hieros Gamos Web site. Figure 16 shows some of the more popular U.S. Government Web sites.

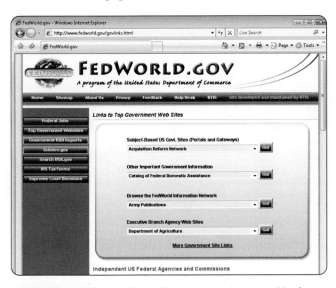

FIGURE 15 The FedWorld Web site contains a wealth of information disseminated by the federal government.

GOVERNMENT RESOURCES WEB SITES

Postage	Web Address
Endicia	endicia.com
Pitney Bowes	pb.com
Stamps.com	stamps.com

Government	Web Address
FedWorld	www.fedworld.gov
Hieros Gamos — Worldwide Legal Directories	hg.org
The Library of Congress	loc.gov
National Agricultural Library	nal.usda.gov
Smithsonian Institution	smithsonian.org
THOMAS (Library of Congress)	thomas.loc.gov
Time Service Department	tycho.usno.navy.mil
U.S. Department of Education	ed.gov
United States Department of the Treasury	treas.gov
U.S. Government Printing Office	www.access.gpo.gov
United States National Library of Medicine	nlm.nih.gov
United States Patent and Trademark Office	uspto.gov
USAJOBS	usajobs.opm.gov
The White House	whitehouse.gov

For more information about government Web sites, visit scsite.com/dcf5e/ch2/web.

FIGURE 16 These Web sites offer information about buying U.S.-approved postage online and researching federal agencies.

GOVERNMENT WEB EXERCISES

1. View the three postage Web sites listed in Figure 16. Compare and contrast the available services on each one. Consider postage cost, necessary equipment, shipping services, security techniques, and tracking capability. Explain why you would or would not like to use this service.

2. Visit the Hieros Gamos Web site listed in Figure 16. What are the names, addresses, and telephone numbers of your two state senators and your local congressional representative? On what committees do they serve? Who is the chief justice of the Supreme Court, and what has been this justice's opinion on two recently decided cases? Who are the members of the president's cabinet? Then, visit two other Web sites listed in Figure 16. Write a paragraph about each Web site describing its content and features.

Shopping and Auctions
BARGAINS GALORE

Let Your Mouse Do Your Shopping

From groceries to clothing to computers, you can buy just about everything you need with just a few clicks of your mouse. Electronic retailers (e-tailers) are cashing in on cybershoppers' purchases. Books, computer software and hardware, and music are the hottest commodities.

The two categories of Internet shopping Web sites are those with physical counterparts, such as Wal-Mart and Best Buy, and those with only a Web presence, such as Amazon and Buy (Figure 17). Popular Web shopping sites are listed in Figure 18.

Another method of shopping for the items you need, and maybe some you really do not need, is to visit auction Web sites, including those listed in Figure 18. Categories include antiques and collectibles, automotive, computers, electronics, music, sports, sports cards and memorabilia,

and toys. Online auction Web sites can offer unusual items, including *Star Wars* props and memorabilia and a round of golf with Tiger Woods. eBay is one of thousands of Internet auction Web sites and is the world's largest personal online trading community.

SHOPPING AND AUCTIONS WEB SITES

Auctions	Web Address
craigslist	craigslist.org
eBay	ebay.com
Sotheby's	sothebys.com
uBid	ubid.com
U.S. Treasury — Seized Property Auctions	ustreas.gov/auctions
Books and Music	**Web Address**
Amazon	amazon.com
Barnes & Noble	bn.com
BookFinder	bookfinder.com
Computers and Electronics	**Web Address**
BestBuy	bestbuy.com
Buy	buy.com
Crutchfield	crutchfield.com
Miscellaneous	**Web Address**
drugstore	drugstore.com
Google Product Search	google.com/products
Sharper Image	sharperimage.com
Wal-Mart	walmart.com

For more information about shopping and auctions Web sites, visit scsite.com/dcf5e/ch2/web

FIGURE 17 Buy is a popular electronic retailer that sells a variety of products.

FIGURE 18 Making online purchases can help ease the burden of driving to and fighting the crowds in local malls.

SHOPPING AND AUCTIONS WEB EXERCISES

1 Visit two of the computers and electronics and two of the miscellaneous Web sites listed in Figure 18. Write a paragraph describing the features these Web sites offer compared with the same offerings from stores. In another paragraph, describe any disadvantages of shopping at these Web sites instead of actually visiting a store. Then, describe their policies for returning unwanted merchandise and for handling complaints.

2 Using one of the auction Web sites listed in Figure 18, search for two objects pertaining to your hobbies. For example, if you are a sports fan, you can search for a complete set of Upper Deck cards. If you are a car buff, search for your dream car. Describe these two items. How many people have bid on these items? Who are the sellers? What are the opening and current bids?

Weather, Sports, and News
WHAT'S NEWS?

Weather, Sports, and News Web Sites Score Big Hits

Rain or sun? Hot or cold? Weather is the leading online news item, with at least 10,000 Web sites devoted to this field. Millions of people view the WX Web site (Figure 19) each month.

Baseball may be the national pastime, but sports aficionados yearn for everything from auto racing to cricket. The Internet has more than one million pages of multimedia sports news, entertainment, and merchandise.

The Internet has emerged as a major source for news, with one-third of Americans going online at least once a week and 15 percent going online daily for reports of major news events. Many of these viewers are using Really Simple Syndication (RSS) technology to be notified when new stories about their favorite topics are available on the Internet. Popular weather, sports, and news Web sites are listed in Figure 20.

FIGURE 19 Local, national, and international weather conditions and details about breaking weather stories are available on WX.

WEATHER, SPORTS, AND NEWS WEB SITES

Weather	Web Address
Infoplease Weather	infoplease.com/weather.html
Intellicast	intellicast.com
National Weather Service	www.crh.noaa.gov
STORMFAX	stormfax.com
The Weather Channel	weather.com
WX	wx.com

Sports	Web Address
CBS SportsLine	cbs.sportsline.com
ESPN	espn.com
NCAAsports	ncaasports.com
OFFICIAL WEBSITE OF THE OLYMPIC MOVEMENT	olympic.org
SIRC — A World of Sport Information	sirc.ca
Sporting News Radio	radio.sportingnews.com

News	Web Address
Google News	news.google.com
MSNBC	msnbc.com
New York Post Online Edition	nypost.com
Onlinenewspapers	onlinenewspapers.com
Privacy	privacy.org
SiliconValley	siliconvalley.com
Starting Page	startingpage.com/html/news.html
USA TODAY	usatoday.com
Washington Post	washingtonpost.com

For more information about weather, sports, and news Web sites, visit scsite.com/dcf5e/ch2/web.

FIGURE 20 Keep informed about the latest weather, sports, and news events with these Web sites.

WEATHER, SPORTS, AND NEWS WEB EXERCISES

1 Visit two of the sports Web sites in Figure 20 and write a paragraph describing the content these Web sites provide concerning your favorite sport. Visit Google News and then search for stories about this sport team or athlete. Then, create a customized news page with stories about your sports interests. Include RSS feeds to get regularly updated summaries on this subject.

2 Visit the Onlinenewspapers and Starting Page Web sites listed in Figure 20 and select two newspapers from each site. Write a paragraph describing the top national news story featured in each of these four Web pages. Then, write another paragraph describing the top international news story displayed at each Web site. In the third paragraph, discuss which of the four Web sites is the most interesting in terms of story selection, photographs, and Web page design.

Learning
YEARN TO LEARN

Discover New Worlds Online

While you may believe your education ends when you finally graduate from college, learning is a lifelong process. You can increase your technological knowledge by visiting several Web sites (Figure 21) with tutorials about building your own Web sites, the latest news about the Internet, and resources for visually impaired users.

LEARNING WEB SITES

Learning How To's	Web Address
Bartleby: Great Books Online	bartleby.com
Blue Web'n	www.kn.pacbell.com/ wired/bluewebn
CBT Nuggets	cbtnuggets.com
How Stuff Works	howstuffworks.com
Learn the Net	learnthenet.com
Internet Public Library	ipl.org
ScienceMaster	sciencemaster.com
Search Engine Watch	searchenginewatch.com
Wiredguide	wiredguide.com
Cooking	**Web Address**
Betty Crocker	bettycrocker.com
RecipeCenter.com	recipecenter.com

For more information about learning Web sites, visit scsite.com/dcf5e/ ch2/web.

FIGURE 21 The information gleaned from these Web sites can help you learn about many aspects of our existence.

Enhancing your culinary skills can be a rewarding endeavor. No matter if you are a gourmet chef or a weekend cook, you will be cooking in style with the help of online resources, including those listed in Figure 21.

Have you ever wondered how to make a key lime pie? How about learning how to cook some easy, low-calorie dishes? Are you seeking advice from expert chefs? The RecipeCenter Web site (Figure 22) is filled with information related to recipes.

FIGURE 22 The RecipeCenter Web site provides access to more than 100,000 recipes, as well as software to help manage your recipes.

LEARNING WEB EXERCISES

1 Using one of the Learning How To's Web sites listed in Figure 21, search for information about installing a computer's hard disk. Write a paragraph about your findings. Then, review the material in the How Stuff Works Web site listed in Figure 21, and write a paragraph describing articles on this Web site that are pertinent to your major.

2 Visit one of the cooking Web sites listed in Figure 21 and find two recipes or cooking tips that you can use when preparing your next meal. Write a paragraph about each one, summarizing your discoveries. What are the advantages and disadvantages of accessing these Web sites on the new Web appliances that might someday be in your kitchen?

Science
$E = MC^2$

Rocket Science on the Web

For some people, space exploration is a hobby. Building and launching model rockets allow these at-home scientists to participate in exploring the great frontier of space. For others, space exploration is their life. Numerous Web sites, including those in Figure 23, provide in-depth information about the universe.

SCIENCE WEB SITES

Periodicals	Web Address
Archaeology Magazine	archaeology.org
Astronomy Magazine	astronomy.com
New Scientist	newscientist.com
OceanLink	oceanlink.island.net
Science Magazine	sciencemag.org
Scientific American	sciam.com

Resources	Web Address
Department of Education and Early Childhood Development, Victoria, Australia	www.education.vic.gov.au
National Science Foundation (NSF)	nsf.gov
Science.gov: USA.gov for Science	science.gov
Thomson Scientific	scientific.thomson.com/free/

Science Community	Web Address
American Scientist, The Magazine of Sigma Xi, The Scientific Research Society	amsci.org
Federation of American Scientists	fas.org
NASA	www.nasa.gov
Sigma Xi, The Scientific Research Society	sigmaxi.org

For more information about science Web sites, visit scsite.com/dcf5e/ch2/web.

FIGURE 23 Resources available on the Internet offer a wide range of subjects for enthusiasts who want to delve into familiar and unknown territories in the world of science.

NASA's Astronaut Flight Lounge Web site contains information about rockets, the space shuttle, the International Space Station, space transportation, and communications. Other science resources explore space-related questions about astronomy, physics, the earth sciences, microgravity, and robotics.

Rockets and space are not the only areas to explore in the world of science. Where can you find the latest pictures taken with the Hubble Space Telescope? Do you know which cities experienced an earthquake today? Have you ever wondered what a 3-D model of the amino acid glutamine looks like? You can find the answers to these questions and many others through the Science.gov Web site (science.gov) shown in Figure 24.

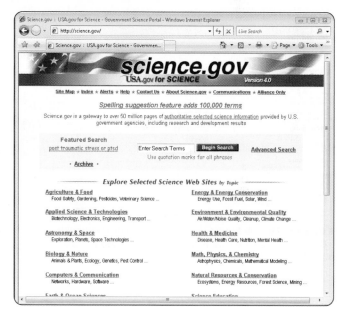

FIGURE 24 The Science.gov Web site provides easy access to the information in various federal science databases.

SCIENCE WEB EXERCISES

1. Visit the NASA Web site listed in the table in Figure 23. View the links about spacecraft, the universe, or tracking satellites and spacecraft, and then write a summary of your findings.

2. Visit the NASA Web site listed in the table in Figure 23. Click the Latest News link and then click the Launches topic. When are the next two launches scheduled? What are the purposes of these missions? Click the Work for NASA topic and then write a paragraph describing the internships, cooperative programs, and summer employment opportunities. Then, view two of the science community Web sites listed in Figure 23 and write a paragraph about each of these Web sites describing the information each contains.

Health
NO PAIN, ALL GAIN

Store Personal Health Records Online

More than 70 million consumers use the Internet yearly to search for health information, so using the Web to store personal medical data is a natural extension of the Internet's capabilities. Internet health services and portals are available to store your personal health history, including prescriptions, lab test results, doctor visits, allergies, and immunizations. Web sites such as MedlinePlus (Figure 25) provide free health information to consumers.

In minutes, you can register with a health Web site by choosing a user name and password. Then, you create a record to enter your medical history. You also can store data for your emergency contacts, primary care physicians,

specialists, blood type, cholesterol levels, blood pressure, and insurance plan. No matter where you are in the world, you and medical personnel can obtain records via the Internet or fax machine. Some popular online health database management systems are shown in Figure 26.

HEALTH WEB SITES

Medical History	Web Address
PersonalMD	personalmd.com
Practice Solutions	practicesolutions.ca
Records for Living, Inc — Personal Health and Living Management	recordsforliving.com
WebMD	webmd.com
General Health	**Web Address**
Centers for Disease Control and Prevention	cdc.gov
familydoctor	familydoctor.org
healthfinder	healthfinder.gov
HealthWeb	healthweb.org
Medical Library Association Consumer and Patient Health Information Section (CAPHIS)	caphis.mlanet.org/consumer
MedlinePlus	medlineplus.gov
PEC: Health and Nutrition Web Sites	pecentral.org/websites/healthsites.html
Physical Activity Guidelines	health.gov/paguidelines

For more information about health Web sites, visit scsite.com/dcf5e/ch2/web.

FIGURE 25 The MedlinePlus Web site provides health information from the U.S. National Library of Medicine and the National Institutes of Health.

FIGURE 26 These health Web sites allow you to organize your medical information and store it in an online database and also obtain information about a variety of medical conditions and treatments.

HEALTH WEB EXERCISES

1 Access one of the health Web sites listed in Figure 26. Register yourself or a family member, and then enter the full health history. Create an emergency medical card if the Web site provides the card option. Submit this record and emergency card to your instructor. If you feel uncomfortable disclosing medical information for yourself or a family member, you may enter fictitious information.

2 Visit three of the health Web sites listed in Figure 26. Describe the features of each. Which of the three is the most user-friendly? Why? Describe the privacy policies of these three Web sites. Submit your analysis of these Web sites to your instructor.

Careers
IN SEARCH OF THE PERFECT JOB

Web Helps Career Hunt

While your teachers give you valuable training to prepare you for a career, they rarely teach you how to begin that career. You can broaden your horizons by searching the Internet for career information and job openings.

First, examine some of the job search Web sites. These resources list thousands of openings in hundreds of fields, companies, and locations. For example, the U.S. Department of Labor Web site, shown in Figure 27, allows you to find information for different types of jobs. This information may include the training and education required, salary data, working conditions, job descriptions, and more. In addition, many companies advertise careers on their Web sites.

When a company contacts you for an interview, learn as much about it and the industry as possible before the interview. Many of the Web sites listed in Figure 28 include detailed company profiles and links to their corporate Web sites.

CAREER WEB SITES

Job Search	Web Address
BestJobsUSA	bestjobsusa.com
CareerBuilder	careerbuilder.com
CareerNet	careernet.com
CAREERXCHANGE	careerxchange.com
College Grad Job Hunter	collegegrad.com
The Employment Guide	employmentguide.com
Job	job.com
Job Bank USA	jobbankusa.com
JobWeb	jobweb.com
Monster	monster.com
Spherion	spherion.com
USAJOBS	usajobs.opm.gov
VolunteerMatch	volunteermatch.org
Yahoo! HotJobs	hotjobs.yahoo.com
Company/Industry Information	**Web Address**
Career ResourceCenter	resourcecenter.com
Forbes	forbes.com/leadership/careers
Fortune	fortune.com
Hoover's	hoovers.com
Occupational Outlook Handbook	stats.bls.gov/oco

For more information about career Web sites, visit scsite.com/dcf5e/ch2/web.

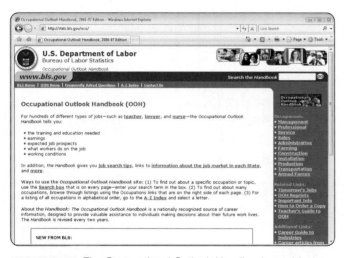

FIGURE 27 The Occupational Outlook Handbook provides career information to those searching for jobs.

FIGURE 28 Career Web sites provide a variety of job openings and information about major companies worldwide.

CAREERS WEB EXERCISES

1 Use two of the job search Web sites listed in Figure 28 to find three companies with job openings in your field. Make a table listing the Web site name, position available, description, salary, location, desired education, and desired experience.

2 It is a good idea to acquire information before graduation about the industry in which you would like to work. Are you interested in the automotive manufacturing industry, the restaurant service industry, or the financial industry? Use two of the company/industry information Web sites listed in Figure 28 to research a particular career related to your major. Write a paragraph naming the Web sites and the specific information you found, such as the nature of the work, recommended training and qualifications, employment outlook, and earnings. Then, use two other Web sites to profile three companies with positions available in this field. Write a paragraph about each of these companies, describing the headquarters' location, sales and earnings for the previous year, total number of employees, working conditions, perks, and competitors.

Arts and Literature
FIND SOME CULTURE

Get Ready to Read, Paint, and Dance

Brush up your knowledge of Shakespeare, grab a canvas, and put on your dancing shoes. Visual arts and literature Web sites, including those in Figure 29, are about to sweep you off your cyberfeet.

The full text of hundreds of books is available online from the Bibliomania and Project Gutenberg Web sites. The Complete Review provides summaries, reviews, and Web links about a variety of books and their authors. The Bartleby Web site features biographies, definitions, quotations, dictionaries, and indexes.

When you are ready to absorb more culture, you can turn to various art Web sites. Many museums have images of their collections online. Among them are the Getty Museum in Los Angeles (Figure 30), the Montreal Museum of Fine Arts, and the Louvre Museum in Paris.

The accessplace Web site focuses on the arts and humanities and provides fascinating glimpses into the worlds of dance, music, performance, cinema, and other topics pertaining to creative expression.

ARTS AND LITERATURE WEB SITES

Arts	Web Address
accessplace	accessplace.com/arts.htm
Art News — absolutearts	absolutearts.com
The Children's Museum of Indianapolis	childrensmuseum.org
Gallery Guide	galleryguide.com
The Getty	getty.edu
Louvre Museum	louvre.fr
Montreal Museum of Fine Arts	mmfa.qc.ca
The Museum of Online Museums	coudal.com/moom
Virtual Library museums pages (VLmp)	vlmp.museophile.com
Literature	**Web Address**
Bartleby	bartleby.com
Bibliomania	bibliomania.com
The Complete Review	complete-review.com
Fantastic Fiction	fantasticfiction.co.uk
Literary History	literaryhistory.com
The Modern Library eBook List	randomhouse.com/modernlibrary/ebookslist.html
Project Gutenberg	gutenberg.org
For more information about arts and literature Web sites, visit scsite.com/dcf5e/ch2/web.	

FIGURE 29 Discover culture throughout the world by visiting these arts and literature Web sites.

FIGURE 30 Permanent and temporary exhibitions, educational activities, and a bookstore are featured on the Getty Museum Web site.

ARTS AND LITERATURE WEB EXERCISES

1. Visit The Modern Library eBook List Web site listed in Figure 29 and view one book in the 20th CENTURY NOVELS, 19th CENTURY NOVELS, BRITISH LITERATURE, and HISTORY sections. Create a table with columns for the book name, author, cost, online store, local store, and description. Then, read the excerpt from each of the four books and write a paragraph describing which of these four books is the most interesting to you. What are the advantages and disadvantages of reading classic literature electronically?

2. Using the arts Web sites listed in Figure 29, search for three temporary exhibitions in galleries throughout the world. Describe the venues, the artists, and the works. What permanent collections are found in these museums? Some people shop for gifts in the museums' stores. View and describe three items for sale.

CHAPTER 3

Application Software

OBJECTIVES

After completing this chapter, you will be able to:

1. Identify the categories of application software

2. Explain how to work with application software

3. Identify the key features of widely used business programs

4. Identify the key features of widely used graphics and multimedia programs

5. Identify the key features of widely used home, personal, and educational programs

6. Identify the types of application software used in communications

7. Describe the function of several utility programs

8. Describe Web-based software and the learning aids available for application software

CONTENTS

APPLICATION SOFTWARE

With the proper software, a computer is a valuable tool. Software allows users to create letters, reports, and other documents; design Web pages and diagrams; draw images; enhance audio and video clips; prepare taxes; play games; compose e-mail messages and instant messages; and much more. To accomplish these and many other tasks, users work with application software. **Application software** consists of programs designed to make users more productive and/or assist them with personal tasks. Application software has a variety of uses:

1. To make business activities more efficient
2. To assist with graphics and multimedia projects
3. To support home, personal, and educational tasks
4. To facilitate communications

The table in Figure 3-1 categorizes popular types of application software by their general use. Although many types of communications software exist, the ones listed in Figure 3-1 are application software oriented. Successful use of application software often requires the use of one or more of the utility programs identified at the bottom of Figure 3-1.

Application software is available in a variety of forms: packaged, custom, Web-based, open source, shareware, freeware, and public domain.

FOUR CATEGORIES OF APPLICATION SOFTWARE
(and some popular utility programs)

1 Business	**2 Graphics and Multimedia**	**3 Home/Personal/Educational**
• Word Processing • Spreadsheet • Database • Presentation Graphics • Note Taking • Personal Information Manager (PIM) • Personal Mobile Device Business Software • Software Suite • Project Management • Accounting • Document Management • Enterprise Computing	• Computer-Aided Design (CAD) • Desktop Publishing (for the Professional) • Paint/Image Editing (for the Professional) • Photo Editing (for the Professional) • Video and Audio Editing (for the Professional) • Multimedia Authoring • Web Page Authoring	• Software Suite (for Personal Use) • Personal Finance • Legal • Tax Preparation • Desktop Publishing (for Personal Use) • Paint/Image Editing (for Personal Use) • Photo Editing and Photo Management (for Personal Use) • Clip Art/Image Gallery • Video and Audio Editing (for Personal Use) • Home Design/Landscaping • Travel and Mapping • Reference and Educational • Entertainment

4 Communications

• Web Browser	• E-Mail	• Instant Messaging	• Chat Room	• Text Messaging
• RSS Aggregator	• Blogging	• Newsgroup/Message Board	• FTP	• VoIP • Video Conferencing

Popular Utility Programs

• Antivirus	• Personal Firewall	• Spyware Remover	• Internet Filters	• File Manager
• File Compression	• Backup	• Media Player	• CD/DVD Burning	• Personal Computer Maintenance

(left margin vertical: APPLICATION SOFTWARE)

FIGURE 3-1   The four major categories of popular application software are outlined in this table. Communications software often is bundled with other application or system software. Also identified at the bottom of the figure are widely used utility programs.

- **Packaged software** is mass-produced, copyrighted retail software that meets the needs of a wide variety of users, not just a single user or company. Microsoft Office 2007 is an example of packaged software. Packaged software is available in retail stores or on the Web.

- **Custom software** performs functions specific to a business or industry. Sometimes a company cannot find packaged software that meets its unique requirements. In this case, the company may use programmers to develop tailor-made custom software.

- **Web-based software** refers to programs hosted by a Web site. Users access and interact with Web-based software from any computer or device that is connected to the Internet. Types of Web-based software include e-mail, word processing, and game programs.

- **Open source software** is software provided for use, modification, and redistribution. This software has no restrictions from the copyright holder regarding modification of the software's internal instructions and redistribution of the software. Open source software usually can be downloaded from the Internet, sometimes at no cost.

- **Shareware** is copyrighted software that is distributed at no cost for a trial period. To use a shareware program beyond that period, you send payment to the program developer.

- **Freeware** is copyrighted software provided at no cost to a user by an individual or a company that retains all rights to the software.

- **Public-domain software** has been donated for public use and has no copyright restrictions. Anyone can copy or distribute public-domain software to others at no cost.

Thousands of shareware, freeware, and public-domain programs are available on the Internet for users to download. Examples include communications programs, graphics programs, and games.

The Role of System Software

System software serves as the interface between the user, the application software, and the computer's hardware (Figure 3-2). To use application software, such as a word processing program, your computer must be running system software — specifically, an operating system. Four popular personal computer operating systems are Windows Vista, Windows XP, Linux, and Mac OS X.

Each time you start a computer, the operating system is loaded (copied) from the computer's hard disk into memory. Once the operating system is loaded, it coordinates all the activities of the computer. This includes starting application software and transferring data among input and output devices and memory. While the computer is running, the operating system remains in memory.

Application Software

System Software

FIGURE 3-2 A user does not communicate directly with the computer hardware. Instead, system software is the interface between the user, the application software, and the hardware. For example, when a user instructs the application software to print, the application software sends the print instruction to the system software, which in turn sends the print instruction to the hardware.

Working with Application Software

To use application software, you must instruct the operating system to start the program. The steps in Figure 3-3 illustrate how to start and interact with the Paint program, which is included with the Windows Vista operating system. The following paragraphs explain the steps in Figure 3-3.

Personal computer operating systems often use the concept of a desktop to make the computer easier to use. The **desktop** is an on-screen work area that has a graphical user interface (read Looking Ahead 3-1 for a look at the next generation of user interfaces). Step 1 of Figure 3-3 shows icons, a button, a pointer, and a menu on the Windows Vista desktop. An **icon** is a small image displayed on the screen that represents a program, a document, or some other object. A **button** is a

FIGURE 3-3   HOW TO START A PROGRAM FROM WINDOWS VISTA

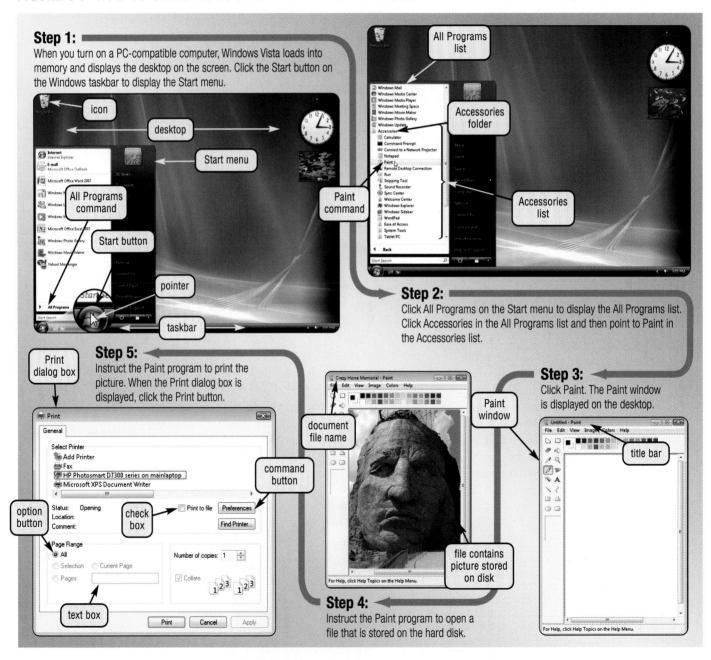

Step 1:
When you turn on a PC-compatible computer, Windows Vista loads into memory and displays the desktop on the screen. Click the Start button on the Windows taskbar to display the Start menu.

icon

desktop

Start menu

All Programs command

Start button

pointer

taskbar

All Programs list

Accessories folder

Paint command

Accessories list

Step 2:
Click All Programs on the Start menu to display the All Programs list. Click Accessories in the All Programs list and then point to Paint in the Accessories list.

Step 5:
Instruct the Paint program to print the picture. When the Print dialog box is displayed, click the Print button.

Print dialog box

option button

check box

command button

text box

document file name

file contains picture stored on disk

Paint window

Step 3:
Click Paint. The Paint window is displayed on the desktop.

title bar

Step 4:
Instruct the Paint program to open a file that is stored on the hard disk.

LOOKING AHEAD 3-1

Touch Drive Your Computer Screen

Computer users soon may discard the mouse and let their fingers do the work with an innovative user interface system that displays images in thin air.

The virtual touch screen uses a rear projector system to create images that look three dimensional and appear to float in midair. Users interact with projected objects with their hands, so that there is no need for a mouse, monitor, physical surface, or special gloves or eyeglasses. In specialized environments, users also can use a scalpel, scissors, pen, or pencil to move objects.

The only hardware required to project these images is a standard video source, such as a computer, television, DVD player, or video game console. The projected images can be as large as 30 inches diagonally and are viewed best against a black background to emphasize the color contrast. For more information, visit scsite.com/dcf5e/ch3/looking and then click Gesture Recognition.

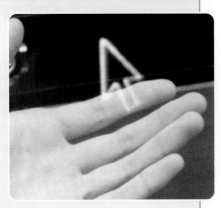

graphical element that you activate to cause a specific action to take place. One way to activate a button is to click it. To **click** a button on the screen requires moving the pointer to the button and then pressing and releasing a button on the mouse (usually the left mouse button). The **pointer** is a small symbol displayed on the screen that moves as you move the mouse. Common pointer shapes are an I-beam (I), a block arrow ($\mathbb{k}$), and a pointing hand ($\mathbetween{}$).

The Windows Vista desktop contains a Start button on the lower-left corner of the taskbar. When you click the Start button, the Start menu is displayed on the desktop. A **menu** contains a list of commands from which you make selections. A **command** is an instruction that causes a program to perform a specific action.

As illustrated in Steps 1 and 2 of Figure 3-3, when you click the Start button and click the All Programs command on the Start menu, the All Programs list is displayed on the Start menu. Clicking the Accessories folder in the All Programs list displays the Accessories list.

To start a program, you can click its program name on a menu or in a list. This action instructs the operating system to start the program, which means the program's instructions load from a storage medium (such as a hard disk) into memory. For example, when you click Paint in the Accessories list, Windows Vista loads the Paint program instructions from the computer's hard disk into memory.

Once loaded into memory, the program is displayed in a window on the desktop (Step 3 of Figure 3-3). A **window** is a rectangular area of the screen that displays data and information. The top of a window has a **title bar**, which is a horizontal space that contains the window's name.

With the program loaded, you can create a new file or open an existing one. A **file** is a named collection of stored data, instructions, or information. A file can contain text, images, audio, and video. To distinguish among various files, each file has a file name. The title bar of the document window usually displays a document's file name. Step 4 of Figure 3-3 shows the contents of the file, Crazy Horse Memorial, displaying in the Paint window.

In some cases, when you instruct a program to perform an activity such as printing, the program displays a dialog box. A dialog box is a window that provides information, presents available options, or requests a response. Dialog boxes, such as the one shown in Step 5 of Figure 3-3 often contain option buttons, text boxes, check boxes, and command buttons.

FAQ 3-1

What programs are included with Windows Vista?

Every version of Windows Vista includes Calculator, Notepad, WordPad, Internet Explorer, Windows Photo Gallery, Windows Mail, Windows Calendar, and a variety of games. For more information, visit scsite.com/dcf5e/ch3/faq and then click Windows Vista Programs.

Test your knowledge of pages 100 through 103 in Quiz Yourself 3-1.

QUIZ YOURSELF 3-1

Instructions: Find the true statement below. Then, rewrite the remaining false statements so they are true.

1. Application software is used to make business activities more efficient; assist with graphics and multimedia projects; support home, personal, and educational tasks; and facilitate communications.

2. Public-domain software is mass-produced, copyrighted retail software that meets the needs of a wide variety of users, not just a single user or company.

3. To use system software, your computer must be running application software.

4. When a program is started, its instructions load from memory into a storage medium.

Quiz Yourself Online: To further check your knowledge of application software categories and working with application software, visit scsite.com/dcf5e/ch3/quiz and then click Objectives 1 – 2.

BUSINESS SOFTWARE

Business software is application software that assists people in becoming more effective and efficient while performing their daily business activities. Business software includes programs such as word processing, spreadsheet, database, presentation graphics, note taking, personal information manager, personal mobile device business software, software suites, project management, accounting, document management, and enterprise computing software. Figure 3-4 lists popular programs for each of these categories.

POPULAR BUSINESS PROGRAMS

Application Software	Manufacturer	Program Name
Word Processing	Microsoft	Word 2007
	Apple	Pages
	Corel	WordPerfect
Spreadsheet	Microsoft	Excel 2007
	Apple	Numbers
	Corel	Quattro Pro
Database	Microsoft	Access 2007
	Corel	Paradox
	Oracle	Oracle Database
	MySQL AB	MySQL
Presentation Graphics	Microsoft	PowerPoint 2007
	Apple	Keynote
	Corel	Presentations
Note Taking	Microsoft	OneNote 2007
	Agilix	GoBinder
	Corel	Grafigo
Personal Information Manager (PIM)	Microsoft	Outlook 2007
	IBM	Organizer
	Palm	Desktop
	Mozilla	Thunderbird
Personal Mobile Device Business Software	CNetX	Pocket SlideShow
	Microsoft	Word Mobile Excel Mobile Outlook Mobile
	Mobile Systems	MobiSystems Office Suite
	Ultrasoft	Money

Application Software	Manufacturer	Program Name
Software Suite (for the Professional)	Microsoft	Office 2007 Office for Mac
	Apple	iWorks
	Sun	StarOffice Office Suite
	Corel	WordPerfect Office
	IBM	Lotus SmartSuite
Project Management	CS Odessa	ConceptDraw Project
	Microsoft	Project 2007
	Primavera	SureTrak Project Manager
Accounting	Intuit	QuickBooks
	Microsoft	Accounting 2007
	Sage Software	Peachtree
Document Management	Adobe	Acrobat
	Enfocus	PitStop
	Nuance	PDF Converter
Enterprise Computing	Oracle	PeopleSoft Enterprise Human Resources
	Sage Software	Sage MAS 500
	MSC Software	MSC.SimManager
	Oracle	Oracle Manufacturing
	SAP	mySAP Customer Relationship Management
	NetSuite	NetERP
	Syntellect	Syntellect Interaction Management Suite

FIGURE 3-4   Popular business software.

Word Processing Software

Word processing software, sometimes called a word processor, allows users to create and manipulate documents containing mostly text and sometimes graphics (Figure 3-5). Millions of people use word processing software every day to develop documents such as letters, memos, reports, fax cover sheets, mailing labels, newsletters, and Web pages.

Word processing software has many features to make documents look professional and visually appealing. Some of these features include the capability of changing the shape and size of characters, changing the color of characters, applying special effects such as three-dimensional shadows, and organizing text in newspaper-style columns.

Most word processing software allows users to incorporate in documents many types of graphical images, such as digital pictures and clip art. **Clip art** is a collection of drawings, photos, and other images that you can insert in documents. In Figure 3-5, a user inserted an image of the Statue of Liberty in the document. With current word processing software, you easily can modify the appearance of an image after inserting it in the document.

All word processing software provides at least some basic capabilities to help users create and modify documents. Defining the size of the paper on which to print and specifying the margins are examples of some of these capabilities. If you type text that extends beyond the right page margin, the word processing software automatically positions text at the beginning of the next line. This feature, called wordwrap, allows users to type words in a paragraph continually without pressing the ENTER key at the end of each line. As you type more lines of text than can be displayed on the screen, the top portion of the document moves upward, or scrolls, off the screen.

A major advantage of using word processing software is that users easily can change what they have written. For example, a user can insert, delete, or rearrange words, sentences, paragraphs, or entire sections. Current word processing programs also have a feature that automatically corrects errors and makes word substitutions as users type text. For instance, when you type the abbreviation asap, the word processing software replaces the abbreviation with the phrase, as soon as possible.

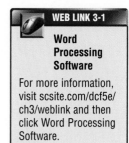

WEB LINK 3-1

Word Processing Software

For more information, visit scsite.com/dcf5e/ch3/weblink and then click Word Processing Software.

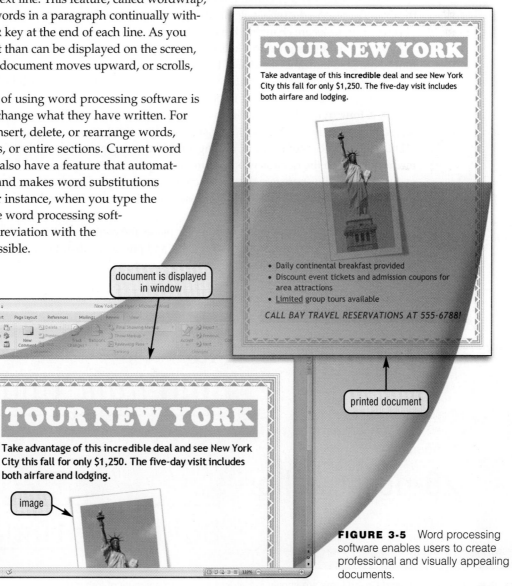

document is displayed in window

printed document

image

FIGURE 3-5 Word processing software enables users to create professional and visually appealing documents.

Word processing software typically includes a spelling checker, which reviews the spelling of individual words, sections of a document, or the entire document. The spelling checker compares the words in the document with an electronic dictionary that is part of the word processing software. Some word processing programs also check for contextual spelling errors, such as a misuse of homophones (words pronounced the same but have different spellings or meanings, such as one and won).

Developing a Document

With application software, such as word processing, users create, edit, format, save, and print documents. When you **create** a document, you enter text or numbers, insert images, and perform other tasks using an input device such as a keyboard, mouse, or digital pen. If you are using Microsoft Office Word 2007 to design a flyer, for example, you are creating a document.

To **edit** a document means to make changes to its existing content. Common editing tasks include inserting, deleting, cutting, copying, and pasting. Inserting text involves adding text to a document. Deleting text means that you are removing text or other content.

Cutting is the process of removing a portion of the document and storing it in a temporary storage location, sometimes called a clipboard. Pasting is the process of transferring an item from a clipboard to a specific location in a document.

When users **format** a document, they change its appearance. Formatting is important because the overall look of a document significantly can affect its ability to communicate clearly. Examples of formatting tasks are changing the font, font size, or font style of text.

A **font** is a name assigned to a specific design of characters. Cambria and Calibri are examples of fonts. **Font size** indicates the size of the characters in a particular font. Font size is gauged by a measurement system called points. A single point is about 1/72 of an inch in height. The text you are reading in this book is about 10 point. Thus, each character is about 5/36 (10/72) of an inch in height. A **font style** adds emphasis to a font. Bold, italic, and underline are examples of font styles. Figure 3-6 illustrates fonts, font sizes, and font styles.

During the process of creating, editing, and formatting a document, the computer holds it in memory. To keep the document for future use requires that you save it. When you **save** a document, the computer transfers the document from memory to a storage medium such as a USB flash drive, hard disk, CD, or DVD. Once saved, a document is stored permanently as a file on the storage medium.

When you **print** a document, the computer places the contents of the document on paper or some other medium. Instead of printing a document and physically distributing it, some users e-mail the document to others on a network such as the Internet.

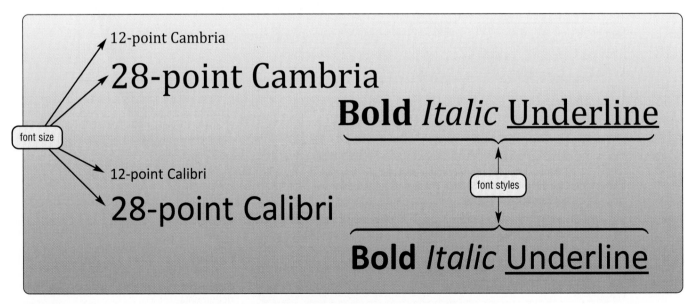

FIGURE 3-6   The Cambria and Calibri fonts are shown in two font sizes and a variety of font styles.

Spreadsheet Software

Spreadsheet software allows users to organize data in rows and columns and perform calculations on the data. These rows and columns collectively are called a **worksheet** (Figure 3-7). Most spreadsheet software has basic features to help users create, edit, and format worksheets. The following sections describe the features of most spreadsheet programs.

SPREADSHEET ORGANIZATION

Typically, a spreadsheet file is similar to a notebook that can contain more than 1,000 related individual worksheets. Data is organized vertically in columns and horizontally in rows on each worksheet (Figure 3-7). Each worksheet usually can have more than 16,000 columns and 1 million rows. One or more letters identify each column, and a number identifies each row. Only a small fraction of these columns and rows are displayed on the screen at one time. Scrolling through the worksheet displays different parts of it on the screen.

A cell is the intersection of a column and row. The spreadsheet software identifies cells by the column and row in which they are located. For example, the intersection of column B and row 8 is referred to as cell B8. As shown in Figure 3-7, cell B8 contains the number, 614,754, which represents the advertising expenses for the first year.

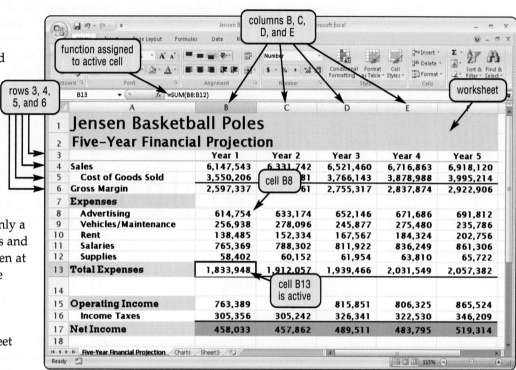

FIGURE 3-7   With spreadsheet software, you create worksheets that contain data arranged in rows and columns, and you can perform calculations on the data in the worksheets.

Cells may contain three types of data: labels, values, and formulas. The text, or label, entered in a cell identifies the worksheet data and helps organize the worksheet. Using descriptive labels, such as Total Expenses and Net Income, helps make a worksheet more meaningful.

CALCULATIONS   Many of the worksheet cells shown in Figure 3-7 contain a number, called a value, that can be used in a calculation. Other cells, however, contain formulas that generate values. A formula performs calculations on the data in the worksheet and displays the resulting value in a cell, usually the cell containing the formula. When creating a worksheet, you can enter your own formulas.

In many spreadsheet programs, you begin a formula with an equal sign, a plus sign, or a minus sign. Next, you enter the formula, separating cell references (e.g., B8) with operators. Common operators are + for addition, - for subtraction, * for multiplication, and / for division. In Figure 3-7, for example, cell B13 could contain the formula =B8+B9+B10+B11+B12, which would add together (sum) the contents of cells B8, B9, B10, B11, and B12. That is, this formula calculates the total expenses for the first year.

A function is a predefined formula that performs common calculations such as adding the values in a group of cells or generating a value such as the time or date. For example, instead of using the formula =B8+B9+B10+B11+B12 to calculate the total expenses for the first year, you could use the SUM function. This function requires you to identify the starting cell and the ending cell in a group to be summed, separating these two cell references with a colon. For example, the function =SUM(B8:B12) instructs the spreadsheet program to add all of the numbers in cells B8 through B12.

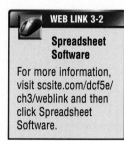

WEB LINK 3-2

Spreadsheet Software

For more information, visit scsite.com/dcf5e/ch3/weblink and then click Spreadsheet Software.

RECALCULATION   One of the more powerful features of spreadsheet software is its capability of recalculating the rest of the worksheet when data in a worksheet changes. When you enter a new value to change data in a cell, any value affected by the change is updated automatically and instantaneously.

CHARTING   Another standard feature of spreadsheet software is charting, which depicts the data in graphical form. A visual representation of data through charts often makes it easier for users to see at a glance the relationship among the numbers. Three popular chart types are line charts, column charts, and pie charts. Figure 3-8 shows examples of these charts that were plotted using the five types of expenses for each of the years shown in the worksheet in Figure 3-7 on the previous page. A line chart shows a trend during a period of time, as indicated by a rising or falling line. A column chart, also called a bar chart, displays bars of various lengths to show the relationship of data. The bars can be horizontal, vertical, or stacked on top of one another. A pie chart, which has the shape of a round pie cut into slices, shows the relationship of parts to a whole.

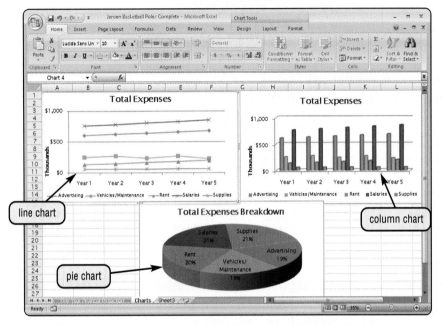

FIGURE 3-8   Three basic types of charts provided with spreadsheet software are line charts, column charts, and pie charts. The charts shown here were created using the data in the worksheet in Figure 3-7.

Database Software

A **database** is a collection of data organized in a manner that allows access, retrieval, and use of that data. In a manual database, you might record data on paper and store it in a filing cabinet. With a computerized database, such as the one shown in Figure 3-9, the computer stores the data in an electronic format on a storage medium such as a hard disk.

Database software is application software that allows users to create, access, and manage a database. Using database software, you can add, change, and delete data in a database; sort and retrieve data from the database; and create forms and reports using the data in the database.

With most popular personal computer database programs, a database consists of a collection of tables, organized in rows and columns. Each row, called a record, contains data about a given person, product, object, or event. Each column, called a field, contains a specific category of data within a record.

The Beauty Supply database shown in Figure 3-9 consists of two tables: a Customer table and a Sales Rep table. The Customer table contains eleven records (rows), each storing data about one customer. The customer data is grouped into six fields (columns): Customer Number, Customer Name, Telephone, Balance, Amount Paid,

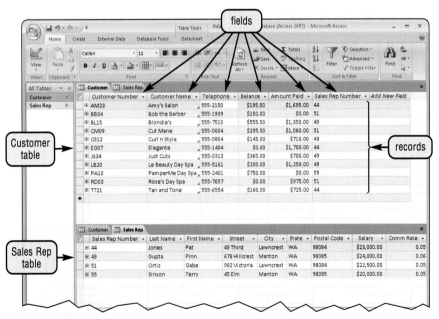

FIGURE 3-9   This database contains two tables: one for the customers and one for the sales representatives. The Customer table has eleven records and six fields; the Sales Rep table has four records and nine fields.

and Sales Rep Number. The Balance field, for instance, contains the balance due from the customer. The Customer and Sales Rep tables relate to one another through a common field, Sales Rep Number.

Users run queries to retrieve data. A query is a request for specific data from the database. For example, a query might request a list of customers whose balance is greater than $500. Database software can take the results of a query and present it in a window on the screen or send it to the printer.

Presentation Graphics Software

Presentation graphics software is application software that allows users to create visual aids for presentations to communicate ideas, messages, and other information to a group. The presentations can be viewed as slides, sometimes called a slide show, that are displayed on a large monitor or on a projection screen (Figure 3-10).

Presentation graphics software typically provides a variety of predefined presentation formats that define complementary colors for backgrounds, text, and graphical accents on the slides. This software also provides a variety of layouts for each individual slide such as a title slide, a two-column slide, and a slide with clip art, a chart, a table, a diagram, or animation. In addition, you can enhance any text, charts, and graphical images on a slide with 3-D and other special effects such as shading, shadows, and textures.

When building a presentation, users can set the slide timing so that the presentation automatically displays the next slide after a preset delay. Presentation graphics software allows you to apply special effects to the transition between slides. One slide, for example, might fade away as the next slide is displayed.

You can view or print a finished presentation in a variety of formats, including an outline of text from each slide and audience handouts that show completed slides.

Presentation graphics software typically includes a clip gallery that provides images, pictures, video clips, and audio clips to enhance multimedia presentations. Some audio and video editing programs work with presentation graphics software, providing users with an easy means to record and insert video, music, and audio commentary in a presentation. Presentation graphics software incorporates features such as checking spelling, formatting, research, ink input, and converting an existing slide show into a format for the World Wide Web.

FIGURE 3-10 This presentation created with presentation graphics software consists of five slides.

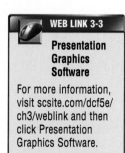

WEB LINK 3-3

Presentation Graphics Software

For more information, visit scsite.com/dcf5e/ch3/weblink and then click Presentation Graphics Software.

Note Taking Software

Note taking software is application software that enables users to enter typed text, handwritten comments, drawings, or sketches anywhere on a page and then save the page as part of a notebook (Figure 3-11). Users also can include audio recordings as part of their notes. Once the notes are captured (entered and saved), users easily can organize them, reuse them, and share them.

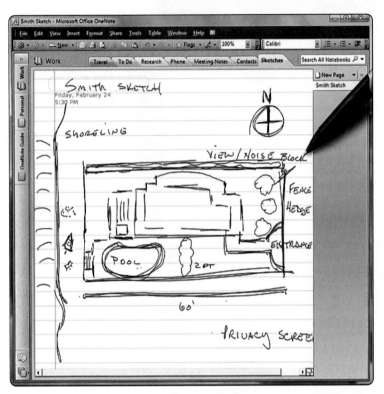

FIGURE 3-11   With note taking software, mobile users can handwrite notes, draw sketches, and type text.

On a desktop or notebook computer, users enter notes primarily via the keyboard or microphone. On a Tablet PC, however, the primary input device is a digital pen. Users find note taking software convenient during meetings, class lectures, conferences, in libraries, and other settings that previously required a pencil and tablet of paper for recording thoughts and discussions.

Personal Information Manager Software

A **personal information manager (PIM)** is application software that includes an appointment calendar, address book, notepad, and other features to help users organize personal information. The appointment calendar allows you to schedule activities for a particular day and time. With the address book, you can enter and maintain names, addresses, telephone numbers, and e-mail addresses of customers, coworkers, family members, and friends. You can use the notepad to record ideas, reminders, and other important information.

Most mobile devices, such as smart phones and PDAs, include, among many other features, PIM functionality. You can synchronize, or coordinate, information so that both the mobile device and your personal computer and/or organization's server have the latest version of any updated information.

Personal Mobile Device Business Software

A huge variety of business software is available for mobile devices, such as smart phones. Some software is preloaded on the device, while other software can be downloaded or accessed on miniature storage media, such as memory cards. Nearly all mobile devices include PIM software. Other business software for mobile devices allows users to create documents and worksheets, manage databases and lists, create slide shows, take notes, manage budgets and finances, view and edit photos, read electronic books, plan travel routes, compose and read e-mail messages, send instant messages, and browse the Web. A variety of other programs are available for mobile devices, which enable you to send text and picture messages, take digital pictures, record videos, listen to music, view maps and directions, customize your background, change your ringtones, and play games.

Software Suite

A **software suite** is a collection of individual programs sold as a single package. Business software suites typically include, at a minimum, the following programs: word processing, spreadsheet, e-mail, and presentation graphics. Popular software suites are Microsoft Office 2007 and Apple iWork.

Software suites offer two major advantages: lower cost and ease of use. Buying a collection of programs in a software suite usually costs significantly less than purchasing them individually. Software suites provide ease of use because the programs within a software suite normally use a similar interface and share features such as clip art and a spelling checker.

Project Management Software

Project management software allows a user to plan, schedule, track, and analyze the events, resources, and costs of a project (Figure 3-12). Project management software helps users manage project variables, allowing them to complete a project on time and within budget. An engineer, for example, might use project management software to manage new product development to schedule timing of market analysis, product design, marketing, and public relations activities.

Accounting Software

Accounting software helps companies record and report their financial transactions (Figure 3-13). With accounting software, business users perform accounting activities related to the general ledger, accounts receivable, accounts payable, purchasing, invoicing, and payroll functions. Accounting software also enables business users to write and print checks, track checking account activity, and update and reconcile balances on demand.

Most accounting software supports online credit checks, billing, direct deposit, and payroll services. Some accounting software offers more complex features such as job costing and estimating, time tracking, multiple company reporting, foreign currency reporting, and forecasting the amount of raw materials needed for products. The cost of accounting software for small businesses ranges from less than one hundred to several thousand dollars. Accounting software for large businesses can cost several hundred thousand dollars.

Document Management Software

Document management software provides a means for sharing, distributing, and searching through documents by converting them into a format that can be viewed by any user (Figure 3-14). The converted document, which mirrors the original document's appearance, can be viewed and printed without the software that created the original document. A popular file format used by document management software to save converted documents is **PDF** (Portable Document Format), developed by Adobe Systems. To view and print a PDF file, you need Acrobat Reader software, which can be downloaded free from Adobe's Web site.

FIGURE 3-12 Project management software allows users to track, control, and manage the events, resources, and costs of a project.

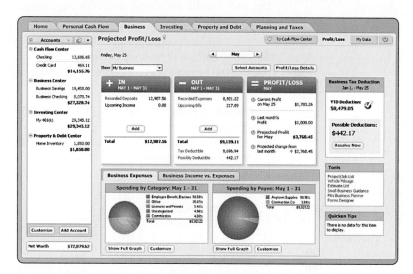

FIGURE 3-13 Accounting software helps companies record and report their financial transactions.

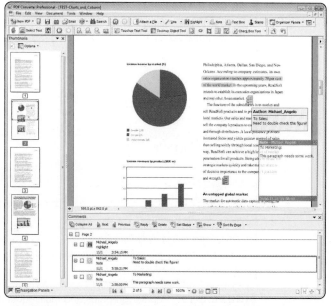

FIGURE 3-14 Document management software allows users to create and edit PDF files.

Enterprise Computing Software

A large organization, commonly referred to as an enterprise, requires special computing solutions because of its size and large geographical distribution. A typical enterprise consists of a wide variety of departments, centers, and divisions — collectively known as functional units. Nearly every enterprise has the following functional units: human resources, accounting and finance, engineering or product development, manufacturing, marketing, sales, distribution, customer service, and information technology. Each of these functional units has specialized software requirements.

GRAPHICS AND MULTIMEDIA SOFTWARE

In addition to business software, many people work with software designed specifically for their field of work. Power users such as engineers, architects, desktop publishers, and graphic artists often use sophisticated software that allows them to work with graphics and multimedia. This software includes computer-aided design, desktop publishing, paint/image editing, photo editing, video and audio editing, multimedia authoring, and Web page authoring. Figure 3-15 lists the more popular programs for each of these categories, specifically designed for professional or more technically astute users. Some of these programs incorporate user-friendly interfaces, or scaled-down versions, making it possible for the home and small business users to create documents using these programs. The following sections discuss the features and functions of graphics and multimedia software.

POPULAR GRAPHICS AND MULTIMEDIA SOFTWARE

Application Software	Manufacturer	Program Name
Computer-Aided Design (CAD)	Autodesk	AutoCAD
	Chief Architect	Chief Architect
	Microsoft	Visio 2007
Desktop Publishing (for the Professional)	Adobe	InDesign
	Corel	Ventura
	Quark	QuarkXPress
Paint/Image Editing (for the Professional)	Adobe	Illustrator
	Corel	Painter
	Microsoft	Expression Design
Photo Editing (for the Professional)	Adobe	Photoshop
	Nik Software	Nik Professional Suite
Video and Audio Editing (for the Professional)	Adobe	Audition Encore DVD Premiere Pro Soundbooth
	Avid Technology	Avid Xpress Pro
	Cakewalk	SONAR
	Sony	ACID Pro
	Corel	Ulead MediaStudio Pro
Multimedia Authoring	Adobe	Director
	Agilix	BrainHoney
	SumTotal Systems	ToolBook Instructor
Web Page Authoring	Adobe	Dreamweaver Fireworks Flash GoLive
	Microsoft	Expression Web SharePoint Designer 2007

FIGURE 3-15 Popular graphics and multimedia programs — for the professional.

Computer-Aided Design

Computer-aided design (CAD) software is a sophisticated type of application software that assists a professional user in creating engineering, architectural, and scientific designs. For example, engineers create design plans for vehicles and security systems. Architects design building structures and floor plans (Figure 3-16). Scientists design drawings of molecular structures.

Desktop Publishing Software (for the Professional)

Desktop publishing (DTP) software enables professional designers to create sophisticated documents that contain text, graphics, and many colors (Figure 3-17). Professional DTP software is ideal for the production of high-quality color documents such as textbooks, corporate newsletters, marketing literature, product catalogs, and annual reports. Today's DTP software also allows designers to convert a color document into a format for use on the World Wide Web.

Paint/Image Editing Software (for the Professional)

Graphic artists, multimedia professionals, technical illustrators, and desktop publishers use paint software and image editing software to create and modify graphical images such as those used in DTP documents and Web pages. **Paint software**, also called illustration software, allows users to draw pictures (Figure 3-18), shapes, and other graphical images with various on-screen tools such as a pen, brush, eyedropper, and paint bucket. **Image editing software** provides the capabilities of paint software and also includes the capability to enhance and modify existing pictures and images. Modifications can include adjusting or enhancing image colors, adding special effects such as shadows and glows, creating animations, and image stitching, which is the process of combining multiple images into a larger image.

Professional photo editing software is a type of image editing software that allows photographers, videographers, engineers, scientists, and other high-volume digital photo users to edit and customize digital photos. With professional photo editing software, users can retouch photos, crop images, remove red-eye, change image shapes, color-correct images, straighten images, remove or rearrange objects in a photo, and apply filters.

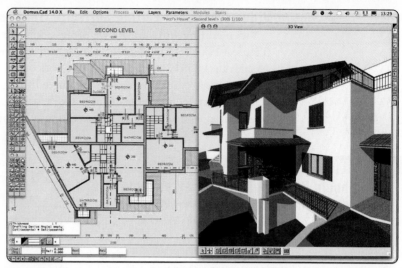

FIGURE 3-16   Architects use CAD software to design building structures and floor plans.

FIGURE 3-17   Professional designers and graphic artists use DTP software to produce sophisticated publications such as a printed magazine article.

FIGURE 3-18   With paint software, artists can create and modify any type of graphical image.

Video and Audio Editing Software (for the Professional)

Video editing software allows professionals to modify a segment of a video, called a clip (Figure 3-19). For example, users can reduce the length of a video clip, reorder a series of clips, or add special effects such as words that move horizontally across the screen. Video editing software typically includes audio editing capabilities. **Audio editing software** lets users modify audio clips, produce studio-quality soundtracks, and add audio to video clips. Most television shows and movies are created or enhanced using video and audio editing software. Read Ethics & Issues 3-1 for a related discussion.

ETHICS & ISSUES 3-1

Should It Be Legal to Share Copyrighted Music or Video Files over a Network?

It is usually illegal to use networks to share copyrighted music or video files. Despite this, a number of file-sharing networks exist, and millions of Americans use file-sharing software to locate and download copyrighted music and videos without paying. Much of this illegal activity takes place at colleges and universities. To combat illegal file sharing, some schools have turned to new programs that intentionally slow the performance of file-sharing software. Other schools have accepted the trend and subscribed to large collections of music for all students to share legally. The Recording Industry Association of America (RIAA) has been filing lawsuits against people suspected of downloading copyrighted music. Those found guilty can be liable for fines up to $150,000 for every stolen song. The RIAA maintains that downloading copyrighted music steals from both the recording artist and the recording industry. Yet, many people feel that the response to sharing copyrighted music and video files is excessive. They argue that copying music from the radio to an audio cassette is legal and insist that downloading copyrighted music is no different. Besides, someone who downloads a copyrighted song later may be inspired to purchase an artist's CD. Are slowing file-sharing software and filing lawsuits unwarranted reactions to what some people consider a victimless violation? Why? Is it a good idea for schools to subscribe to music collections?

FIGURE 3-19   With video editing software, users modify video clips.

Multimedia Authoring Software

Multimedia authoring software allows users to combine text, graphics, audio, video, and animation into an interactive application (Figure 3-20). With this software, users control the placement of text and images and the duration of sounds, video, and animation. Once created, multimedia presentations often take the form of interactive computer-based presentations or Web-based presentations designed to facilitate learning, demonstrate product functionality, and elicit direct-user participation. Training centers, educational institutions, and online magazine publishers all use multimedia authoring software to develop interactive applications. These applications may be available on a CD or DVD, over a local area network, or via the Internet.

Web Page Authoring Software

Web page authoring software helps users of all skill levels create Web pages that include graphical images, video, audio, animation, and special effects with interactive content. In addition, many Web page authoring programs allow users to organize, manage, and maintain Web sites.

Application software, such as Word and Excel, often includes Web page authoring features. This allows home users to create basic Web pages using application software they already own. For more sophisticated Web pages, users work with Web page authoring software.

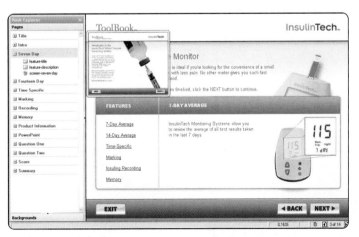

FIGURE 3-20   Multimedia authoring software allows you to create dynamic presentations that include text, graphics, video, sound, and animation.

Test your knowledge of pages 104 through 114 in Quiz Yourself 3-2.

SOFTWARE FOR HOME, PERSONAL, AND EDUCATIONAL USE

A large amount of application software is designed specifically for home, personal, and educational use. Most of the programs in this category are relatively inexpensive, often priced less than $100. Figure 3-21 lists popular programs for many of these categories. The following sections discuss the features and functions of this application software.

POPULAR PROGRAMS FOR HOME/PERSONAL/EDUCATIONAL USE

Application Software	Manufacturer	Program Name
Software Suite (for Personal Use)	Microsoft	Works
	Sun	OpenOffice.org
Personal Finance	Intuit	Quicken
	Microsoft	Money
Legal	Broderbund	Home and Business Lawyer / WillWriter
	Cosmi	Perfect Attorney
	Nolo	Quicken Legal Business / Quicken WillMaker
Tax Preparation	2nd Story Software	TaxACT
	H&R Block	TaxCut
	Intuit	TurboTax
Desktop Publishing (for Personal Use)	Broderbund	The Print Shop / PrintMaster
	Microsoft	Publisher 2007
Paint/Image Editing (for Personal Use)	Corel	CorelDRAW
	The GIMP Team	The Gimp

Application Software	Manufacturer	Program Name
Photo Editing and Photo Management (for Personal Use)	Adobe	Photoshop Elements
	Corel	Paint Shop Pro Photo / Ulead PhotoImpact / Ulead Photo Express
	Google	Picasa
	Microsoft	Photo Story
	Roxio	PhotoSuite
Clip Art/Image Gallery	Broderbund	ClickArt
	Nova Development	Art Explosion
Video and Audio Editing (for Personal Use)	Corel	Ulead VideoStudio
	Microsoft	Movie Maker
	Pinnacle Systems	Studio MovieBox
	Roxio	VideoWave
Home Design/ Landscaping	Broderbund	Instant Architect / Better Homes & Gardens Home Designer
Travel and Mapping	DeLorme	Street Atlas
	Microsoft	Streets & Trips
Reference	Fogware Publishing	Merriam-Webster Collegiate Dictionary & Thesaurus
	Microsoft	Encarta

FIGURE 3-21 Many popular programs are available for home, personal, and educational use.

Software Suite (for Personal Use)

A software suite (for personal use) combines application software such as word processing, spreadsheet, database, and other programs in a single, easy-to-use package. Many computer vendors install a software suite for personal use, such as Microsoft Works, on new computers sold to home users.

As mentioned earlier, the programs in a software suite use a similar interface and share some common features. For many home users, the capabilities of software suites for personal use more than meet their needs.

Personal Finance Software

Personal finance software is a simplified accounting program that helps home users and small office/home office users balance their checkbooks, pay bills, track personal income and expenses (Figure 3-22), track investments, and evaluate financial plans.

Most personal finance software includes financial planning features, such as analyzing home and personal loans, preparing income taxes, and managing retirement savings. Other features include managing home inventory and setting up budgets. Most of these programs also offer a variety of online services, such as online banking, which require access to the Internet.

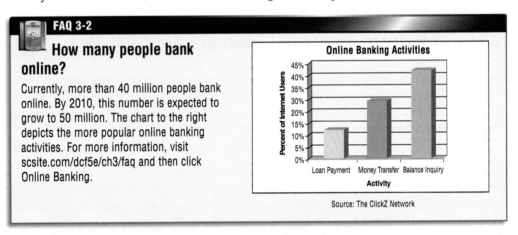

FAQ 3-2

How many people bank online?

Currently, more than 40 million people bank online. By 2010, this number is expected to grow to 50 million. The chart to the right depicts the more popular online banking activities. For more information, visit scsite.com/dcf5e/ch3/faq and then click Online Banking.

Online Banking Activities

Source: The ClickZ Network

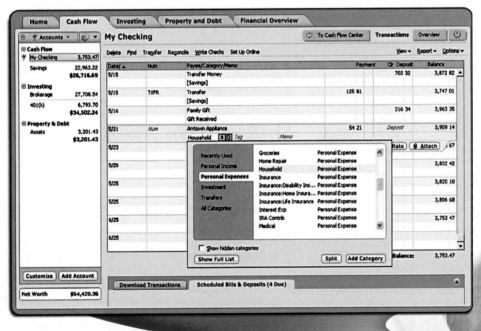

FIGURE 3-22 Personal finance software assists home users with tracking personal income and expenses.

Legal Software

Legal software assists in the preparation of legal documents and provides legal information to individuals, families, and small businesses (Figure 3-23). Legal software provides standard contracts and documents associated with buying, selling, and renting property; estate planning; marriage and divorce; and preparing a will or living trust. By answering a series of questions or completing a form, the legal software tailors the legal document to specific needs.

FIGURE 3-23 Legal software provides legal information and assists in record keeping and the preparation of legal documents.

Tax Preparation Software

Tax preparation software, which is available both as packaged software and Web-based software, can guide individuals, families, or small businesses through the process of filing federal taxes (Figure 3-24). These programs forecast tax liability and offer money-saving tax tips, designed to lower your tax bill. After you answer a series of questions and complete basic forms, the software creates and analyzes your tax forms to search for missed potential errors and deduction opportunities.

Once the forms are complete, you can print any necessary paperwork, and then they are ready for filing. Some tax preparation programs also allow you to file your tax forms electronically.

FIGURE 3-24 Tax preparation software guides individuals, families, or small businesses through the process of filing federal taxes.

Desktop Publishing Software (for Personal Use)

Personal DTP software helps home and small business users create newsletters, brochures, flyers (Figure 3-25), advertisements, postcards, greeting cards, letterhead, business cards, banners, calendars, logos, and Web pages.

Personal DTP programs provide hundreds of thousands of graphical images. You also can import (bring in) your own digital photos into the documents. These programs typically guide you through the development of a document by asking a series of questions. Then, you can print a finished publication on a color printer or post it on the Web.

Many personal DTP programs also include paint/image editing software and photo editing and photo management software.

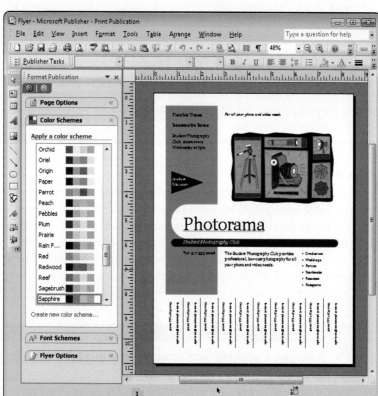

FIGURE 3-25 With desktop publishing software, home and small business users can create flyers.

Paint/Image Editing Software (for Personal Use)

Personal paint/image editing software provides an easy-to-use interface; includes various simplified tools that allow you to draw pictures, shapes, and other images; and provides the capability of modifying existing graphics and photos. These products also include many templates to assist you in adding an image to documents such as greeting cards, banners, calendars, signs, labels, business cards, and letterhead.

Personal photo editing software, a popular type of image editing software, allows users to edit digital photos by removing red-eye, erasing blemishes, restoring aged photos, adding special effects, enhancing image quality (Figure 3-26), or creating electronic photo albums. When you purchase a digital camera, it usually includes photo editing software. You can print edited photos on labels, calendars, business cards, and banners; or post them on a Web page.

With **photo management software**, you can view, organize, sort, catalog, print, and share digital photos. Some software includes both photo editing and photo management functionality.

FIGURE 3-26 As shown here, home users can lighten digital pictures with personal photo editing software.

FAQ 3-3

How do I print my pictures from my digital camera?

Your digital camera may connect with a cable directly to your computer or to a kiosk at a store. You also may be able to remove the media card from the digital camera and transfer pictures from the card to your computer and/or printer for printing. Online services also are available that allow you to transfer your pictures to them electronically, and they will mail you the prints. For more information, visit scsite.com/dcf5e/ch3/faq and then click Printing Digital Pictures.

Clip Art/Image Gallery

Application software often includes a **clip art/image gallery**, which is a collection of clip art and photos. Some applications have links to additional clips available on the Web. You also can purchase clip art/image gallery software that contains thousands of images (Figure 3-27).

In addition to clip art, many clip art/image galleries provide fonts, animations, sounds, video clips, and audio clips. You can use the images, fonts, and other items from the clip art/image gallery in all types of documents, including word processing, desktop publishing, spreadsheet, and presentation graphics.

FIGURE 3-27 Clip art/image gallery software contains thousands of images.

FAQ 3-4

How can I archive and manage my digital photos?

Many free and fee-based Web sites exist on the Internet that allow users to upload and manage their digital photos. People can choose either to upload their photos so that others can view them or to archive the photos for personal use. For more information, visit scsite.com/dcf5e/ch3/faq and then click Digital Photos.

Video and Audio Editing Software (for Personal Use)

Many home users work with easy-to-use video and audio editing software, which is much simpler to use than its professional counterpart, for small-scale movie making projects (Figure 3-28). With these programs, home users can edit home movies, add music or other sounds to the video, and share their movies on the Web. Some operating systems include video editing and audio editing software.

Home Design/Landscaping Software

Homeowners or potential homeowners can use **home design/landscaping software** to assist them with the design, remodeling, or improvement of a home, deck, or landscape (Figure 3-29). This software includes hundreds of predrawn plans that you can customize to meet your needs. These programs show changes to home designs and landscapes, allowing homeowners to preview proposed modifications.

Travel and Mapping Software

Travel and mapping software enables users to view maps, determine route directions, and locate points of interest (Figure 3-30). Using travel and mapping software, you can display maps by searching for an address, postal code, telephone number, or point of interest (such as airports, lodging, and historical sites). Most programs also allow you to download construction reports and calculate mileage, time, and expenses.

Educational and Reference Software

Educational software is software that teaches a particular skill. Educational software exists for just about any subject, from learning how to type to learning how to cook to preparing for college entry exams. Educational software often includes games and other content to make the learning experience more fun. Many educational programs use a computer-based training approach. **Computer-based training (CBT)** is a type of education in which students learn by using and completing exercises with instructional software. CBT typically consists of self-directed, self-paced instruction about a topic.

Reference software provides valuable and thorough information for all individuals. Popular reference software includes encyclopedias, dictionaries, and health/medical guides (Figure 3-31).

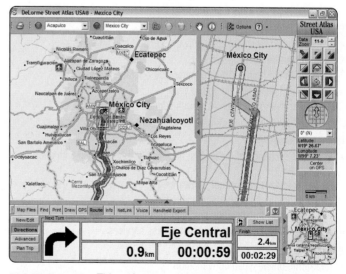

FIGURE 3-28   With personal video and audio editing software, home users can edit their home movies.

FIGURE 3-29   Home design/landscaping software can help you design or remodel a home, deck, or landscape.

FIGURE 3-30   This software provides turn-by-turn directions, along with estimated travel times.

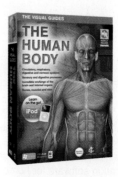

FIGURE 3-31   Reference software provides definitions, illustrations, videos, and more.

Entertainment Software

Entertainment software for personal computers includes interactive games, videos, and other programs designed to support a hobby or provide amusement and enjoyment. For example, you might use entertainment software to play games individually (Figure 3-32) or with others online, make a family tree, or fly an aircraft.

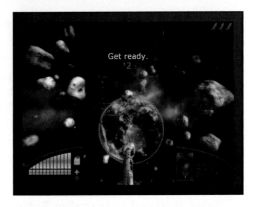

FIGURE 3-32 Entertainment software can provide hours of recreation.

APPLICATION SOFTWARE FOR COMMUNICATIONS

One of the main reasons people use computers is to communicate and share information with others. Some communications software is considered system software because it works with hardware and transmission media. Other communications software performs specific tasks for users, and thus, is considered application software. Chapter 2 presented a variety of application software for communications, which is summarized in the table in Figure 3-33. Read Ethics & Issues 3-2 for a related discussion.

APPLICATION SOFTWARE FOR COMMUNICATIONS

Web Browser
- Allows users to access and view Web pages on the Internet
- Requires a Web browser program
  - Integrated in some operating systems
  - Available for download on the Web free or for a fee

E-Mail
- Messages and files sent via a network such as the Internet
- Requires an e-mail program
  - Integrated in many software suites and operating systems
  - Available free at portals on the Web
  - Included with paid Internet access service
  - Can be purchased separately from retailers

Instant Messaging
- Real-time exchange of messages, files, audio, and/or video with another online user
- Requires instant messenger software
  - Integrated in some operating systems
  - Available for download on the Web, usually at no cost
  - Included with some paid Internet access services

Chat Room
- Real-time, online typed conversation
- Requires chat client software
  - Integrated in some operating systems, e-mail programs, and Web browsers
  - Available for download on the Web, usually at no cost
  - Included with some paid Internet access services
  - Built into some Web sites

Text Messaging
- Short text messages sent and received, mainly on mobile devices
- Requires text messenger software
  - Integrated in most mobile devices
  - Available for download on the Web, usually at no cost, for personal computers

RSS Aggregator
- Keeps track of changes made to Web sites by checking RSS feeds
- Requires RSS aggregator program
  - Integrated in some e-mail programs and Web browsers
  - Available for download on the Web, usually at no cost

Blogging
- Time-stamped articles, or posts, in a diary or journal format, usually listed in reverse chronological order
- Blogger needs blog software, or blogware, to create/maintain blog
  - Some Web sites do not require installation of blog software

Newsgroup/Message Board
- Online area where users have written discussions
- Newsgroup may require a newsreader program
  - Integrated in some operating systems, e-mail programs, and Web browsers
- Built into some Web sites

FTP
- Method of uploading and downloading files with other computers on the Internet
- May require an FTP program
  - Integrated in some operating systems
  - Available for download on the Web for a small fee

VoIP (Internet Telephony)
- Allows users to speak to other users over the Internet
- Requires Internet connection, Internet telephone service, microphone or telephone, and Internet telephone software or telephone adapter

Video Conferencing
- Meeting between geographically separated people who use a network such as the Internet to transmit video/audio
- Requires video conferencing software, a microphone, speakers, and sometimes a video camera attached to your computer

FIGURE 3-33   A summary of application software for home and business communications.

ETHICS & ISSUES 3-2

Should Companies Monitor Employees' E-Mail and Internet Traffic?

Most companies monitor (after transmission) or intercept (during transmission) employees' e-mail messages. Employers can use software to automatically find personal or offensive e-mail messages that have been sent or received, and intercept and filter messages while they are being sent or received. Companies also monitor other Internet traffic such as Web sites visited by employees and how much time employees spend sending instant messages and visiting chat rooms. Companies perform this monitoring to improve productivity, increase security, reduce misconduct, and control liability risks. Few laws regulate employee monitoring, and courts have given employers a great deal of leeway in watching work on company-owned computers. In one case, an employee's termination for using her office e-mail system to complain about her boss was upheld, even though the company allowed e-mail use for personal communications. The court decreed that the employee's messages were inappropriate for workplace communications. Many employees believe that excessive monitoring of software violates their privacy rights. State laws usually favor the privacy of the employee, while federal laws tend to favor the employer's right to perform such monitoring. To reduce employee anxiety about monitoring and to follow some state laws, companies publish written policies called acceptable use policies (AUP). AUPs should provide clear descriptions of acceptable and unacceptable behavior, respect employee needs and time, and establish a balance between security and privacy. Often, the consequence for violating an AUP is that the violator is fired. Should companies monitor or intercept employees' Internet communications? Why or why not? How can a company balance workplace security and productivity with employee privacy? What types of behavior should be covered by an AUP? Why? Should employees have an expectation of free speech in the workplace? Why or why not? Is intercepting and filtering e-mail more offensive than monitoring e-mail? Why?

POPULAR UTILITY PROGRAMS

Utility programs are considered system software because they assist a user with controlling or maintaining the operation of a computer, its devices, or its software. Utility programs typically offer features that provide an environment conducive to successful use of application software. One of the more important utility programs protects a computer against viruses. A computer virus is a potentially damaging computer program that affects, or infects, a computer negatively by altering the way the computer works without the user's knowledge or permission.

Other features of utility programs include protecting a computer against unauthorized intrusions, removing spyware, filtering e-mail and Web content, managing files and disks, compressing files, backing up, playing media files, burning (recording on) a CD or DVD, and maintaining a personal computer. The table in Figure 3-34 briefly describes several types of utility programs.

WIDELY USED UTILITY PROGRAMS

Utility Program	Description
Antivirus Program	An antivirus program protects a computer against viruses by identifying and removing any computer viruses found in memory, on storage media, or in incoming files.
Personal Firewall	A personal firewall detects and protects a personal computer from unauthorized intrusions.
Spyware Remover	A spyware remover detects and deletes spyware, adware, and other similar programs on your computer.
Internet Filters • Anti-Spam Program • Web Filter • Pop-Up Blocker	 An anti-spam program attempts to remove spam (Internet junk mail) before it reaches your e-mail inbox. A Web filter restricts access to specified Web sites. A pop-up blocker stops advertisements from displaying on Web pages and disables pop-up windows.
File Manager	A file manager provides functions related to file and disk management.
File Compression	A file compression utility shrinks the size of a file(s), so that the file takes up less storage space than the original file.
Backup	A backup utility allows users to copy selected files or an entire hard disk to another storage medium.
Media Player	A media player allows you to view images and animation, listen to audio, and watch video files.
CD/DVD Burning	A CD/DVD burner writes text, graphics, audio, and video files on a recordable or rewritable CD or DVD.
Personal Computer Maintenance	A personal computer maintenance utility identifies and fixes operating system problems, detects and repairs disk problems, and includes the capability of improving a computer's performance.

FIGURE 3-34 A summary of widely used utility programs.

WEB-BASED SOFTWARE

As previously mentioned, Web-based software refers to programs hosted by a Web site. Users often interact with Web-based software, sometimes called a **Web application,** directly at the host's Web site. Some Web sites, however, require you download the software to your local computer or device. Web-based software sites often store users' data and information on their servers. Web-based software sites may provide users with an option of storing data locally on their own personal computer or mobile device.

Many of the previously discussed types of application software have Web-based options. For example, Google Docs and Spreadsheets is a Web-based word processing and spreadsheet program, and Windows Live Hotmail is a Web-based e-mail program.

Some Web sites provide free access to the Web-based software, such as the spreadsheet program shown in Figure 3-35. Another site creates a map and driving directions when a user enters a starting and destination point. Others offer part of their Web-based software free and charge for access to a more comprehensive program.

Experts often use the term Web 2.0 to describe Web sites that offer Web-based software. Recall that Web 2.0 refers to Web sites that provide users with a means to share and/or store personal information through Web-based software and may allow users to modify Web site content. Read Looking Ahead 3-2 for a look at the the next generation of Web 2.0.

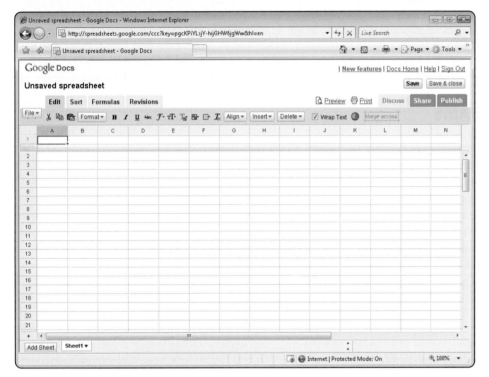

FIGURE 3-35 Shown here is a free Web-based spreadsheet program.

LOOKING AHEAD 3-2

Using Semantics with Web 3.0

When Tim Berners-Lee created the World Wide Web in 1989, he laid the foundation for allowing computers to look at words on the Internet and then make random associations. Fifteen years later, he led a group of researchers who set standards for the semantic Web, also called Web 3.0, which will give the machines the capability to understand the words' meanings.

Such artificial intelligence allows computers to locate and share information on the Internet based on context, so that they automatically can reason and then differentiate between such concepts as a dog bark and tree bark. This classification system has drawn interest in many areas, particularly for entertainment and travel Web sites and in business and scientific databases. The result will be smarter search engines and automated Web tasks such as comparison shopping.

IBM, Google, and Oracle are among the large corporations embracing semantic technology. For more information, visit scsite.com/dcf5e/ch3/looking and then click Web 3.0.

LEARNING AIDS AND SUPPORT TOOLS FOR APPLICATION SOFTWARE

Learning how to use application software effectively involves time and practice. To assist in the learning process, many programs provide online Help (Figure 3-36) and Web-based Help.

Online Help is the electronic equivalent of a user manual. It usually is integrated in a program. In most programs, a function key or a button on the screen starts the Help feature. When using a program, you can use the Help feature to ask a question or access the Help topics in subject or alphabetical order.

Most online Help also links to Web sites that offer Web-based help, which provides updates and more comprehensive resources to respond to technical issues about software. Some Web sites contain chat rooms, in which a user can talk directly with a technical support person.

Many books are available to help you learn to use the features of personal computer programs. These books typically are available in bookstores and software stores.

Web-Based Training

Web-based training (WBT) is a type of CBT (computer-based training) that uses Internet technology and consists of application software on the Web. Similar to CBT, WBT typically consists of self-directed, self-paced instruction about a topic. WBT is popular in business, industry, and schools for teaching new skills or enhancing existing skills of employees, teachers, or students.

Many Web sites offer WBT to the general public. Such training covers a wide range of topics, from how to change a flat tire to creating documents in Word. Many of these Web sites are free. Others require registration and payment to take the complete Web-based course.

WBT often is combined with other materials for distance learning and e-learning. **Distance learning** is the delivery of education at one location while the learning takes place at other locations. **E-learning,** short for electronic learning, is the delivery of education via some electronic method such as the Internet, networks, or CDs/DVDs. To enhance communications, e-learning systems also may include video conferencing, e-mail, blogs, wikis, newsgroups, chat rooms, and groupware (Figure 3-37).

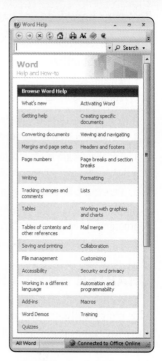

FIGURE 3-36 Many programs include online Help.

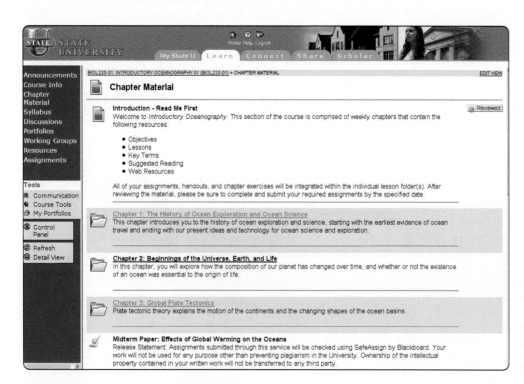

FIGURE 3-37 E-learning systems enable instructors to communicate online with their students.

Test your knowledge of pages 115 through 123 in Quiz Yourself 3-3.

 QUIZ YOURSELF 3-3

Instructions: Find the true statement below. Then, rewrite the remaining false statements so they are true.

1. An anti-spam program protects a computer against viruses by identifying and removing any computer viruses found in memory, on storage media, or in incoming files.

2. Computer-based training is a type of Web-based training that uses Internet technology and consists of application software on the Web.

3. E-mail and Web browsers are examples of communications software that are considered application software.

4. Legal software is a simplified accounting program that helps home users and small office/home office users balance their checkbooks, pay bills, track investments, and evaluate financial plans.

5. Personal DTP software is a popular type of image editing software that allows users to edit digital photos.

Quiz Yourself Online: To further check your knowledge of types and features of home, personal, educational, and communications programs, utility programs, Web-based software, and software learning aids, visit scsite.com/dcf5e/ch3/quiz and then click Objectives 5 – 8.

CHAPTER SUMMARY

This chapter illustrated how to start and use application software. It presented an overview of a variety of business software, graphics and multimedia software, home/personal/educational software, and communications software (read Ethics & Issues 3-3 for a related discussion). Finally, widely used utility programs, Web-based software, and learning aids for application software were presented.

 ETHICS & ISSUES 3-3

Copying Software – A Computer Crime!

Usually, when you buy software, you legally can make one copy of the software for backup purposes. Despite the law, many people make multiple copies, either to share or to sell. Often, the sharing is done online. In a recent survey, more than 50 percent of students and 25 percent of instructors admitted that they illegally had copied, or illegally would copy, software. Microsoft, a leading software manufacturer, estimates that almost 25 percent of software in the United States has been copied illegally. The Business Software Alliance, an industry trade association, believes that 35 percent of all software installed in the world is copied illegally. The illegally copied software is valued at $40 billion, and the amount is increasing annually by up to 15 percent per year. Illegally copied software costs the software industry billions a year in lost revenues, and the law allows fines up to $150,000 for each illegal copy of software. People and companies copy software illegally for a variety of reasons, insisting that software prices are too high, software often is copied for educational or other altruistic purposes, copied software makes people more productive, no restrictions should be placed on the use of software after it is purchased, and everyone copies software. What should be the penalty for copying software? Why? Can you counter the reasons people give for copying software illegally? How? Would you copy software illegally? Why or why not? If you knew a person had copied software illegally, would you report him or her to the authorities? Why or why not?

CAREER CORNER   Help Desk Specialist

A Help Desk specialist position is an entryway into the information technology (IT) field. A **Help Desk specialist** deals with problems in hardware, software, or communications systems. Job requirements may include the following:

- Solve procedural and software questions both in person and over the telephone
- Develop and maintain Help Desk operations manuals
- Assist in training new Help Desk personnel

Usually, a Help Desk specialist must be knowledgeable about the major programs in use. Entry-level positions primarily involve answering calls from people with questions. Other positions provide additional assistance and assume further responsibilities, often demanding greater knowledge and problem-solving skills that can lead to more advanced positions in the IT field. Some Help Desk specialists visit homes and small businesses to act as a personal help desk person. Help Desk specialist is an ideal position for people who must work irregular hours, because many companies need support people to work evenings, weekends, or part-time.

Educational requirements are less stringent than they are for other jobs in the computer field. In some cases, a high school diploma is sufficient. Advancement requires a minimum of a two-year degree, while management generally requires a bachelor's degree in IT or a related field. Certification is another way Help Desk specialists can increase their attractiveness in the marketplace. Entry-level salaries range from $38,000 to $60,000 per year. Managers range from $55,000 to $95,000. For more information, visit scsite.com/dcf5e/ch3/careers and then click Help Desk Specialist.

Adobe Systems
Digital Imaging Leader

Practically every image seen on a computer and in print has been shaped by software developed by Adobe Systems, Inc. The company, based in San Jose, California, is one of the world's largest application software corporations and is committed to helping people communicate effectively.

Adobe's acquisition of Macromedia in 2005 expanded its product line. Print, Internet, and mobile publishers use the software included in Creative Suite, such as Photoshop, Illustrator, and InDesign. Web developers also use Dreamweaver, Flash, Fireworks, Contribute, and FlashPaper. Acrobat software is used to share documents electronically; the free Reader and Flash Player have been downloaded more than 700 million times in 26 different languages, and more than 250 million PDF files reside on the Internet.

Adobe was ranked the 31st best company to work for in America in *FORTUNE* magazine's annual survey. For more information, visit scsite.com/dcf5e/ch3/companies and then click Adobe Systems.

Microsoft
Realizing Potential with Innovative Software

Microsoft's mission is "to enable people and businesses throughout the world to realize their potential." As the largest software company in the world, Microsoft has indeed helped computer users in every field reach their goals.

When Microsoft was incorporated in 1975, the company had three programmers, one product, and revenues of $16,000. The company now employs more than 78,000 people, produces scores of software titles with Office and Windows leading the industry, and has annual revenue of more than $51 billion.

The company's SideWinder Mouse, introduced in 2007, gives customized gaming control for such video games as Halo 3, which was the fastest-selling video game in history. For more information, visit scsite.com/dcf5e/ch3/companies and then click Microsoft.

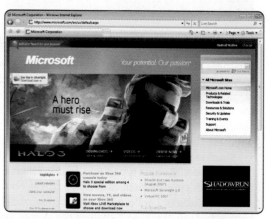

TECHNOLOGY TRAILBLAZERS

Dan Bricklin
VisiCalc Developer

When Dan Bricklin was enrolled at the Harvard Business School in the 1970s, he often used his calculator to determine the effect of changing one value on a balance sheet. He recognized the need to develop a program that would perform a series of calculations automatically when the first number was entered.

He named his creation VisiCalc, short for Visible Calculator. He and a friend formed a company called Software Arts and programmed the VisiCalc prototype using Apple Basic on an Apple II computer. The small program was the first piece of application software that provided a reason for businesses to buy Apple computers. It included many features found in today's spreadsheet software.

As president of Software Garden, Inc., a small consulting and software-development firm, one of his latest projects released in 2007 is wikiCalc, a Web authoring tool that uses a spreadsheet-style interface to operate a browser. For more information, visit scsite.com/dcf5e/ch3/people and then click Dan Bricklin.

Masayoshi Son
Softbank President and CEO

Many students carry photos of family and friends in their wallets and book bags. As a 16-year-old student in the 1970s, Masayoshi Son carried a picture of a microchip. He predicted that the microchip was going to change people's lives, and he wanted to be part of that trend.

While majoring in economics at the University of California, Berkeley, he earned his first million dollars by importing arcade games from Japan to the campus, developing new computer games, and selling a patent for a multilingual pocket translator to Sharp Corporation.

At age 23 he founded Softbank, which is Japan's second-largest broadband Internet service and telephone provider. He ranked 129 on Forbes' The Worlds' Billionaires list with a net worth of $5.8 billion in 2007. For more information, visit scsite.com/dcf5e/ch3/people and then click Masayoshi Son.

Chapter Review

The Chapter Review section summarizes the concepts presented in this chapter. To obtain help from other students regarding any subject in this chapter, visit scsite.com/dcf5e/ch3/forum and post your thoughts or questions.

① What Are the Categories of Application Software?

Application software consists of programs designed to make users more productive and/or assist them with personal tasks. The major categories of application software are business software; graphics and multimedia software; home, personal, and educational software; and communications software.

② How Do You Work with Application Software?

Personal computer operating systems often use the concept of a **desktop**, which is an on-screen work area that has a graphical user interface. To start a program in Windows Vista, move the **pointer** to the Start **button** on the taskbar and **click** the Start button by pressing and releasing a button on the mouse. Then, click the program name on the **menu** or in a list. Once loaded in memory, the program is displayed in a **window** on the desktop.

 Visit scsite.com/dcf5e/ch3/quiz or click the Quiz Yourself button. Click Objectives 1 – 2.

③ What Are the Key Features of Widely Used Business Programs?

Business software assists people in becoming more effective and efficient while performing daily business activities. Business software includes the following programs. **Word processing software** allows users to **create** a document by entering text or numbers and inserting graphical images, **edit** the document by making changes to its existing content, and **format** the document by changing its appearance. **Spreadsheet software** allows users to organize data in rows and columns, perform calculations, recalculate when data changes, and chart the data in graphical form. **Database software** allows users to create a **database**, which is a collection of data organized in a manner that allows access, retrieval, and use of that data. **Presentation graphics software** allows users to create slides that are displayed on a monitor or on a projection screen. **Note taking software** enables users to enter typed text, handwritten comments, drawings, and sketches. A **personal information manager (PIM)** includes an appointment calendar, address book, notepad, and other features to help users organize personal information. A **software suite** is a collection of individual programs sold as a single package. **Project management software** allows users to plan, schedule, track, and analyze the events, resources, and costs of a project. **Accounting software** helps companies record and report their financial transactions. **Document management software** provides a means for sharing, distributing, and searching through documents by converting them into a format that can be viewed by any user.

④ What Are the Key Features of Widely Used Graphics and Multimedia Programs?

Graphics and multimedia software includes the following. **Computer-aided design (CAD) software** assists a professional user in creating engineering, architectural, and scientific designs. **Desktop publishing (DTP) software** enables professional designers to create sophisticated documents that contain text, graphics, and colors. **Paint software** allows users to draw pictures, shapes, and other graphical images with various on-screen tools. **Image editing software** provides the capabilities of paint software and also includes the capability to modify existing images. **Professional photo editing software** is a type of image editing software that allows photographers, videographers, engineers, scientists, and other high-volume digital photo users to edit and customize digital photos. **Video editing software** allows professionals to modify a segment of a video, called a clip. **Audio editing software** lets users modify audio clips, produce studio-quality soundtracks, and add audio to video clips. **Multimedia authoring software** allows users to combine text, graphics, audio, video, and animation into an interactive application. **Web page authoring software** helps users create Web pages and organize and maintain Web sites.

 Visit scsite.com/dcf5e/ch3/quiz or click the Quiz Yourself button. Click Objectives 3 – 4.

⑤ What Are the Key Features of Widely Used Home, Personal, and Educational Programs?

Software for home, personal, and educational use includes the following. A software suite (for personal use) combines application software into a single, easy-to-use package. **Personal finance software** is an accounting program that helps users balance their checkbooks, pay bills, track personal income and expenses, track investments, and evaluate financial plans. **Personal DTP software** helps home and small business users create newsletters, brochures, flyers, advertisements, postcards, greeting cards, letterhead, business cards, banners, calendars, logos, and Web pages. **Personal paint/image editing software** provides an easy-to-use interface and includes various simplified tools that allow you to draw pictures, shapes, and other images and to modify existing graphics and photos. Application software often includes a **clip art/image gallery**, which is a collection of clip art and photos. **Home design/landscaping software** assists users with the design, remodeling, or

Chapter Review

improvement of a home, deck, or landscape. **Travel and mapping software** allows users to view maps, determine routes, and locate points of interest. **Educational software** teaches a particular skill. **Reference software** provides valuable and thorough information for all individuals.

 6   What Are the Types of Application Software Used in Communications?

Application software for communications includes Web browsers to access and view Web pages; e-mail programs to transmit messages via a network; instant messaging software for real-time exchange of messages or files; chat room software to have real-time, online typed conversations; text messaging software; RSS aggregator program to keep track of changes made to Web sites; blog software, or blogware, to create and maintain a blog; newsgroup/message board programs that allow online written discussions; FTP programs to upload and download files on the Internet; VoIP (Internet telephony), which allows users to speak to other users over the Internet; and video conferencing software for meetings on a network.

 7   What Are the Functions of Utility Programs?

Utility programs support the successful use of application software. An antivirus program protects a computer against a computer virus, which is a potentially damaging computer program. A personal firewall detects and protects a personal computer from unauthorized intrusions. A spyware remover detects and deletes spyware, adware, and other similar programs. An anti-spam program removes spam (Internet junk mail). A Web filter restricts access to specified Web sites. A pop-up blocker disables pop-up windows. A file manager provides functions related to file and disk management. A file compression utility shrinks the size of a file. A backup utility allows users to copy selected files or an entire hard disk to another storage medium. A media player allows you to view images and animation, listen to audio, and watch video. A CD/DVD burner writes files to a recordable CD or DVD. A personal computer maintenance utility fixes operating system and disk problems.

8   What Web-Based Software and Learning Aids Are Available for Application Software?

Web-based software, sometimes called a **Web application,** refers to programs hosted by a Web site. Many types of application software have Web-based options. To assist in the learning process, many programs provide **online Help,** which is the electronic equivalent of a user manual. Most online Help also links to Web-based help, which provides updates and more comprehensive resources to respond to technical issues about software.

 Visit scsite.com/dcf5e/ch3/quiz or click the Quiz Yourself button. Click Objectives 5 – 8.

Key Terms

You should know the Key Terms. Use the list below to help focus your study. To further enhance your understanding of the Key Terms in this chapter, visit scsite.com/dcf5e/ch3/terms. See an example of and a definition for each term, and access current and additional information about the term from the Web.

accounting software (111)
application software (100)
audio editing software (114)
business software (104)
button (102)
click (103)
clip art (105)
clip art/image gallery (118)
command (103)
computer-aided design (CAD) software (113)
computer-based training (CBT) (119)
create (106)
custom software (101)
database (108)
database software (108)
desktop (102)
desktop publishing (DTP) software (113)
distance learning (123)

document management software (111)
edit (106)
educational software (119)
e-learning (123)
entertainment software (120)
file (103)
font (106)
font size (106)
font style (106)
format (106)
freeware (101)
Help Desk specialist (124)
home design/landscaping software (119)
icon (102)
image editing software (113)
legal software (117)
menu (103)
multimedia authoring software (114)

note taking software (110)
online Help (123)
open source software (101)
packaged software (101)
paint software (113)
PDF (111)
personal DTP software (117)
personal finance software (116)
personal information manager (PIM) (110)
personal paint/image editing software (118)
personal photo editing software (118)
photo management software (118)
pointer (103)
presentation graphics software (109)
print (106)
professional photo editing software (113)

project management software (111)
public-domain software (101)
reference software (119)
save (106)
shareware (101)
software suite (110)
spreadsheet software (107)
system software (101)
tax preparation software (117)
title bar (103)
travel & mapping software (119)
video editing software (114)
Web application (122)
Web page authoring software (114)
Web-based software (101)
Web-based training (WBT) (123)
window (103)
word processing software (105)
worksheet (107)

Checkpoint

Use the Checkpoint exercises to check your knowledge level of the chapter. To complete the Checkpoint exercises interactively, visit scsite.com/dcf5e/ch3/check.

True/False

Mark T for True and F for False. (See page numbers in parentheses.)

_____ 1. Open source software has restrictions from the copyright holder regarding modification of the software's internal instructions and redistribution of the software. (101)

_____ 2. Shareware is copyrighted software that is distributed at no cost for a trial period. (101)

_____ 3. The desktop is a graphical element that you activate to cause a specific action to take place. (102)

_____ 4. A menu is an instruction that causes a program to perform a specific action. (103)

_____ 5. Business software includes programs such as word processing, spreadsheet, and presentation graphics. (104)

_____ 6. A font is a name assigned to a specific design of characters. (106)

_____ 7. In a spreadsheet program, a formula performs calculations and displays the resulting value in a chart. (107)

_____ 8. Computer-aided design (CAD) software is a sophisticated type of application software that assists a professional user in creating engineering, architectural, and scientific designs. (113)

_____ 9. All communications software is considered to be application software. (120)

_____ 10. Antivirus programs, personal firewalls, and file managers are all examples of utility programs. (121)

Multiple Choice

Select the best answer. (See page numbers in parentheses.)

1. _____ is mass-produced, copyrighted retail software that meets the needs of a wide variety of users, not just a single user or company. (101)
   a. Custom software
   b. Web-based software
   c. Open source software
   d. Packaged software

2. A feature, called _____, allows users of word processing software to type words continually without pressing the ENTER key at the end of each line. (105)
   a. AutoFormat
   b. AutoCorrect
   c. wordwrap
   d. clipboard

3. When using spreadsheet software, a function _____. (107)
   a. depicts data in graphical form
   b. changes certain values to reveal the effects of the changes
   c. is a predefined formula that performs common calculations
   d. contains the formatting necessary for a specific worksheet type

4. _____ combines application software such as word processing, spreadsheet, presentation graphics, and other programs in a single, easy-to-use package. (110)
   a. Shareware
   b. A software suite
   c. Packaged software
   d. Custom software

5. _____ software provides a means for sharing, distributing, and searching through documents by converting them into a format that can be viewed by any user. (111)
   a. Database
   b. Document management
   c. Portable Document Format (PDF)
   d. Word processing

6. With _____, you can view, organize, sort, catalog, print, and share digital photos. (118)
   a. spreadsheet software
   b. photo management software
   c. clip art
   d. desktop publishing software

7. A(n) _____, which can be used to upload and download files with other computers on the Internet, is integrated in some operating systems. (120)
   a. FTP program
   b. e-mail program
   c. Web browser
   d. chat client

8. _____ is the delivery of education via some electronic method such as the Internet, networks, or CDs/DVDs. (123)
   a. A template
   b. Distance learning
   c. Online help
   d. E-learning

Matching

Match the terms with their definitions. (See page numbers in parentheses.)

_____ 1. command (103)

_____ 2. format (106)

_____ 3. note taking software (110)

_____ 4. multimedia authoring software (114)

_____ 5. clip art/image gallery (118)

a. an instruction that causes a program to perform a specific action

b. allows users to combine text, graphics, audio, video, and animation into an interactive application

c. change the appearance of a document

d. collection of clip art and photos

e. enables users to enter typed text, handwritten comments, drawings, or sketches anywhere on a page

f. delivers applications to meet a specific business need

Short Answer

Write a brief answer to each of the following questions.

1. What are the features of presentation graphics software? _____ What types of media might a person use to enhance a presentation? _____
2. What are the features of personal information manager software? _____ Where might you find personal information manager software? _____
3. How is video editing software used? _____ How is multimedia authoring software used? _____
4. How is travel and mapping software used? _____ What are some examples of reference software? _____
5. How is Web-based training used? _____ What elements are included in e-learning to enhance communications? _____

Working Together

Working in a group of your classmates, complete the following team exercise.

1. In any software application, each program is not exactly the same. Different spreadsheet programs, for example, may have different methods to enter formulas, use functions, and draw charts. Have each member of your team interview someone who works with a program described in this chapter. What specific program is used? Why? For what purpose is the program used? What does the interviewee like, or dislike, about the program? Would the interviewee recommend this program? Why? Meet with the members of your team to discuss the results of your interviews. Then, create a group presentation and share your findings with the class.

Web Research

Use the Internet-based Web Research exercises to broaden your understanding of the concepts presented in this chapter. To discuss any of the Web Research exercises in this chapter with other students, post your thoughts or questions at scsite.com/dcf5e/ch3/forum.

1 **Blogs** Vehicle buyers know that the Internet provides a wealth of information that helps direct them toward the best vehicle for their needs. Those consumers who research blogs can obtain price, safety, performance, and maintenance facts and then employ savvy negotiation techniques that help them make the purchase confidently. Visit several automotive blogs, including those from Popular Mechanics (popularmechanics.com/blogs/automotive_news), Autoblog (autoblog.com), Autoblog Green (autobloggreen.com), Autopia (blog.wired.com/cars), Girl on Cars (cnet.com/girl-on-cars), and Yahoo! Tech (tech.yahoo.com/ci/tech_cartech). What new hybrid, luxury, and high-performance vehicles are profiled? Which are promoted as being environmentally friendly? What gadgets and safety information is available?

2 **Scavenger Hunt** Use one of the search engines listed in Figure 2-8 in Chapter 2 on page 58 or your own favorite search engine to find the answers to the questions below. Copy and paste the Web address from the Web page where you found the answer. Some questions may have more than one answer. If required, submit your answers to your instructor. (1) What are some new features in the latest edition of Microsoft Flight Simulator? (2) What are the names of the two ships controlled in the Spacewar! computer game? (3) What Web site features software that creates a game requiring a player to put numbers in nine rows of nine boxes? (4) How many Americans used e-file to file their federal income taxes electronically this past year?

3 **Search Sleuth** A virus is a potentially damaging computer program that can harm files and the operating system. The United States Computer Emergency Readiness Team (US-CERT) Web site is one of the more comprehensive Internet resources discussing viruses and other threats to computer security. (1) The US-CERT home page provides information about and links to various resources that provide specific details about cyber attacks. Who are members of the US-CERT partnership? What is the agency's purpose? When was US-CERT established? (2) Click Search US-CERT at the top of the page and then type "antivirus" as the keyword in the text box. How many articles provide antivirus information on the US-CERT Web site? Click one of the Cyber Security Tips and read the information provided. (3) Click your browser's Back button or press the BACKSPACE key to return to the US-CERT home page. What are the titles of three articles listed in the Current Activity section? Click one of these links and review the material. Summarize the information you read and then write a 50-word summary.

CHAPTER 3

Learn How To

Use the Learn How To activities to learn fundamental skills when using a computer and accompanying technology. Complete the exercises and submit them to your instructor. Premium Activity: The icon indicates you can see a visual demonstration of the associated Learn How To activity by visiting scsite.com/dcf5e/ch3/howto.

LEARN HOW TO 1: Save a File in Application Software

When you use application software, most of the time you either will be creating a new file or modifying an existing file. For example, if you are using a word processor, when you create a new document, the document is a file.

When you create or modify a file, it is contained in RAM. If you turn off your computer or lose electrical power, the file will not be retained. In order to retain the file, you must save it on disk or other permanent storage, such as a USB drive.

As you create the file, you should save the file often. To save a new file, you must complete several tasks:

1. Initiate an action indicating you want to save the file, such as selecting Save on the File menu.
2. Designate where the file should be stored. This includes identifying both the device (such as drive C) and the folder (such as Documents).
3. Specify the name of the file, using the file name rules as specified by the application or operating system.
4. Click the Save button to save the file.

Tasks 2 through 4 normally can be completed using a dialog box such as the one shown in Figure 3-38.

If you use application software to create or modify a file and attempt to close the program prior to saving the new or modified file, the program may display a dialog box that asks if you want to save the file. If you click the Yes button, a modified file will be saved using the same file name in the same location from which it was retrieved. Saving a new file requires that you complete tasks 2 through 4.

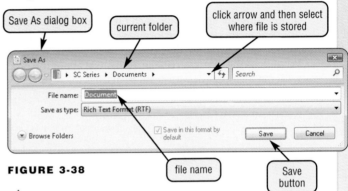

FIGURE 3-38

Exercise

1. Start the WordPad program from the Accessories list in the All Programs list.
2. Type Saving a file is the best insurance against losing work.
3. Click the Save button on the WordPad toolbar. What dialog box is displayed? Where will the file be saved? What is the default file name? If you wanted to save the file on the desktop, what would you do? Click the Cancel button in the dialog box. Submit your answers to your instructor.
4. Click the Close button in the upper-right corner of the WordPad window. What happened? Click the Yes button in the WordPad dialog box. What happened? Connect a USB flash drive to one of the computer's USB ports. Select the USB drive as the location for saving the file. Name the file, Chapter 3 How To 1. Save the file. What happened when you clicked the Save button? Submit your answers to your instructor.

LEARN HOW TO 2: Install and Uninstall Application Software

When you purchase application software, you must install the software on the computer where you want to run it. The exact installation process varies with each program, but generally you must complete the following steps:

1. Insert the CD or DVD containing the application software into a drive.
2. The opening window will appear. If the CD or DVD contains more than one program, choose the program you want to install. Click the Continue or Next button.
3. Some file extractions will occur and then an Install Wizard will begin. The method for using this wizard will vary, but you normally must accomplish the following steps by completing the directions within the wizard:
   a. Accept the terms of the license agreement.
   b. Identify where on your computer the software will be stored. The software usually selects a default location on drive C, and you normally will accept the default location.
   c. Select any default options for the software.
   d. Click a button to install the software.
4. A Welcome/Help screen often will be displayed. It might provide help or documentation. Click a button to finish the installation process.

After you have installed software, use it in the manner you require. At some point, you may want to remove software from your computer. Most application software includes uninstall programming that will remove the program and all its software

Learn How To

components from the computer. To uninstall a program, complete the following steps:

1. Click the Start button on the Windows taskbar.
2. Click Control Panel on the Start menu.
3. Click 'Uninstall a program' to open the Programs and Features window (Figure 3-39).
4. Select the program you wish to remove. In Figure 3-39, Corel Paint Shop Pro Photo XI is selected as the program to remove.
5. Click the Uninstall button.
6. A dialog box will be displayed informing you that the software is being prepared for uninstall. You then will be informed that the process you are following will remove the program. You will be asked if you want to continue. To uninstall the program, click the Yes button.

The program will be removed from the computer. Sometimes, all the shortcut icons for the program might not be removed. If you discover a shortcut icon after a program has been removed, delete the shortcut icon.

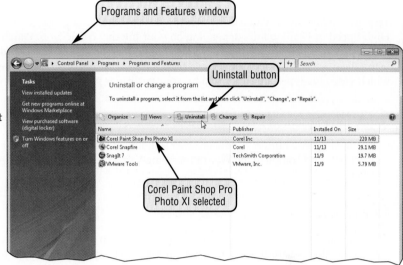

FIGURE 3-39

Exercise

1. Optional: Insert the CD or DVD containing the software you want to install into a drive and follow the instructions for installing the software. **Warning: If you are using a computer other than your own, particularly in a school laboratory, do not perform this exercise unless you have specific permission from your instructor.**
2. Optional: Follow the steps above to uninstall software you want to remove. Be aware that if you uninstall software, the software will not be available for use until you reinstall it. **Warning: If you are using a computer other than your own, particularly in a school laboratory, do not perform this exercise unless you have specific permission from your instructor.**

 LEARN HOW TO 3: Check Application Software Version

Most application software will be modified from time to time by its developer to enable it to work better and faster or to correct errors. Each time the software is changed, it acquires a new version number and sometimes an entirely new name. To determine what version of software you have available on a computer, perform the following steps:

1. Start the application program.
2. Click Help on the menu bar and then click About on the Help menu (the program name often follows the word, About) to open the About window (Figure 3-40).
3. To close the About window, click the OK button.

Depending on the software, in the About window you also might be able to determine further copyright or patent protection for the software, people who developed the software, registration and serial number information, and other facts.

Exercise

1. Start your Web browser and open the About window for the browser. What is the name of the browser? What version of the browser are you using? What is the product ID? What does the copyright notice say? Submit your answers to your instructor.
2. Start any other application software on the computer you are using. Open the About window. What is the name of the application software? What is the version of the software? What information do you find that you did not see in Exercise 1? What did you find in Exercise 1 that you do not see now? Which window do you find more useful? Why? Submit your answers to your instructor.

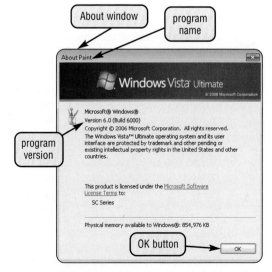

FIGURE 3-40

Learn It Online

Use the Learn It Online exercises to reinforce your understanding of the chapter concepts. To access the Learn It Online exercises, visit scsite.com/dcf5e/ch3/learn.

(1) At the Movies — MediaCell Video Converter

To view the MediaCell Video Converter movie, click the number 1 button. Locate your video and click the corresponding High-Speed or Dial-Up link, depending on your Internet connection. Watch the movie to learn how to use the MediaCell Video Converter. You must know the video file types you are converting from and the video file types you are converting to when using the MediaCell Video Converter. Then, complete the exercise by answering the question that follows: How do you ascertain which video file types are supported by your particular personal mobile device?

(2) Student Edition Labs — Word Processing

Click the number 2 button. A new browser window will open, displaying the Student Edition Labs. Follow the on-screen instructions, and complete the Word Processing Lab. When finished, click the Exit button. If required, submit your results to your instructor.

(3) Practice Test

Click the number 3 button. Answer each question. When completed, enter your name and click the Grade Test button to submit the quiz for grading. Make a note of any missed questions. If required, submit your score to your instructor.

(4) Who Wants To Be a Computer Genius[2]?

Click the number 4 button to find out if you are a computer genius. Directions about how to play the game will be displayed. When you are ready to play, click the Play button. Submit your score to your instructor.

(5) Google Home Page

Click the number 5 button to learn how to make the Google home page your default home page. Explore the different sections of the Google home page (Images, Groups, News, Froogle, Local, and more). On the News page, use the Customize this page feature to rearrange the page and to add other sections. Print the Google News page and then step through the exercise. If required, submit your results to your instructor.

(6) Student Edition Labs — Spreadsheets

Click the number 6 button. A new browser window will open, displaying the Student Edition Labs. Follow the on-screen instructions, and complete the Spreadsheets Lab. When finished, click the Exit button. If required, submit your results to your instructor.

(7) Crossword Puzzle Challenge

Click the number 7 button, then click the Crossword Puzzle Challenge link. Directions about how to play the game will be displayed. Complete the puzzle to reinforce skills you learned in this chapter. When you are ready to play, click the Continue button. Submit the completed puzzle to your instructor.

(8) Vista Exercises

Click the number 8 button. When the Vista Exercises menu appears, click the exercise assigned by your instructor. A new browser window will open. Follow the on-screen instructions to complete the exercise. When finished, click the Exit button. If required, submit your results to your instructor.

The Components of the System Unit

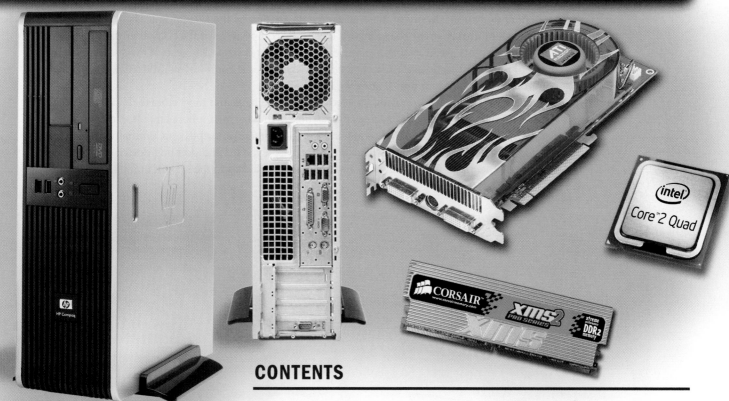

OBJECTIVES

After completing this chapter, you will be able to:

1. Differentiate among various styles of system units
2. Describe the components of a processor and how they complete a machine cycle
3. Define a bit and describe how a series of bits represents data
4. Differentiate among the various types of memory
5. Describe the types of expansion slots and adapter cards
6. Explain the differences among a serial port, a parallel port, a USB port, and other ports
7. Describe how buses contribute to a computer's processing speed
8. Identify components in mobile computers and mobile devices
9. Understand how to clean a system unit

CONTENTS

THE SYSTEM UNIT

Whether you are a home user or a business user, you most likely will make the decision to purchase a new computer or upgrade an existing computer within the next several years. Thus, you should understand the purpose of each component in a computer. As Chapter 1 discussed, a computer includes devices used for input, processing, output, storage, and communications. Many of these components are part of the system unit.

The **system unit** is a case that contains electronic components of the computer used to process data. System units are available in a variety of shapes and sizes. The case of the system unit is made of metal or plastic and protects the internal electronic components from damage. All computers have a system unit (Figure 4-1).

On desktop personal computers, the electronic components and most storage devices are part of the system unit. Other devices, such as the keyboard, mouse, microphone, monitor, printer, USB flash drive, portable media player, scanner, PC video camera, and speakers, normally occupy space outside the system unit. On notebook computers, the keyboard and pointing device often occupy the area on the top of the system unit, and the display attaches to the system unit by hinges. The

FIGURE 4-1   All sizes of computers have a system unit.

location of the system unit on a Tablet PC varies, depending on the design of the Tablet PC. Some models build the system unit behind the display (as shown in Figure 4-1), while others position the system unit below the keyboard (shown later in the chapter). The system unit on an Ultra-Mobile PC, a smart phone, and a PDA usually consumes the entire device. On these mobile computers and devices, the display often is built into the system unit. With game consoles, the input and output devices, such as controllers and a television, reside outside the system unit. On handheld game consoles and portable media players, by contrast, the packaging around the system unit houses the input devices and display.

At some point, you might have to open the system unit on a desktop personal computer to replace or install a new electronic component. For this reason, you should be familiar with the electronic components of a system unit. Figure 4-2 identifies some of these components, which include the processor, memory, adapter cards, drive bays, and the power supply.

The processor interprets and carries out the basic instructions that operate a computer. Memory typically holds data waiting to be processed and instructions waiting to be executed. The electronic components and circuitry of the system unit, such as the processor and memory, usually are part of or are connected to a circuit board called the motherboard. Many motherboards also integrate sound, video, modem, and networking capabilities.

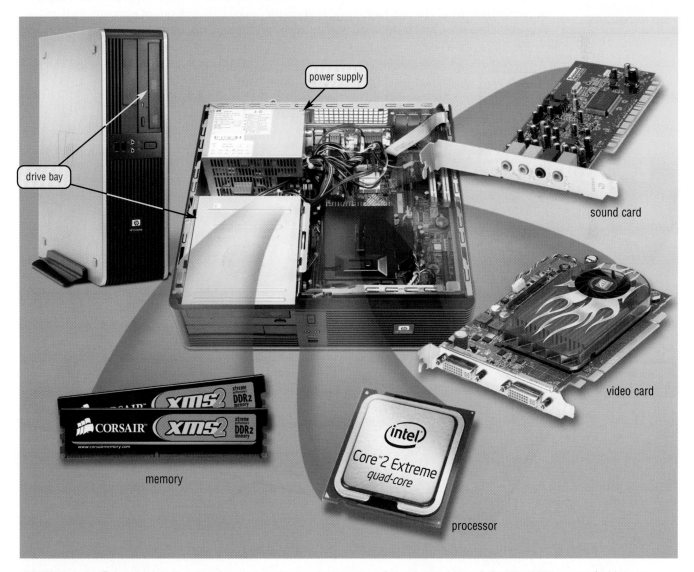

FIGURE 4-2 The system unit on a typical personal computer consists of numerous electronic components, some of which are shown in this figure. The sound card and video card are two types of adapter cards.

Adapter cards are circuit boards that provide connections and functions not built into the motherboard or expand on the capability of features integrated into the motherboard. For example, a sound card and a video card are two types of adapter cards found in some desktop personal computers today.

Devices outside the system unit often attach to ports on the system unit by a connector on a cable. These devices may include a keyboard, mouse, microphone, monitor, printer, scanner, USB flash drive, card reader/writer, digital camera, PC video camera, and speakers. A drive bay holds one or more disk drives. The power supply allows electricity to travel through a power cord from a wall outlet into a computer.

The Motherboard

The **motherboard**, sometimes called a system board, is the main circuit board of the system unit. Many electronic components attach to the motherboard; others are built into it. Figure 4-3 shows a photo of a current desktop personal computer motherboard and identifies its expansion slots, processor chip, and memory slots. Memory chips are installed on memory cards (modules) that fit in a slot on the motherboard.

A computer **chip** is a small piece of semiconducting material, usually silicon, on which integrated circuits are etched. An integrated circuit contains many microscopic pathways capable of carrying electrical current. Each integrated circuit can contain millions of elements such as resistors, capacitors, and transistors. Specific types of chips are discussed later in the chapter.

WEB LINK 4-1

Motherboards

For more information, visit scsite.com/dcf5e/ ch4/weblink and then click Motherboards.

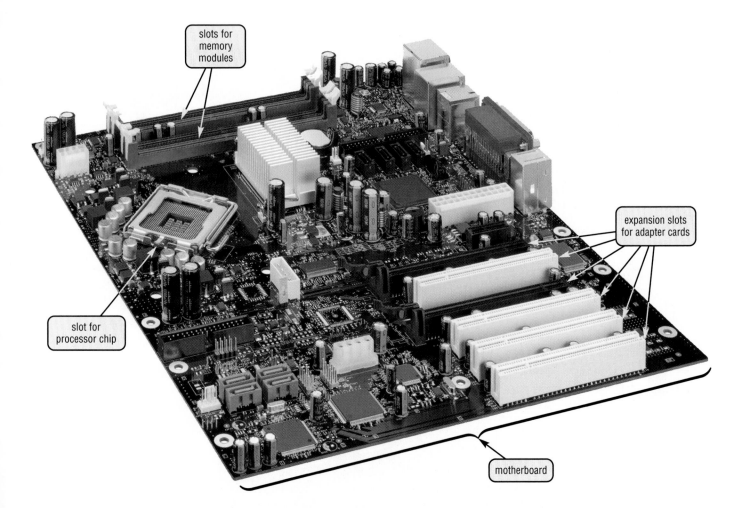

slots for memory modules

expansion slots for adapter cards

slot for processor chip

motherboard

FIGURE 4-3   Many electronic components attach to the motherboard in a desktop personal computer, including a processor chip, memory modules, and adapter cards.

PROCESSOR

The **processor**, also called the **central processing unit (CPU)**, interprets and carries out the basic instructions that operate a computer. The processor significantly impacts overall computing power and manages most of a computer's operations. On a personal computer, all functions of the processor usually are on a single chip. Some computer and chip manufacturers use the term **microprocessor** to refer to a personal computer processor chip.

Most processor chip manufacturers now offer multi-core processors. A **multi-core processor** is a chip with two or more separate processors. Two common multi-core processors used today are dual-core and quad-core. A **dual-core processor** is a chip that contains two separate processors. Similarly, a **quad-core processor** is a chip with four separate processors. Each processor on a multi-core chip generally runs at a slower clock speed than a single-core processor, but multi-core chips typically increase overall performance. For example, although a dual-core processor does not double the processing speed of a single-core processor, it can approach those speeds. Multi-core processors also are energy efficient, requiring lower levels of power consumption and emitting less heat in the system unit.

Processors contain a control unit and an arithmetic logic unit (ALU). These two components work together to perform processing operations. Figure 4-4 illustrates how other devices that are connected to the computer communicate with the processor to carry out a task.

WEB LINK 4-2

Quad-Core Processors

For more information, visit scsite.com/dcf5e/ch4/weblink and then click Quad-Core Processors.

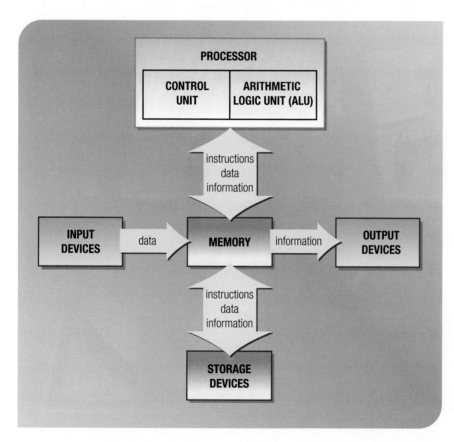

FIGURE 4-4 Most devices connected to the computer communicate with the processor to carry out a task. When a user starts a program, for example, its instructions transfer from a storage device to memory. Data needed by programs enters memory from either an input device or a storage device. The control unit interprets and executes instructions in memory, and the ALU performs calculations on the data in memory. Resulting information is stored in memory, from which it can be sent to an output device or a storage device for future access, as needed.

The Control Unit

The **control unit** is the component of the processor that directs and coordinates most of the operations in the computer. The control unit has a role much like a traffic cop: it interprets each instruction issued by a program and then initiates the appropriate action to carry out the instruction. Types of internal components that the control unit directs include the arithmetic/logic unit and buses, each discussed in this chapter.

The Arithmetic Logic Unit

The **arithmetic logic unit** (ALU), another component of the processor, performs arithmetic, comparison, and other operations. Arithmetic operations include basic calculations such as addition, subtraction, multiplication, and division. Comparison operations involve comparing one data item with another to determine whether the first item is greater than, equal to, or less than the other item. Depending on the result of the comparison, different actions may occur.

Machine Cycle

For every instruction, a processor repeats a set of four basic operations, which comprise a machine cycle (Figure 4-5): (1) fetching, (2) decoding, (3) executing, and, if necessary, (4) storing. Fetching is the process of obtaining a program instruction or data item from memory. The term decoding refers to the process of translating the instruction into signals the computer can execute. Executing is the process of carrying out the commands. Storing, in this context, means writing the result to memory (not to a storage medium).

FIGURE 4-5 THE STEPS IN A MACHINE CYCLE

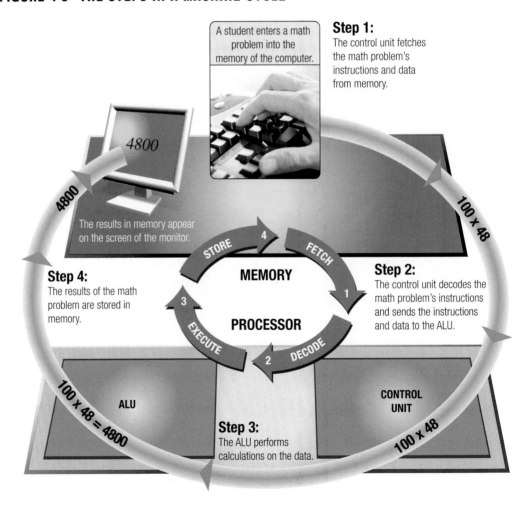

A student enters a math problem into the memory of the computer.

Step 1:
The control unit fetches the math problem's instructions and data from memory.

The results in memory appear on the screen of the monitor.

Step 4:
The results of the math problem are stored in memory.

Step 2:
The control unit decodes the math problem's instructions and sends the instructions and data to the ALU.

Step 3:
The ALU performs calculations on the data.

MEMORY

PROCESSOR

STORE FETCH

EXECUTE DECODE

ALU

CONTROL UNIT

The System Clock

The processor relies on a small quartz crystal circuit called the **system clock** to control the timing of all computer operations. Just as your heart beats at a regular rate to keep your body functioning, the system clock generates regular electronic pulses, or ticks, that set the operating pace of components of the system unit.

The pace of the system clock, called the **clock speed**, is measured by the number of ticks per second. Current personal computer processors have clock speeds in the gigahertz range. Giga is a prefix that stands for billion, and a hertz is one cycle per second. Thus, one **gigahertz** (**GHz**) equals one billion ticks of the system clock per second. A computer that operates at 3 GHz has 3 billion (giga) clock cycles in one second (hertz). The faster the clock speed, the more instructions the processor can execute per second. The speed of the system clock is just one factor that influences a computer's performance. Other factors, such as the type of processor chip, amount of cache, memory access time, bus width, and bus clock speed, are discussed later in this chapter. Read Looking Ahead 4-1 for a look at the future speeds of supercomputers.

Comparison of Personal Computer Processors

The leading processor chip manufacturers for personal computers are Intel, AMD (Advanced Micro Devices), IBM, and Motorola. These manufacturers often identify their processor chips by a model name or model number.

With its earlier processors, Intel used a model number to identify the various chips. After learning that processor model numbers could not be trademarked and protected from use by competitors, Intel began identifying its processors with names. Most high-performance desktop PCs today use a processor in the Intel Core family. Less expensive, basic PCs today use a brand of Intel processor in the Pentium or Celeron family. The Xeon and Itanium families of processors are ideal for workstations and low-end servers.

AMD is the leading manufacturer of Intel-compatible processors, which have an internal design similar to Intel processors, perform the same functions, and can be as powerful, but often are less expensive. Intel and Intel-compatible processors are used in PCs.

Originally, Apple computers used only an IBM processor or a Motorola processor, which had a design different from the Intel-style processor. Today's Apple computers, however, use Intel processors.

In the past, chip manufacturers listed a processor's clock speed in marketing literature and advertisements. As previously mentioned, though, clock speed is only one factor that impacts processing speed in today's computers. To help consumers evaluate various processors, manufacturers such as Intel and AMD now use a numbering scheme that more accurately reflects the processing speed of their chips.

Buying a Personal Computer

If you are ready to buy a new computer, the processor you select should depend on how you plan to use the computer. If you purchase an IBM-compatible PC or Apple computer, you will choose an Intel processor or, in some cases, an Intel-compatible processor.

For detailed computer purchasing guidelines, read the Buyer's Guide feature that follows Chapter 7. Read Ethics & Issues 4-1 for a related discussion.

LOOKING AHEAD 4-1

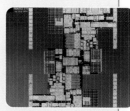

Fastest Supercomputer Will Have Petaflop Speed

Blue Waters should become the world's fastest supercomputer when IBM completes building the machine, scheduled for 2011. The $208 million computer will be housed at the University of Illinois's National Center for Supercomputing Applications in Urbana and will operate at speeds of one petaflop, which is 1,000-trillion mathematical operations per second.

Funding will come from the National Science Foundation. Scientists and engineers have proposed projects that use Blue Waters's hundreds of thousands of processors, such as weather modeling associated with hurricanes and storm surge effects, the impact of global warming, the formation and evolution of galaxies, and the physical and chemical reactions in living cells.

The current world's fastest supercomputer, IBM's Blue Gene, has only one-third of Blue Waters's expected processing power. For more information, visit scsite.com/dcf5e/ch4/looking and then click BlueWaters.

ETHICS & ISSUES 4-1

Discarded Computer Components: Whose Problem Is It?

Experts estimate that about 1 billion computers will be discarded by 2010. The discarded items often are known as e-waste. As technology advances and prices fall, many people think of computers as disposable items. Computers contain several toxic elements, including lead, mercury, and barium. Computers thrown into landfills or burned in incinerators can pollute the ground and the air. A vast amount of e-waste ends up polluting third world countries. One solution is to recycle old computers. Some lawmakers prefer a more aggressive approach, such as setting up a recycling program that would be paid for by adding a $10 fee to the purchase price of computers and computer equipment, or forcing computer makers to be responsible for collecting and recycling their products. California already requires a recycling fee for any products sold that include old monitors and other equipment. Manufacturers have taken steps, such as offering to recycle old computers and using energy efficient and environmentally friendly manufacturing techniques, but some claim that consumers should bear the responsibility of disposing of their old computer parts. Several have reduced the amount of toxic material in their products, and manufacturers have set up their own recycling programs, for which users pay a fee. What can be done to ensure that computers are disposed of safely? Should government, manufacturers, or users be responsible for safe disposal? Why? How can computer users be motivated to recycle obsolete equipment? How can society make it easier to donate used equipment?

Test your knowledge of pages 134 through 139 in Quiz Yourself 4-1.

QUIZ YOURSELF 4-1

Instructions: Find the true statement below. Then, rewrite the remaining false statements so they are true.

1. A computer chip is a small piece of semiconducting material, usually silicon, on which integrated circuits are etched.

2. Four basic operations in a machine cycle are: (1) comparing, (2) decoding, (3) executing, and, if necessary, (4) pipelining.

3. Processors contain a motherboard and an arithmetic logic unit (ALU).

4. The central processing unit, sometimes called a system board, is the main circuit board of the system unit.

5. The leading processor chip manufacturers for personal computers are Microsoft, AMD, IBM, and Motorola.

6. The system unit is a case that contains mechanical components of the computer used to process data.

Quiz Yourself Online: To further check your knowledge of system unit styles, processor components, and machine cycles, visit scsite.com/dcf5e/ch4/quiz and then click Objectives 1 – 2.

DATA REPRESENTATION

To understand fully the way a computer processes data, you should know how a computer represents data. Most computers are **digital**. They recognize only two discrete states: on and off. The two digits, 0 and 1, easily can represent these two states (Figure 4-6). The digit 0 represents the electronic state of off (absence of an electronic charge). The digit 1 represents the electronic state of on (presence of an electronic charge).

The computer uses a binary system because it recognizes only two states. The **binary system** is a number system that has just two unique digits, 0 and 1, called bits. A **bit** (short for binary digit) is the smallest unit of data the computer can process. By itself, a bit is not very informative.

When 8 bits are grouped together as a unit, they form a **byte**. A byte provides enough different combinations of 0s and 1s to represent 256 individual characters. These characters include numbers, uppercase and lowercase letters of the alphabet, punctuation marks, and others, such as the letters of the Greek alphabet.

The combinations of 0s and 1s that represent characters are defined by patterns called a coding scheme. In one coding scheme, the number 4 is represented as 00110100, the number 6 as 00110110, and the capital letter E as 01000101 (Figure 4-7). Two popular coding schemes are ASCII and EBCDIC (Figure 4-8). The American Standard Code for Information Interchange (ASCII pronounced ASK-ee) scheme is the most widely used coding system to represent data. Most personal computers and servers use the ASCII coding scheme. The Extended Binary Coded Decimal Interchange Code (EBCDIC pronounced EB-see-dik) scheme is used primarily on mainframe computers and high-end servers.

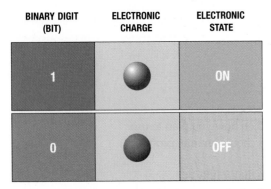

BINARY DIGIT (BIT)	ELECTRONIC CHARGE	ELECTRONIC STATE
1		ON
0		OFF

FIGURE 4-6 A computer circuit represents the 0 or the 1 electronically by the presence or absence of an electronic charge.

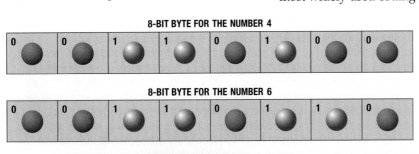

8-BIT BYTE FOR THE NUMBER 4

| 0 | 0 | 1 | 1 | 0 | 1 | 0 | 0 |

8-BIT BYTE FOR THE NUMBER 6

| 0 | 0 | 1 | 1 | 0 | 1 | 1 | 0 |

8-BIT BYTE FOR THE LETTER E

| 0 | 1 | 0 | 0 | 0 | 1 | 0 | 1 |

FIGURE 4-7 Eight bits grouped together as a unit are called a byte. A byte represents a single character in the computer.

ASCII	SYMBOL	EBCDIC
00110000	0	11110000
00110001	1	11110001
00110010	2	11110010
00110011	3	11110011
00110100	4	11110100
00110101	5	11110101
00110110	6	11110110
00110111	7	11110111
00111000	8	11111000
00111001	9	11111001
01000001	A	11000001
01000010	B	11000010
01000011	C	11000011
01000100	D	11000100
01000101	E	11000101
01000110	F	11000110
01000111	G	11000111
01001000	H	11001000
01001001	I	11001001
01001010	J	11010001
01001011	K	11010010
01001100	L	11010011
01001101	M	11010100
01001110	N	11010101
01001111	O	11010110
01010000	P	11010111
01010001	Q	11011000
01010010	R	11011001
01010011	S	11100010
01010100	T	11100011
01010101	U	11100100
01010110	V	11100101
01010111	W	11100110
01011000	X	11100111
01011001	Y	11101000
01011010	Z	11101001
00100001	!	01011010
00100010	"	01111111
00100011	#	01111011
00100100	$	01011011
00100101	%	01101100
00100110	&	01010000
00101000	(	01001101
00101001	)	01011101
00101010	*	01011100
00101011	+	01001110

FIGURE 4-8 Two popular coding schemes are ASCII and EBCDIC.

Coding schemes such as ASCII make it possible for humans to interact with a digital computer that processes only bits. When you press a key on a keyboard, a chip in the keyboard converts the key's electronic signal into a scan code that is sent to the system unit. Then, the system unit converts the scan code into a binary form the computer can process and is stored in memory. Every character is converted to its corresponding byte. The computer then processes the data as bytes, which actually is a series of on/off electrical states. When processing is finished, software converts the byte into a human-recognizable number, letter of the alphabet, or special character that is displayed on a screen or is printed (Figure 4-9). All of these conversions take place so quickly that you do not realize they are occurring.

Standards, such as those defined by ASCII and EBCDIC, also make it possible for components in computers to communicate successfully with each other.

FIGURE 4-9   HOW A LETTER IS CONVERTED TO BINARY FORM AND BACK

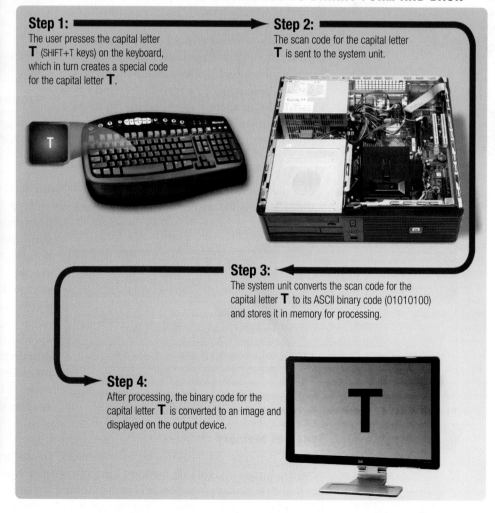

Step 1:
The user presses the capital letter **T** (SHIFT+T keys) on the keyboard, which in turn creates a special code for the capital letter **T**.

Step 2:
The scan code for the capital letter **T** is sent to the system unit.

Step 3:
The system unit converts the scan code for the capital letter **T** to its ASCII binary code (01010100) and stores it in memory for processing.

Step 4:
After processing, the binary code for the capital letter **T** is converted to an image and displayed on the output device.

MEMORY

Memory consists of electronic components that store instructions waiting to be executed by the processor, data needed by those instructions, and the results of processed data (information). Memory usually consists of one or more chips on the motherboard or some other circuit board in the computer.

Memory stores three basic categories of items: (1) the operating system and other system software that control or maintain the computer and its devices; (2) application programs that carry out a specific task such as word processing; and (3) the data being processed by the application programs and resulting information. This role of memory to store both data and programs is known as the stored program concept.

Bytes and Addressable Memory

A byte (character) is the basic storage unit in memory. When application program instructions and data are transferred to memory from storage devices, the instructions and data exist as bytes. Each byte resides temporarily in a location in memory that has an address. An address simply is a unique number that identifies the location of the byte in memory. The illustration in Figure 4-10 shows how seats in an opera house are similar to addresses in memory: (1) a seat, which is identified by a unique seat number, holds one person at a time, and a location in memory, which is identified by a unique address, holds a single byte; and (2) both a seat, identified by a seat number, and a byte, identified by an address, can be empty. To access data or instructions in memory, the computer references the addresses that contain bytes of data.

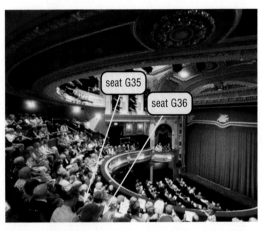

FIGURE 4-10   Seats in an opera house are similar to addresses in memory: a seat holds one person at a time, and a location in memory holds a single byte; and both a seat and a byte can be empty.

Memory Sizes

Manufacturers state the size of memory chips (Figure 4-11) and storage devices in terms of the number of bytes the chip or device has available for storage. Recall that storage devices hold data, instructions, and information for future use, while most memory holds these items temporarily. A **kilobyte** (**KB** or **K**) is equal to exactly 1,024 bytes. To simplify memory and storage definitions, computer users often round a kilobyte down to 1,000 bytes. For example, if a memory chip can store 100 KB, it can hold approximately 100,000 bytes (characters). A **megabyte** (**MB**) is equal to approximately 1 million bytes. A **gigabyte** (**GB**) equals approximately 1 billion bytes. A **terabyte** (**TB**) is equal to approximately 1 trillion bytes.

MEMORY SIZES

Term	Abbreviation	Approximate Number of Bytes	Exact Amount of Bytes	Approximate Number of Pages of Text
Kilobyte	KB or K	1 thousand	1,024	1/2
Megabyte	MB	1 million	1,048,576	500
Gigabyte	GB	1 billion	1,073,741,824	500,000
Terabyte	TB	1 trillion	1,099,511,627,776	500,000,000

FIGURE 4-11   Terms commonly used to define memory sizes.

Types of Memory

The system unit contains two types of memory: volatile and nonvolatile. When the computer's power is turned off, **volatile memory** loses its contents. **Nonvolatile memory**, by contrast, does not lose its contents when power is removed from the computer. Thus, volatile memory is temporary and nonvolatile memory is permanent. RAM is the most common type of volatile memory. Examples of nonvolatile memory include ROM, flash memory, and CMOS. The following sections discuss these types of memory.

RAM

Users typically are referring to RAM when discussing computer memory. **RAM** (random access memory), also called main memory, consists of memory chips that can be read from and written to by the processor and other devices. When you turn on power to a computer, certain operating system files (such as the files that determine how the Windows Vista desktop appears) load into RAM from a storage device such as a hard disk. These files remain in RAM as long as the computer has continuous power. As additional programs and data are requested, they also load into RAM from storage.

The processor interprets and executes a program's instructions while the program is in RAM. During this time, the contents of RAM may change (Figure 4-12). RAM can hold multiple programs simultaneously, provided the computer has enough RAM to accommodate all the programs.

Most RAM is volatile, which means it loses its contents when the power is removed from the computer. For this reason, you must save any items you may need in the future. Saving is the process of copying items from RAM to a storage device such as a hard disk.

FIGURE 4-12 HOW PROGRAM INSTRUCTIONS TRANSFER IN AND OUT OF RAM

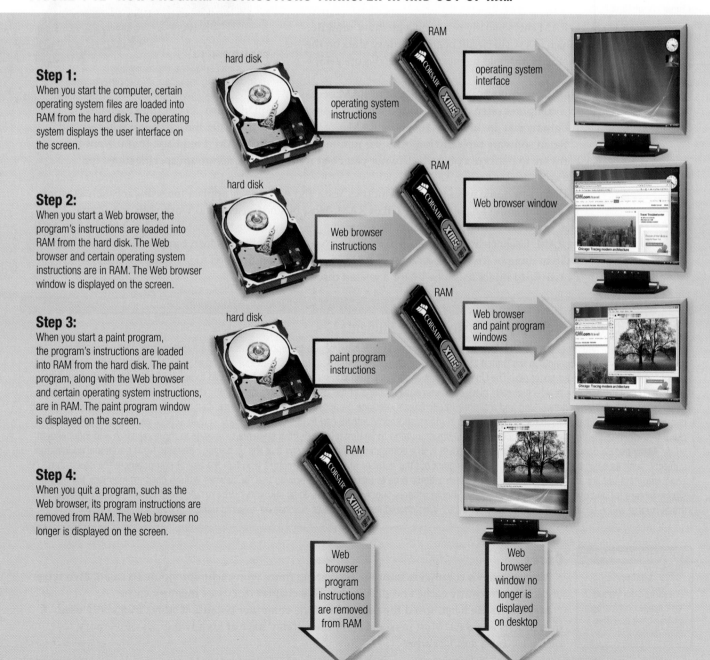

Step 1:
When you start the computer, certain operating system files are loaded into RAM from the hard disk. The operating system displays the user interface on the screen.

Step 2:
When you start a Web browser, the program's instructions are loaded into RAM from the hard disk. The Web browser and certain operating system instructions are in RAM. The Web browser window is displayed on the screen.

Step 3:
When you start a paint program, the program's instructions are loaded into RAM from the hard disk. The paint program, along with the Web browser and certain operating system instructions, are in RAM. The paint program window is displayed on the screen.

Step 4:
When you quit a program, such as the Web browser, its program instructions are removed from RAM. The Web browser no longer is displayed on the screen.

hard disk
RAM
operating system instructions
operating system interface

hard disk
RAM
Web browser instructions
Web browser window

hard disk
RAM
paint program instructions
Web browser and paint program windows

RAM
Web browser program instructions are removed from RAM

Web browser window no longer is displayed on desktop

Three basic types of RAM chips exist: dynamic RAM, static RAM, and magnetoresistive RAM.

- Dynamic RAM (DRAM pronounced DEE-ram) chips must be re-energized constantly or they lose their contents.
- Static RAM (SRAM pronounced ESS-ram) chips are faster and more reliable than any variation of DRAM chips. These chips do not have to be re-energized as often as DRAM chips, thus, the term static.
- A newer type of RAM, called magnetoresistive RAM (MRAM pronounced EM-ram), stores data using magnetic charges instead of electrical charges. Manufacturers claim that MRAM has greater storage capacity, consumes less power, and has faster access times than electronic RAM.

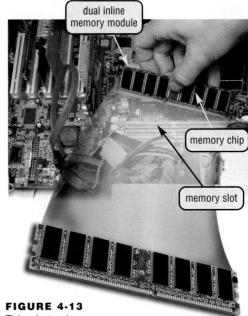

FIGURE 4-13
This photo shows a memory module being inserted in a motherboard.

RAM chips usually reside on a **memory module**, which is a small circuit board. **Memory slots** on the motherboard hold memory modules (Figure 4-13).

RAM CONFIGURATIONS The amount of RAM necessary in a computer often depends on the types of software you plan to use. A computer executes programs that are in RAM. The more RAM a computer has, the faster the computer will respond.

Retail software typically indicates the minimum amount of RAM it requires. If you want the software to perform optimally, usually you need more than the minimum specifications for the software.

Generally, home users running Windows Vista and using basic application software such as word processing should have at least 1 GB of RAM. Most business users who work with accounting, financial, or spreadsheet programs, and programs requiring multimedia capabilities should have 1 to 4 GB of RAM. Users creating professional Web sites or using graphics-intensive applications will want 4 GB or more of RAM. The amount of RAM in computers purchased today ranges from 1 GB to 64 GB. Read Ethics & Issues 4-2 for a related discussion.

ETHICS & ISSUES 4-2

Should Schools Supply Computers to All Students?

Around the country and around the world, local and national governments have begun to supply schoolchildren with inexpensive notebook computers. Many school districts in the United States purchase notebook computers for each student and hope to recoup some of the cost by purchasing lower-cost CD-based textbooks. The United Nations endorses a plan known as One Laptop per Child to supply $100 notebook computers to developing countries, some of which already pledged to purchase millions of the devices for schoolchildren. The device, which recharges with a hand crank, includes Wi-Fi networking and a simple, intuitive user interface. Supporters of these plans maintain that computer literacy and electronic communications are vital skills in today's world, and students should be introduced to computers as early in their school years as possible. Others claim that when students use notebook computers, instructors tend to lecture less, requiring students to engage in more research and independent study. Many people oppose plans to equip every student with a computer because they say that the technology detracts from traditional educational subjects, such as basic reading and math. They also point out the number of college instructors who ban the use of computers in the classroom. The computers require maintenance, support, and instructional time to teach students how to use the devices. Young children may lack the responsibility to care for and use the computers properly. Should schools supply computers to all students? Why or why not? What is the appropriate grade level at which to require computer literacy? Why? Who should bear the cost of purchasing required computers for students? Why?

Cache

Most of today's computers improve processing times with **cache** (pronounced cash). Two types of cache are memory cache and disk cache. This chapter discusses memory cache.

Memory cache helps speed the processes of the computer because it stores frequently used instructions and data. Most personal computers today have at least two types of memory cache: L1 cache and L2 cache.

- **L1 cache** is built directly in the processor chip. L1 cache usually has a very small capacity, ranging from 8 KB to 128 KB.
- **L2 cache** is slightly slower than L1 cache but has a much larger capacity, ranging from 64 KB to 16 MB. Current processors include **advanced transfer cache**, a type of L2 cache built directly on the processor chip. Processors that use advanced transfer cache perform at much faster rates than those that do not use it. Personal computers today typically have from 512 KB to 8 MB of advanced transfer cache.

Cache speeds up processing time because it stores frequently used instructions and data. When the processor needs an instruction or data, it searches memory in this order: L1 cache, then L2 cache, then RAM — with a greater delay in processing for each level of memory it must search. If the instruction or data is not found in memory, then it must search a slower speed storage medium such as a hard disk, CD, or DVD.

ROM

Read-only memory (**ROM** pronounced rahm) refers to memory chips storing permanent data and instructions. The data on most ROM chips cannot be modified — hence, the name read-only. ROM is nonvolatile, which means its contents are not lost when power is removed from the computer.

Manufacturers of ROM chips often record data, instructions, or information on the chips when they manufacture the chips. These ROM chips, called **firmware**, contain permanently written data, instructions, or information.

Flash Memory

Flash memory is a type of nonvolatile memory that can be erased electronically and rewritten. Most computers use flash memory to hold their startup instructions because it allows the computer easily to update its contents. For example, when the computer changes from standard time to daylight savings time, the contents of a flash memory chip (and the real-time clock chip) change to reflect the new time.

Flash memory chips also store data and programs on many mobile computers and devices, such as smart phones, portable media players, PDAs, printers, digital cameras, automotive devices, digital voice recorders, and pagers. Some portable media players store music on flash memory chips (Figure 4-14). Others store music on tiny hard disks or flash memory cards. A later section in this chapter discusses flash memory cards, which contain flash memory on a removable device instead of a chip.

FIGURE 4-14 HOW A PORTABLE MEDIA PLAYER MIGHT STORE MUSIC IN FLASH MEMORY

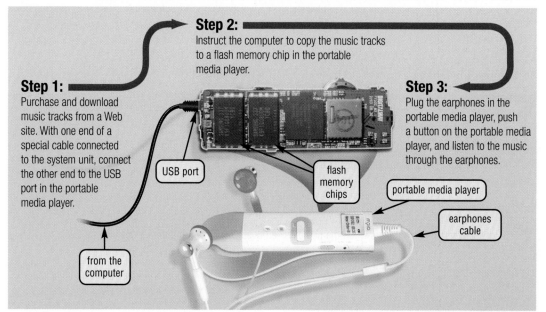

Step 1:
Purchase and download music tracks from a Web site. With one end of a special cable connected to the system unit, connect the other end to the USB port in the portable media player.

Step 2:
Instruct the computer to copy the music tracks to a flash memory chip in the portable media player.

Step 3:
Plug the earphones in the portable media player, push a button on the portable media player, and listen to the music through the earphones.

USB port

flash memory chips

portable media player

earphones cable

from the computer

CMOS

Some RAM chips, flash memory chips, and other types of memory chips use complementary metal-oxide semiconductor (**CMOS** pronounced SEE-moss) technology because it provides high speeds and consumes little power. CMOS technology uses battery power to retain information even when the power to the computer is off. Battery-backed CMOS memory chips, for example, can keep the calendar, date, and time current even when the computer is off. The flash memory chips that store a computer's startup information often use CMOS technology.

Memory Access Times

Access time is the amount of time it takes the processor to read data, instructions, and information from memory. A computer's access time directly affects how fast the computer processes data. Accessing data in memory can be more than 200,000 times faster than accessing data on a hard disk because of the mechanical motion of the hard disk.

Today's manufacturers use a variety of terminology to state access times (Figure 4-15). Some use fractions of a second, which for memory occurs in nanoseconds. A **nanosecond** (abbreviated ns) is one billionth of a second. A nanosecond is extremely fast (Figure 4-16). Other manufacturers state access times in MHz; for example, 800 MHz RAM.

While access times of memory greatly affect overall computer performance, manufacturers and retailers usually list a computer's memory in terms of its size, not its access time.

ACCESS TIME TERMINOLOGY

Term	Abbreviation	Speed
Millisecond	ms	One-thousandth of a second
Microsecond	μs	One-millionth of a second
Nanosecond	ns	One-billionth of a second
Picosecond	ps	One-trillionth of a second

FIGURE 4-15 Access times are measured in fractions of a second. This table lists the terms used to define access times.

10 million operations = 1 blink

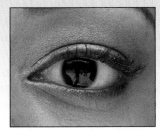 

FIGURE 4-16 It takes about one-tenth of a second to blink your eye, which is the equivalent of 100 million nanoseconds. In the time it takes to blink your eye, a computer can perform some operations 10 million times.

Test your knowledge of pages 140 through 146 in Quiz Yourself 4-2.

QUIZ YOURSELF 4-2

Instructions: Find the true statement below. Then, rewrite the remaining false statements so they are true.

1. A computer's memory access time directly affects how fast the computer processes data.
2. A gigabyte (GB) equals approximately 1 trillion bytes.
3. Memory cache helps speed the processes of the computer because it stores seldom used instructions and data.
4. Most computers are analog, which means they recognize only two discrete states: on and off.
5. Most RAM retains its contents when the power is removed from the computer.
6. Read-only memory (ROM) refers to memory chips storing temporary data and instructions.

Quiz Yourself Online: To further check your knowledge of bits, bytes, data representation, and types of memory, visit scsite.com/dcf5e/ch4/quiz and then click Objectives 3 – 4.

EXPANSION SLOTS AND ADAPTER CARDS

An **expansion slot** is a socket on the motherboard that can hold an adapter card. An **adapter card**, sometimes called an **expansion card**, is a circuit board that enhances functions of a component of the system unit and/or provides connections to peripherals. A **peripheral** is a device that connects to the system unit and is controlled by the processor in the computer. Examples of peripherals are modems, disk drives, printers, scanners, and keyboards.

Figure 4-17 lists a variety of types of adapter cards. Sometimes, all functionality is built into the adapter card. With others, a cable connects the adapter card to a device, such as a digital video camera, outside the system unit. Figure 4-18 shows an adapter card being inserted in an expansion slot on a personal computer motherboard.

Some motherboards include all necessary capabilities and do not require adapter cards. Other motherboards may require adapter cards to provide capabilities such as sound and video. A **sound card** enhances the sound-generating capabilities of a personal computer by allowing sound to be input through a microphone and output through external speakers or headphones. A **video card**, also called a **graphics card**, converts computer output into a video signal that travels through a cable to the monitor, which displays an image on the screen.

WEB LINK 4-6

Video Cards

For more information, visit scsite.com/dcf5e/ch4/weblink and then click Video Cards.

TYPES OF ADAPTER CARDS

Adapter Card	Purpose
Disk controller	Connects disk drives
FireWire	Connects to FireWire devices
HDTV tuner	Allows viewing of HDTV broadcasts on the monitor
MIDI	Connects musical instruments
Modem	Connects other computers through telephone or cable television lines
Network	Connects other computers and peripherals
PC-to-TV converter	Connects a television
Sound	Connects speakers or a microphone
TV tuner	Allows viewing of television channels on the monitor
USB 2.0	Connects to USB 2.0 devices
Video	Connects a monitor
Video capture	Connects a video camera

FIGURE 4-17   Currently used adapter cards and their functions.

FIGURE 4-18   An adapter card being inserted in an expansion slot on the motherboard of a personal computer.

Flash Memory Cards, USB Flash Drives, PC Cards, and ExpressCard Modules

Four widely used types of removable flash memory devices include flash memory cards, USB flash drives, PC Cards, and ExpressCard modules.

- A **flash memory card** is a removable flash memory device (Figure 4-19), usually no bigger than 1.5" in height or width, that you insert and remove from a slot in a computer, mobile device, or card reader/writer. Many mobile and consumer devices, such as smart phones, digital cameras, portable media players, and PDAs use these memory cards. Some printers and computers have built-in card readers/writers or slots that read flash memory cards. In addition, you can purchase an external card reader/writer that attaches to any computer. The type of flash memory card you have will determine the type of card reader/writer you need. Storage capacities of flash memory cards range from 64 MB to 16 GB.

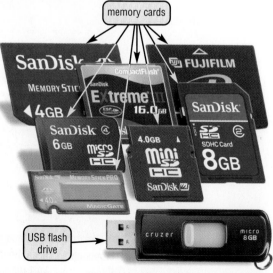

FIGURE 4-19   Removable flash memory devices are available in a range of sizes.

• A **USB flash drive** is a flash memory storage device that plugs in a USB port on a computer or portable device. A special type of USB flash drive, called a **U3 smart drive**, includes preinstalled software accessed through a Windows-type interface. (The next section discusses USB ports.) Storage capacities of USB flash drives range from 256 MB to 64 GB, with the latter being extremely expensive.

• Many computers have a **PC Card slot** or an **ExpressCard slot**, which is a special type of expansion slot that holds a PC Card or an ExpressCard module, respectively. A **PC Card** is a thin, credit card-sized removable flash memory device that primarily is used today to enable notebook computers to access the Internet wirelessly. An **ExpressCard module**, which can be used as a removable flash memory device, is about one-half the size of a PC Card and adds memory, communications, multimedia, and security capabilities to computers (Figure 4-20).

WEB LINK 4-7

ExpressCard Modules

For more information, visit scsite.com/dcf5e/ ch4/weblink and then click ExpressCard Modules.

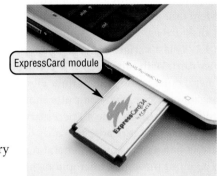

ExpressCard module

FIGURE 4-20   An ExpressCard module slides in an ExpressCard slot on a computer.

PORTS AND CONNECTORS

A **port** is the point at which a peripheral attaches to or communicates with a system unit so that the peripheral can send data to or receive information from the computer. An external device, such as a keyboard, monitor, printer, mouse, and microphone, often attaches by a cable to a port on the system unit. Instead of port, the term jack sometimes is used to identify audio and video ports. The front and back of the system unit contain many ports (Figure 4-21).

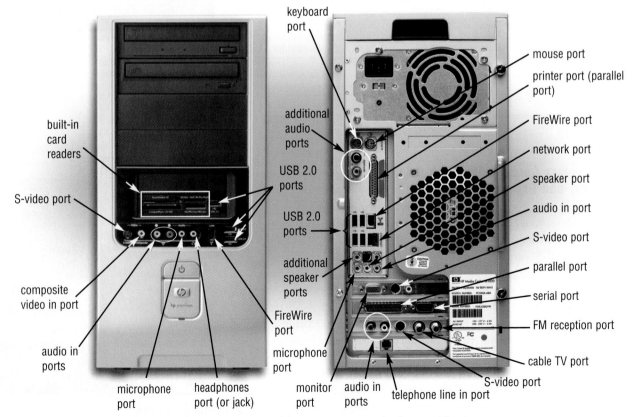

FIGURE 4-21   A system unit has many ports on its front and back.

A **connector** joins a cable to a port. A connector at one end of a cable attaches to a port on the system unit, and a connector at the other end of the cable attaches to a port on the peripheral.

Desktop personal computers may have a serial port, a parallel port, several USB ports, and a FireWire port. The next section discusses these and other ports.

Serial Ports

A **serial port** is a type of interface that connects a device to the system unit by transmitting data one bit at a time (Figure 4-22). Serial ports usually connect devices that do not require fast data transmission rates, such as a mouse, keyboard, or modem. The COM port (short for communications port) on the system unit is one type of serial port.

Parallel Ports

Unlike a serial port, a **parallel port** is an interface that connects devices by transferring more than one bit at a time (Figure 4-23). Parallel ports originally were developed as an alternative to the slower speed serial ports. Some printers can connect to the system unit using a parallel port. This parallel port can transfer eight bits of data (one byte) simultaneously through eight separate lines in a single cable.

USB Ports

A **USB port**, short for universal serial bus port, can connect up to 127 different peripherals together with a single connector. Devices that connect to a USB port include the following: mouse, printer, digital camera, scanner, speakers, portable media player, CD, DVD, smart phone, PDA, game console, and removable hard disk. Personal computers typically have six to eight USB ports on the front and/or back of the system unit (Figure 4-21). The latest version of USB, called USB 2.0, is a more advanced and faster USB, with speeds 40 times higher than that of its predecessor.

To attach multiple peripherals using a single port, you can use a USB hub. A **USB hub** is a device that plugs in a USB port on the system unit and contains multiple USB ports in which you plug cables from USB devices. Some newer peripherals may attach only to a USB port. Others attach to either a serial or parallel port, as well as a USB port.

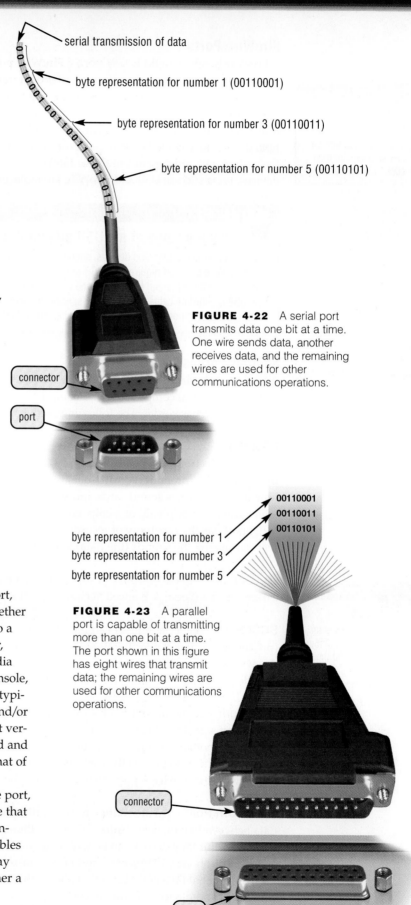

serial transmission of data

byte representation for number 1 (00110001)

byte representation for number 3 (00110011)

byte representation for number 5 (00110101)

FIGURE 4-22 A serial port transmits data one bit at a time. One wire sends data, another receives data, and the remaining wires are used for other communications operations.

connector

port

00110001
00110011
00110101

byte representation for number 1
byte representation for number 3
byte representation for number 5

FIGURE 4-23 A parallel port is capable of transmitting more than one bit at a time. The port shown in this figure has eight wires that transmit data; the remaining wires are used for other communications operations.

connector

port

FireWire Ports

Previously called an IEEE 1394 port, a **FireWire port** is similar to a USB port in that it can connect multiple types of devices that require faster data transmission speeds, such as digital video cameras, digital VCRs, color printers, scanners, digital cameras, and DVD drives, to a single connector. A FireWire port allows you to connect up to 63 devices together. The latest version, called FireWire 800, is much more advanced than the original FireWire. You can use a FireWire hub to attach multiple devices to a single FireWire port. A **FireWire hub** is a device that plugs in a FireWire port on the system unit and contains multiple FireWire ports in which you plug cables from FireWire devices. Ports such as USB and FireWire are replacing all other types of ports.

WEB LINK 4-8

FireWire Ports

For more information, visit scsite.com/dcf5e/ch4/weblink and then click FireWire Ports.

FAQ 4-4

Why are some of my USB and FireWire cables different?

Some smaller computers and devices, such as digital cameras and game consoles, have a mini-USB or mini-FireWire port that requires the USB or FireWire cable have a mini connector at one end and a standard connector at the other end to attach to the computer. Other devices, such as some smart phones, may require the USB or FireWire cable have a device-specific connector at one end for special uses such as wireless Internet connections. For more information, visit scsite.com/dcf5e/ch4/faq and then click USB and FireWire Cables.

Special-Purpose Ports

Five special-purpose ports are MIDI, eSATA, SCSI, IrDA, and Bluetooth. These ports are not included in typical computers. For a computer to have these ports, you often must customize the computer purchase order. The following sections discuss each of these ports.

MIDI PORT   A special type of serial port that connects the system unit to a musical instrument, such as an electronic keyboard, is called a **MIDI port**. Short for Musical Instrument Digital Interface, MIDI (pronounced MID-dee) is the electronic music industry's standard that defines how devices, such as sound cards and synthesizers, represent sounds electronically. A synthesizer, which can be a peripheral or a chip, creates sound from digital instructions. A system unit with a MIDI port has the capability of recording sounds that have been created by a synthesizer and then processing the sounds (the data) to create new sounds.

eSATA PORT   An **eSATA port**, or external SATA port, allows you to connect a high-speed external SATA (Serial Advanced Technology Attachment) hard disk to a computer.

WEB LINK 4-9

SAS

For more information, visit scsite.com/dcf5e/ch4/weblink and then click SAS.

SCSI PORT   A special high-speed parallel port, called a **SCSI port**, allows you to attach SCSI (pronounced skuzzy) peripherals such as disk drives and printers. **SAS** (serial-attached SCSI) is a newer type of SCSI that transmits at much faster speeds than parallel SCSI. Some computers include a SCSI port. Others have a slot that supports a SCSI card.

IrDA PORT   Some devices can transmit data via infrared light waves. For these wireless devices to transmit signals to a computer, both the computer and the device must have an **IrDA port**.

To ensure nothing obstructs the path of the infrared light wave, you must align the IrDA port on the device with the IrDA port on the computer, similarly to the way you operate a television remote control. Devices that use IrDA ports include a smart phone, PDA, keyboard, mouse, printer, and pager.

BLUETOOTH PORT   An alternative to IrDA, **Bluetooth** technology uses radio waves to transmit data between two devices. Unlike IrDA, the Bluetooth devices do not have to be aligned with each other but they do have to be within about 33 feet of each other. Many computers, peripherals, smart phones, PDAs, cars, and other consumer electronics are Bluetooth-enabled, which means they contain a small chip that allows them to communicate with other Bluetooth-enabled computers and devices. If you have a computer that is not Bluetooth enabled, you can purchase a Bluetooth wireless port adapter that will convert an existing USB port or serial port into a Bluetooth port. Also available are Bluetooth PC Cards and ExpressCard modules for notebook computers and Bluetooth cards for smart phones and PDAs.

BUSES

As explained earlier in this chapter, a computer processes and stores data as a series of electronic bits. These bits transfer internally within the circuitry of the computer along electrical channels. Each channel, called a **bus**, allows the various devices both inside and attached to the system unit to communicate with each other. Just as vehicles travel on a highway to move from one destination to another, bits travel on a bus (Figure 4-24).

Buses are used to transfer bits from input devices to memory, from memory to the processor, from the processor to memory, and from memory to output or storage devices. Buses consist of two parts: a data bus and an address bus. The data bus is used to transfer actual data and the address bus is used to transfer information about where the data should reside in memory.

The size of a bus, called the bus width, determines the number of bits that the computer can transmit at one time. For example, a 32-bit bus can transmit 32 bits (4 bytes) at a time. On a 64-bit bus, bits transmit from one location to another 64 bits (8 bytes) at a time. The larger the number of bits handled by the bus, the faster the computer transfers data. Most personal computers today use a 64-bit bus.

Every bus also has a clock speed. Just like the processor, manufacturers state the clock speed for a bus in hertz. Recall that one megahertz (MHz) is equal to one million ticks per second. Most of today's processors have a bus clock speed of 400, 533, 667, 800, 1066, or 1333 MHz. The higher the bus clock speed, the faster the transmission of data, which results in programs running faster.

A computer has two basic types of buses: a system bus and an expansion bus. A **system bus** is part of the motherboard and connects the processor to main memory. When computer professionals use the term bus by itself, they usually are referring to the system bus.

An **expansion bus** allows the processor to communicate with peripherals. Some peripherals outside the system unit connect to a port on an adapter card, which is inserted in an expansion slot on the motherboard. This expansion slot connects to the expansion bus, which allows the processor to communicate with the peripheral attached to the adapter card.

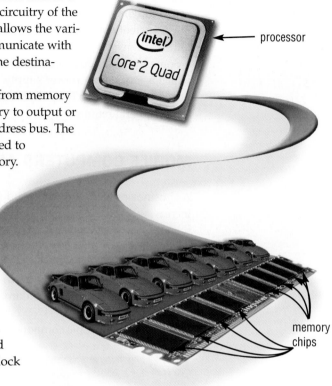

FIGURE 4-24 Just as vehicles travel on a highway, bits travel on a bus. Buses are used to transfer bits from input devices to memory, from memory to the processor, from the processor to memory, and from memory to output or storage devices.

BAYS

After you purchase a computer, you may want to install an additional storage device such as a disk drive in the system unit. A **bay** is an opening inside the system unit in which you can install additional equipment. A bay is different from a slot, which is used for the installation of adapter cards. A **drive bay** is a rectangular opening that typically holds disk drives. Other bays house card readers and widely used ports such as USB, FireWire, and audio ports.

An external bay allows a user to access openings in the bay from outside the system unit (Figure 4-25). CD drives and DVD drives are examples of devices installed in external bays. An internal bay is concealed entirely within the system unit. Hard disk drives are installed in internal bays.

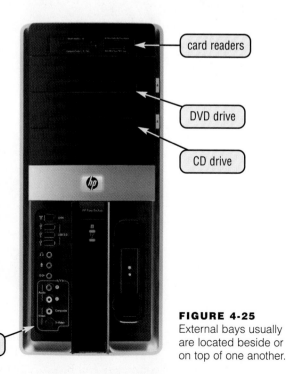

FIGURE 4-25
External bays usually are located beside or on top of one another.

POWER SUPPLY

Many personal computers plug in standard wall outlets, which supply an alternating current (AC) of 115 to 120 volts. This type of power is unsuitable for use with a computer, which requires a direct current (DC) ranging from 5 to 12 volts. The **power supply** is the component of the system unit that converts the wall outlet AC power into DC power.

Some external peripherals such as a cable modem, speakers, or a printer have an **AC adapter**, which is an external power supply. One end of the AC adapter plugs in the wall outlet and the other end attaches to the peripheral. The AC adapter converts the AC power into DC power that the peripheral requires.

MOBILE COMPUTERS AND DEVICES

As businesses and schools expand to serve people across the country and around the world, increasingly more people need to use a computer while traveling to and from a main office or school to conduct business, communicate, or do homework. Users with such mobile computing needs often have a mobile computer, such as a notebook computer or Tablet PC, or a mobile device such as a smart phone, PDA, or portable media player (Figure 4-26).

Weighing on average from 2.5 to more than 10 pounds, notebook computers can run either using batteries or using a standard power supply. Smaller smart phones and PDAs run strictly on batteries. Like their desktop counterparts, mobile computers and devices have a motherboard that contains electronic components that process data.

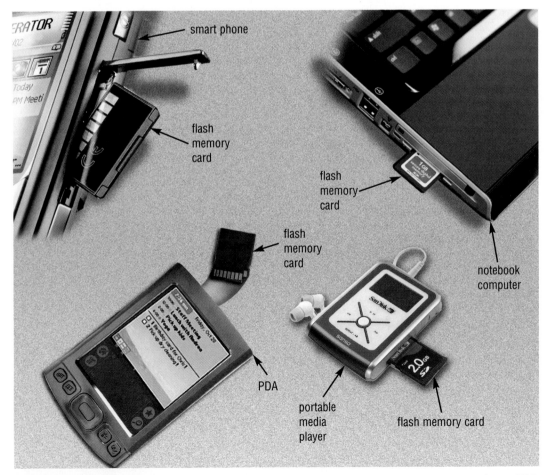

FIGURE 4-26   Users with mobile computing needs often have a notebook computer, smart phone, PDA, and portable media player.

A notebook computer usually is more expensive than a desktop computer with the same capabilities because it is more costly to miniaturize the components. Notebook computers may have video, modem, network, FireWire, USB, headphones, and microphone ports (Figure 4-27). Some mobile users prefer connecting peripherals to a port replicator. A **port replicator**, which is an external device that attaches to a mobile computer, provides connections to peripherals through ports built into the replicator.

Two basic designs of Tablet PC are available: slate and convertible. With the slate Tablet PC (shown in Figure 4-1 on page 134), all hardware is behind the display — much like a smart phone or PDA. Users can attach a removable keyboard to the slate Tablet PC. The display on the convertible Tablet PC, which is attached to a keyboard, can be rotated 180 degrees and folded down over the keyboard. Tablet PCs usually include several slots and ports (Figure 4-28).

Smart phones, portable music players, and PDAs are quite affordable, usually priced at a few hundred dollars or less. These mobile devices often have an IrDA port or are Bluetooth enabled so that users can communicate wirelessly with other computers or devices such as a printer.

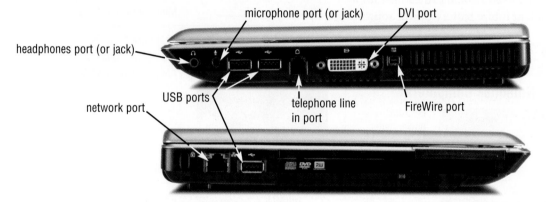

FIGURE 4-27   Ports on a typical notebook computer.

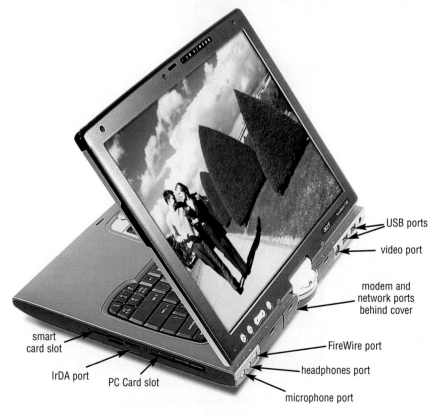

FIGURE 4-28   Ports and slots on a convertible Tablet PC.

PUTTING IT ALL TOGETHER

When you purchase a computer, it is important to understand how the components of the system unit work. Many components of the system unit influence the speed and power of a computer. These include the type of processor, the clock speed of the processor, the amount of RAM, bus width, and the clock speed of the bus. The configuration you require depends on your intended use.

The table in Figure 4-29 lists the suggested minimum processor and RAM requirements based on the needs of various types of computer users. Read Looking Ahead 4-2 for a look at future battery power sources.

LOOKING AHEAD 4-2

Body Heat May Power Notebook Computers

Electrical power generated by the body's natural heat may supplement battery power for your notebook computer, according to engineers working in the field of electronic power sources. Many companies are searching to perfect new power sources for portable electronics in efforts to replace the lithium-ion batteries, which are one of the heaviest notebook computer components.

Another possible power source is a fuel cell, which uses a chemical reaction to generate electricity for several days or even months. The most common reactants are hydrogen and oxygen, but methanol and alcohol also are being explored. Byproducts from the chemical reaction are water vapor and possibly carbon dioxide.

The micro fuel cell industry is predicted to be a $126 million market by 2010, with as many as 80 million devices being powered by a fuel cell cartridge by 2012. For more information, visit scsite.com/dcf5e/ch4/looking and then click Alternate Batteries.

SUGGESTED MINIMUM CONFIGURATIONS BY USER

User	Processor and RAM
HOME 	Intel Celeron D or AMD Sempron or Intel Pentium Dual-Core or Intel Core 2 Duo or AMD Athlon 64 X2 Dual-Core Minimum RAM: 1 GB
SMALL OFFICE/ HOME OFFICE 	Intel Core 2 Duo or Intel Core 2 Quad or AMD Athlon 64 X2 Dual-Core Minimum RAM: 2 GB
MOBILE 	Intel Core 2 Extreme or AMD Turion 64 X2 Minimum RAM: 1 GB
POWER	Intel Itanium 2 or AMD Quad Core Opteron or Intel Quad Core Xeon Minimum RAM: 4 GB
LARGE BUSINESS 	Intel Core 2 Duo or Intel Core 2 Quad or AMD Athlon 64 X2 Dual-Core Minimum RAM: 2 GB

FIGURE 4-29 Suggested processor and RAM configurations by user.

KEEPING YOUR COMPUTER CLEAN

Over time, the system unit collects dust — even in a clean environment. Built up dust can block airflow in the computer, which can cause it to overheat, corrode, or even stop working. By cleaning your computer once or twice a year, you can help extend its life. This preventive maintenance requires a few basic products (Figure 4-30):

- can of compressed air — removes dust and lint from difficult-to-reach areas
- lint-free antistatic wipes and swabs
- bottle of rubbing alcohol
- small computer vacuum (or small attachments on your house vacuum)
- antistatic wristband — to avoid damaging internal components with static electricity
- small screwdriver (may be required to open the case or remove adapter cards)

Before cleaning the computer, turn it off, unplug it from the electrical outlet, and unplug all cables from the ports. Blow away any dust from all openings on the computer case, such as drives, slots, and ports. Vacuum the power supply fan on the back of the computer case to remove any dust that has accumulated on it. Next, release short blasts of compressed air on the power supply fan. Then, use an antistatic wipe to clean the exterior of the case.

If you need assistance opening the computer case, refer to the instructions that came with the computer. Before opening the case, though, check with the computer manufacturer to be sure you will not void a warranty. Once the case is open, put the antistatic wristband on your wrist and attach its clip to the case of the computer. Use the antistatic wipes to clean dust and grime inside the walls of the computer case.

Vacuum as much dust as possible from the interior of the case, including the wires, chips, adapter cards, and fan blades. Next, release short blasts of compressed air in areas the vacuum cannot reach. If the motherboard and adapter cards still look dirty, gently clean them with lint-free wipes or swabs lightly dampened with alcohol.

When finished, be sure all adapter cards are set tightly in their expansion slots. Then close the case, plug in all cables, and attach the power cord. Write down the date you cleaned the computer so that you have a record for your next cleaning.

If you do not feel comfortable cleaning the system unit yourself, have a local computer company clean it for you.

FIGURE 4-30 With a few products, this computer user keeps his computer clean.

Test your knowledge of pages 147 through 155 in Quiz Yourself 4-3.

QUIZ YOURSELF 4-3

Instructions: Find the true statement below. Then, rewrite the remaining false statements so they are true.

1. A bus is the point at which a peripheral attaches to or communicates with a system unit so that the peripheral can send data to or receive information from the computer.

2. An AC adapter is a socket on the motherboard that can hold an adapter card.

3. Serial ports can connect up to 127 different peripherals together with a single connector.

4. The higher the bus clock speed, the slower the transmission of data.

5. When cleaning the inside of the system unit, wear an antistatic wristband to avoid damaging internal components with static electricity.

Quiz Yourself Online: To further check your knowledge of expansion slots, adapter cards, ports, buses, components of mobile computers and devices, and cleaning a computer, visit scsite.com/dcf5e/ch4/quiz and then click Objectives 5 – 9.

CHAPTER SUMMARY

Chapter 4 presented the components of the system unit; described how memory stores data, instructions, and information; and discussed the sequence of operations that occur when a computer executes an instruction. The chapter included a comparison of various personal computer processors on the market today. It also discussed how to clean a system unit.

CAREER CORNER   Computer Engineer

A **computer engineer** designs and develops the electronic components found in computers and peripheral devices. They also can work as researchers, theorists, and inventors. Companies may hire computer engineers for permanent positions or as consultants, with jobs that extend from a few months to a few years, depending on the project. Engineers in research and development often work on projects that will not be released to the general public for two years.

Responsibilities vary from company to company. All computer engineering work, however, demands problem-solving skills and the ability to create and use new technologies. The ability to handle multiple tasks and concentrate on detail is a key component. Assignments often are taken on as part of a team. Therefore, computer engineers must be able to communicate clearly with both computer personnel and computer users, who may have little technical knowledge.

Before taking in-depth computer engineering design and development classes, students usually take mathematics, physics, and basic engineering. Computer engineering degrees include B.S., M.S., and Ph.D. Because computer engineers employed in private industry often advance into managerial positions, many computer engineering graduates obtain a master's degree in business administration (M.B.A.). Most computer engineers earn between $70,000 and $115,000 annually, depending on their experience and employer, but salaries can exceed $150,000. For more information, visit scsite.com/dcf5e/ch4/careers and then click Computer Engineer.

AMD
PC Processor Supplier

Customer needs influence the integrated circuits Advanced Micro Devices (AMD) develops for the computing, communications, and consumer electronics industries. AMD calls this philosophy "customer-centric innovation."

As a global supplier of PC processors, AMD engineers its technologies at its Submicron Development Center (SDC) in Sunnyvale, California. The technologies are put into production at manufacturing facilities in the United States, Europe, Asia, and Japan.

Among the company's more successful line of processors is the AMD 64 family, which is composed of the AMD Athlon 64 processor for desktop and personal computers, the AMD Opteron processor for servers and workstations, and the AMD Turion mobile technology for notebook computers. The company's CoolCore Technology, which saves energy by turning off blocks of memory when not in use, and Barcelona quad-core processors were introduced in 2007. For more information, visit scsite.com/dcf5e/ch4/companies and then click AMD.

Intel
Chip Maker Dominates the Computer Market

When Gordon Moore and Robert Noyce started Intel in 1968, their goal was to replace magnetic core memory with semiconductor memory. Noyce and Moore, together with Andy Grove, refined the process of placing thousands of tiny electronic devices on a silicon chip. In 1971, the company introduced the Intel 4004, the first single-chip microprocessor.

When IBM chose the Intel 8008 chip for its new personal computer in 1980, Intel chips became standard for all IBM-compatible personal computers. Today, Intel's microprocessors are the building blocks in countless personal computers, servers, networks, and communications devices. The company in 2007 joined the One Laptop per Child initiative, which plans to equip children in third-world countries with notebook computers that cost approximately $100. For more information, visit scsite.com/dcf5e/ch4/companies and then click Intel.

TECHNOLOGY TRAILBLAZERS

Jack Kilby
Integrated Circuit Inventor

Jack Kilby was awarded more than 60 patents during his lifetime, but one has changed the world. His integrated circuit, or microchip, invention made microprocessors possible. He was awarded the Nobel Prize in physics in 2000 for his part in the invention of the integrated circuit.

Kilby started his work with miniature electrical components at Centralab, where he developed transistors for hearing aids. He then took a research position with Texas Instruments and developed a working model of the first integrated circuit, which was patented in 1959. Kilby applied this invention to various industrial, military, and commercial applications, including the first pocket calculator, called the Pocketronic.

Kilby is considered one of the more influential people in the world who has had the greatest impact on business computing in the past 50 years. Kilby died in 2005, but his legacy lives on. His first circuit has fostered a worldwide integrated circuit market with sales of nearly $200 billion annually. For more information, visit scsite.com/dcf5e/ch4/people and then click Jack Kilby.

Gordon Moore
Intel Cofounder

More than 40 years ago, Gordon Moore predicted that the number of transistors and resistors placed on computer chips would double every year, with a proportional increase in computing power and decrease in cost. This bold forecast, now known as Moore's Law, proved amazingly accurate for 10 years. Then, Moore revised the estimate to doubling every two years.

Convinced of the future of silicon chips, Moore cofounded Intel in 1968. Moore's lifelong interest in technology was kindled at an early age when he experimented with a neighbor's chemistry set. Even then, he displayed the passion for practical outcomes that has typified his work as a scientist and engineer.

The San Jose Tech Museum of Innovation honored Moore in 2007 with its Global Humanitarian Award for the more than $1 billion donated by his Gordon and Betty Moore Foundation. For more information, visit scsite.com/dcf5e/ch4/people and then click Gordon Moore.

Chapter Review

The Chapter Review section summarizes the concepts presented in this chapter. To obtain help from other students regarding any subject in this chapter, visit scsite.com/dcf5e/ch4/forum and post your thoughts or questions.

(1) How Are Various Styles of System Units Different?

The **system unit** is a case that contains electronic components of the computer used to process data. On desktop personal computers, most storage devices also are part of the system unit. On notebook computers, the keyboard and pointing device often occupy the area on top of the system unit, and the display attaches to the system unit by hinges. On mobile computers and devices, the display often is built into the system unit. With game consoles, the input and output devices, such as controllers and a television, reside outside the system unit. On handheld game consoles and portable media players, by contrast, the packaging around the system unit also houses the input devices and display.

(2) What Are the Components of a Processor, and How Do They Complete a Machine Cycle?

The **processor** interprets and carries out the basic instructions that operate a computer. Processors contain a **control unit** that directs and coordinates most of the operations in the computer and an **arithmetic logic unit** (ALU) that performs arithmetic, comparison, and other operations. The machine cycle is a set of four basic operations — fetching, decoding, executing, and storing — that the processor repeats for every instruction. The control unit fetches program instructions and data from memory and decodes the instructions into commands the computer can execute. The ALU executes the commands, and the results are stored in memory.

 Visit scsite.com/dcf5e/ch4/quiz or click the Quiz Yourself button. Click Objectives 1 – 2.

(3) What Is a Bit, and How Does a Series of Bits Represent Data?

Most computers are **digital** and recognize only two discrete states: off and on. To represent these two states, computers use the **binary system**, which is a number system that has just two unique digits — 0 (for off) and 1 (for on) — called bits. A **bit** is the smallest unit of data a computer can process. Grouped together as a unit, 8 bits form a **byte**, which provides enough different combinations of 0s and 1s to represent 256 individual characters. The combinations are defined by patterns, called coding schemes, such as ASCII and EBCDIC.

(4) What Are the Various Types of Memory?

The system unit contains volatile and nonvolatile memory. **Volatile memory** loses its contents when the computer's power is turned off. **Nonvolatile memory** does not lose its contents when the computer's power is turned off. RAM is the most common type of volatile memory. ROM, flash memory, and CMOS are examples of nonvolatile memory. **RAM** consists of memory chips that can be read from and written to by the processor and other devices. **ROM** refers to memory chips storing permanent data and instructions that usually cannot be modified. **Flash memory** can be erased electronically and rewritten. **CMOS** technology uses battery power to retain information even when the power to the computer is turned off.

 Visit scsite.com/dcf5e/ch4/quiz or click the Quiz Yourself button. Click Objectives 3 – 4.

(5) What Are the Types of Expansion Slots and Adapter Cards?

An **expansion slot** is a socket on the motherboard that can hold an adapter card. An **adapter card** is a circuit board that enhances functions of a component of the system unit and/or provides a connection to a **peripheral** such as a modem, disk drive, printer, scanner, or keyboard. Several types of adapter cards exist. A **sound card** enhances the sound-generating capabilities of a personal computer. A **video card**, also called a **graphics card**, converts computer output into a video signal that displays an image on the screen.

6 How Are a Serial Port, a Parallel Port, a USB Port, and Other Ports Different?

A **port** is the point at which a peripheral attaches to or communicates with a system unit so that the peripheral can send data to or receive information from the computer. A **serial port**, which transmits data one bit at a time, usually connects devices that do not require fast data transmission, such as a mouse, keyboard, or modem. A **parallel port**, which transfers more than one bit at a time, sometimes connects a printer to the system unit. A **USB port** can connect up to 127 different peripherals together with a single connector. A **FireWire port** can connect multiple types of devices that require faster data transmission speeds. Five special-purpose ports are MIDI, eSATA, SCSI, IrDA, and Bluetooth. A **MIDI port** connects the system unit to a musical instrument. An **eSATA port** connects a high-speed external SATA hard disk to a computer. A **SCSI port** attaches the system unit to SCSI peripherals, such as disk drives. An **IrDA port** and **Bluetooth** technology allow wireless devices to transmit signals to a computer via infrared light waves or radio waves.

 7 How Do Buses Contribute to a Computer's Processing Speed?

A **bus** is an electrical channel along which bits transfer within the circuitry of a computer, allowing devices both inside and attached to the system unit to communicate. The size of a bus, called the bus width, determines the number of bits that the computer can transmit at one time. The larger the bus width, the faster the computer transfers data.

 8 What Are the Components in Mobile Computers and Mobile Devices?

Mobile computers and devices have a motherboard that contains electronic components that process data. The system unit for a typical notebook computer often has video, modem, network, FireWire, USB, headphones, and microphone ports. Tablet PCs usually include several slots and ports. Smart phones, portable music players, and PDAs often have an IrDA port or are Bluetooth enabled so that users can communicate wirelessly.

 9 How Do You Clean a System Unit?

Before cleaning a system unit, turn off the computer and unplug it from the wall. Use a small vacuum and a can of compressed air to remove external dust. After opening the case, wear an antistatic wristband and vacuum the interior. Wipe away dust and grime using lint-free antistatic wipes and rubbing alcohol.

 Visit scsite.com/dcf5e/ch4/quiz or click the Quiz Yourself button. Click Objectives 5 – 9.

Key Terms

You should know each key term. Use the list below to help focus your study. To further enhance your understanding of the Key Terms in this chapter, visit scsite.com/dcf5e/ch4/terms. See an example of and a definition for each term, and access current and additional information about the term from the Web.

AC adapter (152)
access time (146)
adapter card (147)
advanced transfer cache (145)
arithmetic logic unit (138)
bay (151)
binary system (140)
bit (140)
Bluetooth (150)
bus (151)
byte (140)
cache (144)
central processing unit (CPU) (137)
chip (136)

clock speed (138)
CMOS (146)
connector (149)
control unit (137)
digital (140)
drive bay (151)
dual-core processor (137)
eSATA port (150)
expansion bus (151)
expansion card (147)
expansion slot (147)
ExpressCard module (148)
ExpressCard slot (148)
FireWire hub (150)
FireWire port (150)

firmware (145)
flash memory (145)
flash memory card (147)
gigabyte (GB) (142)
gigahertz (GHz) (139)
graphics card (147)
IrDA port (150)
kilobyte (KB or K) (142)
L1 cache (145)
L2 cache (145)
megabyte (MB) (142)
memory (142)
memory cache (144)
memory module (144)
memory slots (144)
microprocessor (137)
MIDI port (150)

motherboard (136)
multi-core processor (137)
nanosecond (146)
nonvolatile memory (142)
parallel port (149)
PC Card (148)
PC Card slot (148)
peripheral (147)
port (148)
port replicator (153)
power supply (152)
processor (137)
quad-core processor (137)
RAM (143)

read-only memory (ROM) (145)
SAS (150)
SCSI port (150)
serial port (149)
sound card (147)
system bus (151)
system clock (138)
system unit (134)
terabyte (TB) (142)
U3 smart drive (148)
USB flash drive (148)
USB hub (149)
USB port (149)
video card (147)
volatile memory (142)

Checkpoint

Use the Checkpoint exercises to check your knowledge level of the chapter.

True/False

Mark T for True and F for False. (See page numbers in parentheses.)

_____ 1. The system unit is a case that contains electronic components of the computer used to process data. (134)

_____ 2. The motherboard is the main circuit board of the system unit. (136)

_____ 3. The control unit directs and coordinates most of the operations in the computer. (137)

_____ 4. The speed of the system clock is the only factor that influences a computer's performance. (139)

_____ 5. A byte is the smallest unit of data the computer can process. (140)

_____ 6. When the computer's power is turned off, volatile memory retains its contents. (142)

_____ 7. Current processors include advanced transfer cache (ATC), a type of L2 cache built directly on the processor chip. (145)

_____ 8. CMOS uses battery power to retain information even when the power to the computer is off. (146)

_____ 9. Access time is the amount of time it takes the processor to read data, instructions, and information from memory. (146)

_____ 10. Serial ports usually connect devices that require fast transmission rates, such as printers. (149)

_____ 11. SAS (serial-attached SCSI) is a newer type of SCSI that transmits more reliably, but at slower speeds, than parallel SCSI. (150)

Multiple Choice

Select the best answer. (See page numbers in parentheses.)

1. On _____, the display often is built into the system unit. (135)
   a. desktop personal computers
   b. notebook computers
   c. mobile computers and devices
   d. all of the above

2. The _____ is the component of the processor that directs and coordinates most of the operations in the computer. (137)
   a. control unit
   b. arithmetic logic unit
   c. register
   d. machine cycle

3. Each processor on a multi-core chip generally runs at _____ clock speed than a single-core processor. (137)
   a. a faster   b. the same
   c. twice the   d. a slower

4. The term decoding refers to the process of _____. (138)
   a. obtaining a program instruction or data item from memory
   b. translating an instruction into signals a computer can execute
   c. carrying out commands
   d. writing a result to memory

5. ROM chips, called _____, contain permanently written data, instructions, or information. (145)
   a. memory cache
   b. registers
   c. firmware
   d. transistors

6. A(n) _____ is a socket on the motherboard that can hold an adapter card. (147)
   a. expansion slot
   b. parallel port
   c. drive bay
   d. front side bus

7. A(n) _____ is a device that connects to the system unit and is controlled by the processor in the computer. (147)
   a. adapter card
   b. peripheral
   c. serial port
   d. synthesizer

8. A(n) _____ is part of the motherboard and connects the processor to main memory. (151)
   a. expansion bus
   b. system clock
   c. memory module
   d. system bus

Matching

Match the terms with their definitions. (See page numbers in parentheses.)

_____ 1. processor (137)

_____ 2. memory module (144)

_____ 3. read-only memory (ROM) (145)

_____ 4. expansion slot (147)

_____ 5. IrDA port (150)

_____ 6. bay (151)

a. socket on the motherboard that can hold an adapter card

b. interprets and carries out the basic instructions that operate a computer

c. small ceramic or metal component that absorbs and ventilates heat

d. small circuit board on which RAM chips usually reside

e. opening inside the system unit in which additional equipment can be installed

f. memory chips storing permanent data and instructions

g. allows devices to transmit data via infrared light waves

Checkpoint

Short Answer

Write a brief answer to each of the following questions.

1. What is the motherboard? _____ What is a computer chip? _____
2. What is the binary system? _____ What is the difference between a bit and a byte? _____
3. What is memory cache? _____ How are the two types of cache (L1 cache and L2 cache) different? _____
4. What are four types of removable flash memory devices? _____ How are they different? _____
5. What types of ports might you find on a notebook computer? _____ What is the purpose of a port replicator? _____

Working Together

Working in a group of your classmates, complete the following team exercise.

1. Prepare a report about the different types of ports and the way you connect peripheral devices to a computer. As part of your report, include the following subheadings and an overview of each subheading topic: (1) What is a port? (2) What is a connector? (3) What is a serial port and how does it work? (4) What is a parallel port and how does it work? (5) What is a USB port and how does it work? Expand your report so that it includes information beyond that in your textbook. Create a presentation from your report. Share your presentation with your class.

Web Research

Use the Internet-based Web Research exercises to broaden your understanding of the concepts presented in this chapter. To discuss any of the Web Research exercises in this chapter with other students, post your thoughts or questions at scsite.com/dcf5e/ch4/forum.

1 **Blogs**   Technology news blogs offer information about new products, trends, and issues facing information technology professionals. Visit several technology blogs, including those from CNET (news.com), Geekzone (geekzone.co.nz/blogindex.asp), Good Morning Silicon Valley (svextra.com/blogs/gmsv), Lifehacker (lifehacker.com), TechnoClicks (technoclicks.com), and WordPress (wordpress.com/tag/technology/). What are bloggers discussing in their more recent posts? What top news stories are featured? What products are reviewed? What questions are members asking about computer chips, flash memory, and Bluetooth products? Which stories have generated more than 20 comments?

2 **Scavenger Hunt**   Use one of the search engines listed in Figure 2-8 in Chapter 2 on page 58 or your own favorite search engine to find the answers to the questions below. Copy and paste the Web address from the Web page where you found the answer. Some questions may have more than one answer. If required, submit your answers to your instructor. (1) What is an ultracapacitator? (2) What Carnegie Mellon University professor was the first person to use :-) as a horizontal smiley face in a computer message in 1982? (3) What are rune stones and their connection to Danish King Harald Blatand (Bluetooth)?

3 **Search Sleuth**   Ask.com, a popular search engine, uses natural language, which allows researchers to type millions of questions each day using words a human would use rather than code a computer understands. Visit this Web site and then use your word processing program to answer the following questions. Then, if required, submit your answers to your instructor. (1) Click the Search text box, type `What is the central processing unit?`, and then click the Search button. Review the Narrow Your Search links on the right side of the page. Click the How Does the Central Processing Unit Work link, and then scroll through the links and click one to find the answer to this question. (2) Click your browser's Back button or press the BACKSPACE key to return to the Ask.com home page. Review the list of Search Tools on the page. In addition to Web, what are the names of the other available tools? (3) Click the News search tool and then click one of the links about the central processing unit and review the material. If required, submit to your instructor a 50-word summary of the information.

Learn How To

Use the Learn How To activities to learn fundamental skills when using a computer and accompanying technology. Complete the exercises and submit them to your instructor.

LEARN HOW TO 1: Purchase and Install Memory in a Computer

One of the less expensive and more effective ways to speed up a computer, make it capable of processing more programs at the same time, and enable it to handle graphics, gaming, and other high-level programs is to increase the amount of memory. The process of increasing memory is accomplished in two phases — purchasing the memory and installing the memory. To purchase memory for a computer, complete the following steps:

1. Determine the amount of memory currently in the computer. For a method to do this, see Learn How To number 3 in Chapter 3.
2. Determine the maximum amount of memory your computer can contain. This value can change for different computers, based primarily on the number of slots on the motherboard available for memory and the size of the memory modules you can place in each slot. On most computers, different size memory modules can be inserted in slots. A computer, therefore, might allow a 128 MB, 256 MB, 512 MB, 1 GB, or 2 GB memory module to be inserted in each slot. To determine the maximum memory for a computer, in many cases you can multiply the number of memory slots on the computer by the maximum size memory module that can be inserted in each slot.

    For example, if a computer contains four memory slots and is able to accept memory modules of 128 MB, 256 MB, 512 MB, or 1 GB in each of its memory slots, the maximum amount of memory the computer can contain is 4 GB (4 x 1 GB).

    You can find the number of slots and the allowable sizes of each memory module by contacting the computer manufacturer, looking in the computer's documentation, or contacting sellers of memory such as Kingston (www.kingston.com) or Crucial (www.crucial.com) on the Web. These sellers have documentation for most computers, and even programs you can download to run on your computer that will specify how much memory your computer currently has and how much you can add.
3. Determine how much memory you want to add, which will be somewhere between the current memory and the maximum memory allowed on the computer.
4. Determine the current configuration of memory on the computer. For example, if a computer with four memory slots contains 512 MB of memory, it could be using one memory module of 512 MB in a single slot and the other three slots would be empty; two memory modules of 256 MB each in two slots with two slots empty; one memory module of 256 MB and two memory modules of 128 MB each in three slots with one slot empty; or four memory modules of 128 MB each in four slots with no slots empty. You may be required to look inside the system unit to make this determination. The current memory configuration on a computer will determine what new memory modules you should buy to increase the memory to the amount determined in Step 3.

    You also should be aware that a few computers require memory to be installed in the computer in matching pairs. This means that a computer with four slots could obtain 512 MB of memory with two memory modules of 256 MB each in two slots, or four memory modules of 128 MB each in four slots.
5. Determine the number of available memory slots on your computer and the number and size memory modules you must buy to fulfill your requirement. Several scenarios can occur (in the following examples, assume you can install memory one module at a time).
    a. Scenario 1: The computer has one or more open slots. In this case, you might be able to purchase a memory module that matches the amount of memory increase you desire. For example, if you want to increase memory by 256 MB, you should purchase a 256 MB memory module for insertion in the open slot. Generally, you should buy the maximum size module you can for an open slot. So, if you find two empty slots and wish to increase memory by 256 MB, it is smarter to buy one 256 MB module and leave one empty slot rather than buy two 128 MB memory modules and use both slots. This allows you to increase memory again without removing currently used modules.
    b. Scenario 2: The computer has no open slots. For example, a computer containing 512 MB of memory could have four slots each containing 128 MB memory modules. If you want to increase the memory on the computer to 1 GB, you will have to remove some of the 128 MB memory modules and replace them with the new memory modules you purchase. In this example, you want to increase the memory by 512 MB. You would have several options: (1) You could replace all four 128 MB memory modules with 256 MB memory modules; (2) You could replace all four 128 MB memory modules with two 512 MB memory modules; (3) You could replace one 128 MB memory module with a 512 MB memory module, and replace a second 128 MB module with a 256 MB memory module. Each of these options results in a total memory of 1 GB. The best option will depend on the price of memory and whether you anticipate increasing the memory size at a later time. The least expensive option probably would be number 3.

   c. Scenario 3: Many other combinations can occur. You may have to perform arithmetic calculations to decide the combination of memory modules that will work for the number of slots on the computer and the desired additional memory.

6. Determine the type of memory to buy for the computer. Computer memory has many types and configurations, and it is critical that you buy the kind of memory for which the computer was designed. It is preferable to buy the same type of memory that currently is found in the computer. That is, if the memory is DDR3 SDRAM with a certain clock speed, then that is the type of additional memory you should place in the computer. The documentation for the computer should specify the memory type. In addition, the Web sites cited on the previous page, and others as well, will present a list of memory modules that will work with your computer. Enough emphasis cannot be placed on the fact that the memory you buy must be compatible with the type of memory usable on your computer. Because there are so many types and configurations, you must be especially diligent to ensure you purchase the proper memory for your computer.

7. Once you have determined the type and size of memory to purchase, buy it from a reputable dealer. Buying poor or mismatched memory is a major reason for a computer's erratic performance and is one of the more difficult problems to troubleshoot.

After purchasing the memory, you must install it on your computer. Complete the following steps to install memory on a computer:

1. Unplug the computer, and remove all electrical cords and device cables from the ports on the computer. Open the case of the system unit. You may want to consult the computer's documentation to determine the exact procedure for opening the system unit.

2. Ground yourself so that you do not generate static electricity that can cause memory or other components within the system unit to be damaged. To do this, wear an antistatic wristband you can purchase inexpensively in a computer or electronics store; or, before you touch any component within the system unit, touch an unpainted metal surface such as the metal on the back of the computer. If you are not wearing an antistatic wristband, periodically touch an unpainted metal surface to dissipate any static electricity.

3. Within the system unit, find the memory slots on the motherboard. The easiest way to do this is look for memory modules that are similar to those you purchased. The memory slots often are located near the processor. If you cannot find the slots, consult the documentation. A diagram often is available to help you spot the memory slots.

4. Insert the memory module in the next empty slot. Orient the memory module in the slot to match the modules currently installed. A notch or notches on the memory module will ensure you do not install the module backwards. If your memory module is a DIMM, insert the module straight down into grooves on the clips and then apply gentle pressure to seat the modules properly (see Figure 4-13 on page 144). If your memory is SIMM, which is used on older computers, insert the module at a 45 degree angle and then rotate it to a vertical position until the module snaps into place.

5. If you must remove one or more memory modules before inserting the new memory, carefully release the clips before lifting the memory module out of the memory slot.

6. Plug in the machine and replace all the device cables without replacing the cover.

7. Start the computer. In most cases, the new memory will be recognized and the computer will run normally. If an error message appears, determine the cause of the error. In most cases, if you turn off the computer, remove the chords and cables, ground yourself, and then reinstall the memory, everything will be fine.

8. Replace the computer cover.

Adding memory to a computer can extend its usefulness and increase its processing power.

Exercise

1. Assume you have a computer that contains 512 MB of memory. It contains four memory slots. Each slot can contain 128 MB, 256 MB, or 512 MB memory modules. Two of the slots contain 256 MB memory modules. What memory chip(s) would you buy to increase the memory on the computer to 1 GB? What is the maximum memory on the computer? Submit your answers to your instructor.

2. Assume you have a computer that contains 1 GB of memory. It contains four memory slots. Each slot can contain 128 MB, 256 MB, 512 MB, or 1 GB memory modules. Currently, the four slots each contain a 256 MB memory module. What combinations of memory modules will satisfy your memory upgrade to 2 GB? Visit an appropriate Web site to determine which of these combinations is the least expensive. What is your recommendation? Submit your answers to your instructor.

Learn It Online

Use the Learn It Online exercises to reinforce your understanding of the chapter concepts. To access the Learn It Online exercises, visit scsite.com/dcf5e/ch4/learn.

(1) At the Movies — The Leopard with a Time Machine

To view the The Leopard with a Time Machine movie, click the number 1 button. Locate your video and click the corresponding High-Speed or Dial-Up link, depending on your Internet connection. Watch the movie to learn about Apple Computer's "Time Machine" software, which allows users to travel through time by scrolling through different windows that represent days, to help them find the files that they need. Then, complete the exercise by answering the question that follows. What does Time Machine do for your Mac?

(2) Student Edition Labs — Understanding the Motherboard

Click the number 2 button. A new browser window will open, displaying the Student Edition Labs. Follow the on-screen instructions to complete the Understanding the Motherboard Lab. When finished, click the Exit button. If required, submit your results to your instructor.

(3) Practice Test

Click the number 3 button. Answer each question. When completed, enter your name and click the Grade Test button to submit the quiz for grading. Make a note of any missed questions. If required, submit your score to your instructor.

(4) Who Wants To Be a Computer Genius^2?

Click the number 4 button to find out if you are a computer genius. Directions about how to play the game will be displayed. When you are ready to play, click the Play button. Submit your score to your instructor.

(5) Configuring and Pricing Computers

Click the number 5 button to learn how to configure and price a custom computer. Research at least two different types of computers by visiting the manufacturers' Web sites, and then specify a computer configuration and obtain a quote from each site you visit. Make sure you include any software you may require. Also, add any upgrade items that you would like with your computer including protection plans, peripherals (printer, scanner, etc.), installation services, and recycling options. Print the quotes from each site and submit the results to your instructor.

(6) Student Edition Labs — Binary Numbers

Click the number 6 button. A new browser window will open, displaying the Student Edition Labs. Follow the on-screen instructions to complete the Binary Numbers Lab. When finished, click the Exit button. If required, submit your results to your instructor.

(7) Crossword Puzzle Challenge

Click the number 7 button, then click the Crossword Puzzle Challenge link. Directions about how to play the game will be displayed. Complete the puzzle to reinforce skills you learned in this chapter. When you are ready to play, click the Continue button. Submit the completed puzzle to your instructor.

(8) Vista Exercises

Click the number 8 button. When the Vista Exercises menu appears, click the exercise assigned by your instructor. A new browser window will open. Follow the on-screen instructions to complete the exercise. When finished, click the Exit button. If required, submit your results to your instructor.

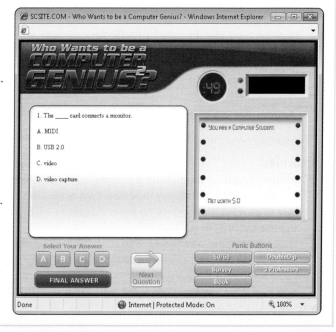

Input and Output

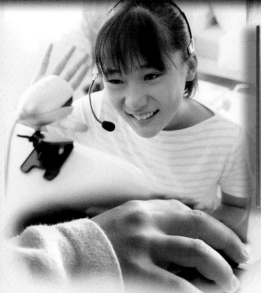

OBJECTIVES

After completing this chapter, you will be able to:

1. List the characteristics of a keyboard
2. Summarize how these pointing devices work: mouse, trackball, touchpad, pointing stick, light pen, touch screen, stylus, digital pen, and gaming and media player controllers
3. Describe other types of input, including voice input; input devices for smart phones, PDAs, and Tablet PCs; digital cameras; video input; scanners and reading devices; terminals; and biometric input
4. Describe the characteristics of LCD monitors, LCD screens, and CRT monitors
5. Summarize the various types of printers
6. Explain the characteristics of speakers, headphones, and earphones; fax machines and fax modems; multifunction peripherals; data projectors; and interactive whiteboards
7. Identify input and output options for physically challenged users

CONTENTS

WHAT IS INPUT

Input is any data and instructions entered into the memory of a computer. As shown in Figure 5-1, people have a variety of options for entering input into a computer.

An **input device** is any hardware component that allows users to enter data and instructions into a computer. The following pages discuss a variety of input devices.

FIGURE 5-1   Users can enter data and instructions into a computer in a variety of ways.

KEYBOARD AND POINTING DEVICES

Two of the more widely used input devices are the keyboard and the mouse. Most computers include a keyboard or keyboarding capabilities.

The mouse is a **pointing device** because it allows a user to control a pointer on the screen. In a graphical user interface, a **pointer** is a small symbol on the screen whose location and shape change as a user moves a pointing device. A pointing device can select text, graphics, and other objects; and click buttons, icons, links, and menu commands.

The following pages discuss the keyboard and a variety of pointing devices.

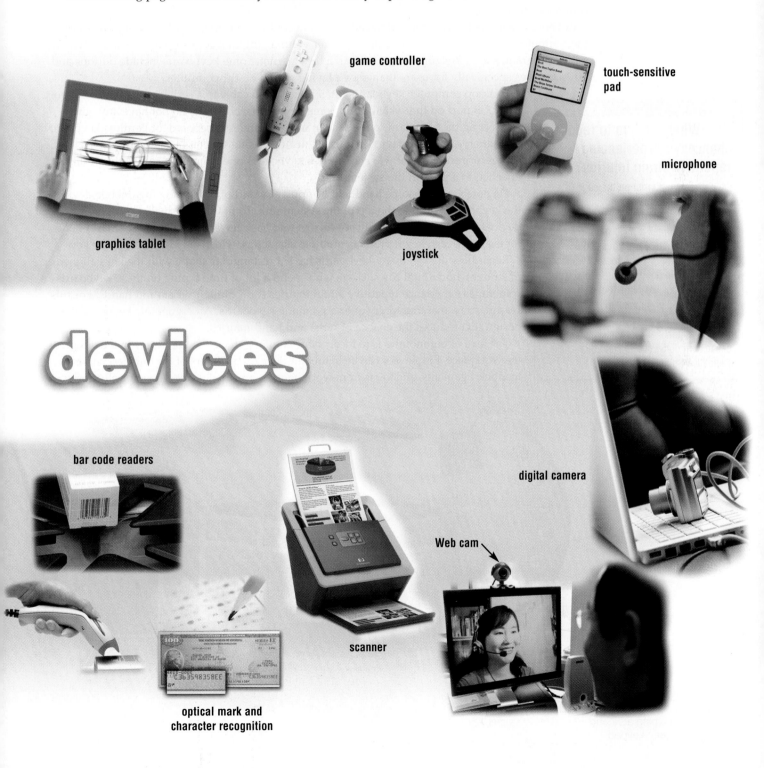

game controller

touch-sensitive pad

microphone

graphics tablet

joystick

devices

bar code readers

digital camera

Web cam

scanner

optical mark and character recognition

The Keyboard

Many people use a keyboard as one of their input devices. A **keyboard** is an input device that contains keys users press to enter data and instructions into a computer (Figure 5-2).

All computer keyboards have a typing area that includes the letters of the alphabet, numbers, punctuation marks, and other basic keys. Many desktop computer keyboards also have a numeric keypad on the right side of the keyboard.

Most of today's desktop computer keyboards are enhanced keyboards. An enhanced keyboard has 12 or more function keys along the top and a set of arrow and additional keys between the typing area and the numeric keypad (Figure 5-2). Function keys are special keys programmed to issue commands to a computer.

Keyboards with media control buttons allow you to control your media player program, access the computer's CD/DVD drive, and adjust speaker volume. Internet controls allow you to open an e-mail program, start a Web browser, and search the Internet. Some keyboards include buttons and other features specifically for users that enjoy playing games on the computer.

Desktop computer keyboards often attach via a cable to a serial port, a keyboard port, or a USB port on the system unit. Some keyboards, however, do not have any wires connecting the keyboard to the system unit. A wireless keyboard, or cordless keyboard, is a battery-powered device that transmits data using wireless technology, such as radio waves or infrared light waves. Wireless keyboards often communicate with a receiver attached to a port on the system unit.

On notebook and some handheld computers, smart phones, and other mobile devices, the keyboard is built in the top of the system unit. To fit in these smaller computers and devices, the keyboards usually are smaller and have fewer keys. On many smart phones, for example, each key represents multiple characters, which are identified on the key.

Regardless of size, many keyboards have a rectangular shape with the keys aligned in straight, horizontal rows. Users who spend a lot of time typing on these keyboards sometimes experience repetitive strain injuries (RSI) of their wrists and hands. For this reason, some manufacturers offer ergonomic keyboards. An ergonomic keyboard has a design that reduces the chance of wrist and hand injuries.

The goal of **ergonomics** is to incorporate comfort, efficiency, and safety in the design of the workplace. Employees can be injured or develop disorders of the muscles, nerves, tendons, ligaments, and joints from working in an area that is not ergonomically designed.

FAQ 5-1

What can I do to reduce chances of experiencing repetitive strain injuries?

Do not rest your wrist on the edge of a desk; use a wrist rest. Keep your forearm and wrist level so that your wrist does not bend. Take a break and do hand exercises every 15 minutes. Keep your shoulders, arms, hands, and wrists relaxed while you work. Maintain good posture. Keep feet flat on the floor, with one foot slightly in front of the other. Immediately stop using the computer if you begin to experience pain or fatigue. For more information, visit scsite.com/dcf5e/ch5/faq and then click Repetitive Strain Injuries.

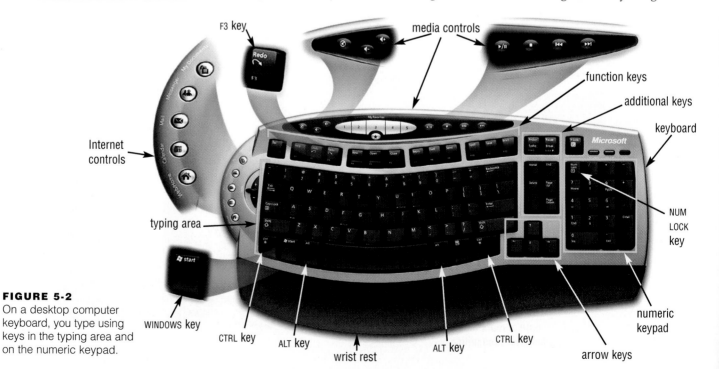

FIGURE 5-2
On a desktop computer keyboard, you type using keys in the typing area and on the numeric keypad.

Mouse

A **mouse** is a pointing device that fits comfortably under the palm of your hand. With a mouse, users control the movement of the pointer. As you move a mouse, the pointer on the screen also moves. Generally, you use the mouse to move the pointer on the screen to an object such as a button, a menu, an icon, a link, or text. Then, you press a mouse button to perform a certain action associated with that object.

A mechanical mouse, which was the first type of mouse used with personal computers, has a rubber or metal ball on its underside. Electronic circuits in the mouse translate the movement of the mouse into signals the computer can process. A mechanical mouse is placed on a **mouse pad,** which is a rectangular rubber or foam pad that provides better traction than the top of a desk.

Most computer users today have some type of optical mouse, which has no moving mechanical parts inside. Instead, an **optical mouse** uses devices that emit and sense light to detect the mouse's movement. Some use optical sensors, and others use a laser (Figure 5-3a). The latter type often is referred to as a **laser mouse**, which usually is more expensive than the former. An optical mouse is more precise than a mechanical mouse and does not require cleaning as does a mechanical mouse, but it also is more expensive.

The mobile user who makes presentations may prefer a mouse that has additional buttons on the bottom for running a slide show and controlling media, similar to a remote control. An **air mouse** is a newer type of motion-sensing mouse that, in addition to the typical buttons, allows you to control objects, media players, and slide shows by moving the mouse in predetermined directions through the air (Figure 5-3b). For example, raising the mouse up would increase the volume on your media player.

A mouse connects to a computer in several ways. Many types connect with a cable that attaches to a serial port, mouse port, or USB port on the system unit. A wireless mouse, or cordless mouse, is a battery-powered device that transmits data using wireless technology, such as radio waves or infrared light waves. Read Ethics & Issues 5-1 for a related discussion.

WEB LINK 5-1

Air Mouse

For more information, visit scsite.com/dcf5e/ch5/weblink and then click Air Mouse.

FIGURE 5-3a   (optical mouse that uses laser)

FIGURE 5-3b   (air mouse)

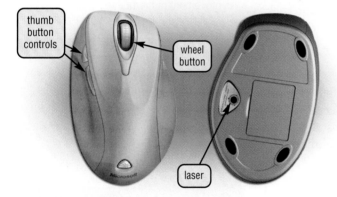

FIGURE 5-3   The top and sides of a mouse have one to four buttons; some also have a small wheel.

ETHICS & ISSUES 5-1

Are Employers Responsible for Medical Problems Related to Computer Use?

When you consider the causes of workplace injuries, you might not put clicking a mouse or using a cell phone in the same category with lifting a bag of concrete, but perhaps you should. According to the chairman of a National Academy of Sciences panel that investigated workplace injuries, every year one million Americans lose workdays because of repetitive strain injuries, including the latest malady known as cell phone elbow. Repetitive strain injuries are caused when muscle groups perform the same actions over and over again. Once, repetitive strain injuries were common among factory workers who performed the same tasks on an assembly line for hours a day. Today, these injuries, which often result from prolonged use of a computer mouse and keyboard or overuse of cell phones and other personal mobile devices, are the largest job-related injury and illness problem in the United States and are almost completely avoidable with proper computer and mobile device use. OSHA proposed standards whereby employers would have to establish programs to prevent workplace injuries with respect to computer use. Yet, Congress rejected the standards, accepting the argument that the cost to employers would be prohibitive and unfair. Some argue that it is each employee's responsibility to be aware of preventative measures against repetitive strain injuries. Should the government establish laws regarding computer use? Why or why not? Are employees, employers, or the government responsible for repetitive strain injuries? Why? Who should be responsible for the costs of prevention and medical care? Why?

Trackball

A **trackball** is a stationary pointing device with a ball on its top or side (Figure 5-4). To move the pointer using a trackball, you rotate the ball with your thumb, fingers, or the palm of your hand. In addition to the ball, a trackball usually has one or more buttons that work just like mouse buttons.

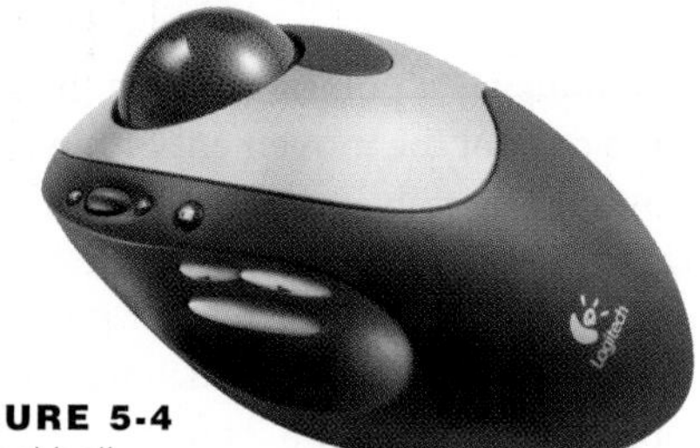

FIGURE 5-4
A trackball.

Touchpad

A **touchpad** is a small, flat, rectangular pointing device that is sensitive to pressure and motion (Figure 5-5). To move the pointer using a touchpad, slide your fingertip across the surface of the pad. Some touchpads have one or more buttons around the edge of the pad that work like mouse buttons. On most touchpads, you also can tap the pad's surface to imitate mouse operations such as clicking. Touchpads are found most often on notebook computers.

Pointing Stick

A **pointing stick** is a pressure-sensitive pointing device shaped like a pencil eraser that is positioned between keys on a keyboard (Figure 5-6). To move the pointer using a pointing stick, you push the pointing stick with a finger. The pointer on the screen moves in the direction you push the pointing stick. By pressing buttons below the keyboard, users can click and perform other mouse-type operations with a pointing stick.

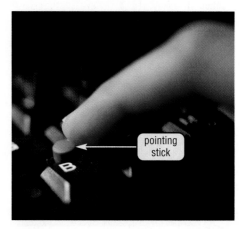

FIGURE 5-5   Most notebook computers have a touchpad that allows users to control the movement of the pointer.

Light Pen

A **light pen** is a handheld input device that can detect the presence of light. To select objects on the screen, a user presses the light pen against the surface of the screen or points the light pen at the screen and then presses a button on the pen.

Touch Screen

A **touch screen** is a touch-sensitive display device. Users can interact with these devices by touching areas of the screen. Because touch screens require a lot of arm movements, you do not enter large amounts of data using a touch screen. Instead, users touch words, pictures, numbers, letters, or locations identified on the screen.

FIGURE 5-6   Some notebook computers include a pointing stick to allow a user to control the movement of the pointer.

With some smart phones, portable media players, and other personal mobile devices, you can touch the screen to perform tasks such as dialing telephone numbers, entering text, and making on-screen selections. Many handheld game consoles also have touch screens. Kiosks, which are freestanding computers, have touch screens (Figure 5-7).

FIGURE 5-7 This user looks up an address on a public kiosk.

FIGURE 5-8 This user organizes photos by touching and dragging them across the Microsoft Surface display.

A recently developed touch screen, called **Microsoft Surface**, is a 30-inch tabletop display that allows one or more people to interact with the screen using their fingers or hands (Figure 5-8). The Microsoft Surface display also allows devices that are not digital, such as an everyday paintbrush, to be used as an input device.

Pen Input

Mobile users often enter data and instructions with a pen-type device. With **pen input**, users write, draw, and tap on a flat surface to enter input. The surface may be a monitor, a screen, a special type of paper, or a graphics tablet. Two devices used for pen input are the stylus and digital pen. A **stylus** is a small metal or plastic device that looks like a tiny ink pen but uses pressure instead of ink. A **digital pen**, which is slightly larger than a stylus, is available in two forms: some are pressure-sensitive; others have built-in digital cameras.

Some mobile computers and nearly all mobile devices have touch screens that recognize pen input. Instead of using a finger to enter data and instructions, most of these devices include a pressure-sensitive digital pen or stylus. You write, draw, or make selections on the screen by touching it with the pen or stylus. For example, Tablet PCs use a pressure-sensitive digital pen and many smart phones and other personal mobile devices use a stylus. Pressure-sensitive digital pens, often simply called pens, typically provide more functionality than a stylus, featuring electronic erasers and programmable buttons.

Pen input is possible on computers without touch screens by attaching a graphics tablet to the computer. A **graphics tablet** is a flat, rectangular, electronic, plastic board. Architects, mapmakers, designers, artists, and home users create drawings and sketches by using a pressure-sensitive pen on a graphics tablet (Figure 5-9).

Digital pens that have built-in digital cameras work differently from pressure-sensitive digital pens. These pens look very much like a ballpoint pen and typically do not contain any additional buttons. As you write or draw on special digital paper with the pen, it captures every handwritten mark and then stores the images in the pen's memory. You then can transfer the images from the pen to a computer or mobile device, such as a smart phone.

pen

graphics tablet

FIGURE 5-9 Artist using a pen on a graphics tablet.

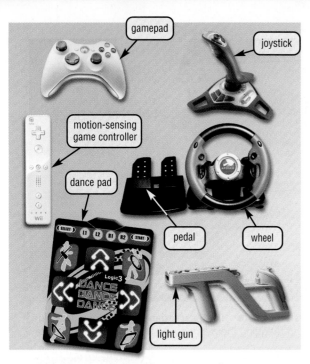

FIGURE 5-10   A variety of game controllers.

GAMING AND MEDIA PLAYER CONTROLLERS

Video games and computer games use a **game controller** as the input device that directs movements and actions of on-screen objects (Figure 5-10). Game controllers include gamepads, joysticks and wheels, light guns, dance pads, and a variety of motion-sensing controllers. Portable media players use a touch-sensitive pad as their input device.

Gamepads

A **gamepad**, which is held with both hands, controls the movement and actions of players or objects in video games or computer games. On the gamepad, users press buttons with their thumbs or move sticks in various directions to trigger events. Gamepads communicate with a game console or a personal computer via wired or wireless technology.

Joysticks and Wheels

Users running game software or flight and driving simulation software often use a joystick or wheel to control an airplane, vehicle, or player. A **joystick** is a handheld vertical lever mounted on a base. You move the lever in different directions and press buttons to control the actions of the simulated vehicle or player. A **wheel** is a steering-wheel-type input device that you turn to simulate driving a car, truck, or other vehicle. Most wheels also include foot pedals for acceleration and braking actions. Joysticks and wheels typically attach via a cable to a personal computer or game console.

Light Guns

A **light gun** is used to shoot targets and moving objects after you pull the trigger on the weapon. Light guns typically attach via a cable to a game console or personal computer.

Dance Pads

A **dance pad** is a flat electronic device divided into panels that users press with their feet in response to instructions from a music video game. These games test the user's ability to step on the correct panel at the correct time, following a pattern that is synchronized with the rhythm or beat of a song. Dance pads communicate with a game console or a personal computer via wired or wireless technology.

Motion-Sensing Game Controllers

Motion-sensing game controllers allow the user to guide on-screen elements by moving a handheld input device in predetermined directions through the air. Sports games, for example, use motion-sensing game controllers, such as baseball bats and golf clubs, as their input device. These types of controllers communicate with a game console or a personal computer via wired or wireless technology.

A popular general-purpose, motion-sensing game controller is Nintendo's Wii Remote. Shaped like a television remote control and operated with one hand, the **Wii Remote** is a motion-sensing input device that uses Bluetooth wireless technology to communicate with the Wii game console. Users point the Wii Remote in different directions and rotate it to control on-screen players, vehicles, and other objects.

Touch-Sensitive Pads

The touch-sensitive pad on a portable media player is an input device that enables users to scroll through and play music, view pictures, watch videos or movies, adjust volume, and customize settings. Touch-sensitive pads typically contain buttons and/or wheels that are operated with a thumb or finger. For example, users rotate a **Click Wheel** to browse through its song, picture, or movie lists and press the Click Wheel's buttons to play or pause media, display a menu, and other actions (Figure 5-11).

WEB LINK 5-3

Wii Remote

For more information, visit scsite.com/dcf5e/ch5/weblink and then click Wii Remote.

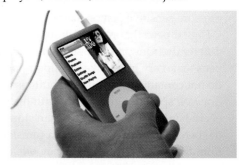

FIGURE 5-11   You use your thumb to rotate or press buttons on a Click Wheel.

Test your knowledge of pages 166 through 172 in Quiz Yourself 5-1.

 QUIZ YOURSELF 5-1

Instructions: Find the true statement below. Then, rewrite the remaining false statements so they are true.

1. A keyboard is an output device that contains keys users press to enter data and instructions into a computer.
2. A trackball is a small, flat, rectangular pointing device commonly found on notebook computers.
3. Input is any data and instructions entered into the memory of a computer.
4. An optical mouse has moving mechanical parts inside.
5. Many smart phones and other personal mobile devices use a pressure-sensitive digital pen, and Tablet PCs use a stylus.

Quiz Yourself Online: To further check your knowledge of the keyboard, the mouse and other pointing devices, and gaming and media player controllers, visit scsite.com/dcf5e/ch5/quiz and then click Objectives 1 – 2.

OTHER TYPES OF INPUT

In addition to the keyboard, mouse, and pointing devices just discussed, users have a variety of other options available to enter data and instructions into a computer. These include voice input; input for smart phones, PDAs, and Tablet PCs; digital cameras; video input; scanners and reading devices; terminals; and biometric input. Read Looking Ahead 5-1 for a look at the next generation of input devices.

Voice Input

Voice input is the process of entering input by speaking into a microphone. Uses of voice input include instant messaging that supports voice conversations, chat rooms that support voice chats, VoIP, and voice recognition. Recall that VoIP (Voice over IP) enables users to speak to other users over the Internet. **Voice recognition**, also called **speech recognition**, is the computer's capability of distinguishing spoken words. Voice recognition programs recognize a vocabulary of preprogrammed words. The vocabulary of voice recognition programs can range from two words to millions of words.

LOOKING AHEAD 5-1

Controlling Games by Thinking

Putting on your thinking cap one day may take on a whole new meaning for gamers. Scientists are envisioning a gamer wearing a baseball-cap device or a headband and then having a wireless connection with a computer.

One product uses tiny, metal sensors to detect brainwave activity without skin contact. Using special software, the wearer must calibrate his individual brainwaves with the computer by imagining moving his left or right hand or foot or rotating an object. Electrodes then pick up these thought signals. Once the person is in sync with the computer, he can imagine moving his hands or feet to trigger an action in the game.

Another gaming interface prototype uses three sensor pads embedded in a headband actuator to receive facial muscle activity, eye movement, and brain activity cues. Eleven specific signals then are assigned to a specific keystroke or mouse button.

The thought-controlled devices also could be used as communication tools for people who cannot speak or sign by translating their brainwave electrical impulses into letters and words. For more information, visit scsite.com/dcf5e/ch5/looking and then click Thought-Controlled Input.

AUDIO INPUT Voice input is part of a larger category of input called audio input. **Audio input** is the process of entering any sound into the computer such as speech, music, and sound effects. To enter high-quality sound into a personal computer, the computer must have a sound card. Users enter sound into a computer via devices such as microphones, tape players, CD/DVD players, or radios, each of which plugs in a port on the sound card.

Some users also enter music and other sound effects using external MIDI devices such as an electronic piano keyboard (Figure 5-12). MIDI (musical instrument digital interface) is the electronic music industry's standard that defines how digital musical devices represent sounds electronically. Software that conforms to the MIDI standard allows users to compose and edit music and many other sounds.

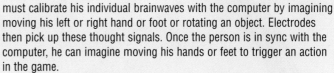

FIGURE 5-12 An electronic piano keyboard is an external MIDI device that allows users to record music, which can be stored in the computer.

Input for Smart Phones, PDAs, and Tablet PCs

Mobile devices, such as smart phones and PDAs, and mobile computers, such as the Tablet PC, offer convenience for the mobile user. A variety of alternatives for entering data and instructions is available for these devices and computers.

SMART PHONES   Users enter data and instructions into a smart phone using a variety of techniques (Figure 5-13). You can talk directly into the smart phone's microphone or into a Bluetooth headset that wirelessly communicates with the smart phone to receive audio. Some smart phones have digital cameras that take pictures and touch-sensitive pads that enable you to interact with media, such as music and pictures. Others can receive GPS signals to provide maps and directions to users and include card readers.

Some smart phones have a built-in mini keyboard. For those that do not, users can enter data and messages into the smart phone using its keypad. Types of messages users send with smart phones include text messages, instant messages, and picture/video messages.

obtain maps and directions on the phone by attaching this GPS receiver to your vehicle's window

speak into the microphone that wirelessly communicates with the phone

take a picture using the digital camera built into the phone

draw or write on special paper with a digital pen and then wirelessly transmit the message to the phone

transfer data and instructions to and from the computer and smart phone by connecting it to the computer with a cable

enter text-based messages via a wireless keyboard

store pictures taken with the phone's camera by inserting the memory card in the phone's card slot

FIGURE 5-13   Users input data into a smart phone using a variety of techniques.

PDAs A user enters data and instructions into a PDA in many ways. PDAs ship with a basic stylus, which is the primary input device (Figure 5-14). As with the smart phone, you can use the stylus to enter data in two ways: using an on-screen keyboard or using handwriting recognition software.

For users who prefer typing to handwriting, some PDAs have a built-in mini keyboard. For PDAs without a keyboard, users can purchase a keyboard that snaps on the bottom of the device. Other users type on a desktop computer or notebook computer keyboard and transfer the data to the PDA.

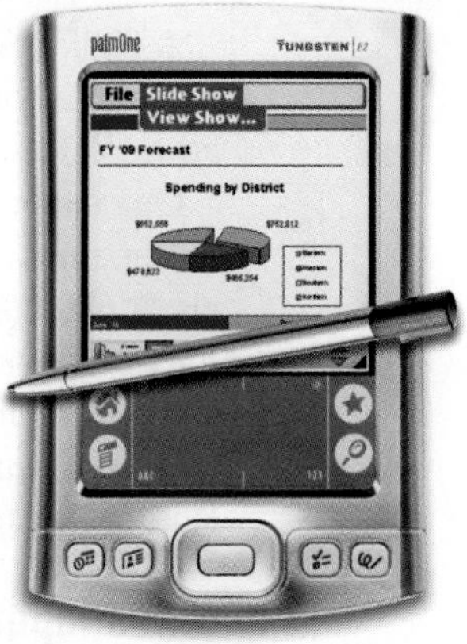

Because today's smart phones provide PDA functions, it is becoming increasingly difficult to differentiate between the two devices. This convergence trend has led manufacturers to refer to PDAs and/or smart phones simply as handhelds.

FIGURE 5-14 As shown in this figure, you can work with business software on a PDA.

TABLET PCs The primary input device for a Tablet PC is a pressure-sensitive digital pen, which allows users to write on the device's screen. Both the slate and convertible designs of a Tablet PC provide a means for keyboard input.

To access peripherals at their home or office, users can slide their Tablet PC in a docking station. A docking station, which is an external device that attaches to a mobile computer, contains a power connection and provides connections to peripherals and usually also includes slots for memory cards, CD/DVD drives, and other devices (Figure 5-15). The design of docking stations varies depending on the type of mobile computer or device to which they attach.

FIGURE 5-15 To use a slate Tablet PC while working at a desk, simply insert the Tablet PC in a docking station. Devices such as a keyboard and CD drive can be plugged in the docking station.

Digital Cameras

A **digital camera** allows users to take pictures and store the photographed images digitally, instead of on traditional film (Figure 5-16). Most digital cameras have some amount of internal flash memory to store images. Many also can store additional images on mobile storage media, including a flash memory card, memory stick, and mini disc.

Digital cameras typically allow users to review, and sometimes edit, images while they are in the camera. Some digital cameras can connect to or communicate wirelessly with a computer or printer, allowing users to print or view images directly from the camera. Most cameras can connect with a cable to a computer's USB port, so that you can use the computer to access the media in the camera just like you access any other drive on the computer.

Often users prefer to download, or transfer a copy of, the images from the digital camera to the computer's hard disk, where the images are available for editing with photo editing software, printing, faxing, sending via e-mail, including in another document, or posting to a Web site or photo community for everyone to see.

FIGURE 5-16 Users can view photographed images immediately through a small screen on the digital camera to see if the picture is worth keeping.

A digital camera often features flash, zoom, automatic focus, and special effects. Some allow users to record short audio narrations for photographed images. Others even record short video clips in addition to still images.

One factor that affects the quality of a digital camera is its resolution. **Resolution** is the number of horizontal and vertical pixels in a display device. A digital camera's resolution is defined in pixels. A **pixel** (short for picture element) is the smallest element in an electronic image. The greater the number of pixels the camera uses to capture an image, the better the quality of the image. Digital camera resolutions range from about 4 million to more than 16 million pixels (MP). For additional information about digital cameras, read the Digital Imaging and Video Technology feature that follows this chapter.

Video Input

Video input is the process of capturing full-motion images and storing them on a computer's storage medium such as a hard disk or DVD. Some video devices use analog video signals. A **digital video (DV) camera**, by contrast, records video as digital signals instead of analog signals. Many DV cameras have the capability of capturing still frames, as well as motion. To transfer recorded images to a hard disk or CD or DVD, users connect DV cameras directly to a USB port or a FireWire port on the system unit. After saving the video on a storage medium, such as a hard disk or DVD, you can play it or edit it using video editing software on a computer.

WEB CAMS A **Web cam**, also called a **PC video camera**, is a type of digital video camera that enables a home or small business user to capture video and still images, send e-mail messages with video attachments, add live images to instant messages, broadcast live images over the Internet, and make video telephone calls. During a **video telephone call**, both parties see each other as they communicate over the Internet (Figure 5-17). The cost of Web cams usually is less than $100.

Some Web cams display their output on a Web page. This use of a Web cam attracts Web site visitors by showing images that change regularly. Home or small business users might use Web cams to show a work in progress, weather and traffic information, employees at work, photos of a vacation, and countless other images.

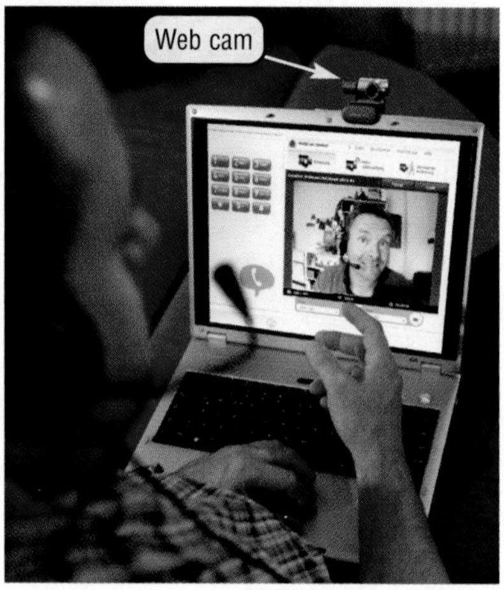

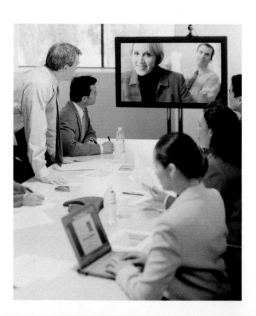

FIGURE 5-17 Using a Web cam, home users can see each other as they communicate over the Internet.

WEB LINK 5-4

Web Cams

For more information, visit scsite.com/dcf5e/ch5/weblink and then click Web Cams.

VIDEO CONFERENCING A **video conference** is a meeting between two or more geographically separated people who use a network or the Internet to transmit audio and video data (Figure 5-18). To participate in a video conference, you need video conferencing software along with a microphone, speakers, and a video camera attached to a computer. As you speak, members of the meeting hear your voice on their speakers. Any image in front of the video camera, such as a person's face, appears in a window on each participant's screen.

As the costs of video conferencing hardware and software decrease, increasingly more business meetings, corporate training, and educational classes will be conducted as video conferences.

FIGURE 5-18 To save on travel expenses, many large businesses are turning to video conferencing.

Scanners and Reading Devices

Some input devices save users time by capturing data directly from a source document, which is the original form of the data. Examples of source documents include time cards, order forms, invoices, paychecks, advertisements, brochures, photos, inventory tags, or any other document that contains data to be processed.

Devices that can capture data directly from a source document include optical scanners, optical readers, bar code readers, RFID readers, magnetic stripe card readers, and magnetic-ink character recognition readers.

OPTICAL SCANNERS   An optical scanner, usually called a **scanner**, is a light-sensing input device that reads printed text and graphics and then translates the results into a form the computer can process. A **flatbed scanner** works in a manner similar to a copy machine except it creates a file of the document in memory instead of a paper copy (Figure 5-19). Once you scan a picture or document, you can display the scanned object on the screen, modify its appearance, store it on a storage medium, print it, fax it, attach it to an e-mail message, include it in another document, or post it to a Web site or photo community for everyone to see.

Many scanners include OCR (optical character recognition) software, which can read and convert text documents into electronic files. OCR software converts a scanned image into a text file that can be edited, for example, with a word processing program.

FIGURE 5-19   A flatbed scanner.

OPTICAL READERS   An optical reader is a device that uses a light source to read characters, marks, and codes and then converts them into digital data that a computer can process. Two technologies used by optical readers are optical character recognition and optical mark recognition.

• **Optical character recognition** (OCR) involves reading typewritten, computer-printed, or hand-printed characters from ordinary documents and translating the images into a form the computer can process. Most **OCR devices** include a small optical scanner for reading characters and sophisticated software to analyze what is read. OCR devices range from large machines that can read thousands of documents per minute to handheld wands that read one document at a time.

Many companies use OCR characters on turnaround documents. A **turnaround document** is a document that you return (turn around) to the company that creates and sends it. For example, when consumers receive a bill, they often tear off a portion of the bill and send it back to the company with their payment (Figure 5-20). The portion of the bill they return usually has their payment amount, account number, and other information printed in OCR characters.

• **Optical mark recognition** (OMR) devices read hand-drawn marks such as small circles or rectangles. A person places these marks on a form, such as a test, survey, or questionnaire answer sheet.

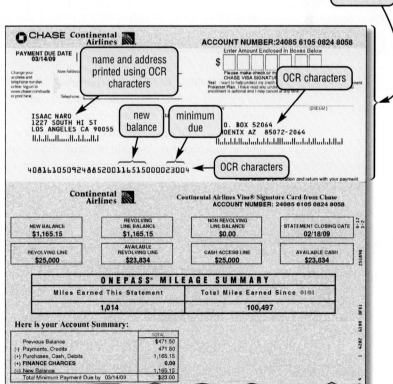

FIGURE 5-20   OCR characters frequently are used with turnaround documents. With this bill, you tear off the top portion and return it with a payment.

BAR CODE READERS   A **bar code reader**, also called a bar code scanner, is an optical reader that uses laser beams to read bar codes (Figure 5-21). A **bar code** is an identification code that consists either of a set of vertical lines and spaces of different widths or a two-dimensional pattern of dots, squares, and other images. A 2-D bar code can store much more data than the traditional linear bar code. The bar code represents data that identifies the manufacturer and the item.

Manufacturers print a bar code either on a product's package or on a label that is affixed to a product. Read Ethics & Issues 5-2 for a related discussion.

FIGURE 5-21   A bar code reader uses laser beams to read bar codes on products such as books and food.

RFID READERS   RFID (radio frequency identification) is a technology that uses radio signals to communicate with a tag placed in or attached to an object, an animal, or a person. RFID tags, which contain a memory chip and an antenna, are available in many shapes and sizes. An **RFID reader** reads information on the tag via radio waves. RFID readers can be handheld devices or mounted in a stationary object such as a doorway.

Many retailers see RFID as an alternative to bar code identification because it does not require direct contact or line-of-site transmission. Each product in a store would contain a tag that identifies the product (Figure 5-22). As consumers remove products from the store shelves and walk through a checkout area, an RFID reader reads the tag(s) and communicates with a computer that calculates the amount due.

Other uses of RFID include tracking times of runners in a marathon; tracking location of soldiers, employee wardrobes, airline baggage, and misplaced or stolen goods; checking lift tickets of skiers; managing inventory; gauging temperature and pressure of tires on a

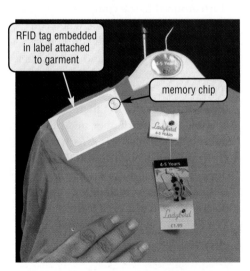

FIGURE 5-22   RFID readers read information stored on an RFID tag and then communicate this information to computers, which instantaneously compute payments and update inventory records. In this example, the RFID tag is embedded in a label attached to the garment.

vehicle; checking out library books; and tracking payment as vehicles pass through booths on tollway systems. Read Looking Ahead 5-2 for a look at the next generation of RFID.

MAGNETIC STRIPE CARD READERS

A **magnetic stripe card reader**, often called a magstripe reader, reads the magnetic stripe on the back of credit cards, entertainment cards, bank cards, and other similar cards. The stripe contains information identifying you and the card issuer (Figure 5-23). Some information stored in the stripe includes your name, account number, the card's expiration date, and a country code.

When a consumer swipes a credit card through a magstripe reader, it reads the information stored on the magnetic stripe on the card. If the magstripe reader rejects the card, it is possible that the magnetic stripe is scratched, dirty, or erased. Exposure to a magnet or magnetic field can erase the contents of a card's magnetic stripe.

MICR READERS

MICR (magnetic-ink character recognition) devices read text printed with magnetized ink. An **MICR reader** converts MICR characters into a form the computer can process. The banking industry almost exclusively uses MICR for check processing. Each check in your checkbook has precoded MICR characters beginning at the lower-left edge (Figure 5-24).

LOOKING AHEAD 5-2

Clothing, Appliances Show RFID Uses

New business and consumer applications for RFID tags are likely to continue as manufacturing costs continue to decline to as little as five cents per tag. Clothing, for example, could have a unique RFID tag embedded in the label. When you purchase apparel and then desire to return an item to the store for a refund, a clerk would scan the RFID tag and then reference a record of when you purchased the item, the original price, and the method of payment.

This same clothing tag automatically could tell your washing machine which settings to use to launder the fabric properly. It also could keep an inventory of which clothes are in your closet and which are at the dry cleaners or in the laundry basket.

Your refrigerator could monitor its contents and alert you when expiration dates are near. It also could create shopping lists and search the Internet to locate recipes that use items on hand. For more information, visit scsite.com/dcf5e/ch5/looking and then click RFID.

FIGURE 5-23 A magnetic stripe card reader reads information encoded on the stripe on the back of your credit card.

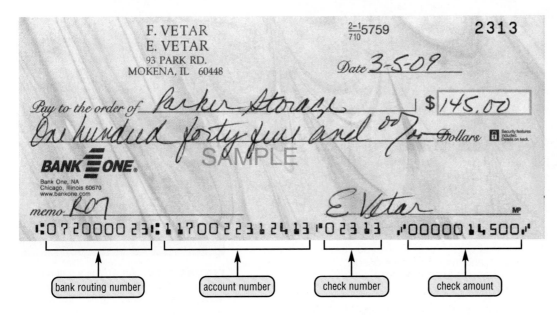

FIGURE 5-24
The MICR characters preprinted on the check represent the bank routing number, the customer account number, and the check number. The amount of the check in the lower-right corner is added after the check is cashed.

When a bank receives a check for payment, it uses an MICR inscriber to print the amount of the check in MICR characters in the lower-right corner. The check then is sorted or routed to the customer's bank, along with thousands of others. Each check is inserted in an MICR reader, which sends the check information — including the amount of the check — to a computer for processing.

Terminals

A **terminal** consists of a keyboard, a monitor, a video card, and memory. These components often are housed in a single unit. Users enter data and instructions into a terminal and then transmit some or all of the data over a network to a host computer.

Special-purpose terminals perform specific tasks and contain features uniquely designed for use in a particular industry. Two special-purpose terminals are point-of-sale (POS) terminals and automated teller machines.

- **Point-of-Sale (POS) Terminals** — The location in a retail or grocery store where a consumer pays for goods or services is the point of sale (POS). Most retail stores use a **POS terminal** to record purchases, process credit or debit cards, and update inventory.

  Many POS terminals handle credit card or debit card payments and thus also include a magstripe reader. Some have fingerprint readers (discussed in the next section) that read your fingerprint, which is linked to a payment method such as a checking account or credit card. Once the transaction is approved, the terminal prints a receipt for the customer. A self-service POS terminal allows consumers to perform all checkout-related activities (Figure 5-25). That is, they scan the items, bag the items, and pay for the items themselves.

- **Automated Teller Machines** — An **automated teller machine** (**ATM**) is a self-service banking machine that connects to a host computer through a network (Figure 5-26). Banks place ATMs in convenient locations, including grocery stores, convenience stores, retail outlets, shopping malls, and gas stations.

  Using an ATM, people withdraw cash, deposit money, transfer funds, or inquire about an account balance. Some ATMs have a touch screen; others have special buttons or keypads for entering input. To access a bank account, you insert a plastic bankcard in the ATM's magstripe reader. The ATM asks you to enter a password, called a personal identification number (PIN), which verifies that you are the holder of the bankcard. When your transaction is complete, the ATM prints a receipt for your records.

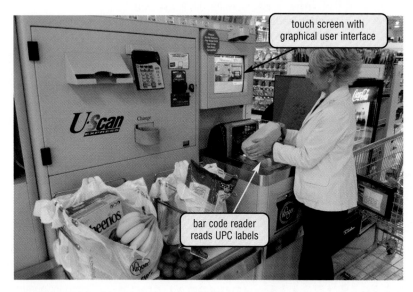

FIGURE 5-25   Many grocery stores offer self-serve checkouts, where the consumers themselves use the POS terminals to scan purchases, scan their store saver card and coupons, and then pay for the goods.

FIGURE 5-26   An ATM is a self-service banking terminal that allows customers to access their bank accounts.

Biometric Input

Biometrics is the technology of authenticating a person's identity by verifying a personal characteristic. Biometric devices grant users access to programs, systems, or rooms by analyzing some physiological (related to physical or chemical activities in the body) or behavioral characteristic. Examples include fingerprints, hand geometry, facial features, voice, signatures, and eye patterns.

WEB LINK 5-5

Biometric Input

For more information, visit scsite.com/dcf5e/ch5/weblink and then click Biometric Input.

The most widely used biometric device today is a fingerprint reader. A **fingerprint reader** captures curves and indentations of a fingerprint. To save on desk space, some newer keyboards and notebook computers have a fingerprint reader built into them, which allows users to log on to programs and Web sites via their fingerprint instead of entering a user name and password (Figure 5-27). Grocery and retail stores now use fingerprint readers as a means of payment, where the customer's fingerprint is linked to a payment method such as a checking account or credit card.

A face recognition system captures a live face image and compares it with a stored image to determine if the person is a legitimate user. Some buildings use face recognition systems to secure access to rooms. Law enforcement, surveillance systems, and airports use face recognition to protect the public.

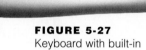

FIGURE 5-27
Keyboard with built-in fingerprint reader.

Biometric devices measure the shape and size of a person's hand using a hand geometry system. Because their cost is more than $1,000, larger companies typically use these systems as time and attendance devices or as security devices.

A voice verification system compares a person's live speech with their stored voice pattern. Larger organizations sometimes use voice verification systems as time and attendance devices. Many companies also use this technology for access to sensitive files and networks.

A signature verification system recognizes the shape of your handwritten signature, as well as measures the pressure exerted and the motion used to write the signature. Signature verification systems use a specialized pen and tablet.

High security areas use iris recognition systems. The camera in an iris recognition system uses iris recognition technology to read patterns in the iris of the eye (Figure 5-28). These patterns are as unique as a fingerprint. Iris recognition systems are quite expensive and are used by government security organizations, the military, and financial institutions that deal with highly sensitive data. Some organizations use retinal scanners, which work similarly but instead scan patterns of blood vessels in the back of the retina.

Sometimes, fingerprint, iris, retina, and other biometric data are stored on a smart card. A **smart card**, which is comparable in size to a credit card or ATM card, stores the personal data on a thin microprocessor that is embedded in the card.

FIGURE 5-28 An iris recognition system.

Test your knowledge of pages 173 through 181 in Quiz Yourself 5-2.

QUIZ YOURSELF 5-2

Instructions: Find the true statement below. Then, rewrite the remaining false statements so they are true.

1. A digital camera allows users to take pictures and store the photographed images digitally, instead of on traditional film.
2. A fingerprint reader captures curves and indentations of a signature.
3. After swiping a credit card through an MICR reader, it reads the information stored on the magnetic stripe on the card.
4. Instant messaging is the computer's capability of distinguishing spoken words.
5. Many smart phones today have POS capabilities.
6. RFID is a technology that uses laser signals to communicate with a tag placed in an object, an animal, or a person.

Quiz Yourself Online: To further check your knowledge of voice input; input devices for smart phones, PDAs, and Tablet PCs; digital cameras; video input; scanners and reading devices; terminals; and biometric devices, visit scsite.com/dcf5e/ch5/quiz and then click Objective 3.

WHAT IS OUTPUT?

Output is data that has been processed into a useful form. That is, computers process data (input) into information (output). Users view or watch output on a screen, print it, or hear it through speakers, headphones, or earphones. While working with a computer, a user encounters four basic categories of output: text, graphics, audio, and video (Figure 5-29). Very often, a single form of output, such as a Web page, includes more than one of these categories.

An **output device** is any hardware component that conveys information to one or more people. Commonly used output devices include display devices; printers; speakers, headphones, and earphones; fax machines and fax modems; multifunction peripherals; data projectors; and interactive whiteboards.

FIGURE 5-29   Four categories of output are text, graphics, audio, and video.

DISPLAY DEVICES

A **display device** is an output device that visually conveys text, graphics, and video information. Desktop computers typically use a monitor as their display device. A **monitor** is a display device that is packaged as a separate peripheral. Some monitors have a tilt-and-swivel base that allows users to adjust the angle of the screen to minimize neck strain and reduce glare from overhead lighting. With some, you can rotate the screen. Monitor controls permit users to adjust the brightness, contrast, positioning, height, and width of images.

Most mobile computers and devices integrate the display and other components into the same physical case.

Display devices usually show text, graphics, and video information in color. Some, however, are monochrome. Monochrome means the information appears in one color (such as white, amber, green, black, blue, or gray) on a different color background (such as black or grayish-white). Some mobile devices use monochrome displays because they require less battery power.

Types of display devices include LCD monitors and LCD screens, plasma monitors, and CRT monitors. The following pages discuss each of these display devices.

LCD Monitors and LCD Screens

An **LCD monitor**, also called a flat panel monitor, is a desktop monitor that uses a liquid crystal display to produce images (Figure 5-30). These monitors produce sharp, flicker-free images. LCD monitors have a small footprint; that is, they do not take up much desk space. LCD monitors are available in a variety of sizes, with the more common being 17, 19, 20, 22, and 27 inches — some are 45 or 65 inches. Many are widescreen, which are much wider than they are tall. You measure a monitor the same way you measure a television, that is, diagonally from one corner to the other.

Mobile computers, such as notebook computers and Tablet PCs, and mobile devices, such as Ultra-Mobile PCs, portable media players, and smart phones often have built-in LCD screens (Figure 5-31). Notebook computer screens are available in a variety of sizes, with the more common being 14.1, 15.4, 17, and 20.1 inches. Tablet PC screens range from 8.4 inches to 14.1 inches. Typical screen sizes of Ultra-Mobile PCs are 5 inches to 7 inches. Portable media players usually have screen sizes from 1.5 inches to 3.5 inches. On smart phones, screen sizes range from 2.5 inches to 3.5 inches.

FIGURE 5-30
A widescreen LCD monitor.

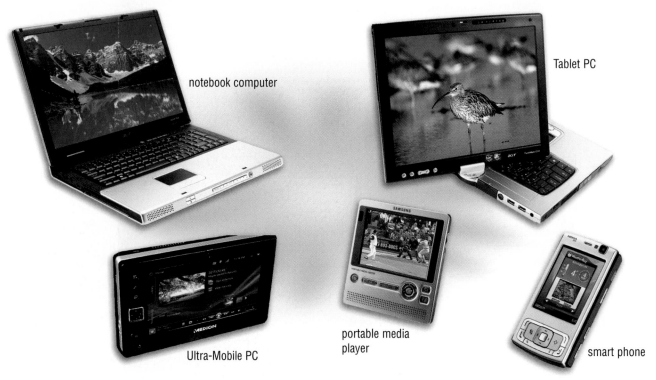

notebook computer

Tablet PC

Ultra-Mobile PC

portable media player

smart phone

FIGURE 5-31 Many people use their notebook computers, Tablet PCs, Ultra-Mobile PCs, portable media players, and smart phones to view pictures or watch videos and movies.

LCD TECHNOLOGY AND **Q**UALITY   A **liquid crystal display** (**LCD**) uses a liquid compound to present information on a display device. Computer LCDs typically contain fluorescent tubes that emit light waves toward the liquid-crystal cells, which are sandwiched between two sheets of material.

The quality of an LCD monitor or LCD screen depends primarily on its resolution, response time, brightness, dot pitch, and contrast ratio.

- Resolution is the number of horizontal and vertical pixels in a display device. For example, a monitor that has a 1440 × 900 resolution displays up to 1440 pixels per horizontal row and 900 pixels per vertical row, for a total of 1,296,000 pixels to create a screen image. A higher resolution uses a greater number of pixels and thus provides a smoother, sharper, and clearer image. As the resolution increases, however, some items on the screen appear smaller.

  With LCD monitors and screens, resolution generally is proportional to the size of the device. That is, the resolution increases for larger monitors and screens. For example, a widescreen 19-inch LCD monitor typically has a resolution of 1440 × 900, while a widescreen 22-inch LCD monitor has a resolution of 1680 × 1050. LCDs are geared for a specific resolution.

- Response time of an LCD monitor or screen is the time in milliseconds (ms) that it takes to turn a pixel on or off. LCD monitors' and screens' response times range from 3 to 16 ms. The lower the number, the faster the response time.

- Brightness of an LCD monitor or LCD screen is measured in nits. A nit is a unit of visible light intensity. The higher the nits, the brighter the images.

- Dot pitch, sometimes called pixel pitch, is the distance in millimeters between pixels on a display device. Average dot pitch on LCD monitors and screens should be .30 mm or lower. The lower the number, the sharper the image.

- Contrast ratio describes the difference in light intensity between the brightest white and darkest black that can be displayed on an LCD monitor. Contrast ratios today range from 500:1 to 2000:1. Higher contrast ratios represent colors better.

WEB LINK 5-6

Widescreen LCD Monitors

For more information, visit scsite.com/ dcf5e/ch5/weblink and then click Widescreen LCD Monitors.

PORTS AND **LCD M**ONITORS   A cable on a monitor plugs in a port on the system unit. LCD monitors use a digital signal to produce a picture. To display the highest quality images, an LCD monitor should plug in a DVI or an HDMI port. A DVI (Digital Video Interface) port enables digital signals to transmit directly to an LCD monitor. An HDMI (High-Definition Media Interface) port combines DVI with high-definition (HD) television and video.

Plasma Monitors

A **plasma monitor** is a display device that uses gas plasma technology, which sandwiches a layer of gas between two glass plates (Figure 5-32).

Plasma monitors offer screen sizes up to 60 inches wide and richer colors than LCD monitors but are more expensive. Like LCD monitors, plasma monitors can hang directly on a wall.

FIGURE 5-32 Large plasma monitors can measure more than 60 inches wide.

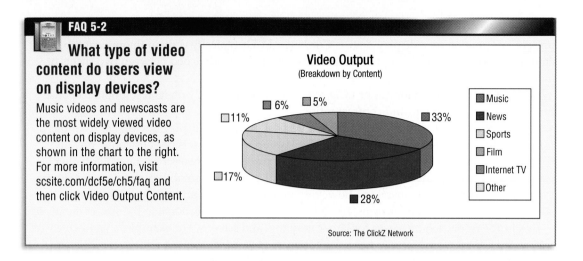

What type of video content do users view on display devices?

Music videos and newscasts are the most widely viewed video content on display devices, as shown in the chart to the right. For more information, visit scsite.com/dcf5e/ch5/faq and then click Video Output Content.

Video Output
(Breakdown by Content)

6%　5%　11%　33%　17%　28%

Music　News　Sports　Film　Internet TV　Other

Source: The ClickZ Network

CRT Monitors

A **CRT monitor** is a desktop monitor that contains a cathode-ray tube (Figure 5-33). A cathode-ray tube (CRT) is a large, sealed glass tube. The front of the tube is the screen.

CRT monitors for desktop computers are available in various sizes, with the more common being 15, 17, 19, 21, and 22 inches. In addition to monitor size, advertisements also list a CRT monitor's viewable size. The viewable size is the diagonal measurement of the actual viewing area provided by the screen in the CRT monitor. A 21-inch monitor, for example, may have a viewable size of 20 inches.

A CRT monitor usually costs less than an LCD monitor but also generates more heat and uses more power than an LCD monitor. To help reduce the amount of electricity used by monitors and other computer components, the United States Department of Energy (DOE) and the United States Environmental Protection Agency (EPA) developed the **ENERGY STAR program**. This program encourages manufacturers to create energy-efficient devices that require little power when the devices are not in use. Monitors and devices that meet ENERGY STAR guidelines display an ENERGY STAR label.

FIGURE 5-33 The core of a CRT monitor is a cathode-ray tube.

CRT monitors produce a small amount of electromagnetic radiation. Electromagnetic radiation (EMR) is a magnetic field that travels at the speed of light. Excessive amounts of EMR can pose a health risk. To be safe, all high-quality CRT monitors comply with a set of standards that defines acceptable levels of EMR for a monitor. To protect yourself even further, sit at arm's length from the CRT monitor because EMR travels only a short distance.

Test your knowledge of pages 182 through 187 in Quiz Yourself 5-3.

QUIZ YOURSELF 5-3

Instructions: Find the true statement below. Then, rewrite the remaining false statements so they are true.

1. A lower resolution uses a greater number of pixels and thus provides a smoother image.

2. An output device is any type of software component that conveys information to one or more people.

3. LCD monitors have a larger footprint than CRT monitors.

4. You measure a monitor diagonally from one corner to the other.

Quiz Yourself Online: To further check your knowledge of LCD monitors, LCD screens, and CRT monitors, visit scsite.com/dcf5e/ch5/quiz and then click Objective 4.

PRINTERS

A **printer** is an output device that produces text and graphics on a physical medium such as paper or transparency film. Many different printers exist with varying speeds, capabilities, and printing methods. Figure 5-34 presents a list of questions to help you decide on the printer best suited to your needs.

The following pages discuss producing printed output and the various printer types including ink-jet printers, photo printers, laser printers, thermal printers, mobile printers, plotters, and large format printers.

1. What is my budget?
2. How fast must my printer print?
3. Do I need a color printer?
4. What is the cost per page for printing?
5. Do I need multiple copies of documents?
6. Will I print graphics?
7. Do I want to print photos?
8. Do I want to print directly from a memory card or other type of miniature storage media?
9. What types of paper does the printer use?
10. What sizes of paper does the printer accept?
11. Do I want to print on both sides of the paper?
12. How much paper can the printer tray hold?
13. Will the printer work with my computer and software?
14. How much do supplies such as ink, toner, and paper cost?
15. Can the printer print on envelopes and transparencies?
16. How many envelopes can the printer print at a time?
17. How much do I print now, and how much will I be printing in a year or two?
18. Will the printer be connected to a network?
19. Do I want wireless printing capability?

FIGURE 5-34   Questions to ask when purchasing a printer.

Producing Printed Output

Although many users today print by connecting a computer to a printer with a cable, a variety of printing options are available as shown in Figure 5-35.

Today, wireless printing technology makes the task of printing from a notebook computer, Tablet PC, smart phone, or digital camera much easier. Two wireless technologies for printing are Bluetooth and infrared. With Bluetooth printing, a computer or other device transmits output to a printer via radio waves. With infrared printing, a printer communicates with a computer or other device using infrared light waves.

Instead of downloading images from a digital camera to a computer, users can print images using a variety of other techniques. Some cameras connect directly to a printer via a cable. Others store images on media cards that can be removed and inserted in the printer. Some printers have a docking station, into which the user inserts the camera to print pictures stored in the camera.

Finally, many home and business users print to a central printer on a network. Their computer may communicate with the network printer via cables or wirelessly.

WEB LINK 5-7

**Printing
Wirelessly**

For more information, visit scsite.com/dcf5e/ch5/weblink and then click Printing Wirelessly.

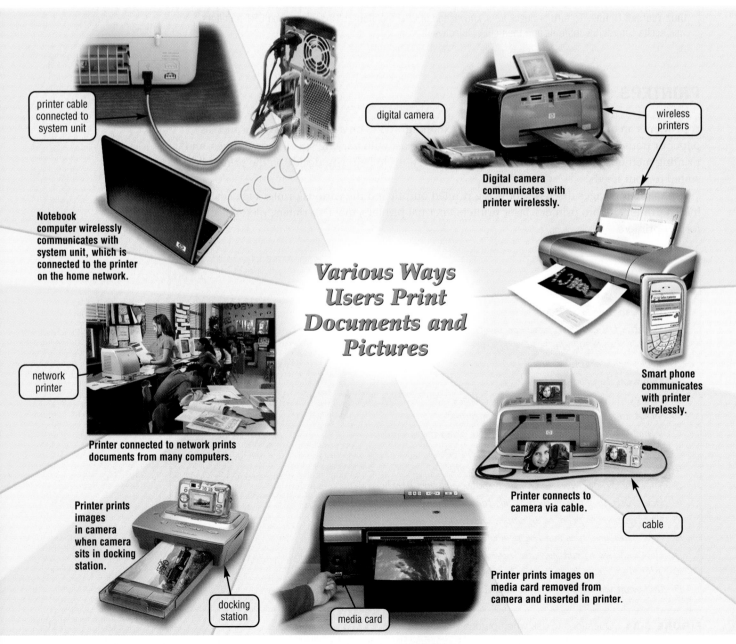

printer cable connected to system unit

digital camera

wireless printers

Digital camera communicates with printer wirelessly.

Notebook computer wirelessly communicates with system unit, which is connected to the printer on the home network.

Various Ways Users Print Documents and Pictures

network printer

Smart phone communicates with printer wirelessly.

Printer connected to network prints documents from many computers.

Printer connects to camera via cable.

cable

Printer prints images in camera when camera sits in docking station.

docking station

media card

Printer prints images on media card removed from camera and inserted in printer.

FIGURE 5-35   Users print documents and pictures using a variety of printing methods.

Nonimpact Printers

A **nonimpact printer** forms characters and graphics on a piece of paper without actually striking the paper. Some nonimpact printers spray ink, while others use heat or pressure to create images. Commonly used nonimpact printers are ink-jet printers, photo printers, laser printers, thermal printers, mobile printers, plotters, and large-format printers.

Ink-Jet Printers

An **ink-jet printer** is a type of nonimpact printer that forms characters and graphics by spraying tiny drops of liquid ink onto a piece of paper. Ink-jet printers have become a popular type of color printer for use in the home. Ink-jet printers produce text and graphics in both black-and-white and color on a variety of paper types (Figure 5-36). A reasonable quality ink-jet printer costs less than $100.

As with many other input and output devices, one factor that determines the quality of an ink-jet printer is its resolution. Printer resolution is measured by the number of dots per inch (dpi) a printer can print. Most ink-jet printers can print from 1200 to 4800 dpi.

The speed of an ink-jet printer is measured by the number of pages per minute (ppm) it can print. Most ink-jet printers print from 12 to 36 ppm. Graphics and colors print at a slower rate.

FIGURE 5-36 Ink-jet printers are a popular type of color printer used in the home.

The print head mechanism in an ink-jet printer contains ink-filled print cartridges. Each cartridge has fifty to several hundred small ink holes, or nozzles. The ink propels through any combination of the nozzles to form a character or image on the paper. When the print cartridge runs out of ink, you simply replace the cartridge. Most ink-jet printers have two or more print cartridges: one containing black ink and the other(s) containing colors. Consider the number of ink cartridges a printer requires, along with the cost of the cartridges, when purchasing a printer.

Photo Printers

A **photo printer** is a color printer that produces photo-lab-quality pictures (Figure 5-37). Some photo printers print just one or two sizes of images, for example, 3 × 5 inches and 4 × 6 inches. Others print up to letter size, legal size, or even larger. Many photo printers use ink-jet technology. With models that can print letter-sized documents, users connect the photo printer to their computer and use it for all their printing needs. Read Looking Ahead 5-3 for a look at the next generation of paper.

Most photo printers are PictBridge enabled, so that you can print pictures without a computer. **PictBridge** is a standard technology that allows you to print pictures directly from a digital camera by connecting a cable from the digital camera to a USB port on the printer.

prints 4 × 6, 5 × 7, 8 × 10, 8½ × 11, and panoramic sizes

FIGURE 5-37   Photo printers print in a range of sizes.

Photo printers also usually have a built-in card slot(s) so that the printer can print digital photos directly from a media card. That is, you do not need to transfer the images from the media card to the computer to print them. Some photo printers have built-in LCD color screens, allowing users to view and enhance the pictures before printing them.

Laser Printers

A **laser printer** is a high-speed, high-quality nonimpact printer (Figure 5-38). Laser printers for personal computers ordinarily use individual sheets of paper stored in one or more removable trays that slide in the printer case.

Laser printers print text and graphics in high-quality resolutions, usually ranging from 1200 to 2400 dpi. While laser printers usually cost more than ink-jet printers, many models are available at affordable prices for the home user. Laser printers usually print at faster speeds than ink-jet printers. A laser printer for the home and small office user typically prints black-and-white text at speeds of 12 to 37 ppm. Color laser printers print 8 to 35 ppm. Laser printers for large business users print more than 150 ppm.

Depending on the quality, speed, and type of laser printer, the cost ranges from a few hundred to a few thousand dollars for the home and small office user, and several hundred thousand dollars for the large business user. Color laser printers are slightly higher priced than otherwise equivalent black-and-white laser printers.

Operating in a manner similar to a copy machine, a laser printer creates images using a laser beam and powdered ink, called toner. Black-and-white laser printers use one toner cartridge. Color laser printers use multiple cartridges — one for black and one or more for colors. When the toner runs out, you replace the toner cartridge.

WEB LINK 5-9

Laser Printers

For more information, visit scsite.com/dcf5e/ch5/weblink and then click Laser Printers.

black-and-white laser printer

color laser printer

FIGURE 5-38   Laser printers are available in both black-and-white and color models.

 FAQ 5-3

How do I dispose of toner cartridges?

Do not throw them in the garbage. The housing contains iron, metal, and aluminum that is not biodegradable. The ink toner inside the cartridges contains toxic chemicals that pollute water and soil if discarded in dumps. Instead, recycle empty toner cartridges. Recycling programs in which some schools and organizations participate offer discounts or cash to customers who bring in depleted cartridges. If you are unable to find a recycling program in your area, contact your printer manufacturer to see if it has a recycling program. For more information, visit scsite.com/dcf5e/ch5/faq and then click Recycling Toner Cartridges.

Thermal Printers

A **thermal printer** generates images by pushing electrically heated pins against heat-sensitive paper. Basic thermal printers are inexpensive, but the print quality is low and the images tend to fade over time. Self-service gas pumps often print gas receipts using a built-in lower-quality thermal printer. Many point-of-sale terminals in retail and grocery stores also print purchase receipts on thermal paper.

Some thermal printers have high print quality. A dye-sublimation printer, sometimes called a digital photo printer, uses heat to transfer colored dye to specially coated paper. Professional applications requiring high image quality, such as photography studios, medical labs, and security identification systems, use dye-sublimation printers. These high-end printers cost thousands of dollars and print images in a wide range of sizes.

Dye-sublimation printers for the home or small business user, by contrast, typically print images in only one or two sizes and are much slower than their professional counterparts. These lower-end dye-sublimation printers are comparable in cost to a photo printer based on ink-jet technology (Figure 5-39).

FIGURE 5-39   The printer shown in this figure uses dye-sublimation technology to create photographic-quality output for the home or small office user.

Mobile Printers

A **mobile printer** is a small, lightweight, battery-powered printer that allows a mobile user to print from a notebook computer, Tablet PC, or smart phone or other personal mobile device while traveling (Figure 5-40). Barely wider than the paper on which they print, mobile printers fit easily in a brief-case alongside a notebook computer. Mobile printers mainly use ink-jet or thermal technology.

Plotters and Large-Format Printers

Plotters are sophisticated printers used to produce high-quality drawings such as blueprints, maps, and circuit diagrams. These printers are used in special-ized fields such as engineering and drafting and usually are very costly.

Using ink-jet printer technology, but on a much larger scale, a **large-format printer** creates photo-realistic-quality color prints. Graphic artists use these high-cost, high-performance printers for signs, posters, and other professional quality displays (Figure 5-41).

FIGURE 5-40
A mobile printer.

FIGURE 5-41   Graphic artists use large-format printers to print signs, posters, and other professional quality displays.

Impact Printers

An **impact printer** forms characters and graphics on a piece of paper by striking a mechanism against an inked ribbon that physically contacts the paper. Impact printers are ideal for printing multipart forms because they easily print through many layers of paper. Two commonly used types of impact printers are dot-matrix printers and line printers.

A **dot-matrix printer** is an impact printer that produces printed images when tiny wire pins on a print head mechanism strike an inked ribbon (Figure 5-42). When the ribbon presses against the paper, it creates dots that form characters and graphics.

Dot-matrix printers typically use continuous-form paper, in which thousands of sheets of paper are connected together end to end. The pages have holes along the sides to help feed the paper through the printer. The speed of most dot-matrix printers ranges from 375 to 1100 characters per second (cps), depending on the desired print quality.

A **line printer** is a high-speed impact printer that prints an entire line at a time. The speed of a line printer is measured by the number of lines per minute (lpm) it can print. Some line printers print as many as 3,000 lpm.

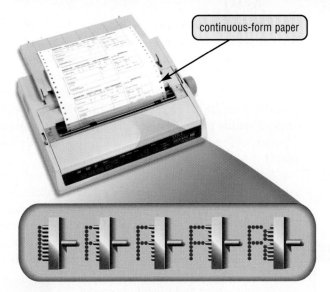

FIGURE 5-42 A dot-matrix printer produces printed images when tiny pins strike an inked ribbon.

OTHER OUTPUT DEVICES

In addition to monitors and printers, other output devices are available for specific uses and applications. These include speakers, headphones, and earphones; fax machines and fax modems; multifunction peripherals; data projectors; and interactive whiteboards.

Speakers, Headphones, and Earphones

An **audio output device** is a component of a computer that produces music, speech, or other sounds, such as beeps. Three commonly used audio output devices are speakers, headphones, and earphones.

Most personal computers have a small internal speaker that usually emits only low-quality sound. Thus, many personal computer users attach surround sound **speakers** or speaker systems to their computers to generate higher-quality sounds (Figure 5-43). Most surround sound computer speaker systems include one or two center speakers and two or more satellite speakers that are positioned so that sound emits from all directions. Speakers typically have tone and volume controls, allowing users to adjust settings. To boost the low bass sounds, surround sound speaker systems also include a subwoofer. In many cases, a cable connects the speakers or the subwoofer to a port on the sound card. With wireless speakers, however, a transmitter connects to the sound card, which wirelessly communicates with the speakers.

Many users opt for a wireless music system, where you can play any CD, DVD, or media file on your computer and transmit the audio to a home or office stereo or television. You also can plug a portable media player, such as an iPod, into the computer to hear its songs on the stereo or television speakers.

FIGURE 5-43 Most personal computer users attach high-quality surround sound speaker systems to their computers.

In a computer laboratory or other crowded environment, speakers might not be practical. Instead, users can plug headphones or earphones in a port on the sound card, in a speaker, or in the front of the system unit. With headphones or earphones, only the individual wearing the headphones or earphones hears the sound from the computer. The difference is that **headphones** cover or are placed outside of the ear, whereas **earphones**, or **earbuds**, rest inside the ear canal.

Portable media players usually include a set of earphones. As an alternative, you can listen to audio from the portable media player through speakers in a vehicle or on a stereo system at home or work. Or, you can purchase speakers specifically designed to play audio from a portable media player.

Electronically produced voice output is growing in popularity. **Voice output** occurs when you hear a person's voice or when the computer talks to you through the speakers on the computer. In some programs, the computer can speak the contents of a document through voice output. On the Web, you can listen to (or download and then listen to) interviews, talk shows, sporting events, news, recorded music, and live concerts from many radio and television stations. Some Web sites and programs, such as media players, dedicate themselves to providing voice output, such as those that allow you to listen to and then purchase and download songs. VoIP allows users to speak and listen to others over the Internet using their computer or mobile device.

Fax Machines and Fax Modems

A **fax machine** is a device that codes and encodes documents so that they can be transmitted over telephone lines (Figure 5-44). The documents can contain text, drawings, or photos, or can be handwritten. The term fax refers to a document that you send or receive via a fax machine.

Many computers include fax capability by using a fax modem. A fax modem transmits computer-prepared documents, such as a word processing letter, or documents that have been digitized with a scanner or digital camera. A fax modem transmits these faxes to a fax machine or to another fax modem.

FIGURE 5-44   A stand-alone fax machine.

Multifunction Peripherals

A **multifunction peripheral** is a single device that looks like a copy machine but provides the functionality of a printer, scanner, copy machine, and perhaps a fax machine (Figure 5-45). Some use color ink-jet printer technology, while others include a black-and-white or color laser printer. An advantage of these devices is they are significantly less expensive than if you purchase each device separately. If the device breaks down, however, you lose all four functions, which is the primary disadvantage.

FIGURE 5-45   This multifunction peripheral is a color printer, scanner, copy machine, and fax machine.

Data Projectors

A **data projector** is a device that takes the text and images displaying on a computer screen and projects them on a larger screen so that an audience can see the image clearly. Some data projectors are large devices that attach to a ceiling or wall in an auditorium. Others, designed for the mobile user, are small portable devices that can be transported easily (Figure 5-46).

computer

data projector

FIGURE 5-46 Data projectors can produce sharp, bright images.

Interactive Whiteboards

An **interactive whiteboard** is a touch-sensitive device, resembling a dry-erase board, that displays the image on a connected computer screen. A presenter controls the computer program by clicking a remote control, touching the whiteboard, drawing on or erasing the whiteboard with a special digital pen and eraser, or writing on a special tablet. Notes written on the interactive whiteboard can be saved directly on the computer. Interactive whiteboards are used frequently in classrooms as a teaching tool (Figure 5-47), during meetings as a collaboration tool, and to enhance delivery of presentations.

Interactive whiteboards, which are hung on the wall or mounted on a stand, range in size from 48 to 94 inches. A widely used interactive whiteboard is the SMART Board.

FIGURE 5-47 Teachers and students can write directly on an interactive whiteboard, or they can write on a wireless slate that communicates with the whiteboard.

PUTTING IT ALL TOGETHER

Many factors influence the type of input and output devices you should use: the type of input and output desired, the hardware and software in use, and the anticipated cost. Figure 5-48 outlines several suggested input and output devices for various types of computer users.

SUGGESTED INPUT AND OUTPUT DEVICES BY USER

User	Input Device	Output Device
HOME 	• Enhanced keyboard or ergonomic keyboard • Mouse • Stylus for smart phone or other personal mobile device • Game controller • Color scanner • 4-megapixel digital camera • Headphones that include a microphone • Web cam • Fingerprint reader	• 17- or 19-inch color LCD monitor, or 17-inch LCD screen on notebook computer • Ink-jet color printer; or • Photo printer • Speakers • Headphones or earphones
SMALL OFFICE/ HOME OFFICE	• Enhanced keyboard or ergonomic keyboard • Mouse • Stylus and portable keyboard for smart phone or other personal mobile device, or digital pen for Tablet PC • Color scanner • 5-megapixel digital camera • Headphones that include a microphone • Web cam	• 19- or 22-inch LCD monitor • LCD screen on Tablet PC, smart phone, or other personal mobile device • Multifunction peripheral; or • Ink-jet color printer; or • Laser printer (black-and-white or color) • Fax machine • Speakers
MOBILE	• Wireless mouse for notebook computer • Touchpad or pointing stick on notebook computer • Stylus and portable keyboard for smart phone or other personal mobile device, or digital pen for Tablet PC • 4- or 5-megapixel digital camera • Headphones that include a microphone • Fingerprint reader for notebook computer	• 17-inch LCD screen on notebook computer • LCD screen on smart phone or other personal mobile device • Mobile color printer • Ink-jet color printer; or • Laser printer, for in-office use (black-and-white or color) • Photo printer • Fax modem • Headphones or earphones • Data projector
POWER	• Enhanced keyboard or ergonomic keyboard • Mouse • Stylus and portable keyboard for smart phone or other personal mobile device • Pen for graphics tablet • Color scanner • 6- to 12-megapixel digital camera • Headphones that include a microphone • Web cam	• 27-inch LCD monitor • Laser printer (black-and-white or color) • Plotter or large-format printer; or • Photo printer; or • Dye-sublimation printer • Fax machine or fax modem • Speakers • Headphones or earphones
LARGE BUSINESS	• Enhanced keyboard or ergonomic keyboard • Mouse • Stylus and portable keyboard for smart phone or other personal mobile device, or digital pen for Tablet PC • Touch screen • Light pen • Color scanner • 6- to 12-megapixel digital camera • OCR/OMR readers, bar code readers, or MICR reader • Microphone • Video camera for video conferences • Fingerprint reader or other biometric device	• 19- or 22-inch LCD monitor • LCD screen on Tablet PC, smart phone, or other personal mobile device • High-speed laser printer • Laser printer, color • Line printer (for large reports from a mainframe) • Fax machine or fax modem • Speakers • Headphones or earphones • Data projector • Interactive whiteboard

FIGURE 5-48   This table recommends suggested input and output devices for various types of users.

INPUT AND OUTPUT DEVICES FOR PHYSICALLY CHALLENGED USERS

The ever-increasing presence of computers in everyone's lives has generated an awareness of the need to address computing requirements for those who have or may develop physical limitations. The **Americans with Disabilities Act (ADA)** requires any company with 15 or more employees to make reasonable attempts to accommodate the needs of physically challenged workers. Read Ethics and Issues 5-3 for a related discussion.

Besides voice recognition, which is ideal for blind or visually impaired users, several other input devices are available. Users with limited hand mobility who want to use a keyboard have several options. Keyboards with larger keys are available. Still another option is the on-screen keyboard, in which a graphic of a standard keyboard is displayed on the user's screen. As the user clicks letters on the on-screen keyboard, they appear in the document at the location of the insertion point. An option for people with limited hand movement is a head-mounted pointer to control the pointer or insertion point (Figure 5-49). To simulate the functions of a mouse button, a user works with switches that control the pointer. The switch might be a hand pad, a foot pedal, a receptor that detects facial motions, or a pneumatic instrument controlled by puffs of air.

For users with mobility, hearing, or vision disabilities, many different types of output devices are available. Hearing-impaired users, for example, can instruct programs to display words instead of sounds.

Visually impaired users can change Windows Vista settings, such as increasing the size or changing the color of the text to make the words easier to read. Instead of using a monitor, blind users can work with voice output. That is, the computer reads the information that appears on the screen. Another alternative is a Braille printer, which outputs information on paper in Braille (Figure 5-50).

reflective tracking surface attached to brim of hat

camera/receiver

FIGURE 5-49 A camera/receiver mounted on the monitor tracks the position of the head-mounted pointer, which is reflective material that this user is wearing on the brim of her hat. As the user moves her head, the pointer on the screen also moves.

ETHICS & ISSUES 5-3

Should Web Sites Be Held Accountable for Accessibility Levels for Physically Challenged People?

The World Wide Web Consortium (W3C) has published accessibility guidelines for Web sites. The guidelines specify measures that Web site designers can take to increase accessibility for physically challenged users. Among its guidelines, the W3C urges Web site designers to provide equivalent text for audio or visual content, include features that allow elements to be activated and understood using a variety of input and output devices, and make the user interface follow principles of accessible design. A recent report found that most Web sites do not meet all of the W3C guidelines. This failure is disappointing, because many physically challenged users could benefit from the Web's capability to bring products and services into the home. Ironically, a survey discovered that more than 50 percent of the Web sites run by disability organizations also fail to meet the W3C guidelines. Critics contend that these Web sites neglect the needs of their users and fail to lead by example. The Web site supporters contend, however, that many sponsoring organizations lack the funding necessary to comply with the guidelines. Should the government require that all Web sites meet the W3C accessibility guidelines? Why or why not? Do Web sites run by disability organizations have a moral obligation to meet the guidelines? Why? What can be done to encourage people and organizations to make their Web sites more accessible?

FIGURE 5-50
A Braille printer.

Test your knowledge of pages 187 through 197 in Quiz Yourself 5-4.

QUIZ YOURSELF 5-4

Instructions: Find the true statement below. Then, rewrite the remaining false statements so they are true.

1. A laser printer generates images by pushing electrically heated pins against heat-sensitive paper.

2. A photo printer creates images using a laser beam and powdered ink, called toner.

3. An ink-jet printer is a type of impact printer that forms characters and graphics by spraying tiny drops of liquid nitrogen onto a piece of paper.

4. Many personal computer users attach surround sound printer systems to their computers to generate a higher-quality sound.

5. Multifunction peripherals require more space than having a separate printer, scanner, copy machine, and fax machine.

6. The Americans with Disabilities Act (ADA) requires any company with 15 or more employees to make reasonable attempts to accommodate the needs of physically challenged workers.

Quiz Yourself Online: To further check your knowledge of types of printers, other output devices, and input and output options for physically challenged users, visit scsite.com/dcf5e/ch5/quiz and then click Objectives 5 – 7.

CHAPTER SUMMARY

Input is any data and instructions you enter into the memory of a computer. This chapter described the various techniques of entering input and several commonly used input devices. Topics included the keyboard; mouse and other pointing devices; controllers for gaming and media players; voice input; input for smart phones, PDAs, and Tablet PCs; digital cameras; video input; scanners and reading devices; terminals; and biometric input.

Computers process and organize data (input) into information (output). This chapter also described the various methods of output and several commonly used output devices. Output devices presented included display devices; printers; speakers, headphones, and earphones; fax machines and fax modems; multifunction peripherals; data projectors; and interactive whiteboards.

CAREER CORNER

Graphic Designer/Illustrator

Graphic designers and **graphic illustrators** are artists, but many do not create original works. Instead, they portray visually the ideas of their clients. Illustrators create pictures for books and other publications and sometimes for commercial products, such as greeting cards. They work in fields such as fashion, technology, medicine, animation, or even cartoons. Illustrators often prepare their images on a computer. Designers combine practical skills with artistic talent to convert abstract concepts into designs for products and advertisements. Many use computer-aided design (CAD) tools to create, visualize, and modify designs. Designer careers usually are specialized in particular areas, such as:

- Graphic designers — book covers, stationery, and CD covers
- Commercial and industrial designers — products and equipment
- Costume and theater designers — costumes and settings for theater and television
- Interior designers — layout, decor, and furnishings of homes and buildings
- Merchandise displayers — commercial displays
- Fashion designers — clothing, shoes, and other fashion accessories

Certificate, two-year, four-year, and masters-level educational programs are available within design areas. About 30 percent of graphic designers/illustrators choose to freelance, while others work with advertising agencies, publishing companies, design studios, or specialized departments within large companies. Salaries range from $40,000 to $100,000-plus, based on experience and educational background. For more information, visit scsite.com/dcf5e/ch5/careers and then click Graphic Designer/Illustrator.

Logitech
Personal Interface Products Leader

The average Internet user has more than 40 inches of cords on his desktop, according to a Logitech survey. This company is working to reduce desktop clutter with a variety of cordless peripherals.

A market leader, Logitech has sold more than 50 million wireless devices. It also designs, manufactures, and markets corded devices. The company's retail sales account for more than 85 percent of its revenue.

Two engineering students from Stanford University, Italian-born Pierluigi Zappacosta and Swiss-born Daniel Borel, launched Logitech in 1981. Today, the corporation is the world's largest manufacturer of the mouse. In 2008, it expanded its notebook product portfolio with its VX Nano mouse devices, Alto product line of keyboards and stands, Web cams, speakers, headphones, earphones, and USB hubs. For more information, visit scsite.com/dcf5e/ch5/companies and then click Logitech.

Hewlett-Packard
Technology for Business and Life

If you have printed a document recently, chances are the printer manufacturer was Hewlett-Packard (HP). Market analysts estimate that 60 percent of printers sold today bear the HP logo, and HP says it ships one million printers each week.

HP is noted for a range of high-quality printers, disk storage systems, UNIX and Windows servers, and notebook, desktop, and handheld computers. The company is the only technology vendor listed in *Fortune* magazine's 10 Green Giants, which lists the companies that have exceeded the minimum legal requirements of operating in an environmentally responsible manner in 2007.

William Hewlett and David Packard started the company in a one-car garage in 1939 with the goal of manufacturing test and measurement equipment. HP has been developing personal information devices, including calculators and computers, for more than 30 years. For more information, visit scsite.com/dcf5e/ch5/companies and then click Hewlett-Packard.

TECHNOLOGY TRAILBLAZERS

Douglas Engelbart
Creator of the Mouse

The phrase "point and click" might not be part of every computer user's vocabulary if Douglas Engelbart had not pursued his engineering dreams. In 1964, he developed the first prototype computer mouse with the goal of making it easier to move a cursor around a computer screen.

Ten years later, engineers at Xerox refined Engelbart's prototype and showed the redesigned product to Apple's Steve Jobs, who applied the concept to his graphical Macintosh computer. The mouse was mass produced in the mid-1980s, and today it is the most widely used pointing device.

Engelbart currently is refining his Collective IQ philosophy at his Bootstrap Institute; this concept optimizes collaboration, creativity, and competition to solve problems. For more information, visit scsite.com/dcf5e/ch5/people and then click Douglas Engelbart.

Donna Dubinsky
Palm, Handspring, and Numenta Cofounder

The human brain stores and analyzes data to make predictions and reach conclusions. Donna Dubinsky believes her newest company, Numenta, can create a computer memory system that allows researchers to develop applications that mimic the human brain's workings.

Dubinsky is passionate about creating companies that produce ground-breaking technologies. In the mid-1990s, she sensed that people wanted to own an electronic version of their paper appointment books. She and Jeff Hawkins introduced the original Palm Pilot at Palm Computing in 1996. Sales of more than two million units made the Palm Pilot the most rapidly adopted new computing product ever manufactured.

Dubinsky and Hawkins left Palm in 1998 to cofound Handspring, where they introduced several successful products, including the Treo smart phone. In 2003, Handspring merged with the Palm hardware group to create palmOne, now called Palm.

In 2007, Palm shareholders elected Dubinsky as a Class II director to serve until 2010. For more information, visit scsite.com/dcf5e/ch5/people and then click Donna Dubinsky.

Chapter Review

The Chapter Review section summarizes the concepts presented in this chapter. To obtain help from other students regarding any subject in this chapter, visit scsite.com/dcf5e/ch5/forum and post your thoughts or questions.

 What Are the Characteristics of a Keyboard?

Any hardware component that allows users to enter data and instructions into a computer is an **input device**. A **keyboard** is an input device that contains keys users press to enter data and instructions into a computer. Computer keyboards have a typing area that includes letters of the alphabet, numbers, punctuation marks, and other basic keys. An enhanced keyboard also has function keys programmed to issue commands, a numeric keypad, arrow keys, and additional keys and buttons.

 How Do Pointing Devices and Gaming and Media Player Controllers Work?

A **pointing device** allows users to control a small symbol, called a **pointer**, on the screen. A **mouse** is a pointing device that fits under the palm of your hand. As you move the mouse, the pointer on the screen also moves. A **trackball** is a stationary pointing device with a ball that you rotate to move the pointer. A **touchpad** is a flat, pressure-sensitive device that you slide your fingertip across to move the pointer. A **pointing stick** is a pointing device positioned on the keyboard that you push to move the pointer. A **light pen** is a light-sensitive device that you press against or point at the screen to select objects. A **touch screen** is a touch-sensitive display device that you interact with by touching areas of the screen. A **stylus** and **digital pen** use pressure to write text and draw lines. Video and computer games use a **game controller** as the input device. Game controllers include a **gamepad**, which controls the movement and actions of players or objects in video games or computer games; a **joystick**, which is a handheld vertical lever mounted on a base; a **wheel**, which is a steering-wheel-type input device; a **light gun**, which is used to shoot targets; and a **dance pad,** which users press with their feet in response to instructions. The **Wii Remote** is a type of motion-sensing game controller that communicates via Bluetooth wireless technology. A **Click Wheel** is a type of touch-sensitive pad on a portable media player.

 Visit scsite.com/dcf5e/ch5/quiz or click the Quiz Yourself button. Click Objectives 1 – 2.

 What Are Other Types of Input?

Voice input is the process of entering input by speaking into a microphone. Users can enter data and instructions into a smart phone with a microphone or headset, with a digital camera or touch-sensitive pad, or with the smart phone's keypad. Mobile users employ a basic stylus to enter data and instructions into a PDA, or sometimes use a built-in keyboard or snap-on keyboard. The primary input device for a Tablet PC is a digital pen. A **digital camera** allows users to take pictures, store the images digitally, and download the images to a computer's hard disk. **Video input** is the process of capturing full-motion pictures and storing them on a computer's storage medium. A **Web cam**, also called a **PC video camera**, is used for video input. A **scanner** is a light-sensing input device that reads printed text and graphics and translates the results into a form a computer can process. An optical reader is a device that uses a light source to read characters, marks, and codes and converts them into digital data. **OCR (optical character recognition) devices** use a small optical scanner and software to analyze characters from ordinary documents. **OMR (optical mark recognition)** devices read hand-drawn marks on a form. A **bar code reader** uses laser beams to read bar codes. An **RFID device** reads information on an embedded tag via radio waves. A **magnetic stripe card reader** reads the magnetic stripe on the back of credit cards and other similar cards. **MICR** (magnetic-ink character recognition) devices read text printed with magnetized ink. A **terminal** consists of a keyboard, a monitor, a video card, and memory and often is used to perform specific tasks for a particular industry. **Biometrics** is the technology of authenticating a person's identity by verifying a physical characteristic. Biometric input can include fingerprints, hand geometry, facial features, voice, signatures, and eye patterns.

 Visit scsite.com/dcf5e/ch5/quiz or click the Quiz Yourself button. Click Objective 3.

4 **What Are the Characteristics of LCD Monitors, LCD Screens, and CRT Monitors?**

Any hardware component that conveys information to one or more people is an **output device**. A **display device** is a commonly used output device that visually conveys text, graphics, and video information. An **LCD monitor**, also called a flat panel monitor, is a desktop monitor that uses a liquid crystal display. A **liquid crystal display** (**LCD**) uses a liquid compound to present information on a display device. A **CRT monitor** is a desktop monitor that contains a cathode-ray tube.

 Visit scsite.com/dcf5e/ch5/quiz or click the Quiz Yourself button. Click Objective 4.

5 **What Are Various Types of Printers?**

A **printer** is an output device that produces text and graphics on a physical medium. A **nonimpact printer** forms characters and graphics without striking the paper. Several types of nonimpact printers are available. An **ink-jet printer** forms characters and graphics by spraying tiny drops of ink onto paper. A **photo printer** produces photo-lab-quality pictures. A **laser printer** is a high-speed, high-quality printer that operates in a manner similar to a copy machine. A **thermal printer** generates images by pushing electrically heated pins against heat-sensitive paper. A **mobile printer** is a small, battery-powered printer used to print from a notebook computer, Tablet PC, smart phone, or other personal mobile devices. **Plotters** are used to produce high-quality drawings in specialized fields. A **large-format printer** creates large, photo-realistic-quality color prints. An **impact printer** forms characters and graphics by striking a mechanism against an inked ribbon that physically contacts the paper. A **dot-matrix printer** is an impact printer that produces an image when tiny wire pins on a print head strike an inked ribbon. A **line printer** is a high-speed impact printer that prints an entire line at a time.

6 **What Are the Characteristics of Speakers, Headphones, and Earphones; Fax Machines and Fax Modems; Multifunction Peripherals; Data Projectors; and Interactive Whiteboards?**

Speakers are a type of **audio output device** added to computers to generate higher-quality sound. With headphones and earphones, only the individual wearing the headphones or earphones hears the sound from the computer. The difference is that **headphones** cover or are placed outside of the ear, whereas **earphones**, or **earbuds**, rest inside the ear canal. A **fax machine** is a device that codes and encodes documents so they can be transmitted over telephone lines. Many computers have a fax modem that transmits computer-prepared documents. A **multifunction peripheral** is a single device that provides the functionality of a printer, scanner, copy machine, and perhaps a fax machine. A **data projector** is a device that takes the text and images displaying on a computer screen and projects them on a larger screen for an audience. An **interactive whiteboard** is a touch-sensitive device, resembling a dry-erase board, that displays the image on a connected computer screen.

7 **What Are Input and Output Options for Physically Challenged Users?**

Voice recognition, which is the computer's capability of distinguishing spoken words, is an ideal input option for visually impaired users. Input options for people with limited hand mobility include keyboards with larger keys, on-screen keyboards, and head-mounted pointers. Hearing-impaired users can instruct programs to display words instead of sound. Visually impaired users can change Windows Vista settings such as the size and color of text to make words easier to read. Instead of a monitor, blind users can use voice output and a Braille printer.

 Visit scsite.com/dcf5e/ch5/quiz or click the Quiz Yourself button. Click Objectives 5 – 7.

Key Terms

You should know each key term. Use the list below to help focus your study. To further enhance your understanding of the Key Terms in this chapter, visit scsite.com/dcf5e/ch5/terms. See an example of and a definition for each term, and access current and additional information about the term from the Web.

air mouse (169)
Americans with Disabilities Act
 (ADA) (197)
audio input (173)
audio output device (193)
automated teller machine (ATM) (180)
bar code (178)
bar code reader (178)
biometrics (181)
Click Wheel (172)
CRT monitor (186)
dance pad (172)
data projector (195)
digital camera (175)
digital pen (171)
digital video (DV) camera (176)
display device (183)
dot-matrix printer (192)
earbuds (194)
earphones (194)
ENERGY STAR program (186)
ergonomics (168)
fax machine (194)
fingerprint reader (181)
flatbed scanner (177)
game controller (172)
gamepad (172)
graphic designers (198)
graphic illustrators (198)
graphics tablet (171)
headphones (194)
impact printer (192)
ink-jet printer (189)
input (166)
input device (166)

interactive whiteboard (195)
joystick (172)
keyboard (168)
large-format printer (192)
laser mouse (169)
laser printer (190)
LCD monitor (184)
light gun (172)
light pen (170)
line printer (193)
liquid crystal display (LCD) (185)
magnetic stripe card reader (179)
MICR (179)
MICR reader (179)
Microsoft Surface (171)
mobile printer (192)
monitor (183)
mouse (169)
mouse pad (169)
multifunction peripheral (194)
nonimpact printer (189)
OCR devices (177)
optical character recognition (OCR)
 (177)
optical mark recognition (OMR) (177)
optical mouse (169)
output (182)
output device (182)
PC video camera (176)
pen input (171)
photo printer (190)
PictBridge (190)
pixel (176)
plasma monitor (185)
plotters (192)

pointer (167)
pointing device (167)
pointing stick (170)
POS terminal (180)
printer (187)
resolution (176)
RFID (178)
RFID reader (178)
scanner (177)
smart card (181)
speakers (193)
speech recognition (173)
stylus (171)
terminal (180)
thermal printer (191)
touch screen (170)
touchpad (170)
trackball (170)
turnaround document (177)
video conference (176)
video input (176)
video telephone call (176)
voice input (173)
voice output (194)
voice recognition (173)
Web cam (176)
wheel (172)
Wii Remote (172)

Checkpoint

Use the Checkpoint exercises to check your knowledge level of the chapter. To complete the Checkpoint exercises interactively, visit scsite.com/dcf5e/ch5/check.

True/False
Mark T for True and F for False. (See page numbers in parentheses.)

_____ 1. A laser mouse is a newer type of motion-sensing mouse that allows you to control objects, media players, and slide shows by moving the mouse in predetermined directions through the air. (169)

_____ 2. A trackball is a stationary pointing device with a ball on its top or side. (170)

_____ 3. A Click Wheel is a motion-sensing input device that uses Bluetooth wireless technology to communicate with a game console. (172)

_____ 4. A scanner is a light-sensing input device that reads printed text and graphics and then translates the results into a form the computer can process. (177)

_____ 5. Plasma monitors use a liquid compound to present information on a display device. (185)

_____ 6. Most photo printers are PictBridge enabled, which requires the use of a computer to print pictures. (190)

_____ 7. A line printer is a high-speed impact printer that prints an entire line at a time. (193)

_____ 8. The advantage of a multifunction peripheral is that it is significantly more expensive than if you purchase each device separately. (194)

Multiple Choice
Select the best answer. (See page numbers in parentheses.)

1. An ergonomic keyboard _____. (168)
   a. is used to enter data into a biometric device
   b. transmits data using wireless technology
   c. has a design that reduces wrist and hand injuries
   d. is built into the top of a handheld computer

2. Two types of pen input are _____. (171)
   a. digital pen and touch screen
   b. stylus and digital pen
   c. trackball and stylus
   d. pointing stick and digital pen

3. Architects, mapmakers, designers, artists, and home users create drawings and sketches on a _____. (171)
   a. trackball
   b. smart terminal
   c. graphics tablet
   d. touchpad

4. A _____ controls the movement and actions of players or objects in video games or computer games. (172)
   a. control pad
   b. pointing stick
   c. gamepad
   d. touchpad

5. RFID is a technology that uses _____ to communicate with a tag placed in or attached to an object, an animal, or a person. (178)
   a. a thin wire   b. pixels
   c. light waves   d. radio signals

6. The speed of an ink-jet printer is measured by the number of _____ it can print. (189)
   a. lines per page (lpp)
   b. dots per inch (dpi)
   c. characters per second (cps)
   d. pages per minute (ppm)

7. Basic _____ are inexpensive, but the print quality is low and the images tend to fade over time. (191)
   a. laser printers   b. thermal printers
   c. dot-matrix printers   d. line printers

8. A(n) _____ is a touch-sensitive device, resembling a dry-erase board, that displays the image on a connected computer screen. (195)
   a. flatbed scanner
   b. data projector
   c. interactive whiteboard
   d. video conference

Matching
Match the terms with their definitions. (See page numbers in parentheses.)

_____ 1. pointing stick (170)

_____ 2. turnaround document (177)

_____ 3. POS terminal (180)

_____ 4. smart card (181)

_____ 5. plotter (192)

a. pressure-sensitive pointing device shaped like a pencil eraser that is positioned between keys on a keyboard

b. sophisticated printers used to produce high-quality drawings such as blueprints, maps, and circuit diagrams

c. self-service banking machine that connects to a host computer through a network

d. a document that you return to the company that creates and sends it

e. stores data on a thin microprocessor that is embedded in a credit-card-sized card

f. used by most retail stores to record purchases, process credit or debit cards, and update inventory

Checkpoint

Short Answer   Write a brief answer to each of the following questions.

1. How are a mechanical mouse, an optical mouse, and a wireless mouse different? _____ What is a mouse pad? _____

2. How does voice recognition work? _____ What are some different ways in which users input audio into a computer? _____

3. How are optical character recognition (OCR), optical mark recognition (OMR), and magnetic ink character recognition (MICR) different? _____ How is an RFID reader used? _____

4. What type of monitor emits electromagnetic radiation? _____ What can you do to protect yourself from electromagnetic radiation from a monitor? _____

5. How does an ink-jet printer work? _____ What are the differences between dye-sublimation printers used by professionals as compared to home or small business users? _____

Working Together   Working in a group of your classmates, complete the following team exercise.

1. Stores, libraries, parcel carriers, and other organizations use optical codes. Some people mistakenly believe that an optical code contains the name of a product or its price, but the codes are only a link to a database in which this information, and more, is stored. Have each member of your team visit an organization that uses optical codes. How are the optical codes read? What information is obtained when the code is read? What information is recorded? How is the information used? Meet with the members of your team to discuss the results of your investigations. Then, create a group presentation and share your findings with the class.

Web Research

Use the Internet-based Web Research exercises to broaden your understanding of the concepts presented in this chapter. To discuss any of the Web Research exercises in this chapter with other students, post your thoughts or questions at scsite.com/dcf5e/ch5/forum.

(1) Blogs   Whether you are listening to the radio, watching television, or drinking a beverage at the local coffee shop, the world of sports is likely to surface. People are passionate about their favorite athletes and sporting events, from the community Little League game to the NFL Super Bowl. Visit several sports blogs, including those from Fanblogs (fanblogs.com), BlogCritics Sports (blogcritics.org/sports), Deadspin (deadspin.com), Full Throttle (cranialcavity.net/fullthrottle/wp), ESPN (sports.espn.go.com/espn/blog), and Fox Sports (community.foxsports.com/blogs). What are the more popular discussions? What college football and basketball stories are featured? Who are the professional athletes receiving much criticism? What NASCAR teams are analyzed?

(2) Scavenger Hunt   Use one of the search engines listed in Figure 2-8 in Chapter 2 on page 58 or your own favorite search engine to find the answers to the questions below. Copy and paste the Web address from the Web page where you found the answer. Some questions may have more than one answer. If required, submit your answers to your instructor. (1) Consumers use touch screens at bank ATMs, airport check-ins, and mall kiosks. What did Dr. Samuel C. Hurst invent in 1971 that led to the development of touch screen technology? (2) What are some of the services available from providers, such as Yahoo! Photo, to help consumers store and share digital photos online? What are the costs of some of these services? (3) Who holds patents awarded in the 1950s for automatic video scanning and inspection methods, which led to bar code technology?

(3) Search Sleuth   Typical search Web sites, such as Google and ask.com, maintain their own internal databases of links to Web pages. MetaCrawler (metacrawler.com) is a different type of search Web site because it returns combined results from these and other leading search engines. Visit this Web site and then use your word processing program to answer the following questions. Then, if required, submit your answers to your instructor. (1) Click the About MetaCrawler link at the bottom of the page. Which search engines are you searching when you use MetaCrawler? (2) Click your browser's Back button or press the BACKSPACE key to return to the MetaCrawler home page. Locate the Popular Searches section. What are the six most popular searches today? (3) Click the Images link on the home page, type sunset in the search text box, and then click the Search button. How many results did your search yield? Click the Audio link above the search text box to search for audio files of sunsets. How many results did your search yield? (4) Click your browser's Back button or press the BACKSPACE key three times to return to the MetaCrawler home page. Click the Tools & Tips link at the bottom of the page. Click the FAQ link. Click several question links concerning conducting searches on this Web site and read the answers to these questions. Summarize the information you read and then write a 50-word summary that may be submitted to your instructor.

Use the Learn How To activities to learn fundamental skills when using a computer and accompanying technology. Complete the exercises and submit them to your instructor. Premium Activity: The icon indicates you can see a visual demonstration of the associated Learn How To activity by visiting scsite.com/dcf5e/ch5/howto.

LEARN HOW TO 1: Adjust the Sound on a Computer

Every computer today contains a sound card and associated hardware and software that allow you to play and record sound. You can adjust the sound by completing the following steps:

1. Click the Start button on the Windows taskbar and then click Control Panel on the Start menu to open the Control Panel window.
2. Click Hardware and Sound and then click 'Adjust the system volume' to display the Volume Mixer dialog box (Figure 5-51).
3. To adjust the volume for all devices connected to the sound card, drag the Device Volume slider down or up to decrease or increase the volume.
4. If you want to mute the sound on the computer, click the Mute button so it contains a red x, and then click the Close button on the title bar.
5. To remove the volume icon from the Windows taskbar, right-click an empty area on the Windows taskbar and then click Properties to display the Taskbar and Start Menu Properties dialog box. Click the Notification Area tab, click the Volume check box to remove the check mark, and then click the OK button or the Apply button. You can click the icon on the taskbar to set the volume level or mute the sound.
6. To make sound and other adjustments for each device on the computer, click the 'Manage audio devices' link on the Hardware and Sound page of the Control Panel to display the Sound dialog box, and then click the Properties button to display the Speakers Properties dialog box.
7. Click the Levels tab to display the volume controls (Figure 5-52).
8. To adjust volumes, drag the Volume Control slider left or right for each device. To adjust speaker balance, click the Balance button to display the Balance dialog box (Figure 5-53), drag the Balance sliders, and then click the OK button.
9. If you click the Advanced tab in the Speakers Properties dialog box, you can control the sample rate and bit depth by using the drop-down list in the Default Format area of the Speakers Properties dialog box.

Exercise

1. Open the Control Panel window, click Hardware and Sound, and then click the 'Manage audio devices' link to display the Sound dialog box. What kind of sound card is on the computer? Click the Place volume icon in the taskbar check box and then click the Apply button. What change did you notice on the Windows taskbar? Repeat these steps again. What change occurred on the Windows taskbar? Click Speakers, click the Properties button, and then click the Levels tab. What volumes are you able to control? How would you change the balance? How do you hide the Volume icon from the Notification Area on the Windows taskbar? Submit your answers to your instructor.

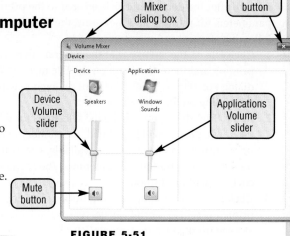
FIGURE 5-51

FIGURE 5-52

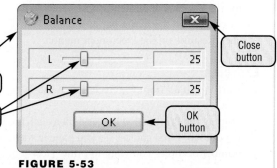
FIGURE 5-53

Learn How To

When you print using a computer, you control printing at two different points: first, before the printing actually begins, and second, after the document has been sent to the printer and either is physically printing or is waiting to be printed. To set the parameters for printing and then print the document, complete the following steps:

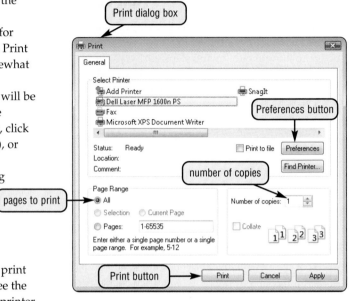

1. Click File on the menu bar of the program that will be used for printing and then click Print on the File menu to display the Print dialog box (Figure 5-54). The Print dialog box will vary somewhat depending on the program used.
2. In the Print dialog box, make the selections for what printer will be used, what pages will be printed, the number of copies to be printed, and any other choices available. For further options, click the Preferences button (or, sometimes, the Properties button), or click the Options button.
3. Click the OK button or the Print button. The document being printed is sent to a print queue, which is an area on disk storage from which documents actually are printed. This process occurs so that you can continue to use the program even while printing is taking place on the printer.

When you click the Print button to send the document to the print queue, a printer icon may appear on the Windows taskbar. To see the print queue and control the actual printing of documents on the printer, complete the following steps:

FIGURE 5-54

1. If the printer icon appears on the Windows taskbar, double-click it; otherwise, click the Start button on the Windows taskbar, click Control Panel on the Start menu, click the Printers link, and then double-click the printer icon with the check mark. The check mark indicates the default printer. A window opens with the name of the printer on the title bar (Figure 5-55). All documents either printing or waiting to be printed are listed in the window. The Status column indicates whether the document is printing or waiting. In addition, the owner of the file, number of pages, size, date and time submitted, and printer port are listed.
2. If you click Printer on the menu bar in the printer window, you can set printing preferences from the Printer menu. In addition, you can pause all printing and cancel all printing jobs from the Printer menu.
3. If you select a document in the document list and then click Document on the menu bar, you can cancel the selected document for printing, or you can pause the printing for the selected document. To continue printing for the selected document, click Document on the menu bar and then click Resume on the Document menu.

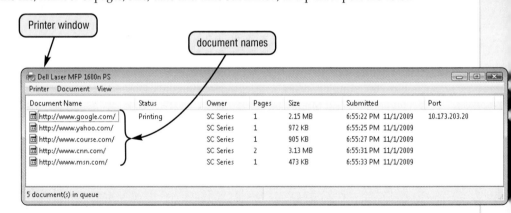

FIGURE 5-55

Exercise

1. Start WordPad from the Accessories list. Type `Click Print on the File menu to display the Print dialog box`.
2. Display the Print dialog box and then click the Preferences button. When the Printing Preferences dialog box appears, click the Layout tab. What choices do you have in the Layout sheet? Close the Printing Preferences dialog box. How do you select the number of copies you want to print? How would you print pages 25–35 of a document? Submit your answers to your instructor.

Learn It Online

Use the Learn It Online exercises to reinforce your understanding of the chapter concepts. To access the Learn It Online exercises, visit scsite.com/dcf5e/ch5/learn.

 At the Movies — Video Editing on Your Computer

To view the Video Editing on Your Computer movie, click the number 1 button. Locate your video and click the corresponding High-Speed or Dial-Up link, depending on your Internet connection. Watch the movie to learn simple editing tips for converting raw video footage into interesting videos that will hold the interest of your audience. Then, complete the exercise by answering the questions that follow. What is the most important point to keep in mind when editing a video? During video editing, why does the audio portion of the clip require close attention?

 Student Edition Labs — Peripheral Devices

Click the number 2 button. A new browser window will open, displaying the Student Edition Labs. Follow the on-screen instructions to complete the Peripheral Devices Lab. When finished, click the Exit button. If required, submit your results to your instructor.

 Practice Test

Click the number 3 button. Answer each question. When completed, enter your name and click the Grade Test button to submit the quiz for grading. Make a note of any missed questions. If required, submit your results to your instructor.

(4) Who Wants To Be a Computer Genius²?

Click the number 4 button to find out if you are a computer genius. Directions about how to play the game will be displayed. When you are ready to play, click the Play button. Submit your score to your instructor.

(5) Howstuffworks.com

Click the number 5 button to learn how to use Howstuffworks.com. Use this Web site to discover how a laser printer works in comparison to an ink-jet printer. Follow the instructions to display the computer peripherals page. Read the articles about how both types of printers work. Write a report listing the major differences between the printers. Which type of printer would you recommend to your fellow students? Why? Print your report and submit it to your instructor.

(6) Student Edition Labs — Working with Graphics

Click the number 6 button. A new browser window will open, displaying the Student Edition Labs. Follow the on-screen instructions to complete the Working with Graphics Lab. When finished, click the Exit button. If required, submit your results to your instructor.

 Crossword Puzzle Challenge

Click the number 7 button, then click the Crossword Puzzle Challenge link. Directions about how to play the game will be displayed. Complete the puzzle to reinforce skills you learned in this chapter. When you are ready to play, click the Continue button. Continue the completed puzzle to your instructor.

 Vista Exercises

Click the number 8 button. When the Vista Exercises menu appears, click the exercise assigned by your instructor. A new browser window will open. Follow the on-screen instructions to complete the exercise. When finished, click the Exit button. If required, submit your results to your instructor.

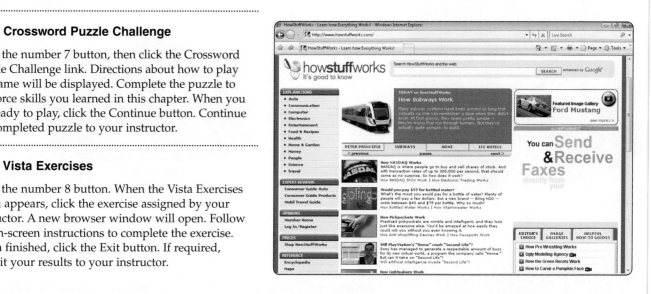

Digital Imaging
and Video Technology

Everywhere you look, people are capturing moments they want to remember. They take pictures or make movies of their vacations, birthday parties, activities, accomplishments, sporting events, weddings, and more. Because of the popularity of digital cameras and digital video cameras, increasingly more people desire to capture their memories digitally, instead of on film. With digital technology, photographers have the ability to modify and share the digital images and videos they create. When you use special hardware and/or software, you can copy, manipulate, print, and distribute digital images and videos using your personal computer and the Internet. Amateurs can achieve professional quality results by using more sophisticated hardware and software.

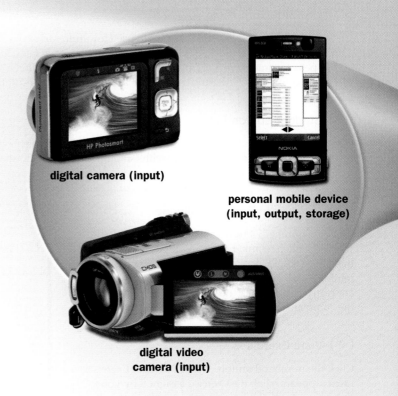

digital camera (input)

personal mobile device
(input, output, storage)

digital video
camera (input)

FIGURE 1 A variety of input, output, and storage devices are used by home users to process and edit digital photos and video.

Digital photography and recordings deliver significant benefits over film-based photography and movie making. With digital cameras, no developing is needed. Instead, the images reside on storage media such as a hard disk, CD, DVD, or flash memory card. Unlike film, storage media can be reused, which reduces costs, saves time, and provides immediate results. Digital technology allows greater control over the creative process, both while taking pictures and video and in the editing process. You can check results immediately after capturing a picture or video to determine whether it meets your expectations. If you are dissatisfied with a picture or video, you can erase it and recapture it, again and again. Today, many personal mobile devices, such as smart phones and PDAs, allow you to capture pictures and video.

As shown in Figure 1, digital cameras, personal mobile devices, and digital video cameras function as input devices when they transmit pictures or video to a personal computer. You can transmit pictures and video by connecting the video camera or mobile device to your personal computer using a FireWire or USB 2.0 port, or by placing the storage media used on the camera or personal mobile device in the computer. Some cameras and devices also can transmit wirelessly to a computer.

When you transmit images that were captured with a digital camera or personal mobile device to a computer, you can edit the pictures on the computer, save them on the computer's storage media, and print them on a photo printer via a USB or FireWire port or wirelessly.

When you transmit images or video that were captured with a digital video camera to a computer, you can edit the video using video editing software. If desired, you can preview the video during the editing process on a television. Finally, you save the finished result to the desired media, such as a DVD or, perhaps, e-mail the edited video or post it to a video sharing Web site. In this example, a DVD drive also can be used to input video from a DVD.

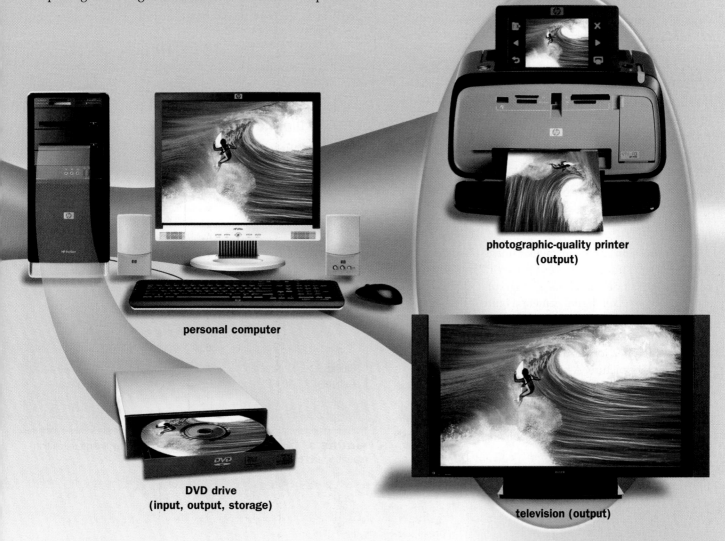

personal computer

photographic-quality printer (output)

DVD drive (input, output, storage)

television (output)

DIGITAL IMAGING TECHNOLOGY

Digital imaging technology involves capturing and manipulating still photographic images in an electronic format. The following sections outline the steps involved in the process of using digital imaging technology.

1 Select a Digital Camera

A **digital camera** is a type of camera that stores photographed images electronically instead of on traditional film. Digital cameras are divided into three categories (Figure 2) based mainly on image resolution, features, and of course, price. The image resolution is measured in pixels (short for picture element). The image quality increases with the number of pixels. The image resolution usually is measured in **megapixels** (million of pixels), often abbreviated as **MP**. Features of digital cameras include red-eye reduction, zoom, autofocus, flash, self-timer, and manual mode for fine-tuning settings. You also may choose to use a personal mobile device to take your digital pictures. Figure 3 summarizes the three categories of digital cameras.

2 Take Pictures

Digital cameras provide you with several options that are set before a picture is taken. Three of the more important options are the resolution, compression, and image file format in which the camera should save the picture. While a camera may allow for a very high resolution for a large print, you may choose to take a picture at a lower resolution if the image does not require great detail or must be a small size. For example, you may want to use the image on a Web page where smaller image file sizes are beneficial.

Compression results in smaller image file sizes. Figure 4 illustrates the image file sizes for varying resolutions and compressions under standard photographic conditions using a 6-megapixel digital camera. Figure 4 also shows the average picture size for a given resolution. The camera may take more time to save an image at lower compression, resulting in a longer delay before the camera is ready to take another picture. A higher compression, however, may result in some loss of image quality. If a camera has a 64 MB flash memory card, you can determine the number of pictures the card can hold by dividing 64 MB by the file size. Flash memory cards are available in sizes from 64 MB to 16 GB or more.

Most digital cameras also allow you to choose an image file format. Two popular file formats are TIFF and JPEG.

FIGURE 2 The point-and-shoot digital camera usually allows, but does not require, adjustments before shooting. The field digital camera offers improved quality and features that allow you to make manual adjustments before shooting and use a variety of lenses. The studio digital camera offers better color and resolution and greater control over exposure and lenses.

TYPES OF DIGITAL CAMERAS

Type	Resolution Range	Features	Price
Point-and-shoot cameras	Usually less than 10 MP	Fully automatic; fits in your pocket; easy to use; ideal for average consumer usage.	Less than $400
Field cameras	Greater than 10 MP	Used by photojournalists; portable but flexible; provides ability to change lenses and use other attachments; great deal of control over exposure and other photo settings.	$400 to $2,000
Studio cameras	Greater than 10 MP	Stationary camera used for professional studio work; flexible; widest range of lenses and settings.	$1,500 and up

FIGURE 3 Digital cameras often are categorized by image resolution, features, and price.

The **TIFF** file format saves the image uncompressed. All of the image detail is captured and stored, but the file sizes can be large. Some cameras include a **RAW** format, which varies by manufacturer. RAW formats are similar to the TIFF format in that no compression is done, but, in some cases, the image is slightly enhanced. The **JPEG** file format is compressed. The resolution of the image may be the same as a TIFF file, but some detail may be lost in the image.

Finally, before you take a picture, you should choose the type of media on which to store the resulting image file. Some cameras allow for a choice of media to which you can store the image, such as a CompactFlash card or Memory Stick, while others allow for only one type of storage media. One major advantage of a digital camera is that you easily can erase pictures from its media, freeing up space for new pictures.

IMAGE FILE SIZE WITH A 6-MEGAPIXEL DIGITAL CAMERA

Resolution in Pixels	COMPRESSION			Picture Size in Inches
	Low	Medium	High	
	Resulting Image File Size			
3000 × 2000	8.9 MB	3.3 MB	780 KB	16 × 20
2272 × 1704	2 MB	1.1 MB	556 KB	11 × 17
1600 × 1200	1 MB	558 KB	278 KB	8 × 10
1024 × 768	570 KB	320 KB	170 KB	4 × 6

FIGURE 4 Image file sizes for varying resolutions and compressions under standard photographic conditions using a 6-megapixel digital camera.

③ Transfer and Manage Image Files

The method of transferring images from the camera to the personal computer differs greatly depending on the capabilities of both. Digital cameras, including personal mobile devices, use a variety of storage media (Figure 5). If your camera uses a flash memory card such as CompactFlash, Memory Stick, SmartMedia, xD Picture card, Secure Digital (SD), or Mini HD card you can remove the media from the camera and place it in a slot on the personal computer or in a device, such as a card reader, connected to the personal computer. Your camera, card reader, or personal mobile device also may connect to the personal computer using a USB, USB 2.0, or FireWire (Figure 6) port. Other cameras may connect to a computer using a camera dock or wireless connection. Some personal computers include an internal card reader. When you insert the memory card or connect the camera, software on the personal computer guides you through the process of transferring the images to the hard disk.

Some operating systems and software recognize a memory card or camera as though it is another hard disk on the computer. This feature allows you to access the files, navigate them, and then copy, delete, or rename the files while the media still is in the camera.

After you transfer the files to the hard disk on your personal computer, you should organize the files by sorting them or renaming them so that information, such as the subject, date, time, and purpose, is saved along with the image. Finally, before altering the images digitally or using the images for other purposes, you should back up the images to another location, such as a CD or DVD, so that the original image is recoverable.

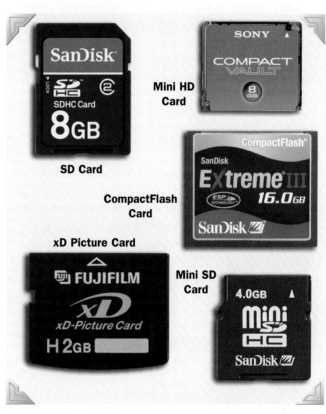

FIGURE 5 SD Cards, mini HD cards, CompactFlash Cards, xD Picture Cards, and mini SD cards are popular storage devices for digital cameras.

FIGURE 6 Using a USB or FireWire connection, you can add a card reader to your personal computer.

④ Edit Images

Image editing software allows you to edit digital images. You should edit a copy, not the original image file, so that you always have the original file to use as a backup or for other editing projects. The following list summarizes the more common image enhancements or alterations:

- Adjust the contrast and brightness; correct lighting problems; or help give the photo a particular feeling, such as warm or stark.
- Remove red-eye.
- Crop an image to remove unnecessary elements and resize it.
- Rotate the image to change its orientation.
- Add elements to the image, such as descriptive text, a date, a logo, or decorative items; create collages or add missing elements.
- Replace individual colors with a new color.
- Add special effects, such as texture, motion blurring or reflections to enhance the image.
- Add aging to make the image appear as if it was taken a long time ago.
- Stitch images together to create a larger image.

Some popular image editing programs are Adobe Photoshop, Microsoft Photo Story, and Corel Paint Shop Pro Photo. Figure 7 shows some of the effects available in Corel Paint Shop Pro X on the Effects submenu.

⑤ Print Images

Once an image is altered digitally, it is ready to be printed. You can print images on a personal color printer or send them to a professional service that specializes in digital photo printing.

When printing the images yourself, make sure that the resolution used to create the image was high enough for the size of the print you want to create. For example, if the camera used a resolution of 640 × 480 pixels, then the ideal print size is a wallet size. If you print such an image at a size of 8 × 10 inches, then the image will appear **pixilated**, or blurry. Use high-quality photo paper for the best results. A photo printer gives the best results when printing digital photography.

Many services print digital images, either over the Internet or through traditional photo developing locations and kiosks (Figure 8), such as those found in drug stores or shopping marts. Some services allow you to e-mail or upload the files to the service; specify the size, quality, and quantity of print; and then receive the finished prints via the postal service. Other services allow you to drop off flash memory cards or CDs at a photo shop and later pick up the prints, just as you do with traditional photo developing shops.

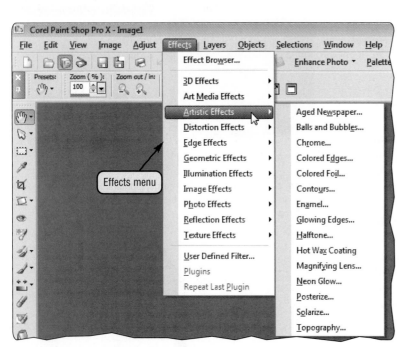

FIGURE 7 The capability of applying effects separates digital photography from film photography.

FIGURE 8 A kiosk allows you to print digital images in high resolution on photo paper.

6 Distribute Images Electronically

Rather than printing images, you often need to use the images electronically. Depending on the electronic use of the image, the image may require additional processing. If you use the images on a Web site or want to e-mail a photo, you probably want to send a lower-resolution image because a lower resolution image will be downloaded faster. Image editing software allows you to lower the resolution of the image, resulting in a smaller file size. Some photo sharing Web sites automatically will change the resolution of your photos for you. You also should use standard file formats when distributing an electronic photo. The JPEG format is viewable using most personal computers or Web browsers. Some online services allow you to upload and share your photos free of charge and automatically will change your photos to a lower resolution and JPEG format. Some personal mobile devices allow you to send images directly from the device to an e-mail address, another personal mobile device, or a printer.

You can store very high resolution photos on a DVD or a CD. **DVD and CD mastering software** allows you to create slide show presentations on a recordable DVD or CD that can play in many home DVD players or personal computer DVD drives. Photo sharing Web sites, such as Fotki and Flickr (Figure 9), allow you to share your photos with acquaintances or with the whole world. You also can search for and view photos of others.

Finally, you should back up and store images that you distribute electronically with the same care as you store your traditional film negatives.

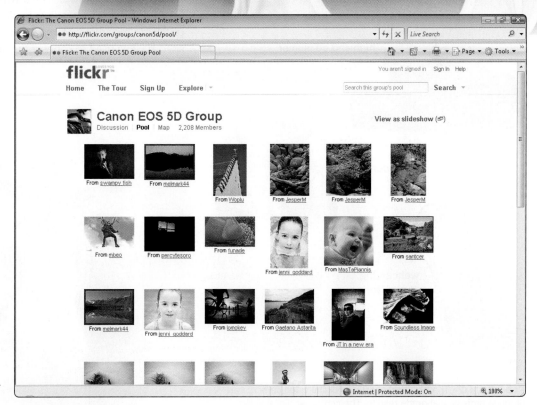

FIGURE 9 The Flickr photo sharing Web site allows you to share your photos, organize your photos, and search for photos.

DIGITAL VIDEO TECHNOLOGY

Digital video technology allows you to input, edit, manage, publish, and share your videos using a personal computer. With digital video technology, you can transform home videos into Hollywood-style movies by enhancing the videos with scrolling titles and transitions, cutting out or adding scenes, and adding background music and voice-over narration. The following sections outline the steps involved in the process of using digital video technology.

① Select a Video Camera

Video cameras record in either analog or digital format. **Analog formats** include 8mm, Hi8, VHS-C, and Super VHS-C. **Digital formats** include Mini-DV, MICROMV, Digital8, DVD, and HDV (high-definition video format). Some digital video cameras record to an internal hard disk. Others may allow you to record directly on a DVD. Digital video cameras fall into three general categories: high-end consumer, consumer, and webcasting and monitoring (Figure 10). Consumer digital video cameras are by far the most popular type among consumers. High-end consumer models may support the HDV standard. A video recorded

FIGURE 10 The high-end consumer digital video camera can produce professional-grade results. The consumer digital video camera produces amateur-grade results. The webcasting and monitoring digital video camera is appropriate for webcasting and security monitoring.

in high-definition can be played back on a high-definition display. Many personal mobile devices allow you to record video that you later can transmit to your computer or e-mail from the device. Digital video cameras provide more features than analog video cameras, such as a higher level of zoom, better sound, or greater control over color and lighting.

② Record a Video

Most video cameras provide you with a choice of recording programs, which sometimes are called automatic settings. Each recording program includes a different combination of camera settings, so that you can adjust the exposure and other functions to match the recording environment. Usually, several different programs are available, such as point-and-shoot, point-and-shoot with manual adjustment, sports, portrait, spotlit scenes, and low light. You also have the ability to select special digital effects, such as fade, wipe, and black and white. If you are shooting outside on a windy day, then you can enable the windscreen to prevent wind noise. If you are shooting home videos or video meant for a Web site, then the point-and-shoot recording program is sufficient.

③ Transfer and Manage Videos

After recording the video, the next step is to transfer the video to your personal computer. Most video cameras connect directly to a USB 2.0 or FireWire port on your personal computer (Figure 11). Transferring video with a digital camera is easy, because the video already is in a digital format that the computer can recognize. Many personal mobile devices include a special cable used to connect the device to a personal computer.

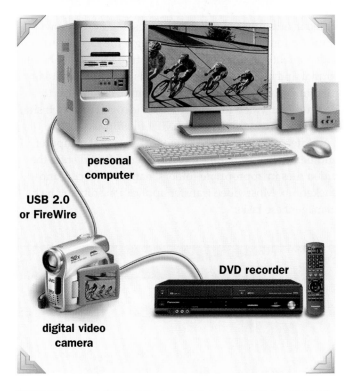

FIGURE 11 A digital video camera is connected to the personal computer or DVD recorder via a FireWire or USB 2.0 port. No additional hardware is needed.

Many people own analog format video tapes that require additional hardware to convert the analog signals to a digital format before the video can be manipulated on a personal computer. The additional hardware includes a special video capture card using a standard RCA video cable or an S-video cable (Figure 12). **S-video** cables provide sharper images and greater overall quality. A personal computer also can record video to a CD or DVD, or it can be connected to an external DVD recorder to record videos.

When transferring video, plan to use approximately 15 to 30 GB of hard disk storage space per hour of digital video. A typical video project requires about four times the amount of raw footage as the final product. Therefore, at the high end, a video that lasts an hour may require up to 120 GB of storage for the raw footage, editing process, and final video. This storage requirement can vary depending on the software you use to copy the video from the video camera to the hard disk and the format you select to save the video. For example, Microsoft's Windows Movie Maker can save 15 hours of standard video in 10 GB when creating video for playback on a computer, but saves only 1 hour of video in 10 GB when creating video for playback on a DVD. A high-definition video file may require over 10 GB per hour.

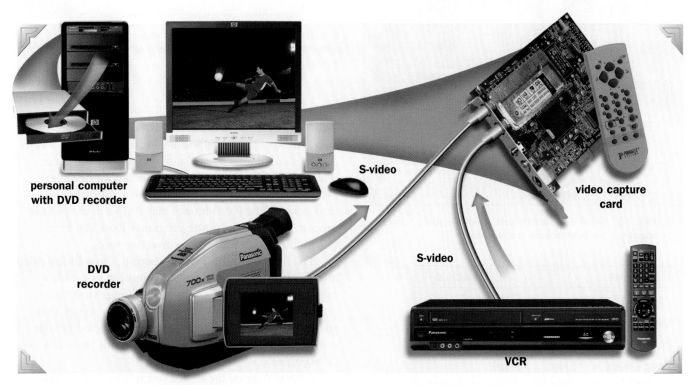

FIGURE 12 An analog camcorder or VCR is connected to the personal computer via an S-video port on a video capture card.

The video transfer requires application software on the personal computer (Figure 13). Windows Vista includes the Windows Movie Maker software that allows you to transfer the video from your video camera. Depending on the length of video and the type of connection used, the video may take a long time to transfer. Make certain that no other programs are running on your personal computer while transferring the video.

The frame rate of a video refers to the number of frames per second (fps) that are captured in the video. The most widely used frame rate is 30 fps. A smaller frame rate results in a smaller file size for the video, but playback of the video will not be as smooth as one recorded with a higher frame rate.

When transferring video, the software may allow you to choose a file format and a codec to store the video. A video **file format** holds the video information in a manner specified by a vendor, such as Apple or Microsoft. Four of the more popular file formats are listed in Figure 14.

File formats support codecs to encode the audio and video into the file formats. A **codec** specifies how the audio and video is compressed and stored within the file. A particular file format may be able to store audio and

video in a number of different codecs. Figure 15 shows some options available for specifying a file format and video quality settings in a video capture program. The file format and codec you choose often is based on what you plan to do with the movie. For example, if you plan to upload your video to the YouTube video sharing Web site, the best choices are DivX and MP4 file formats.

After transferring the video to a personal computer, and before manipulating the video, you should store the video files in appropriate folders, named correctly, and backed up. Most video transfer application software helps manage these tasks.

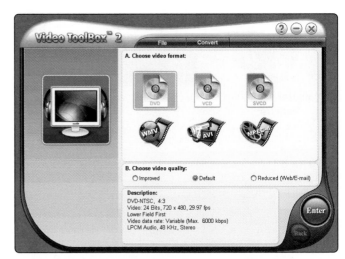

FIGURE 15   Video editing software allows you to specify a combination of file format and video quality settings when saving a video.

④ Edit a Video

Once the video is stored on your hard disk, the next step is to edit, or manipulate, the video. If you used a video capture card to transfer analog video to your computer (Figure 12 on the previous page), the files may require extra initial processing. When you use a video capture card, some of the video frames may be lost in the transfer process. Some video editing programs allow you to fix this problem with **frame rate correction** tools.

The first step in the editing process is to split the video into smaller pieces, or scenes, that you can manipulate more easily. This process is called splitting. Most video software automatically splits the video into scenes, thus sparing you the task. After splitting, you should cut out unwanted scenes or portions of scenes. This process is called pruning.

After you create the scenes you want to use in your final production, you edit each individual scene. You can crop, or change the size of, scenes. That is, you may want to

FIGURE 13   Some video editing software allows you to transfer your video from any video source to a hard disk.

File Format	File Extensions
Apple QuickTime	.MOV or .QT
DivX	.DIVX
Microsoft Windows Media Video	.WMV or .ASF
MPEG-4 Part 4	.MP4
Real RealMedia	.RM or .RAM

FIGURE 14   Apple, DivX, Microsoft, and Real offer the more popular video file formats.

cut out the top or a side of a scene that is irrelevant. You also can resize the scene. For example, you may be creating a video that will be displayed in a Web browser. Making a smaller video, such as 320 × 200 pixels instead of 640 × 480 pixels, results in a smaller file that transmits faster over the Internet. Some video sharing Web sites recommend smaller video resolutions, such as 320 × 200 pixels.

If video has been recorded over a long period, using different cameras or under different lighting conditions, the video may need color correction. Color correction tools (Figure 16) analyze your video and match brightness, colors, and other attributes of video clips to ensure a smooth look to the video.

You can add logos, special effects, or titles to scenes. You can place a company logo or personal logo in a video to identify yourself or the company producing the video. Logos often are added on the lower-right corner of a video and remain for the duration of the video. Special effects include warping, changing from color to black and white, morphing, or zoom motion. Morphing is a special effect in which one video image is transformed into another image over the course of several frames of video, creating the illusion of metamorphosis. You usually add titles at the beginning and end of a video to give the video context. A training video may have titles throughout the video to label a particular scene, or each scene may begin with a title.

The next step in editing a video is to add audio effects, including voice-over narration

and background music. Many video editing programs allow you to add additional tracks, or layers, of sound to a video in addition to the sound that was recorded on the video camera. You also can add special audio effects.

The final step in editing a video is to combine the scenes into a complete video (Figure 17). This process involves ordering scenes and adding transition effects between scenes. Video editing software allows you to combine scenes and separate each scene with a transition. Transitions include fading, wiping, blurry, bursts, ruptures, erosions, and more.

FIGURE 17 Scenes are combined into a sequence on the bottom of the screen.

FIGURE 16 Color correction tools in video editing software allow a great deal of control over the mood of your video creation.

⑤ Distribute the Video

After editing the video, the final step is to distribute it or save it on an appropriate medium. You can save video in a variety of formats. Using special hardware, you can save the video on standard video tape. A digital-to-analog converter is necessary to allow your personal computer to transmit video to a VCR. A digital-to-analog converter may be an external device that connects to both the computer and input device, or may be a video capture card inside the computer.

Video also can be stored in digital formats in any of several DVD formats, on CD, on a media sharing Web site, or on video CD (VCD). **DVD** or **CD creation software**, which often is packaged with video editing software, allows you to create, or master, DVDs and CDs. You can add interactivity to your DVDs. For example, you can allow viewers to jump to certain scenes using a menu. A video CD (VCD) is a CD format that stores video on a CD-R that can be played in many DVD players.

You also can save your video creation in electronic format for distribution over the Web, via e-mail, or to a personal mobile device. Popular media sharing Web sites, such as YouTube (Figure 18), have recommendations for the best file format and codecs to use for video that you upload to them (Figure 19). Your video editing software must support the file format and codec you want to use. Apple's iMovie software typically saves files in the QuickTime file format.

Professionals use hardware and software that allow them to create a film version of digital video that can be played in movie theaters. This technology is becoming increasingly popular. The cost of professional video editing software ranges from thousands to hundreds of thousands of dollars. Video editing software for the home user is available for a few hundred dollars or less. Some Hollywood directors believe that eventually, all movies will be recorded and edited digitally.

After creating your final video for distribution or your personal video collection, you should back up the final video file. You can save your scenes for inclusion in other video creations or create new masters using different effects, transitions, and ordering of scenes.

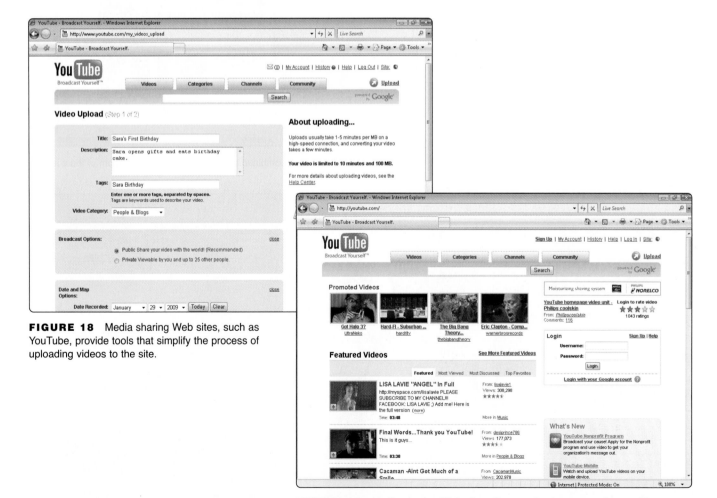

FIGURE 18 Media sharing Web sites, such as YouTube, provide tools that simplify the process of uploading videos to the site.

FIGURE 19 Media sharing Web sites allow you to share your videos with acquaintances or the entire world.

CHAPTER 6

Storage

OBJECTIVES

After completing this chapter, you will be able to:

1. Describe the characteristics of magnetic disks
2. Describe the characteristics of a hard disk
3. Discuss various types of miniature, external, and removable hard disks
4. Describe the characteristics of optical discs
5. Differentiate among various CD and DVD formats
6. Identify the uses of tape
7. Discuss PC Cards, ExpressCard modules, and the various types of miniature mobile storage media
8. Identify uses of microfilm and microfiche

CONTENTS

STORAGE

Storage holds data, instructions, and information for future use. For example, the home user might store letters, budgets, bank statements, a household inventory, records of stock purchases, tax data, addresses of friends and relatives, daily schedules, e-mail messages, homework assignments, recipes, digital photos, music, and videos. A business user accesses many stored items, including customer orders and invoices, vendor payments, payroll records, tax data, inventory records, presentations, digital photos, contracts, marketing literature, contacts, appointments, schedules, e-mail messages, and Web pages. Other users store diagrams, drawings,

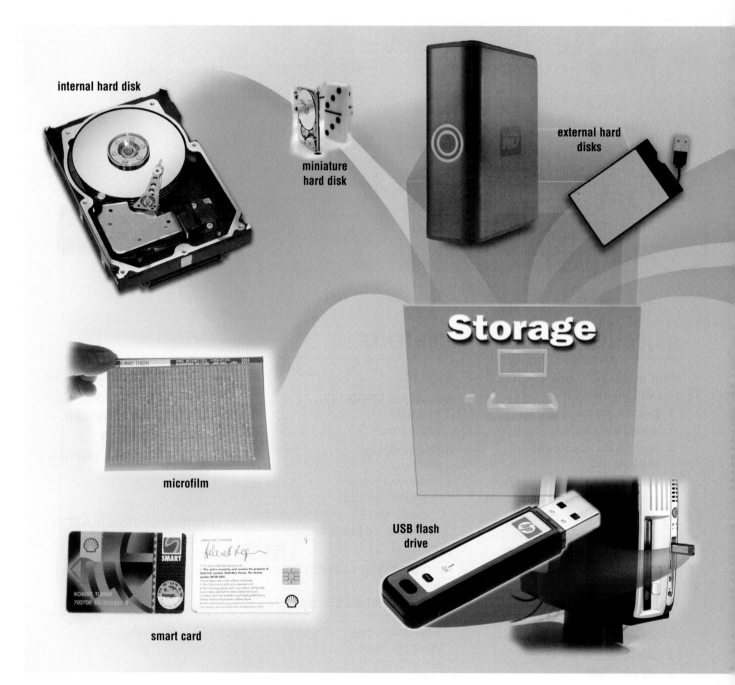

FIGURE 6-1 A variety of storage media.

blueprints, designs, marketing literature, corporate newsletters, product catalogs, and multimedia presentations. All computers also store system and application software.

Storage requirements among users vary greatly. Home users typically have much smaller storage requirements than business users. For example, a home user may need 320 billion bytes of storage, while large businesses may require 50 quadrillion bytes of storage.

A **storage medium** (media is the plural), also called **secondary storage**, is the physical material on which a computer keeps data, instructions, and information. Examples of storage media are hard disks, CDs and DVDs, PC Cards and ExpressCard modules, flash memory cards, USB flash drives, smart cards, and microfilm (Figure 6-1).

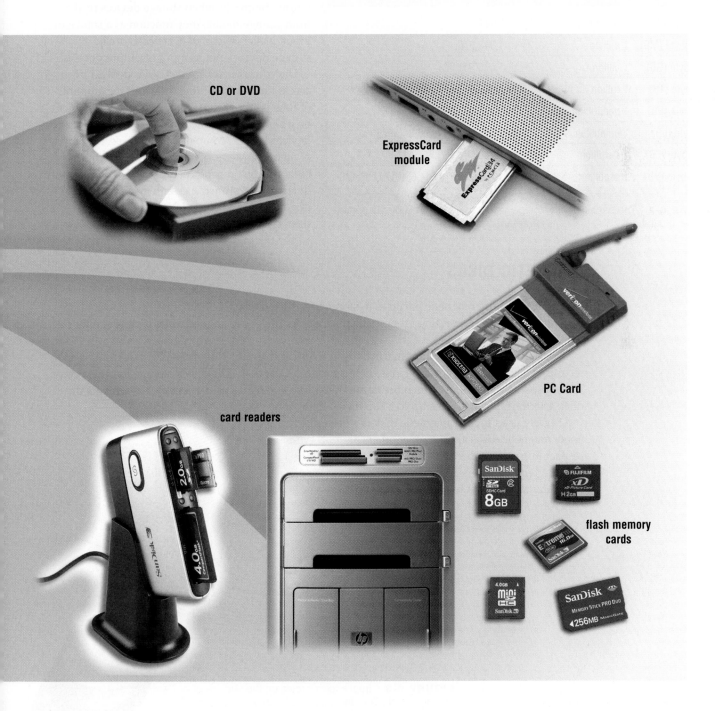

CD or DVD

ExpressCard module

PC Card

card readers

flash memory cards

Capacity is the number of bytes (characters) a storage medium can hold. Figure 6-2 identifies the terms manufacturers use to define the capacity of storage media. For example, a reasonably priced USB flash drive can store up to 1 GB of data (approximately one billion bytes) and a typical hard disk has 320 GB (approximately 320 billion bytes) of storage capacity.

A **storage device** is the computer hardware that records and/or retrieves items to and from storage media. **Writing** is the process of transferring data, instructions, and information from memory to a storage medium. **Reading** is the process of transferring these items from a storage medium into memory. When storage devices write data on storage media, they are creating output. Similarly, when storage devices read from storage media, they function as a source of input. Nevertheless, they are categorized as storage devices, not as input or output devices.

The speed of storage devices is defined by access time. **Access time** measures the amount of time it takes a storage device to locate an item on a storage medium. The access time of storage devices is slow, compared with the access time of memory. Memory (chips) accesses items in billionths of a second (nanoseconds). Storage devices, by contrast, access items in thousandths of a second (milliseconds) or millionths of a second (microseconds).

STORAGE TERMS

Storage Term	Approximate Number of Bytes	Exact Number of Bytes
Kilobyte (KB)	1 thousand	2^{10} or 1,024
Megabyte (MB)	1 million	2^{20} or 1,048,576
Gigabyte (GB)	1 billion	2^{30} or 1,073,741,824
Terabyte (TB)	1 trillion	2^{40} or 1,099,511,627,776
Petabyte (PB)	1 quadrillion	2^{50} or 1,125,899,906,842,624
Exabyte (EB)	1 quintillion	2^{60} or 1,152,921,504,606,846,976
Zettabyte (ZB)	1 sextillion	2^{70} or 1,180,591,620,717,411,303,424
Yottabyte (YB)	1 septillion	2^{80} or 1,208,925,819,614,629,174,706,176

FIGURE 6-2 The capacity of a storage medium is measured by the number of bytes it can hold.

MAGNETIC DISKS

Magnetic disks use magnetic particles to store items such as data, instructions, and information on a disk's surface. Depending on how the magnetic particles are aligned, they represent either a 0 bit or a 1 bit.

Magnetic disks store data and instructions in tracks and sectors (Figure 6-3). A track is a narrow recording band that forms a full circle on the surface of the disk. The disk's storage locations consist of pie-shaped sections, which break the tracks into small arcs called sectors. On a magnetic disk, a sector typically stores up to 512 bytes of data.

A widely used type of magnetic disk is a hard disk. Some magnetic disks are portable; others are not. With respect to a storage medium, the term portable means you can remove the medium from one computer and carry it to another computer.

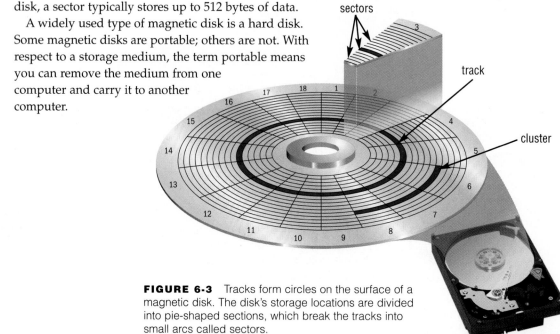

FIGURE 6-3 Tracks form circles on the surface of a magnetic disk. The disk's storage locations are divided into pie-shaped sections, which break the tracks into small arcs called sectors.

Hard Disks

A **hard disk** is a storage device that contains one or more inflexible, circular platters that store data, instructions, and information. People use hard disks to store all types of documents, spreadsheets, presentations, databases, e-mail messages, Web pages, digital photos, music, videos, and software. Businesses use hard disks to store correspondence, reports, financial records, e-mail messages, customer orders and invoices, payroll records, inventory records, presentations, contracts, marketing literature, schedules, and Web sites.

The system unit on most desktop and notebook computers contains at least one hard disk. The entire device is enclosed in an airtight, sealed case to protect it from contamination. A hard disk that is mounted inside the system unit sometimes is called a fixed disk because it is not portable (Figure 6-4).

Current personal computer hard disks have storage capacities from 160 GB to 1 TB and more. Traditionally, hard disks stored data using **longitudinal recording**, which aligned the magnetic particles horizontally around the surface of the disk. With **perpendicular recording**, by contrast, hard disks align the magnetic particles vertically, or perpendicular to the disk's surface, making much greater storage capacities possible. Experts estimate that hard disks using perpendicular recording will provide storage capacities about 10 times greater than disks that use longitudinal recording. Read Looking Ahead 6-1 for a look at the next generation of hard disk storage capacities.

Hard disks are read/write storage media. That is, you can read from and write on a hard disk any number of times.

hard disk mounted inside system unit

FIGURE 6-4   The hard disk in a desktop computer is enclosed inside an airtight, sealed case inside the system unit. (In this and other hard disk photos in the book, the top plate is removed from the hard disk for illustration purposes.)

WEB LINK 6-1

Perpendicular Recording

For more information, visit scsite.com/dcf5e/ch6/weblink and then click Perpendicular Recording.

LOOKING AHEAD 6-1

Heat Increases Disk Capacity

Things are heating up in the data storage industry. Engineers at IBM Research are testing the use of heat to record data inexpensively on magnetic media, such as hard disks.

Within the next few years, the researchers predict that this new technique will allow storage of more than one terabit per square inch, which is the equivalent of 25 DVDs on an area the size of a postage stamp. With this capacity, a hard disk that can store seven terabits will be commonplace.

IBM calls this new storage system Millipede. It uses heated tips mounted on the ends of cantilevers, in a fashion similar to the way the stylus on an old phonograph sat on the grooves of vinyl records. For more information, visit scsite.com/dcf5e/ch6/looking and then click Heated Storage.

CHARACTERISTICS OF A HARD DISK Characteristics of a hard disk include capacity, platters, read/write heads, cylinders, sectors and tracks, revolutions per minute, transfer rate, and access time. Figure 6-5 shows sample characteristics of a 500 GB hard disk. The following paragraphs discuss each of these characteristics.

The capacity of a hard disk is determined from the number of platters it contains, together with composition of the magnetic coating on the platters. A platter is made of aluminum, glass, or ceramic and is coated with an alloy material that allows items to be recorded magnetically on its surface. The coating usually is three millionths of an inch thick.

On desktop computers, platters most often have a size of approximately 3.5 inches in diameter. A typical hard disk has multiple platters stacked on top of one another. Each platter has two read/write heads, one for each side. The hard disk has arms that move the read/write heads to the proper location on the platter (Figure 6-6).

SAMPLE HARD DISK CHARACTERISTICS

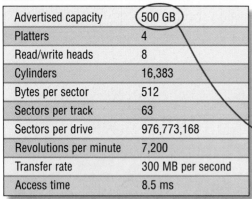

Advertised capacity	500 GB
Platters	4
Read/write heads	8
Cylinders	16,383
Bytes per sector	512
Sectors per track	63
Sectors per drive	976,773,168
Revolutions per minute	7,200
Transfer rate	300 MB per second
Access time	8.5 ms

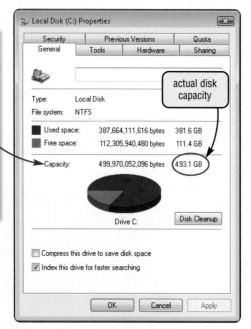

FIGURE 6-5 Characteristics of a sample 500 GB hard disk. The actual disk's capacity sometimes is different from the advertised capacity because of bad sectors on the disk.

FIGURE 6-6 HOW A HARD DISK WORKS

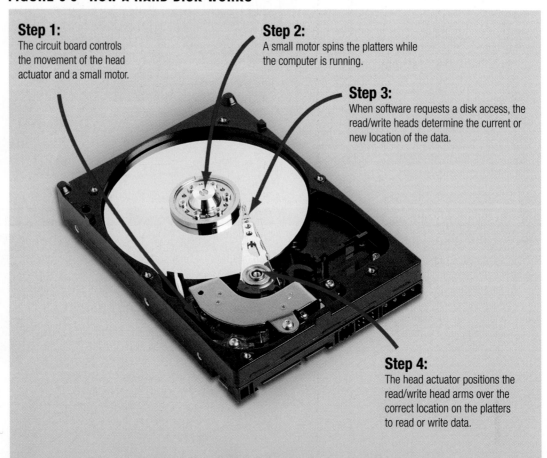

Step 1:
The circuit board controls the movement of the head actuator and a small motor.

Step 2:
A small motor spins the platters while the computer is running.

Step 3:
When software requests a disk access, the read/write heads determine the current or new location of the data.

Step 4:
The head actuator positions the read/write head arms over the correct location on the platters to read or write data.

The location of the read/write heads often is referred to by its cylinder. A cylinder is the vertical section of a track that passes through all platters (Figure 6-7). A single movement of the read/write head arms accesses all the platters in a cylinder. If a hard disk has two platters (four sides), each with 1,000 tracks, then it will have 1,000 cylinders with each cylinder consisting of 4 tracks (2 tracks for each platter).

While the computer is running, the platters in the hard disk rotate at a high rate of speed. This spinning, which usually is 5,400 to 15,000 revolutions per minute (rpm), allows nearly instant access to all tracks and sectors on the platters. The platters typically continue to spin until power is removed from the computer. (On many computers, the hard disk stops spinning or slows down after a specified time to save power.) The spinning motion creates a cushion of air between the platter and its read/write head. This cushion ensures that the read/write head floats above the platter instead of making direct contact with the platter surface. The distance between the read/write head and the platter is about two millionths of one inch.

As shown in Figure 6-8, this close clearance leaves no room for any type of contamination. Dirt, hair, dust, smoke, and other particles could cause the hard disk to have a head crash. A head crash occurs when a read/write head touches the surface of a platter, usually resulting in a loss of data or sometimes loss of the entire drive. Thus, it is crucial that you back up your hard disk regularly. A **backup** is a duplicate of a file, program, or disk placed on a separate storage medium that you can use in case the original is lost, damaged, or destroyed. Chapter 7 discusses backup techniques. Access time for today's hard disks ranges from approximately 3 to 12 ms (milliseconds).

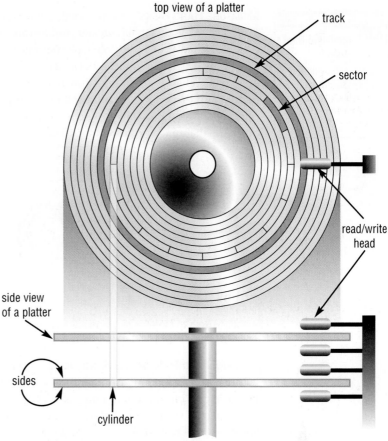

FIGURE 6-7 A cylinder is the vertical section of track through all platters on a hard disk.

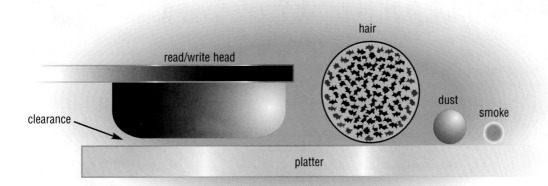

FIGURE 6-8 The clearance between a disk read/write head and the platter is about two millionths of an inch. A smoke particle, dust particle, human hair, or other contaminant could render the drive unusable.

RAID Some personal computer manufacturers provide a hard disk configuration that connects multiple smaller disks into a single unit that acts like a single large hard disk. A group of two or more integrated hard disks is called a **RAID** (redundant array of independent disks). RAID is an ideal storage solution for users who must have the data available when they attempt to access it.

MINIATURE HARD DISKS Many mobile devices and consumer electronics include miniature hard disks to provide users with greater storage capacities than flash memory. These tiny hard disks, which are smaller than the notebook computer hard disks, often have form factors of 1.8 inch, 1 inch, and 0.85 inch (Figure 6-9). Devices such as portable media players, digital cameras, and smart phones often have built-in miniature hard disks. Another type of miniature hard disk, often called a **pocket hard drive**, is a self-contained unit that you insert in and remove from a slot in a device or a computer or plug in a USB port on a computer (Figure 6-10). Miniature hard disks have storage capacities that range from 4 GB to 250 GB.

earbuds for portable media player

FIGURE 6-9 This miniature hard disk is used in portable media players and other small devices, enabling users to store music, videos, movies, and any other type of files on the disk.

pocket hard drive

FIGURE 6-10 Users easily can transport data from one computer to another with a pocket hard drive.

EXTERNAL AND REMOVABLE HARD DISKS An **external hard disk**, shown in the left picture in Figure 6-11, is a separate free-standing hard disk that connects with a cable to a USB port or FireWire port on the system unit. As with the internal hard disk, the entire hard disk is enclosed in an airtight, sealed case. External hard disks have storage capacities of up to 2 TB and more. Some external hard disk units include multiple hard disks that you can use for different purposes, if desired.

A **removable hard disk** is a hard disk that you insert and remove from a drive. A removable hard disk drive, shown in the right picture in Figure 6-11, reads from and writes on the removable hard disk. Removable hard disks have storage capacities up to 750 GB.

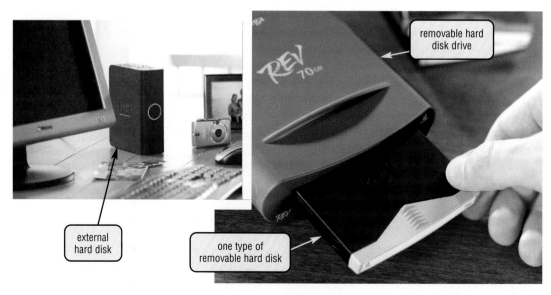

removable hard disk drive

external hard disk

one type of removable hard disk

FIGURE 6-11 Examples of external and removable hard disks.

External and removable hard disks offer the following advantages over internal hard disks (fixed disks):

- Transport a large number of files
- Back up important files or an entire internal hard disk (several external hard disk models allow you to back up simply by pushing a button on the disk)
- Easily store large audio and video files
- Secure your data; for example, at the end of a work session, remove the hard disk and lock it up, leaving no data in the computer
- Add storage space to a notebook computer or Tablet PC
- Add storage space to a desktop computer without having to open the system unit
- Share a drive with multiple computers

As the prices of external and removable hard disks drop, increasingly more users are purchasing one to supplement a home or office internal hard disk.

FAQ 6-1

Can airport security screening equipment damage or erase the data on my hard disk or other media?

The Transportation Security Administration's Web site states that their screening (x-ray) equipment will not damage or erase the data stored on hard disks CDs, DVDs, or the miniature storage media used in digital cameras. Although your media is equally safe whether you carry it onto the airplane or leave it in checked baggage, packing it with your carry-on items is a better safeguard against physical damage. If you are uneasy about your media passing through the airport screening equipment, you may be able to request that the items be manually (hand) searched. It is important to note that the equipment used to screen checked baggage will not harm electronic media, but it will damage undeveloped film. As a safeguard, you should carry all film onto the airplane and request a manual search. For more information, visit scsite.com/dcf5e/ch6/faq and then click Airport Screening Equipment.

HARD DISK CONTROLLERS A **disk controller** consists of a special-purpose chip and electronic circuits that control the transfer of data, instructions, and information from a disk to and from the system bus and other components in the computer. That is, it controls the interface between the hard disk and the system bus. A disk controller for a hard disk, called the hard disk controller, may be part of a hard disk or the motherboard, or it may be a separate adapter card inside the system unit.

In their personal computer advertisements, vendors usually state the type of hard disk interface supported by the hard disk controller. Thus, you should understand the types of available hard disk interfaces. In addition to USB and FireWire (external hard disk interfaces), four other types of hard disk interfaces for internal use in personal computers are SATA, EIDE, SCSI, and SAS.

- SATA (Serial Advanced Technology Attachment) uses serial signals to transfer data, instructions, and information. The primary advantage of SATA interfaces is their cables are thinner, longer, more flexible, and less susceptible to interference than cables used by hard disks that use parallel signals. SATA interfaces also support connections to CD and DVD drives.
- EIDE (Enhanced Integrated Drive Electronics) is a hard disk interface that uses parallel signals to transfer data, instructions, and information. EIDE interfaces can support up to four hard disks at 137 GB per disk. EIDE interfaces also provide connections for CD and DVD drives and tape drives.
- SCSI interfaces, which also use parallel signals, can support up to eight or fifteen peripheral devices. Supported devices include hard disks, CD and DVD drives, tape drives, printers, scanners, network cards, and much more. Some computers have a built-in SCSI interface, while others use an adapter card to add a SCSI interface.
- SAS (serial-attached SCSI) is a newer type of SCSI that uses serial signals to transfer data, instructions, and information. Advantages of SAS over parallel SCSI include thinner, longer cables; reduced interference; less expensive; support for many more connected devices at once; and faster speeds. In addition to hard disks, SAS interfaces support connections to CD and DVD drives, printers, scanners, digital cameras, and other devices. Experts predict that SAS eventually will replace parallel SCSI.

WEB LINK 6-3

SAS

For more information, visit scsite.com/dcf5e/ch6/weblink and then click SAS.

ONLINE STORAGE Some users choose online storage instead of storing data locally on a hard disk. **Online storage** is a service on the Web that provides hard disk storage to computer users, for free or for a minimal monthly fee (Figure 6-12). Fee arrangements vary. For example, one online storage service provides 5 GB of storage free to registered users; another charges $10 per month for 5 GB of storage.

Users subscribe to an online storage service for a variety of reasons:

- To access files on the Internet hard disk from any computer or device that has Internet access
- To allow others to access files on their Internet hard disk so that others can listen to an audio file, watch a video clip, or view a picture — instead of e-mailing the file to them
- To view time-critical data and images immediately while away from the main office or location; for example, doctors can view x-ray images from another hospital, home, or office
- To store offsite backups of data

Once users subscribe to the online storage service, they can save on the Internet hard disk in the same manner they save on their local hard disk.

FIGURE 6-12 An example of one Web site advertising its online storage service.

Floppy Disks

A **floppy disk**, also called a **diskette**, is a portable, inexpensive storage medium that consists of a thin, circular, flexible plastic Mylar film with a magnetic coating enclosed in a square-shaped plastic shell. A typical floppy disk is 3.5 inches wide and has storage capacities up to 1.44 MB. Floppy disks are not as widely used as they were 15 years ago because of their low storage capacity.

A **floppy disk drive** is a device that reads from and writes on a floppy disk. A user inserts a floppy disk in and removes it from a floppy disk drive. Because computers today do not include a floppy disk drive as standard equipment, you can use an external floppy disk drive, in which the drive is a separate device with a cable that plugs in a port on the system unit (Figure 6-13). These external drives are attached to the computer only when the user needs to access items on a floppy disk. You can read from and write on a floppy disk any number of times.

FIGURE 6-13 An external floppy disk drive attached to a computer with a cable.

Test your knowledge of pages 220 through 228 in Quiz Yourself 6-1.

OPTICAL DISCS

An **optical disc** is a type of optical storage media that consists of a flat, round, portable, disc made of metal, plastic, and lacquer. These discs usually are 4.75 inches in diameter and less than one-twentieth of an inch thick.

Optical discs primarily store software, data, digital photos, movies, and music. Some optical disc formats are read only, meaning users cannot write (save) on the media. Others are read/write, which allows users to save on the disc just as they save on a hard disk.

Nearly every personal computer today includes some type of optical disc drive installed in a drive bay. On these drives, you push a button to slide out a tray, insert the disc, and then push the same button to close the tray (Figure 6-14). Other convenient features on most of these drives include a volume control button and a headphone port (or jack) so that you can use headphones to listen to audio without disturbing others nearby.

With some discs, you can read and/or write on one side only. Manufacturers usually place a silk-screened label on the top layer of these single-sided discs. You insert a single-sided disc in the drive with the label side up. Other discs are double-sided. Simply remove the disc from the drive, flip it over, and reinsert it in the drive to use the other side of the disc. Double-sided discs often have no label; instead each side of the disc is identified with small writing around the center of the disc. Some drives use **LightScribe technology**, which works with specially coated optical discs, to etch labels directly on the disc (as opposed to placing an adhesive label on the disc).

Optical discs store items by using microscopic pits (indentations) and lands (flat areas) that are in the middle layer of the disc. A high-powered laser light creates the pits. A lower-powered laser light reads items from the disc by reflecting light through the bottom of the disc, which usually is either solid gold or silver in color. The reflected light is converted into a series of bits the computer can process.

Push the button to slide out the tray.

Insert the disc.

Push the same button to close the tray.

FIGURE 6-14 On optical disc drives, you push a button to slide out a tray, insert the disc and then push the same button to close the tray.

Manufacturers claim that a properly cared for high-quality optical disc will last 5 years but could last up to 100 years. Figure 6-15 offers some guidelines for the proper care of optical discs.

Many different formats of optical discs exist today. Figure 6-16 identifies a variety of optical disc formats and specifies whether a user can read from the disc, write to the disc, and/or erase the disc. The following sections describe characteristics unique to each of these disc formats. Read Looking Ahead 6-2 for a look at the future of optical disc technology.

OPTICAL DISC FORMATS

Optical Disc		Read	Write	Erase
	CD-ROM	Y	N	N
	CD-R	Y	Y	N
	CD-RW	Y	Y	Y
	DVD-ROM BD-ROM HD DVD-ROM	Y	N	N
	DVD-R DVD+R BD-R HD DVD-R	Y	Y	N
	DVD-RW DVD+RW DVD-RAM BD-RE HD DVD-RW	Y	Y	Y

FIGURE 6-16 Manufacturers sell CD-ROM and DVD-ROM media prerecorded (written) with audio, video, and software. Users cannot change the contents of these discs. Users, however, can purchase the other formats of CDs and DVDs as blank media and record (write) their own data, instructions, and information on these discs.

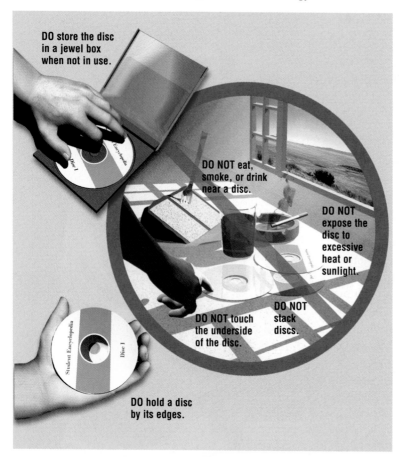

FIGURE 6-15 Some guidelines for the proper care of optical discs.

DO store the disc in a jewel box when not in use.

DO NOT eat, smoke, or drink near a disc.

DO NOT expose the disc to excessive heat or sunlight.

DO NOT touch the underside of the disc.

DO NOT stack discs.

DO hold a disc by its edges.

 FAQ 6-2

Can I clean a disc?

Yes, you can remove dust, dirt, smudges, and fingerprints from the bottom surface of a CD or DVD. Moisten a nonabrasive cloth with warm water or rubbing alcohol and then wipe the disc in straight lines from the center outward. You also can repair scratches on the bottom surface with a specialized disc repair kit. For more information, visit scsite.com/dcf5e/ch6/faq and then click Cleaning and Repairing Discs.

LOOKING AHEAD 6-2

Interactive Gift Cards Provide Marketing Opportunities

Finding the perfect gift for a finicky friend or for a person who seems to have everything can be quite a problem. Gift cards can solve this dilemma. Consumers spend more than $25 million on gift cards during the holiday season, making this item the most popular present among consumers of all ages.

Today's plastic gift cards may one day become optical discs, complete with interactive activities for the recipient. EnXnet is developing ThinDisc technology to create a Multimedia Gift Card that, when played on a computer, can display detailed product information, games, online promotions, printable coupons, and Web links.

The optical disc gift card also may have other uses, including functioning as an interactive room key at hotels and resorts. Guests can open their hotel door and then play the key on their computer to view content provided by the hotel, such as a destination video and exclusive online discounts and promotions. For more information, visit scsite.com/dcf5e/ch6/looking and then click Optical Discs.

CD-ROMs

A **CD-ROM** (pronounced SEE-DEE-rom), or compact disc read-only memory, is a type of optical disc that users can read but not write (record) or erase — hence, the name read-only. Manufacturers write the contents of standard CD-ROMs. A standard CD-ROM is called a single-session disc because manufacturers write all items on the disc at one time. Software manufacturers often distribute programs using CD-ROMs (Figure 6-17).

A typical CD-ROM holds from 650 MB to 1 GB of data, instructions, and information. To read a CD-ROM, insert the disc in a **CD-ROM drive** or a CD-ROM player. Because audio CDs and CD-ROMs use the same laser technology, you may be able to use a CD-ROM drive to listen to an audio CD while using the computer.

WEB LINK 6-4

CD-ROMs

For more information, visit scsite.com/dcf5e/ch6/weblink and then click CD-ROMs.

FIGURE 6-17 Encyclopedias, games, simulations, and many other programs are distributed on CD-ROM.

ARCHIVE CDs AND PICTURE CDs   Many people use Archive CDs or Picture CDs to preserve their photos. When you post and share photos online on a photo sharing community, you can choose to save your collection of online photos on an **Archive CD**, which stores photos in the jpg file format (Figure 6-18). The cost of Archive CDs is determined by the number of photos being stored. One service, for example, charges $7 for every hundred pictures.

A Kodak **Picture CD** stores digital versions of film using a jpg file format. Many photo centers offer Picture CD service for consumers when they drop off film to be developed. The additional cost for a Picture CD is about $3 per roll of film.

Most optical disc drives can read an Archive CD and a Picture CD. You can print copies of the photos from the CD on paper with an ink-jet printer. If you do not have a printer to print the images, many stores have kiosks at which you can print pictures from an Archive CD, a Picture CD, or other media.

WEB LINK 6-5

Archive CDs

For more information, visit scsite.com/dcf5e/ ch6/weblink and then click Archive CDs.

FIGURE 6-18 HOW AN ARCHIVE CD WORKS

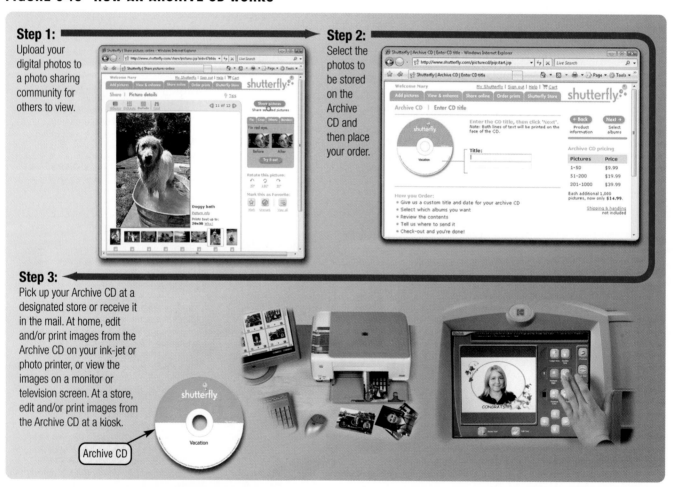

Step 1:
Upload your digital photos to a photo sharing community for others to view.

Step 2:
Select the photos to be stored on the Archive CD and then place your order.

Step 3:
Pick up your Archive CD at a designated store or receive it in the mail. At home, edit and/or print images from the Archive CD on your ink-jet or photo printer, or view the images on a monitor or television screen. At a store, edit and/or print images from the Archive CD at a kiosk.

Archive CD

CD-Rs and CD-RWs

Many personal computers today include either a CD-R or CD-RW drive as a standard feature. Unlike standard CD-ROM drives, users record, or write, their own data on a disc with a CD-R or CD-RW drive. The process of writing on an optical disc is called **burning**.

A **CD-R** (compact disc-recordable) is a multisession optical disc on which users can write, but not erase, their own items such as text, graphics, and audio. Multisession means you can write on part of the disc at one time and another part at a later time. Each part of a CD-R can be written on only one time, and the disc's contents cannot be erased. Writing on the CD-R requires a CD recorder or a **CD-R drive**. A CD-R drive usually can read both audio CDs and standard CD-ROMs.

A **CD-RW** (compact disc-rewritable) is an erasable multisession disc you can write on multiple times. To write on a CD-RW disc, you must have CD-RW software and a **CD-RW drive**. A popular use of CD-RW and CD-R discs is to create audio CDs. For example, users can record their own music and save it on a CD, purchase and download songs from the Web, or rearrange tracks on a purchased music CD. The process of copying audio and/or video data from a purchased disc and saving it on digital media is called **ripping**.

DVD-ROMs, BD-ROMs, and HD DVD-ROMs

A **DVD-ROM** (digital versatile disc-read-only memory or digital video disc-read-only memory) is a high-capacity optical disc on which users can read but not write or erase. Manufacturers write the contents of DVD-ROMs and distribute them to consumers. DVD-ROMs store movies, music, huge databases, and complex software (Figure 6-19).

To read a DVD-ROM, you must have a **DVD-ROM drive** or DVD player. Most DVD-ROM drives also can read audio CDs, CD-ROMs, CD-Rs, and CD-RWs. Some drives, called DVD/CD-RW drives, are combination drives that read DVD and CD media.

A DVD-ROM uses one of three storage techniques. The first involves making the disc denser by packing the pits closer together. The second involves using two layers of pits. For this technique to work, the lower layer of pits is semitransparent so that the laser can read through it to the upper layer. This technique doubles the capacity of the disc. Finally, some DVD-ROMs are double-sided. Two newer, more expensive competing DVD formats are Blu-ray and HD DVD, both of which are higher capacity and better quality than standard DVDs. A **Blu-ray Disc** (BD) has storage capacities of 100 GB, with expectations of exceeding 200 GB in the future. The **HD DVD disc**, which stands for high-density-DVD, has storage capacities up to 60 GB with future projections of 90 GB capacities. Figure 6-20 compares the current storage capacities of DVD-ROM, BD-ROM, and HD DVD-ROM media (read Ethics & Issues 6-1 for a related discussion). Another high density format, called **HD VMD** (Versatile Multilayer Disc) potentially will contain up to 20 layers, each with a capacity of 5 GB. Current HD VMDs have capacities of 40 GB and more.

FIGURE 6-19 A DVD-ROM is a high-capacity optical disc.

DVD, BD, AND HD DVD STORAGE CAPACITIES

Sides	Layers	DVD-ROM	BD-ROM	HD DVD-ROM
1	1	4.7 GB	25 GB	15 GB
1	2	8.5 GB	50 GB	30 GB
2	1	9.4 GB	50 GB	30 GB
2	2	17 GB	100 GB	60 GB

FIGURE 6-20 Storage capacities of DVDs, BDs, and HD DVDs.

ETHICS & ISSUES 6-1

Is the Blu-ray and HD DVD Competition Good for Consumers?

In the early 1980s, a battle raged over the VHS and Betamax video tape formats. Eventually, the VHS format won over the hearts and dollars of consumers despite experts' claims of the superiority of the Betamax format, and the Betamax format remains a footnote in the history of consumer electronics. Today, a similar rivalry exists between the Blu-ray and HD DVD formats as two competing groups of consumer electronic corporate giants vie to get their players and discs in your home.

Some differences exist between the standards. While a Blu-ray Disc (BD) can hold more data than an HD DVD disc, the HD DVD players are much less expensive and still include enough capacity to hold a high-definition movie. HD DVD discs are less expensive to make, though more movie studios have announced support for Blu-ray. Some consumer advocates claim that the competition between the standards will benefit consumers as each side tries to win through lower prices and more features. Others claim that two standards hurt consumers because some movie studios, computer companies, and software providers will choose to support only one format. If this happens, consumers may choose to purchase both types of devices or, in frustration, not purchase a player at all. Recently, though, some manufacturers released players that support both formats. Is the availability of two high-definition DVD formats good for consumers? Why or why not? Do you think that prices will go up if one format eventually wins over the other? Why or why not? With limited shelf space, how should video rental and retail stores cope with keeping both formats for a movie in stock?

A mini-DVD that has grown in popularity is the UMD, which works specifically with the PlayStation Portable handheld game console. The **UMD** (Universal Media Disc), which has a diameter of about 2.4 inches, can store up to 1.8 GB of games, movies, or music.

Recordable and Rewritable DVDs

WEB LINK 6-6

Blu-ray and HD DVD

For more information, visit scsite.com/dcf5e/ch6/weblink and then click Blu-ray and HD DVD.

Many types of recordable and rewritable DVD formats are available. DVD-R, DVD+R, BD-R, and HD DVD-R allow users to write on the disc once and read (play) it many times. **DVD-RW**, **DVD+RW**, and **DVD+RAM** are three competing rewritable DVD formats. Similarly, **BD-RE** and **HD DVD-RW** are competing high-capacity rewritable DVD formats. To write on these discs, you must have a compatible drive or recorder.

Rewritable DVD drives usually can read a variety of DVD and CD media. Before investing in equipment, check to be sure it is compatible with the media on which you intend to record.

As the cost of DVD technologies becomes more reasonable, many industry professionals expect that DVD eventually will replace all CD media.

Test your knowledge of pages 229 through 234 in Quiz Yourself 6-2.

QUIZ YOURSELF 6-2

Instructions: Find the true statement below. Then, rewrite the remaining false statements so they are true.

1. A CD-RW is a type of optical disc on which users can read but not write (record) or erase.
2. A DVD-RAM is a single-session disc that stores digital versions of film using a jpg file format.
3. DVDs have the same storage capacities as CDs.
4. Optical discs are written and read by mirrors.
5. Three competing rewritable DVD formats are DVD-RW, DVD+RW, and DVD+RAM.

Quiz Yourself Online: To further check your knowledge of optical discs and various optical disc formats, visit scsite.com/dcf5e/ch6/quiz and then click Objectives 4 – 5.

TAPE

One of the first storage media used with mainframe computers was tape. **Tape** is a magnetically coated ribbon of plastic capable of storing large amounts of data and information at a low cost. Tape no longer is used as a primary method of storage. Instead, business users utilize tape most often for long-term storage and backup.

A **tape drive** reads and writes data and information on a tape. Although older computers used reel-to-reel tape drives, today's tape drives use tape cartridges. A tape cartridge is a small, rectangular, plastic housing for tape (Figure 6-21). Tape cartridges that contain quarter-inch-wide tape are slightly larger than audiocassette tapes.

FIGURE 6-21   A tape drive and a tape cartridge.

Business users sometimes back up personal computer hard disks to tape, often using an external tape drive. On larger computers, tape cartridges are mounted in a separate cabinet called a tape library.

Tape storage requires sequential access, which refers to reading or writing data consecutively. As with a music tape, you must forward or rewind the tape to a specific point to access a specific piece of data.

Hard disks, CDs, and DVDs all use direct access. Direct access means that the device can locate a particular data item or file immediately, without having to move consecutively through items stored in front of the desired data item or file. When writing or reading specific data, direct access is much faster than sequential access.

PC CARDS AND EXPRESSCARD MODULES

A **PC Card** is a thin, credit-card-sized removable flash memory device that fits into a PC Card slot. An **ExpressCard module** is a removable device, smaller than a PC Card, that fits in an ExpressCard slot. PC Cards and ExpressCard modules can be used to add memory, storage, communications, multimedia, and security capabilities to a computer. PC Cards and ExpressCard modules commonly are used in notebook computers.

PC Cards are about 86 mm long and 54 mm wide. ExpressCard modules, by contrast, are either rectangular at 75 mm long and 34 mm wide or L-shaped with a width of 54 mm (Figure 6-22).

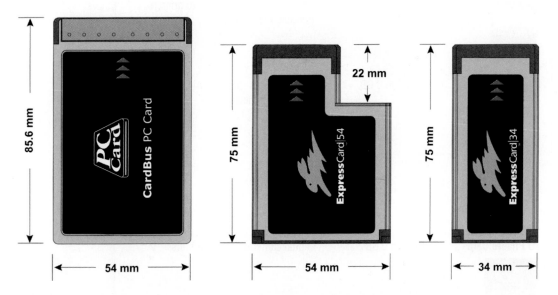

FIGURE 6-22   Comparison of PC Card and ExpressCard module form factors.

MINIATURE MOBILE STORAGE MEDIA

Miniature mobile storage media allow mobile users easily to transport digital images, music, or documents to and from computers and other devices. Many desktop computers, notebook computers, Tablet PCs, digital cameras, portable media players, smart phones, and other personal mobile devices have built-in ports or slots to hold miniature mobile storage media. For computers or devices without built-in slots, users insert the media in separate peripherals such as card reader/writers, which typically plugs in a USB port. Three types of miniature mobile storage media include flash memory cards, USB flash drives, and smart cards.

Flash Memory Cards

Common types of flash memory cards include **CompactFlash (CF)**, **Secure Digital (SD)**, **microSD**, **miniSD**, **xD Picture Card**, and **Memory Stick**. The table in Figure 6-23 compares storage capacities and uses of these miniature mobile storage media. Depending on the device, manufacturers claim miniature mobile storage media can last from 10 to 100 years.

To view, edit, or print images and information stored on miniature mobile storage media, you transfer the contents to your desktop computer or other device. Some printers have slots to read flash memory cards. If your computer or printer does not have a built-in slot, you can purchase a **card reader/writer**, which is a device that reads and writes data, instructions, and information stored on flash memory cards. Card reader/writers usually connect to the USB port or FireWire port on the system unit. The type of card you have will determine the type of card reader/writer needed.

VARIOUS FLASH MEMORY CARDS

Media Name	Storage Capacity	Use
CompactFlash 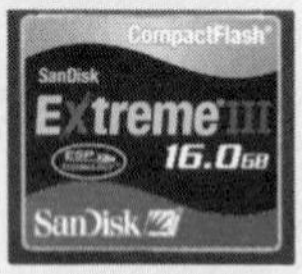	64 MB to 16 GB	Digital cameras, smart phones, PDAs, photo printers, portable media players, notebook computers, desktop computers
Secure Digital (SD) 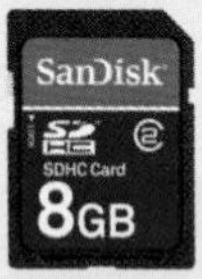	64 MB to 8 GB	Digital cameras, digital video cameras, smart phones, PDAs, photo printers, portable media players
microSD 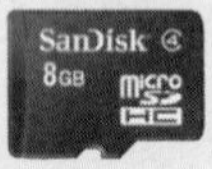	512 MB to 6 GB	Smart phones, portable media players, handheld game consoles, handheld navigation devices
miniSD 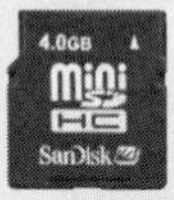	512 MB to 4 GB	Smart phones, portable media players, digital cameras
xD Picture Card 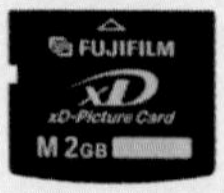	64 MB to 2 GB	Digital cameras, photo printers
Memory Stick 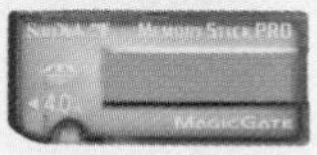	256 MB to 4 GB	Digital cameras, digital video cameras, photo printers, smart phones, PDAs, handheld game consoles, notebook computers
Memory Stick PRO Duo 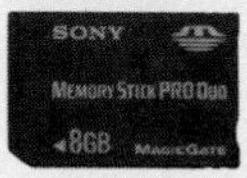	128 MB to 8 GB	Digital cameras, smart phones, handheld game consoles

FIGURE 6-23
A variety of flash memory cards.

FAQ 6-3

Can I take pictures faster if I use a high-speed memory card?

When you take a picture with a digital camera, the camera captures the image, processes the image, and then saves the image to the memory card. High-speed memory cards only decrease the time that it takes to save the image to the card, and not the time necessary to capture and process the image. A high-speed memory card, however, will allow you to take more photos in a short amount of time. For more information, visit scsite.com/dcf5e/ch6/faq and then click Memory Card Speed.

USB Flash Drives

A **USB flash drive**, sometimes called a pen drive or thumb drive, is a flash memory storage device that plugs in a USB port on a computer or mobile device (Figure 6-24). USB flash drives are convenient for mobile users because they are small and lightweight enough to be transported on a keychain or in a pocket. USB flash drives have become the mobile user's primary storage device, making the floppy disk nearly obsolete because they have much greater storage capacities and are much more convenient to carry. Current USB flash drives have storage capacities ranging from 256 MB to 64 GB, with the latter being extremely expensive.

FIGURE 6-24
A USB flash drive.

Smart Cards

A **smart card**, which is similar in size to a credit card or ATM card (Figure 6-25), stores data on a thin microprocessor embedded in the card. Smart cards contain a processor and have input, process, output, and storage capabilities. When you insert the smart card in a specialized card reader, the information on the smart card is read and, if necessary, updated. Uses of smart cards include storing medical records, vaccination data, and other health care or identification information; tracking information such as customer purchases or employee attendance; storing a prepaid amount of money, such as for student purchases on campus; and authenticating users such as for Internet purchases or building access. In addition, smart cards can double as an ID card. Read Ethics & Issues 6-2 for a related discussion.

FIGURE 6-25 Motorists use their smart cards to pay parking fees.

ETHICS & ISSUES 6-2

Should the World Become a Cashless Society?

Do you toss your loose change in a jar with the hopes of making a special purchase with the savings someday? This habit may become futile if the world goes cashless. One form of payment that could end the need for cash is the smart card, which can store a dollar amount on a thin microprocessor and update the amount whenever a transaction is made. Advocates claim that smart cards would eliminate muggings and robberies, make it difficult to purchase illegal goods, and reduce taxes by identifying tax cheats. Also, payment using biometrics, such as fingerprints, is becoming more common. Several high-profile security breaches at credit reporting and credit card companies, however, have heightened concerns over privacy. In a recent survey, most Americans said that they would not use a smart card even if privacy was guaranteed. Another survey shows that most Americans believe that fingerprints are a trustworthy form of identification. A cash purchase usually is anonymous. Yet, a smart card purchase preserves a record of the transaction that could become available to other merchants, advertisers, government agencies, or hackers. Considering the advantages and disadvantages, should the world become a cashless society? Why or why not? Would you be comfortable using a smart card or fingerprint instead of cash for all transactions? Why?

MICROFILM AND MICROFICHE

Microfilm and microfiche store microscopic images of documents on roll or sheet film. **Microfilm** is a 100- to 215-foot roll of film. **Microfiche** is a small sheet of film, usually about 4 × 6 inches. A computer output microfilm recorder is the device that records the images on the film. The stored images are so small that you can read them only with a microfilm or microfiche reader (Figure 6-26).

Microfilm and microfiche use is widespread, with many companies allowing you to search through and view microfilm images online. Libraries use these media to store back issues of newspapers, magazines, and genealogy records. Some large organizations use microfilm and microfiche to archive inactive files. Some banks use them to store transactions and canceled checks. The U.S. Army uses them to store personnel records.

The use of microfilm and microfiche provides a number of advantages. They greatly reduce the amount of paper firms must handle. They are inexpensive and have the longest life of any storage media (Figure 6-27).

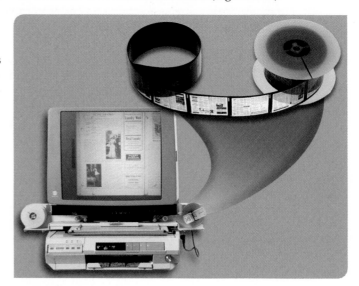

FIGURE 6-26   Images on microfilm can be read only with a microfilm reader.

MEDIA LIFE EXPECTANCIES* (when using high-quality media)

Media Type	Guaranteed Life Expectancy	Potential Life Expectancy
Magnetic disks	3 to 5 years	20 to 30 years
Optical discs	5 to 10 years	50 to 100 years
Microfilm	100 years	500 years

* according to manufacturers of the media

FIGURE 6-27   Microfilm is the medium with the longest life.

ENTERPRISE STORAGE

A large business, commonly referred to as an enterprise, has hundreds or thousands of employees in offices across the country or around the world. Enterprises use computers and computer networks to manage and store huge volumes of data and information about customers, suppliers, and employees.

To meet their large-scale needs, enterprises use special hardware geared for heavy use, maximum availability, and maximum efficiency. One or more servers on the network have the sole purpose of providing storage to connected users. For high-speed storage access, entire networks are dedicated exclusively to connecting devices that provide storage to other servers. In an enterprise, some storage systems can provide more than 185 TB of storage capacity. CD servers and DVD servers hold hundreds of CDs or DVDs.

An enterprise's storage needs usually grow daily. Thus, the storage solutions an enterprise chooses must be able to store its data and information requirements today and tomorrow. Read Ethics & Issues 6-3 for a related discussion.

PUTTING IT ALL TOGETHER

Many factors influence the type of storage devices you should use: the amount of data, instructions, and information to be stored; the hardware and software in use; and the desired cost. The table in Figure 6-28 outlines several suggested storage devices for various types of computer users.

CATEGORIES OF USERS

User	Typical Storage Devices
HOME 	• 320 GB hard disk • Online storage • CD or DVD drive • Card reader/writer • USB flash drive
SMALL OFFICE/ HOME OFFICE 	• 1 TB hard disk • Online storage • CD or DVD drive • External hard disk for backup • USB flash drive
MOBILE 	• 250 GB hard disk • Online storage • CD or DVD drive • Card reader/writer • Portable hard disk for backup • USB flash drive
POWER	• 2.5 TB hard disk • Online storage • CD or DVD drive • Portable hard disk for backup • USB flash drive

LARGE BUSINESS 	• Desktop Computer
	  - 1 TB hard disk
	  - CD or DVD drive
	  - Smart card reader
	  - Tape drive
	  - USB flash drive
	• Server or Mainframe
	  - Network storage server
	  - 40 TB hard disk system
	  - CD or DVD server
	  - Microfilm or microfiche

FIGURE 6-28 Recommended storage devices for various users.

Test your knowledge of pages 234 through 239 in Quiz Yourself 6-3.

 QUIZ YOURSELF 6-3

Instructions: Find the true statement below. Then, rewrite the remaining false statements so they are true.

1. A USB flash drive is a flash memory storage device that plugs in a parallel port on a computer or mobile device.

2. CompactFlash and Memory Sticks are two types of flash memory cards.

3. Microfilm and microfiche have the shortest life of any storage media.

4. Tape storage requires direct access, which refers to reading or writing data consecutively.

Quiz Yourself Online: To further check your knowledge of tape, PC Cards and ExpressCard modules, miniature mobile storage media, and microfilm and microfiche, visit scsite.com/dcf5e/ch6/quiz and then click Objectives 6 – 8.

CHAPTER SUMMARY

Storage holds data, instructions, and information, which includes pictures, music, and videos, for future use. Users depend on storage devices to provide access to their storage media for years and decades to come. Read Ethics & Issues 6-4 for a related discussion.

This chapter identified and discussed various storage media and storage devices. Storage media covered included internal hard disks, external and removable hard disks, floppy disks, CD-ROMs, recordable and rewritable CDs, DVD-ROMs, Blu-ray Discs (BDs), HD DVD discs, recordable and rewritable DVDs, tape, PC Cards and ExpressCard modules, flash memory cards, USB flash drives, smart cards, and microfilm and microfiche.

 ETHICS & ISSUES 6-4

Who Is Responsible for Maintaining Your Online Storage?

In recent years, online storage services, such as Google Gmail or Google Documents, began offering greater capacity and security to users for storing and managing their data. Gmail offers users several gigabytes of free e-mail storage, while Yahoo!'s mail service provides unlimited storage of e-mail messages. Other services offer storage for images, video, and nearly any type of document. Those advocating online storage services maintain that one's data is safer with an online storage company because the company specializes in such technology. The professionals who maintain these services are much more knowledgeable about security, backups, and availability of the service than people typically are about their own personal computers.

Others oppose the use of such services, claiming that the services should not be used to store sensitive documents because they could be more susceptible to security breaches. They also stress that a person always should make regular backups of what they keep stored on the service because if the storage company goes out of business or suffers a power outage, then a person's or company's data may be at risk of becoming unavailable. Who should be responsible for maintaining your online storage? Why? How can people protect their data if an online storage system becomes unavailable or the online storage company goes out of business? What role should the government play in protecting consumers' online storage? What rights should consumers demand from online storage companies? Why?

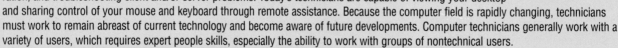

CAREER CORNER   Computer Technician

The demand for computer technicians is growing in every organization and industry. For many, this is the entry point for a career in the computer/information technology field. The responsibilities of a **computer technician**, also called a computer service technician, include a variety of duties. Most companies that employ someone with this title expect the technician to have basic across-the-board knowledge of concepts in the computer electronics field. Some of the tasks are hardware repair and installation; software installation, upgrade, and configuration; and troubleshooting client and/or server problems. Today's technicians are capable of viewing your desktop and sharing control of your mouse and keyboard through remote assistance. Because the computer field is rapidly changing, technicians must work to remain abreast of current technology and become aware of future developments. Computer technicians generally work with a variety of users, which requires expert people skills, especially the ability to work with groups of nontechnical users.

Most entry-level computer technicians possess the A+ certification. This certification attests that a computer technician has demonstrated knowledge of core hardware and operating system technology including installation, configuration, diagnosing, preventive maintenance, and basic networking that meets industry standards and has at least six months of experience in the field. The Electronics Technicians Association also provides a Computer Service Technician (CST) certification program.

Because this is an entry-level position, the pay scale is not as high as other more demanding and skilled positions. Individuals can expect an average annual starting salary of around $36,000 to $50,000. Companies pay more for computer technicians with experience and certification. For more information, visit scsite.com/dcf5e/ch6/careers and then click Computer Technician.

Seagate Technology
Information Storage Supplier

Consumers understand the need to back up their data, but fewer than 25 percent of computer users back up their data on a weekly basis. Hard-disk manufacturer Seagate has been persuading people to save copies of their important documents so that they will suffer less data loss in the event of a fire or natural disaster.

Seagate is a leading manufacturer of hard disks and storage solutions for desktop computers, high-performance servers, and consumer electronics, including digital video recorders and game consoles.

Seagate unveiled the world's first 1 TB hard disk in 2007. In that year, the company also was named the CRN Channel Champion, an honor bestowed to the top vendor in the server-class disk drive category. For more information, visit scsite.com/dcf5e/ch6/companies and then click Seagate.

SanDisk Corporation
World's Largest Flash Memory Card Supplier

The next time you buy milk at the grocery store or shampoo at the drug store, you might want to purchase a flash memory card for your digital camera, too. SanDisk Corporation products can be found in more than 200,000 retail stores across the United States. SanDisk teamed with Sony in 2007 to develop the SxS memory card specification for high-speed data transfer of large digital video camera files.

With retail sales of flash memory cards soaring, SanDisk executives believe consumers buy multiple flash memory cards to store their digital photos in much the same manner as they formerly stored film negatives in shoe boxes. They also prefer to take a separate flash memory card to digital photo processing centers, which produce high-quality prints.

SanDisk is the only company with the rights to manufacture and sell every flash card format. For more information, visit scsite.com/dcf5e/ch6/companies and then click SanDisk.

TECHNOLOGY TRAILBLAZERS

Al Shugart
Storage Expert

Al Shugart enjoyed fixing broken items and developing new technology. The day after receiving his bachelor's degree in 1951, he went to work at IBM to repair broken machines. IBM then promoted him to supervisor of the product development team that developed the first removable rigid read/write disk drive.

He left IBM in 1969 and went to work as vice president of product development for Memorex. In 1973, he started Shugart Associates, a pioneer in the manufacture of floppy disks. Six years later he and some associates founded Seagate Technology, Inc., which is a leader in designing and manufacturing storage products.

He served as president and CEO of Al Shugart International, a venture capital firm in California, until his death in 2006. For more information, visit scsite.com/dcf5e/ch6/people and then click Al Shugart.

Mark Dean
IBM Inventor

The next generation of IBM's hardware and software might be the work of Mark Dean. As vice president of IBM's Almaden Research Center lab in California, Dean is responsible for developing innovative products.

His designs are used in more than 40 million personal computers manufactured each year. He has more than 40 patents or patents pending, including four of the original seven for the architecture of the original personal computer.

Dean joined IBM in 1979 after graduating at the top of his class at the University of Tennessee. Dean earned his Ph.D. degree at Stanford, and he headed a team at IBM that invented the first CMOS microprocessor to operate at 1 gigahertz. For more information, visit scsite.com/dcf5e/ch6/people and then click Mark Dean.

Chapter Review

The Chapter Review section summarizes the concepts presented in this chapter. To obtain help from other students regarding any subject in this chapter, visit scsite.com/dcf5e/ch6/forum and post your thoughts or questions.

① What Are the Characteristics of Magnetic Disks?

Magnetic disks use magnetic particles to store items such as data, instructions, and information, which includes pictures, music, and videos, on a disk's surface. They store data and instructions in tracks and sectors. A widely used type of magnetic disk is a hard disk. Some magnetic disks are portable; others are not.

② What Are the Characteristics of a Hard Disk?

A **hard disk** is a storage device that contains one or more inflexible, circular platters that store data, instructions, and information. A platter is made of aluminum, glass, or ceramic and is coated with a material that allows items to be recorded magnetically on its surface. Each platter has two read/write heads, one for each side. The location of a read/write head often is referred to by its cylinder. A cylinder is the vertical section of a track that passes through all platters. While the computer is running, the platters rotate at 5,400 to 15,000 revolutions per minute (rpm), which allows nearly instant access to all tracks and sectors on the platters. The spinning creates a cushion of air between the platters and the read/write heads. A head crash occurs when a read/write head touches the surface of a platter, usually resulting in a loss of data. A **backup** is a duplicate of a file, program, or disk placed on a separate storage medium that you can use in case the original is lost, damaged, or destroyed.

③ What Are the Various Types of Miniature, External, and Removable Hard Disks?

Many mobile devices include miniature hard disks that provide greater storage capacities than flash memory. A type of miniature hard disk called a **pocket hard drive** is a self-contained unit that fits in a slot in a device or computer or plugs in a USB port on a computer. Miniature hard disks have storage capacities that range from 4 GB to 250 GB. An **external hard disk** is a separate free-standing hard disk that connects with a cable to a USB or FireWire port. External hard disks have storage capacities up to 2 TB or more. A **removable hard disk** can be inserted or removed from a drive. Removable hard disks have storage capacities up to 750 GB.

 Visit scsite.com/dcf5e/ch6/quiz or click the Quiz Yourself button. Click Objectives 1 – 3.

④ What Are the Characteristics of Optical Discs?

An **optical disc** is a type of storage media that consists of a flat, round, portable disc made of metal, plastic, and lacquer. Optical discs store items by using microscopic pits (indentations) and lands (flat areas). A high-powered laser light creates the pits, and a lower-powered laser light reads items by reflecting light through the bottom of the disc.

⑤ What Are the Various CD and DVD Formats?

A **CD-ROM** is an optical disc that users can read but not write (record) or erase. A **CD-R** is a multisession disc on which users can write, but not erase. A **CD-RW** is erasable. An **Archive CD** is used to store photos from a photo sharing community in the jpg file format. A **Picture CD** stores digital versions of film using a jpg file format. A **DVD-ROM** is a high-capacity disc which users can read but not write on or erase. A **Blu-ray Disc** (BD) currently has storage capacities of 100 GB. The **HD DVD disc** has storage capacities up to 60 GB. The **HD VMD** (Versatile Multilayer Disc) is a high-density format with a capacity of 40 GB or more. The **UMD** can store up to 1.8 GB of games, movies, or music. DVD-R, DVD+R, BD-R, and HD DVD-R formats can be written on once. **DVD-RW, DVD+RW,** and **DVD+RAM** are three competing high-capacity rewritable DVD formats. **BD-RE** and **HD DVD-RW** are competing rewritable DVD formats.

 Visit scsite.com/dcf5e/ch6/quiz or click the Quiz Yourself button. Click Objectives 4 – 5.

Chapter Review

(6) How Is Tape Used?

Tape is a magnetically coated ribbon of plastic capable of storing large amounts of data and information at a low cost. A **tape drive** reads and writes data and information on tape. Businesses and home users sometimes back up personal computer hard disks to tape.

(7) What Are PC Cards, ExpressCard Modules, and Other Types of Miniature Mobile Storage Media?

A **PC Card** is a thin, credit-card-sized removable flash memory device that fits into a PC Card slot. An **ExpressCard module** is a removable device, smaller than a PC Card, that fits in an ExpressCard slot. PC Cards and ExpressCard modules add storage or other capabilities to a computer. Tablet PCs, digital cameras, portable media players, smart phones, and other personal mobile devices use some form of miniature mobile storage media to store digital images, music, or documents. Common types of miniature flash memory cards include **CompactFlash** (**CF**), **Secure Digital** (**SD**), **microSD**, **miniSD**, **xD Picture Card**, and **Memory Stick**. A **USB flash drive** is a flash memory storage device that plugs in a USB port on a computer or mobile device. A **smart card**, which is similar in size to a credit card, stores data on a thin microprocessor embedded in the card.

(8) How Are Microfilm and Microfiche Used?

Microfilm is a 100- to 215-foot roll of film. **Microfiche** is a small sheet of film, usually about 4 × 6 inches. Libraries use microfilm and microfiche to store back issues of newspapers, magazines, and records; some large organizations use them to archive inactive files; some banks use them to store transactions and canceled checks; and the U.S. Army uses them to store personnel records.

 Visit scsite.com/dcf5e/ch6/quiz or click the Quiz Yourself button. Click Objectives 6 – 8.

Key Terms

You should know each key term. Use the list below to help focus your study. To further enhance your understanding of the Key Terms in this chapter, visit scsite.com/dcf5e/ch6/terms. See an example of and a definition for each term, and access current and additional information about the term from the Web.

access time (222)
Archive CD (232)
backup (225)
BD-RE (234)
Blu-ray Disc (233)
burning (232)
capacity (222)
card reader/writer (236)
CD-R (232)
CD-R drive (232)
CD-ROM (231)
CD-ROM drive (231)
CD-RW (233)
CD-RW drive (233)
CompactFlash (CF) (236)
computer technician (240)
disk controller (227)
diskette (228)
DVD+RAM (234)
DVD+RW (234)
DVD-ROM (233)
DVD-ROM drive (233)
DVD-RW (234)

ExpressCard module (235)
external hard disk (226)
floppy disk (228)
floppy disk drive (228)
hard disk (223)
HD DVD disc (233)
HD DVD-RW (234)
HD VMD (233)
LightScribe technology (229)
longitudinal recording (223)
magnetic disks (222)
Memory Stick (236)
microfiche (238)
microfilm (238)
microSD (236)
miniSD (236)
online storage (228)
optical disc (229)
PC Card (235)
perpendicular recording (223)
Picture CD (232)
pocket hard drive (226)

RAID (226)
reading (222)
removable hard disk (226)
ripping (233)
secondary storage (221)
Secure Digital (SD) (236)
smart card (237)
storage device (222)
storage medium (221)
tape (234)
tape drive (234)
UMD (234)
USB flash drive (237)
writing (222)
xD Picture Card (236)

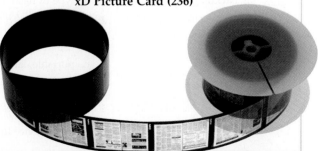

Checkpoint

Use the Checkpoint exercises to check your knowledge level of the chapter. To complete the Checkpoint exercises interactively, visit scsite.com/dcf5e/ch6/check.

True/False

Mark T for True and F for False. (See page numbers in parentheses.)

_____ 1. Secondary storage is the physical material on which a computer keeps data, instructions, and information. (221)

_____ 2. A sector is a narrow recording band that forms a full circle on the surface of the disk. (222)

_____ 3. A typical hard disk usually contains multiple platters. (224)

_____ 4. A removable hard disk is a separate, free-standing hard disk that connects with a cable to a port on the system unit. (226)

_____ 5. A CD-ROM can be read from and written on any number of times. (231)

_____ 6. HD VMDs have a capacity of 400 GB and more. (233)

_____ 7. A UMD can store up to 4.8 GB of games, movies, or music. (234)

_____ 8. BD-RE and HD DVD-RW are competing high-capacity rewritable DVD formats. (234)

_____ 9. Unlike PC Cards, ExpressCard modules can be used to add memory, storage, communications, multimedia, and security capabilities to a computer. (235)

_____ 10. microSD and miniSD are common types of removable hard disks. (236)

Multiple Choice

Select the best answer. (See page numbers in parentheses.)

1. _____ measures the amount of time it takes a storage device to locate an item on a storage medium. (222)
   a. Access time
   b. Capacity
   c. A storage medium
   d. Reading

2. A group of two or more integrated hard disks is called a _____. (226)
   a. backup
   b. platter
   c. RAID
   d. portable hard disk

3. A _____ consists of a special-purpose chip and electronic circuits that control the transfer of data, instructions, and information from a disk to and from the system bus and other components in the computer. (227)
   a. pocket hard drive
   b. removable hard disk
   c. magnetic disk
   d. disk controller

4. Users subscribe to an online storage service to _____. (228)
   a. access files from any computer that has Internet access
   b. allow others to access files
   c. store offsite backups of data
   d. all of the above

5. _____ technology works with specially coated optical discs to etch labels directly on the disc. (229)
   a. SCSI
   b. SATA
   c. LightSaber
   d. LightScribe

6. _____ storage requires sequential access. (235)
   a. Hard disk
   b. Tape
   c. Floppy disk
   d. DVD

7. A _____ is a memory storage device that plugs in a USB port on a computer or mobile device. (237)
   a. PC Card
   b. UMD
   c. USB flash drive
   d. Memory Stick

8. A(n) _____, which is similar in size to a credit card or ATM card, stores data on a thin microprocessor embedded in the card. (237)
   a. CompactFlash card
   b. ExpressCard module
   c. smart card
   d. PC Card

Matching

Match the terms with their definitions. (See page numbers in parentheses.)

_____ 1. backup (225)

_____ 2. online storage (228)

_____ 3. burning (232)

_____ 4. Secure Digital (236)

_____ 5. card reader/writer (236)

a. type of flash memory card often used in digital cameras, digital video cameras, smart phones, PDAs, photo printers, and portable media players

b. duplicate of a file, program, or disk placed on a separate storage medium that you can use in case the original is lost, damaged, or destroyed

c. portable, large-capacity magnetic medium that can store from 100 MB to 750 MB of data

d. device that reads and writes data, instructions, and information stored on flash memory cards

e. the process of writing on an optical disc

f. Web service that provides storage to computer users for free or for a monthly fee

Short Answer

Write a brief answer to each of the following questions.

1. What is longitudinal recording? _____ What is the benefit of perpendicular recording over longitudinal recording? _____

2. What is the purpose of Archive CDs and Picture CDs? _____ What are the approximate costs of Archive CDs and Picture CDs? _____

3. How is a single-session disc different from a multisession disc? _____ What is a CD-RW? _____

4. Why might you use miniature mobile storage? _____ What types of devices might include miniature mobile storage? _____

5. What is one difference between microfilm and microfiche? _____ What are some uses of microfilm and microfiche? _____

Working Together

Working in a group of your classmates, complete the following team exercise.

1. Data and information backup is as important for people with personal computers as it is for companies. Develop a report detailing what your group would consider to be the ideal backup system and required devices for the following scenarios: (1) a home computer for personal use, (2) a computer used in a home-based business, (3) a small business with 6 to 8 computers, (4) a business or organization with up to 100 computers, and (5) a business or organization with more than 100 computers. Include information that supports why you selected the particular options. Develop a presentation to share the information with your class.

Web Research

Use the Internet-based Web Research exercises to broaden your understanding of the concepts presented in this chapter. To discuss any of the Web Research exercises in this chapter with other students, post your thoughts or questions at scsite.com/dcf5e/ch6/forum.

① Blogs One effective method of staying healthy and fit is to obtain sound exercise and nutrition advice from experts who post firsthand experiences in their blogs. These authorities may be people who share a particular experience, such as losing weight or training for a marathon, or who have specialized training in the fitness field. For example, noted author Lou Schuler discusses nutrition, weight training, and issues of particular interest to men (malepatternfitness.com), and runner Scott Dunlop features trail running and triathlon topics (runtrails.blogspot.com). Other popular fitness blogs are featured by The Families.com (fitness.families.com/blog), Getfitsource.com (getfitsource.blogware.com), and Diet-Blog (diet-blog.com). Visit these sites and read the posts. What products are featured? What news stories received more than 25 comments? Which foods are recommended? Which exercises and programs are featured?

② Scavenger Hunt Use one of the search engines listed in Figure 2-8 in Chapter 2 on page 58 or your own favorite search engine to find the answers to the questions that follow. Copy and paste the Web address from the Web page where you found the answer. Some questions may have more than one answer. If required, submit your answers to your instructor. (1) In what year was USB 1.0 introduced? (2) What companies are sponsor members of the USB Flash Drive Alliance? (3) Who did Al Shugart attempt to elect to Congress in 1996?

③ Search Sleuth Many computer users search the World Wide Web by typing words in the search text box, and often they are overwhelmed when the search engine returns thousands of possible Web sites. You can narrow your search by typing quotation marks around phrases and by adding words that give details about the phrase. Go.com is a Web portal developed by the Walt Disney Internet Group. Visit this Web site and then use your word processing program to answer the following questions. Then, if required, submit your answers to your instructor. (1) Locate the Weather section. Type your postal code in the text box. What are the predicted high and low temperatures for your area tomorrow? (2) Click your browser's Back button or press the BACKSPACE key to return to the Go.com home page. (3) Click the Find text box at the top of the page. Type "HD VMD" in the box. How many pages of search results are returned? (4) Click the Search for text box after the words, "HD VMD". Add the search term, +"Blu-ray". How many pages of search results are returned? (5) Review your search results and then write a 50-word summary of your findings.

Learn How To

Use the Learn How To activities to learn fundamental skills when using a computer and accompanying technology. Complete the exercises and submit them to your instructor. Premium Activity: The icon indicates you can see a visual demonstration of the associated Learn How To activity by visiting scsite.com/dcf5e/ch6/howto.

LEARN HOW TO 1: Maintain a Hard Disk

A computer's hard disk is used for the majority of storage requirements. It is important, therefore, to ensure that each hard disk on a computer is operating at peak efficiency, both to use the available storage space effectively and to make disk operations as fast as possible.

Three tasks that maximize disk operations are detecting and repairing disk errors by using the Check Disk utility program; removing unused or unnecessary files and folders by using the Disk Cleanup utility program; and, consolidating files and folders into contiguous storage areas using the Disk Defragmenter utility program. Defragmenting allows your system to access stored files and folders more efficiently.

A. Check Disk

To detect and repair disk errors using the Check Disk utility program, complete the following steps:

1. Click the Start button on the Windows taskbar and then click Computer on the Start menu.
2. When the Computer window opens, right-click the hard disk icon for drive C (or any other hard disk you want to select), and then click Properties on the shortcut menu.
3. In the Properties dialog box, if necessary click the Tools tab to display the Tools sheet. The Tools sheet contains buttons to start the Check Disk program, the Defragment program, and the Backup program (Figure 6-29).
4. Click the Check Now button to display the Check Disk dialog box.
5. To do a complete scan of the disk and correct any errors that are found, place a check mark in the 'Scan for and attempt recovery of bad sectors' check box, and then click the Start button. Four phases of checking the disk will occur. While the checking is in progress, the disk being checked cannot be used for any purpose whatsoever; furthermore, once it has started, the process cannot be stopped.
6. When the four phases are complete (this may take more than one-half hour, depending on the size of the hard disk and how many corrections must occur), a dialog box is displayed with the message, Disk Check Complete. Click the OK button in the dialog box to complete the disk check.

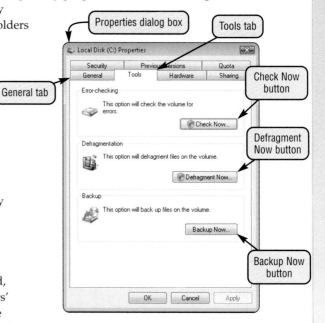

FIGURE 6-29

B. Cleanup Disk

After checking the disk, your next step can be to clean up the disk by removing any programs and data that are not required for the computer. To do so, complete the following steps:

1. Click the General tab (Figure 6-29) in the disk drive Properties dialog box to display the General sheet.
2. Click the Disk Cleanup button in the General sheet to display the Disk Cleanup Options dialog box. When the Disk Cleanup Options dialog box is displayed, click My files only.
3. The Disk Cleanup dialog box is displayed and contains a message that indicates the amount of space that can be freed up is being calculated.
4. After the calculation is complete, the Disk Cleanup dialog box specifies the amount of space that can be freed up and the files to delete, some of which are checked automatically (Figure 6-30). Select those items from which you wish to delete files.

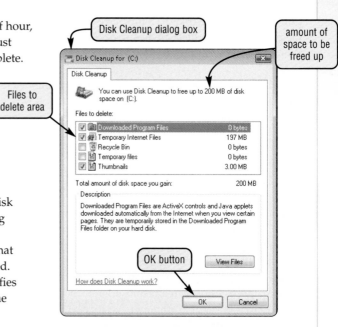

FIGURE 6-30

5. Click the OK button in the Disk Cleanup dialog box.
6. A dialog box asks if you are sure you want to perform these actions. Click the Delete Files button. The Disk Cleanup dialog box illustrates the progress of the cleanup. When the cleanup is complete, the dialog box closes.

C. Defragment Disk

After removing all the unnecessary files from the hard disk, the next step in disk maintenance is to defragment all the files on the disk. When a file is stored on disk, the data in the file sometimes is stored contiguously, and other times is stored in a noncontiguous manner. The greater the amount of data on a disk, the more likely files will be stored noncontiguously. When a file is stored in a noncontiguous manner, it can take significantly longer to find and retrieve data from the file. Therefore, one of the more useful utilities to speed up disk operations is the defragmentation program, which combines all files so that no files are stored in a noncontiguous manner. To use the defragmentation program, complete the following steps:

1. If necessary, click the Tools tab in the Properties dialog box for the hard disk to be defragmented.
2. Click the Defragment Now button in the Tools sheet to display the Disk Defragmenter dialog box (Figure 6-31). This window displays the Disk Defragmenter schedule, when Disk Defragmenter was last run, and when Disk Defragmenter is next scheduled to run.
3. Click the Defragment now button. The defragmentation process begins. During the defragmentation process, the Cancel defragmentation button replaces the Defragment now button. The defragmentation process can consume more than one hour in some cases, depending on the size of the hard disk and the amount of processing that must occur. You can cancel the operation at any time by clicking the Cancel defragmentation button in the Disk Defragmenter window.
4. When the process is complete, the Defragment now button will replace the Cancel defragmentation button.
5. Click the Close button to close the Disk Defragmenter dialog box.

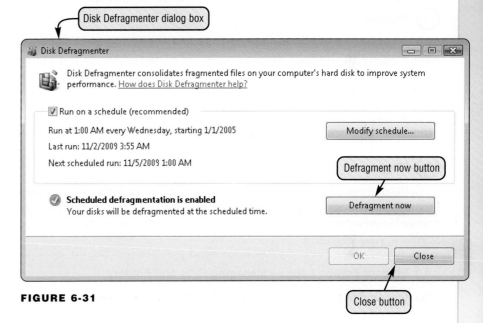

FIGURE 6-31

Proper disk maintenance is critically important so that disk operation is as efficient as possible.

Exercise

Caution: The exercises for this chapter that require the actual disk maintenance are optional. If you are performing these exercises on a computer that is not your own, obtain explicit permission to complete these exercises. Keep in mind that these exercises can require significant computer time and the computer may be unusable during this time.

1. Display the Properties dialog box for a hard disk found on the computer. Display the Tools sheet. Click the Check Now button and then place a check mark in the 'Scan for and attempt recovery of bad sectors' check box. Click the Start button. How long did it take to complete the check of the hard disk? Were any errors discovered and corrected? Submit your answers to your instructor.
2. Display the Properties dialog box for a hard disk found on the computer. Display the General sheet. What is the capacity of the hard disk? How much space is used? How much free space is available? Click the Disk Cleanup button. How much space can be freed up if you use the Disk Cleanup program? Click the OK button to clean up the disk. How long did it take to perform the disk cleanup? Submit your answers to your instructor.
3. Display the Properties dialog box for a hard disk found on the computer. Display the Tools sheet. Click the Defragment now button. In the Disk Defragmenter window, click the Defragment now button. How could you tell when the defragmentation process was completed? How long did defragmentation require? Submit your answers to your instructor.

Learn It Online

Use the Learn It Online exercises to reinforce your understanding of the chapter concepts. To access the Learn It Online exercises, visit scsite.com/dcf5e/ch6/learn.

1 At the Movies — Got Your Video Right Here

To view the Got Your Video Right Here movie, click the number 1 button. Locate your video and click the corresponding High-Speed or Dial-Up link, depending on your Internet connection. Watch the movie to see why the Sling Media Slingbox is the best way to beam your favorite shows to any broadband-connected computer or Windows Mobile device in the world. Then, complete the exercise by answering the questions that follow. How does the Slingbox work? What is one function that it currently is not able to support?

2 Student Edition Labs — Maintaining a Hard Drive

Click the number 2 button. A new browser window will open, displaying the Student Edition Labs. Follow the on-screen instructions to complete the Maintaining a Hard Drive Lab. When finished, click the Exit button. If required, submit your results to your instructor.

3 Practice Test

Click the number 3 button. Answer each question. When completed, enter your name and click the Grade Test button to submit the quiz for grading. Make a note of any missed questions. If required, submit your results to your instructor.

4 Who Wants To Be a Computer Genius²?

Click the number 4 button to find out if you are a computer genius. Directions about how to play the game will be displayed. When you are ready to play, click the Play button. Submit your score to your instructor.

5 Blogs

Click the number 5 button to learn how to use blogs to find information about a topic. Follow the instructions to use MSNBC.com's Blogs Etc. to find a blog about a popular topic, such as the hottest national news story or another topic of national interest. Write a report comparing opinions of two different people about the selected topic. Print your report and submit to your instructor.

6 Student Edition Labs — Managing Files and Folders

Click the number 6 button. A new browser window will open, displaying the Student Edition Labs. Follow the on-screen instructions to complete the Managing Files and Folders Lab. When finished, click the Exit button. If required, submit your results to your instructor.

7 Crossword Puzzle Challenge

Click the number 7 button, then click the Crossword Puzzle Challenge link. Directions about how to play the game will be displayed. Complete the puzzle to reinforce skills you learned in this chapter. When you are ready to play, click the Continue button. Submit the completed puzzle to your instructor.

8 Vista Exercises

Click the number 8 button. When the Vista Exercises menu appears, click the exercise assigned by your instructor. A new browser window will open. Follow the on-screen instructions to complete the exercise. When finished, click the Exit button. If required, submit your results to your instructor.

CHAPTER 7

Operating Systems and Utility Programs

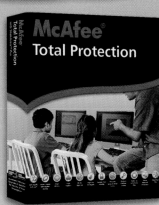

CONTENTS

OBJECTIVES

After completing this chapter, you will be able to:

1. Identify the types of system software

2. Describe the functions of an operating system

3. Explain the purpose of the utilities included with most operating systems

4. Summarize the features of several stand-alone operating systems

5. Identify devices that use embedded operating systems

6. Explain the purpose of several stand-alone utility programs

SYSTEM SOFTWARE

When you purchase a personal computer, it usually has system software installed on its hard disk. **System software** consists of the programs that control or maintain the operations of the computer and its devices. System software serves as the interface between the user, the application software, and the computer's hardware.

Two types of system software are operating systems and utility programs. This chapter discusses the operating system and its functions, as well as several types of utility programs for personal computers.

FIGURE 7-1   Most operating systems perform similar functions, which are illustrated with Windows Vista in this figure.

OPERATING SYSTEMS

An **operating system (OS)** is a set of programs containing instructions that work together to coordinate all the activities among computer hardware resources. Most operating systems perform similar functions that include starting a computer, providing a user interface, managing programs, managing memory, coordinating tasks, configuring devices, establishing an Internet connection, monitoring performance, and providing file management utilities. Some operating systems also allow users to control a network and administer security (Figure 7-1).

In most cases, the operating system is installed and resides on the computer's hard disk. On handheld computers and many mobile devices, however, the operating system may reside on a ROM chip.

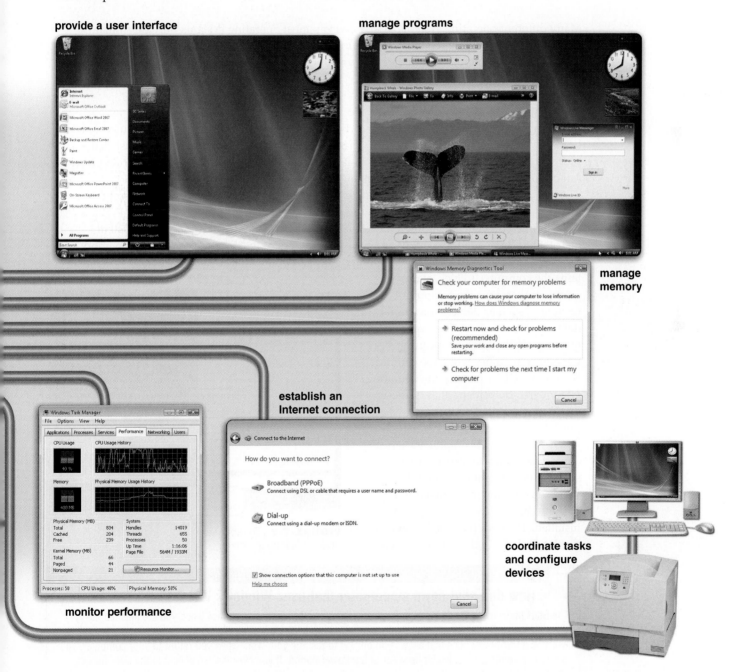

provide a user interface

manage programs

manage memory

establish an Internet connection

monitor performance

coordinate tasks and configure devices

Different sizes of computers typically use different operating systems. For example, a mainframe computer does not use the same operating system as a personal computer. Even the same types of computers, such as desktop computers, may not use the same operating system. Some, however, can run multiple operating systems. When purchasing application software, you must ensure that it works with the operating system installed on your computer.

The operating system that a computer uses sometimes is called the platform. On purchased application software, the package identifies the required platform (operating system). A cross-platform program is one that runs the same on multiple operating systems.

OPERATING SYSTEM FUNCTIONS

Many different operating systems exist; however, most operating systems provide similar functions. The following sections discuss functions common to most operating systems. The operating system handles many of these functions automatically, without requiring any instruction from a user.

Starting a Computer

Booting is the process of starting or restarting a computer. When turning on a computer that has been powered off completely, you are performing a **cold boot**. A **warm boot**, by contrast, is the process of using the operating system to restart a computer. With Windows Vista, for example, you can perform a warm boot by clicking a menu command (Figure 7-2).

When you install new software or update existing software, often an on-screen prompt instructs you to restart the computer. In this case, a warm boot is appropriate.

Each time you boot a computer, the kernel and other frequently used operating system instructions are loaded, or copied, from the hard disk (storage) into the computer's memory (RAM). The kernel is the core of an operating system that manages memory and devices, main-

tains the computer's clock, starts programs, and assigns the computer's resources, such as devices, programs, data, and information. The kernel is memory resident, which means it remains in memory while the computer is running. Other parts of the operating system are nonresident, that is, these instructions remain on the hard disk until they are needed.

When you boot a computer, a series of messages may be displayed on the screen. The actual information displayed varies depending on the make and type of the computer and the equipment installed. The boot process, however, is similar for large and small computers.

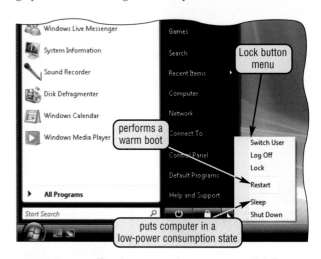

FIGURE 7-2 To reboot a running computer, click Restart on the Lock button menu.

FAQ 7-1

How do I shut down a computer that uses Windows Vista?

The Start menu in Windows Vista provides many options from which to choose when you are finished using your computer. By default, clicking the Power button on the Start menu will place your computer in sleep mode, which is a low-power state that allows you quickly to resume your work when you return to your computer. You are able to configure the default behavior of the Power button. If you click the arrow next to the Lock button, you can select commands that allow you to switch users, log off, lock the computer, restart the computer, put the computer to sleep, put the computer in hibernate mode (allows you to power off the computer, and then resume from where you left off when you turn it on again), and shut down (power off) the computer. For more information, visit scsite.com/dcf5e/ch7/faq and then click Shut Down Options.

Providing a User Interface

You interact with software through its user interface. That is, a **user interface** controls how you enter data and instructions and how information is displayed on the screen. Two types of user interfaces are command-line and graphical. Operating systems sometimes use a combination of these interfaces to define how a user interacts with a computer.

COMMAND-LINE INTERFACE   To configure devices, manage system resources, and troubleshoot network connections, network administrators and other advanced users work with a command-line interface. In a **command-line interface**, a user types commands or presses special keys on the keyboard to enter data and instructions (Figure 7-3a). Command-line interfaces often are difficult to use because they require exact spelling, grammar, and punctuation.

GRAPHICAL USER INTERFACE   Most users today work with a graphical user interface. With a **graphical user interface** (**GUI**), you interact with menus and visual images such as buttons and other graphical objects to issue commands (Figure 7-3b). Many current GUI operating systems incorporate features similar to those of a Web browser. Windows Vista offers two different GUIs, depending on your hardware configuration. Computers with less than 1 GB of RAM work with the **Windows Vista Basic** interface. Computers with more than 1 GB of RAM work with the Windows Vista Aero interface, known as **Windows Aero**, shown in Figure 7-3b, which provides an enhanced visual look, additional navigation options, and animation.

FIGURE 7-3a   (command-line interface)

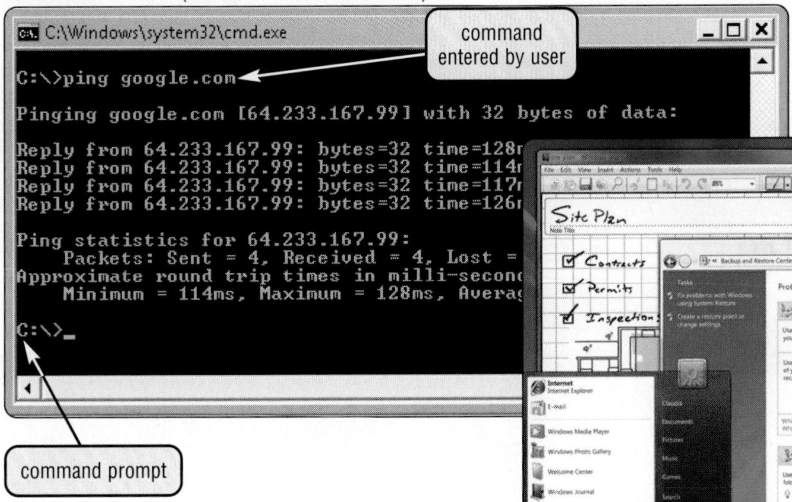

FIGURE 7-3b   (graphical user interface)

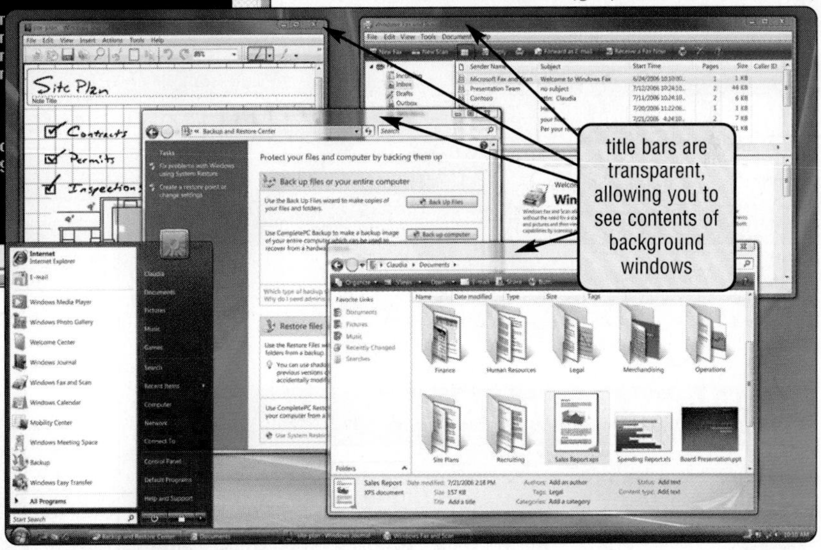

FIGURE 7-3   Examples of command-line and graphical user interfaces.

Managing Programs

Some operating systems support a single user and only one running program at a time. Others support thousands of users running multiple programs. How an operating system handles programs directly affects your productivity.

A single user/single tasking operating system allows only one user to run one program at a time. Smart phones and other personal mobile devices often use a single user/single tasking operating system.

A single user/multitasking operating system allows a single user to work on two or more programs that reside in memory at the same time. Users today typically run multiple programs concurrently. It is common to have an e-mail program and Web browser open at all times, while working with application programs such as word processing or graphics.

When a computer is running multiple programs concurrently, one program is in the foreground and the others are in the background. The one in the foreground is the active program, that is, the one you currently are using. The other programs running but not in use are in the background. In Figure 7-4, the Microsoft PowerPoint program, which is showing a slide show, is in the foreground, and three other programs are running in the background (Microsoft Excel, Windows Media Player, and Chess Titans).

The foreground program typically is displayed on the desktop but the background programs often are hidden partially or completely behind the foreground program. You easily can switch between foreground and background programs. To make a program active (in the foreground) in Windows Vista, click its program button on the taskbar. This causes the operating system to place all other programs in the background.

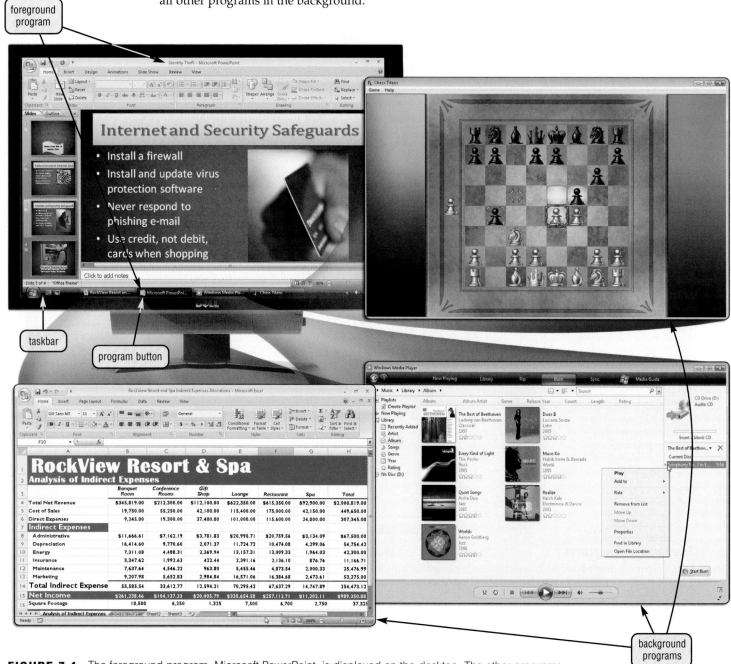

FIGURE 7-4   The foreground program, Microsoft PowerPoint, is displayed on the desktop. The other programs (Windows Media Player, Microsoft Excel, and Chess Titans) are in the background.

A multiuser operating system enables two or more users to run programs simultaneously. Networks, servers, mainframes, and supercomputers allow hundreds to thousands of users to connect at the same time, and thus are multiuser.

A multiprocessing operating system supports two or more processors running programs at the same time. Multiprocessing involves the coordinated processing of programs by more than one processor. Multiprocessing increases a computer's processing speed.

A computer with separate processors also can serve as a fault-tolerant computer. A **fault-tolerant computer** continues to operate when one of its components fails, ensuring that no data is lost. Fault-tolerant computers have duplicate components such as processors, memory, and disk drives. If any one of these components fails, the computer switches to the duplicate component and continues to operate. Airline reservation systems, communications networks, automated teller machines, and other systems that must be operational at all times use fault-tolerant computers.

Managing Memory

The purpose of **memory management** is to optimize the use of random access memory (RAM). RAM consists of one or more chips on the motherboard that hold items such as data and instructions while the processor interprets and executes them. The operating system allocates, or assigns, data and instructions to an area of memory while they are being processed. Then, it carefully monitors the contents of memory. Finally, the operating system releases these items from being monitored in memory when the processor no longer requires them.

Virtual memory is a concept in which the operating system allocates a portion of a storage medium, usually the hard disk, to function as additional RAM. As you interact with a program, part of it may be in physical RAM, while the rest of the program is on the hard disk as virtual memory. Because virtual memory is slower than RAM, users may notice the computer slowing down while it uses virtual memory.

The operating system uses an area of the hard disk for virtual memory, in which it swaps (exchanges) data, information, and instructions between memory and storage. The technique of swapping items between memory and storage is called paging. When an operating system spends much of its time paging, instead of executing application software, it is said to be thrashing. If application software, such as a Web browser, has stopped responding and the hard disk's LED blinks repeatedly, the operating system probably is thrashing.

Instead of using a hard disk as virtual memory, Windows Vista users can increase size of memory through **Windows ReadyBoost**, which can allocate up to 4 GB of removable flash memory devices as additional memory cache. Users notice better performance with Windows ReadyBoost versus hard disk virtual memory because the operating system accesses a flash memory device, such as a USB flash drive or SD memory card, more quickly than it accesses a hard disk.

Coordinating Tasks

The operating system determines the order in which tasks are processed. A task, or job, is an operation the processor manages. Tasks include receiving data from an input device, processing instructions, sending information to an output device, and transferring items from storage to memory and from memory to storage.

A multiuser operating system does not always process tasks on a first-come, first-served basis. Sometimes, one user may have a higher priority than other users. In this case, the operating system adjusts the schedule of tasks.

Sometimes, a device already may be busy processing one task when it receives a second task. This occurs because the processor operates at a much faster rate of speed than peripheral devices. For example, if the processor sends five documents to a printer, the printer can print only one document at a time and store as many documents as its memory can handle.

While waiting for devices to become idle, the operating system places items in buffers. A **buffer** is a segment of memory or storage in which items are placed while waiting to be transferred from an input device or to an output device.

The operating system commonly uses buffers with printed documents. This process, called **spooling**, sends documents to be printed to a buffer instead of sending them immediately to the printer. The buffer holds the information waiting to print while the printer prints from the buffer at its own rate of speed. By spooling documents to a buffer, the processor can continue interpreting and executing instructions while the printer prints. This allows users to work on the computer for other tasks while a printer is printing. Multiple print jobs line up in a **queue** (pronounced Q) in the buffer. A program, called a print spooler, intercepts documents to be printed from the operating system and places them in the queue (Figure 7-5).

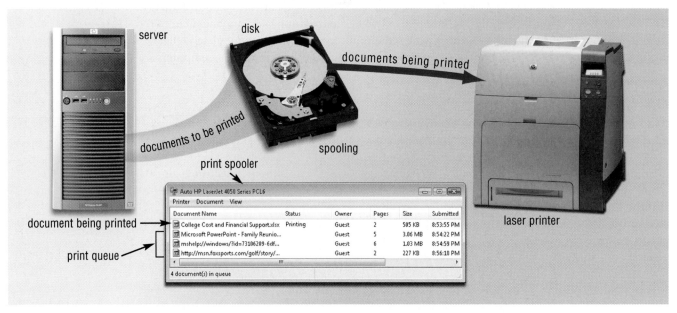

FIGURE 7-5 Spooling increases both processor and printer efficiency by placing documents to be printed in a buffer on disk before they are printed. This figure illustrates three documents in the queue with one document printing.

Configuring Devices

A **driver** is a small program that tells the operating system how to communicate with a specific device. Each device on a computer, such as the mouse, keyboard, monitor, printer, and scanner, has its own specialized set of commands and thus requires its own specific driver. When you boot a computer, the operating system loads each device's driver.

If you attach a new device to a computer, such as a printer or scanner, its driver must be installed before you can use the device. For many devices, the computer's operating system includes the necessary drivers. If it does not, you can install the drivers from the CD provided with the purchased device.

Today, many devices and operating systems support Plug and Play. **Plug and Play** means the operating system automatically configures new devices as you install them. With Plug and Play, a user can plug in a device, turn on the computer, and then use the device without having to configure the system manually.

WEB LINK 7-1

Plug and Play

For more information, visit scsite.com/dcf5e/ch7/weblink and then click Plug and Play.

Establishing an Internet Connection

Operating systems typically provide a means to establish Internet connections. For example, Windows Vista includes a 'Connect to a network' wizard that guides users through the process of setting up a connection between a computer and an Internet access provider (Figure 7-6).

Some operating systems also include a Web browser and an e-mail program, enabling you to begin using the Web and communicate with others as soon as you set up the Internet connection. Some also include utilities to protect computers from unauthorized intrusions and unwanted software such as viruses and spyware.

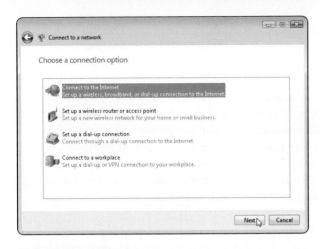

FIGURE 7-6 To connect to a network using Windows Vista, click the Start button, click Connect To, and then click 'Set up a connection or network'.

Monitoring Performance

Operating systems typically contain a performance monitor. A **performance monitor** is a program that assesses and reports information about various computer resources and devices.

The information in performance reports helps users and administrators identify a problem with resources so that they can try to resolve any problems. If a computer is running extremely slow, for example, the performance monitor may determine that the computer's memory is being used to its maximum. Thus, you might consider installing additional memory in the computer.

Providing File Management and Other Utilities

Operating systems often provide users with the capability of managing files, searching for files, viewing images, securing a computer from unauthorized access, uninstalling programs, scanning disks, defragmenting disks, diagnosing problems, backing up files and disks, and setting up screen savers. A later section in the chapter discusses these utilities in depth.

Controlling a Network

Some operating systems are network operating systems. A **network operating system**, or **network OS**, is an operating system that organizes and coordinates how multiple users access and share resources on a network. Resources include hardware, software, data, and information. For example, a network OS allows multiple users to share a printer, Internet access, files, and programs.

Some operating systems have network features built into them. In other cases, the network OS is a set of programs separate from the operating system on the client computers that access the network. When not connected to the network, the client computers use their own operating system. When connected to the network, the network OS may assume some of the operating system functions.

The **network administrator**, the person overseeing network operations, uses the network OS to add and remove users, computers, and other devices to and from the network. The network administrator also uses the network operating system to install software and administer network security.

Administering Security

The network administrator uses the network OS to establish permissions to resources. These permissions define who can access certain resources and when they can access those resources.

For each user, the network administrator establishes a user account, which enables a user to access, or **log on** to, a computer or a network. Each user account typically consists of a user name and password (Figure 7-7). A **user name**, or **user ID**, is a unique combination of characters, such as letters of the alphabet or numbers, that identifies one specific user. Many users select a combination of their first and last names as their user name. A user named Henry Baker might choose H Baker as his user name.

FIGURE 7-7 Most multiuser operating systems allow each user to log on, which is the process of entering a user name and a password into the computer.

A **password** is a private combination of characters associated with the user name that allows access to certain computer resources. Some operating systems allow the network administrator to assign passwords to files and commands, restricting access to only authorized users.

To prevent unauthorized users from accessing computer resources, keep your password confidential. While entering your password, most computers hide the actual password characters by displaying some other characters, such as asterisks (*) or dots. After entering a user name and password, the operating system compares the user's entry with a list of authorized user names and passwords. If the entry matches the user name and password kept on file, the operating system grants the user access. If the entry does not match, the operating system denies access to the user.

The operating system records successful and unsuccessful logon attempts in a file. This allows the network administrator to review who is using or attempting to use the computer. Network administrators also use these files to monitor computer usage.

To protect sensitive data and information as it travels over the network, a network operating system may encrypt it. Encryption is the process of encoding data and information into an unreadable form. Network administrators can set up a network to encrypt data as it travels over the network to prevent unauthorized users from reading the data. When an authorized user attempts to read the data, it automatically is decrypted, or converted back into a readable form. Read Ethics & Issues 7-1 for a related discussion.

FAQ 7-2

What are the guidelines for selecting a good password?

Choose a password that is easy to remember, and that no one could guess. Do not use any part of your first or last name, your spouse's or child's name, telephone number, street address, license plate number, Social Security number, birthday, and so on. Be sure your password is at least eight characters long, mixed with uppercase and lowercase letters, numbers, and special characters. You also should avoid using single-word passwords that are found in the dictionary. For more information, visit scsite.com/dcf5e/ch7/faq and then click Passwords.

ETHICS & ISSUES 7-1

Who Should Be Responsible for Notebook Computer Security?

As notebook computers now outsell desktop computers, they increasingly have become the focus of security breaches. A notebook computer's greatest asset, portability, also may be its greatest weakness. Recently, the theft of a notebook computer from an employee's home resulted in information regarding more than 25 million veterans falling into the wrong hands. The information included Social Security numbers, and the resulting fallout cost the organization millions of dollars. Security experts claim that organizations have become lax about allowing employees to store sensitive information on notebook computers. Too often, they argue, organizations allow employees to take computers home on a daily basis when no such need exists. Employers, on the other hand, feel that workers are more productive when allowed to work during the evenings and weekends using notebook computers. One possible solution is the use of full-disk encryption, which scrambles all of the notebook computer's data on its hard disk and requires a password to unlock. If the computer is stolen, the thief cannot access the data on the hard disk. Those who opposed the widespread use of full-disk encryption say that its use results in slower system performance, is still vulnerable when users are lax with securing their passwords, and may result in lost data when an employee leaves the organization without disclosing the password. Who should be responsible for notebook computer security? Why? Should employees be allowed to take their notebook computers home every night or should the computers be taken offsite only for legitimate, preapproved business purposes? Why or why not? Should more organizations use full-disk encryption? Why or why not?

Test your knowledge of pages 250 through 258 in Quiz Yourself 7-1.

QUIZ YOURSELF 7-1

Instructions: Find the true statement below. Then, rewrite the remaining false statements so they are true.

1. A buffer is a small program that tells the operating system how to communicate with a specific device.

2. A warm boot is the process of using the operating system to restart a computer.

3. A password is a public combination of characters associated with the user name that allows access to certain computer resources.

4. The program you currently are using is in the background, and the other programs running but not in use are in the foreground.

5. Two types of system software are operating systems and application programs.

Quiz Yourself Online: To further check your knowledge of system software and functions common to most operating systems, visit scsite.com/dcf5e/ch7/quiz and then click Objectives 1 – 2.

OPERATING SYSTEM UTILITY PROGRAMS

A **utility program**, also called a **utility**, is a type of system software that allows a user to perform maintenance-type tasks, usually related to managing a computer, its devices, or its programs. Most operating systems include several built-in utility programs (Figure 7-8). Users often buy stand-alone utilities, however, because they offer improvements over those included with the operating system.

Utility programs included with most operating systems provide the following functions: managing files, searching for files, viewing images, securing a computer from unauthorized access, uninstalling programs, scanning disks, defragmenting disks, diagnosing problems, backing up files and disks, and setting up screen savers. The following sections briefly discuss each of these utilities.

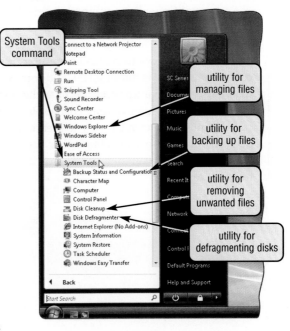

FIGURE 7-8
To display the utilities available in the Windows Vista System Tools list, click the Start button, click All Programs, click Accessories, and then click System Tools.

File Manager

A **file manager** is a utility that performs functions related to file management. Some of the file management functions that a file manager performs are displaying a list of files on a storage medium (Figure 7-9); organizing files in folders; and copying, renaming, deleting, moving, and sorting files. A **folder** is a specific named location on a storage medium that contains related documents.

Search Utility

A **search utility** is a program that attempts to locate a file on your computer based on criteria you specify. The criteria could be a word or words contained in a file, date the file was created or modified, size of the file, location of the file, file name, author/artist, and other similar properties. Search utilities can look through documents, pictures, music, and other files. Windows Vista has a built-in search utility. All the Explorer windows, as well as the Start menu, contain a Search box where you enter the search criteria.

Image Viewer

An **image viewer** is a utility that allows users to display, copy, and print the contents of a graphics file. With an image viewer, users can see images without having to open them in a paint or image editing program. Windows Vista includes an image viewer called Windows Photo Gallery (Figure 7-10). To display a file in this image viewer, simply double-click the thumbnail of the image in the file manager, such as the thumbnail shown in Figure 7-9.

FIGURE 7-9 Windows Vista includes file managers that allow you to view documents, pictures, and music. In this case, thumbnails of pictures are displayed.

FIGURE 7-10 Windows Photo Gallery allows users to see the contents of a picture file.

Personal Firewall

A **personal firewall** is a utility that detects and protects a personal computer from unauthorized intrusions. Personal firewalls constantly monitor all transmissions to and from a computer.

When connected to the Internet, your computer is vulnerable to attacks from a hacker. A hacker is someone who tries to access a computer or network illegally. Users with broadband Internet connections, such as through DSL and Internet cable television service, are even more susceptible than those with dial-up access because the Internet connection always is on.

Windows Vista automatically enables its built-in personal firewall upon installation. This firewall, called Windows Firewall, is easy to access and configure (Figure 7-11). If your operating system does not include a personal firewall or you want additional protection, you can purchase a stand-alone personal firewall utility or a hardware firewall, which is a device such as a router that has a built-in firewall.

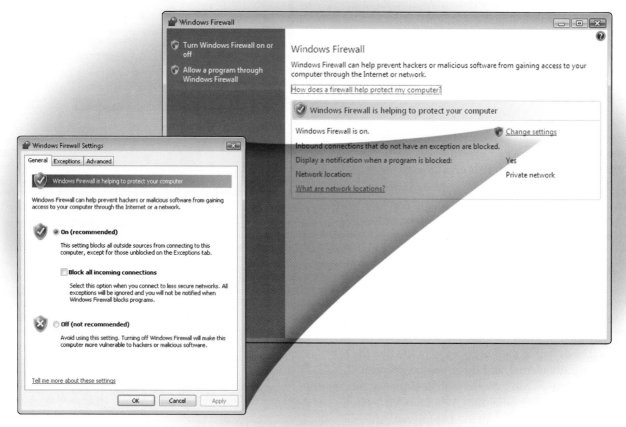

FIGURE 7-11   Through the Security Center in the Control Panel of Windows Vista, users can configure Windows Firewall, which is a personal firewall utility included with Windows Vista.

Uninstaller

An **uninstaller** is a utility that removes a program, as well as any associated entries in the system files. When you install a program, the operating system records the information it uses to run the software in the system files. The uninstaller deletes files and folders from the hard disk, as well as removes program entries from the system files.

Disk Scanner

A **disk scanner** is a utility that searches for and removes unnecessary files. Windows Vista includes a disk scanner utility called Disk Cleanup.

Disk Defragmenter

A **disk defragmenter** is a utility that reorganizes the files and unused space on a computer's hard disk so that the operating system accesses data more quickly and programs run faster. When an operating system stores data on a disk, it places the data in the first available sector on the disk. It attempts to place data in sectors that are contiguous (next to each other), but this is not always possible. When the contents of a file are scattered across two or more noncontiguous sectors, the file is fragmented.

Fragmentation slows down disk access and thus the performance of the entire computer. **Defragmenting** the disk, or reorganizing it so that the files are stored in contiguous sectors, solves this problem (Figure 7-12). Windows Vista includes a disk defragmenter available on the System Tools list.

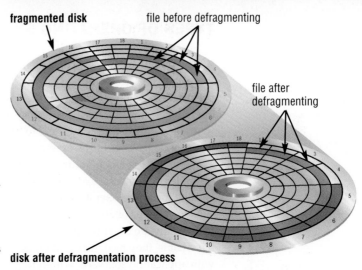

FIGURE 7-12 A fragmented disk has many files stored in noncontiguous sectors. Defragmenting reorganizes the files so that they are located in contiguous sectors, which speeds access time.

Diagnostic Utility

A **diagnostic utility** compiles technical information about your computer's hardware and certain system software programs and then prepares a report outlining any identified problems. Information in the report assists technical support staff in remedying any problems.

Backup Utility

A **backup utility** allows users to copy, or back up, selected files or an entire hard disk to another storage medium such as CD, DVD, external hard disk, USB flash drive, or tape. During the backup process, the backup utility monitors progress and alerts you if it needs additional media, such as another CD. Many backup programs compress, or shrink the size of, files during the backup process. By compressing the files, the backup program requires less storage space for the backup files than for the original files.

Because they are compressed, you usually cannot use backup files in their backed up form. In the event you need to use a backup file, a **restore program** reverses the process and returns backed up files to their original form. Backup utilities include restore programs.

You should back up files and disks regularly in the event your originals are lost, damaged, or destroyed. Instead of backing up to a local disk storage device, some users opt to use online storage to back up their files. Online storage is a service on the Web that provides hard disk storage to computer users, usually for free or for a minimal monthly fee.

Screen Saver

A **screen saver** is a utility that causes a display device's screen to show a moving image or blank screen if no keyboard or mouse activity occurs for a specified time (Figure 7-13). When you press a key on the keyboard or move the mouse, the screen saver disappears and the screen returns to the previous state.

Screen savers originally were developed to prevent a problem called ghosting, in which images could be etched permanently on a monitor's screen. Although ghosting is not as severe of a problem with today's displays, manufacturers continue to recommend that users install screen savers for this reason. Screen savers also are popular for security, business, and entertainment purposes. To secure a computer, users configure their screen saver to require a password to deactivate. Many of the Windows Vista screen savers require Windows Aero. In addition to those included with the operating system, many screen savers are available for a minimal fee in stores and on the Web.

FIGURE 7-13 Windows Vista includes several screen savers.

TYPES OF OPERATING SYSTEMS

When you purchase a new computer, it typically has an operating system preinstalled. As new versions of the operating system are released, users upgrade their existing computers to incorporate features of the new version. Purchasing an operating system upgrade usually costs less than purchasing the entire operating system.

New versions of an operating system usually are downward compatible. That is, they recognize and work with application software written for an earlier version of the operating system (or platform). By contrast, the application software is said to be upward compatible, meaning it will run on new versions of the operating system.

The three basic categories of operating systems that exist today are stand-alone, network, and embedded. The table in Figure 7-14 lists names of operating systems in each category. The following pages discuss the operating systems listed in the table.

CATEGORIES OF OPERATING SYSTEMS

Category	Operating System Name
Stand-alone	• DOS • Early Windows versions (Windows 3.x, Windows 95, Windows NT Workstation, Windows 98, Windows 2000 Professional, Windows Millennium Edition) • Windows XP • Windows Vista • Mac OS X • UNIX • Linux
Network	• Early Windows Server versions (Windows NT Server, Windows 2000 Server, Windows Server 2003) • Windows Server 2008 • UNIX • Linux • Solaris • NetWare
Embedded	• Windows Embedded CE • Windows Mobile • Palm OS • Embedded Linux • Symbian OS

FIGURE 7-14 Examples of stand-alone, network, and embedded operating systems. Some stand-alone operating systems include the capability of configuring small home or office networks.

STAND-ALONE OPERATING SYSTEMS

A **stand-alone operating system** is a complete operating system that works on a desktop computer, notebook computer, or mobile computing device. Some stand-alone operating systems are called client operating systems because they also work in conjunction with a network operating system. Client operating systems can operate with or without a network. Other stand-alone operating systems include networking capabilities, allowing the home and small business user to set up a small network. Examples of currently used stand-alone operating systems are Windows XP, Windows Vista, Mac OS X, UNIX, and Linux.

FAQ 7-3

What was Microsoft's first operating system?

In the early 1980s, Microsoft introduced **DOS** (Disk Operating System) as its first operating system. The two more widely used versions of DOS were PC-DOS and MS-DOS. At first, DOS used a command-line interface, but later versions introduced a menu-driven interface. DOS once was used on an estimated 70 million computers, but rarely is used today because it lacks a graphical user interface and does not take full advantage of modern personal computer processors. For more information, visit scsite.com/dcf5e/ch7/faq and then click DOS.

Windows XP

In the mid-1980s, Microsoft developed its first version of Windows, which provided a graphical user interface (GUI). Since then, Microsoft continually has updated its Windows operating system, incorporating innovative features and functions with each new version. **Windows XP** is a fast, reliable Windows operating system, providing quicker startup, better performance, increased security, and a simpler visual look than previous Windows versions (Figure 7-15). Windows XP is available in five editions: Home Edition, Professional Edition, Media Center Edition, Tablet PC Edition, and Professional x64 Edition.

Windows Vista

Windows Vista, the successor to Windows XP, is Microsoft's fastest, most reliable and efficient operating system to date, offering quicker program start up, built-in diagnostics, automatic recovery, improved security, and enhanced searching and organizing capabilities (Figure 7-16).

Windows Vista is available in five editions: Windows Vista Home Basic, Windows Vista Home Premium, Windows Vista Ultimate, Windows Vista Business, and Windows Vista Enterprise. Windows Vista Home Basic, designed for the basic home user, uses the Windows Vista Basic interface and allows users easily to search

FIGURE 7-15 Windows XP, with its simplified look, is a fast, reliable Windows operating system.

for files, protect their computer from unauthorized intruders and unwanted programs, and set parental controls to monitor the use of games, the Internet, instant messaging, and other communications programs. Windows Vista Home Premium includes all the capabilities of Windows Vista Home Basic and also includes Windows Aero with its Flip 3D feature and provides tools to create DVDs and edit movies, record and watch television shows, connect to a game console, securely connect to Wi-Fi networks, work with a Tablet PC, and quickly view messages on a powered-off, specially equipped notebook computer. Windows Vista Ultimate includes all features of Windows Vista Home

Premium and provides additional features designed to make mobile users' computers more secure and easier to network. With Windows Vista Business, users in all sizes of businesses are provided a secure operating environment that uses Windows Aero where they easily can search for files, protect their computers from unauthorized intruders and unwanted programs, use improved backup technologies, securely connect to Wi-Fi networks, quickly view messages on a powered-off, specially equipped notebook computer, and easily share documents and collaborate with other users. Windows Vista Enterprise includes all the features of Windows Vista Business and also offers greater levels of data protection and a multi-language interface.

Windows Vista adapts to the hardware configuration on which it is installed. Thus, two users with the same edition of Windows Vista may experience different functionality and interfaces.

FIGURE 7-16 Windows Vista has a new interface, easier navigation and searching techniques, and improved security.

WEB LINK 7-5

Mac OS X

For more information, visit scsite.com/dcf5e/ch7/weblink and then click Mac OS X.

Mac OS X

Since it was released with Macintosh computers in 1984, Apple's **Macintosh operating system** has set the standard for operating system ease of use and has been the model for most of the new GUIs developed for non-Macintosh systems. The latest version, **Mac OS X**, is a multitasking operating system available only for computers manufactured by Apple (Figure 7-17).

FIGURE 7-17 Mac OS X is the operating system used with Apple Macintosh computers.

UNIX

UNIX (pronounced YOU-nix) is a multitasking operating system. Several versions of this operating system exist, each slightly different. Although some versions of UNIX have a command-line interface, most versions of UNIX offer a graphical user interface (Figure 7-18). Today, a version of UNIX is available for most computers of all sizes. Power users often work with UNIX because of its flexibility and power.

FIGURE 7-18 Many versions of UNIX have a graphical user interface.

Linux

Linux is one of the faster growing operating systems. **Linux** (pronounced LINN-uks) is a popular, multitasking UNIX-type operating system. In addition to the basic operating system, Linux also includes many free programming languages and utility programs. Linux is not proprietary software like the operating systems discussed thus far. Instead, Linux is open source software, which means its code is available to the public for use, modification, and redistribution. Read Ethics & Issues 7-2 for a related discussion, and read Looking Ahead 7-1 for a look at a future use of open source software.

WEB LINK 7-6

Linux

For more information, visit scsite.com/dcf5e/ch7/weblink and then click Linux.

Linux is available in a variety of forms, or distributions. Some distributions of Linux are command-line. Others are GUI (Figure 7-19). Users obtain Linux in a variety of ways. Some people download it free from the Web. Others purchase it from vendors, who bundle their own software with the operating system. Linux CDs are included in many Linux books and also are available for purchase from vendors. For purchasers of new personal computers, some retailers such as Dell will preinstall Linux on the hard disk on request. Another option is Live CD or Live USB, where the CD or USB flash drive is bootable. In this case, the CD or USB drive contains files necessary to boot and work with the Linux operating system, which allows users to preview the operating system without installing it.

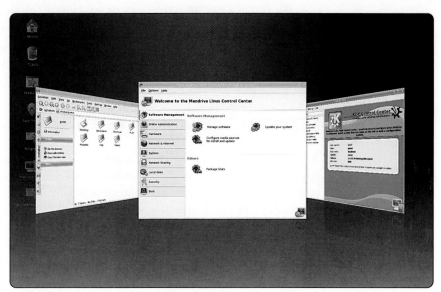

FIGURE 7-19   This distribution of Linux has a graphical user interface.

Closed Source vs. Open Source Operating Systems

Linux is a fast-growing, innovative operating system. One of the features that make it different from other operating systems is that Linux is open source and its source code, along with any changes, remains public. Since its introduction in 1991, Linux has been altered, adapted, and improved by thousands of programmers. Unlike Linux, most operating systems are proprietary, and their program code often is a zealously guarded secret. At one large software developer, an employee reported that application programmers had little opportunity to contribute to operating system programs because they had no access to the operating system program source code. Supporters of open source maintain that source code should be open to the public so that it can be scrutinized, corrected, and enhanced. In light of concerns about security and fears of possible virus problems, however, some people are not sure open source software is a good idea. Besides, they argue, companies and programmers should be able to control, and profit from, the operating systems they create. On the other hand, open source software can be scrutinized for errors by a much larger group of people and changes can be made immediately. Are open source operating systems a good idea? Why or why not? How can the concerns about open source software be addressed? What are the advantages and disadvantages of open versus closed source operating systems? Does the open source model lead to better software?

Open Source Projects Promote Digital Identity Sharing

A typical Internet user may need dozens of passwords to conduct business and view particular Web pages. This need for a unique identity at each Web site may be eliminated with several new projects Microsoft is funding.

Under the company's Identity Selector Interoperability Profile (ISIP), Web users will log on once, verify their identity, and then access multiple Web sites without needing to log on at each one. ISIP should be useful in online transactions and other circumstances where user information is shared over a network.

Microsoft will allow programmers to access the open-source code the company has developed for its ISIP technology. Programmers will not need a license or fear patent infringement lawsuits under Microsoft's Open Specification Promise (OSP) project. OSP's goal is to encourage a wide range of developers to use Microsoft's open source software in a simple, clear manner. For more information, visit scsite.com/dcf5e/ch7/looking and then click Open Source Digital Identity.

Test your knowledge of pages 259 through 265 in Quiz Yourself 7-2.

NETWORK OPERATING SYSTEMS

As discussed earlier in this chapter, a network operating system is an operating system that is designed specifically to support a network. A network operating system typically resides on a server. The client computers on the network rely on the server(s) for resources. Many of the client operating systems discussed in the previous section work in conjunction with a network operating system.

Some of the stand-alone operating systems discussed in the previous section include networking capability; however, network operating systems are designed specifically to support all sizes of networks, including medium- to large-sized businesses and Web servers.

Examples of network operating systems include Windows Server 2008.

- Windows Server 2008 is an upgrade to Windows Server 2003.
- UNIX and Linux often are called multipurpose operating systems because they are both stand-alone and network operating systems.
- Solaris, a version of UNIX developed by Sun Microsystems, is a network operating system designed specifically for e-commerce applications.
- Novell's Netware is a network operating system designed for client/server networks.

EMBEDDED OPERATING SYSTEMS

The operating system on most smart phones and small devices, called an **embedded operating system**, resides on a ROM chip. Popular embedded operating systems include Windows Embedded CE, Windows Mobile, Palm OS, BlackBerry (Figure 7-20), embedded Linux, and Symbian OS.

- Windows Embedded CE is a scaled-down Windows operating system designed for use on communications, entertainment, and computing devices with limited functionality. Examples of devices that use Windows Embedded CE include VoIP telephones, point-of-sale terminals, digital cameras, navigation systems, portable media players, ticket machines, and computerized sewing machines.
- Windows Mobile, an operating system based on Windows Embedded CE, works on specific types of devices. Window Mobile-based devices include smart phones and PDAs, called the Pocket PC. With the Windows Mobile operating system and a compatible device, users have access to the basic PIM (personal information manager) functions such as contact lists, schedules, tasks, calendars, and notes.
- Palm OS, which is a competing operating system to Windows Mobile, runs on smart phones and PDAs. With Palm OS and a compatible device, users manage schedules and contacts, phone messages, project notes, reminders, tasks and address lists, and important dates and appointments.

- The BlackBerry operating system runs on handheld devices supplied by RIM (Research In Motion). BlackBerry devices provide PIM, phone, and wireless capabilities. Some also allow you to take pictures, play music, and access maps and directions.
- Embedded Linux is a scaled-down Linux operating system designed for smart phones, PDAs, smart watches, set-top boxes, Internet telephones, and many other types of devices and computers requiring an embedded operating system. Devices with embedded Linux offer calendar and address book and other PIM functions, touch screens, and handwriting recognition.
- Symbian OS is an open source multitasking operating system designed for smart phones. Users enter data by pressing keys on the keypad or keyboard, touching the screen, and writing on the screen with a stylus.

WEB LINK 7-7

BlackBerry

For more information, visit scsite.com/dcf5e/ch7/weblink and then click BlackBerry.

FIGURE 7-20
A smart phone that uses the BlackBerry operating system.

STAND-ALONE UTILITY PROGRAMS

Although operating systems typically include some built-in utilities, many stand-alone utility programs are available for purchase. For example, you can purchase personal firewalls, backup utilities, and screen savers. These stand-alone utilities typically offer improvements over those features built into the operating system or provide features not included in an operating system.

Other functions provided by stand-alone utilities include protecting against viruses, removing spyware and adware, filtering Internet content, compressing files, converting files, playing media files, burning CDs and DVDs, and maintaining a personal computer. The following sections discuss each of these utilities.

Antivirus Programs

The term, computer **virus**, describes a potentially damaging computer program that affects, or infects, a computer negatively by altering the way the computer works without the user's knowledge or permission. More specifically, a computer virus is a segment of program code from some outside source that implants itself in a computer. Once the virus is in a computer, it can spread throughout and may damage your files and operating system.

Computer viruses do not generate by chance. The programmer of a virus, known as a virus author, intentionally writes a virus program. Some virus authors find writing viruses a challenge. Others write them to cause destruction. Writing a virus program usually requires significant programming skills.

Some viruses are harmless pranks that simply freeze a computer temporarily or display sounds or messages. The Music Bug virus, for example, instructs the computer to play a few chords of music.

Other viruses destroy or corrupt data stored on the hard disk of the infected computer. If you notice any unusual changes in your computer's performance, it may be infected with a virus. Figure 7-21 outlines some common symptoms of virus infection.

A **worm** copies itself repeatedly, for example, in memory or over a network, using up system resources and possibly shutting the system down. A **Trojan horse** hides within or looks like a legitimate program such as a screen saver. A certain condition or action usually triggers the Trojan horse. Unlike a virus or worm, a Trojan horse does not replicate itself to other computers. Currently, more than 180,000 known viruses, worms, Trojan horses, and similar threats exist.

SIGNS OF VIRUS INFECTION

- An unusual message or image is displayed on the computer screen
- An unusual sound or music plays randomly
- The available memory is less than what should be available
- A program or file suddenly is missing
- An unknown program or file mysteriously appears
- The size of a file changes without explanation
- A file becomes corrupted
- A program or file does not work properly
- System properties change
- The operating system runs much slower than usual

FIGURE 7-21 Viruses attack computers in a variety of ways. This list indicates some of the more common signs of virus infection.

To protect a computer from virus attacks, users should install an antivirus program and update it frequently. An **antivirus program** protects a computer against viruses by identifying and removing any computer viruses found in memory, on storage media, or on incoming files (Figure 7-22). Most antivirus programs also protect against worms and Trojan horses. When you purchase a new computer, it often includes antivirus software.

Three more popular antivirus programs are McAfee VirusScan, Norton AntiVirus, and Windows Live OneCare, the latter of which also contains spyware removers, Internet filters, PC maintenance, and backup utilities. As an alternative to purchasing these products on CD, both McAfee and Norton offer Web-based antivirus programs.

FIGURE 7-22   An antivirus program scans memory, disks, and incoming e-mail messages and attachments for viruses and attempts to remove any viruses it finds.

Spyware and Adware Removers

Spyware is a program placed on a computer without the user's knowledge that secretly collects information about the user, often related to Web browsing habits. The spyware program communicates information it collects to some outside source while you are online. **Adware** is a program that displays an online advertisement in a banner or pop-up window on Web pages, e-mail, or other Internet services. Sometimes, spyware is hidden in adware. A **spyware remover** is a program that detects and deletes spyware, and similar programs. An **adware remover** is a program that detects and deletes adware. Most spyware and adware removers cost less than $50; some are available on the Web at no cost. Some operating systems include spyware and adware removers.

Internet Filters

Filters are programs that remove or block certain items from being displayed. Four widely used Internet filters are anti-spam programs, Web filters, phishing filters, and pop-up blockers.

ANTI-SPAM PROGRAMS   **Spam** is an unsolicited e-mail message or newsgroup posting sent to many recipients or newsgroups at once. Spam is Internet junk mail. An **anti-spam program** is a filtering program that attempts to remove spam before it reaches your inbox. Internet access providers often filter spam as a service for their subscribers.

WEB FILTERS   **Web filtering software** is a program that restricts access to certain material on the Web. Some restrict access to specific Web sites; others filter sites that use certain words or phrases. Many businesses use Web filtering software to limit employee's Web access. Some schools, libraries, and parents use this software to restrict access to minors.

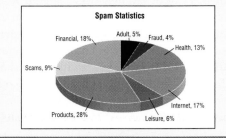

PHISHING FILTERS   **Phishing** is a scam in which a perpetrator attempts to obtain your personal and/or financial information. A **phishing filter** is a program that warns or blocks you from potentially fraudulent or suspicious Web sites. Some Web browsers include phishing filters.

POP-UP BLOCKERS   A pop-up ad is an Internet advertisement that suddenly appears in a new window in the foreground of a Web page displayed in your browser. A **pop-up blocker** is a filtering program that stops pop-up ads from displaying on Web pages. Many Web browsers include a pop-up blocker. You also can download pop-up blockers from the Web at no cost.

WEB LINK 7-8

Phishing Filters

For more information, visit scsite.com/dcf5e/ ch7/weblink and then click Phishing Filters.

File Compression

A **file compression utility** shrinks the size of a file(s). A compressed file takes up less storage space than the original file. Compressing files frees up room on the storage media and improves system performance. Attaching a compressed file to an e-mail message, for example, reduces the time needed for file transmission. Uploading and downloading compressed files to and from the Internet reduces the file transmission time.

Compressed files sometimes are called **zipped files**. When you receive or download a compressed file, you must uncompress it. To **uncompress**, or unzip, a file, you restore it to its original form. Some operating systems such as Windows Vista include file compression and uncompression capabilities. To compress a file, however, you need a stand-alone file compression utility. Two popular stand-alone file compression utilities are PKZIP and WinZip.

File Conversion

A **file conversion utility** transforms the contents of a file or data from one format to another. When a business develops a new system, often the data in the current system is not in the correct format for the new system. Thus, part of the system development process is to convert data — instead of having users re-enter all the existing data in the new system. On a smaller scale, when home users purchase new software, they may need to convert files so that the files will be displayed properly in the new software.

Media Player

A **media player** is a program that allows you to view images and animation, listen to audio, and watch video files on your computer (Figure 7-23). Media players may also include the capability to organize media files, convert them to different formats, connect to and purchase media from an online media store, download podcasts and vodcasts, burn audio CDs, and transfer media to portable media players. Windows Vista includes Windows Media Player. Three other popular media players are iTunes, RealPlayer, and Rhapsody.

FIGURE 7-23   A popular media player.

CD/DVD Burning

CD/DVD burning software writes text, graphics, audio, and video files on a recordable or rewritable CD or DVD, including Blu-ray and HD DVD. This software enables the home user easily to back up contents of their hard disk on a CD/DVD and make duplicates of uncopyrighted music or movies. CD/DVD burning software usually also includes photo editing, audio editing, and video editing capabilities (Figure 7-24).

When you buy a recordable or rewritable CD or DVD, it typically includes CD/DVD burning software. You also can buy CD/DVD burning software for a cost of less than $100.

FIGURE 7-24   Using CD/DVD burning software, you can copy text, graphics, audio, and video files on a CD or DVD, provided you have the correct type of CD/DVD drive and media.

Personal Computer Maintenance

Operating systems typically include a diagnostic utility that diagnoses computer problems but does not repair them. A **personal computer maintenance utility** identifies and fixes operating system problems, detects and repairs disk problems, and includes the capability of improving a computer's performance. Additionally, some personal computer maintenance utilities continuously monitor a computer while you use it to identify and repair problems before they occur. Norton SystemWorks is a popular personal computer maintenance utility designed for Windows operating systems (Figure 7-25).

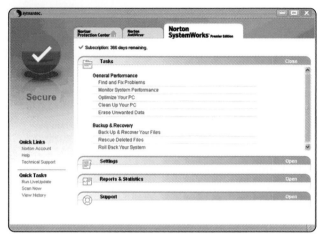

FIGURE 7-25 A popular maintenance program for Windows users.

Test your knowledge of pages 266 through 270 in Quiz Yourself 7-3.

QUIZ YOURSELF 7-3

Instructions: Find the true statement below. Then, rewrite the remaining false statements so they are true.

1. A pop-up blocker shrinks the size of a file(s).

2. An anti-spam program protects a computer against viruses.

3. Examples of network operating systems include Windows Server 2008, UNIX, Linux, Solaris, and Netware.

4. Pocket PCs use Palm OS as their operating system.

5. Web filtering software writes text, graphics, audio, and video files to a recordable or rewritable CD or DVD.

Quiz Yourself Online: To further check your knowledge of embedded operating systems and stand-alone utility programs, visit scsite.com/dcf5e/ch7/quiz and then click Objectives 5 – 6.

CHAPTER SUMMARY

This chapter defined an operating system and then discussed the functions common to most operating systems. Next, it introduced several utility programs commonly found in operating systems. The chapter discussed a variety of stand-alone operating systems, network operating systems, and embedded operating systems. Finally, the chapter described several stand-alone utility programs.

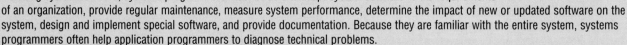

CAREER CORNER — Systems Programmer

System software is a key component in any computer. A **systems programmer** evaluates, installs, and maintains system software and provides technical support to the programming staff.

Systems programmers work with the programs that control computers, such as operating systems, network operating systems, and database systems. They identify current and future processing needs and then recommend the software and hardware necessary to meet those needs. In addition to selecting and installing system software, systems programmers must be able to adapt system software to the requirements of an organization, provide regular maintenance, measure system performance, determine the impact of new or updated software on the system, design and implement special software, and provide documentation. Because they are familiar with the entire system, systems programmers often help application programmers to diagnose technical problems.

Systems programmers must be acquainted thoroughly with a variety of operating systems. They must be able to think logically, pay attention to detail, work with abstract concepts, and devise solutions to complex problems. Systems programmers often work in teams and interact with programmers and nontechnical users, so communications skills are important.

Most systems programmers have a four-year B.S. degree in Computer Science or Information Technology. Depending on responsibilities and experience, salaries range from $65,000 to as much as $120,000. For more information, visit scsite.com/dcf5e/ch7/careers and then click Systems Programmer.

Red Hat
Open Source Software Distributor

When you were young, you were taught to share. University professors share their research with colleagues throughout the world; and Red Hat shares software code, or instructions, with computer users.

Red Hat is the world's largest supplier of open source software, which allows buyers to view, modify, and perhaps improve, the software. The company delivers the software improvements to customers through the Red Hat Network, the company's Internet service.

Bob Young and Marc Ewing founded Red Hat in 1994 and started distributing a version of the Red Hat Linux operating system complete with documentation and support. Today, Linux is Red Hat's most well-known product. Subscriptions to the company's premium Linux software have helped boost the company to profitability. The company launched the Red Hat Exchange in 2007 to offer a Web site where customers can buy a range of open-source software from the company's business partners. For more information, visit scsite.com/dcf5e/ch7/companies and then click Red Hat.

Research In Motion (RIM)
Wireless Mobile Communication Devices Manufacturer

In today's mobile world, people often need to access their e-mail wirelessly. Chances are they find Research In Motion (RIM)'s products valuable. More than 4 million people are using RIM's popular BlackBerry models, which combine e-mail, phone, Internet browsing, and organizer features. The built-in keyboards allow users to send and receive text messages.

Mike Lazaridis, the current co-CEO, founded RIM in 1984 in Waterloo, Ontario. His passion for wireless technology emerged in high school as a member of the local amateur radio and television club. He developed RIM's first major product, the Inter@ctive Pager, in 1996. Two years later, the same hardware was used in the first BlackBerry; this product's success was due to its capability to combine a wireless mailbox with a corporate mailbox so that users could access e-mail continuously.

In 2007, RIM was the only wireless technology company named one of Canada's Top 100 Employers for its exceptional work atmosphere, performance management, and community involvement. For more information, visit scsite.com/dcf5e/ch7/companies and then click RIM.

TECHNOLOGY TRAILBLAZERS

Alan Kay
Computer Pioneer

Chances are that every time you use your computer you use one of Alan Kay's ideas. More than 35 years ago — long before the personal computer became ubiquitous — he was developing a notebook computer complete with a flat screen, wireless network, and storage. More than 20 years ago, he engineered a graphical user interface, object-oriented languages, and personal computer networks.

Kay did much of his early work at the U.S. Defense Department's Advance Research Project Agency (DARPA) and Xerox's Palo Alto Research Center (PARC). Today he is a computer science professor at UCLA and president of the Viewpoints Research Institute, a nonprofit organization involved in the One Laptop per Child project and in developing a new user interface that helps users learn. For more information, visit scsite.com/dcf5e/ch7/people and then click Alan Kay.

Linus Torvalds
Linux Creator

When Linus Torvalds developed a new operating system in 1991, he announced his project in an Internet newsgroup, made the source code available, and asked for suggestions. Computer users responded by reviewing the system and offering enhancements. Three years later, Torvalds released a much-enhanced version of an open source operating system he called Linux.

Torvalds developed the innovative operating system when he was a 21-year-old computer science student in Finland. Today, Linux is estimated to be running on at least 10 percent of computers and is Microsoft's main competitor. Torvalds leads the development of Linux as a fellow at OSDL (Open Source Development Labs), a not-for-profit consortium of companies dedicated to developing and promoting the operating system. Torvalds says his day-to-day involvement with Linux involves merging the lines of code so that the software runs smoothly. For more information, visit scsite.com/dcf5e/ch7/people and then click Linus Torvalds.

Chapter Review

The Chapter Review section summarizes the concepts presented in this chapter. To obtain help from other students regarding any subject in this chapter, visit scsite.com/dcf5e/ch7/forum and post your thoughts or questions.

(1) What Are the Types of System Software?

System software consists of the programs that control or maintain the operations of a computer and its devices. Two types of system software are operating systems and utility programs. An **operating system (OS)** contains instructions that work together to coordinate all the activities among computer hardware resources. A **utility program** performs maintenance-type tasks, usually related to managing a computer, its devices, or its programs.

(2) What Are the Functions of an Operating System?

The operating system provides a user interface, manages programs, manages memory, coordinates tasks, configures devices, establishes an Internet connection, and monitors performance. The **user interface** controls how data and instructions are entered and how information is displayed. Two types of user interfaces are a **command-line interface** and a **graphical user interface (GUI)**. Managing programs refers to how many users, and how many programs, an operating system can support at one time. An operating system can be single user/single tasking, single user/multitasking, multi-user, or multiprocessing. **Memory management** optimizes the use of random access memory (RAM). **Virtual memory** allocates a portion of a storage medium to function as additional RAM. Coordinating tasks determines the order in which tasks are processed. Configuring devices involves loading each device's driver when a user boots the computer. A **driver** is a program that tells the operating system how to communicate with a specific device. Establishing an Internet connection sets up a connection between a computer and an Internet access provider. A **performance monitor** is a program that assesses and reports information about computer resources and devices.

 Visit scsite.com/dcf5e/ch7/quiz or click the Quiz Yourself button. Click Objectives 1 – 2.

(3) What Is the Purpose of the Utilities Included with Most Operating Systems?

Most operating systems include several built-in utility programs. A **file manager** performs functions related to file management. A **search utility** attempts to locate a file on your computer based on criteria you specify. An **image viewer** displays, copies, and prints the contents of a graphics file. A **personal firewall** detects and protects a personal computer from unauthorized intrusions. An **uninstaller** removes a program and any associated entries in the system files. A **disk scanner** searches for and removes unnecessary files. A **disk defragmenter** reorganizes the files and unused space on a computer's hard disk. A **diagnostic utility** compiles and reports technical information about a computer's hardware and certain system software programs. A **backup utility** is used to copy, or back up, selected files or an entire hard disk to another storage medium. A **screen saver** displays a moving image or blank screen if no keyboard or mouse activity occurs for a specified time.

(4) What Are Features of Several Stand-Alone Operating Systems?

A **stand-alone operating system** is a complete operating system that works on a desktop computer, notebook computer, or mobile computing device. Stand-alone operating systems include Windows XP, Windows Vista, Mac OS X, UNIX, and Linux. **Windows XP** is a fast, reliable Windows operating system, providing better performance, increased security, and a simpler look than previous Windows versions. **Windows Vista**, successor to Windows XP, is Microsoft's fastest, most reliable and efficient operating system to date, offering quicker program start up, built-in diagnostics, automatic recovery, improved security, and enhanced searching and organizing capabilities. **Mac OS X** is a multitasking GUI operating system available only for Apple computers. **UNIX** is a multitasking operating system that is flexible and powerful. **Linux** is a popular, multitasking UNIX-type operating system that is open source software, which means its code is available to the public for use, modification, and redistribution.

 Visit scsite.com/dcf5e/ch7/quiz or click the Quiz Yourself button. Click Objectives 3 – 4.

Chapter Review

(5) What Devices Use Embedded Operating Systems?

Most smart phones and small devices have an **embedded operating system** that resides on a ROM chip. Popular embedded operating systems include Windows Embedded CE, Windows Mobile, Palm OS, BlackBerry, embedded Linux, and Symbian OS. Windows Embedded CE is a scaled-down Windows operating system designed for use on communications, entertainment, and computing devices with limited functionality. Windows Mobile, an operating system based on Windows Embedded CE, works on specific types of devices, such as smart phones and PDAs, called a Pocket PC. Palm OS is an operating system used on smart phones and PDAs. The BlackBerry operating system runs on handheld devices supplied by RIM. Embedded Linux is a scaled-down Linux operating system for smart phones, PDAs, and other devices. Symbian OS is an open source multitasking operating system designed for smart phones.

(6) What Is the Purpose of Several Stand-Alone Utility Programs?

Stand-alone utility programs offer improvements over features built into the operating system or provide features not included in the operating system. An **antivirus program** protects computers against a **virus**, or potentially damaging computer program, by identifying and removing any computer viruses. A **spyware remover** detects and deletes spyware and similar programs. An **adware remover** detects and deletes adware. An **anti-spam program** attempts to remove **spam** before it reaches your inbox. **Web filtering software** restricts access to certain material on the Web. A **phishing filter** warns or blocks you from potentially fraudulent or suspicious Web sites. A **pop-up blocker** stops pop-up ads from displaying on Web pages. A **file compression utility** shrinks the size of a file. A **file conversion utility** transforms the contents of a file from one format to another. A **media player** allows you to view images and animation, listen to audio, and watch video files on a computer. **CD/DVD burning software** writes on a recordable or rewritable CD or DVD. A **personal computer maintenance utility** identifies and fixes operating system or disk problems and improves a computer's performance.

 Visit scsite.com/dcf5e/ch7/quiz or click the Quiz Yourself button. Click Objectives 5 – 6.

Key Terms

You should know each key term. Use the list below to help focus your study. To further enhance your understanding of the Key Terms in this chapter, visit scsite.com/dcf5e/ch7/terms. See an example of and a definition for each term, and access current and additional information about the term from the Web.

adware (268)
adware remover (268)
anti-spam program (268)
antivirus program (268)
backup utility (261)
booting (252)
buffer (255)
CD/DVD burning software (269)
cold boot (252)
command-line interface (253)
defragmenting (261)
diagnostic utility (261)
disk defragmenter (261)
disk scanner (260)
driver (256)
embedded operating system (266)
fault-tolerant computer (255)

file compression utility (269)
file conversion utility (269)
file manager (259)
folder (259)
graphical user interface (GUI) (253)
image viewer (259)
Linux (265)
log on (257)
Mac OS X (264)
Macintosh operating system (264)
media player (269)
memory management (255)
network administrator (257)
network operating system (257)
network OS (257)
operating system (OS) (251)
password (258)

performance monitor (257)
personal computer maintenance utility (270)
personal firewall (260)
phishing (269)
phishing filter (269)
Plug and Play (256)
pop-up blocker (269)
queue (256)
restore program (261)
screen saver (261)
search utility (259)
spam (268)
spooling (256)
spyware (268)
spyware remover (268)
stand-alone operating system (262)
system software (250)
systems programmer (270)
Trojan horse (267)

uncompress (269)
uninstaller (260)
UNIX (264)
user ID (257)
user interface (253)
user name (257)
utility (259)
utility program (259)
virtual memory (255)
virus (267)
warm boot (252)
Web filtering software (268)
Windows Aero (253)
Windows ReadyBoost (255)
Windows Vista (263)
Windows Vista Basic (253)
Windows XP (262)
worm (267)
zipped files (269)

Checkpoint

Use the Checkpoint exercises to check your knowledge level of the chapter. To complete the Checkpoint exercises interactively, visit scsite.com/dcf5e/ch7/check.

True/False

Mark T for True and F for False. (See page numbers in parentheses.)

_____ 1. The operating system that a computer uses sometimes is called the level. (252)

_____ 2. Booting is the process of permanently removing a computer from operation. (252)

_____ 3. In a command-line interface, you interact with menus and visual images such as buttons and other graphical objects to issue commands. (253)

_____ 4. A folder is a specific named location on a storage medium that contains related documents. (259)

_____ 5. A personal firewall is a utility program that detects and protects a personal computer from unauthorized intrusions. (260)

_____ 6. A disk defragmenter is a utility that reorganizes the files and unused space on a computer's hard disk so that the operating system accesses data more quickly and programs run faster. (261)

_____ 7. Linux is open source software, which means its code can be modified and redistributed. (265)

_____ 8. An adware remover is a program that detects and deletes spam. (268)

_____ 9. Web filtering software is a program that secretly collects information about a user, often related to the user's Web browsing habits. (268)

_____ 10. Phishing is a scam in which a perpetrator attempts to obtain your personal and/or financial information. (269)

Multiple Choice

Select the best answer. (See page numbers in parentheses.)

1. In the Windows Vista operating system, _____ provides an enhanced visual look, additional navigation options, and animation. (253)
   a. Plug and Play
   b. Windows Aero
   c. Mac OS X
   d. Windows Vista Basic

2. Windows Vista users can increase the size of memory through _____, which can allocate up to 4 GB of removable flash memory devices as additional memory cache. (255)
   a. Windows Aero
   b. Plug and Play
   c. Windows ReadyBoost
   d. a disk defragmenter

3. A _____ is a small program that tells the operating system how to communicate with a specific device. (256)
   a. buffer
   b. driver
   c. performance monitor
   d. device

4. A _____ is a program that attempts to locate a file on your computer based on criteria you specify. (259)
   a. file manager
   b. search utility
   c. Startup folder
   d. worm

5. Defragmenting reorganizes the files on a disk so that they are located in _____ access time. (261)
   a. noncontiguous sectors, which slows
   b. contiguous sectors, which speeds
   c. contiguous sectors, which slows
   d. noncontiguous sectors, which speeds

6. The operating system on most smart phones and small devices, called a(n) _____, resides on a ROM chip. (266)
   a. network operating system
   b. embedded operating system
   c. stand-alone operating system
   d. stand-alone utility program

7. A(n) _____ is a program that warns or blocks you from potentially fraudulent or suspicious Web sites. (269)
   a. phishing filter
   b. Web filter
   c. adware remover
   d. Trojan horse

8. A _____ is a program that allows you to view images and animation, listen to audio, and watch video files on your computer. (269)
   a. file manager
   b. media player
   c. service pack
   d. Media Center PC

Matching

Match the terms with their definitions. (See page numbers in parentheses.)

_____ 1. fault-tolerant computer (255)

_____ 2. virus (267)

_____ 3. worm (267)

_____ 4. adware (268)

_____ 5. file conversion utility (269)

a. continues to operate when one of its components fails

b. program that displays an online advertisement in a banner or pop-up window on Web pages, e-mail, or other Internet services

c. transforms the contents of a file or data from one format to another

d. a potentially damaging computer program that affects, or infects, a computer negatively by altering the way the computer works without the user's knowledge or permission

e. hides within or looks like a legitimate program such as a screen saver

f. copies itself repeatedly using up system resources and possibly shutting the system down

Short Answer

Write a brief answer to each of the following questions.

1. How is a cold boot different from a warm boot? _____ How is a memory-resident part of an operating system different from a nonresident part of an operating system? _____

2. What is the purpose of memory management? _____ What is the purpose of virtual memory, and where is virtual memory stored? _____

3. What is a performance monitor? _____ How do users and administrators use performance reports? _____

4. What is a backup utility, and what happens during a backup? _____ What is the purpose of a restore program? _____

5. What are the differences between Windows Vista Home Basic and Windows Vista Home Premium? _____ What is the difference between Windows Vista Business and Windows Vista Enterprise? _____

Working Together

Working in a group of your classmates, complete the following team exercise.

1. The Buyer's Guide on page 279 offers tips on buying a computer. Each member of your team should answer the three questions presented in the Buyer's Guide to determine the type of computer he or she needs. Then, each team member should visit one or more computer vendors and, using the guidelines and tools presented in the Buyer's Guide, find the "perfect" computer. Later, meet with the members of your team and compare your results. How are the computers similar? How are they different? Create a group presentation and share your findings with the class.

Web Research

Use the Internet-based Web Research exercises to broaden your understanding of the concepts presented in this chapter. To discuss any of the Web Research exercises in this chapter with other students, post your thoughts or questions at scsite.com/dcf5e/ch7/forum.

1 Blogs

Search engines help locate Web pages about certain topics based on the search text specified. A number of the search engine Web sites feature blogs describing popular search topics. For example, Ask.com's blog (blog.ask.com) lists Smart Answers, which are paragraphs containing links to news, the entertainment industry, holiday events, and fitness. The Yahoo! Search blog (ysearchblog.com) includes news about consumer search trends (Yahoo! Buzz) and innovations in Web search technology. Google Blog Search (blogsearch.google.com) and Ask.com have search engines to help users find blogs about particular topics. Visit these sites and read the posts. What topics are discussed? Compose search queries about issues and products discussed in this chapter, such as Windows Vista or antivirus programs, and read a few of the blogs describing these topics. Summarize the information you read.

2 Scavenger Hunt

Use one of the search engines listed in Figure 2-8 in Chapter 2 on page 58 or your own favorite search engine to find the answers to the questions that follow. Copy and paste the Web address from the Web page where you found the answer. Some questions may have more than one answer. If required, submit your answers to your instructor. (1) What did David Bradley invent? (2) The term, spool, is an acronym for what words? (3) What is the origin of the term, booting? (4) From what television program is the term, spam, derived?

3 Search Sleuth

A search engine using a concept-based search system seeks Web sites containing a search term along with related concepts. Google Book Search (books.google.com) has been created to help individuals locate books on a broad range of topics. Visit this Web site and then use your word processing program to answer the following questions. Then, if required, submit your answers to your instructor. (1) Type "anti-spam program" in the search text box. How many search results are returned that are not sponsored links? (2) Click one of these book titles and review the information. Click the 'Find this book in a library' link on the right side of the page. Type your postal code in the Enter Location Information text box and then click the Go button. How many libraries within a 25-mile radius carry this book? (3) Click your browser's Back button or press the BACKSPACE key several times to return to the Google Book Search home page. Click the Google Book Search Help link. Read some of the information and then write a 50-word summary of your findings.

Learn How To

Use the Learn How To activities to learn fundamental skills when using a computer and accompanying technology. Complete the exercises and submit them to your instructor. Premium Activity: The 🖼 icon indicates you can see a visual demonstration of the associated Learn How To activity by visiting scsite.com/dcf5e/ch7/howto.

LEARN HOW TO 1: Install a Computer

Once you have purchased a computer, you must install it for use. Based on years of experience, a set of guidelines for installing and using your computer has been developed. To examine these guidelines, complete the following steps:
1. Start the browser on your computer.
2. Type the Web address scsite.com/dcf5e in the Address bar and then press the ENTER key.
3. Click the Chapter 7 link in the top navigation bar.
4. Click Install Computer in the left sidebar below the heading, Features.
5. Read the material presented about how to install a computer.

Exercise
1. Using your Web search skills, research the latest recommendations with respect to proper ergonomics for using a computer. What information did you find that you did not know before? What changes would you make to your current computer setup that might make you more productive? Submit your answers to your instructor.
2. Many people report illnesses or injuries from using computers. Perform research in a library or on the Web to discover the five most common ailments associated with using a computer. Determine the actions people can take to minimize or eliminate these ailments. Submit a report to your instructor describing your findings.
3. Your computer lab at school contains multiple computers for student use. Using the knowledge you have obtained from this Learn How To activity, evaluate the computer installation in your school lab. In a report to your instructor, specify those items you think can be improved in the lab.

LEARN HOW TO 2: Maintain a Computer

While computers are amazingly resilient and reliable, you still should perform certain activities to ensure they maintain peak performance. To learn about these activities, complete the following steps:
1. Start the browser on your computer.
2. Type the Web address scsite.com/dcf5e in the Address bar and then press the ENTER key.
3. Click the Chapter 7 link in the top navigation bar.
4. Click Maintain Computer in the left sidebar below the heading, Features.
5. Read the material presented about how to maintain a computer.

Exercise
1. On either your computer or the computer on which you are working, perform a hardware and software inventory of at least five hardware devices and five application programs. List the vendor, product, vendor Web address, vendor e-mail address, and vendor support telephone number. Submit your inventory to your instructor.
2. Record the serial number of the computer on which you are working. Then, record the serial number for seven different application programs on the computer. Submit this information to your instructor.

LEARN HOW TO 3: Keep Windows Vista Up-to-Date

Keeping Windows Vista up-to-date is a critical part of keeping your computer in good working order. The updates made available by Microsoft for no charge over the Internet will keep errors from occurring on your computer and will ensure that all security safeguards are in place. To update Windows, complete the next steps:

Learn How To

1. Click the Start button on the Windows taskbar, click All Programs, and then click Windows Update in the All Programs list (Figure 7-26) to open the Windows Update window.
2. Click the 'View available updates' link to list the updates that are available for your computer.
3. If necessary, select those updates you wish to install and then click the Install button. Be aware that some updates might take 20 minutes or more to download and install, based primarily on your Internet access speed.
4. Often, after installation of updates, you must restart your computer to allow those updates to take effect. Be sure to save any open files before restarting your computer.

You also can schedule automatic updates for your computer. To do so, complete the following steps:

1. Click the Start button on the Windows taskbar and then click Control Panel on the Start menu.
2. In the Control Panel window, click System and Maintenance to display the System and Maintenance window.
3. In the System and Maintenance window, click 'Turn automatic updating on or off' to display the Change settings window (Figure 7-27).
4. Select the option you want to use for Windows updates. Microsoft, together with all security and operating system experts, strongly recommends you select 'Install updates automatically' so that updates will be installed on your computer automatically. Notice that if you select Install updates automatically, you also should select a time when your computer will be on and be connected to the Internet. A secondary choice is to download the suggested updates and then choose when you want to install them, and a third choice allows you to check for updates and then choose when you want to download and install them.
5. When you have made your selection, click the OK button in the Change settings window.

FIGURE 7-26

Updating Windows on your computer is vital to maintain security and operational integrity.

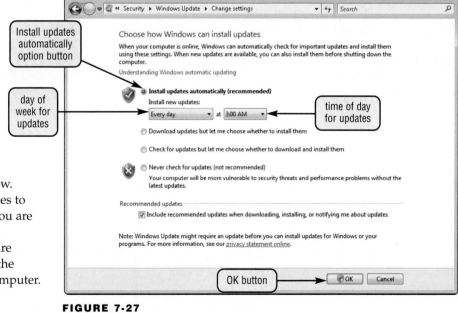

FIGURE 7-27

Exercise

1. Open the Windows Update window. Make a list of the important updates to Windows Vista on the computer you are using. Add to the list the optional updates that are available. If you are using your own computer, install the updates of your choice on your computer. Submit the list of updates to your instructor.
2. Optional: If you are not using your own computer, do not complete this exercise. Open the Control Panel, click System and Maintenance, and then click 'Turn automatic updating on or off'. Select the level of automatic updates you want to use. Write a report justifying your choice of automatic updates and then submit the report to your instructor.

Learn It Online

Use the Learn It Online exercises to reinforce your understanding of the chapter concepts. To access the Learn It Online exercises, visit scsite.com/dcf5e/ch7/learn.

1 At the Movies — Free Online Antivirus

To view the Free Online Antivirus movie, click the number 1 button. Locate your video and click the corresponding High-Speed or Dial-Up link, depending on your Internet connection. Watch the movie and then complete the exercise by answering the questions that follow. If you follow all the rules and guidelines for avoiding computer viruses and other malware, why is it still important to run antivirus software on your computer? How can you scan your computer for malware online for no cost?

2 Student Edition Labs — Installing and Uninstalling Software

Click the number 2 button. A new browser window will open, displaying the Student Edition Labs. Follow the on-screen instructions to complete the Installing and Uninstalling Software Lab. When finished, click the Exit button. If required, submit your results to your instructor.

3 Practice Test

Click the number 3 button. Answer each question. When completed, enter your name and click the Grade Test button to submit the quiz for grading. Make a note of any missed questions. If required, submit your results to your instructor.

4 Who Wants To Be a Computer Genius^2?

Click the number 4 button to find out if you are a computer genius. Directions about how to play the game will be displayed. When you are ready to play, click the Play button. Submit your score to your instructor.

5 Airline Schedules

Click the number 5 button to learn how to use the Internet to price, reserve, and track airline flights. Follow the instructions to use Southwest Airlines' Web site to price a flight from Chicago to Las Vegas. Using the Schedules link, check for available flights for the dates you select. Once you have selected a flight, use the Reservations link to price the flight. Print a copy of the pricing for your selected flight. Check the status of a current flight comparable to the flight you priced. Write a report comparing the different fares available and summarizing what information is available when you check the status of a flight. Include in your report what the circumstances would have to be for you to choose a more expensive flight. Print your report and submit it to your instructor.

6 Student Edition Labs — Keeping Your Computer Virus Free

Click the number 6 button. A new browser window will open, displaying the Student Edition Labs. Follow the on-screen instructions to complete the Keeping Your Computer Virus Free Lab. When finished, click the Exit button. If required, submit your results to your instructor.

7 Crossword Puzzle Challenge

Click the number 7 button, then click the Crossword Puzzle Challenge link. Directions about how to play the game will be displayed. Complete the puzzle to reinforce skills you learned in this chapter. When you are ready to play, click the Continue button. Submit the completed puzzle to your instructor.

8 Vista Exercises

Click the number 8 button. When the Vista Exercises menu appears, click the exercise assigned by your instructor. A new browser window will open. Follow the on-screen instructions to complete the exercise. When finished, click the Exit button. If required, submit your results to your instructor.

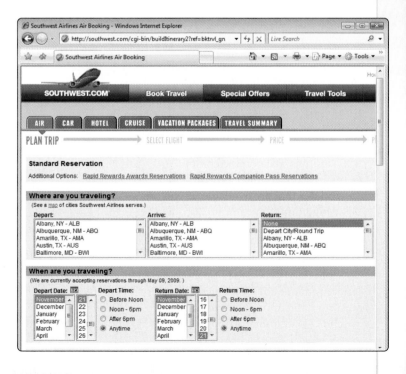

Special Feature

Buyer's Guide
How to Purchase a Personal Computer

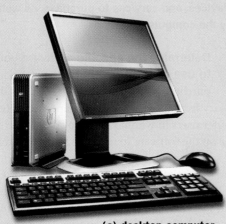

(a) desktop computer

At some point, perhaps while you are taking this course, you may decide to buy a personal computer. The decision is an important one and will require an investment of both time and money. Like many buyers, you may have little computer experience and find yourself unsure of how to proceed. You can get started by talking to your friends, coworkers, and instructors about their computers. What type of computers did they buy? Why? For what purposes do they use their computers? You also should answer the following three questions to help narrow your choices to a specific computer type, before reading this Buyer's Guide.

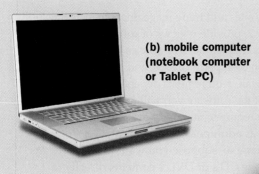

(b) mobile computer (notebook computer or Tablet PC)

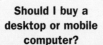

Should I buy a desktop or mobile computer?

For what purposes will I use the computer?

Should the computer I buy be compatible with the computers at school or work?

FIGURE 1

1 **Do you want a desktop computer or mobile computer?** A desktop computer (Figure 1a) is designed as a stationary device that sits on or below a desk or table in a location such as a home, office, or dormitory room. A desktop computer must be plugged in an electrical outlet to operate. A mobile computer, such as a notebook computer or Tablet PC (Figure 1b), is smaller than a desktop computer, more portable, and has a battery that allows you to operate it for a period without an electrical outlet.

Desktop computers are a good option if you work mostly in one place and have plenty of space in your work area. Desktop computers generally give you more performance for your money. Today, manufacturers are putting more emphasis on style by offering bright colors and stylish displays so that your computer looks attractive if it is in an area of high visibility.

Increasingly, more corporations are buying mobile computers to take advantage of their portability while traveling and at home. The past disadvantages of mobile computers, such as lower processor speeds, poor-quality monitors, weight, short battery life, and significantly higher prices, have all but disappeared. Today, hard disk speed, capacity, processor speed, and graphics capability in notebook computers are equal to, if not better than, desktop computers.

Mobile computers used to have several drawbacks, including the lack of high-end capabilities. Today's high-end notebook computers include most of the capabilities of a good desktop computer. Manufacturers have made great strides in improving durability and battery life. Most notebook computers are 1.5 to 2 inches thick and weigh less than 10 pounds, making them very portable and easy to carry.

② For what purposes will you use the computer? Having a general idea of the purposes for which you want to use your computer will help you decide on the type of computer to buy. At this point in your research, it is not necessary to know the exact application software titles or version numbers you might want to use. Knowing that you plan to use the computer primarily to create word processing, spreadsheet, database, and presentation documents, however, will point you in the direction of a desktop or notebook computer. If you want the portability of a smart phone or PDA, but you need more computing power, then a Tablet PC may be the best alternative. You also must consider that some application software runs only on a Mac, while others run only on a PC with the Windows operating system. Still other software may run only on a PC running the Linux operating system.

③ Should the computer be compatible with the computers at school or work? If you plan to bring work home, telecommute, or take distance education courses, then you should purchase a computer that is compatible with those at school or work.

Compatibility is primarily a software issue. If your computer runs the same operating system version, such as Microsoft Windows Vista, and the same application software, such as Microsoft Office 2007, then your computer will be able to read documents created at school or work and vice versa. Incompatible hardware can become an issue if you plan to connect directly to a school or office network using a cable or wireless technology. You usually can obtain the minimum system requirements from the Information Technology department at your school or workplace.

After evaluating the answers to these three questions, you should have a general idea of how you plan to use your computer and the type of computer you want to buy. Once you have decided on the type of computer you want, you can follow the guidelines presented in this Buyer's Guide to help you purchase a specific computer, along with software, peripherals, and other accessories.

Many of the desktop computer guidelines presented also apply to the purchase of a mobile computer. Later sections in this Buyer's Guide address additional purchasing considerations.

This Buyer's Guide concentrates on recommendations for purchasing a desktop computer or mobile computer.

HOW TO PURCHASE A DESKTOP COMPUTER

Once you have decided that a desktop computer is most suited to your computing needs, the next step is to determine specific software, hardware, peripheral devices, and services to purchase, as well as where to buy the computer.

① Determine the specific software you want to use on your computer. Before deciding to purchase software, be sure it contains the features necessary for the tasks you want to perform. Rely on the computer users in whom you have confidence to help you decide on the software to use. The minimum requirements of the software you select may determine the operating system (Microsoft Windows Vista, Linux, Mac OS X) you need. If you have decided to use a particular operating system that does not support software you want to use, you may be able to purchase similar software from other manufacturers.

Many Web sites and trade magazines, such as those listed in Figure 2, provide reviews of software products. These Web sites frequently have articles that rate computers and software on cost, performance, and support.

Your hardware requirements depend on the minimum requirements of the software you will run on your computer. Some software requires more memory and disk space than others, as well as additional input, output, and storage devices. For example, suppose you want to run software that can copy one CD's or DVD's contents directly to

Type of Computer	Web Site	Web Address
PC	CNET Shopper	shopper.cnet.com
	PC World Magazine	pcworld.com
	BYTE Magazine	byte.com
	PC Magazine	pcmag.com
	Yahoo! Computers	shopping.yahoo.com
	MSN Shopping	shopping.msn.com
Mac	Macworld Magazine	macworld.com
	Apple	apple.com
	Switch to Mac Campaign	apple.com/getamac

For an updated list of hardware and software reviews and their Web site addresses, visit scsite.com/dcf5e/ch7/buyers.

FIGURE 2 Hardware and software reviews.

another CD or DVD, without first copying the data to your hard disk. To support that, you should consider a desktop computer or a high-end notebook computer, because the computer will need two CD or DVD drives: one that reads from a CD or DVD, and one that reads from and writes on a CD or DVD. If you plan to run software that allows your computer to work as an entertainment system, then you will need a CD or DVD drive, quality speakers, and an upgraded sound card.

2 **Know the system requirements of the operating system.** After deciding the software you want to run on your new computer, you need to determine the operating system you want to use. If, however, you purchase a new computer, chances are it will have the latest version of your preferred operating system (Windows Vista, Linux, Mac OS X). Figure 3 lists the minimum computer requirements of Windows Vista versions.

Windows Vista Versions	Minimum Computer Requirements
Windows Vista Home Basic	• 1 GHz processor • 512 MB of system memory • DirectX 9 capable graphics processor • 20 GB of hard disk capacity (15 GB free space) • DVD drive • Audio output capability • Internet access capability
Windows Vista Home Premium **Windows Vista Ultimate** **Windows Vista Business** **Windows Vista Enterprise**	• 1 GHz processor • 1 GB of system memory • DirectX 9 capable graphics processor with WDDM driver and 128 MB of graphics memory • 40 GB of hard disk capacity (15 GB free space) • DVD drive • Audio output capability • Internet access capability

FIGURE 3 Hardware requirements for Windows Vista.

3 **Look for bundled software.** When you purchase a computer, it may come bundled with software. Some sellers even let you choose which software you want. Remember, however, that bundled software has value only if you would have purchased the software even if it had not come with the computer. At the very least, you probably will want word processing software and a browser to access the Internet. If you need

additional programs, such as a spreadsheet, a database, or presentation graphics, consider purchasing or downloading Microsoft Office 2007, Microsoft Works, OpenOffice.org, or Sun StarOffice, which include several programs at a reduced price.

4 **Avoid buying the least powerful computer available.** Once you know the application software you want to use, you then can consider the following important criteria about the computer's components: (1) processor speed, (2) size and types of memory (RAM) and storage, (3) types of input/output devices, (4) types of ports and adapter cards, and (5) types of communications devices. You also need to consider if the computer is upgradeable and to what extent you are able to upgrade. For example, all manufacturers limit the amount of memory you can add. The information in Figures 4 and 5 on pages 282 through 284 can help you determine what system components are best for you. Figure 4 outlines considerations for specific hardware components. Figure 5 provides a Base Components worksheet that lists PC recommendations for each category of user discussed in this book: Home User, Small Office/Home Office User, Mobile User, Power User, and Large Business User. In the worksheet, the Home User category is divided into two groups: Application Home User and Game Home User.

Computer technology changes rapidly, meaning a computer that seems powerful enough today may not serve your computing needs in a few years. In fact, studies show that many users regret not buying a more powerful computer. To avoid this, plan to buy a computer that will last you for two to three years. You can help delay obsolescence by purchasing the fastest processor, the most memory, and the largest hard disk you can afford. If you must buy a less powerful computer, be sure you can upgrade it with additional memory, components, and peripheral devices as your computer requirements grow.

5 **Consider upgrades to the mouse, keyboard, monitor, printer, microphone, and speakers.** You use these peripheral devices to interact with your computer, so you should make sure they are up to your standards. Review the peripheral devices listed in Figure 4 and then visit both local computer dealers and large retail stores to test the computers on display. Ask the salesperson what input and output devices would be best for you and whether you should upgrade beyond what comes standard. Consider purchasing a wireless keyboard and wireless mouse to eliminate bothersome wires on your desktop. A few extra dollars spent on these components when you initially purchase a computer can extend its usefulness by years.

CD/DVD Drives: Most computers come with a DVD±RW combination drive and/or Blu-ray or HD DVD drive. A DVD±RW drive allows you to read DVDs and CDs and to write data on (burn) a DVD or CD. It also will allow you to store and share video files, digital photos, and other large files with other people who have access to a DVD±RW drive or Blu-ray HD or DVD drive. A DVD has a capacity of at least 4.7 GB versus the 650 MB capacity of a CD. An HD DVD has a minimum capacity of 45 GB.

Card Reader/Writer: A card reader/writer is useful for transferring data directly to and from a removable flash memory card, such as the ones used in your camera or audio player. Make sure the card reader/writer can read from and write on the flash memory cards that you use.

Digital Camera: Consider an inexpensive point-and-shoot digital camera. They are small enough to carry around, usually operate automatically in terms of lighting and focus, and contain storage cards for storing photos. A 6-megapixel camera with a 512 MB storage card is sufficient for all personal picture taking needs, including creating images for use on the Web or to send via e-mail.

Digital Video Capture Device: A digital video capture device allows you to connect your computer to a camcorder or VCR and record, edit, manage, and then write video back on a VCR tape, a CD, or a DVD. To create quality video (true 30 frames per second, full-sized TV), the digital video capture device should have a USB 2.0 or FireWire port.

External Hard Disk: An external hard disk can serve many purposes: it can serve as extra storage for your computer, provide a way to store and transport large files or large quantities of files, and provide a convenient way to backup data on other internal and external hard disks. External hard disks can be purchased with the same amount of capacity as any internal disk. If you are going to use it as a backup to your internal hard disk, you should purchase an external hard disk with at least as much capacity as your internal hard disk. Many disk controllers come with a RAID option that allows you to replicate data among multiple hard disks.

Fingerprint Reader: For added security, you may want to consider purchasing a fingerprint reader. It helps prevent unauthorized access to your computer and also allows you to log onto Web sites quickly via your fingerprint, rather than entering a user name and password each time you access the site. Most use a USB connection and require software installation.

Hard Disk: It is recommended that you buy a computer with 320 GB if your primary interests are browsing the Web and using e-mail and Office suite-type applications; 1 TB if you also want to edit digital photos; 2.5 TB if you plan to edit digital video or manipulate large audio files even occasionally; and 200 to 500 GB if you will edit digital video, movies, or photography often; store audio files and music; or consider yourself to be a power user. It also is recommended that you use Serial ATA (SATA) as opposed to Parallel ATA (PATA). SATA has many advantages over PATA, including support for Plug and Play devices. Internal hard disk controllers also are available with the RAID option for added data protection.

Joystick/Wheel: If you use your computer to play games, then you will want to purchase a joystick or a wheel. These devices, especially the more expensive ones, provide for realistic game play with force feedback, programmable buttons, and specialized levers and wheels.

Keyboard: The keyboard is one of the more important devices used to communicate with the computer. For this reason, make sure the keyboard you purchase has 101 to 105 keys, is comfortable and easy to use, and has a USB connection. A wireless keyboard should be considered, especially if you have a small desk area.

Microphone: If you plan to record audio or use speech recognition to enter text and commands, then purchase a close-talk headset with gain adjustment support.

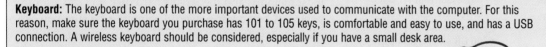

Modem: Most computers come with a modem so that you can use your telephone line to access the Internet. Some modems also have fax capabilities. Your modem should be rated at 56 Kbps.

Monitor: The monitor is where you will view documents, read e-mail messages, and view pictures. A minimum of a 17" screen is recommended, but if you are planning to use your computer for graphic design or game playing, then you may want to purchase a 19" or 21" monitor. The LCD flat panel monitor should be considered, especially if space is an issue. Instead of a large, wide screen monitor, you may want to consider a side-by-side monitor setup.

Mouse: As you work with your computer, you use the mouse constantly. For this reason, spend a few extra dollars, if necessary, and purchase a mouse with an optical or laser sensor and USB connection. The optical or laser sensor replaces the need for a mouse ball, which means you do not need a mouse pad. For a PC, make sure your mouse has a wheel, which acts as a third button in addition to the top two buttons on the left and right. An ergonomic design also is important because your hand is on the mouse most of the time when you are using your computer. A wireless mouse should be considered to eliminate the cord and allow you to work at short distances from your computer.

FIGURE 4 Hardware guidelines.

continued...

Ports: Depending on how you are using your computer, you may need anywhere from 4 to 10 USB 2.0 ports. USB 2.0 ports have become the connection of choice in the computer industry. They offer an easy way to connect peripheral devices such as printers, digital cameras, portable media players, etc. Many computers intended for home or professional audio/video use have built-in FireWire ports. Most personal computers come with a minimum of six USB 2.0 ports, two FireWire ports, and an Ethernet port.

Port Hub Expander: If you plan to connect several peripheral devices to your computer at the same time, then you need to be concerned with the number of ports available on your computer. If your computer does not have enough ports, then you should purchase a port hub expander. A port hub expander plugs in a single FireWire port or USB port and provides several additional ports.

Printer: Your two basic printer choices are ink-jet and laser. Color ink-jet printers cost on average between $50 and $300. Laser printers cost from $200 to $2,000. In general, the cheaper the printer, the lower the resolution and speed, and the more often you are required to change the ink cartridge or toner. Laser printers print faster and with a higher quality than an ink-jet, and their toner on average costs less. If you want color, then go with a high-end ink-jet printer to ensure quality of print. Duty cycle (the number of pages you expect to print each month) also should be a determining factor. If your duty cycle is on the low end — hundreds of pages per month — then stay with a high-end ink-jet printer, rather than purchasing a laser printer. If you plan to print photos taken with a digital camera, then you should purchase a photo printer. A photo printer is a dye-sublimation printer or an ink-jet printer with higher resolution and features that allow you to print quality photos.

Processor: For a PC, an Intel Core 2 Quad processor at 2.40 GHz is more than enough processor power for application home and small office/home office users. Game home, large business, and power users should upgrade to faster processors.

RAM: RAM plays a vital role in the speed of your computer. Make sure the computer you purchase has at least 1 GB of RAM. If you have extra money to invest in your computer, then consider increasing the RAM. The extra money for RAM will be well spent because more RAM typically translates into more speed.

Scanner: The most popular scanner purchased with a computer today is the flatbed scanner. When evaluating a flatbed scanner, check the color depth and resolution. Do not buy anything less than a color depth of 48 bits and a resolution of 1200 x 2400 dpi. The higher the color depth, the more accurate the color. A higher resolution picks up the more subtle gradations of color.

Sound Card: Many computers come with a standard sound card that supports Dolby 5.1 surround and are capable of recording and playing digital audio. Make sure they are suitable in the event you decide to use your computer as an entertainment or gaming system.

Speakers: Once you have a good sound card, quality speakers and a separate subwoofer that amplifies the bass frequencies of the speakers can turn your computer into a premium stereo system.

Web Cam: A Web cam is a small digital video camera used to capture and display live video (in some cases with sound), on a Web page. You also can capture, edit, and share video and still photos. The camera sits on your monitor or desk. Recommended minimum specifications include 640 x 480 resolution, a video with a rate of 30 frames per second, and a USB 2.0 or FireWire port.

USB Flash Drive: If you work on different computers and need access to the same data and information, then this portable miniature mobile storage device is ideal. USB flash drive capacity varies from 64 MB to 16 GB.

Video Card: Most standard video cards satisfy the monitor display needs of application home and small office users. If you are a game home user or a graphic designer, you will want to upgrade to a higher quality video card. The higher refresh rates will further enhance the display of games, graphics, and movies.

Wireless LAN Access Point: A wireless LAN access point allows you to network several computers, so that they can share files and access the Internet through a single cable modem or DSL connection. Each device that you connect requires a wireless card. A wireless LAN access point can offer a range of operations up to several hundred feet, so be sure the device has a high-powered antenna.

FIGURE 4 (continued)   Hardware guidelines.

BASE COMPONENTS

	Application Home User	Game Home User	Small Office/Home Office	Mobile User	Power User	Large Business User
HARDWARE						
Processor	Intel Core 2 Duo	Intel Core 2 Quad	Intel Core 2 Quad	Intel Core 2 Extreme	Intel Quad Core Xeon	Intel Core 2 Quad
RAM	1 GB	4 GB	2 GB	1 GB	4 GB	2 GB
Cache	512 KB L2	512 KB L2	512 KB L2	512 KB L2	2 MB L3	512 KB L2
Hard Disk	250 GB	300 GB	500 GB	100 GB	1.5 TB	500 GB
LCD Flat Panel	17" or 19"	21"	19" or 21"	17" Wide Display	23"	19" or 21"
Video Card	256 MB	512 MB	256 MB	256 MB	256 MB	256 MB
CD/DVD Bay 1	CD-RW	Blu-ray or HD DVD reader/writer	CD-RW	CD-RW/DVD	Blu-ray or HD DVD Reader/Writer	CD-RW
CD/DVD Bay 2	DVD+_RW	DVD±RW	DVD±RW	DVD±RW	DVD±RW	DVD±RW
Printer	Color Ink-Jet	Color Ink-Jet	18 ppm Laser	Portable Ink-Jet	10 ppm Color Laser	50 ppm Laser
Web Cam	Yes	Yes	Yes	Yes	Yes	Yes
Fax/Modem	Yes	Yes	Yes	Yes	Yes	Yes
Microphone	Close-Talk Headset with Gain Adjustment	Close-Talk Headset with Gain Adjustment	Close-Talk Headset with Gain Adjustment	Close-Talk Headset with Gain Adjustment	Close-Talk Headset with Gain Adjustment	Close-Talk Headset with Gain Adjustment
Speakers	5.1 Dolby Surround	5.1 Dolby Surround	5.1 Dolby Surround	Stereo	5.1 Dolby Surround	5.1 Dolby Surround
Pointing Device	IntelliMouse or Optical Mouse	Laser Mouse and Joystick	IntelliMouse or Optical Mouse	Touchpad or Pointing Stick and Laser Mouse	IntelliMouse or Laser Mouse and Joystick	IntelliMouse or Optical Mouse
Keyboard	Yes	Yes	Yes	Built-In	Yes	Yes
Backup Disk/Tape Drive	External or Removable Hard Disk	External or Removable Hard Disk	External or Removable Hard Disk	External or Removable Hard Disk	External or Removable Hard Disk	Tape Drive
USB Flash Drive	256 MB	512 MB	512 MB	512 MB	2 GB	4 GB
Sound Card	Sound Blaster Compatible	Sound Blaster Audigy 2	Sound Blaster Compatible	Built-In	Sound Blaster Audigy 2	Sound Blaster Compatible
Network Card	Yes	Yes	Yes	Yes	Yes	Yes
TV-Out Connector	Yes	Yes	Yes	Yes	Yes	Yes
USB 2.0 Port	6	8	6	4	10	9
FireWire Port	2	2	2	1	2	2
Ethernet Port	1	1	1	1	1	1
SOFTWARE						
Operating System	Windows Vista Home Basic	Windows Vista Home Premium	Windows Vista Business	Windows Vista Business	Windows Vista Ultimate	Windows Vista Enterprise
Office Suite	Office Standard 2007	Office Standard 2007	Office Small Business 2007	Office Small Business 2007	Office Professional 2007	Office Professional 2007
Antivirus	Yes, 12-Mo. Subscription	Yes, 12-Mo. Subscription	Yes, 12-Mo. Subscription	Yes, 12-Mo. Subscription	Yes, 12-Mo. Subscription	Yes, 12-Mo. Subscription
Internet Access	Cable, DSL, or Dial-up	Cable or DSL	Cable or DSL	Wireless or Dial-up	Cable or DSL	LAN/WAN (T1/T3)
OTHER						
Surge Protector	Yes	Yes	Yes	Portable	Yes	Yes
Warranty	3-Year Limited, 1-Year Next Business Day On-Site Service	3-Year Limited, 1-Year Next Business Day On-Site Service	3-year On-Site Service	3-Year Limited, 1-Year Next Business Day On-Site Service	3-year On-Site Service	3-year On-Site Service
Other		Wheel	Postage Printer	Docking Station Carrying Case Fingerprint Reader Portable Data Projector	Graphics Tablet Plotter or Large-Format Printer	

Optional Components for All Categories	
802.11a/b/g/n Wireless Card	Graphics Tablet
Bluetooth Enabled	Portable Media Player
Biometric Input Device	IrDA Port
Card Reader/Writer	Multifunction Peripheral
Digital Camera	Photo Printer
Digital Video Capture Device	Port Hub Expander
Digital Video Camera	Portable Data Projector
Dual-Monitor Support with Second Monitor	Scanner
Ergonomic Keyboard	TV/FM Tuner
External Hard Disk	Uninterruptible Power Supply
Fingerprint Reader	

FIGURE 5 Base desktop and mobile computer components and optional components. A copy of the Base Components worksheet is part of the Data Files for Students. To obtain a copy of the Data Files for Students, see the inside back cover of this book for instructions.

6 Determine whether you want to use telephone lines or broadband (cable or DSL) to access the Internet. If your computer has a modem, then you can access the Internet using a standard telephone line. Ordinarily, you call a local or toll-free 800 number to connect to an ISP (see Guideline 7). Using a dial-up Internet connection usually is relatively inexpensive but slow.

DSL and cable connections provide much faster Internet connections, which are ideal if you want faster file download speeds for software, digital photos, and music. As you would expect, they can be more expensive than a dial-up connection. DSL also may require that you subscribe to an ISP. DSL works just like a dial-up connection from a users point of view, but is always connected and has a much faster connection speed. Cable is available through your local cable television provider and some online service providers (OSPs). If you get cable, then you would not use a separate Internet service provider or online service provider.

7 **If you are using a dial-up or wireless connection to connect to the Internet, then select an ISP or OSP.**   You can access the Internet in one of two ways: an ISP or an OSP. Both provide Internet access for a monthly fee that ranges from $10 to $55. Local ISPs offer Internet access to users in a limited geographic region, through local telephone numbers. National ISPs provide access for users nationwide (including mobile users), through local and toll-free telephone numbers, cable, and DSL. Because of their size, national ISPs generally offer more services and have a larger technical support staff than local ISPs. OSPs furnish Internet access as well as members-only features for users nationwide. Figure 6 lists several national ISPs and OSPs. Before you choose an ISP or OSP, compare such features as the number of access hours, monthly fees, available services (e-mail, Web page hosting, chat), and reliability.

Company	Service	Web Address
America Online	OSP	aol.com
AT&T Worldnet	ISP	www.att.net
Comcast	OSP	comcast.net
CompuServe	OSP	compuserve.com
EarthLink	ISP	earthlink.net
Juno	OSP	juno.com
NetZero	OSP	netzero.com
MSN	OSP	msn.com
Prodigy	ISP/OSP	myhome.prodigy.net

For an updated list of national ISPs and OSPs and their Web site addresses, visit scsite.com/dcf5e/ch7/buyers.

FIGURE 6   National ISPs and OSPs.

8 **Use a worksheet to compare computers, services, and other considerations.**   You can use a separate sheet of paper to take notes on each vendor's computer and then summarize the information on a worksheet, such as the one shown in Figure 7. You can use Figure 7 to compare prices for either a PC or a Mac. Most companies advertise a price for a base computer that includes components housed in the system unit (processor, RAM, sound card, video card), disk drives (hard disk, CD-ROM, CD-RW, DVD-ROM, and DVD±RW), a keyboard, mouse, monitor, printer, speakers, and modem. Be aware, however, that some advertisements list prices for computers with only some of these components. Monitors and printers, for example, often are not included in a base computer's price. Depending on how you plan to use the computer, you may want to invest in additional or more powerful components. When you are comparing the prices of computers, make sure you are comparing identical or similar configurations.

PC or MAC Cost Comparison Worksheet

Dealers list prices for computers with most of these components (instead of listing individual component costs). Some dealers do not supply a monitor. Some dealers offer significant discounts, but you must subscribe to an Internet service for a specified period to receive the dicounted price. To compare computers, enter overall system price at top and enter a 0 (zero) for components _included in the computer cost._ For any additional components not covered in the computer price, enter the cost in the appropriate cells.

Items to Purchase	Desired Computer (PC)	Desired Computer (Mac)	Local Dealer #1	Local Dealer #2	Online Dealer #1	Online Dealer #2	Comments
OVERALL COMPUTER							
Overall Computer Price	< $2,000	< $2,000					
HARDWARE							
Processor	Intel Core 2 Quad	Intel Core 2 Quad					
RAM	1 GB	1 GB					
Cache	512 KB L2	512 KB L2					
Hard Disk	250 GB	250 GB					
Monitor/LCD Flat Panel	20 Inch	20 Inch					
Video Card	256 MB	256 MB					
USB Flash Drive	1 GB	1 GB					
CD/DVD Bay 1	CD-RW	DVD+RW					
CD/DVD Bay 2	DVD+RW	NA					
Speakers	Dolby 5.1 Surround	Dolby 5.1 Surround					
Sound Card	Sound Blaster Compatible	Sound Blaster Compatible					
USB 2.0 Port	6	6					
FireWire Port	2	2					
Ethernet Port	1	1					
Network Card	Yes	Yes					
Fax/Modem	56 Kbps	56 Kbps					
Keyboard	Standard	Apple Pro Keyboard					
Pointing Device	IntelliMouse	Intellimouse or Apple Pro Mouse					
Microphone	Close-Talk Headset with Gain Adjustment	Close-Talk Headset with Gain Adjustment					
Printer	Color Ink-Jet	Color Ink-Jet					
SOFTWARE							
Operating System	Windows Vista Ultimate	Mac OS X					
Application Software	Office 2007 Small Business	Office 2007 for Mac					
Antivirus	Yes - 12 Mo. Subscription	Yes - 12 Mo. Subscription					
OTHER							
Card Reader							
Digital Camera	5-Megapixel	5-Megapixel					
Internet Connection	1-Year Subscription	1-Year Subscription					
Joystick	Yes	Yes					
Web Cam	With Microphone	With Microphone					
Port Hub Expander							
Scanner	30-bit 600x1200 ppi Color	30-bit 600x1200 ppi Color					
Surge Protector							
Warranty	3-Year On-Site Service	3-Year On-Site Service					
Wireless Card	Internal	Internal					
Wireless LAN Access Point	LinkSys	Apple AirPort					
Total Cost			$.	$.	$.	$.	

FIGURE 7   A worksheet is an effective tool for summarizing and comparing components and prices of different computer vendors. A copy of the Computer Cost Comparison Worksheet is part of the Data Files for Students. To obtain a copy of the Data Files for Students, see the inside back cover of this book for instructions.

9 **If you are buying a new computer, you have several purchasing options: buying from your school bookstore, a local computer dealer, a local large retail store, or ordering by mail via telephone or the Web.** Each purchasing option has certain advantages. Many college bookstores, for example, sign exclusive pricing agreements with computer manufacturers and, thus, can offer student discounts. Local dealers and local large retail stores, however, more easily can provide hands-on support. Mail-order companies that sell computers by telephone or online via the Web (Figure 8) often provide the lowest prices, but extend less personal service. Some major mail-order companies, however, have started to provide next-business-day, on-site services. A credit card usually is required to buy from a mail-order company. Figure 9 lists some of the more popular mail-order companies and their Web site addresses.

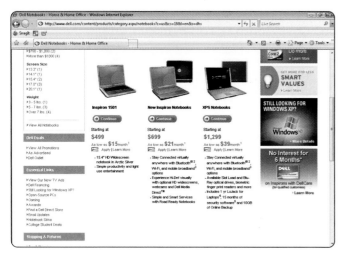

FIGURE 8 Mail-order companies, such as Dell, sell computers online.

Type of Computer	Company	Web Address
PC	CNET Shopper	shopper.cnet.com
	Hewlett-Packard	hp.com
	CompUSA	compusa.com
	TigerDirect	tigerdirect.com
	Dell	dell.com
	Acer	global.acer.com
Macintosh	Apple Computer	store.apple.com
	ClubMac	clubmac.com
	MacConnection	macconnection.com
	PC & MacExchange	macx.com
For an updated list of mail-order computer companies and their Web site addresses, visit scsite.com/dcf5e/ch7/buyers.		

FIGURE 9 Computer mail-order companies.

10 **If you are buying a used computer, stay with name brands such as Dell, Acer, Hewlett-Packard, and Apple.** Although brand-name equipment can cost more, most brand-name computers have longer, more comprehensive warranties, are better supported, and have more authorized centers for repair services. As with new computers, you can purchase a used computer from local computer dealers, local large retail stores, or mail order via the telephone or the Web. Classified ads and used computer sellers offer additional outlets for purchasing used computers. Figure 10 lists several major used computer brokers and their Web site addresses.

Company	Web Address
Amazon.com	amazon.com
TECHAGAIN	techagain.com
American Computer Express	americancomputerex.com
U.S. Computer Exchange	usce.org
eBay	ebay.com
For an updated list of mail-order computer companies and their Web site addresses, visit scsite.com/dcf5e/ch7/buyers.	

FIGURE 10 Used computer mail-order companies.

11 **If you have a computer and are upgrading to a new one, then consider selling or trading in the old one.** If you are a replacement buyer, your older computer still may have value. If you cannot sell the computer through the classified ads, via a Web site, or to a friend, then ask if the computer dealer will buy your old computer. An increasing number of companies are taking trade-ins, but do not expect too much money for your old computer. Other companies offer free disposal of your old PC.

12 **Be aware of hidden costs.** Before purchasing, be sure to consider any additional costs associated with buying a computer, such as an additional telephone line, a cable or DSL modem, an uninterruptible power supply (UPS), computer furniture, a USB flash drive, paper, and computer training classes you may want to take. Depending on where you buy your computer, the seller may be willing to include some or all of these in the computer purchase price.

13 **Consider more than just price.** The lowest-cost computer may not be the best long-term buy. Consider such intangibles as the vendor's time in business, the vendor's regard for quality, and the vendor's reputation for support. If you need to upgrade your computer often, you may want to consider a leasing arrangement, in which you pay monthly lease fees, but can upgrade or add on to your computer as your equipment needs change. No matter what type of buyer you are, insist on a 30-day, no-questions-asked return policy on your computer.

14 **Avoid restocking fees.** Some companies charge a restocking fee of 10 to 20 percent as part of their money-back return policy. In some cases, no restocking fee for hardware is applied, but it is applied for software. Ask about the existence and terms of any restocking policies before you buy.

15 **Use a credit card to purchase your new computer.** Many credit cards offer purchase protection and extended warranty benefits that cover you in case of loss of or damage to purchased goods. Paying by credit card also gives you time to install and use the computer before you have to pay for it. Finally, if you are dissatisfied with the computer and are unable to reach an agreement with the seller, paying by credit card gives you certain rights regarding withholding payment until the dispute is resolved. Check your credit card terms for specific details.

16 **Consider purchasing an extended warranty or service plan.** If you use your computer for business or require fast resolution to major computer problems, consider purchasing an extended warranty or a service plan through a local dealer or third-party company. Most extended warranties cover the repair and replacement of computer components beyond the standard warranty. Most service plans ensure that your technical support calls receive priority response from technicians. You also can purchase an on-site service plan that states that a technician will come to your home, work, or school within 24 hours. If your computer includes a warranty and service agreement for a year or less, think about extending the service for two or three years when you buy the computer.

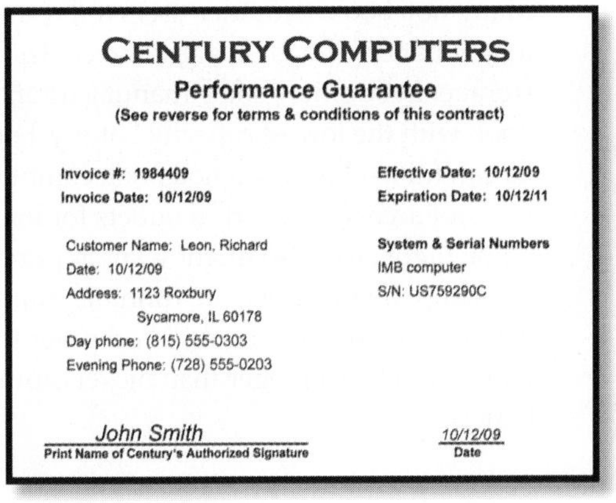

CENTURY COMPUTERS
Performance Guarantee
(See reverse for terms & conditions of this contract)

Invoice #: 1984409   Effective Date: 10/12/09
Invoice Date: 10/12/09   Expiration Date: 10/12/11

Customer Name: Leon, Richard   System & Serial Numbers
Date: 10/12/09   IMB computer
Address: 1123 Roxbury   S/N: US759290C
              Sycamore, IL 60178
Day phone: (815) 555-0303
Evening Phone: (728) 555-0203

John Smith   *10/12/09*
Print Name of Century's Authorized Signature   Date

HOW TO PURCHASE A NOTEBOOK COMPUTER

If you need computing capability when you travel or to use in lecture or meetings, you may find a notebook computer to be an appropriate choice. The guidelines mentioned in the previous section also apply to the purchase of a notebook computer. The following are additional considerations unique to notebook computers.

1 **Purchase a notebook computer with a sufficiently large screen.** Active-matrix screens display high-quality color that is viewable from all angles. Less expensive, passive-matrix screens sometimes are difficult to see in low-light conditions and cannot be viewed from an angle.

Notebook computers typically come with a 12.1-inch, 13.3-inch, 14.1-inch, 15.4-inch, or 17-inch display. For most users, a 14.1-inch display is satisfactory. If you intend to use your notebook computer as a desktop computer replacement, however, you may opt for a 15.7-inch or 17-inch display. The WSXGA+ standard (1680 × 1050) is popular with 17" displays, so if you intend to watch HD movies on your computer, take this into consideration. Dell offers a notebook computer with a 20.1-inch display that looks like a briefcase when closed. Notebook computers with these larger displays weigh seven to ten pounds, however, so if you travel a lot and portability is essential, you might want a lighter computer with a smaller display. The lightest notebook computers, which weigh less than 3 pounds, are equipped with a 12.1-inch display. Regardless of size, the resolution of the display should be at least 1024 × 768 pixels. To compare the monitor size on various notebook computers, visit the company Web sites in Figure 11.

Type of Notebook	Company	Web Address
PC	Acer	global.acer.com
	Dell	dell.com
	Fujitsu	fujitsu.com
	Hewlett-Packard	hp.com
	Lenovo	lenovo.com/us/en/
	NEC	nec.com
	Sony	sony.com
	Toshiba	toshiba.com
Mac	Apple	apple.com

For an updated list of companies and their Web site addresses, visit scsite.com/dcf5e/ch7/buyers.

FIGURE 11 Companies that sell notebook computers.

2 **Experiment with different keyboards and pointing devices.**   Notebook computer keyboards are far less standardized than those for desktop computers. Some notebook computers, for example, have wide wrist rests, while others have none, and keyboard layouts on notebook computers often vary. Notebook computers also use a range of pointing devices, including pointing sticks, touchpads, and trackballs. Before you purchase a notebook computer, try various types of keyboard and pointing devices to determine which is easiest for you to use. Regardless of the pointing device you select, you also may want to purchase a regular mouse to use when you are working at a desk or other large surface.

3 **Make sure the notebook computer you purchase has a CD and/or DVD drive.**   Most notebook computers come with a CD and/or a DVD drive. Although DVD drives are slightly more expensive, they allow you to play CDs and DVD movies using your notebook computer and hear the sound through headphones

4 **If necessary, upgrade the processor, memory, and disk storage at the time of purchase.**   As with a desktop computer, upgrading your notebook computer's memory and disk storage usually is less expensive at the time of initial purchase. Some disk storage is custom designed for notebook computer manufacturers, meaning an upgrade might not be available in the future. If you are purchasing a lightweight notebook computer, then it should include at least an Intel Core 2 Quad processor, 1 GB RAM, and 250 GB of storage.

5 **The availability of built-in ports and slots and a port extender on a notebook computer is important.**   A notebook computer does not have much room to add adapter cards. If you know the purpose for which you plan to use your notebook computer, then you can determine the ports you will need. Most notebooks come with common ports, such as a mouse port, IrDA port, serial port, parallel port, video port, a FireWire port, multiple USB ports, and a network port. If you plan to connect your notebook computer to a TV, however, then you will need a PCtoTV port. To optimize TV viewing, you may want to consider DVI or HDMI interfaces. If you want to connect to networks at school or in various offices via a network cable, make sure the notebook computer you purchase has a network port. If your notebook computer does not contain a network port, then you will have to purchase an external network card that slides into an expansion slot in your notebook computer, as well as a network cable. You also may want to consider adding a card reader. While newer portable media players connect to a USB port, older ones require a FireWire port.

6 **If you plan to use your notebook computer for note-taking at school or in meetings, consider a notebook computer that converts to a Tablet PC.**   Some computer manufacturers have developed convertible Tablet PCs that allow the screen to rotate 180 degrees on a central hinge and then fold down to cover the keyboard (Figure 12). You then can use a digital pen to enter text or drawings into the computer by writing on the screen. Some notebook computers have wide screens for better viewing and editing, and some even have a screen on top of the unit in addition to the regular screen.

FIGURE 12
A convertible Tablet PC.

7 **Purchase a notebook computer with a built-in wireless network connection.**   A wireless network connection (Bluetooth, Wi-Fi a/b/g/n, WiMAX, etc.) can be useful when you travel or as part of a home network. Increasingly more airports, hotels, and cafes have wireless networks that allow you to connect to the Internet. Many users today are setting up wireless home networks. With a wireless home network, the desktop computer functions as the server, and your notebook computer can access the desktop computer from any location in the house to share files and hardware, such as a printer, and browse the Web. Most home wireless networks allow connections from distances of 150 to 800 feet.

8 **If you are going to use your notebook computer for long periods without access to an electrical outlet, purchase a second battery.**   The trend among notebook computer users today is power and size over battery life, and notebook computer manufacturers have picked up on this. Many notebook computer users today are willing to give up longer battery life for a larger screen, faster processor, and more storage. In addition, some manufacturers typically sell the notebook with the lowest capacity battery. For this reason, you need to be careful in choosing a notebook computer if you plan to use it without access to electrical outlets for long periods, such as an airplane flight. You also might want to purchase a second battery as a backup. If you anticipate running your notebook computer on batteries frequently, choose a computer that uses lithium-ion batteries, which last longer than nickel cadmium or nickel hydride batteries.

9 **Purchase a well-padded and well-designed carrying case.** An amply padded carrying case will protect your notebook computer from the bumps it will receive while traveling. A well-designed carrying case will have room for accessories such as spare CDs and DVDs, a user manual, pens, and paperwork (Figure 13).

FIGURE 13
A well-designed notebook computer carrying case.

10 **If you travel, obtain a set of electrical and telephone adapters and purchase an accident and theft protection plan.** When traveling overseas, it is important to know that different countries use different outlets for electrical and telephone connections. Several manufacturers sell sets of adapters that will work in most countries. You also may want to consider accident and theft protection by purchasing a protection plan or insurance. Some devices contain built-in recovery mechanisms (like LoJack for cars) that make tracking and recovery possible.

11 **If you plan to connect your notebook computer to a video projector, make sure the notebook computer is compatible with the video projector.** You should check, for example, to be sure that your notebook computer will allow you to display an image on the computer screen and projection device at the same time (Figure 14). Also, ensure that your notebook computer has the ports required to connect to the video projector. You also may consider purchasing a notebook computer with a built-in Web cam for video conferencing purposes.

12 **For improved security and convenience, consider a fingerprint reader.** More than half a million notebook computers are stolen or lost each year. If you have critical information stored on your notebook computer, then consider purchasing one with a fingerprint reader (Figure 15) to protect the data if your computer is stolen or lost. Fingerprint security offers a level of protection that extends well beyond the standard password protection. If your notebook computer is stolen, the odds of recovering it improve dramatically with anti-theft tracking software. Manufacturers claim recovery rates of 90 percent or more for notebooks using their product. For convenience, fingerprint readers also allow you to log onto several Web sites via your fingerprint, rather than entering a user name and password information.

FIGURE 15 Fingerprint reader technology offers greater security than passwords.

FIGURE 14 A notebook computer connected to a video projector projects the image displayed on the screen.

HOW TO PURCHASE A TABLET PC

The Tablet PC (Figure 16) combines the mobility features of a traditional notebook computer with the simplicity of pencil and paper, because you can create and save Office-type documents by writing and drawing directly on the screen with a digital pen. Tablet PCs use the Windows Tablet Technology in the Windows Vista operating system. A notebook computer and a Tablet PC have many similarities. For this reason, if you are considering purchasing a Tablet PC, review the guidelines for purchasing a notebook computer, as well as the guidelines below.

Company	Web Address
Fujitsu	fujitsu.com
Hewlett-Packard	hp.com
Microsoft	microsoft.com/windowsxp/tabletpc
ViewSonic	viewsonic.com

For an updated list of companies and their Web site addresses, visit scsite.com/dcf5e/ch7/buyers.

FIGURE 17 Companies involved with Tablet PCs and their Web sites.

2 **Decide whether you want a convertible or pure Tablet PC.** Convertible Tablet PCs have an attached keyboard and look like a notebook computer. You rotate the screen and lay it flat against the computer for note-taking. The pure Tablet PCs are slim and lightweight, weighing less than four pounds. They have the capability of easily docking at a desktop to gain access to a large monitor, keyboard, and mouse. If you spend a lot of time attending lectures or meetings, then the pure Tablet PC is ideal. Acceptable specifications for a Tablet PC are shown in Figure 18.

TABLET PC SPECIFICATIONS

Dimensions	12" × 9" × 1.2"
Weight	Less than 4 Pounds
Processor	Pentium M Processor at 2 GHz
RAM	1 GB
Hard Disk	60 GB
Display	12.1" TFT
Digitizer	Electromagnetic Digitizer
Battery	6-Cell High Capacity Lithium-Ion
USB	3
FireWire	1
Docking Station	Grab and Go with CD-ROM, Keyboard, and Mouse
Bluetooth Port	Yes
Wireless	802.11a/b/g/n Card
Network Card	10/100 Ethernet
Modem	56 Kbps
Speakers	Internal
Microphone	Internal
Operating System	Windows Vista
Application Software	Office Small Business Edition
Antivirus Software	Yes – 12 Month Subscription
Warranty	1-Year Limited Warranty Parts and Labor

FIGURE 18 Tablet PC specifications.

FIGURE 16 The lightweight Tablet PC, with its handwriting capabilities, is the latest addition to the family of mobile computers.

1 **Make sure the Tablet PC fits your mobile computing needs.** The Tablet PC is not for every mobile user. If you find yourself in need of a computer in class or you are spending more time in meetings than in your office, then the Tablet PC may be the answer. Before you invest money in a Tablet PC, however, determine the programs you plan to use on it. You should not buy a Tablet PC simply because it is an interesting type of computer. For additional information on the Tablet PC, visit the Web sites listed in Figure 17. You may have to use the search capabilities on the home page of the companies listed to locate information about the Tablet PC.

3 **Be sure the weight and dimensions are conducive to portability.** The weight and dimensions of the Tablet PC are important because you carry it around like a notepad. The Tablet PC you buy should weigh four pounds or less. Its dimensions should be approximately 12 inches by 9 inches by 1.2 inches.

4 **Port availability, battery life, and durability are even more important with a Tablet PC than they are with a notebook computer.** Make sure the Tablet PC you purchase has the ports required for the applications you plan to run. As with any mobile computer, battery life is important especially if you plan to use your Tablet PC for long periods without access to an electrical outlet. A Tablet PC must be durable because if you use it the way it was designed to be used, then you will be handling it much like you handle a pad of paper.

5 **Experiment with different models of the Tablet PC to find the digital pen that works best for you.** The key to making use of the Tablet PC is to be comfortable with its handwriting capabilities and on-screen keyboard. Not only is the digital pen used to write on the screen (Figure 19), you also use it to make gestures to complete tasks, in a manner similar to the way you use a mouse. Figure 20 compares the standard point-and-click of a mouse with the gestures made with a digital pen. Other gestures with the digital pen replicate some of the commonly used keys on a keyboard.

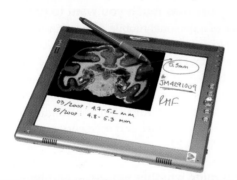

FIGURE 19 A Tablet PC lets you handwrite notes and draw on the screen using a digital pen.

Mouse	Digital Pen
Point	Point
Click	Tap
Double-click	Double-tap
Right-click	Tap and hold
Click and drag	Drag

FIGURE 20 Standard point-and-click of a mouse compared with the gestures made with a digital pen.

6 **Check out the comfort level of handwriting in different positions.** You should be able to handwrite on a Tablet PC with your hand resting on the screen. You also should be able to handwrite holding the Tablet PC in one hand, as well as with it sitting in your lap.

7 **Make sure the LCD display device has a resolution high enough to take advantage of Microsoft's ClearType technologies.** Tablet PCs use a digitizer under a standard 10.4-inch motion-sensitive LCD display to make the writing experience on the screen feel like writing on paper. To ensure you get the maximum benefits from the new ClearType technology, make sure the LCD display has a resolution of 800×600 in landscape mode and a 600×800 in portrait mode.

8 **Test the built-in Tablet PC microphone and speakers.** Although most application software, including Microsoft Office, recognizes human speech, it is important that the Tablet PC's built-in microphone operates at an acceptable level. If the microphone is not to your liking, you may want to purchase a close-talk headset with your Tablet PC. Increasingly more users are sending information as audio files, rather than relying solely on text. For this reason, you also should check the speakers on the Tablet PC to make sure they meet your standards.

9 **Consider a Tablet PC with a built-in Web cam.** A Web cam adds streaming video and still photography capabilities to your Tablet PC, while still allowing you to take notes in lectures or meetings.

10 **Review the docking capabilities of the Tablet PC.** The Tablet Technology in the Windows Vista operating system supports a grab-and-go form of docking, so you can pick up and take a docked Tablet PC with you, just as you would pick up a notepad on your way to a meeting (Figure 21).

FIGURE 21 A Tablet PC docked to create a desktop computer with the Tablet PC as the monitor.

11 **Wireless access to the Internet and your e-mail is essential with a Tablet PC.** Make sure the Tablet PC has wireless networking (Bluetooth, Wi-Fi a/b/g/n, WiMAX, etc.), so you can access the Internet and your e-mail anytime and anywhere. Your Tablet PC also should include standard network connections, such as dial-up and Ethernet connections.

12 **Review available accessories to purchase with your Tablet PC.** Tablet PC accessories include docking stations, mouse units, keyboards, security cables, additional memory and storage, protective handgrips, screen protectors, and various types of digital pens.

HOW TO PURCHASE A PERSONAL MOBILE DEVICE

Whether you choose a smart phone, Ultra-Mobile PC, or portable media player, handheld navigation device, or handheld game console depends on where, when, and how you will use the device. If you need to stay organized and in touch when on the go, then a smart phone or Ultra-Mobile PC may be the right choice. Choose a handheld navigation device if you often need directions or information about your surroundings. If you plan to relax and play games, then a handheld game console may be right for you. Busy professionals who are on the move often carry more than one personal mobile device.

This section lists guidelines you should consider when purchasing a smart phone, Ultra-Mobile PC, portable media player, handheld navigation device, handheld game console, or any other personal mobile device. You also should visit the Web sites listed in Figure 22 to gather more information about the type of personal mobile device that best suits your computing needs.

1 **Determine the programs you plan to run on your device.** Most smart phones and other personal mobile devices can handle basic organizer-type software such as a calendar, address book, and notepad. Portable media players and handheld navigation devices usually have the fewest programs available to run on them. Ultra-Mobile PCs usually have the most programs available because the devices can run almost any personal computer software. The availability of other software depends on the operating system you choose. The depth and breadth of software for the Palm OS is significant, with more than 20,000 basic programs and more than 600 wireless programs. Devices that run Windows-based operating systems, such as Windows Mobile, may have fewer programs available, but the operating system and application software are similar to those with which you are familiar, such as Word and Excel. When choosing a handheld game console, consider whether your favorite games are available for the device. Consider if you want extras on the device, such as the capability of playing media files.

2 **Consider how much you want to pay.** The price of a personal mobile device can range from $100 to more than $2,000, depending on its capabilities. Some Palm OS devices are at the lower end of the cost spectrum, and Ultra-Mobile PCs often are at the higher end. A personal mobile device will be less expensive than a smart phone with a similar configuration. For the latest prices, capabilities, and accessories, visit the Web sites listed in Figure 22.

3 **Determine whether you need wireless Internet access and e-mail or mobile phone capabilities with your device.** Smart phones often give you access to e-mail and other data and Internet services. Some smart phones, Ultra-Mobile PCs, and handheld game consoles include wireless networking capability to allow you to connect to the Internet wirelessly. These wireless features and services allow personal mobile device users to access real-time information from anywhere to help make decisions while on the go. Most portable media players do not include the capability to access Internet services.

Web Site	Web Address
CNET Shopper	shopper.cnet.com
iPod	apple.com/itunes
Palm	palm.com
Microsoft	windowsmobile.com pocketpc.com microsoft.com/smartphone
Oqo	oqo.com
MobileTechReview	mobiletechreview.com
Nintendo	nintendo.com/channel/ds
Research in Motion	rim.com
Garmin	garmin.com
Symbian	symbian.com
Wireless Developer Network	wirelessdevnet.com
Sharp	www.myzaurus.com

For an updated list of reviews and information about personal mobile devices and their Web addresses, visit scsite.com/dcf5e/ch7/buyers.

FIGURE 22 Web site reviews and information about personal mobile devices.

4 **For wireless devices, determine how and where you will use the service.**   When purchasing a wireless device, you must subscribe to a wireless service. Determine if the wireless network (carrier) you choose has service in the area where you plan to use the device. Some networks have high-speed data networks only in certain areas, such as large cities or business districts. Also, a few carriers allow you to use your device in other countries.

When purchasing a smart phone, determine if you plan to use the device more as a telephone or wireless data device. Some smart phones, such as those based on the Pocket PC Phone edition or the Palm OS, are geared more for use as a personal mobile device and have a personal mobile device form factor. Other smart phones, such as those based on Microsoft Smartphone or Symbian operating systems, mainly are telephone devices that include robust PIM functionality. Research in Motion Blackberry-based smart phones include robust data features that are oriented to accessing e-mail and wireless data services.

5 **Make sure your device has enough memory and storage.**   Memory is a major issue for high-end devices that, for example, have color displays and wireless features. Without enough memory, the performance level of your device will drop dramatically. If you plan to purchase a high-end device running the Palm OS operating system, the device should have at least 32 MB of RAM. If you plan to purchase a high-end device running the Windows Mobile operating system, the device should have at least 64 MB of RAM. An Ultra-Mobile PC can have 512 MB of RAM or more, while a handheld navigation device may have over 2 GB of flash memory.

Many personal mobile devices include a hard disk for storage. Portable media players, Ultra-Mobile PC, and some smart phones include hard disks to store media and other data. Consider how much media and other data you need to store on your device. The hard disk size may range from 4 GB to more than 80 GB.

6 **Practice with the touch screen, handwriting recognition, and built-in keyboard.**   To enter data into a smart phone and some Ultra-Mobile PCs and handheld game consoles, you use a pen-like stylus to handwrite on the screen or a keyboard. The keyboard either slides out or is mounted on the front of the device. With handwriting recognition, the device translates the handwriting into a computerized font. You also can use the stylus as a pointing device to select items on the screen and enter data by tapping on an on-screen keyboard. By practicing data entry before buying a device, you can learn if one device may be easier for you to use than another. You also can buy third-party software to improve a device's handwriting recognition.

7 **Compare battery life.**   Any mobile device is good only if it has the power required to run. The use of wireless networking will shorten battery time considerably. To help alleviate this problem, most devices have incorporated rechargeable batteries that can be recharged by placing the device in a cradle or connecting it to a charger.

8 **Seriously consider the importance of ergonomics.** Will you put the device in your pocket, a carrying case, or wear it on your belt? How does it feel in your hand? Will you use it indoors or outdoors? Many screens are unreadable outdoors. Do you need extra ruggedness, such as would be required in construction, in a plant, or in a warehouse? A smart phone with a PDA form factor may be larger than a typical PDA. A smart phone with a phone form factor may be smaller, but have fewer capabilities.

9 **Check out the accessories.** Determine which accessories you want for your personal mobile device. Accessories include carrying cases, portable mini- and full-sized keyboards, removable storage, modems, synchronization cradles and cables, car chargers, wireless communications, global positioning system modules, digital camera modules, expansion cards, dashboard mounts, replacement styli, headsets, microphones, and more.

10 **Decide whether you want additional functionality.** In general, off-the-shelf Microsoft operating system-based devices have broader functionality than devices with other operating systems. For example, voice-recording capability, e-book players, and media players are standard on most Windows Mobile devices. If you are leaning towards a Palm OS device

and want these additional functions, you may need to purchase additional software or expansion modules to add them later. Determine whether your employer permits devices with cameras on the premises, and if not, do not consider devices with cameras. Some handheld game consoles include the capability to access the Web. High-end handheld navigation devices may include destination information, such as information about restaurants and points of interest, an e-book reader, a media player, and currency converter.

11 **Determine whether synchronization of data with other devices or personal computers is important.** Most devices include a cradle that connects to the USB or serial port on your computer so that you can synchronize data on your device with your desktop or notebook computer. Increasingly more devices are Bluetooth and/or wireless networking enabled, which gives them the capability of synchronizing wirelessly. Many devices today also have an infrared port that allows you to synchronize data with any device that has a similar infrared port, including desktop and notebook computers or other personal mobile devices.

CHAPTER 8

Communications and Networks

OBJECTIVES

After completing this chapter, you will be able to:

1. Discuss the components required for successful communications
2. Describe uses of computer communications
3. Differentiate among types of networks
4. Explain the purpose of communications software
5. Describe various types of lines for communications over the telephone network
6. Describe commonly used communications devices
7. Discuss different ways to set up a home network
8. Identify various physical and wireless transmission media

CONTENTS

COMMUNICATIONS

Computer **communications** describes a process in which two or more computers or devices transfer data, instructions, and information. Figure 8-1 shows a sample communications system. Some communications involve cables and wires; others are sent wirelessly through the air. As illustrated in this figure, communications systems contain all types of computers and computing devices. For successful communications, you need the following:

- A **sending device** that initiates an instruction to transmit data, instructions, or information.
- A communications device that connects the sending device to a communications channel.
- A **communications channel**, or transmission media on which the data, instructions, or information travel.
- A communications device that connects the communications channel to a receiving device.
- A **receiving device** that accepts the transmission of data, instructions, or information.

FIGURE 8-1   An example of a communications system. The communications channel consists of telephone and power lines, cable television and other underground lines, microwave stations, and satellites.

All types of computers and mobile devices serve as sending and receiving devices in a communications system. This includes mainframe computers, servers, desktop computers, notebook computers, Tablet PCs, smart phones, portable media players, and GPS receivers. One type of communications device that connects a communications channel to a sending or receiving device such as a computer is a modem. Two examples of communications channels are cable television lines and telephone lines.

USES OF COMPUTER COMMUNICATIONS

Computer communications are everywhere. Many require that users subscribe to an Internet access provider. With other computer communications, an organization such as a business or school provides communications services to employees, students, or customers. The following pages discuss a variety of computer communications.

system

Internet, Web, E-Mail, Instant Messaging, Chat Rooms, Newsgroups, Blogs, Wikis, RSS, VoIP, FTP, Web Folders, Video Conferencing, and Fax

Previous chapters discussed many uses of computer communications as they related to a particular topic. In the course of a day, it is likely you use, or use information generated by, one or more of the previously discussed communications technologies, which are outlined in Figure 8-2.

The following pages discuss a variety of other uses of communications that have not been discussed previously. These include wireless messaging services, wireless Internet access points, cybercafés, global positioning systems, collaboration, groupware, voice mail, and Web services.

PREVIOUSLY DISCUSSED USES OF COMMUNICATIONS

Internet — Worldwide collection of networks that links millions of businesses, government agencies, educational institutions, and individuals

Web — Worldwide collection of electronic documents on the Internet that users access through a Web browser

E-Mail — Transmission of messages and files via a computer network

Instant Messaging — Real-time one-on-one communications service on the Internet that notifies you when one or more people are online and then allows you to exchange messages, pictures, files, audio, and video

Chat Rooms — Real-time typed conversation among two or more people that takes place on a computer connected to a network that also may allow the exchange of messages, pictures, files, audio, and video

Newsgroups — Online areas in which users have written discussions about a particular subject

Blogs — Time-stamped articles on a network that reflect the author's interests, opinions, and personality

Wikis — Collaborative Web sites that allow users to create, add to, modify, or delete Web site content

RSS — Specification that enables Web content to be distributed to subscribers

VoIP — Conversation that takes place over the Internet using a telephone connected to a computer or mobile device or telephone adapter

FTP — Internet standard that permits users to upload and download files to and from FTP servers on the Internet

Web Folders — Location on a Web server (also known as an HTTP server) to which users publish documents and other files

Video Conferencing — Real-time meeting between two or more geographically separated people who use a network to transmit audio and video data

Fax Machine or Computer Fax/Modem — Transmits and receives documents over telephone lines

FIGURE 8-2   Uses of communications discussed in earlier chapters.

Wireless Messaging Services

Users can send and receive wireless messages to and from smart phones, cell phones, handheld game consoles, and other personal mobile devices using three techniques: text messaging, wireless instant messaging, and picture/video messaging (Figure 8-3).

TEXT MESSAGING   A mobile device with **text messaging**, also called SMS (short message service), capability allows users to send and receive short text messages on a phone or other mobile device. Text messaging services typically provide users with several options for sending and receiving messages:

- Mobile to Mobile: send a message from your mobile device to another mobile device
- Mobile to E-Mail: send a message from your mobile device to an e-mail address anywhere in the world
- Web to Mobile: send a message from a text messaging Web site to a mobile device, or request that a Web site alert a mobile device with breaking news and other updates, such as sports scores, stock prices, and weather forecasts
- Mobile to Provider: send a message by entering a four- or five-digit number assigned to a specific content or wireless service provider, followed by the message, such as a vote for a television program contestant

WIRELESS INSTANT MESSAGING   Wireless instant messaging (IM) is a real-time Internet communications service that allows wireless mobile devices to exchange messages with one or more mobile devices or online users. Some wireless Internet service providers partner with IM services so that you can use your smart phone or other mobile device to send and receive wireless instant messages. With a compatible IM service, users have these IM options:

- Mobile to Mobile: use a wireless instant messenger to communicate between two mobile devices
- Mobile to Personal Computer: use a wireless instant messenger to communicate between a mobile device and a personal computer
- Web to Mobile: send or forward messages from a personal computer's instant messenger to a mobile device

PICTURE/VIDEO MESSAGING   With **picture messaging**, users can send pictures and sound files, as well as short text messages, to a phone or other personal mobile device, or a computer. With **video messaging**, users can send short video clips, usually about 30 seconds in length, in addition to all picture messaging services (read Ethics & Issues 8-1 for a related discussion). Picture/video messaging service, also called MMS (multimedia message service), typically provides users these options for sending and receiving messages:

* Mobile to Mobile: send the picture/video from your mobile device to another mobile device
* Mobile to E-Mail: send the picture/video from your mobile device to an e-mail address anywhere in the world

WEB LINK 8-1

Video Messaging

For more information, visit scsite.com/dcf5e/ch8/weblink and then click Video Messaging.

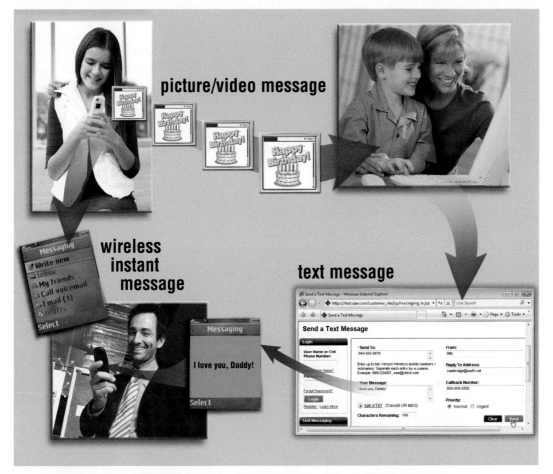

FIGURE 8-3   Users can send and receive text messages, wireless instant messages, and picture/video messages to and from their smart phones and other computers and devices.

ETHICS & ISSUES 8-1

High-Tech Cheating via Wireless Messaging Services

Several schools have banned student smart phones claiming that they disrupt classes and sometimes are used for illegal activities, such as drug sales. Now, schools may have another reason to prohibit smart phones and other wireless devices among students. Once, teachers had to watch test-takers only to make sure that no one was copying from a neighbor's paper or secretly referring to notes concealed under a desk. Recently, however, some students have been caught using their smart phones' messaging service to send each other answers to test questions. Others have been caught using camera phones to take pictures of tests and forwarding the images to other students who were scheduled to take the test at a later time. Some teachers fear that more students soon may be using wireless devices, such as gaming devices, to communicate covertly with classmates during a test, or even to receive messages from sources outside the classroom. Some schools have gone as far as installing electronic jamming equipment to stop wireless communications. To eliminate this high-tech method of cheating, should smart phones, digital cameras, notebook computers, Tablet PCs, and other wireless devices be banned during lectures and exams? Why or why not? Short of banning these devices, what, if anything, can schools do to prevent students from using them to cheat? Is it possible for schools to seek a point of compromise so that they can both embrace the new technology and control it?

Wireless Internet Access Points

At home, work, school, and in many public locations, people connect wirelessly to the Internet through a **wireless Internet access point** using mobile computers, smart phones, handheld game consoles, or other devices. Users access wireless Internet access points with computers or devices that have the necessary built-in wireless capability or the appropriate wireless network card, PC Card, ExpressCard module, or USB network adapter (Figure 8-4). Two types of wireless Internet access points are hot spots and mobile wireless networks.

A **hot spot** is a wireless network that provides Internet connections to mobile computers and other devices. Through the hot spot, mobile users check e-mail, browse the Web, and access any service on the Internet. Three hot spot technologies are Wi-Fi, WiMAX, and Bluetooth. Wi-Fi hot spots provide wireless network connections to users in public locations such as airports, train stations, hotels, convention centers, schools, campgrounds, shopping malls, bookstores, libraries, restaurants, and coffee shops. The coverage range for WiMAX hot spots, can be much wider than Wi-Fi; for example, they can cover an entire city. Bluetooth hot spots provide location-based services, such as sending coupons or menus, to users whose enabled devices enter the coverage range. Sections later in this chapter discuss Wi-Fi, WiMAX, and Bluetooth in more detail.

Some hot spots provide free Internet access, some charge a per-use fee, and others require users to subscribe to a wireless Internet service provider, to which they pay per access fees, daily fees, or a monthly fee. Per access fees average $3, daily fees range from $5 to $20, and monthly fees range from $20 to $60 for unlimited access, with the higher monthly fee providing greater coverage areas.

A mobile wireless network provides users with high-speed Internet connections, as long as they are in the network's range. A mobile wireless network usually includes most major cities and airports. Subscription fees for unlimited monthly Internet access to a mobile wireless network through a cell phone range from $30 to $50. Fees for notebook computer access are higher, ranging from $60 to $80 per month.

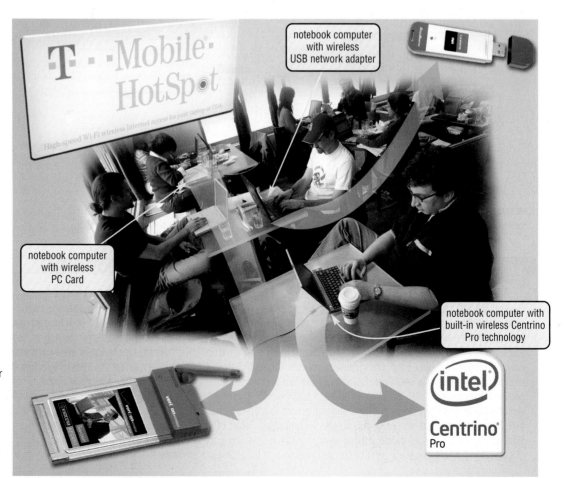

FIGURE 8-4 Mobile users in this hot spot access the Internet through their notebook computers. One computer uses a wireless USB network adapter; another uses a wireless PC Card. Others have Intel's built-in wireless Centrino, Centrino Duo, or Centrino Pro technology.

Cybercafés

When mobile users travel without their notebook computer or Internet-enabled mobile device, they can visit a cybercafé to access e-mail, the Web, and other Internet services. A **cybercafé**, or Internet cafe, is a coffeehouse, restaurant, or other location that provides personal computers with Internet access to its customers. Cybercafés exist in cities around the world. Although some provide free Internet access, most charge a per-hour or per-minute fee. Some cybercafés also are hot spots.

Global Positioning Systems

A **global positioning system** (**GPS**) is a navigation system that consists of one or more earth-based receivers that accept and analyze signals sent by satellites in order to determine the receiver's geographic location (Figure 8-5). A GPS receiver is a handheld, mountable, or embedded device that contains an antenna, a radio receiver, and a processor. Many include a screen display that shows an individual's location on a map. Some also function as a portable media player.

Many mobile devices such as smart phones have GPS capability built into the device or as an add-on feature. Some users carry a handheld GPS receiver; others mount a receiver to an object such as an automobile, boat, airplane, farm and construction equipment, or computer.

The first and most used application of GPS technology is to assist people with determining where they are located. The data obtained from a GPS, however, can be applied to a variety of other uses: creating a map, ascertaining the best route between two points, locating a lost person or stolen object, monitoring the movement of a person or object, determining altitude, and calculating speed. Many vehicles use GPSs to provide drivers with directions or other information.

WEB LINK 8-2

GPS

For more information, visit scsite.com/dcf5e/ch8/weblink and then click GPS.

FIGURE 8-5 HOW A GPS WORKS

Step 1:
GPS satellites orbit Earth. Every thousandth of a second, each satellite sends a signal that indicates its current position to the GPS receiver.

L O C A T E   M E

Step 2:
A GPS receiver (such as in a car, a wearable device, a smart phone, a handheld device, or a collar) determines its location on Earth by analyzing at least 3 separate satellite signals from the 24 satellites in orbit.

Collaboration

Many software products provide a means to **collaborate**, or work online, with other users connected to a server. Two methods of collaboration include collaborative software and document management systems. **Collaborative software** includes tools that enable users to share documents via online meetings and communicate with other connected users. An online meeting allows users to share documents with others in real time (Figure 8-6). When the online meeting takes place on the Web, it is called a **Web conference**. In an online meeting, all participants see a document(s) at the same time. As someone changes the document, everyone in the meeting sees the changes being made. Collaborative software often has chat, whiteboard, and video/audio conferencing capabilities.

Some companies use document management systems to make collaboration possible among employees. A **document management system** provides for storage and management of a company's documents, such as word processing documents, presentations, and spreadsheets. Users then access these documents, depending on their needs. A document management system can track all changes made to a document. It also can store additional information such as the document's creation date, the user who created the document, a summary of the document, and any keywords associated with the document. Google Docs is a Web-based document management system that provides basic services to its subscribers at no cost.

FIGURE 8-6 Through an online meeting, all participants see a document at the same time.

WEB LINK 8-3

Web Conferences

For more information, visit scsite.com/dcf5e/ch8/weblink and then click Web Conferences.

Groupware

Groupware is software that helps groups of people work together on projects and share information over a network. Groupware is a component of a broad concept called workgroup computing, which includes network hardware and software that enables group members to communicate, manage projects, schedule meetings, and make group decisions. To assist with these activities, most groupware provides personal information manager (PIM) functions, such as an electronic appointment calendar, an address book, and a notepad. A major feature of groupware is group scheduling, in which a group calendar can track the schedules of multiple users and help coordinate appointments and meeting times.

Voice Mail

Voice mail, which functions much like an answering machine, allows someone to leave a voice message for one or more people. Unlike answering machines, however, a computer in the voice mail system converts an analog voice message into digital form. Once digitized, the message is stored in a voice mailbox. A voice mailbox is a storage location on a hard disk in the voice mail system. Some voice mail systems can send digital voice mail files to e-mail addresses. Others can convert a voice mail message to a text message for display on a computer or mobile device.

Web Services

Web services describe standardized software that enables programmers to create applications that communicate with other remote computers over the Internet or over an internal business network. Businesses are the primary users of Web services because this technology provides a means for departments to communicate with each other, suppliers, vendors, and with clients. For example, third-party vendors can use Web services to communicate with their online retailer's Web site to manage their inventory levels.

Test your knowledge of pages 296 through 302 in Quiz Yourself 8-1.

QUIZ YOURSELF 8-1

Instructions: Find the true statement below. Then, rewrite the remaining false statements so they are true.

1. A cybercafé is a wireless network that provides Internet connections to mobile computers and devices.

2. GPS is a navigation system that consists of one or more earth-based receivers that accept and analyze signals sent by satellites in order to determine the receiver's geographic location.

3. Receiving devices initiate an instruction to transmit data, instructions, or information.

4. Users can send pictures and sound files, as well as short text messages, with text messaging.

Quiz Yourself Online: To further check your knowledge of required components for communications and uses of computer communications, visit scsite.com/dcf5e/ch8/quiz and then click Objectives 1 – 2.

NETWORKS

As discussed in Chapter 1, a **network** is a collection of computers and devices connected together via communications devices and transmission media. Many businesses network their computers together to facilitate communications, share hardware, share data and information, share software, and transfer funds.

A network can be internal to an organization or span the world by connecting to the Internet. Instead of using the Internet or an internal network, some companies hire a value-added network provider for network functions. A **value-added network** (**VAN**) is a third-party business that provides networking services for a fee.

Networks facilitate communications among users and allow users to share resources with other users. Some examples of resources are data, information, hardware, and software.

LANs, MANs, and WANs

Networks usually are classified as a local area network, metropolitan area network, or wide area network. The main differentiation among these classifications is their area of coverage, as described in the following paragraphs.

LAN A **local area network** (**LAN**) is a network that connects computers and devices in a limited geographical area such as a home, school computer labora-tory, office building, or closely positioned group of buildings. Each computer or device on the network, called a node, often shares resources such as printers, large hard disks, and programs. Often, the nodes are connected via cables. A **wireless LAN** (**WLAN**) is a LAN that uses no physical wires. Very often, a WLAN com-municates with a wired LAN for access to its resources (Figure 8-7).

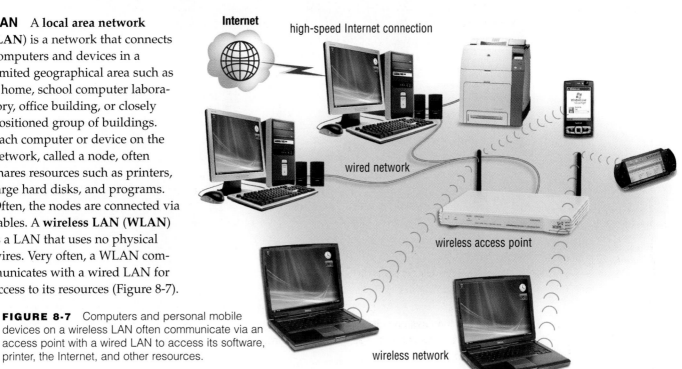

Internet

high-speed Internet connection

wired network

wireless access point

wireless network

FIGURE 8-7 Computers and personal mobile devices on a wireless LAN often communicate via an access point with a wired LAN to access its software, printer, the Internet, and other resources.

MAN A **metropolitan area network** (**MAN**) is a high-speed network that connects local area networks in a metropolitan area such as a city or town and handles the bulk of communications activity across that region. A MAN typically includes one or more LANs, but covers a smaller geographic area than a WAN.

A MAN usually is managed by a consortium of users or by a single network provider that sells the service to the users. Local and state governments, for example, regulate some MANs. Telephone companies, cable television operators, and other organizations provide users with connections to the MAN.

WAN A **wide area network** (**WAN**) is a network that covers a large geographic area (such as a city, country, or the world) using a communications channel that combines many types of media such as telephone lines, cables, and radio waves (Figure 8-8). A WAN can be one large network or can consist of two or more LANs connected together. The Internet is the world's largest WAN.

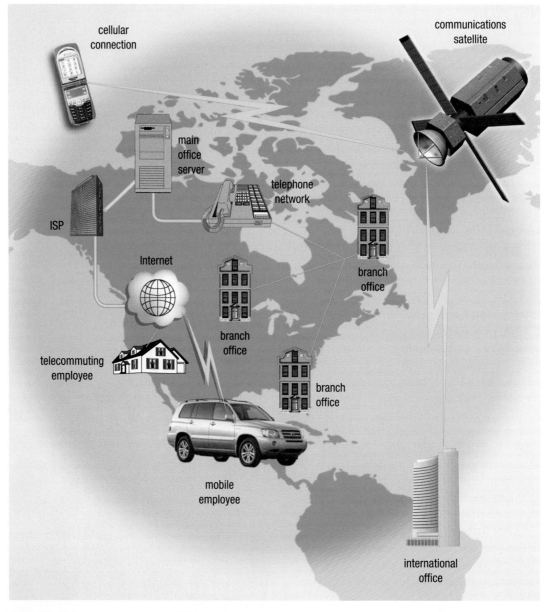

FIGURE 8-8 An example of a WAN.

Network Architectures

The design of computers, devices, and media in a network, sometimes called the network architecture, is categorized as either client/server or peer-to-peer.

CLIENT/SERVER   On a **client/server network**, one or more computers act as a server; the other computers on the network request services from the server (Figure 8-9). A **server** controls access to the hardware, software, and other resources on the network and provides a centralized storage area for programs, data, and information. The **clients** are other computers and mobile devices on the network that rely on the server for its resources. For example, a server might store a database of customers. Clients on the network (company employees) access the customer database on the server.

Some servers, called dedicated servers, perform a specific task and can be placed with other dedicated servers to perform multiple tasks. For example, a file server stores and manages files. A print server manages printers and documents being printed. A database server stores and provides access to a database. A network server manages network traffic (activity).

A client/server network typically provides an efficient means to connect 10 or more computers. Most client/server networks require a person to serve as a network administrator because of the large size of the network.

PEER-TO-PEER   One type of **peer-to-peer network** is a simple, inexpensive network that typically connects fewer than 10 computers. Each computer, called a peer, has equal responsibilities and capabilities, sharing hardware (such as a printer), data, or information with other computers on the peer-to-peer network (Figure 8-10). Each computer stores files on its own storage devices. Thus, each computer on the network contains both the network operating system and application software. All computers on the network share any peripheral device(s) attached to any computer. For example, one computer may have a laser printer and a scanner, while another has an ink-jet printer and an external hard disk. Peer-to-peer networks are ideal for very small businesses and home users.

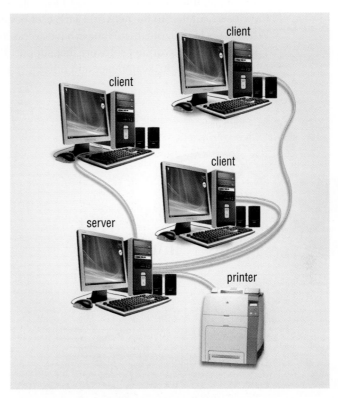

FIGURE 8-9   On a client/server network, one or more computers act as a server, and the clients access the server(s).

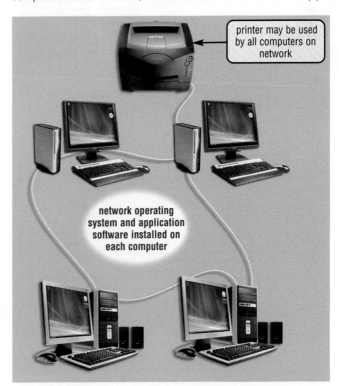

FIGURE 8-10   Each computer on a peer-to-peer network shares its hardware and software with other computers on the network.

INTERNET PEER-TO-PEER   Another type of peer-to-peer, called **P2P**, describes an Internet network, on which users access each other's hard disks and exchange files directly (Figure 8-11). This type of peer-to-peer network sometimes is called a file sharing network because users with compatible software and an Internet connection copy files from someone else's hard disk to their hard disks. As more users connect to the network, each user has access to shared files on other users' hard disks. When users log off, others no longer have access to their hard disks.

Examples of networking software that support P2P are BitTorrent, Gnutella, Kazaa, and LimeWire which allow users to swap music and other files via the Web.

FIGURE 8-11   P2P describes an Internet network on which users connect to each other's hard disks and exchange files directly.

Network Topologies

A **network topology** refers to the layout of the computers and devices in a communications network. Three commonly used network topologies are bus, ring, and star. Networks usually use combinations of these topologies.

BUS NETWORK   A **bus network** consists of a single central cable, to which all computers and other devices connect (Figure 8-12). The bus is the physical cable that connects the computers and other devices. The bus in a bus network transmits data, instructions, and information in both directions. When a sending device transmits data, the address of the receiving device is included with the transmission so that the data is routed to the appropriate receiving device.

Bus networks are popular on LANs because they are inexpensive and easy to install. One advantage of the bus network is that computers and other devices can be attached and detached at any point on the bus without disturbing the rest of the network. Another advantage is that failure of one device usually does not affect the rest of the bus network. The greatest risk to a bus network is that the bus itself might become inoperable. If that happens, the network remains inoperative until the bus is back in working order.

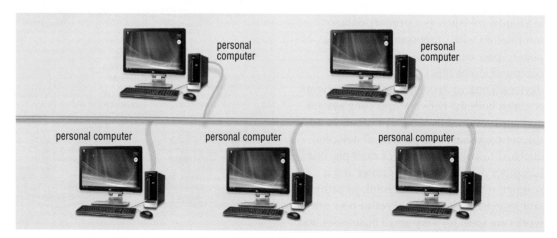

FIGURE 8-12   Devices in a bus network share a single data path.

RING NETWORK On a **ring network**, a cable forms a closed loop (ring) with all computers and devices arranged along the ring (Figure 8-13). Data transmitted on a ring network travels from device to device around the entire ring, in one direction. When a computer or device sends data, the data travels to each computer on the ring until it reaches its destination.

If a computer or device on a ring network fails, all devices before the failed device are unaffected, but those after the failed device cannot function. A ring network can span a larger distance than a bus network, but it is more difficult to install. The ring topology primarily is used for LANs, but also is used in WANs.

STAR NETWORK On a **star network**, all of the computers and devices (nodes) on the network connect to a central device, thus forming a star (Figure 8-14). Two types of devices that provide a common central connection point for nodes on the network are a hub and a switch. All data that transfers from one node to another passes through the hub/switch.

Star networks are fairly easy to install and maintain. Nodes can be added to and removed from the network with little or no disruption to the network.

On a star network, if one node fails, only that node is affected. The other nodes continue to operate normally. If the hub/switch fails, however, the entire network is inoperable until the device is repaired.

Intranets

Recognizing the efficiency and power of the Internet, many organizations apply Internet and Web technologies to their own internal networks. An **intranet** (intra means within) is an internal network that uses Internet technologies. Intranets generally make company information accessible to employees and facilitate working in groups.

Simple intranet applications include electronic publishing of organizational materials such as telephone directories, event calendars, procedure manuals, employee benefits information, and job postings. Additionally, an intranet typically includes a connection to the Internet. More sophisticated uses of intranets include groupware applications such as project management, chat rooms, newsgroups, group scheduling, and video conferencing.

An intranet essentially is a small version of the Internet that exists within an organization. Users update information on the intranet by creating and posting a Web page, using a method similar to that used on the Internet.

Sometimes a company uses an extranet, which allows customers or suppliers to access part of its intranet. Package shipping companies, for example, allow customers to access their intranet to print air bills, schedule pickups, and even track shipped packages as the packages travel to their destinations.

FIGURE 8-13 On a ring network, all connected devices form a continuous loop.

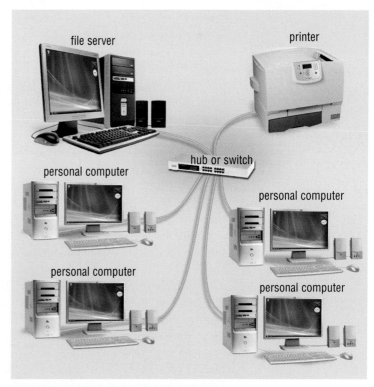

FIGURE 8-14 A star network contains a single, centralized hub or switch through which all the devices in the network communicate.

Network Communications Standards

Today's networks connect terminals, devices, and computers from many different manufacturers across many types of networks, such as wide area, local area, and wireless. For the different devices on various types of networks to be able to communicate, the network must use similar techniques of moving data through the network from one application to another.

To alleviate the problems of incompatibility and ensure that hardware and software components can be integrated into any network, various organizations such as ANSI and IEEE (pronounced I triple E) propose, develop, and approve network standards. A **network standard** defines guidelines that specify the way computers access the medium to which they are attached, the type(s) of medium used, the speeds used on different types of networks, and the type(s) of physical cable and/or the wireless technology used. A standard that outlines characteristics of how two network devices communicate is called a protocol. Hardware and software manufacturers design their products to meet the guidelines specified in a particular standard, so that their devices can communicate with the network.

The following sections discuss some of the more widely used network communications standards for both wired and wireless networks including Ethernet, token ring, TCP/IP, 802.11 (Wi-Fi), Bluetooth, UWB, IrDA, RFID, WiMAX, and WAP.

WEB LINK 8-4

Ethernet

For more information, visit scsite.com/dcf5e/ ch8/weblink and then click Ethernet.

ETHERNET   **Ethernet** is a network standard that specifies no central computer or device on the network (nodes) should control when data can be transmitted; that is, each node attempts to transmit data when it determines the network is able to receive communications. If two computers on an Ethernet network attempt to send data at the same time, a collision occurs, and the computers must attempt to send their messages again.

Ethernet is based on a bus topology, but Ethernet networks can be wired in a star pattern. The Ethernet standard defines guidelines for the physical configuration of the network, e.g., cabling, network cards, and nodes. Today, Ethernet is the most popular LAN standard because it is relatively inexpensive and easy to install and maintain. Ethernet networks often use cables to transmit data.

TOKEN RING   The **token ring** standard specifies that computers and devices on the network share or pass a special signal, called a token, in a unidirectional manner and in a preset order. A token is a special series of bits that function like a ticket. The device with the token can transmit data over the network. Only one token exists per network. This ensures that only one computer transmits data at a time. Token ring is based on a ring topology (although it can use a star topology). The token ring standard defines guidelines for the physical configuration of a network. Some token ring networks connect up to 72 devices. Others use a special type of wiring that allows up to 260 connections.

TCP/IP   Short for Transmission Control Protocol/Internet Protocol, **TCP/IP** is a network standard, specifically a protocol, that defines how messages (data) are routed from one end of a network to the other. TCP/IP describes rules for dividing messages into small pieces, called packets; providing addresses for each packet; checking for and detecting errors; sequencing packets; and regulating the flow of messages along the network.

TCP/IP has been adopted as a network standard for Internet communications. Thus, all hosts on the Internet follow the rules defined in this standard. Internet communications also use other standards, such as the Ethernet standard, as data is routed to its destination.

When a computer sends data over the Internet, the data is divided into packets. Each packet contains the data, as well as the recipient (destination), the origin (sender), and the sequence information used to reassemble the data at the destination. Each packet travels along the fastest individual available path to the recipient's computer via communications devices called routers.

802.11 (WI-FI)   Developed by IEEE, **802.11** also known as **Wi-Fi** (**wireless fidelity**) and wireless Ethernet, is a series of network standards that specifies how two wireless devices communicate over the air with each other. Using Wi-Fi, computers or devices that have the appropriate wireless capability communicate via radio waves with other computers or devices. The Wi-Fi standard uses techniques similar to the Ethernet standard to specify how physically to configure a wireless network. Most of today's computers and many personal mobile devices, such as smart phones and handheld game consoles, are Wi-Fi enabled.

One popular use of the Wi-Fi standard is in hot spots that offer mobile users the ability to connect to the Internet with their Wi-Fi enabled wireless computers and devices. Many homes and small businesses also use Wi-Fi to network computers and devices together wirelessly.

BLUETOOTH **Bluetooth** is a standard, specifically a protocol, that defines how two Bluetooth devices use short-range radio waves to transmit data. To communicate with each other, Bluetooth devices often must be within about 10 meters (about 33 feet) but can be extended to 100 meters with additional equipment. Examples of Bluetooth devices can include desktop computers, notebook computers, handheld computers, smart phones, PDAs, headsets, microphones, digital cameras, and printers.

UWB **UWB**, which stands for **ultra-wideband**, is a network standard that specifies how two UWB devices use short-range radio waves to communicate at high speeds with each other. For optimal communications, the devices should be within 2 to 10 meters (about 6.5 to 33 feet) of each other. Examples of UWB uses include wirelessly transferring video from a digital video camera, printing pictures from a digital camera, downloading media to a portable media player, or displaying a slide show on a projector.

IrDA Some computers and devices use the **IrDA** specification to transmit data wirelessly to each other via infrared (IR) light waves. Infrared requires a line-of-sight transmission; that is, the sending device and the receiving device must be in line with each other so that nothing obstructs the path of the infrared light wave.

RFID **RFID** (radio frequency identification) is a standard, specifically a protocol, that defines how a network uses radio signals to communicate with a tag placed in or attached to an object, an animal, or a person. The tag consists of an antenna and a memory chip that contains the information to be transmitted via radio waves. Through an antenna, an RFID reader reads the radio signals and transfers the information to a computer or computing device. Readers can be handheld or embedded in an object such as a doorway or tollbooth.

WiMAX **WiMAX** (Worldwide Interoperability for Microwave Access), also known as **802.16**, is a newer network standard developed by IEEE that specifies how wireless devices communicate over the air in a wide area. Using the WiMAX standard, computers or devices with the appropriate WiMAX wireless capability communicate via radio waves with other computers or devices via a WiMAX tower. The WiMAX tower, which can cover up to a 30-mile radius, connects to the Internet or to another WiMAX tower. Read Ethics & Issues 8-2 for a discussion related to wireless antennas and towers.

Two types of WiMAX specifications are fixed wireless and mobile wireless. With fixed wireless WiMAX, a customer accesses the Internet from a desktop computer at home or other permanent location. Mobile wireless WiMAX, by contrast, enables users to access the WiMAX network with mobile computers and mobile devices such as smart phones.

The WiMAX standard provides wireless broadband Internet access at a reasonable cost over long distances to business and home users. The WiMAX standard, similar to the Wi-Fi standard, connects mobile users to the Internet via hot spots. The next generation of game consoles also plans to support the WiMAX standard.

ETHICS & ISSUES 8-2

Should You Worry about Cell Phone and Cellular Antenna Radiation?

Well over two billion people use cell phones, and more than 80 percent of the world's population has access to cell phone service from cellular antennas. These numbers are expected to rise sharply in coming years, and many are concerned about potential health effects from cell phones and cellular antennas. Some cell phone users who suffered rare illnesses have filed lawsuits against cell phone companies, but the cases usually are lost due to lack of scientific evidence linking the use of the phones to the illnesses. While debates rage in communities over placement of cellular antennas, the consideration of health effects on residents is muted because the federal government's Telecommunications Act of 1996 prohibits local governments from considering health effects when making decisions about antenna placement. As cellular providers begin offering faster Internet services, they estimate that they may need to more than double the current number of antennas in the United States. It generally is agreed that no studies conclusively demonstrate negative health effects from cell phones and cellular antennas, but skeptics claim that digital cellular technology is too new to have endured long-term studies on humans. Long-term studies that are underway may not provide results for decades. Are you concerned about cell phone and cellular antenna radiation? Why or why not? Do you or anyone you know minimize use of cell phones due to health concerns? Should more studies be done on potential health effects, and if so, who should pay for the studies? Why? Would you live next to a cellular antenna? Why or why not?

WAP The **Wireless Application Protocol (WAP)** is a standard, specifically a protocol, that specifies how some mobile devices such as smart phones can display the content of Internet services such as the Web, e-mail, and chat rooms. For example, users can check weather, sports scores, and headline news from their WAP-enabled smart phone. To display a Web page on a smart phone, the phone should contain a microbrowser. WAP uses a client/server network. The wireless device contains the client software, which connects to the Internet access provider's server.

COMMUNICATIONS SOFTWARE

Communications software consists of programs that (1) help users establish a connection to another computer or network; (2) manage the transmission of data, instructions, and information; and (3) provide an interface for users to communicate with one another. The first two are system software and the third is application software. Chapter 3 presented a variety of examples of application software for communications: e-mail, FTP, Web browser, newsgroup/message boards, chat rooms, instant messaging, video conferencing, and VoIP.

Some communications devices are preprogrammed to accomplish communications tasks. Other communications devices require separate communications software to ensure proper transmission of data. Communications software works with the network standards and protocols defined earlier to ensure data moves correctly through a network. Communications software usually is bundled with the operating system or purchased network devices.

Often, a computer has various types of communications software, each serving a different purpose. One type of communications software helps users establish a connection to the Internet using wizards, dialog boxes, and other on-screen messages. Communications software also allows home and small office users to configure wired and wireless networks and connect devices to an existing network.

COMMUNICATIONS OVER THE TELEPHONE NETWORK

The public switched telephone network (PSTN) is the worldwide telephone system that handles voice-oriented telephone calls (Figure 8-15). Nearly the entire telephone network today uses digital technology, with the exception of the final link from the local telephone company to a home, which often is analog.

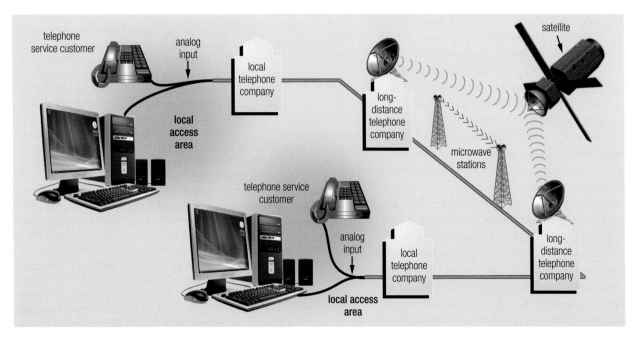

FIGURE 8-15 A sample telephone network configuration.

The telephone network is an integral part of computer communications. Data, instructions, and information are transmitted over the telephone network using dial-up lines or dedicated lines. The following sections discuss dial-up lines and the various types of dedicated lines that use the telephone network for data communications.

Dial-Up Lines

A **dial-up line** is a temporary connection that uses one or more analog telephone lines for communications. A dial-up connection is not permanent. Using a dial-up line to transmit data is similar to using the telephone to make a call. A modem at the sending end dials the telephone number of a modem at the receiving end. When the modem at the receiving end answers the call, a connection is established and data can be transmitted. When either modem hangs up, the communications end.

Using a dial-up line to connect computers costs no more than making a regular telephone call. Computers at any two locations establish an Internet or network connection using modems and the telephone network.

Dedicated Lines

A **dedicated line** is a type of always-on connection that is established between two communications devices (unlike a dial-up line where the connection is reestablished each time it is used). The quality and consistency of the connection on a dedicated line are better than a dial-up line because dedicated lines provide a constant connection.

Businesses often use dedicated lines to connect geographically distant offices. Dedicated lines can be either analog or digital. Digital lines increasingly are connecting home and business users to networks around the globe because they transmit data and information at faster rates than analog lines.

Five types of digital dedicated lines are ISDN lines, DSL, FTTP, T-carrier lines, and ATM. Although cable television (CATV) lines and fixed wireless are not a type of standard telephone line, they are very popular ways for the home user to connect to the Internet. Fixed wireless Internet connections use an antenna on your house or business to communicate with a tower location via radio signals. Later sections in this chapter discuss the use of CATV lines and radio signals to connect to the Internet.

The table in Figure 8-16 lists the approximate monthly costs of various types of Internet connections and transfer rates (speeds), as compared with dial-up lines. The following sections discuss ISDN lines, DSL, FTTP, T-carrier lines, and ATM.

ISDN LINES   For the small business and home user, an ISDN line provides faster transfer rates than dial-up telephone lines. Not as widely used today as in the past, **ISDN** (Integrated Services Digital Network) is a set of standards for digital transmission of data over standard copper telephone lines. ISDN requires that both ends of the connection have an ISDN modem. The ISDN modem at your location must be within about 3.5 miles of the telephone company's ISDN modem. Thus, ISDN may not be an option for rural residents.

DSL   DSL is a popular digital line alternative for the small business or home user. **DSL** (Digital Subscriber Line) transmits at fast speeds on existing standard copper telephone wiring. Some DSL installations include a dial tone, providing users with both voice and data communications.

To connect to DSL, a customer must have a special network card and a DSL modem. Not all areas offer DSL service because the local telephone company or the lines in the area may not be capable of supporting DSL technology. As with ISDN, DSL may not be an

SPEEDS OF VARIOUS INTERNET CONNECTIONS

Type of Line	Approximate Monthly Cost	Transfer Rates*
Dial-up	Local or long-distance rates	Up to 56 Kbps
ISDN	$10 to $40	Up to 1.54 Mpbs
DSL	$13 to $70	128 Kbps to 8.45 Mbps
Cable TV (CATV)	$20 to $50	128 Kbps to 52 Mbps
FTTP	$35 to $180	5 Mbps to 100 Mbps
Fixed Wireless	$35 to $80	256 Kbps to 10 Mbps
Fractional T1	$200 to $700	128 Kbps to 768 Kbps
T1	$400 to $1,600	1.544 Mbps
T3	$5,000 to $15,000	44.736 Mbps
ATM	$3,000 or more	155 Mbps to 622 Mbps, can reach 10 Gbps

*Kbps = thousand bits per second
Mbps = million bits per second
Gbps = billion bits per second

FIGURE 8-16   The speeds of various lines that can be used to connect to the Internet.

option for rural residents because the user's location (and DSL modem) and the telephone company's DSL modem must be located within about 3.5 miles of each other.

ADSL is one of the more popular types of DSLs. ADSL (asymmetric digital subscriber line) is a type of DSL that supports faster transfer rates when receiving data (the downstream rate) than when sending data (the upstream rate). ADSL is ideal for Internet access because most users download more information from the Internet than they upload.

FTTP   FTTP, which stands for **Fiber to the Premises**, uses fiber-optic cable to provide extremely high-speed Internet access to a user's physical permanent location. Two specific types of FTTP are FTTH (Fiber to the Home) and FTTB (Fiber to the Building). With FTTP service, an optical terminal at your premises receives the signals and transfers them to a router connected to your computer. As the cost of installing fiber decreases, increasingly more homes and businesses will opt for this high-speed Internet access.

T-CARRIER LINES   A **T-carrier line** is any of several types of long-distance digital telephone lines that carry multiple signals over a single communications line. T-carrier lines provide very fast data transfer rates. Only medium to large companies usually can afford the investment in T-carrier lines because these lines are so expensive.

The most popular T-carrier line is the **T1 line**. Businesses often use T1 lines to connect to the Internet. Many Internet access providers use T1 lines to connect to the Internet backbone. Home and small business users purchase fractional T1, in which they share a connection to the T1 line with other users. Fractional T1 is slower than a dedicated T1 line, but it also is less expensive.

A T3 line is equal in speed to 28 T1 lines. T3 lines are quite expensive. Main users of T3 lines include large companies, telephone companies, and Internet access providers connecting to the Internet backbone. The Internet backbone itself also uses T3 lines.

ATM   ATM (Asynchronous Transfer Mode) is a service that carries voice, data, video, and multimedia at extremely high speeds. Telephone networks, the Internet, and other networks with large amounts of traffic use ATM. Some experts predict that ATM eventually will become the Internet standard for data transmission, replacing T3 lines.

Test your knowledge of pages 303 through 312 in Quiz Yourself 8-2.

QUIZ YOURSELF 8-2

Instructions: Find the true statement below. Then, rewrite the remaining false statements so they are true.

1. A wireless LAN is a LAN that uses physical wires.

2. An intranet is an internal network that uses video conferencing technologies.

3. Five types of digital dial-up lines are ISDN lines, DSL, FTTP, T-carrier lines, and ATM.

4. In a client/server network, servers on the network access resources on the client.

5. P2P describes an Internet network on which users access each other's hard disks and exchange files directly over the Internet.

Quiz Yourself Online: To further check your knowledge of networks, communications software, and communications over the telephone network, visit scsite.com/dcf5e/ch8/quiz and then click Objectives 3 – 5.

COMMUNICATIONS DEVICES

A **communications device** is any type of hardware capable of transmitting data, instructions, and information between a sending device and a receiving device. One type of communications device that connects a communications channel to a sending or receiving device such as a computer is a modem. Computers process data as digital signals. Data, instructions, and information travel along a communications channel in either analog or digital form, depending on the communications channel. An analog signal consists of a continuous electrical wave. A digital signal consists of individual electrical pulses that represent bits grouped together into bytes.

For communications channels that use digital signals (such as cable television lines), the modem transfers the digital signals between the computer and the communications channel (Figure 8-17a). If a communications channel uses analog signals (such as some telephone lines), however, the modem first converts between analog and digital signals (Figure 8-17b).

The following pages describe the following types of communications devices: dial-up modems, ISDN and DSL modems, cable modems, wireless modems, network cards, wireless access points, and routers.

FIGURE 8-17a (all digital communications channel)

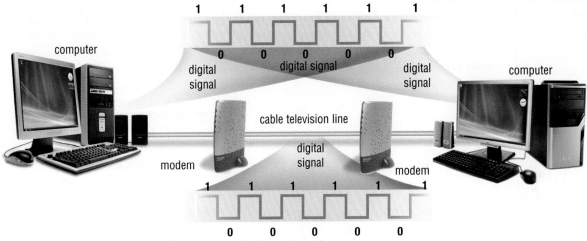

FIGURE 8-17b (digital to analog to digital communications channel)

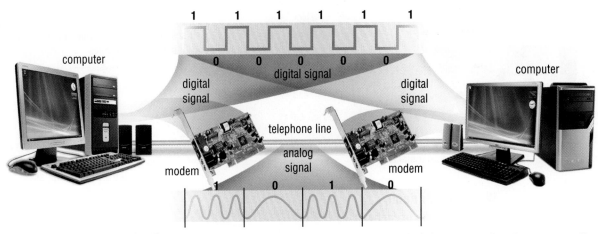

FIGURE 8-17 A modem connects a communications channel, such as a cable television line or a telephone line, to a sending or receiving device, such as a computer. Depending on the type of communications channel, a modem may need to convert digital signals to analog signals (and vice versa) before transferring data, instructions, and information to or from a sending or receiving device.

Dial-Up Modems

As previously discussed, a computer's digital signals must be converted to analog signals before they are transmitted over standard telephone lines. The communications device that performs this conversion is a **modem**, sometimes called a dial-up modem. The word, modem, is derived from the combination of the words, modulate, to change into an analog signal, and demodulate, to convert an analog signal into a digital signal.

A modem usually is in the form of an adapter card that you insert in an expansion slot on a computer's motherboard. One end of a standard telephone cord attaches to a port on the modem card and the other end plugs into a telephone outlet.

ISDN and DSL Modems

If you access the Internet using ISDN or DSL, you need a communications device to send and receive the digital ISDN or DSL signals. An **ISDN modem** sends digital data and information from a computer to an ISDN line and receives digital data and information from an ISDN line. A **DSL modem** sends digital data and information from a computer to a DSL line and receives digital data and information from a DSL line. ISDN and DSL modems usually are external devices, in which one end connects to the telephone line and the other end connects to a port on the system unit.

Cable Modems

A **cable modem** is a digital modem that sends and receives digital data over the cable television (CATV) network (Figure 8-18). With more than 110 million homes wired for cable television, cable modems provide a faster Internet access alternative to dial-up for the home user and have speeds similar to DSL. Cable modems currently can transmit data at speeds that are much faster than either a dial-up modem or ISDN.

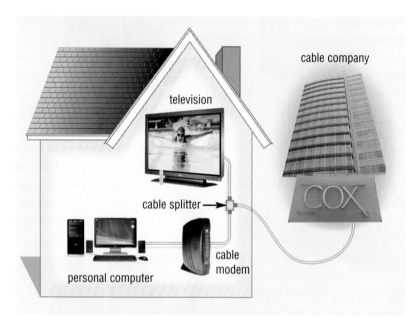

cable company

television

cable splitter →

cable modem

personal computer

FIGURE 8-18 A typical cable modem installation.

FAQ 8-1

Which is better, DSL or cable Internet service?

Each has its own advantages. DSL uses a line that is not shared with other users in the neighborhood. With cable Internet service, by contrast, users share the node with up to hundreds of other cable Internet users. Simultaneous access by many users can cause the cable Internet service to slow down. Cable Internet service, however, has widespread availability. For more information, visit scsite.com/dcf5e/ch8/faq and then click DSL and Cable Internet Service.

Wireless Modems

Some mobile users have a **wireless modem** that uses the cell phone network to connect to the Internet wirelessly from a notebook computer, a smart phone, or other mobile device (Figure 8-19). Wireless modems, which have an external or built-in antenna, are available as PC Cards, ExpressCard modules, and flash cards.

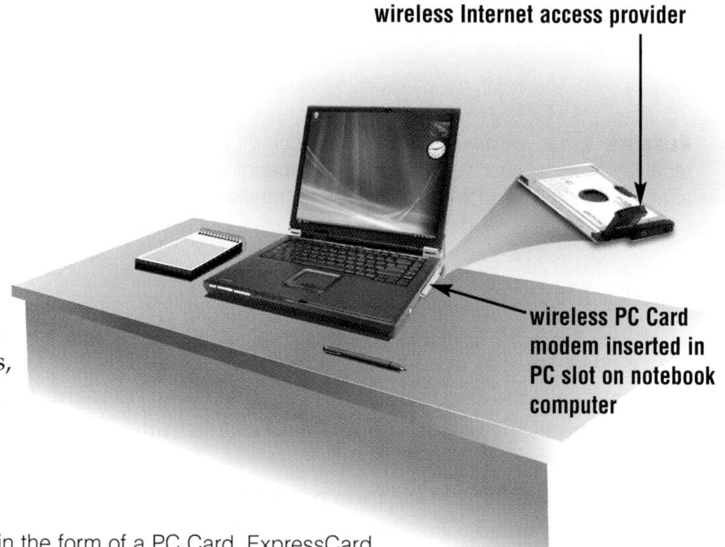

antenna on wireless PC Card modem communicates with wireless Internet access provider

wireless PC Card modem inserted in PC slot on notebook computer

FIGURE 8-19 Wireless modems, in the form of a PC Card, ExpressCard module, or flash card, allow users to access the Internet wirelessly using the cell phone network.

Network Cards

A **network card** is an adapter card, PC Card, ExpressCard module, USB network adapter, or flash card that enables a computer or device that does not have networking capability to access a network. The network card coordinates the transmission and receipt of data, instructions, and information to and from the computer or device containing the network card.

Network cards are available in a variety of styles (Figure 8-20). A network card for a desktop computer is an adapter card that has a port to which a cable connects. A network card for mobile computers and devices is in the form of a PC Card, ExpressCard module, USB network adapter, or a flash card. Network cards that provide wireless data transmission also are available. This type of card, sometimes called a wireless network card, often has an antenna.

A network card follows the guidelines of a particular network communications standard, such as Ethernet or token ring. An Ethernet card is the most common type of network card.

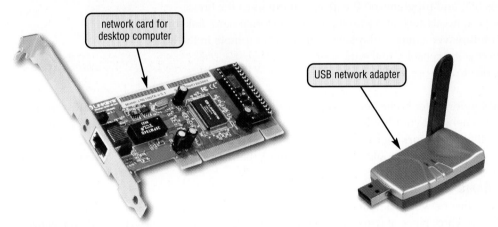

network card for desktop computer

USB network adapter

FIGURE 8-20   Network cards are available for both desktop and notebook computers.

Wireless Access Points

A **wireless access point** is a central communications device that allows computers and devices to transfer data wirelessly among themselves or to transfer data wirelessly to a wired network (Figure 8-7 on page 303). Wireless access points have high-quality antennas for optimal signals.

Routers

A **router** is a communications device that connects multiple computers or other routers together and transmits data to its correct destination on the network. A router can be used on any size of network. On the largest scale, routers along the Internet backbone forward data packets to their destination using the fastest available path. For smaller business and home networks, a router allows multiple computers to share a single high-speed Internet connection such as a cable modem or DSL modem (Figure 8-21). These routers connect from 2 to 250 computers.

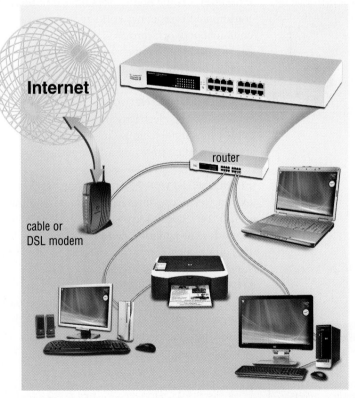

Internet

router

cable or DSL modem

FIGURE 8-21   Through a router, home and small business networks can share access to a high-speed Internet connection such as through a cable or DSL modem.

To prevent unauthorized users from accessing files and computers, many routers are protected by a built-in firewall, called a hardware firewall. Some also have built-in antivirus protection. Today's routers or combination wireless access point/routers are easy to configure and secure against unauthorized access.

HOME NETWORKS

Many home users are connecting multiple computers and devices together in a **home network**. Each networked computer in the house has the following capabilities:
- Connect to the Internet at the same time
- Share a single high-speed Internet connection
- Access files and programs on the other computers in the house
- Share peripherals such as a printer, scanner, external hard disk, or DVD drive
- Play multiplayer games with players on other computers in the house
- Connect game consoles to the Internet
- Subscribe to and use VoIP

Many vendors offer home networking packages that include all the necessary hardware and software to network your home using wired or wireless techniques. Some of these packages also offer intelligent networking capabilities. An intelligent home network extends the basic home network to include features such as lighting control, thermostat adjustment, and a security system.

Wired Home Networks

As with other networks, a home network can use wires, be wireless, or use a combination of wired and wireless. Three types of wired home networks are Ethernet, powerline cable, and phoneline.

ETHERNET   Some home users have an Ethernet network. As discussed earlier in this chapter, traditional Ethernet networks require that each computer have built-in networking capabilities or contain a network card, which connects to a central network hub or similar device with a physical cable. This may involve running cable through walls, ceilings, and floors in the house. For the average home user, the hardware and software of an Ethernet network can be difficult to configure.

POWERLINE CABLE NETWORK   A home powerline cable network is a network that uses the same lines that bring electricity into the house. This network requires no additional wiring. One end of a cable plugs in the computer's parallel or USB port and the other end of the cable plugs in a wall outlet. The data transmits through the existing power lines in the house.

PHONELINE NETWORK   A phoneline network is an easy-to-install and inexpensive network that uses existing telephone lines in the home. With this network, one end of a cable connects to an adapter card or PC Card in the computer and the other end plugs in a wall telephone jack. The phoneline network does not interfere with voice and data transmissions on the telephone lines. That is, you can talk on the telephone and use the same line to connect to the Internet.

Wireless Home Networks

To network computers and devices that span multiple rooms or floors in a home, it may be more convenient to use a wireless strategy. One advantage of wireless networks is that you can take a mobile computer outside, for example in the backyard, and connect to the Internet through the home network as long as you are in the network's range.

Most home networks use a Wi-Fi network, which sends signals through the air at distances of up to 1,500 feet in some configurations. Home users set up Wi-Fi networks in their homes because Wi-Fi networks are fairly easy to configure. Each computer that accesses the network must have the appropriate built-in wireless networking capabilities or a wireless network card, which communicates with a wireless access point or a combination router/wireless access point (Figure 8-22).

WEB LINK 8-6

Home Networks

For more information, visit scsite.com/dcf5e/ch8/weblink and then click Home Networks.

FIGURE 8-22   HOW TO SET UP HARDWARE FOR A WI-FI HOME NETWORK

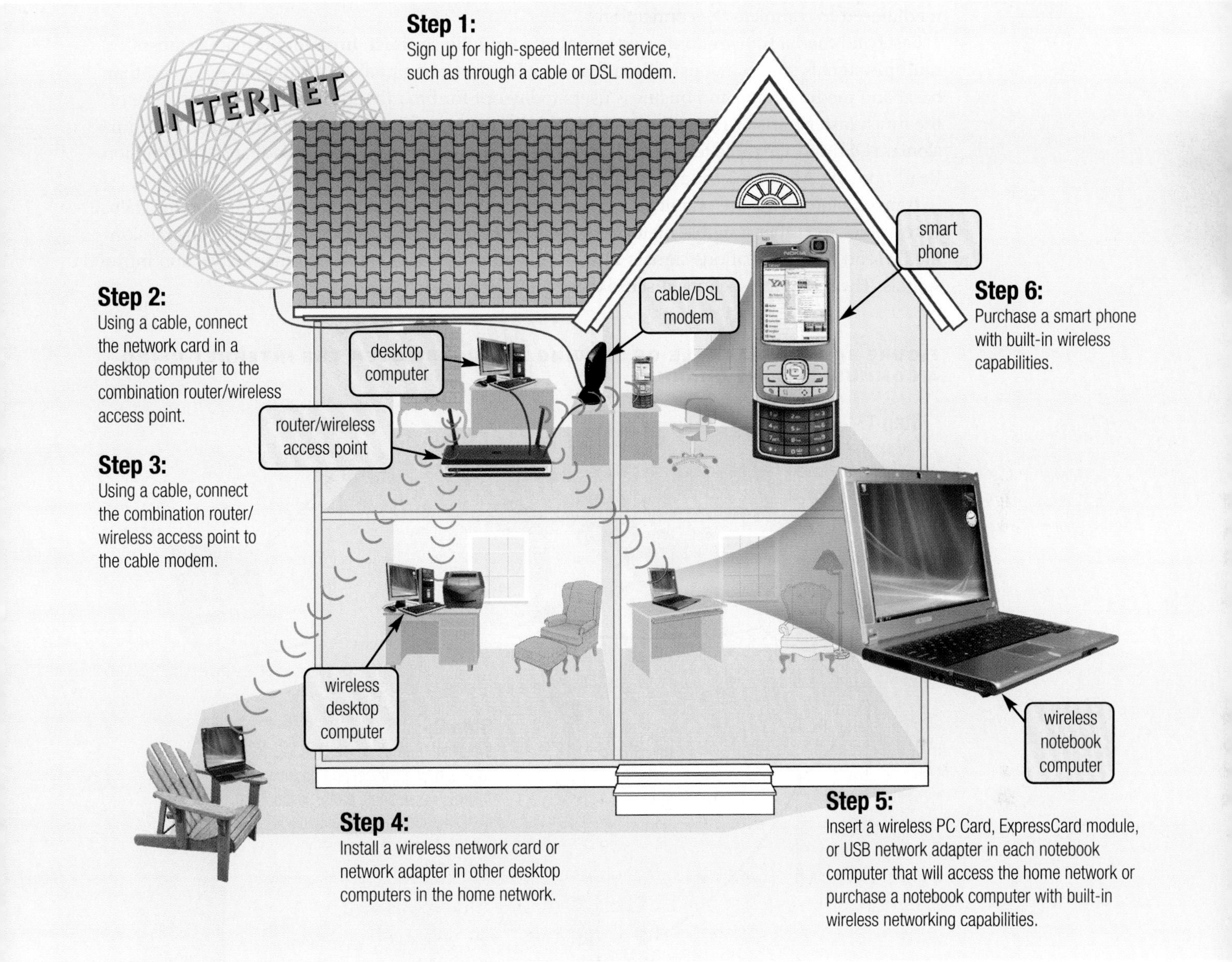

Step 1:
Sign up for high-speed Internet service, such as through a cable or DSL modem.

Step 2:
Using a cable, connect the network card in a desktop computer to the combination router/wireless access point.

Step 3:
Using a cable, connect the combination router/wireless access point to the cable modem.

Step 6:
Purchase a smart phone with built-in wireless capabilities.

INTERNET

smart phone

cable/DSL modem

desktop computer

router/wireless access point

wireless desktop computer

wireless notebook computer

Step 4:
Install a wireless network card or network adapter in other desktop computers in the home network.

Step 5:
Insert a wireless PC Card, ExpressCard module, or USB network adapter in each notebook computer that will access the home network or purchase a notebook computer with built-in wireless networking capabilities.

COMMUNICATIONS CHANNEL

As described at the beginning of the chapter, a communications channel is the transmission media on which data, instructions, or information travel in a communications system. The amount of data, instructions, and information that can travel over a communications channel sometimes is called the **bandwidth**. The higher the bandwidth, the more the channel transmits. For example, a cable modem has more bandwidth than a dial-up modem.

For transmission of text only, a lower bandwidth is acceptable. For transmission of music, graphics, photos, virtual reality images, or 3-D games, however, you need a higher bandwidth. When the bandwidth is too low for the application, you will notice a considerable slow-down in system performance.

A communications channel consists of one or more transmission media. **Transmission media** consist of materials or substances capable of carrying one or more signals. When you send data from a computer, the signal that carries the data may travel over various transmission media. This is especially true when the transmission spans a long distance.

Figure 8-23 illustrates a typical communications channel and shows the variety of transmission media used to complete the connection.

Baseband media transmit only one signal at a time. By contrast, **broadband** media transmit multiple signals simultaneously. Broadband media transmit signals at a much faster speed than baseband media. Home and business users today opt for broadband Internet access because of the much faster transfer rates. Two previously discussed services that offer broadband transmission are DSL and the cable television Internet service. Satellites also offer broadband transmission. Read Looking Ahead 8-1 for a look at the future of communications.

Transmission media are one of two types: physical or wireless. Physical transmission media use wire, cable, and other tangible materials to send communications signals. Wireless transmission media send communications signals through the air or space using radio, microwave, and infrared signals. The following sections discuss these types of media.

FIGURE 8-23   AN EXAMPLE OF SENDING A REQUEST OVER THE INTERNET USING A COMMUNICATIONS CHANNEL

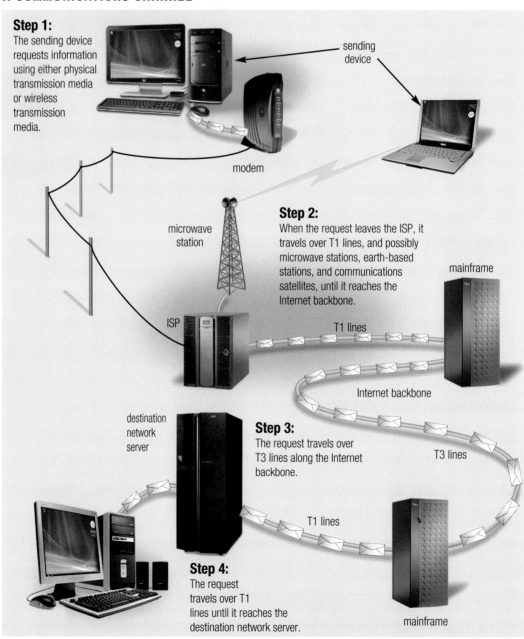

Step 1:
The sending device requests information using either physical transmission media or wireless transmission media.

sending device

modem

microwave station

Step 2:
When the request leaves the ISP, it travels over T1 lines, and possibly microwave stations, earth-based stations, and communications satellites, until it reaches the Internet backbone.

mainframe

ISP

T1 lines

Internet backbone

destination network server

Step 3:
The request travels over T3 lines along the Internet backbone.

T3 lines

T1 lines

Step 4:
The request travels over T1 lines until it reaches the destination network server.

mainframe

LOOKING AHEAD 8-1

Technology Curbs Impaired Drivers

In an effort to stop impaired drivers from getting behind the wheel, Nissan has installed three prototype features designed to detect a person's level of sobriety in a concept car.

A sensor in the transmission shift knob detects alcohol escaping the body through perspiration. Three other sensors in the driver's and passengers' seats detect alcohol in the cabin air. If the alcohol level exceeds a predetermined threshold, the transmission is locked and the car's navigation system issues a voice alert and displays a warning message.

Another feature uses a camera mounted on the dashboard to monitor eye blinking. When drowsiness is detected, the driver's seat belt tightens and voice and visual alerts activate in efforts to encourage the driver to pull off the road and rest. A third feature senses when the car is weaving in the driving lane and consequently issues visual and auditory alerts along with tugs on the seat belt. For more information, visit scsite.com/dcf5e/ch8/looking and then click Sobriety Technology.

FAQ 8-2

Do many home users have a broadband Internet connection?

As shown in the chart to the right, the number of home users with a broadband Internet connection has grown to approximately 90 percent. For more information, visit scsite.com/dcf5e/ch8/faq and then click Broadband Usage.

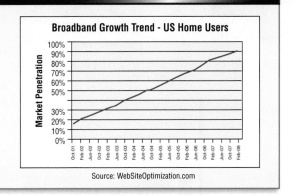

Broadband Growth Trend - US Home Users

Source: WebSiteOptimization.com

PHYSICAL TRANSMISSION MEDIA

Physical transmission media used in communications include twisted-pair cable, coaxial cable, and fiber-optic cable. These cables typically are used within or underground between buildings. Ethernet and token ring LANs often use physical transmission media.

Twisted-Pair Cable

One of the more commonly used transmission media for network cabling and telephone systems is twisted-pair cable. **Twisted-pair cable** consists of one or more twisted-pair wires bundled together (Figure 8-24). Each twisted-pair wire consists of two separate insulated copper wires that are twisted together. The wires are twisted together to reduce noise. **Noise** is an electrical disturbance that can degrade communications.

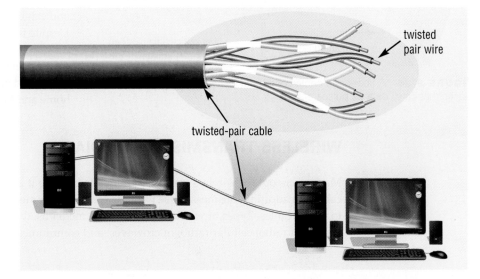

FIGURE 8-24 A twisted-pair cable consists of one or more twisted-pair wires. Each twisted-pair wire usually is color coded for identification.

Coaxial Cable

Coaxial cable, often referred to as coax (pronounced KO-ax), consists of a single copper wire surrounded by at least three layers: (1) an insulating material, (2) a woven or braided metal, and (3) a plastic outer coating (Figure 8-25).

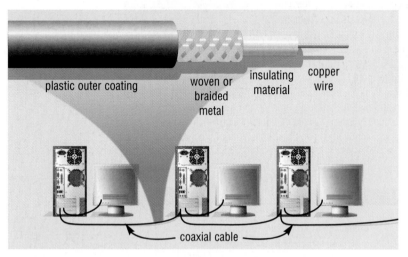

plastic outer coating

woven or braided metal

insulating material

copper wire

coaxial cable

FIGURE 8-25 On a coaxial cable, data travels through a copper wire. This illustration shows computers networked together with coaxial cable.

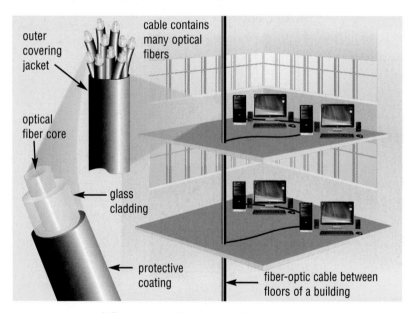

outer covering jacket

cable contains many optical fibers

optical fiber core

glass cladding

protective coating

fiber-optic cable between floors of a building

FIGURE 8-26 A fiber-optic cable consists of hair-thin strands of glass or plastic that carry data as pulses of light.

Cable television (CATV) network wiring often uses coaxial cable because it can be cabled over longer distances than twisted-pair cable. Most of today's computer networks, however, do not use coaxial cable because other transmission media such as fiber-optic cable transmit signals at faster rates.

Fiber-Optic Cable

The core of a **fiber-optic cable** consists of dozens or hundreds of thin strands of glass or plastic that use light to transmit signals. Each strand, called an optical fiber, is as thin as a human hair. Inside the fiber-optic cable, an insulating glass cladding and a protective coating surround each optical fiber (Figure 8-26).

Fiber-optic cables have the following advantages over cables that use wire, such as twisted-pair and coaxial cables:

- Capability of carrying significantly more signals than wire cables
- Faster data transmission
- Less susceptible to noise (interference) from other devices such as a copy machine
- Better security for signals during transmission because they are less susceptible to noise
- Smaller size (much thinner and lighter weight)

Disadvantages of fiber-optic cable are it costs more than twisted-pair or coaxial cable and can be difficult to install and modify. Despite these limitations, many local and long-distance telephone companies are replacing existing telephone lines with fiber-optic cables, enabling them to offer fiber Internet access to home and business users.

WIRELESS TRANSMISSION MEDIA

Many users opt for wireless transmission media because it is more convenient than installing cables. In addition, businesses use wireless transmission media in locations where it is impossible to install cables. Types of wireless transmission media used in communications include infrared, broadcast radio, cellular radio, microwaves, and communications satellites.

Infrared

As discussed earlier in the chapter, infrared (IR) is a wireless transmission medium that sends signals using infrared light waves. Mobile computers and devices, such as a mouse, printer, and smart phone, often have an IrDA port that enables the transfer of data from one device to another using infrared light waves.

Broadcast Radio

Broadcast radio is a wireless transmission medium that distributes radio signals through the air over long distances such as between cities, regions, and countries and short distances such as within an office or home. Bluetooth, UWB, Wi-Fi, and WiMAX communications technologies discussed earlier in this chapter use broadcast radio signals.

Cellular Radio

Cellular radio is a form of broadcast radio that is used widely for mobile communications, specifically wireless modems and cell phones. A cell phone is a telephone device that uses high-frequency radio waves to transmit voice and digital data messages.

Some mobile users connect their notebook computer or other mobile computer to a cell phone to access the Web, send and receive e-mail, enter a chat room, or connect to an office or school network while away from a standard telephone line. Read Looking Ahead 8-2 for a look at the next generation of cellular communications.

Personal Communications Services (**PCS**) is the term used by the United States Federal Communications Commission (FCC) to identify all wireless digital communications. Devices that use PCS include cell phones, PDAs, pagers, and fax machines.

WEB LINK 8-7

Cellular Communications

For more information, visit scsite.com/dcf5e/ch8/weblink and then click Cellular Communications.

LOOKING AHEAD 8-2

Femto Base Stations Enhance Cell Phone Signals

Your cell phone may work fine when you are in your backyard, but sometimes it barely can receive a signal when you walk into your house. This frustrating coverage problem may disappear when major communications companies, such as Alcatel-Lucent and Sony, develop a femto base station that will increase the signal strength in an indoor residence.

The femto access point, also called a femtocell, will be approximately the size of a cable converter box and will function as a hot spot. A cell phone automatically will switch to this indoor base station when the user walks into the home. Consumers are expected to welcome this enhanced signal strength because one-half of cell phone calls originate from inside a home.

Engineers claim the low-power femto signal causes no health concerns because it has only one percent of the transmitting strength of a Wi-Fi network. For more information, visit scsite.com/dcf5e/ch8/looking and then click Femto Base Station.

Microwaves

Microwaves are radio waves that provide a high-speed signal transmission. Microwave transmission, often called fixed wireless, involves sending signals from one microwave station to another (shown in Figure 8-1 on page 296). Microwaves can transmit data at rates up to 4,500 times faster than a dial-up modem.

A microwave station is an earth-based reflective dish that contains the antenna, transceivers, and other equipment necessary for microwave communications. Microwaves use line-of-sight transmission. To avoid possible obstructions, such as buildings or mountains, microwave stations often sit on the tops of buildings, towers, or mountains.

Microwave transmission is used in environments where installing physical transmission media is difficult or impossible and where line-of-sight transmission is available. For example, microwave transmission is used in wide-open areas such as deserts or lakes; between buildings in a close geographic area; or to communicate with a satellite. Current users of microwave transmission include universities, hospitals, city governments, cable television providers, and telephone companies. Home and small business users who do not have other high-speed Internet connections available in their area also opt for lower-cost fixed wireless plans.

Communications Satellite

A **communications satellite** is a space station that receives microwave signals from an earth-based station, amplifies (strengthens) the signals, and broadcasts the signals back over a wide area to any number of earth-based stations (shown in Figure 8-1 on page 296).

These earth-based stations often are microwave stations. Other devices, such as smart phones and GPS receivers, also can function as earth-based stations. Transmission from an earth-based station to a satellite is an uplink. Transmission from a satellite to an earth-based station is a downlink.

Applications such as air navigation, television and radio broadcasts, weather forecasting, video conferencing, paging, global positioning systems, and Internet connections use communications satellites. With the proper satellite dish and a satellite modem card, consumers access the Internet using satellite technology. With satellite Internet connections, however, uplink transmissions usually are slower than downlink transmissions. This difference in speeds usually is acceptable to most Internet satellite users because they download much more data than they upload. Although a satellite Internet connection is more expensive than cable Internet or DSL connections, sometimes it is the only high-speed Internet option in remote areas.

Test your knowledge of pages 312 through 322 in Quiz Yourself 8-3.

QUIZ YOURSELF 8-3

Instructions: Find the true statement below. Then, rewrite the remaining false statements so they are true.

1. A cable modem converts a computer's digital signals to analog signals before they are transmitted over standard telephone lines.

2. A network card is an adapter card, PC Card, ExpressCard module, USB network adapter, or flash card that enables the computer or device to access a network.

3. Analog signals consist of individual electrical pulses that represent bits grouped together into bytes.

4. Physical transmission media send communications signals through the air or space using radio, microwave, and infrared signals.

5. Most wireless home networks use powerline cables.

Quiz Yourself Online: To further check your knowledge of communications devices, home networks, and transmission media, visit scsite.com/dcf5e/ch8/quiz and then click Objectives 6 – 8.

CHAPTER SUMMARY

This chapter provided an overview of communications terminology and applications. It also discussed how to join computers into a network, allowing them to communicate and share resources such as hardware, software, data, and information. It also explained various types of communications devices, media, and procedures as they relate to computers.

CAREER CORNER   Network Specialist

As more companies rely on networks, the demand for network specialists will continue to grow. A **network specialist** must have a working knowledge of local area networks and their application within wide area networks. A network specialist also must be familiar with the Internet, its connectivity to LANs and WANs, and Web server management. Responsibilities of a network specialist include installing, configuring, and troubleshooting network systems. Other responsibilities may include managing system and client software, Web page integration and creation, network security measures, user accounting, and monitoring network event logs for problem resolution. A network specialist must possess good problem-solving skills and the ability to work independently. They also must have the ability to concentrate on detailed projects for long periods of time. Good oral, written, and team-oriented interpersonal skills also are beneficial.

Many institutions offer two-year network specialist programs. In addition to a college degree, industry certifications are available for further career enhancement. Two of the more notable certifications are the Novell CNA (Certified Novell Administrator) and the Cisco CCNA (Certified Cisco Networking Associate). Network specialist salaries will vary depending on education, certifications, and experience. Individuals with certifications can expect an approximate starting salary between $55,000 and $95,000. For more information, visit scsite.com/dcf5e/ch8/careers and then click Network Specialist.

Cisco Systems
Networking the Internet

As the world leader in networking equipment, Cisco Systems strives to empower the Internet generation by connecting people and networks regardless of differences in locations, time, or types of computers. The company offers a broad line of networking equipment for transporting data within a building, across a campus, or across the globe.

A group of computer scientists from Stanford University founded Cisco in 1984. From the start, the company focused on communicating over networks. Today, Cisco's Internet Protocol-based (IP) networking equipment is the basis of the Internet and most networks.

Its key products focus on the areas of home and wireless networking, network security, and communications. Cisco's CEO, John Chambers, received the first-ever Clinton Global Citizen Award for partnering with nonprofit organizations to alleviate poverty across Africa. For more information, visit scsite.com/dcf5e/ch8/companies and then click Cisco.

Qualcomm
Wireless Communications Leader

When you speak into your cell phone, your voice is converted into digital information that is transmitted as a radio signal with a unique code. This wireless communications process is based on Code Division Multiple Access (CDMA), which Qualcomm engineers first conceptualized in 1988.

Commercial CDMA networks were unveiled in 1995, and they provided about 10 times the capacity of analog networks. Today, Qualcomm is the world's largest provider of 3G technology and has shipped more than 1 million chips to the 125 telecommunications equipment manufacturers using the CDMA standard.

Qualcomm's work environment earned it a place on FORTUNE 's list of 100 Best Companies to Work for in America for nine consecutive years in 2007. For more information, visit scsite.com/dcf5e/ch8/companies and then click Qualcomm.

TECHNOLOGY TRAILBLAZERS

Robert Metcalfe
Ethernet Inventor

While studying for his doctorate degree at Harvard and working at Xerox's Palo Alto Research Center (PARC), Robert Metcalfe combined hardware with a high-speed network interface and envisioned that his invention would be used widely. This network technology developed into Ethernet, today's most popular LAN technology that links millions of computers worldwide.

In 1979, Metcalfe left Xerox to found 3Com Corporation and make Ethernet the standard for computer communications. After he retired from that company, he became a general partner in the venture capital firm, Polaris Ventures, which invests in the early stages of information technology and life sciences companies. In 2007, he was inducted into the National Inventors Hall of Fame for his Ethernet innovations. For more information, visit scsite.com/dcf5e/ch8/people and then click Robert Metcalfe.

Patricia Russo
Alcatel-Lucent Technologies CEO

As captain of her high school cheerleading squad, Patricia Russo had to project a spirit of optimism, build teamwork, and solve problems. She uses these same skills in her current job as chief executive officer of Alcatel-Lucent Technologies, which designs and delivers voice, data, and video communications services worldwide.

Russo helped found Lucent in 1996 and oversaw various critical corporate functions, including global sales, strategy and business development, human resources, and public relations. She left Lucent to serve as CEO for Eastman Kodak, but nine months later Lucent asked her to return and appointed her CEO in 2002 and chairman the following year. Under her leadership, Lucent merged with Alcatel in 2006. Forbes.com listed Russo as the tenth most powerful woman in the world in its 2007 rankings. For more information, visit scsite.com/dcf5e/ch8/people and then click Patricia Russo.

CHAPTER 8

Chapter Review

The Chapter Review section summarizes the concepts presented in this chapter. To obtain help from other students regarding any subject in this chapter, visit scsite.com/dcf5e/ch8/forum and post your thoughts or questions.

1 **What Components Are Required for Successful Communications?**

Computer **communications** describes a process in which two or more computers or devices transfer data, instructions, and information. Successful communications require a **sending device** that initiates a transmission instruction, a communications device that connects the sending device to a communications channel, a **communications channel** on which the data travels, a communications device that connects the communications channel to a receiving device, and a **receiving device** that accepts the transmission.

2 **How Are Computer Communications Used?**

Communications technologies include the Internet, Web, e-mail, instant messaging, chat rooms, newsgroups, blogs, wikis, RSS, VoIP, FTP, Web folders, video conferencing, and fax machine or computer fax/modem. People also use communications for other purposes. Users send and receive wireless messages to and from smart phones, cell phones, handheld game consoles, and other personal mobile devices using **text messaging**, wireless instant messaging, **picture messaging,** and **video messaging**. At home, work, school, and in many public locations, people connect wirelessly to the Internet through a **wireless Internet access point**, either a **hot spot** or a mobile wireless network. A **cybercafé** is a coffeehouse, restaurant, or other location that provides personal computers with Internet access. A **global positioning system** (**GPS**) analyzes signals sent by satellites to determine an earth-based receiver's geographic location. Many software products allow users to **collaborate**, or work online, with other users connected to a server. A **document management system** provides for storage and management of a company's documents, such as word processing documents, presentations, and spreadsheets. **Groupware** is software that helps people work together and share information over a network. **Voice mail** allows someone to leave a voice message for one or more people.

 Visit scsite.com/dcf5e/ch8/quiz or click the Quiz Yourself button. Click Objectives 1 – 2.

3 **What Are Different Types of Networks?**

A **network** is a collection of computers and devices connected together via communications devices and media. Networks usually are classified as a local area network, metropolitan area network, or wide area network. A **local area network** (**LAN**) connects computers and devices in a limited geographical area or closely positioned group of buildings. A **wireless LAN** (**WLAN**) is a LAN that uses no physical wires. A **metropolitan area network** (**MAN**) connects local area networks in a metropolitan area and handles the bulk of communications activity across that region. A **wide area network** (**WAN**) covers a large geographic area using a communications channel that combines many types of media.

4 **What Is the Purpose of Communications Software?**

Communications software helps users establish a connection to another computer or network, manages the transmission of data, and provides an interface for users to communicate with one another.

5 **What Are Various Types of Lines for Communications Over the Telephone Network?**

The telephone network uses dial-up lines or dedicated lines. A **dial-up line** is a temporary connection that uses one or more analog telephone lines for communications. A **dedicated line** is an always-on connection established between two communications devices. Dedicated lines include ISDN lines, DSL, FTTP, T-carrier lines, and ATM. **ISDN** is a set of standards for digital transmission over standard copper telephone lines. **DSL** transmits at fast speeds on existing standard copper telephone wiring. **FTTP** (**Fiber to the Premises**) uses fiber-optic cable to provide extremely high-speed Internet access to a user's physical permanent location. A **T-carrier line** is a long-distance digital telephone line that carries multiple signals over a single communications line. **ATM** (Asynchronous Transfer Mode) is a service that carries voice, data, video, and multimedia at extremely high speeds.

 Visit scsite.com/dcf5e/ch8/quiz or click the Quiz Yourself button. Click Objectives 3 – 5.

Chapter Review

⑥ What Are Commonly Used Communications Devices?

A **communications device** is any hardware capable of transmitting data between a sending device and a receiving device. A **modem** converts a computer's digital signals to analog signals for transmission over standard telephone lines. An **ISDN modem** transmits digital data to and from an ISDN line, while a **DSL modem** transmits digital data to and from a DSL line. A **cable modem** is a digital modem that sends and receives digital data over the cable television network. A **wireless modem** uses the cell phone network to connect to the Internet wirelessly from a smart phone, a mobile computer, or mobile device. A **network card** is an adapter card, PC Card, ExpressCard module, USB network adapter, or flash card that enables a computer or device that does not have networking capability to access a network. A **wireless access point** allows computers and devices to transfer data wirelessly. A **router** connects multiple computers together and transmits data to its correct destination on the network.

⑦ How Can a Home Network Be Set Up?

A **home network** connects multiple computers and devices in a home. An Ethernet network connects each computer to a central hub with a physical cable. A home powerline cable network uses the same lines that bring electricity into the house. A phoneline network uses existing telephone lines in a home. Most home networks use a Wi-Fi network, which sends signals through the air at distances of up to 1,500 feet in some configurations.

⑧ What Are Various Physical and Wireless Transmission Media?

Transmission media consist of materials or substances capable of carrying one or more signals. Physical transmission media use tangible materials to send communications signals. **Twisted-pair cable** consists of one or more twisted-pair wires bundled together. **Coaxial cable** consists of a single copper wire surrounded by at least three layers: an insulating material, a woven or braided metal, and a plastic outer coating. **Fiber-optic cable** consists of thin strands of glass or plastic that use light to transmit signals. Wireless transmission media send communications signals through the air or space. Infrared (IR) sends signals using infrared light waves. **Broadcast radio** distributes radio signals through the air over long and short distances. **Cellular radio** is a form of broadcast radio that is used widely for mobile communications. **Microwaves** are radio waves that provide a high-speed signal transmission. A **communications satellite** is a space station that receives microwave signals from an earth-based station, amplifies the signals, and broadcasts the signals back over a wide area.

 Visit scsite.com/dcf5e/ch8/quiz or click the Quiz Yourself button. Click Objectives 6 – 8.

Key Terms

You should know each key term. Use the list below to help focus your study. To further enhance your understanding of the Key Terms in this chapter, visit scsite.com/dcf5e/ch8/terms. See an example of and a definition for each term, and access current and additional information about the term from the Web.

802.11 (308)
802.16 (309)
ATM (312)
bandwidth (317)
Bluetooth (309)
broadband (318)
broadcast radio (321)
bus network (306)
cable modem (314)
cellular radio (321)
client/server network (305)
clients (305)
coaxial cable (320)
collaborate (302)
collaborative software (302)
communications (296)
communications channel (296)
communications device (312)
communications satellite (322)
communications software (310)
cybercafé (301)
dedicated line (311)

dial-up line (311)
document management system (302)
DSL (311)
DSL modem (314)
Ethernet (308)
fiber-optic cable (320)
FTTP (Fiber to the Premises) (312)
global positioning system (GPS) (301)
groupware (302)
home network (316)
hot spot (300)
intranet (307)
IrDA (309)
ISDN (311)
ISDN modem (314)
local area network (LAN) (303)
metropolitan area network (MAN) (305)
microwaves (321)

modem (313)
network (303)
network card (315)
network specialist (322)
network standard (308)
network topology (306)
noise (319)
P2P (306)
peer-to-peer network (305)
Personal Communications Services (PCS) (321)
picture messaging (299)
receiving device (296)
RFID (309)
ring network (307)
router (315)
sending device (296)
server (305)
star network (307)
T1 line (312)
T-carrier line (312)
TCP/IP (308)

text messaging (298)
token ring (308)
transmission media (317)
twisted-pair cable (319)
UWB (ultra-wideband) (309)
value-added network (VAN) (303)
video messaging (299)
voice mail (302)
Web conference (302)
Web services (302)
wide area network (WAN) (304)
Wi-Fi (wireless fidelity) (308)
WiMAX (309)
wireless access point (315)
Wireless Application Protocol (WAP) (310)
wireless Internet access point (300)
wireless LAN (WLAN) (303)
wireless modem (314)

Checkpoint

Use the Checkpoint exercises to check your knowledge level of the chapter. To complete the Checkpoint exercises interactively, visit scsite.com/dcf5e/ch8/check.

True/False

Mark T for True and F for False. (See page numbers in parentheses.)

_____ 1. Computer communications describes a process in which two or more computers or devices transfer data, instructions, and information. (296)

_____ 2. A network is a collection of computers and devices connected together via communications devices and transmission media. (303)

_____ 3. A metropolitan area network (MAN) is a network that covers a small geographic area using a communications channel that uses a single type of media. (304)

_____ 4. On a client/server network, clients are computers and mobile devices on the network that rely on the server for its resources. (305)

_____ 5. Ethernet is a network standard that specifies no central computer or device on the network (nodes) should control when data can be transmitted. (308)

_____ 6. For optimal communications, UWB devices should be within 2 to 100 meters (about 6.5 to 330 feet) of each other. (309)

_____ 7. A dial-up line is a temporary connection that uses one or more analog telephone lines for communications. (311)

_____ 8. Fiber to the Premises (FTTP) uses fiber-optic cable to provide extremely high-speed Internet access to a user's physical permanent location. (312)

_____ 9. A cable modem is a digital modem that sends and receives digital data over the cable television network. (314)

_____ 10. Hubs along the Internet backbone forward data packets to their destination using the fastest available path. (315)

_____ 11. Noise is an electrical disturbance that can degrade communications. (319)

Multiple Choice

Select the best answer. (See page numbers in parentheses.)

1. A _____ is a coffeehouse, restaurant, or other location that provides personal computers with Internet access to its customers. (301)
   a. GPS
   b. wireless messaging service
   c. cybercafé
   d. none of the above

2. When an online meeting takes place on the Web, it is called _____. (302)
   a. video messaging
   b. a peer-to-peer network
   c. a Web meeting
   d. a Web conference

3. A _____ network is a third-party business that provides networking services for a fee. (303)
   a. star
   b. client/server
   c. value-added
   d. file sharing

4. _____ is a standard, specifically a protocol, that defines how a network uses radio signals to communicate with a tag placed in or attached to an object, an animal, or a person. (309)
   a. RFID
   b. WiMAX
   c. Bluetooth
   d. UWB

5. _____ is a newer network standard developed by IEEE that specifies how wireless devices communicate over the air in a wide area. (309)
   a. Wi-Fi
   b. WiMAX
   c. 802.16
   d. Both b and c

6. Communications software consists of programs that do all of the following, except _____. (310)
   a. help users establish a connection to another computer or network
   b. manage the transmission of data, instructions, and information
   c. provide an interface for users to communicate with one another
   d. convert a computer's analog signals into digital signals for transmission

7. DSL, cable television Internet service, and satellites offer _____ transmission. (318)
   a. baseband
   b. IrDA
   c. microwave
   d. broadband

8. _____ consists of a single copper wire surrounded by at least three layers. (320)
   a. Fiber-optic cable
   b. Coaxial cable
   c. Twisted-pair cable
   d. Infrared

Matching

Match the terms with their definitions. (See page numbers in parentheses.)

_____ 1. collaborate (302)

_____ 2. Bluetooth (309)

_____ 3. dedicated line (311)

_____ 4. transmission media (317)

_____ 5. fiber-optic cable (320)

a. work online with other users connected to a server
b. dozens or hundreds of thin strands of glass or plastic that use light to transmit signals
c. materials or substances capable of carrying one or more signals
d. type of always-on connection that is established between two communications devices
e. online area in which users have written discussions about a subject
f. a protocol that defines how two devices use short-range radio waves to transmit data

Checkpoint

1. What is text messaging? _____ What are some options for sending and receiving text messages? _____

2. How are a local area network (LAN), a metropolitan area network (MAN), and a wide area network (WAN) different? _____ What is a wireless LAN? _____

3. Describe P2P networking. _____ What are some examples of P2P networking software? _____

4. What is a network topology? _____ How are a bus network, a ring network, and a star network different? _____

5. What is UWB and what are its benefits? _____ What are some uses of UWB? _____

Working Together Working in a group of your classmates, complete the following team exercise.

1. Assume you are part of a group hired as consultants to recommend a network plan for a small company of 20 employees. Using the Internet and other available resources, develop a network plan for the company. Include the following components in your plan: (1) the type of network — peer-to-peer or client/server, (2) the suggested topology, (3) the type and number of servers, (4) the peripheral devices, and (5) the communications media. Prepare a written report and presentation to share with the class.

Web Research

Use the Internet-based Web Research exercises to broaden your understanding of the concepts presented in this chapter. To discuss any of the Web Research exercises in this chapter with other students, post your thoughts or questions at scsite.com/dcf5e/ch8/forum.

① Blogs

The blogosphere has captured the attention of mainstream America, for more than half of its citizens visit blogs on a regular basis. According to a Synovate/Marketing Daily survey, nearly one-half of these readers turn to blogs for entertainment value, while one-fourth read the online content for information about hobbies and other interests. Bloglines can help blog readers monitor changes to their favorite Web sites by notifying subscribers when a particular blog has been updated. Visit Bloglines (bloglines.com) and then read the information in the About link at the bottom of the home page. What are Bloglines' features? How does Bloglines examine RSS feeds? How does the Web site help readers organize their subscriptions? What forums and playlists are featured?

② Scavenger Hunt

Use one of the search engines listed in Figure 2-8 in Chapter 2 on page 58 or your own favorite search engine to find the answers to the questions that follow. Copy and paste the Web address from the Web page where you found the answer. Some questions may have more than one answer. If required, submit your answers to your instructor. (1) How is Boeing using RFID in its aircraft? (2) What is geocaching? (3) What are some of the products featured on the International Symposium on Wearable Computing Web site?

③ Search Sleuth

Subject directories are used to find specialized topics, such as information about automobiles, travel, and real estate. Most subject directories are arranged by topic and then displayed in a series of menus. Yahoo! is one of the more popular directories. Visit this Web site (yahoo.com) and then use your word processing program to answer the following questions. Then, if required, submit your answers to your instructor. (1) Click the Tech link in the Yahoo! Services area at the top of the page to display the Yahoo! Tech page. Click the Tech Search text box and type "GPS" and "MP3" in the box. Sort the products by lowest price by clicking the Lowest Price link near the top of the page. Which product is the least expensive? (2) Scroll down to the bottom of the page and then click one of the links in the Wi-Fi & Networking Product Categories area. Read one of the How-To articles and then write a 50-word summary of your findings.

Learn How To

Use the Learn How To activities to learn fundamental skills when using a computer and accompanying technology. Complete the exercises and submit them to your instructor. Premium Activity: The icon indicates you can see a visual demonstration of the associated Learn How To activity by visiting scsite.com/dcf5e/ch8/howto.

LEARN HOW TO 1: **Set Up and Install a Wi-Fi Home Network**

In this chapter you learned about home networks and their advantages (see page 316, Home Networks). Creating a Wi-Fi home network consists of four phases: 1) subscribe to a high-speed Internet access provider; 2) purchase the Wi-Fi equipment; 3) connect the physical devices; and 4) create the network through the use of software.

SUBSCRIBE TO A HIGH-SPEED INTERNET ACCESS PROVIDER   A high-speed Internet access provider is advisable to connect all computers on the home network to the Internet. The three primary ways for home users to obtain a fast connection to the Internet are DSL, cable, and satellite. DSL is provided by telephone companies, cable is provided by cable TV companies, and satellite connections are provided by satellite TV providers. Each has its advantages and disadvantages, including the minimum and maximum speed of Internet access, cost, and availability.

Determining the optimal high-speed Internet access provider depends largely on where the network will be located, local costs, and service availability. The way to obtain the best high-speed Internet access provider is to research the options available in your area.

Exercise

1. Assume you live near Coeur d'Alene, Idaho. You have decided that a high-speed Internet access provider and a Wi-Fi network would be advantageous for your at-home business. Find answers to the following questions for this Idaho town or a town specified by your instructor: What high-speed Internet access providers are available? Which provides the best service? Which is the cheapest? Based on the information you gather, write a plan for subscribing to a high-speed Internet access provider. Submit the answers to the questions and your plan to your instructor.

PURCHASE THE WI-FI EQUIPMENT   As part of the service when you subscribe to a high-speed Internet access provider, you receive a modem that is capable of connecting to the Internet. In most cases, the modem is not a wireless transmitter. So, in order to establish a wireless connection between the Internet and the home network, you will need a wireless router that establishes the wireless access point.

You can visit any retail electronics store and find a wide variety of wireless routers. A key to purchasing the correct router is to ensure it will work with your modem and Internet access provider. Some Internet access providers support only certain brands of routers and, while it is true that other routers may work, you might be taking a risk if you purchase an unsupported router. With the popularity of wireless home networks, though, some Internet access providers now provide a wireless router as part of the subscription service, often for an additional fee. You should investigate closely the needs for the Wi-Fi router to ensure compatibility with your Internet access provider.

In addition to the router, each computer that is to be part of the Wi-Fi network needs a wireless network adapter. This device allows the computers to communicate with one another. Most external wireless network adapters plug in either a PC Card slot, ExpressCard slot, or a USB connection. Many notebook computers have a built-in wireless network adapter.

Finally, some home networks have a combination of wired and wireless devices. In these networks, the modem connects to the wireless router, and computers on the network either connect to the wireless router using a wireless or wired connection.

Once the Wi-Fi equipment is assembled, you are ready to connect your home network.

Exercise

1. Using your Web research skills, determine the type of IEEE 802.11 standard used by modems available from Internet access providers. What percentage use 802.11b? What percentage use 802.11g? If your modem uses 802.11b but your wireless network router is 802.11g, what happens? Based on your research, which router do you recommend? Submit your answers to your instructor.

CONNECT THE PHYSICAL DEVICES   Once you have assembled your equipment, you can connect the devices in the network. Usually, the modem will be connected to the source of the Internet transmission (DSL, cable, or satellite). Then the modem is connected to the wireless router, which in turn is connected to the computers on your network.

After these connections are completed, each of the computers that will be used in the network that do not have a built-in wireless network adapter must have the adapter attached, often by using a USB connection. Once these connections are made, the network can be created.

CREATE THE NETWORK To establish a network, operating system software must be configured based on the design of your network. To begin the process on a Windows Vista computer, you should run the 'Set up a wireless router or access point' wizard by completing the following steps:

1. Click the Start button on the Windows taskbar and then click Control Panel on the Start menu.
2. In Classic View, double-click Network and Sharing Center to open the Network and Sharing Center window, and then click the 'Set up a connection or network' link below the Tasks heading to display the 'Set up a connection or network' dialog box.
3. Click 'Set up a wireless router or access point' and then click the Next button.
4. Click the Next button to start the wizard. If the User Account Control dialog box appears, click the Continue button. After Windows detects your network hardware and settings, click 'Create wireless network settings and save to USB drive'.
5. In the Network name (SSID) text box (Figure 8-27), type a name for the wireless network you are creating. Use a name that you will recognize as the name for the network, and then click the Next button.
6. In the Passphrase text box (Figure 8-28), type a passphrase you would like others to provide, who wish to connect to your wireless network. Use a passphrase that is easy for you to remember, but difficult for others to guess. Click the Next button. If the User Account Control dialog box appears, click the Continue button.
7. If necessary, click 'Allow sharing with anyone with a user account and password for this computer' and then click the Next button.
8. If you have not already done so, insert your USB flash drive in a USB port and wait for your computer to recognize the drive.
9. Follow the remaining instructions in the wizard to finish creating the network configuration.
10. The network has been created. Your USB flash drive now can be used to configure additional computers you wish to add to your wireless network.

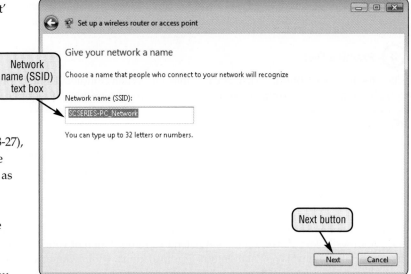

FIGURE 8-27

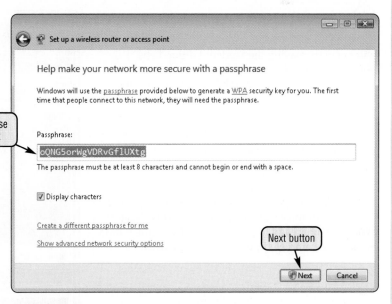

FIGURE 8-28

Exercise

1. Form a three-person team whose responsibility is to create a Wi-Fi network for a small business in your local area. Assign tasks to each member of the team. Write a detailed plan for creating the Wi-Fi network, including the brand and type of equipment to be purchased, costs, and a schedule for completing the work. Explain why your team made each choice, and be prepared to defend your choices. Submit the plan to your instructor.

Learn It Online

Use the Learn It Online exercises to reinforce your understanding of the chapter concepts. To access the Learn It Online exercises, visit scsite.com/dcf5e/ch8/learn.

① At the Movies — Trillian

To view the Trillian movie, click the number 1 button. Locate your video and click the corresponding High-Speed or Dial-Up link, depending on your Internet connection. Watch the movie to learn about Trillian, a chat program for Windows, that can connect to multiple online messaging services, such as AIM, ICQ, Windows Live Messenger, Yahoo! Messenger, and IRC. Then, complete the exercise by answering the question that follows. How does the freeware version of Trillian work?

② Student Edition Labs — Networking Basics

Click the number 2 button. A new browser window will open, displaying the Student Edition Labs. Follow the on-screen instructions to complete the Networking Basics Lab. When finished, click the Exit button. If required, submit your results to your instructor.

③ Practice Test

Click the number 3 button. Answer each question. When completed, enter your name and click the Grade Test button to submit the quiz for grading. Make a note of any missed questions. If required, submit your results to your instructor.

④ Who Wants To Be a Computer Genius^2?

Click the number 4 button to find out if you are a computer genius. Directions about how to play the game will be displayed. When you are ready to play, click the Play button. Submit your score to your instructor.

⑤ Online Radio

Click the number 5 button to learn how to use the Internet to find and listen to various radio stations. Follow the instructions to use Windows Media Player to find and listen to a radio station of your choice. Once you have selected a genre, use the Zip Code search text box to display a list of Internet radio stations within your area. Listen to at least three different radio stations. Write a report comparing the quality of sound of each station. Include in your report any difficulties you may have encountered as well as any features you found interesting. Print your report and submit it to your instructor.

⑥ Student Edition Labs — Wireless Networking

Click the number 6 button. A new browser window will open, displaying the Student Edition Labs. Follow the on-screen instructions to complete the Wireless Networking Lab. When finished, click the Exit button. If required, submit your results to your instructor.

⑦ Crossword Puzzle Challenge

Click the number 7 button, and then click the Crossword Puzzle Challenge link. Directions about how to play the game will be displayed. Complete the puzzle to reinforce skills you learned in this chapter. When you are ready to play, click the Continue button. Submit the completed puzzle to your instructor.

⑧ Vista Exercises

Click the number 8 button. When the Vista Exercises menu appears, click the exercise assigned by your instructor. A new browser window will open. Follow the on-screen instructions to complete the exercise. When finished, click the Exit button. If required, submit your results to your instructor.

Database Management

OBJECTIVES

After completing this chapter, you will be able to:

1. Define the term, database
2. Identify the qualities of valuable information
3. Discuss the terms character, field, record, and file
4. Identify file maintenance techniques
5. Differentiate between a file processing system approach and the database approach
6. Discuss the functions common to most DBMSs
7. Describe characteristics of relational, object-oriented, and multidimensional databases
8. Explain how to interact with Web databases
9. Discuss the responsibilities of database analysts and administrators

CONTENTS

DATABASES, DATA, AND INFORMATION

A database is a collection of data organized in a manner that allows access, retrieval, and use of that data. **Data** is a collection of unprocessed items, which can include text, numbers, images, audio, and video. **Information** is processed data; that is, it is organized, meaningful, and useful.

Computers process data in a database into information. A database at a members-only discount warehouse, for example, contains data about members, e.g., member data, purchases data, etc. As shown in Figure 9-1, a computer at the warehouse processes new member data and then sends receipt and ID card information to the printers.

With **database software**, often called a **database management system** (**DBMS**), users create a computerized database; add, change, and delete data in the database; sort and retrieve data from the database; and create forms and reports from the data in the database. Database software includes many powerful features, as you will discover later in this chapter.

FIGURE 9-1   HOW A MEMBERS-ONLY DISCOUNT WAREHOUSE MIGHT PROCESS DATA INTO INFORMATION

Step 1:
A membership services associate uses a digital camera to take a photo of the new member and uses a keyboard to enter other member data into the computer.

Data Integrity

Most companies realize that data is one of their more valuable assets — because data is used to generate information. Many business transactions take less time when employees have instant access to information. To ensure that data is accessible on demand, a company must manage and protect its data just as it would any other resource. Thus, it is vital that the data has integrity and is kept secure.

For a computer to produce correct information, the data that is entered into a database must have integrity. Data integrity identifies the quality of the data. An erroneous member address in a member database is an example of incorrect data. When a database contains this type of error, it loses integrity. Data integrity is very important because computers and people use information to make decisions and take actions.

Garbage in, garbage out (**GIGO**) is a computing phrase that points out the accuracy of a computer's output depends on the accuracy of the input. If you enter incorrect data into a computer (garbage in), the computer will produce incorrect information (garbage out).

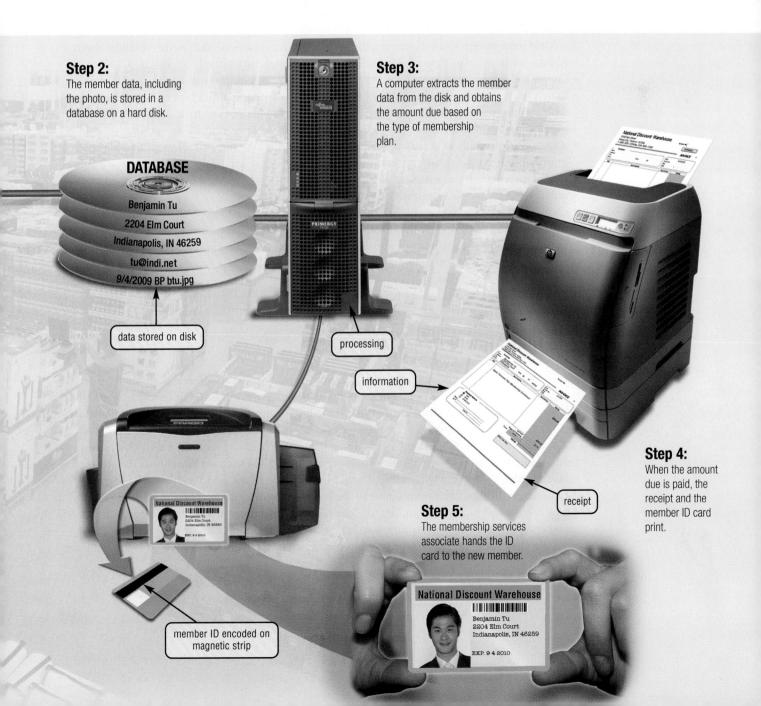

Step 2:
The member data, including the photo, is stored in a database on a hard disk.

Step 3:
A computer extracts the member data from the disk and obtains the amount due based on the type of membership plan.

DATABASE

Benjamin Tu

2204 Elm Court

Indianapolis, IN 46259

tu@indi.net

9/4/2009 BP btu.jpg

data stored on disk

processing

information

receipt

Step 4:
When the amount due is paid, the receipt and the member ID card print.

Step 5:
The membership services associate hands the ID card to the new member.

member ID encoded on magnetic strip

National Discount Warehouse

Benjamin Tu
2204 Elm Court
Indianapolis, IN 46259

EXP. 9 4 2010

Qualities of Valuable Information

The information that data generates also is an important asset. People make decisions daily using all types of information such as receipts, bank statements, pension plan summaries, stock analyses, and credit reports. In a business, managers make decisions based on sales trends, competitors' products and services, production processes, and even employee skills.

To assist with sound decision making, the information must have value. For it to be valuable, information should be accurate, verifiable, timely, organized, accessible, useful, and cost-effective.

* Accurate information is error free. Inaccurate information can lead to incorrect decisions. For example, consumers assume their credit report is accurate. If your credit report incorrectly shows past due payments, a bank may not lend you money for a car or house.

* Verifiable information can be proven as correct or incorrect. For example, security personnel at an airport usually request some type of photo identification to verify that you are the person named on the ticket.

* Timely information has an age suited to its use. A decision to build additional schools in a particular district should be based on the most recent census report — not on one that is 20 years old.

  Most information loses its value with time. Some information, such as information about trends, gains value as time passes and more information is obtained.

* Organized information is arranged to suit the needs and requirements of the decision maker. Different people may need the same information presented in a different manner. For example, an inventory manager may want an inventory report to list out-of-stock items first. The purchasing agent, instead, wants the report alphabetized by vendor.

* Accessible information is available when the decision maker needs it. Having to wait for information may delay an important decision.

* Useful information has meaning to the person who receives it. Most information is important only to certain people or groups of people.

* Cost-effective information should give more value than it costs to produce. A company occasionally should review the information it produces to determine if it still is cost-effective to produce. Sometimes, it is not easy to place a value on information. For this reason, some companies create information only on demand, that is, as people request it, instead of on a regular basis. Many companies make information available online. Users then can access and print online information as they need it.

THE HIERARCHY OF DATA

Data is organized in layers. In the computer profession, data is classified in a hierarchy. Each higher level of data consists of one or more items from the lower level. For example, a member has an address, and an address consists of letters and numbers. Depending on the application and the user, different terms describe the various levels of the hierarchy.

As shown in Figure 9-2, a database contains files, a file contains records, a record contains fields, and a field is made up of one or more characters. The Discount Warehouse database contains four files: Member, Membership Plans, Member Purchases, and Products. The Member file contains records about current members. The Membership Plans file contains records identifying a type of membership and its annual fee. The Member Purchases file contains records about members' purchases at the discount warehouse, and the Products file contains records about items for sale. Each field in a record contains many characteristics, one of which is the field size.

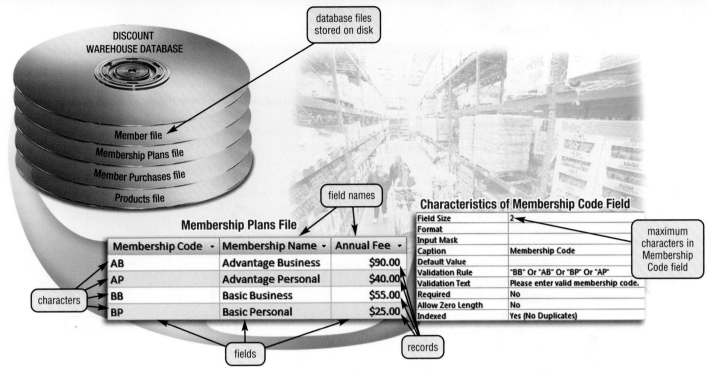

FIGURE 9-2 A sample discount warehouse database with four files: Member, Membership Plans, Member Purchases, and Products. The sample Membership Plans file contains four records. Each record contains three fields. The Membership Code field can contain a maximum of two characters (bytes).

Characters

As Chapter 4 discussed, a bit is the smallest unit of data the computer can process. Eight bits grouped together in a unit comprise a byte. In the ASCII and EBCDIC coding schemes, each byte represents a single **character**, which can be a number (4), letter (R), punctuation mark (?), or other symbol (&).

Fields

A **field** is a combination of one or more related characters or bytes and is the smallest unit of data a user accesses. A **field name** uniquely identifies each field. When searching for data in a database, you often specify the field name. Field names for the data in the Membership Plans file are Membership Code, Membership Name, and Annual Fee.

A database uses a variety of characteristics, such as field size and data type, to define each field. The **field size** defines the maximum number of characters a field can contain. For example, the Membership Code field contains two characters. Valid entries include BB (Basic Business), AB (Advantage Business), BP (Basic Personal), and AP (Advantage Personal). Thus, as shown in Figure 9-2, the Membership Code field has a field size of 2.

The type of data in a field is an important consideration. Figure 9-3 identifies the data types for fields in the Membership Plans and Member files. The **data type** specifies the kind of data a field can contain and how the field is used. Common data types include:

- Text (also called alphanumeric) — letters, numbers, or special characters
- Numeric — numbers only
- AutoNumber — unique number automatically assigned by the DBMS to each added record
- Currency — dollar and cent amounts or numbers containing decimal values
- Date — month, day, year, and sometimes time information
- Memo — lengthy text entries
- Yes/No — only the values Yes or No (or True or False)
- Hyperlink — Web address that links to a document or a Web page
- Object — photo, audio, video, or a document created in other programs

Membership Plans file

Membership Code	Text
Membership Name	Text
Annual Fee	Currency

data types

Member file

Member ID	AutoNumber
First Name	Text
Last Name	Text
Address	Text
City	Text
State	Text
Postal Code	Text
E-mail Address	Hyperlink
Date Joined	Date/Time
Membership Code	Text
Photo	Object

FIGURE 9-3 Data types of fields in the Membership Plans and Member files.

Records

A **record** is a group of related fields. For example, a member record includes a set of fields about one member. A **key field**, or **primary key**, is a field that uniquely identifies each record in a file. The data in a key field is unique to a specific record. For example, the Member ID field uniquely identifies each member because no two members can have the same Member ID.

Files

A **data file** is a collection of related records stored on a storage medium such as a hard disk, CD, or DVD. A Member file at a discount warehouse might consist of hundreds of individual member records. Each member record in the file contains the same fields. Each field, however, contains different data. Figure 9-4 shows a small sample Member file that contains four member records, each with eleven fields.

A database includes a group of related data files. Read Ethics & Issues 9-1 for a discussion related to a use of databases.

SAMPLE MEMBER FILE

Member ID	First Name	Last Name
2295	Milton	Brewer
3876	Louella	Drake
3928	Adelbert	Ruiz
4872	Elena	Gupta

records

key field   fields

ETHICS & ISSUES 9-1

Are Portable Storage Devices a Threat to Businesses?

For years, and to the dismay of many companies, workers have carted home portable storage devices loaded with valuable company information. Today's USB flash drives, portable media players, smart phones, and external hard disks allow employees to pack volumes of valuable information in their pockets. The term podslurping has been coined to refer to the practice of stealing data using such devices. Companies now must be concerned with visitors or disgruntled employees walking off with complete customer lists, employee databases, or secret product designs and strategies on portable storage devices. Almost every instance of such data theft involves a company insider. Some companies have gone as far as banning some portable media players and other portable storage devices from the company premises. Other companies disable USB and FireWire ports on employee computers, thereby preventing the devices from being used at all.

How can companies control employee use of portable storage devices to copy company information? Should companies be allowed to dictate the types of personal devices that visitors and employees bring to the workplace? Why or why not? Is the problem solvable, just manageable, or should a company find other ways to secure its information? Why? Should companies be held legally liable when such data theft occurs? Why or why not?

MAINTAINING DATA

File maintenance refers to the procedures that keep data current. File maintenance procedures include adding records to, changing records in, and deleting records from a file.

Adding Records

Users add new records to a file when they obtain new data. If a new member wants to join the discount warehouse club, a membership services associate adds a new record to the Member file at the discount warehouse. The process required to add this record to the file might include the following steps:

1. A membership services associate uses the database management system (DBMS) to display a Member Maintenance form that gives him or her access to the Member file. The associate then clicks the New button, which begins the process of adding a record to the Member file.
2. The associate fills in the fields of the member record with data (except for the Member ID, which automatically is assigned by the DBMS).
3. The associate takes a picture of the member using a digital camera. The DBMS stores this picture in the Member file and prints it on a member ID card.
4. The membership services associate verifies the data on the screen and then presses a key on the keyboard or clicks a button on the screen to add the new member record to the Member file. The system software determines where to write the record on the disk (Figure 9-5).

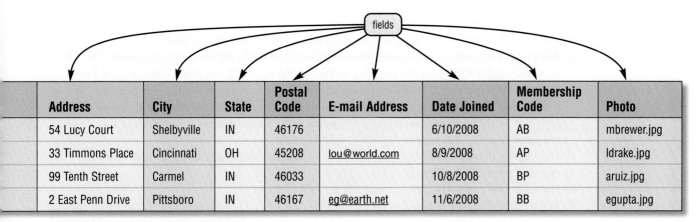

fields								
Address	**City**	**State**	**Postal Code**	**E-mail Address**	**Date Joined**	**Membership Code**	**Photo**
54 Lucy Court	Shelbyville	IN	46176		6/10/2008	AB	mbrewer.jpg
33 Timmons Place	Cincinnati	OH	45208	lou@world.com	8/9/2008	AP	ldrake.jpg
99 Tenth Street	Carmel	IN	46033		10/8/2008	BP	aruiz.jpg
2 East Penn Drive	Pittsboro	IN	46167	eg@earth.net	11/6/2008	BB	egupta.jpg

FIGURE 9-4 A sample data file, stored on a hard disk, that contains four records, each with eleven fields.

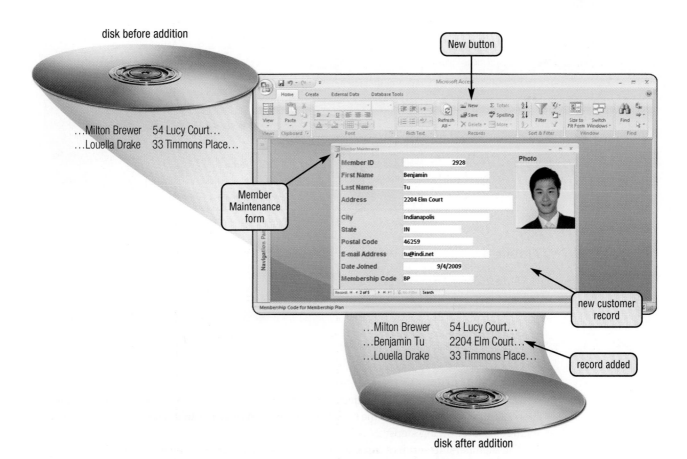

FIGURE 9-5 Using the Member Maintenance form, a membership services associate adds a new member record for Benjamin Tu. After the associate takes the photo with the digital camera and confirms the data is correct, he or she adds the record to the database file.

Changing Records

Generally, users change a record in a file for two reasons: (1) to correct inaccurate data or (2) to update old data with new data.

Suppose, for example, that Benjamin Tu moves from 2204 Elm Court to 76 Ash Street. The process to change the address and update Benjamin Tu's record might include the following steps:

1. The membership services associate displays the Member Maintenance form.
2. Assuming Benjamin Tu is present, the services associate inserts Benjamin's member ID card in a card reader to display his member record on the screen. If Benjamin did not have his ID card or was not present, the associate could enter Benjamin's member ID — if Benjamin knew it. Otherwise, the associate could enter Tu in the Last Name field, which would retrieve all members with that same last name. The associate then would scroll through all of the retrieved records to determine which one is Benjamin's.
3. The DBMS displays data about Benjamin Tu so that the associate can confirm the correct member record is displayed.
4. The associate enters the new street address, 76 Ash Street.
5. The membership services associate verifies the data on the screen and then, if required, clicks the Save button to change the record in the Member file. The DBMS changes the record on the disk (Figure 9-6).

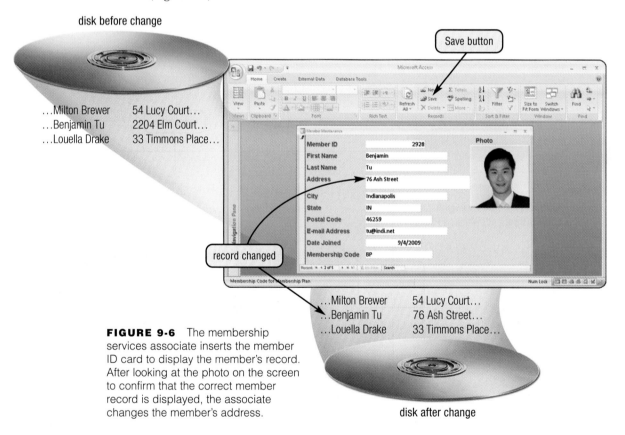

FIGURE 9-6 The membership services associate inserts the member ID card to display the member's record. After looking at the photo on the screen to confirm that the correct member record is displayed, the associate changes the member's address.

Deleting Records

When a record no longer is needed, a user deletes it from a file. Assume a member named Elena Gupta is moving out of the country. The process required to delete a record from a file includes the following steps:

1. The membership services associate displays the Member Maintenance form.
2. The associate displays Elena Gupta's member record on the screen.
3. The associate confirms the correct member record is displayed. Then, the associate clicks the Delete Record command to delete the record from the Member file and then, if required, clicks the Save button to save the modified file.

DBMSs use a variety of techniques to manage deleted records. Sometimes, the DBMS removes the record from the file immediately, which means the deleted record cannot be restored. Other times, the record is flagged, or marked, so the DBMS will not process it again. In this case, the DBMS places an asterisk (*) or some other character at the beginning of the record (Figure 9-7).

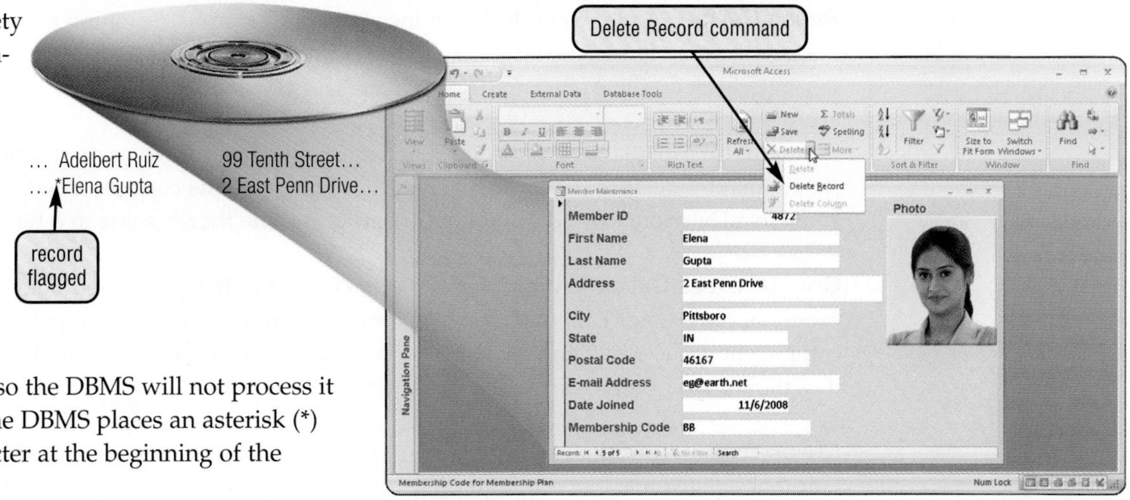

DBMSs that maintain inactive data for an extended period commonly flag records. For example, a discount warehouse might flag canceled memberships. When a DBMS flags a deleted record, the record remains physically on the disk. The record, however, is deleted logically because the DBMS will not process it.

From time to time, users should run a utility program that removes the flagged records and reorganizes current records. For example, the discount warehouse may remove from disk any accounts that have been canceled for more than one year.

FIGURE 9-7 The membership services associate displays the member's record on the screen. After the associate verifies that the correct member record is displayed, he or she deletes the record. The DBMS flags the member record on disk by placing an asterisk in the first position of the record.

Validating Data

Validation is the process of comparing data with a set of rules or values to find out if the data is correct. Many programs perform a validity check that analyzes entered data to help ensure that it is correct. For instance, when a membership services associate adds or changes data in a member record, the DBMS tests the entered data.

With an annual membership fee, you would expect to see numbers before and after a decimal point. For example, a valid annual membership fee is 30.00. An entry of XR.WP clearly is not correct. If the entered data fails a validity check, the computer should display an error message that instructs the user to enter the data again. Validity checks reduce data entry errors.

Various types of validity checks include alphabetic checks, numeric checks, range checks, consistency checks, and completeness checks. Check digits also validate data accuracy. The following paragraphs describe the purpose of these validity checks. The table in Figure 9-8 illustrates several of these validity checks and shows valid data that passes the check and invalid data that fails the check.

SAMPLE VALID AND INVALID DATA

Validity Check	Field(s) Being Checked	Valid Data	Invalid Data
Alphabetic Check	First Name	Karen	Ka24n
Numeric Check	Postal Code	46322	4tr22
Range Check	Annual Fee	$30.00	$120.00
Consistency Check	Date Joined and Birth Date	9/20/2008 8/27/1984	9/20/2008 8/27/2009
Completeness Check	Last Name	Tu	

FIGURE 9-8 In this table of sample valid and invalid data, the first column lists commonly used validity checks. The second column lists the name of the field that contains data being checked. The third column shows valid data that passes the validity checks. The fourth column shows invalid data that fails the validity checks.

ALPHABETIC/NUMBERIC CHECK An **alphabetic check** ensures that users enter only alphabetic data into a field. A **numeric check** ensures that users enter only numeric data into a field. For example, data in a First Name field should contain only characters from the alphabet. Data in a Postal Code field should contain numbers (with the exception of the special characters such as a hyphen).

RANGE CHECK   A **range check** determines whether a number is within a specified range. Assume the lowest annual membership fee at the discount warehouse is $25.00 and the highest is $90.00. A range check on the Annual Fee field ensures it is a value between $25.00 and $90.00.

CONSISTENCY CHECK   A **consistency check** tests the data in two or more associated fields to ensure that the relationship is logical and their data is in the correct format. For example, the value in a Date Joined field cannot occur earlier in time than a value in a Birth Date field.

COMPLETENESS CHECK   A **completeness check** verifies that a required field contains data. For example, some fields cannot be left blank; others require a minimum number of characters. One completeness check can ensure that data exists in a Last Name field. Another can ensure that a day, month, and year are included in a Birth Date field.

CHECK DIGIT   A **check digit** is a number(s) or character(s) that is appended to or inserted in a primary key value. A check digit often confirms the accuracy of a primary key value. Bank account, credit card, and other identification numbers often include one or more check digits.

A program determines the check digit by applying a formula to the numbers in the primary key value. An oversimplified illustration of a check digit formula is to add the numbers in the primary key. For example, if the primary key is 1367, this formula would add these numbers (1 + 3 + 6 + 7) for a sum of 17. Next, the formula would add the numbers in the result (1 + 7) to generate a check digit of 8. The primary key then is 13678. This example began with the original primary key value, 1367, then the check digit, 8, was appended.

When a data entry clerk enters the primary key of 13678, for example, to look up an existing record, the program determines whether the check digit is valid. If the clerk enters an incorrect primary key, such as 13778, the check digit entered (8) will not match the computed check digit (9). In this case, the program displays an error message that instructs the user to enter the primary key value again.

Test your knowledge of pages 332 through 340 in Quiz Yourself 9-1.

 QUIZ YOURSELF 9-1

Instructions: Find the true statement below. Then, rewrite the remaining false statements so they are true.

1. A database is a combination of one or more related characters or bytes and is the smallest unit of data a user accesses.

2. A record is a collection of data organized in a manner that allows access, retrieval, and use of that data.

3. Data is processed information.

4. Hierarchy of data procedures include adding records to, changing records in, and deleting records from a file.

5. To be valuable, information should be accurate, verifiable, timely, organized, accessible, useful, and cost-effective.

Quiz Yourself Online: To further check your knowledge of databases, qualities of valuable information, the hierarchy of data, and file maintenance techniques, visit scsite.com/dcf5e/ch9/quiz and then click Objectives 1 – 4.

FILE PROCESSING VERSUS DATABASES

Almost all application programs use the file processing approach, the database approach, or a combination of both approaches to store and manage data. The following pages discuss these two approaches.

File Processing Systems

In the past, many organizations exclusively used file processing systems to store and manage data. In a typical **file processing system**, each department or area within an organization has its own set of files. The records in one file may not relate to the records in any other file.

Companies have used file processing systems for many years. A lot of these systems, however, have two major weaknesses: they have redundant data and they isolate data.

- Data Redundancy — Each department or area in a company has its own files in a file processing system. Thus, the same fields are stored in multiple files. If a file processing system is used at the discount warehouse, for example, the Member file and the Member Purchases file store the same members' names and addresses.

   Duplicating data in this manner wastes resources such as storage space and people's time. When new members are added or member data is changed, file maintenance tasks consume additional time because people must update multiple files that contain the same data.

   Data redundancy also can increase the chance of errors. If a member changes his or her address, for example, the discount warehouse must update the address wherever it appears. In this example, the Address field is in the Member file and also in the Member Purchases file. If the Address field is not changed in all the files where it is stored, then discrepancies among the files exist.

- Isolated Data — Often it is difficult to access data stored in separate files in different departments. Sharing data from multiple, separate files is a complicated procedure and usually requires the experience of a computer programmer.

The Database Approach

When a company uses the **database approach**, many programs and users share the data in the database. A discount warehouse's database most likely contains data about members, membership plans, member purchases, and products. As shown in Figure 9-9, various areas within the discount warehouse share and interact with the data in this database. The database does secure its data, however, so that only authorized users can access certain data items. While a user is working with the database, the DBMS resides in the memory of the computer.

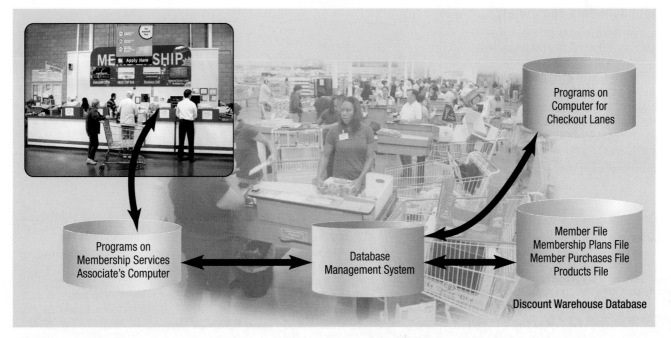

Programs on Computer for Checkout Lanes

Programs on Membership Services Associate's Computer

Database Management System

Member File
Membership Plans File
Member Purchases File
Products File

Discount Warehouse Database

FIGURE 9-9   In a discount warehouse that uses a database, the computer used by a membership services associate and the computer used in a checkout lane access data in a single database through the DBMS.

The database approach addresses many of the weaknesses associated with file processing systems. The following list presents some strengths of the database approach.

- Reduced Data Redundancy — Most data items are stored in only one file, which greatly reduces duplicate data. Figure 9-10 demonstrates the differences between how a database application and a file processing application might store data.
- Improved Data Integrity — When users modify data in the database, they make changes to one file instead of multiple files. Thus, the database approach increases the data's integrity by reducing the possibility of introducing inconsistencies.
- Shared Data — The data in a database environment belongs to and is shared, usually over a network, by the entire organization. Companies that use databases typically have security settings to define who can access, add, change, and delete the data in a database.
- Easier Access — The database approach allows nontechnical users to access and maintain data, providing they have the necessary privileges.
- Reduced Development Time — It often is easier and faster to develop programs that use the database approach.

Databases have many advantages as well as some disadvantages. A database can be more complex than a file processing system. People with special training usually develop larger databases and their associated applications. Databases also require more memory, storage, and processing power than file processing systems.

Data in a database can be more vulnerable than data in file processing systems. A database can store a lot of data in a single file. Many users and programs share and depend on this data. If the database is not operating properly or is damaged or destroyed, users may not be able to perform their jobs. Furthermore, unauthorized users potentially could gain access to a single database file that contains personal and confidential data. To protect their valuable database resource, individuals and companies should establish and follow security procedures. Despite these limitations, many business and home users work with databases because of their tremendous advantages.

FAQ 9-1

Can a database eliminate redundant data completely?

No, a database reduces redundant data — it does not eliminate it. Key fields link data together in a database. For example, a Student ID field will exist in any database file that requires access to student data. Thus, a Student ID is duplicated (exists in many database files) in the database. For more information, visit scsite.com/dcf5e/ch9/faq and then click Database Relationships.

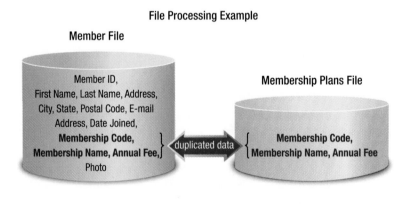

FIGURE 9-10 In the file processing environment, both files contain all three membership plans' data fields. In a database environment, only the Membership Plans file contains the Membership Name and Annual Fee fields. Other files, however, such as the Member file, contain the Membership Code, which links to the Membership Plans file when membership plans data is needed.

DATABASE MANAGEMENT SYSTEMS

WEB LINK 9-1

MySQL

For more information, visit scsite.com/dcf5e/ch9/weblink and then click MySQL.

As previously discussed, a database management system (DBMS), or database program, is software that allows you to create, access, and manage a database. DBMSs are available for many sizes and types of computers (Figure 9-11). Whether designed for a small or large computer, most DBMSs perform common functions. The following pages discuss functions common to most DBMSs.

POPULAR DATABASE MANAGEMENT SYSTEMS

Database	Manufacturer	Computer Type
Access	Microsoft Corporation	Personal computer, server, mobile devices
Adabas	Software AG	Server, mainframe
D³	Raining Data	Personal computer, server
DB2	IBM Corporation	Personal computer, server, mainframe
Essbase	Oracle Corporation	Personal computer, server, mobile devices
Informix	IBM Corporation	Personal computer, server, mainframe
Ingres	Ingres Corporation	Personal computer, server, mainframe
InterBase	Borland Software Corporation	Personal computer, server
ObjectStore	Progress Software Corporation	Personal computer, server
Oracle Database	Oracle Corporation	Personal computer, server, mainframe, mobile devices
SQL Server	Microsoft Corporation	Server, personal computer
Sybase	Sybase Inc.	Personal computer, server, mobile devices
Teradata Database	Teradata	Server
Versant	Versant Corporation	Personal computer, server

FIGURE 9-11 Many database management systems run on multiple types of computers.

FAQ 9-2

Which database vendors have the largest revenue market share?

As shown in the chart below, Oracle has the largest market share in terms of revenue, followed by IBM and Microsoft. For more information, visit scsite.com/dcf5e/ch9/faq and then click Database Market Share.

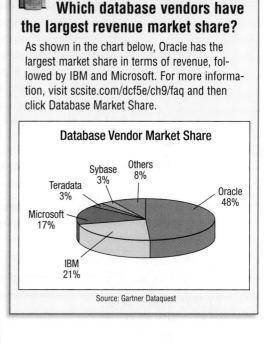

Database Vendor Market Share

Others 8%
Sybase 3%
Teradata 3%
Microsoft 17%
IBM 21%
Oracle 48%

Source: Gartner Dataquest

Data Dictionary

A **data dictionary** contains data about each file in the database and each field within those files. For each file, it stores details such as the file name, description, the file's relationship to other files, and the number of records in the file. For each field, it stores details such as the field name, description, field type, field size, default value, validation rules, and the field's relationship to other fields. Figure 9-12 shows how a data dictionary might list data for a Member file.

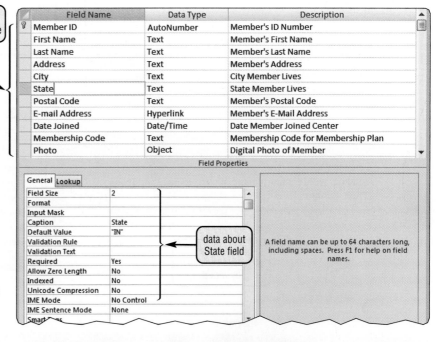

fields in Member file

Field Name	Data Type	Description
Member ID	AutoNumber	Member's ID Number
First Name	Text	Member's First Name
Last Name	Text	Member's Last Name
Address	Text	Member's Address
City	Text	City Member Lives
State	Text	State Member Lives
Postal Code	Text	Member's Postal Code
E-mail Address	Hyperlink	Member's E-Mail Address
Date Joined	Date/Time	Date Member Joined Center
Membership Code	Text	Membership Code for Membership Plan
Photo	Object	Digital Photo of Member

Field Properties

General | Lookup

Field Size	2
Format	
Input Mask	
Caption	State
Default Value	"IN"
Validation Rule	
Validation Text	
Required	Yes
Allow Zero Length	No
Indexed	No
Unicode Compression	No
IME Mode	No Control
IME Sentence Mode	None

data about State field

A field name can be up to 64 characters long, including spaces. Press F1 for help on field names.

FIGURE 9-12 A sample data dictionary entry shows the fields in the Member file and the properties of the State field.

File Retrieval and Maintenance

A DBMS provides several tools that allow users and programs to retrieve and maintain data in the database. To retrieve or select data in a database, you query it. A **query** is a request for specific data from the database. Users can instruct the DBMS to display, print, or store the results of a query. The capability of querying a database is one of the more powerful database features.

A DBMS offers several methods to retrieve and maintain its data. The four more commonly used are query languages, query by example, forms, and report generators. The following paragraphs describe each of these methods. Read Looking Ahead 9-1 for a look at a future use of queries.

QUERY LANGUAGE   A **query language** consists of simple, English-like statements that allow users to specify the data to display, print, or store. Users can retrieve actual data in a query or display the results of calculations performed on the data. Each query language has its own grammar and vocabulary. A person without a programming background usually can learn a query language in a short time.

To simplify the query process, many DBMSs provide wizards to guide users through the steps of creating a query. Figure 9-13 shows how to use the Simple Query Wizard in Microsoft Office Access 2007 to display the First Name, Last Name, and E-mail Address fields from the Member file. Instead of using the wizard, you could enter the query language statement shown in Figure 9-13 directly in the DBMS to display the results shown in Step 3.

FIGURE 9-13 HOW TO USE THE SIMPLE QUERY WIZARD

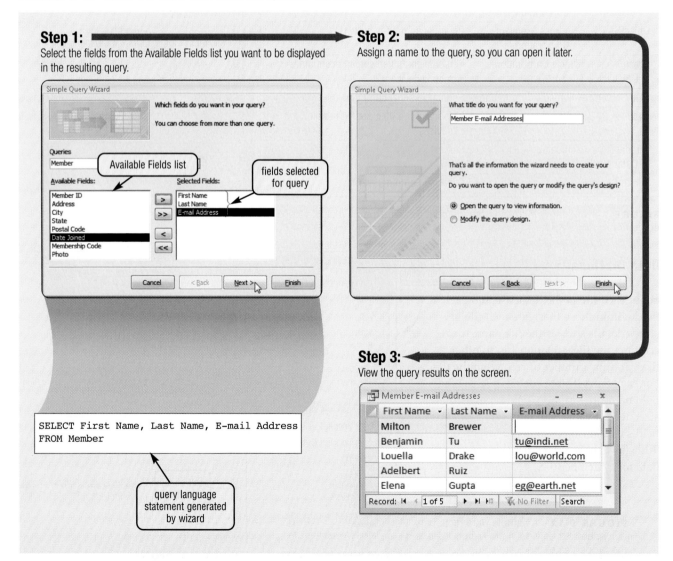

Archive an Entire Lifetime

Photo albums, memory boxes, and notebooks are relics of the past for Microsoft researcher Gordon Bell, and they may be for you, too. Bell is recording practically everything in his entire life and storing these memories in a searchable SQL Server-based database.

Bell's MyLifeBits project is composed of two parts: one that digitizes all aspects of his life experiences, such as telephone calls, faxes, photos, cards, and music files; the second that allows anyone to create a lifetime library on a home computer.

Bell's lifelog, or flog, is one of several storage systems being developed that document conversations, movements, and photos automatically. Telecommunications companies and university researchers are developing tools designed specifically for lifelogging, and many of the projects involve recording and then querying health-related data. Privacy experts are debating the legality of lifelogging in both public and private locations because people's conversations and photos could be recorded without their consent. For more information, visit scsite.com/dcf5e/ch9/looking and then click Lifelog.

QUERY BY EXAMPLE Most DBMSs include a **query by example** (**QBE**) feature that has a graphical user interface to assist users with retrieving data. Figure 9-14 shows a sample QBE screen for a query that searches for and lists members on the Basic Personal plan; that is, their Membership Code field value is equal to BP.

FIGURE 9-14a (all records in Member table)

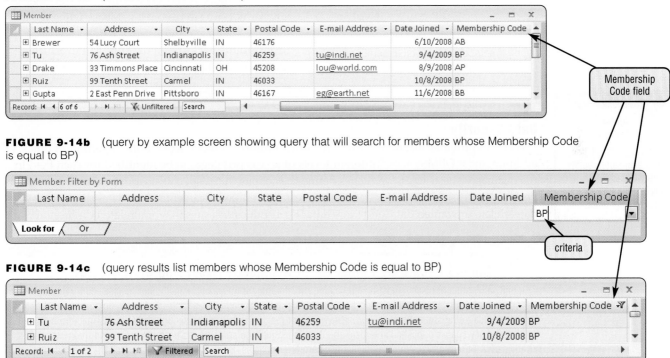

FIGURE 9-14b (query by example screen showing query that will search for members whose Membership Code is equal to BP)

FIGURE 9-14c (query results list members whose Membership Code is equal to BP)

FIGURE 9-14 Access has many QBE capabilities. One QBE technique is Filter by Form, which uses a form to show available fields. The database program retrieves records that match criteria you enter in the form fields. This example searches for members whose Membership Code is equal to BP.

FORM A **form**, sometimes called a data entry form, is a window on the screen that provides areas for entering or changing data in a database. You use forms (such as the Member Maintenance form in Figure 9-5 on page 337) to retrieve and maintain the data in a database.

To reduce data entry errors, well-designed forms should validate data as it is entered. When designing a form using a DBMS, you can make the form attractive and easy to use by incorporating color, shading, lines, boxes, and graphics; varying the fonts and font styles; and using other formatting features.

REPORT GENERATOR   A **report generator**, also called a report writer, allows users to design a report on the screen, retrieve data into the report design, and then display or print the report (Figure 9-15). Report generators usually allow you to format page numbers and dates; titles and column headings; subtotals and totals; and fonts, font sizes, color, and shading.

Member List by Membership Plan

Membership Name	Advantage Business				
	Last Name	First Name	Address	City	Date Joined
	Brewer	Milton	54 Lucy Court	Shelbyville	6/10/2008
Membership Name	Advantage Personal				
	Last Name	First Name	Address	City	Date Joined
	Drake	Louella	33 Timmons Place	Cincinnati	8/9/2008
Membership Name	Basic Business				
	Last Name	First Name	Address	City	Date Joined
	Gupta	Elena	2 East Penn Drive	Pittsboro	11/6/2008
Membership Name	Basic Personal				
	Last Name	First Name	Address	City	Date Joined
	Ruiz	Adelbert	99 Tenth Street	Carmel	10/8/2008
	Tu	Benjamin	76 Ash Street	Indianapolis	9/4/2009

FIGURE 9-15   This report, created in Access 2007, displays member information by the type of membership in which members are enrolled.

Backup and Recovery

Occasionally a database is damaged or destroyed because of hardware failure, a problem with the software, human error, or a catastrophe such as fire or flood. A DBMS provides a variety of techniques to restore the database to a usable form in case it is damaged or destroyed.

- A **backup**, or copy, of the entire database should be made on a regular basis. Some DBMSs have their own built-in backup utilities. Others require users to purchase a separate backup utility, or use one included with the operating system.
- More complex DBMSs maintain a **log**, which is a listing of activities that change the contents of the database.
- A DBMS that creates a log usually provides a recovery utility. A **recovery utility** uses the logs and/or backups to restore a database when it becomes damaged or destroyed.
- **Continuous backup** is a backup plan in which all data is backed up whenever a change is made.

Data Security

A DBMS provides means to ensure that only authorized users access data at permitted times. In addition, most DBMSs allow different levels of access privileges to be identified for each field in the database. These access privileges define the actions that a specific user or group of users can perform. Access privileges for data involve establishing who can enter new data, change existing data, delete unwanted data, and view data. Read Ethics & Issues 9-2 for a related discussion.

ETHICS & ISSUES 9-2

Should People Be Punished for Accidently Accessing Stolen Data?

A university student discovered a file containing private student information, including Social Security numbers and student grades, on a publicly accessible area of a university computer. Instead of notifying authorities, he took the file to the student newspaper in the hopes of making sure that the security breach was made public. After the newspaper published an article about the situation, the student was nearly expelled and the newspaper's adviser was fired for violating the university's computer policies. Some privacy advocates felt that the outcome was a case of shooting the messenger.

More and more often, institutions attempt to resolve security breaches as quietly as possible, fearing that publicity may cause financial loss and loss of public confidence, and may encourage hackers to target the institution. In some cases, an institution may file lawsuits against those who make security breaches public, including reporters. If you find a stolen or lost file that includes personal information, such as Social Security numbers, should you be required to report the incident to pertinent authorities? Why or why not? In the situation described above, should the student and newspaper be praised or punished for making the security breach public knowledge? Why? How would you handle such a situation? Why? Should institutions be required to disclose to the public all security breaches? Why or why not?

Test your knowledge of pages 340 through 346 in Quiz Yourself 9-2.

RELATIONAL, OBJECT-ORIENTED, AND MULTIDIMENSIONAL DATABASES

Every database and DBMS is based on a specific data model. A **data model** consists of rules and standards that define how the database organizes data. A data model defines how users view the organization of the data. It does not define how the operating system actually arranges the data on the disk.

Three popular data models in use today are relational, object-oriented, and multidimensional. A database typically is based on one data model. Some databases, however, combine features of the relational and object-oriented data models. The following sections discuss relational, object-oriented, and multidimensional databases.

FAQ 9-3

How big is the largest commercial database?

The world's largest commercial database stores more than 100 TB of data for Yahoo! Incorporated. This database uses Oracle database software and runs on a UNIX platform. For more information, visit scsite.com/dcf5e/ch9/faq and then click World's Largest Database.

Relational Databases

Today, a relational database is a widely used type of database. A **relational database** is a database that stores data in tables that consist of rows and columns. Each row has a primary key and each column has a unique name.

As discussed earlier in this chapter, a file processing environment uses the terms file, record, and field to represent data. A relational database uses terms different from a file processing system. A developer of a relational database refers to a file as a **relation**, a record as a **tuple**, and a field as an **attribute**. A user of a relational database, by contrast, refers to a file as a **table**, a record as a **row**, and a field as a **column**. Figure 9-16 summarizes this varied terminology.

DATA TERMINOLOGY

File Processing Environment	Relational Database Developer	Relational Database User
File	Relation	Table
Record	Tuple	Row
Field	Attribute	Column

FIGURE 9-16   In this data terminology table, the first column identifies the terms used in a file processing environment. The second column presents the terms used by developers of a relational database. The third column indicates terms to which the users of a relational database refer.

WEB LINK 9-4

Relational Databases

For more information, visit scsite.com/dcf5e/ch9/weblink and then click Relational Databases.

In addition to storing data, a relational database also stores data relationships. A **relationship** is a connection within the data. In a relational database, you can set up a relationship between tables at any time. The tables must have a common column (field). For example, you would relate the Member table and the Membership Plans table using the Membership Code column. Figure 9-17 illustrates these relational database concepts. In a relational database, the only data redundancy (duplication) exists in the common columns (fields). The database uses these common columns for relationships.

Many businesses use relational databases for payroll, accounts receivable, accounts payable, general ledger, inventory, order entry, invoicing, and other business-related functions.

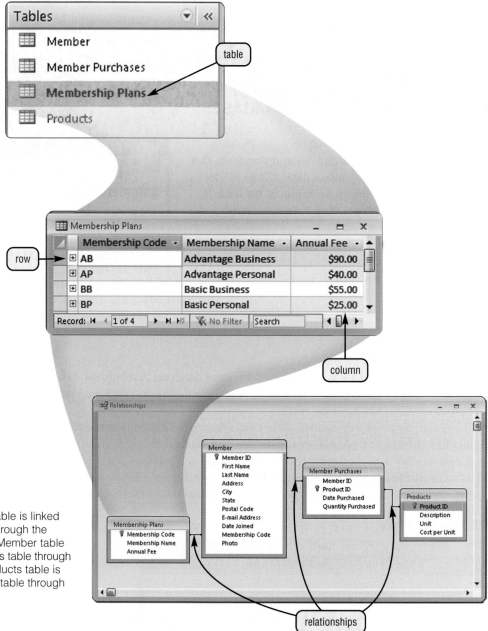

FIGURE 9-17 The Member table is linked to the Membership Plans table through the Membership Code column. The Member table is linked to the Member Purchases table through the Member ID column. The Products table is linked to the Member Purchases table through the Product ID column.

WEB LINK 9-5

SQL

For more information, visit scsite.com/dcf5e/ch9/weblink and then click SQL.

SQL   **Structured Query Language (SQL)** is a query language that allows users to manage, update, and retrieve data. SQL has special keywords and rules that users include in SQL statements. For example, the SQL statement in Figure 9-18a creates the results shown in Figure 9-18b.

Most relational database products for servers and mainframes include SQL. Many personal computer databases also include SQL.

FIGURE 9-18a   (SQL statement)

```
SELECT FIRST NAME, LAST NAME, ANNUAL FEE, ANNUAL FEE * .05
   AS EARLY PAY DISCOUNT
FROM MEMBER, MEMBERSHIP PLANS
WHERE MEMBER.MEMBERSHIP CODE =
   MEMBERSHIP PLANS.MEMBERSHIP CODE
ORDER BY LAST NAME
```

FIGURE 9-18b   (SQL statement results)

First Name ▾	Last Name ◂┤	Annual Fee ▾	EarlyPayDiscount ▾
Milton	Brewer	$90.00	$4.50
Louella	Drake	$40.00	$2.00
Elena	Gupta	$55.00	$2.75
Adelbert	Ruiz	$25.00	$1.25
Benjamin	Tu	$25.00	$1.25

FIGURE 9-18   A sample SQL statement and its results.

Object-Oriented Databases

An **object-oriented database** (OODB) stores data in objects. An **object** is an item that contains data, as well as the actions that read or process the data. A Member object, for example, might contain data about a member such as Member ID, First Name, Last Name, Address, and so on. It also could contain instructions about how to print the member record or the formula required to calculate a member's balance due.

Object-oriented databases have several advantages compared with relational databases: they can store more types of data, access this data faster, and allow programmers to reuse objects. An object-oriented database stores unstructured data more efficiently than a relational database. Unstructured data includes photos, video clips, audio clips, and documents. When users query an object-oriented database, the results often are displayed more quickly than the same query of a relational database. If an object already exists, programmers can reuse it instead of recreating a new object — saving on program development time.

OBJECT QUERY LANGUAGE   Object-oriented databases often use a query language called object query language (OQL) to manipulate and retrieve data. OQL is similar to SQL. OQL and SQL use many of the same rules, grammar, and keywords. Because OQL is a relatively new query language, not all object databases support it.

Multidimensional Databases

A **multidimensional database** stores data in dimensions. Whereas a relational database is a two-dimensional table, a multidimensional database can store more than two dimensions of data. These multiple dimensions allow users to access and analyze any view of the database data.

A Webmaster at a retailing business may want information about product sales and customer sales for each region spanning a given time. A manager at the same business may want information about product sales by department for each sales representative spanning a given time. A multidimensional database can consolidate this type of data from multiple dimensions at very high rates of speed. Nearly every multidimensional database has a dimension of time. The content of other dimensions varies depending on the subject.

No standard query language exists for multidimensional databases. Each database uses its own language. Most are similar to SQL.

DATA WAREHOUSES   One application that typically uses multidimensional databases is a data warehouse. A **data warehouse** is a huge database that stores and manages the data required to analyze historical and current transactions. Through a data warehouse, managers and other users access transactions and summaries of transactions quickly and efficiently. Some major credit card companies monitor and manage customers' credit card transactions using a data warehouse. Additionally, consumers can access their own transactions in the data warehouse via the Web. A data warehouse typically has a user-friendly interface, so that users easily can interact with its data.

A smaller version of a data warehouse is the data mart. A data mart contains a database that helps a specific group or department make decisions. Marketing and sales departments may have their own separate data marts. Individual groups or departments often extract data from the data warehouse to create their data marts.

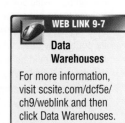

WEB DATABASES

One of the more profound features of the Web is the vast amount of information it provides. The Web offers information about jobs, travel destinations, television programming, pictures, movies, videos, local and national weather, sporting events, and legislative information. You can shop for just about any product or service, buy or sell stocks, search for a job, and make airline reservations. Much of this and other information on the Web exists in databases. Some Web databases are **collaborative databases**, where users store and share photos, videos, recordings, and other personal media with other registered users (Figure 9-19). Read Ethics & Issues 9-3 for a related discussion.

To access data in a Web database, you fill in a form or enter search text on a Web page. Many search engines such as Yahoo! use databases to store Web site descriptions. To access the database, you enter search text into the search engine. A Web database usually resides on a database server. A database server is a computer that stores and provides access to a database.

In addition to accessing information, users provide information to Web databases. Many Web sites request users to enter personal information, such as name, address, telephone number, and preferences, into an e-form (electronic form). The database then stores this personal information for future use. A company, for example, may send e-mail messages to certain groups of customers.

FIGURE 9-19 Media sharing Web sites store users' digital videos, photos, and other media in a collaborative database, the contents of which are shared with other registered users.

ETHICS & ISSUES 9-3

Who Should Be Held Accountable for the Rash of Database Security Breaches?

Over the course of three years, a privacy advocacy group documented the fact that more than 160 million records that contain personal information were accessed illegally or stolen. The records were allowed to be accessed because of carelessness by government agencies, educational institutions, and corporations. Information such as credit card numbers, credit history, and employment information often are involved in such security breaches. In one case, a company determined that a particular data breach cost the company more than $168 million. Institutions typically have their own set of guidelines to manage the security of such information, yet the number of security breaches is escalating. While some have proposed laws requiring stricter controls for how institutions handle private data and provide for harsher penalties for those not properly securing data, corporations resist such efforts. They claim that the costs involved in such measures would hurt their capability of competing with corporations in other states and countries that are not bound by the same rules. Many institutions voluntarily notify individuals whose information was breached, and some even compensate victims; for example, some provide credit monitoring for free. Who should be held accountable for the rash of database security breaches? Why? Should the government enact stronger laws regarding data security? Why or why not? Should institutions be required to notify individuals whose data has been breached, and if so, should they be required to compensate the victims? Why or why not?

DATABASE ADMINISTRATION

WEB LINK 9-8

Database Design Guidelines

For more information, visit scsite.com/dcf5e/ch9/weblink and then click Database Design Guidelines.

Managing a company's database requires a great deal of coordination. The role of coordinating the use of the database belongs to the database analysts and administrators. To carry out their responsibilities, these IT (information technology) professionals follow database design guidelines and need cooperation from all database users.

Database Design Guidelines

A carefully designed database makes it easier for a user to query the database, modify the data, and create reports. The guidelines shown in Figure 9-20 apply to databases of all sizes.

Role of the Database Analysts and Administrators

The database analysts and administrators are responsible for managing and coordinating all database activities. The **database analyst (DA)** decides on the proper placement of fields, defines the relationships among data, and identifies users' access privileges. The **database administrator (DBA)** requires a more technical inside view of the data. The DBA creates and maintains the data dictionary, manages security of the database, monitors the performance of the database, and checks backup and recovery procedures.

In small companies, one person often is both the DA and DBA. In larger companies, the responsibilities of the DA and DBA are split among two or more people.

Role of the Employee as a User

Employees should learn how to use the data in the database effectively. The amount of information available often amazes first-time database users. Instant access to information helps employees perform their jobs more effectively. Today, employees access databases from their office desktop computers, notebook computers, or even smart phones and other mobile devices (Figure 9-21).

The maintenance of a database is an ongoing task that companies measure constantly against their overall goals.

DATABASE DESIGN GUIDELINES

1. Determine the purpose of the database.
2. Design the tables or files.
   - Design tables or files on paper first.
   - Each table or file should contain data about one subject. The Member table, for example, contains data about members.
3. Design the records and fields for each table or file.
   - Be sure every record has a unique primary key.
   - Use separate fields for logically distinct items. For example, a name could be stored in six fields: Title (Mr., Mrs., Dr., etc.), First Name, Middle Name, Last Name, Suffix (Jr., Sr., etc.), and Nickname.
   - Do not create fields for information that can be derived from entries in other fields. For example, do not include a field for Age. Instead, store the birthdate and compute the age.
   - Allow enough space for each field.
   - Set default values for frequently entered data.
4. Determine the relationships among the tables or files.

FIGURE 9-20   Guidelines for developing a database.

FIGURE 9-21   This grocery store employee scans the labels before placing the products on the shelf, so that the inventory accurately reflects product availability.

Test your knowledge of pages 347 through 351 in Quiz Yourself 9-3.

 QUIZ YOURSELF 9-3

Instructions: Find the true statement below. Then, rewrite the remaining false statements so they are true.

1. Object-oriented databases store data in tables.

2. Relational database users refer to a file as a table, a field as a column, and a record as a row.

3. SQL is a data modeling language that allows users to manage, update, and retrieve data.

4. The database analyst requires a more technical inside view of the data than does the database administrator.

Quiz Yourself Online: To further check your knowledge of relational, object-oriented, and multidimensional databases; Web databases; and database administration, visit scsite.com/dcf5e/ch9/quiz and then click Objectives 7 – 9.

CHAPTER SUMMARY

This chapter discussed how data and information are valuable assets to an organization. The chapter also presented methods for maintaining high-quality data and assessing the quality of valuable information. It then discussed the advantages of organizing data in a database and described various types of databases (read Looking Ahead 9-2 for a look at a future use of databases). It also presented the roles of the database analysts and administrators.

 LOOKING AHEAD 9-2

Barcodes Identify World's Animal, Plant Species

Only a few of the 3,500 species of mosquitoes transmit infections such as malaria, dengue fever, and the West Nile virus, so scientists need an easy method of distinguishing the harmful and harmless species. A short DNA sequence, called the barcode of life, can speed identification of known organisms and facilitate recognizing new species.

The Consortium for the Barcode of Life is attempting to build a public database composed of the barcodes of the earth's 1.8 million known animal and plant species. This group of scientists from nearly 50 nations can identify one species in a few hours, and they have logged about 30,000 species since the Consortium's beginnings in 2004.

Along with identifying infection-carrying mosquitoes, the DNA database will be useful to locate the birds that are prone to striking aircraft so that pilots can avoid flying into their paths. In addition the database will help farmers locate and then control fruit flies. For more information, visit scsite.com/dcf5e/ch9/looking and then click DNA Barcode.

CAREER CORNER   Database Administrator

Most businesses and organizations are built around databases. Access to timely, accurate, and relevant information is a company's lifeline. A database administrator (DBA) creates, applies, supports, and administers the policies and procedures for maintaining a company's database. Database administrators construct logical and physical descriptions of the database, establish database parameters, develop data models characterizing data elements, ensure database integrity, and coordinate database security measures including developing and implementing disaster recovery and archiving procedures. They also use query languages to obtain reports of the information in the database. With the large amounts of sensitive data generated, data integrity, backup, and security have become increasingly important aspects of the administrator's responsibilities.

Administering a database requires a great deal of mental work and the ability to focus on finite details. Database administrators must be able to read and comprehend business-related information, organize data in a logical manner, apply general rules to specific problems, identify business principles and practices, and communicate clearly with database users. Being proficient with a particular database such as Oracle, Informix, Sybase, or SQL Server is an added advantage. The real key, however, is learning, understanding, and becoming an expert in database design.

Database administrators usually have a bachelor's or associate's degree and experience with computer programming, relational databases, query languages, and online analytical processing. Typical salaries for database administrators are between $75,000 and $97,000, depending on experience. For more information, visit scsite.com/dcf5e/ch9/careers and then click Database Administrator.

Oracle
Database Software Developer

More than half of the FORTUNE 100 companies use an Oracle product as their primary database, but Oracle's quest, according to CEO Larry Ellison, is to have its customers convert all their database applications to Oracle's software.

Ellison and two partners founded the company in 1977 with the intent of developing a commercially viable relational database. When their Oracle database was released, it was an immediate success and changed the way companies stored and managed information. For the first time, separate data tables could be connected by a common field.

The company is the world's second largest independent software company behind Microsoft. Its 10 actual or proposed acquisitions in 2007 strengthened the company's domination of the database community. For more information, visit scsite.com/dcf5e/ch9/companies and then click Oracle.

Sybase
Managing Data for the Unwired Enterprise

Researchers at the University of California, Berkeley, estimate that 95 percent of the data produced by major corporations never is used after it is stored in a database because it is disorganized and inaccessible.

Sybase helps companies unlock and use this data whenever and wherever needed through its unwired enterprise. This data access solution helps mobile database users tap into corporate networks, often wirelessly. The company focuses especially on Enterprise Portal (EP) solutions, which convert stored data into information that can be used by customers, partners, and suppliers.

For more than 20 years, Sybase has produced software that links platforms, servers, databases, applications, and mobile devices. The company's unique employee perks helped earn it a place on the list of Canada's Top 100 Employers in 2007. For more information, visit scsite.com/dcf5e/ch9/companies and then click Sybase.

TECHNOLOGY TRAILBLAZERS

E. F. Codd
Relational Database Model Inventor

The majority of large and small databases are structured on the relational model, which is considered one of the greatest technological inventions of the 20th Century. E. F. Codd single-handedly is credited with developing and promoting that model in a series of research papers beginning with his 1969 IBM Research Report, "Derivability, Redundancy, and Consistency of Relations Stored in Large Data Banks."

Edgar F. Codd began his career in 1949 when he joined IBM as a programming mathematician after graduating from Oxford University. Throughout the 1950s he helped develop several IBM computers and then turned his attention to database management. Among his achievements is earning the prestigious A. M. Turing Award, which is the Association for Computing Machinery's highest technical achievement honor given to an individual, for his relational database theory. For more information, visit scsite.com/dcf5e/ch9/people and then click E. F. Codd.

Larry Ellison
Oracle CEO

On a visit to Kyoto, Japan, Larry Ellison became intrigued with the country's culture and the citizens' combination of confidence and humility. He says he applies these philosophical principles to his work at Oracle, where he serves as CEO.

As a young man, Ellison was interested in science and mathematics. He was inspired by E. F. Codd's relational database model and founded Oracle in 1977 under the name Software Development Laboratories with a $1,200 investment.

Under Ellison's leadership, the company doubled its sales in 11 of its first 12 years. He is known for his uncanny ability to motivate his employees and business partners toward a common goal. He predicted in 2007 that Oracle would have the best Red Hat Linux support in the world. For more information, visit scsite.com/dcf5e/ch9/people and then click Larry Ellison.

Chapter Review

The Chapter Review section summarizes the concepts presented in this chapter. To obtain help from other students regarding any subject in this chapter, visit scsite.com/dcf5e/ch9/forum and post your thoughts or questions.

(1) What Is a Database?

A **database** is a collection of data organized in a manner that allows access, retrieval, and use of that data. **Database software**, often called a **database management system (DBMS)**, allows users to create a computerized database; add, change, and delete the data; sort and retrieve the data; and create forms and reports from the data.

(2) What Are the Qualities of Valuable Information?

Data is a collection of unprocessed items, which can include text, numbers, images, audio, and video. **Information** is processed data; that is, it is organized, meaningful, and useful. For information to be valuable, it should be accurate, verifiable, timely, organized, accessible, useful, and cost-effective.

(3) What Is Meant by Character, Field, Record, and File?

Data is classified in a hierarchy, with each level of data consisting of one or more items from the lower level. A bit is the smallest unit of data a computer can process. Eight bits grouped together in a unit form a byte, and each byte represents a single **character**. A **field** is a combination of one or more related characters and is the smallest unit of data a user accesses. A **record** is a group of related fields. A **data file** is a collection of related records stored on a storage medium.

(4) How Are Files Maintained?

File maintenance refers to the procedures that keep data current. File maintenance procedures include adding records when new data is obtained, changing records to correct inaccurate data or to update old data with new data, and deleting records when they no longer are needed. **Validation** is the process of comparing data with a set of rules or values to find out if the data is correct. Many programs perform a validity check that analyzes entered data to help ensure that it is correct. Types of validity checks include an **alphabetic check**, a **numeric check**, a **range check**, a **consistency check**, a **completeness check**, and a **check digit**.

Visit scsite.com/dcf5e/ch9/quiz or click the Quiz Yourself button. Click Objectives 1 – 4.

(5) How Is a File Processing System Approach Different from a Database Approach?

In a **file processing system**, each department or area within an organization has its own set of data files. Two major weaknesses of file processing systems are redundant data (duplicated data) and isolated data. With a **database approach**, many programs and users share the data in a database. The database approach reduces data redundancy, improves data integrity, shares data, permits easier access, and reduces development time. A database, however, can be more complex than a file processing system, requiring special training and more computer memory, storage, and processing power. Data in a database also can be more vulnerable than data in file processing systems.

(6) What Functions Are Common to Most DBMSs?

With a DBMS, users can create and manipulate a computerized database. Most DBMSs perform common functions. A **data dictionary** contains data about each file in the database and each field within those files. A DBMS offers several methods to maintain and retrieve data, such as query languages, query by example, forms, and report generators. A **query language** consists of simple, English-like statements that allow users to specify the data to display, print, or store. **Query by example (QBE)** has a graphical user interface that assists users with retrieving data. A **form** is a window on the screen that provides areas for entering or changing data. A **report generator** allows users to design a report on the screen, retrieve data into the report design, and then display or print the report. If a database is damaged or destroyed, a DBMS provides techniques to return the database to a usable form. A **backup** is a copy of the database. A **log** is a listing of activities that change the contents of the database. A **recovery utility** uses the logs and/or backups to restore the database. **Continuous backup** is a backup plan in which all data is backed up whenever a change is made. To supply security, most DBMSs can identify different levels of access privileges that define the actions a specific user or group of users can perform for each field in a database.

Visit scsite.com/dcf5e/ch9/quiz or click the Quiz Yourself button. Click Objectives 5 – 6.

Chapter Review

 7 **What Are Characteristics of Relational, Object-Oriented, and Multidimensional Databases?**

A **data model** consists of rules and standards that define how the database organizes data. Three popular data models are relational, object-oriented, and multidimensional. A **relational database** stores data in tables that consist of rows and columns. A relational database developer refers to a file as a **relation**, a record as a **tuple**, and a field as an **attribute**. A relational database user refers to a file as a **table**, a record as a **row**, and a field as a **column**. A **relationship** is a connection within the data in a relational database. **Structured Query Language** (**SQL**) allows users to manage, update, and retrieve data. An **object-oriented database** (**OODB**) stores data in objects. An **object** is an item that contains data, as well as the actions that read or process the data. Object-oriented databases often use an object query language (OQL) to manipulate and retrieve data. A **multidimensional database** stores data in dimensions. These multiple dimensions allow users to access and analyze any view of the database data. One application that uses multidimensional databases is a **data warehouse**, which is a huge database system that stores and manages the data required to analyze historical and current transactions. No standard query language exists for multidimensional databases. A smaller version of a data warehouse is the data mart.

8 **How Do Web Databases Work?**

A Web database links to a form on a Web page. To access data in a Web database, you fill in the form or enter search text on a Web page. A Web database usually resides on a database server, which is a computer that stores and provides access to a database.

9 **What Are the Responsibilities of Database Analysts and Administrators?**

A **database analyst** (**DA**) focuses on the meaning and usage of data. The DA decides on the placement of fields, defines the relationships among data, and identifies users' access privileges. A **database administrator** (**DBA**) requires a more technical inside view of the data. The DBA creates and maintains the data dictionary, manages database security, monitors database performance, and checks backup and recovery procedures. In small companies, one person often is both the DA and DBA.

 Visit scsite.com/dcf5e/ch9/quiz or click the Quiz Yourself button. Click Objectives 7 – 9.

Key Terms

You should know each key term. Use the list below to help focus your study. To further enhance your understanding of the Key Terms in this chapter, visit scsite.com/dcf5e/ch9/terms. See an example of and a definition for each term, and access current and additional information about the term from the Web.

alphabetic check (339)
attribute (347)
backup (346)
character (335)
check digit (340)
collaborative databases (350)
column (347)
completeness check (340)
consistency check (340)
continuous backup (346)
data (332)
data dictionary (343)
data file (336)
data model (347)
data type (335)

data warehouse (349)
database (332)
database administrator (DBA) (351)
database analyst (DA) (351)
database approach (341)
database management system (DBMS) (332)
database software (332)
field (335)
field name (335)
field size (335)
file maintenance (336)
file processing system (341)

form (345)
garbage in, garbage out (GIGO) (333)
information (332)
key field (336)
log (346)
multidimensional database (349)
numeric check (339)
object (349)
object-oriented database (OODB) (349)
primary key (336)
query (344)
query by example (QBE) (345)

query language (344)
range check (340)
record (336)
recovery utility (346)
relation (347)
relational database (347)
relationship (348)
report generator (346)
row (347)
Structured Query Language (SQL) (348)
table (347)
tuple (347)
validation (339)

Checkpoint

Use the Checkpoint exercises to check your knowledge level of the chapter. To complete the Checkpoint exercises interactively, visit scsite.com/dcf5e/ch9/check.

_____ 1. Information is organized, meaningful, and useful data. (332)

_____ 2. A database management system allows users to create forms and reports from the data in the database. (332)

_____ 3. A data file is a group of related fields. (336)

_____ 4. A check digit often confirms the accuracy of a primary key value. (340)

_____ 5. To retrieve or select data in a database, you create a backup. (344)

_____ 6. A query language consists of simple, English-like statements that allow users to specify the data to display, print, or store. (344)

_____ 7. A recovery utility uses the logs and/or backups to back up a database when it becomes damaged or destroyed. (346)

_____ 8. A multidimensional database is a database that stores data in tables that consist of rows and columns. (347)

_____ 9. A relationship is a connection within the data in a database. (348)

_____ 10. In small companies, the responsibilities of the DA and DBA are split among two or more people. (351)

Multiple Choice   Select the best answer. (See page numbers in parentheses.)

1. A _____ is a field that uniquely identifies each record in a file. (336)
   a. data type
   b. data file
   c. primary key
   d. data character

2. _____ procedures include adding records to, changing records in, and deleting records from a file. (336)
   a. File maintenance
   b. Range check
   c. Backup
   d. Validation

3. A _____ ensures that users enter only numeric data into a field. (339)
   a. range check
   b. completeness check
   c. numeric check
   d. consistency check

4. A _____ verifies that a required field contains data. (340)
   a. completeness check
   b. range check
   c. consistency check
   d. numeric check

5. When a company uses _____, many programs and users share the data in the database. (341)
   a. the database approach
   b. a file processing system
   c. a data model
   d. a check digit

6. All of the following are strengths of the database approach, except _____. (342)
   a. less complexity
   b. improved data integrity
   c. reduced development time
   d. easier access

7. A _____ is a window on the screen that provides areas for entering or changing data in a database. (345)
   a. field
   b. form
   c. report
   d. query

8. The database analyst (DA) _____. (351)
   a. monitors the performance of the database
   b. creates and maintains the data dictionary
   c. decides on the proper placement of fields
   d. checks backup and recovery procedures

Matching   Match the terms with their definitions. (See page numbers in parentheses.)

_____ 1. field name (335)

_____ 2. field size (335)

_____ 3. query by example (QBE) (345)

_____ 4. continuous backup (346)

_____ 5. database administrator (351)

a. DBMS feature that has a graphical user interface to assist users with retrieving data

b. creates and maintains the data dictionary, manages security of the database, monitors the performance of the database, and checks backup and recovery procedures

c. item that contains data and the actions that read or process the data

d. backup plan in which all data is backed up whenever a change is made

e. uniquely identifies each field

f. defines the maximum number of characters a field can contain

Checkpoint

Short Answer

Write a brief answer to each of the following questions.

1. What is data integrity and why is it important? _____ What does the computer phrase, garbage in, garbage out (GIGO), mean? _____

2. What is validation? _____ What are five types of validity checks? _____

3. Why is data redundancy a weakness of file processing systems? _____ Why is isolated data a weakness of file processing systems? _____

4. What is the database approach? _____ Describe five strengths of the database approach. _____

5. Describe multidimensional databases and their uses. _____ What is a data warehouse and how is it used? _____

Working Together

Working in a group of your classmates, complete the following team exercise.

1. Most libraries use databases to keep track of their collections. Each member of your team should visit a library that uses a database. Interview a librarian to find out more about the database. How many items are represented? What information does the database contain? How is the database searched? How frequently is it updated? Meet with the members of your team to discuss the results of your interviews. Create a group presentation and share your findings with the class.

Web Research

Use the Internet-based Web Research exercises to broaden your understanding of the concepts presented in this chapter. To discuss any of the Web Research exercises in this chapter with other students, post your thoughts or questions at scsite.com/dcf5e/ch9/forum.

① Blogs

Scripting News is the longest-running blog on the Internet. Dave Winer developed this Web site in 1997 before the term "Weblog" had been coined, and he continues to post to his blog on a regular basis. Visit the Scripting News blog (scripting.com) and read Winer's biographical information on the home page. What technological breakthroughs did he develop? What are his employment and educational backgrounds? What are the three most recent topics discussed? Click two links listed in the "Things to revisit" column and summarize Winer's viewpoints. What podcasts are listed in the Morning Coffee Notes? Click the Archive link at the top of the page and then click the year and month four years ago from today. What topics were posted at that time?

② Scavenger Hunt

Use one of the search engines listed in Figure 2-8 in Chapter 2 on page 58 or your own favorite search engine to find the answers to the following questions. Copy and paste the Web address from the Web page where you found the answer. Some questions may have more than one answer. If required, submit your answers to your instructor. (1) Who is Charles Bachman? What is the name of the database system he helped to create? (2) What geographic information system (GIS) functions does ArcExplorer perform? (3) What are the ACID rules?

③ Search Sleuth

Major United States newspapers helped design Clusty the Clustering Engine (clusty.com). One of its unique features is returning search results for Web sites, news stories, images, and shopping sites in clusters, which are categories of folders, along with a list of links. Visit this Web site and then use your word processing program to answer the following questions. Then, if required, submit your answers to your instructor. (1) Click the About link at the bottom of the page and then click the What's New? link. What are three stories featured in the What's New? section? (2) Click your browser's Back button or press the BACKSPACE key to return to the Clusty home page. Type Structured Query Language in the box and then click the Search button. Review the listing of clusters on the left side of the page and then click the Tutorial link. Select one of the links and view the tutorial. (3) Click the News link at the top of the page and then click the Tech link. What are two stories listed for today? Write a 50-word summary of your findings.

Learn How To

Use the Learn How To activities to learn fundamental skills when using a computer and accompanying technology. Complete the exercises and submit them to your instructor. Premium Activity: The icon indicates you can see a visual demonstration of the associated Learn How To activity by visiting scsite.com/dcf5e/ch9/howto.

LEARN HOW TO 1: Organize and Manage Files on a Computer

Introduction In Learn How To 1 in Chapter 3 (page 130), you learned the procedure for saving a file. In this Learn How To activity, you will learn how to manage files using folders and how to find a file if you cannot remember where you saved it.

Folders A folder is a virtual container where you can store a file on media. When you store any file, the file must be stored in a folder. The folder symbol, together with the folder name, identifies a folder.

You can create folders in a variety of ways. To create a folder on the desktop, complete the following steps:
1. Right-click the desktop in a location that does not contain an icon or toolbar.
2. Point to New on the shortcut menu that is displayed (Figure 9-22).
3. Click Folder on the New submenu.
4. When the folder icon is displayed on the desktop, type the name you want to assign to the folder and then press the ENTER key. You should choose a name that identifies the contents of the folder.

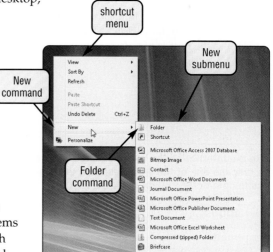

FIGURE 9-22

A folder can contain other folders. This allows you to organize your files in a hierarchical manner so that the highest-level folder contains all the folders for a given subject, and lower-level folders contain more specific files and folders. For example, your highest-level folder could be named Fall Semester. For each class, such as Computer Information Systems 110, you could define a folder within the Fall Semester folder. Within each class folder, you could define folders for each week of the class, or for each project or assignment within the class. In this manner, you would have a set of folders, each designated for a specific use. You then would save your files in the appropriate folder.

To create a folder within a folder, complete the following steps:
1. Double-click the folder name either on the desktop or in the window or dialog box in which the folder name appears.
2. Right-click a blank space in the window that is displayed.
3. Point to New on the shortcut menu that is displayed and then click Folder on the New submenu.
4. When the folder icon is displayed, type the name you want to assign to the folder, and then press the ENTER key.

To delete a folder, complete the following steps:
1. Right-click the folder.
2. On the shortcut menu that is displayed (Figure 9-23), click Delete.
3. In the Delete Folder dialog box, click the Yes button.

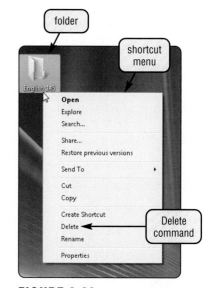

FIGURE 9-23

When you delete a folder, all the files and folders contained in the folder you are deleting, together with all files and folders on the lower hierarchical levels, are deleted. If you accidentally delete a folder, complete the following steps:
1. Double-click the Recycle Bin icon on the desktop.
2. In the Recycle Bin window, select the folder you wish to restore.
3. Click the 'Restore this item' button.

Using folders effectively will aid you in keeping track of files you create for your classes.

Exercise

1. Assume you are taking the following courses: Computer Information Systems 120, History 210, English 145, Marketing 221, and Business Law 120. Define the hierarchy of folders you would create for these classes. In which folder would you store an assignment from English 145 that was assigned in the sixth week of class? Submit your answers to your instructor.

LEARN HOW TO 2: Search for Files and Folders

At times, you might store a file in a folder and then forget where you stored the file. The Search feature of Windows Vista enables you to search storage media on a computer to find the file. To use the Search feature, complete the following steps:

1. Click the Start button on the Windows taskbar.
2. Click Search on the Start menu.
3. If necessary, click the All filter button.
4. In the Search box, type the name of the file for which you are searching. If you do not know the entire file name, enter as much of the file name as you can remember. If you do not know any portion of the file name, click the Advanced Search button to help narrow the search.
5. If you are performing an Advanced Search, click the Search button to begin the search. Otherwise, Windows will search as you type your search criteria into the Search box (Figure 9-24).
6. All items containing the file name or partial file name will be displayed in the Search Results in Indexed Locations window. If the file was not found, a message to that effect is displayed.
7. Double-click the file name in the list to open the file with the appropriate program.
8. Before you close the Search Results in Indexed Locations window, make a note of the location of the file. If this is not the location where you want the file to be stored, store the file in the correct location.

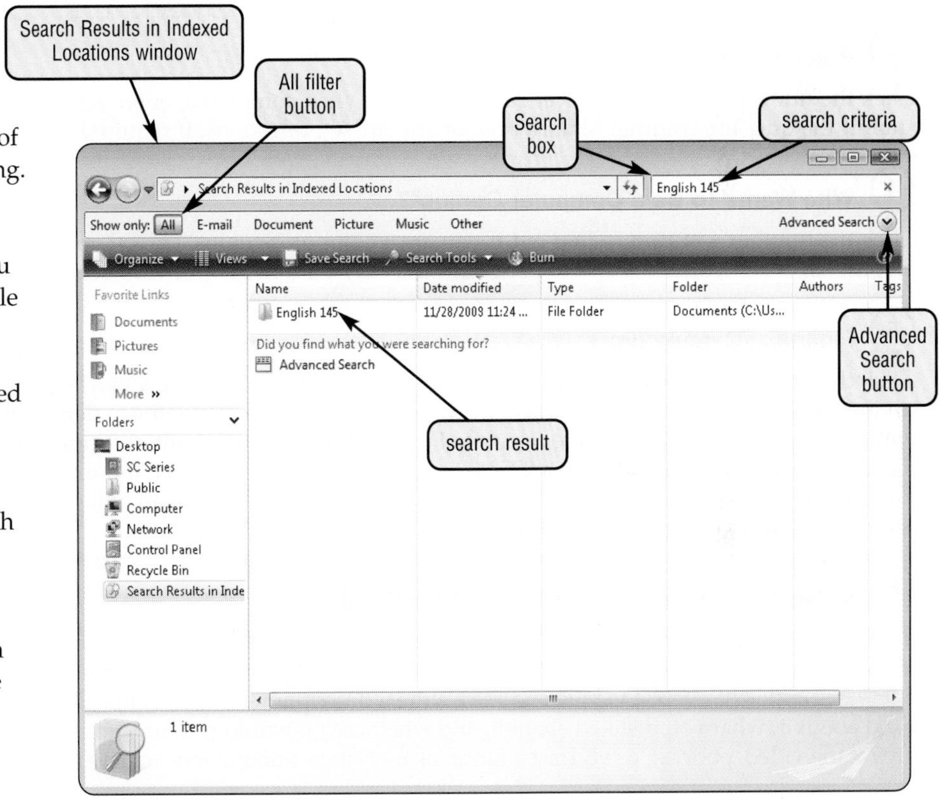

FIGURE 9-24

Exercise

1. Using the Windows Vista Search feature, locate the file named Green Sea Turtle. How many file names were displayed? Which folder contains the Green Sea Turtle file? Submit your answers to your instructor.
2. On the computer you are using, create a hierarchy of folders for your classes. Create a WordPad file that contains the following text: This file will be found using the Search feature. Save the file in one of the folders using a file name of your choice. Using the Search feature, search for the file you just created. How many files were displayed from your search? Delete all folders and files you created in this exercise. Write a paragraph describing the steps you will take to organize your files for the coming semester. Submit your responses to your instructor.

Learn It Online

Use the Learn It Online exercises to reinforce your understanding of the chapter concepts. To access the Learn It Online exercises, visit scsite.com/dcf5e/ch9/learn.

(1) At the Movies — How a Photo Sharing Site Keeps Its Data

To view the How a Photo Sharing Site Keeps Its Data movie, click the number 1 button. Locate your video and click the corresponding High-Speed or Dial-Up link, depending on your Internet connection. Watch the movie to learn about Equinix, the data storage site for Smugmug.com, and learn how photos are uploaded and shared on the Web. Then, complete the exercise by answering the question that follows. How does the photo sharing community Smugmug.com store and allow users to share photos?

(2) Student Edition Labs — Advanced Spreadsheets

Click the number 2 button. A new browser window will open, displaying the Student Edition Labs. Follow the on-screen instructions to complete the Advanced Spreadsheets Lab. When finished, click the Exit button. If required, submit your results to your instructor.

(3) Practice Test

Click the number 3 button. Answer each question. When completed, enter your name and click the Grade Test button to submit the quiz for grading. Make a note of any missed questions. If required, submit your results to your instructor.

(4) Who Wants To Be a Computer Genius^2?

Click the number 4 button to find out if you are a computer genius. Directions about how to play the game will be displayed. When you are ready to play, click the Play button. Submit your score to your instructor.

(5) Financial Calculators

Click the number 5 button to learn how to use the Internet to calculate a mortgage payment, a car payment, or retirement savings. Follow the instructions to use USA Today's Mortgage calculator to determine what your monthly payment would be on a $150,000 mortgage calculated over 30 years using an interest rate of 6.5%. Use the Autos calculator to figure your monthly payment on a $25,000 auto loan calculated over 60 months using an interest rate of 8.0%. Use the Retirement calculator to determine what type of retirement savings plan will provide you with the most income. Submit each calculation to your instructor.

(6) Video and Audio: You Review It — Web Databases

In this chapter you learned about Web databases. Click the number 6 button to view the suggested links and begin your search for videos, podcasts, or vodcasts related to Web databases. Choose a video, podcast, or vodcast that discusses Web databases and is of interest to you, and then write a description of its contents. Explain why you chose this piece, what you liked about it, what you disliked about it, and whether you would recommend it to a fellow student. Finish your review by giving the video, podcast, or vodcast a rating of 1 – 5 stars. Submit your review in the format requested by your instructor.

(7) Crossword Puzzle Challenge

Click the number 7 button, then click the Crossword Puzzle Challenge link. Directions about how to play the game will be displayed. Complete the puzzle to reinforce skills you learned in this chapter. When you are ready to play, click the Continue button. Submit the completed puzzle to your instructor.

(8) Vista Exercises

Click the number 8 button. When the Vista Exercises menu appears, click the exercise assigned by your instructor. A new browser window will open. Follow the on-screen instructions to complete the exercise. When finished, click the Exit button. If required, submit your results to your instructor.

CHAPTER 10

Computer Security, Ethics, and Privacy

OBJECTIVES

After completing this chapter, you will be able to:

1. Identify ways to safeguard against computer viruses, worms, Trojan horses, botnets, denial of service attacks, back doors, and spoofing
2. Discuss techniques to prevent unauthorized computer access and use
3. Identify safeguards against hardware theft and vandalism
4. Explain the ways to protect against software theft and information theft
5. Discuss the types of devices available that protect computers from system failure
6. Identify risks and safeguards associated with wireless communications
7. Discuss issues surrounding information privacy
8. Discuss ways to prevent health-related disorders and injuries due to computer use

CONTENTS

COMPUTER SECURITY RISKS

Today, people rely on computers to create, store, and manage critical information. Thus, it is crucial that users take measures to protect their computers and data from loss, damage, and misuse.

A **computer security risk** is any event or action that could cause a loss of or damage to computer hardware, software, data, information, or processing capability. Some breaches to computer security are accidental. Others are planned intrusions. Some intruders do no damage; they merely access data, information, or programs on the computer. Other intruders indicate some evidence of their presence either by leaving a message or by deliberately altering or damaging data.

An intentional breach of computer security often involves a deliberate act that is against the law. Any illegal act involving a computer generally is referred to as a **computer crime**. The term **cybercrime** refers to online or Internet-based illegal acts. Today, cybercrime is one of the FBI's top three priorities.

Perpetrators of cybercrime and other intrusions fall into seven basic categories: hacker, cracker, script kiddie, corporate spy, unethical employee, cyberextortionist, and cyberterrorist.

Internet and network attacks

VIRUS ATTACK

system failure

LIGHTNING STRIKE

- The term **hacker**, although originally a complimentary word for a computer enthusiast, now has a derogatory meaning and refers to someone who accesses a computer or network illegally. Some hackers claim the intent of their security breaches is to improve security.
- A **cracker** also is someone who accesses a computer or network illegally but has the intent of destroying data, stealing information, or other malicious action. Both hackers and crackers have advanced computer and network skills.
- A **script kiddie** has the same intent as a cracker but does not have the technical skills and knowledge. Script kiddies often are teenagers that use prewritten hacking and cracking programs to break into computers.
- Some corporate spies have excellent computer and network skills and are hired to break into a specific computer and steal its proprietary data and information. Unscrupulous companies hire corporate spies, a practice known as corporate espionage, to gain a competitive advantage.
- Unethical employees break into their employers' computers for a variety of reasons. Some simply want to exploit a security weakness. Others seek financial gains from selling confidential information. Disgruntled employees may want revenge.

- A **cyberextortionist** is someone who uses e-mail as a vehicle for extortion. These perpetrators send a company a threatening e-mail message indicating they will expose confidential information, exploit a security flaw, or launch an attack that will compromise the company's network — if they are not paid a sum of money.
- A **cyberterrorist** is someone who uses the Internet or network to destroy or damage computers for political reasons. The extensive damage might destroy the nation's air traffic control system, electricity-generating companies, or a telecommunications infrastructure. Cyberterrorism usually requires a team of highly skilled individuals, millions of dollars, and several years of planning.

Business and home users must protect, or safeguard, their computers from breaches of security and other computer security risks. The more common computer security risks include Internet and network attacks, unauthorized access and use, hardware theft, software theft, information theft, and system failure (Figure 10-1). The following pages describe these computer security risks and also discuss safeguards users might take to minimize or prevent their consequences.

FIGURE 10-1 Computers are exposed to several types of security risks.

INTERNET AND NETWORK ATTACKS

Information transmitted over networks has a higher degree of security risk than information kept on a company's premises. In a business, network administrators usually take measures to protect a network from security risks. On the Internet, where no central administrator is present, the security risk is greater.

Internet and network attacks that jeopardize security include computer viruses, worms, and Trojan horses; botnets; denial of service attacks; back doors; and spoofing. The following pages address these computer security risks and suggest measures businesses and individuals can take to protect their computers while on the Internet or connected to a network.

Computer Viruses, Worms, and Trojan Horses

Every unprotected computer is susceptible to the first type of computer security risk — a computer virus, worm, and/or Trojan horse.

- A computer **virus** is a potentially damaging computer program that affects, or infects, a computer negatively by altering the way the computer works without the user's knowledge or permission. Once the virus infects the computer, it can spread throughout and may damage files and system software, including the operating system.
- A **worm** is a program that copies itself repeatedly, for example in memory or on a network, using up resources and possibly shutting down the computer or network.
- A **Trojan horse** (named after the Greek myth) is a program that hides within or looks like a legitimate program. A certain condition or action usually triggers the Trojan horse. Unlike a virus or worm, a Trojan horse does not replicate itself to other computers.

Computer viruses, worms, and Trojan horses are classified as **malware** (short for malicious software), which are programs that act without a user's knowledge and deliberately alter the computer's operations. Unscrupulous programmers write malware and then test it to ensure it can deliver its payload. The **payload** is the destructive event or prank the program is intended to deliver. A computer infected by a virus, worm, or Trojan horse often has one or more of the following symptoms:

- Screen displays unusual message or image
- Available memory is less than expected
- Files become corrupted
- Unknown programs or files mysteriously appear

- Music or unusual sound plays randomly
- Existing programs and files disappear
- Programs or files do not work properly
- System properties change
- Operating system runs much slower than usual

Computer viruses, worms, and Trojan horses deliver their payload on a computer in four basic ways: when a user (1) opens an infected file, (2) runs an infected program, (3) boots the computer with infected removable media inserted in a drive or plugged in a port, or (4) connects an unprotected computer to a network. A common way computers become infected with viruses, worms, and Trojan horses is through users opening infected e-mail attachments. Figure 10-2 shows how a virus can spread from one computer to another through an infected e-mail attachment.

Currently, more than 180,000 known viruses, worms, and Trojan horse programs exist.

 FAQ 10-1

How long is an unprotected computer safe from intruders?

One security expert maintains that unprotected computers are compromised by an intruder within 12 minutes, on average. It is possible, however, for an unprotected computer to become infected within seconds of connecting it to a network. Slammer and Nimda, two devastating worms, wreaked worldwide havoc in 10 and 30 minutes, respectively. For more information, visit scsite.com/dcf5e/ch10/faq and then click Viruses and Worms.

FIGURE 10-2 HOW A VIRUS CAN SPREAD THROUGH AN E-MAIL MESSAGE

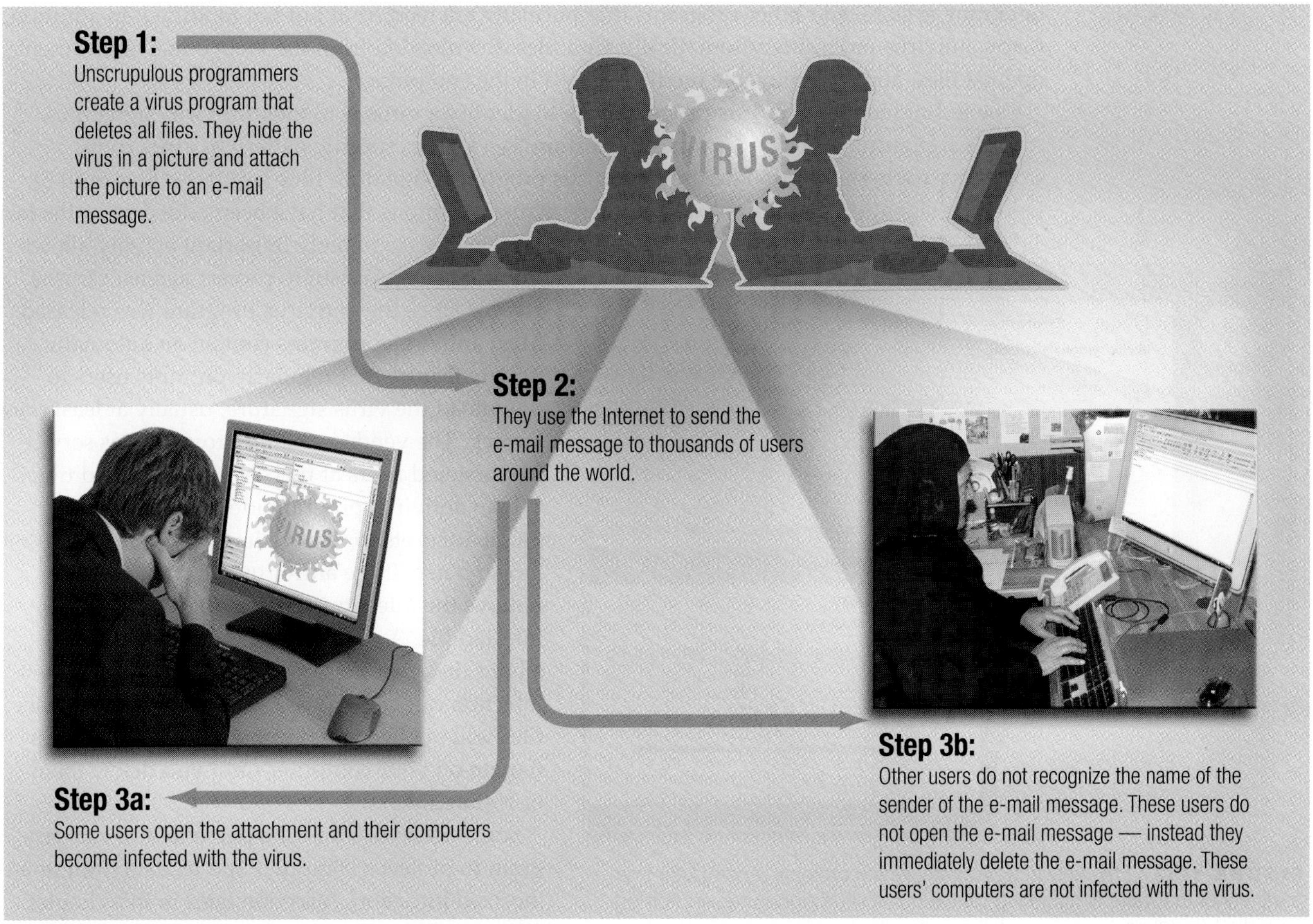

Step 1:
Unscrupulous programmers create a virus program that deletes all files. They hide the virus in a picture and attach the picture to an e-mail message.

Step 2:
They use the Internet to send the e-mail message to thousands of users around the world.

Step 3a:
Some users open the attachment and their computers become infected with the virus.

Step 3b:
Other users do not recognize the name of the sender of the e-mail message. These users do not open the e-mail message — instead they immediately delete the e-mail message. These users' computers are not infected with the virus.

Safeguards against Computer Viruses, Worms, and Trojan Horses

Users can take several precautions to protect their home and work computers from these malicious infections. The following paragraphs discuss these precautionary measures.

Do not start a computer with removable media, such as CDs, DVDs, and USB flash drives, in the drives or ports — unless you are certain the media are uninfected. Never open an e-mail attachment unless you are expecting the attachment *and* it is from a trusted source. If the e-mail message is from an unknown source, delete the e-mail message immediately — without opening or executing any attachments. If the e-mail message is from a trusted source, but you were not expecting an attachment, verify with the source that they intended to send you an attachment — before opening it. Many e-mail programs allow users to preview an e-mail message before or without opening it. Some viruses and worms can deliver their payload when a user simply previews the message. Thus, you should turn off message preview in your e-mail program.

Some viruses are hidden in macros, which are instructions saved in software such as a word processing or spreadsheet program. In programs that allow users to write macros, you should set the macro security level so that the application software warns users that a document they are attempting to open contains a macro. From this warning, a user chooses to disable or enable the macro. If the document is from a trusted source, the user can enable the macro. Otherwise, it should be disabled.

Users should install an antivirus program and update it frequently. An **antivirus program** protects a computer against viruses by identifying and removing any computer viruses found in memory, on storage media, or on incoming files. Most antivirus programs also protect against worms, Trojan horses, and spyware. When you purchase a new computer, it often includes antivirus software. Many e-mail servers also have antivirus programs installed to check incoming and outgoing e-mail messages for malware.

An antivirus program scans for programs that attempt to modify the boot program, the operating system, and other programs that normally are read from but not modified. In addition, many antivirus programs automatically scan files downloaded from the Web, e-mail attachments, opened files, and all removable media inserted in the computer.

One technique that antivirus programs use to identify a virus is to look for virus signatures. A **virus signature**, also called a **virus definition**, is a known specific pattern of virus code. Computer users should update their antivirus program's signature files regularly (Figure 10-3). Updating signature files downloads any new virus definitions that have been added since the last update. This extremely important activity allows the antivirus program to protect against viruses written since the antivirus program was released. Most antivirus programs contain an automatic update feature that regularly prompts users to download the virus signature, usually at least once a week. The vendor usually provides this service to registered users at no cost for a specified time.

If an antivirus program identifies an infected file, it attempts to remove its virus, worm, or Trojan horse. If the antivirus program cannot remove the infection, it often quarantines the infected file. A **quarantine** is a separate area of a hard disk that holds the infected file until the infection can be removed. This step ensures other files will not become infected. Quarantined files remain on your computer until you delete them or restore them.

Some users also install a personal firewall program to protect a computer and its data from unauthorized intrusion. A section later in this chapter discusses firewalls.

Finally, stay informed about new virus alerts and virus hoaxes. A **virus hoax** is an e-mail message that warns users of a nonexistent virus, worm, or Trojan horse. Often, these virus hoaxes are in the form of a chain letter that requests the user to send a copy of the e-mail message to as many people as possible. Instead of forwarding the message, visit a Web site that publishes a list of virus alerts and virus hoaxes.

The list in Figure 10-4 summarizes important tips for protecting your computer from virus, worm, and Trojan horse infections.

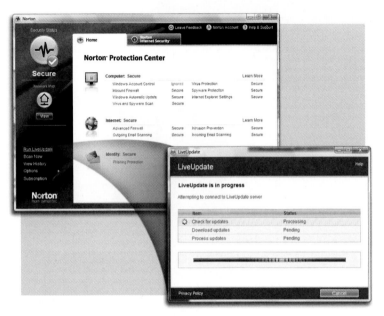

FIGURE 10-3   This antivirus program, which protects a computer from a variety of malware, is checking for the latest virus signatures and other important updates.

WEB LINK 10-1

Virus Hoaxes

For more information, visit scsite.com/dcf5e/ch10/weblink and then click Virus Hoaxes.

TIPS FOR PREVENTING VIRUS, WORM, AND TROJAN HORSE INFECTIONS

1. Never start a computer with removable media inserted in the drives or plugged in the ports, unless the media are uninfected.
2. Never open an e-mail attachment unless you are expecting it *and* it is from a trusted source. Turn off message preview.
3. Set the macro security in programs so that you can enable or disable macros. Enable macros only if the document is from a trusted source and you are expecting it.
4. Install an antivirus program on all of your computers. Update the software regularly. Obtain updates to the virus signature files on a regular basis.
5. Check all downloaded programs for viruses, worms, or Trojan horses. This malware often is placed in seemingly innocent programs, so that it will affect a large number of users.
6. If the antivirus program flags an e-mail attachment as infected, delete the attachment immediately.
7. Before using any removable media, use the antivirus scan program to check the media for infection. Incorporate this procedure even for shrink-wrapped software from major developers. Some commercial software has been infected and distributed to unsuspecting users this way.
8. Install a personal firewall program.
9. Stay informed about new virus alerts and virus hoaxes.

FIGURE 10-4   With the growing number of new viruses, worms, and Trojan horses, it is crucial that users take steps to protect their computers.

Botnets

A **botnet** is a group of compromised computers connected to a network such as the Internet that are used as part of a network that attacks other networks, usually for nefarious purposes. A compromised computer, known as a **zombie**, is one whose owner is unaware the computer is being controlled remotely by an outsider. Cybercriminals use botnets to send spam via e-mail, spread viruses and other malware, or commit a denial of service attack.

Denial of Service Attacks

A **denial of service attack**, or **DoS attack**, is an assault whose purpose is to disrupt computer access to an Internet service such as the Web or e-mail. Perpetrators carry out a DoS attack in a variety of ways. For example, they may use an unsuspecting computer to send an influx of confusing data messages or useless traffic to a computer network. The victim computer network eventually jams, blocking legitimate visitors from accessing the network.

Back Doors

A **back door** is a program or set of instructions in a program that allow users to bypass security controls when accessing a program, computer, or network. Once perpetrators gain access to unsecure computers, they often install a back door or modify an existing program to include a back door, which allows them to continue to access the computer remotely without the user's knowledge.

Spoofing

Spoofing is a technique intruders use to make their network or Internet transmission appear legitimate to a victim computer or network. E-mail spoofing occurs when the sender's address or other components of the e-mail header are altered so that it appears the e-mail originated from a different sender. E-mail spoofing commonly is used for virus hoaxes, spam, and phishing scams. IP spoofing occurs when an intruder computer fools a network into believing its IP address is associated with a trusted source. Perpetrators of IP spoofing trick their victims into interacting with a phony Web site.

Safeguards against Botnets, DoS Attacks, Back Doors, and Spoofing

To defend against botnets, DoS attacks, improper use of back doors, and spoofing, users can implement firewall solutions and install intrusion detection software. The following sections discuss these safeguards.

Firewalls

A **firewall** is hardware and/or software that protects a network's resources from intrusion by users on another network such as the Internet (Figure 10-5). All networked and online computer users should implement a firewall solution.

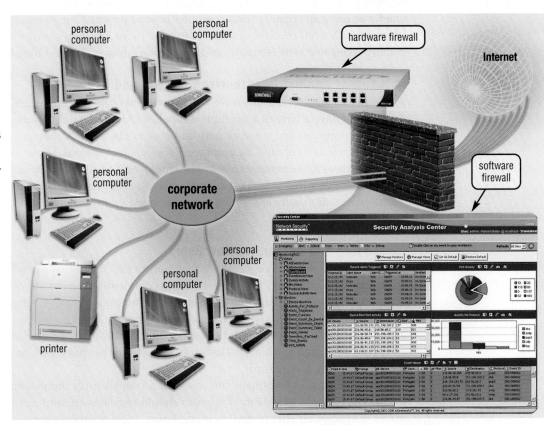

FIGURE 10-5 A firewall is hardware and/or software that protects a network's resources from intrusion by users on another network such as the Internet.

Companies use firewalls to protect network resources from outsiders and to restrict employees' access to sensitive data such as payroll or personnel records. Businesses can implement a firewall solution themselves or outsource their needs to a company specializing in providing firewall protection. Large companies often route all their communications through a proxy server, which is a component of the firewall. A proxy server is a server outside the company's network that controls which communications pass into the company's network.

Home and small office/home office users often protect their computers with a personal firewall utility. A **personal firewall** is a utility that detects and protects a personal computer and its data from unauthorized intrusions. Some operating systems, such as Windows Vista, include personal firewalls.

Some small office/home office users purchase a hardware firewall, such as a router or other device that has a built-in firewall, in addition to or instead of personal firewall software. Hardware firewalls stop intrusions before they break in your computer.

Intrusion Detection Software

To provide extra protection against hackers and other intruders, large companies sometimes use intrusion detection software to identify possible security breaches. **Intrusion detection software** automatically analyzes all network traffic, assesses system vulnerabilities, identifies any unauthorized access (intrusions), and notifies network administrators of suspicious behavior patterns or system breaches.

To utilize intrusion detection software requires the expertise of a network administrator because the programs are complex and difficult to use and interpret. These programs also are quite expensive.

UNAUTHORIZED ACCESS AND USE

Another type of computer security risk is unauthorized access and use. **Unauthorized access** is the use of a computer or network without permission. **Unauthorized use** is the use of a computer or its data for unapproved or possibly illegal activities. Unauthorized use includes a variety of activities: an employee using an organization's computer to send personal e-mail messages, an employee using the organization's word processing software to track his or her child's soccer league scores, or someone gaining access to a bank computer and performing an unauthorized transfer.

Safeguards against Unauthorized Access and Use

Companies take several measures to help prevent unauthorized access and use. At a minimum, they should have a written acceptable use policy (AUP) that outlines the computer activities for which the computer and network may and may not be used. A company's AUP should specify the acceptable use of computers by employees for personal reasons. Some companies prohibit such use entirely. Others allow personal use on the employee's own time such as a lunch hour.

Other measures that safeguard against unauthorized access and use include firewalls and intrusion detection software, which were discussed in the previous section, and identifying and authenticating users.

Identifying and Authenticating Users

Many companies use access controls to minimize the chance that a perpetrator intentionally may access or an employee accidentally may access confidential information on a computer. An **access control** is a security measure that defines who can access a computer, when they can access it, and what actions they can take while accessing the computer. In addition, the computer should maintain an **audit trail** that records in a file both successful and unsuccessful access attempts. An unsuccessful access attempt could result from a user mistyping his or her password, or it could result from a hacker trying thousands of passwords.

Companies should investigate unsuccessful access attempts immediately to ensure they are not intentional breaches of security. They also should review successful access for irregularities, such as use of the computer after normal working hours or from remote computers.

Many systems implement access controls using a two-phase process called identification and authentication. Identification verifies that an individual is a valid user. Authentication verifies that the individual is the person he or she claims to be. Three methods of identification and authentication include user names and passwords, possessed objects, and biometric devices. The technique(s) a company uses should correspond to the degree of risk that is associated with the unauthorized access.

USER NAMES AND PASSWORDS A **user name**, or user ID (identification), is a unique combination of characters, such as letters of the alphabet or numbers, that identifies one specific user. A **password** is a private combination of characters associated with the user name that allows access to certain computer resources.

Most multiuser (networked) operating systems require that users correctly enter a user name and a password before they can access the data, information, and programs stored on a computer or network (Figure 10-6).

Multiuser systems typically require that users select their own passwords. Users typically choose an easy-to-remember word or series of characters for passwords. If your password is too obvious, however, such as your initials or birthday, others can guess it easily. Easy passwords make it simple for hackers and other intruders to break into a system. Hackers use computer automated tools to assist them with guessing passwords. Thus, you should select a password carefully. Longer passwords provide greater security than shorter ones. Each character added to a password significantly increases the number of possible combinations and the length of time it might take for someone or for a hacker's computer to guess the password (Figure 10-7).

Some Web sites use a CAPTCHA to further protect a user's password. A **CAPTCHA**, which stands for Completely Automated Public Turing test to tell Computers and Humans Apart, is a program that verifies user input is not computer generated. A CAPTCHA displays a series of distorted characters and requires the user to enter the characters correctly to continue using the Web site.

FIGURE 10-6 Many Web sites that maintain personal and confidential data require a user to enter a user name and password.

WEB LINK 10-2

CAPTCHAs

For more information, visit scsite.com/dcf5e/ch10/weblink and then click CAPTCHAs.

PASSWORD PROTECTION		AVERAGE TIME TO DISCOVER	
Number of Characters	**Possible Combinations**	**Human**	**Computer**
1	36	3 minutes	.000018 second
2	1,300	2 hours	.00065 second
3	47,000	3 days	.02 second
4	1,700,000	3 months	1 second
5	60,000,000	10 years	30 seconds
10	3,700,000,000,000,000	580 million years	59 years

- *Possible characters include the letters A–Z and numbers 0–9*
- *Human discovery assumes 1 try every 10 seconds*
- *Computer discovery assumes 1 million tries per second*
- *Average time assumes the password would be discovered in approximately half the time it would take to try all possible combinations*

FIGURE 10-7 This table shows the effect of increasing the length of a password that consists of letters and numbers. The longer the password, the more effort required to discover it. Long passwords, however, are more difficult for users to remember.

In addition to a user name and password, some systems ask users to enter one of several pieces of personal information. Such items can include a spouse's first name, a birth date, a place of birth, or a mother's maiden name. As with a password, if the user's response does not match the information on file, the system denies access.

POSSESSED OBJECTS   A possessed object is any item that you must carry to gain access to a computer or computer facility. Examples of possessed objects are badges, cards, smart cards, and keys. The card you use in an automated teller machine (ATM) is a possessed object that allows access to your bank account.

Possessed objects often are used in combination with personal identification numbers. A **personal identification number** (**PIN**) is a numeric password, either assigned by a company or selected by a user. PINs provide an additional level of security. An ATM card typically requires a four-digit PIN. PINs are passwords. Select them carefully and protect them as you do any other password.

BIOMETRIC DEVICES   A **biometric device** authenticates a person's identity by translating a personal characteristic, such as a fingerprint, into a digital code that is then compared with a digital code stored in the computer verifying a physical or behavioral characteristic. If the digital code in the computer does not match the personal characteristic code, the computer denies access to the individual.

Biometric devices grant access to programs, computers, or rooms using computer analysis of some biometric identifier. Examples of biometric devices and systems include fingerprint readers (Figure 10-8), hand geometry systems, face recognition systems, voice verification systems, signature verification systems, iris recognition systems, and retinal scanners. Many grocery stores, retail stores, and gas stations now use **biometric payment**, where the customer's fingerprint is read by a fingerprint reader that is linked to a specific payment method such as a checking account or credit card. Read Looking Ahead 10-1 for a look at biometric software.

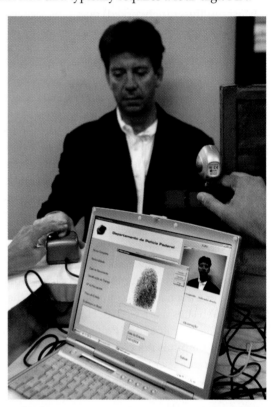

FIGURE 10-8   A fingerprint reader verifies this traveler's identity.

LOOKING AHEAD 10-1

Biometric Software Aids Behavior Detection

Security experts use a technique called behavior detection to recognize suspicious behavior. These specially trained personnel study a person's body language, facial expressions, and speech for specific patterns that criminals commonly exhibit and then alert crime prevention specialists when something looks awry.

IBM has developed a Smart Surveillance System that enhances the security experts' visual checks. It analyzes video footage shot at various locations for specific uncontrollable actions and spoken words. Airports are prime locations for the biometric software as are large urban cities. Chicago already is testing the system.

The Smart Surveillance System project is in its infancy as programmers are attempting to teach the computers to recognize microexpressions, which are the split-second emotions lasting one-fifteenth of a second, on peoples' faces. In the far-distant future, experts predict the software will detect these actions and behaviors automatically. For more information, visit scsite.com/dcf5e/ch10/looking and then click Biometric Software.

Test your knowledge of pages 362 through 370 in Quiz Yourself 10-1.

HARDWARE THEFT AND VANDALISM

Hardware theft and vandalism are other types of computer security risks. **Hardware theft** is the act of stealing computer equipment. **Hardware vandalism** is the act of defacing or destroying computer equipment. Hardware vandalism takes many forms, from someone cutting a computer cable to individuals breaking into a business or school computer lab and aimlessly smashing computers.

Mobile users are susceptible to hardware theft. It is estimated that more than two million notebook computers are stolen each year. The size and weight of these computers make them easy to steal. Thieves often target notebook computers of company executives, so that they can use the stolen computer to access confidential company information illegally. In this case, hardware theft is combined with software and information theft.

Safeguards against Hardware Theft and Vandalism

To help reduce the chances of theft, companies and schools use a variety of security measures. Physical access controls, such as locked doors and windows, usually are adequate to protect the equipment. Many businesses, schools, and some homeowners install alarm systems for additional security. School computer labs and other areas with a large number of semifrequent users often attach additional physical security devices such as cables that lock the equipment to a desk (Figure 10-9), cabinet, or floor. Small locking devices also exist that require a key to access a hard disk or CD/DVD drive.

Some businesses use a **real time location system** (**RTLS**) to track and identify the location of high-risk or high-value items. One implementation of RTLS places RFID tags in items to be tracked.

Mobile computer users must take special care to protect their equipment. Some users attach a physical device such as a cable to lock a mobile computer temporarily to a stationary object. Other mobile users install a mini-security system in the notebook computer. Some of these security systems shut down the computer and sound an alarm if the computer moves outside a specified distance. Notebook computer security systems and tracking software can track the location of a stolen notebook computer.

Some notebook computers use passwords, possessed objects, and biometrics as methods of security. When you start these computers, you must enter a password, slide a card in a card reader, or press your finger on a fingerprint reader before the hard disk unlocks. This type of security does not prevent theft, but it renders the computer useless if it is stolen.

FIGURE 10-9 Using cables to lock computers can help prevent the theft of computer equipment.

WEB LINK 10-3

RTLS

For more information, visit scsite.com/dcf5e/ch10/weblink and then click RTLS.

SOFTWARE THEFT

Another type of computer security risk is software theft. **Software theft** occurs when someone steals software media, intentionally erases programs, or illegally copies a program. One form of software theft involves someone physically stealing the media that contain the software or the hardware that contains the media, as described in the previous section. Another form of software theft occurs when software is stolen from software manufacturers. This type of theft, called piracy, is by far the most common form of software theft. Software **piracy** is the unauthorized and illegal duplication of copyrighted software.

Safeguards against Software Theft

To protect software media from being stolen, owners should keep original software boxes and media in a secure location. All computer users should back up their files and disks regularly, in the event of theft.

To protect themselves from software piracy, software manufacturers issue users license agreements. A **license agreement** is the right to use the software. That is, you do not own the software. The license agreement provides specific conditions for use of the software, which a user must accept before using the software (Figure 10-10). These terms usually are displayed when you install the software.

The most common type of license included with software purchased by individual users is a single-user license agreement, also called an end-user license agreement (EULA). A single-user license agreement typically includes many of the following conditions that specify a user's responsibility upon acceptance of the agreement.

Users are permitted to:
- Install the software on only one computer. (Some license agreements allow users to install the software on one desktop computer and one notebook computer.)
- Make one copy of the software as a backup.
- Give or sell the software to another individual, but only if the software is removed from the user's computer first.

Users are not permitted to:
- Install the software on a network, such as a school computer lab.
- Give copies to friends and colleagues, while continuing to use the software.
- Export the software.
- Rent or lease the software.

Unless otherwise specified by a license agreement, you do not have the right to copy, loan, borrow, rent, or in any way distribute software. Doing so is a violation of copyright law. It also is a federal crime. Despite this, some experts estimate for every authorized copy of software in use, at least one unauthorized copy exists.

In an attempt to prevent software piracy, Microsoft and other manufacturers have incorporated an activation process into many of its consumer products. During the **product activation**, which is conducted either online or by telephone, users provide the software product's 25-character identification number to receive an installation identification number unique to the computer on which the software is installed.

If you are not completely familiar with your school or employer's policies governing installation of software, check with the information technology department or your school's technology coordinator.

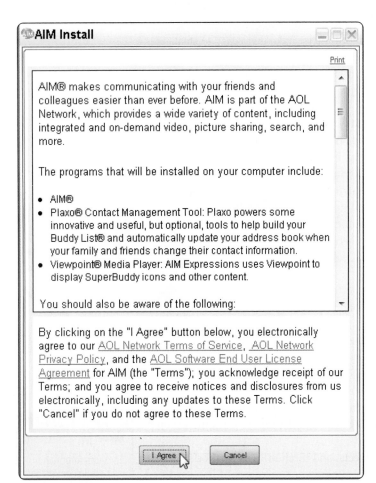

FIGURE 10-10 A user must accept the terms in the license agreement before using the software.

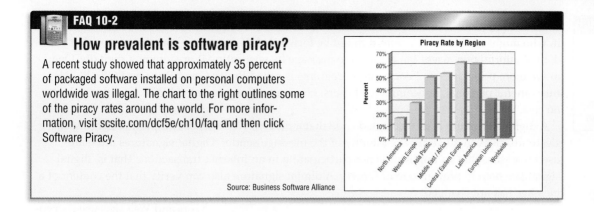

FAQ 10-2

How prevalent is software piracy?

A recent study showed that approximately 35 percent of packaged software installed on personal computers worldwide was illegal. The chart to the right outlines some of the piracy rates around the world. For more information, visit scsite.com/dcf5e/ch10/faq and then click Software Piracy.

Source: Business Software Alliance

INFORMATION THEFT

Information theft is yet another type of computer security risk. **Information theft** occurs when someone steals personal or confidential information. An unethical company executive may steal or buy stolen information to learn about a competitor. A corrupt individual may steal credit card numbers to make fraudulent purchases.

Safeguards against Information Theft

Most companies attempt to prevent information theft by implementing the user identification and authentication controls discussed earlier in this chapter. These controls are best suited for protecting information on computers located on a company's premises. Information transmitted over networks offers a higher degree of risk because unscrupulous users can intercept it during transmission. To protect information on the Internet and networks, companies and individuals use a variety of encryption techniques.

Encryption

Encryption is the process of converting readable data into unreadable characters to prevent unauthorized access. You treat encrypted data just like any other data. That is, you can store it or send it in an e-mail message. To read the data, the recipient must **decrypt**, or decipher, it into a readable form.

In the encryption process, the unencrypted, readable data is called plaintext. The encrypted (scrambled) data is called ciphertext. To encrypt the data, the originator of the data converts the plaintext into ciphertext using an encryption key. In its simplest form, an encryption key is a programmed formula that the recipient of the data uses to decrypt ciphertext.

Many data encryption methods exist. Figure 10-11 shows examples of some simple encryption methods. An encryption key (formula) often uses more than one of these methods, such as a combination of transposition and substitution. Most organizations use available software for encryption. Windows Vista enables you easily to encrypt the contents of files, folders, and drives.

WEB LINK 10-4

Encryption

For more information, visit scsite.com/dcf5e/ch10/weblink and then click Encryption.

SAMPLE ENCRYPTION METHODS

Name	Method	Plaintext	Ciphertext	Explanation
Transposition	Switch the order of characters	SOFTWARE	OSTFAWER	Adjacent characters swapped
Substitution	Replace characters with other characters	INFORMATION	WLDIMXQUWIL	Each letter replaced with another
Expansion	Insert characters between existing characters	USER	UYSYEYRY	Letter Y inserted after each character
Compaction	Remove characters and store elsewhere	ACTIVATION	ACIVTIN	Every third letter removed (T, A, O)

FIGURE 10-11   This table shows four simple methods of encryption. Most encryption programs use a combination of these four methods.

When users send an e-mail message over the Internet, they never know who might intercept it, who might read it, or to whom it might be forwarded. If a message contains personal or confidential information, users can protect the message by encrypting it or signing it digitally. One of the more popular e-mail encryption programs is called **Pretty Good Privacy** (**PGP**). PGP is freeware for personal, noncommercial users. Home users can download PGP from the Web at no cost.

A **digital signature** is an encrypted code that a person, Web site, or company attaches to an electronic message to verify the identity of the message sender. Digital signatures often are used to ensure that an impostor is not participating in an Internet transaction. That is, digital signatures help to prevent e-mail forgery. A digital signature also can verify that the content of a message has not changed.

Many Web browsers and Web sites use encryption. A Web site that uses encryption techniques to secure its data is known as a **secure site** (Figure 10-12). Secure sites often use digital certificates. A **digital certificate** is a notice that guarantees a user or a Web site is legitimate. A **certificate authority** (CA) is an authorized person or a company that issues and verifies digital certificates. Users apply for a digital certificate from a CA. The digital certificate typically contains information such as the user's name, the issuing CA's name and signature, and the serial number of the certificate. The information in a digital certificate is encrypted.

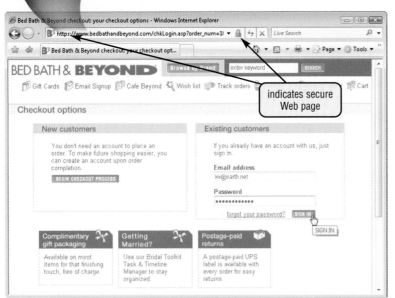

FIGURE 10-12 Web addresses of secure sites often begin with https instead of http. Secure sites also often display a lock symbol in the window.

SYSTEM FAILURE

System failure is yet another type of computer security risk. A **system failure** is the prolonged malfunction of a computer. System failure can cause loss of hardware, software, data, or information. A variety of causes can lead to system failure. These include aging hardware; natural disasters such as fires, floods, or hurricanes; random events such as electrical power problems; and even errors in computer programs.

One of the more common causes of system failure is an electrical power variation. Electrical power variations can cause loss of data and loss of equipment. If the computer equipment is networked, a single power disturbance can damage multiple systems.

Safeguards against System Failure

To protect against electrical power variations, use a surge protector. A **surge protector** uses special electrical components to provide a stable current flow to the computer and other electronic equipment (Figure 10-13). Sometimes resembling a power strip, the computer and other devices plug in the surge protector, which plugs in the power source.

FIGURE 10-13 Circuits inside a surge protector safeguard against electrical power variations.

No surge protectors are 100 percent effective. Typically, the amount of protection offered by a surge protector is proportional to its cost. That is, the more expensive, the more protection the protector offers.

If your computer connects to a network or the Internet, also be sure to have protection for your modem, telephone lines, DSL lines, Internet cable lines, and network lines. Many surge protectors include plug-ins for telephone lines and other cables.

For additional electrical protection, some applications connect an uninterruptible power supply to the computer. An **uninterruptible power supply** (**UPS**) is a device that contains surge protection circuits and one or more batteries that can provide power during a loss of power (Figure 10-14). A UPS connects between your computer and a power source.

As another measure of protection, some companies use duplicate components or computers as a safeguard against system failure.

WEB LINK 10-6

Uninterruptible Power Supply

For more information, visit scsite.com/dcf5e/ ch10/weblink and then click Uninterruptible Power Supply.

FIGURE 10-14
If power fails, an uninterruptible power supply (UPS) uses batteries to provide electricity for a limited amount of time.

BACKING UP — THE ULTIMATE SAFEGUARD

To prevent against data loss caused by a system failure or hardware/software/information theft, computer users should back up files regularly. A **backup** is a duplicate of a file, program, or disk that can be used if the original is lost, damaged, or destroyed. Thus, to **back up** a file means to make a copy of it. In the case of a system failure or the discovery of corrupted files, you **restore** the files by copying the backed up files to their original location on the computer.

You can use just about any media to store backups. A good choice for a home user might be CD-RWs or DVD+RWs. Keep backup copies in a fireproof and heatproof safe or vault, or offsite. Offsite means in a location separate from the computer site. A growing trend is to use online storage as an offsite location. Recall that online storage is a service on the Web that provides storage to computer users.

Most backup programs for the home user provide for a full backup and a selective backup. A full backup copies all of the files in the computer. With a selective backup, users choose which folders and files to include in a backup.

Some users implement a three-generation backup policy to preserve three copies of important files. The grandparent is the oldest copy of the file. The parent is the second oldest copy of the file. The child is the most recent copy of the file.

Most operating systems include a backup program. Backup devices, such as tape and removable disk drives, also include backup programs. Numerous stand-alone backup utilities exist. Many of these can be downloaded from the Web at no cost.

Some companies choose to use an online backup service to handle their backup needs. An **online backup service** is a Web site that automatically backs up files to its online location. These sites usually charge a monthly or annual fee. If the system crashes, the online backup service typically sends the company one or more CD/DVDs that contains all its backed up data.

WIRELESS SECURITY

Wireless technology has made dramatic changes in the way computer users communicate worldwide. Billions of home and business users have notebook computers, smart phones, and other personal mobile devices to access the Internet, send e-mail and instant messages, chat online, or share network connections — all without wires. Home users set up wireless home networks. Mobile users access wireless networks in hot spots at airports, hotels, schools, shopping malls, bookstores, restaurants, and coffee shops. Schools have wireless networks so that students can access the school network using their mobile computers and devices as they move from building to building.

Although wireless access provides many conveniences to users, it also poses additional security risks. One study showed that about 80 percent of wireless networks have no security protection. Some perpetrators connect to other's wireless networks to gain free Internet access; others may try to access a company's confidential data.

To access the network, the individual must be in range of the wireless network. Some intruders intercept and monitor communications as they transmit through the air. Others connect to a network through an unsecured wireless access point (WAP). In one technique, called **war driving**, individuals attempt to detect wireless networks via their notebook computer while driving a vehicle through areas they suspect have a wireless network.

In addition to using firewalls, some safeguards that improve the security of wireless networks include reconfiguring the wireless access point and ensuring equipment uses one or more wireless security standards such as Wi-Fi Protected Access and 802.11i.

- A wireless access point (WAP) should be configured so that it does not broadcast a network name. The WAP also can be programmed so that only certain devices can access it.
- **Wi-Fi Protected Access** (WPA) is a security standard that improves on older security standards by authenticating network users and providing more advanced encryption techniques.
- An **802.11i** network, the most recent network security standard, conforms to the government's security standards and uses more sophisticated encryption techniques than WPA.

By implementing these security measures, you can help to prevent unauthorized access to wireless networks.

Test your knowledge of pages 371 through 376 in Quiz Yourself 10-2.

QUIZ YOURSELF 10-2

Instructions: Find the true statement below. Then, rewrite the remaining false statements so they are true.

1. An end-user license agreement (EULA) permits users to give copies to friends and colleagues, while continuing to use the software.
2. Encryption is a process of converting ciphertext into plaintext to prevent authorized access.
3. Mobile users are not susceptible to hardware theft.
4. Two wireless security standards are Wi-Fi Protected Access and 802.11i.
5. To prevent against data loss caused by a system failure, computer users should restore files regularly.

Quiz Yourself Online: To further check your knowledge of safeguards against hardware theft, software theft, information theft, protection against system failure, and wireless security, visit scsite.com/dcf5e/ch10/quiz and then click Objectives 3 – 6.

ETHICS AND SOCIETY

As with any powerful technology, computers can be used for both good and bad intentions. The standards that determine whether an action is good or bad are known as ethics.

Computer ethics are the moral guidelines that govern the use of computers and information systems. Five frequently discussed areas of computer ethics are unauthorized use of computers and networks, software theft (piracy), information accuracy, intellectual property rights, and information privacy. The questionnaire in Figure 10-15 raises issues in each of these areas.

Previous sections in this chapter discussed unauthorized use of computers and networks, and software theft (piracy). The following pages discuss issues related to information accuracy, intellectual property rights, and information privacy.

	Ethical	Unethical
1. A company requires employees to wear badges that track their whereabouts while at work.	☐	☐
2. A supervisor reads an employee's e-mail.	☐	☐
3. An employee uses his computer at work to send e-mail messages to a friend.	☐	☐
4. An employee sends an e-mail message to several coworkers and blind copies his supervisor.	☐	☐
5. An employee forwards an e-mail message to a third party without permission from the sender.	☐	☐
6. An employee uses her computer at work to complete a homework assignment for school.	☐	☐
7. The vice president of your Student Government Association (SGA) downloads a photo from the Web and uses it in a flier recruiting SGA members.	☐	☐
8. A student copies text from the Web and uses it in a research paper for his English Composition class.	☐	☐
9. An employee sends political campaign material to individuals on her employer's mailing list.	☐	☐
10. As an employee in the registration office, you have access to student grades. You look up grades for your friends, so that they do not have to wait for delivery of grade reports from the postal service.	☐	☐
11. An employee makes a copy of software and installs it on her home computer. No one uses her home computer while she is at work, and she uses her home computer only to finish projects from work.	☐	☐
12. An employee who has been laid off installs a computer virus on his employer's computer.	☐	☐
13. A person designing a Web page finds one on the Web similar to his requirements, copies it, modifies it, and publishes it as his own Web page.	☐	☐
14. A student researches using only the Web to write a report.	☐	☐
15. In a society in which all transactions occur online (a cashless society), the government tracks every transaction you make and automatically deducts taxes from your bank account.	☐	☐
16. Someone copies a well-known novel to the Web and encourages others to read it.	☐	☐
17. A person accesses a company's network and reports to the company any vulnerabilities discovered.	☐	☐

FIGURE 10-15   Indicate whether you think the situation described is ethical or unethical. Discuss your answers with your instructor and other students.

Information Accuracy

Information accuracy today is a concern because many users access information maintained by other people or companies, such as on the Internet. Do not assume that because the information is on the Web that it is correct. Users should evaluate the value of a Web page before relying on its content. Be aware that the company providing access to the information may not be the creator of the information.

In addition to concerns about the accuracy of computer input, some individuals and organizations raise questions about the ethics of using computers to alter output, primarily graphical output such as retouched photos. Using graphics equipment and software, users easily can digitize photos and then add, change, or remove images (Figure 10-16).

One group that completely opposes any manipulation of an image is the National Press Photographers Association. It believes that allowing even the slightest alteration could lead to misrepresentative photos. Others believe that digital photo retouching is acceptable as long as the significant content or meaning of the photo does not change. Digital retouching is an area in which legal precedents so far have not been established.

FIGURE 10-16
A digitally altered photo shows sports legend Michael Jordan (born in 1963) meeting the famous scientist Albert Einstein (who died in 1955).

Intellectual Property Rights

Intellectual property (IP) refers to unique and original works such as ideas, inventions, art, writings, processes, company and product names, and logos. **Intellectual property rights** are the rights to which creators are entitled for their work. Certain issues arise surrounding IP today because many of these works are available digitally.

A **copyright** gives authors and artists exclusive rights to duplicate, publish, and sell their materials. A copyright protects any tangible form of expression.

A common infringement of copyright is piracy. People pirate (illegally copy) software, movies, and music. Many areas are not clear-cut with respect to the law, because copyright law gives the public fair use to copyrighted material. The issues surround the phrase, fair use, which allows use for educational and critical purposes.

This vague definition is subject to widespread interpretation and raises many questions:
• Should individuals be able to download contents of your Web site, modify it, and then put it on the Web again as their own?
• Should a faculty member have the right to print material from the Web and distribute it to all members of the class for teaching purposes only?
• Should someone be able to scan photos or pages from a book, publish them to the Web, and allow others to download them?
• Should students be able to post term papers they have written on the Web, making it tempting for other students to download and submit them as their own work?

WEB LINK 10-7

Digital Rights Management

For more information, visit scsite.com/dcf5e/ch10/weblink and then click Digital Rights Management.

These issues with copyright law led to the development of **digital rights management** (DRM), a strategy designed to prevent illegal distribution of movies, music, and other digital content. Read Ethics & Issues 10-1 for a related discussion.

ETHICS & ISSUES 10-1

Is It Illegal to Delete Some Files from Your Own Computer?

Recently, a man was sued by a company that distributes discount coupons on its Web site because he found a method that allowed him to print more than two copies of each coupon. He then notified others how to do the same. The company placed files and other information on each of the Web site's users' computers that helped to enforce a policy of allowing a person to print two copies of each coupon. By changing these files, the man was able to print more than two copies of a coupon.

The company sued the man because it claimed that he violated a provision of the law known as the DMCA, or Digital Millennium Copyright Act. One provision of the law states that a person cannot circumvent technology intended to protect another's intellectual property. In this case, the circumvention was the man's deletion and changing of files on his computer, and the intellectual property included copied coupons. Many legal scholars argue that the company took an overly broad view of the law. Others claim the law is vague and, in fact, does appear to apply in this situation. Should you legally be prohibited from deleting or changing files on your own computer? Why or why not? Would you delete files on your computer in order to print more coupons than allowed by a company's policy? Why or why not? What sort of common-sense laws can the government enact that could avoid these types of situations?

INFORMATION PRIVACY

Information privacy refers to the right of individuals and companies to deny or restrict the collection and use of information about them. In the past, information privacy was easier to maintain because information was kept in separate locations. Each retail store had its own credit files. Each government agency maintained separate records. Doctors had their own patient files.

Today, huge databases store this data online. Much of the data is personal and confidential and should be accessible only to authorized users. Many individuals and organizations, however, question whether this data really is private.

Figure 10-17 lists measures you can take to make your personal data private. The following pages address techniques companies and employers use to collect your personal data.

HOW TO SAFEGUARD PERSONAL INFORMATION

1. Fill in only necessary information on rebate, warranty, and registration forms.
2. Do not preprint your telephone number or Social Security number on personal checks.
3. Have an unlisted or unpublished telephone number.
4. If Caller ID is available in your area, find out how to block your number from displaying on the receiver's system.
5. Do not write your telephone number on charge or credit receipts.
6. Ask merchants not to write credit card numbers, telephone numbers, Social Security numbers, and driver's license numbers on the back of your personal checks.
7. Purchase goods with cash, rather than credit or checks.
8. Avoid shopping club and buyer cards.
9. If merchants ask personal questions, find out why they want to know before releasing the information.
10. Inform merchants that you do not want them to distribute your personal information.
11. Request, in writing, to be removed from mailing lists.
12. Obtain your credit report once a year from each of the three major credit reporting agencies (Equifax, Experian, and TransUnion) and correct any errors.
13. Request a free copy of your medical records once a year from the Medical Information Bureau.
14. Limit the amount of information you provide to Web sites. Fill in only required information.
15. Install a cookie manager to filter cookies.
16. Clear your history file when you are finished browsing.
17. Set up a free e-mail account. Use this e-mail address for merchant forms.
18. Turn off file and printer sharing on your Internet connection.
19. Install a personal firewall.
20. Sign-up for e-mail filtering through your Internet access provider or use an anti-spam program such as Brightmail.
21. Do not reply to spam for any reason.
22. Surf the Web anonymously with a program such as Freedom WebSecure or through an anonymous Web site such as Anonymizer.com.

FIGURE 10-17 Techniques to keep personal data private.

Electronic Profiles

When you fill out a form such as a magazine subscription, product warranty registration card, or contest entry form, the merchant that receives the form usually enters it into a database. Likewise, every time you click an advertisement on the Web or register software online, your information and preferences enter a database. Merchants then sell the contents of their databases to national marketing firms and Internet advertising firms. By combining this data with information from public sources such as driver's licenses and vehicle registrations, these firms create an electronic profile of individuals.

Critics contend that the information in an electronic profile reveals more about an individual than anyone has a right to know. They also claim that companies should inform people if they plan to provide personal information to others. Many companies today allow people to specify whether they want their personal information distributed.

Cookies

E-commerce and other Web applications often rely on cookies to identify users. A **cookie** is a small text file that a Web server stores on your computer. Cookie files typically contain data about you, such as your user name or viewing preferences.

Many commercial Web sites send a cookie to your browser, and then your computer's hard disk stores the cookie. The next time you visit the Web site, your browser retrieves the cookie from your hard disk and sends the data in the cookie to the Web site. Figure 10-18 illustrates how Web sites work with cookies.

FIGURE 10-18   HOW COOKIES WORK

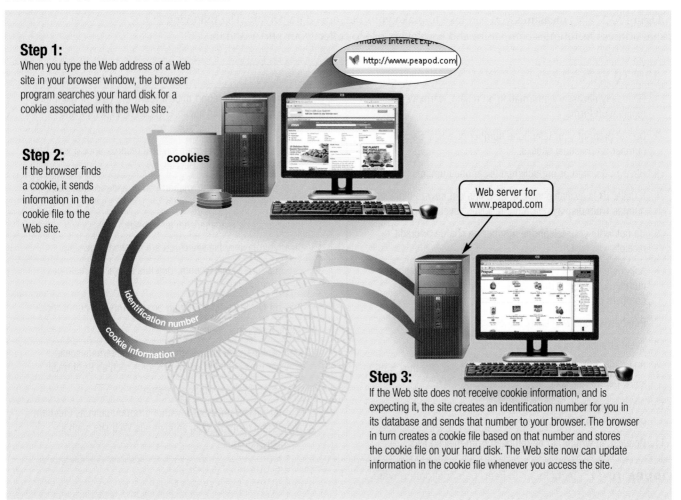

Step 1:
When you type the Web address of a Web site in your browser window, the browser program searches your hard disk for a cookie associated with the Web site.

Step 2:
If the browser finds a cookie, it sends information in the cookie file to the Web site.

cookies

http://www.peapod.com

Web server for www.peapod.com

identification number

cookie information

Step 3:
If the Web site does not receive cookie information, and is expecting it, the site creates an identification number for you in its database and sends that number to your browser. The browser in turn creates a cookie file based on that number and stores the cookie file on your hard disk. The Web site now can update information in the cookie file whenever you access the site.

Web sites use cookies for a variety of purposes:

- Most Web sites that allow for personalization use cookies to track user preferences. On such sites, users may be asked to fill in a form requesting personal information, such as their name, postal code, or site preferences. A news Web site, for example, might allow users to customize their viewing preferences to display certain stock quotes. The Web site stores their preferences in a cookie on the users' hard disks.
- Some Web sites use cookies to store users' passwords, so that they do not need to enter it every time they log in to the Web site.
- Online shopping sites generally use a session cookie to keep track of items in a user's shopping cart. This way, users can start an order during one Web session and finish it on another day in another session. Session cookies usually expire after a certain time, such as a week or a month.
- Some Web sites use cookies to track how regularly users visit a site and the Web pages they visit while at the site.
- Web sites may use cookies to target advertisements. These sites store a user's interests and browsing habits in the cookie.

You can set your browser to accept cookies automatically, prompt you if you want to accept a cookie, or disable cookie use altogether. Keep in mind if you disable cookie use, you will not be able to use many of the e-commerce Web sites.

Spyware and Adware

Spyware is a program placed on a computer without the user's knowledge that secretly collects information about the user. Spyware can enter a computer as a virus or as a result of a user installing a new program. The spyware program communicates information it collects to some outside source while you are online.

Some vendors or employers use spyware to collect information about program usage or employees. Internet advertising firms often collect information about users' Web browsing habits by hiding spyware in adware. **Adware** is a program that displays an online advertisement in a banner or pop-up window on Web pages, e-mail messages, or other Internet services. To remove spyware and adware, you can obtain a spyware and adware remover that can detect and delete spyware and adware. Some operating systems and Web browsers include spyware removers. Read Ethics & Issues 10-2 for a related discussion.

ETHICS & ISSUES 10-2

Should Spyware Be Legal?

Legitimate businesses and illegitimate hackers use a variety of techniques to secretly install spyware on unsecured computers. Spyware can perform a number of tasks, such as monitoring the Web sites that a person visits or controlling a computer remotely. Some Web pages also have cookies that count visitors and gather basic statistical information about a visitor's location and Web browser. Online advertising agencies or Internet access providers frequently place spyware cookies as part of a promotion, sometimes without the knowledge of the Web page's sponsor. When the collected information is stored in a Web database and shared among several sites, the technology can track a visitor's travels around the Web. If a visitor completes a registration, that information also can be distributed to other advertisers. Spyware and cookies help advertisers reach their markets and refine their messages, but opponents say the technology is little more than electronic stalking. Legal experts say that the use of spyware is in a legal gray area, and stronger laws are needed to regulate it. Should spyware and/or cookies be banned, or is it the right of Web page owners and advertisers to collect information about visitors? Why? Should Web page authors and/or Web page visitors be made aware of spyware and cookies? Why or why not?

Phishing

Phishing is a scam in which a perpetrator sends an official looking e-mail message that attempts to obtain your personal and financial information. Some phishing e-mail messages ask you to reply with your information; others direct you to a phony Web site, or a pop-up window that looks like a Web site, that collects the information.

If you receive an e-mail that looks legitimate and requests you update credit card numbers, Social Security numbers, bank account numbers, passwords, or other private information, the FTC recommends you visit the Web site directly to determine if the request is valid. Never click a link in an e-mail message; instead retype the Web address in your browser.

A **phishing filter** is a program that warns or blocks you from potentially fraudulent or suspicious Web sites. Some Web browsers include phishing filters.

Pharming is a scam, similar to phishing, where a perpetrator attempts to obtain your personal and financial information, except they do so via spoofing. That is, when you type a Web address in the Web browser, you are redirected to a phony Web site that looks legitimate. The phony Web site requests you enter confidential information.

FAQ 10-3

What do I do if I have been caught in a phishing scam?

If you have been trapped in a phishing scam, visit http://www.ftc.gov or call the FTC help line at 1-877-FTC-HELP. For more information, visit scsite.com/dcf5e/ch10/faq and then click Phishing Scams.

WEB LINK 10-8

Spam

For more information, visit scsite.com/dcf5e/ch10/weblink and then click Spam.

Spam

Spam is an unsolicited e-mail message or newsgroup posting sent to multiple recipients or newsgroups at once. Spam is Internet junk mail (Figure 10-19). The content of spam ranges from selling a product or service, to promoting a business opportunity, to advertising offensive material. One study indicates the average user receives more than 2,200 spam e-mail messages each year.

FIGURE 10-19   An example of spam.

Users can reduce the amount of spam they receive with a number of techniques. Some e-mail programs have built-in settings that allow users to delete spam automatically. Users also can sign up for e-mail filtering from their Internet access provider. **E-mail filtering** is a service that blocks e-mail messages from designated sources. An alternative to e-mail filtering is to purchase an **anti-spam program** that attempts to remove spam before it reaches your inbox. The disadvantage of e-mail filters and anti-spam programs is that sometimes they remove valid e-mail messages. Thus, users should review the contents of the spam messages periodically to ensure they do not contain valid messages.

Privacy Laws

The concern about privacy has led to the enactment of federal and state laws regarding the storage and disclosure of personal data (Figure 10-20).

Common points in some of these laws include the following:

1. Information collected and stored about individuals should be limited to what is necessary to carry out the function of the business or government agency collecting the data.
2. Once collected, provisions should be made to restrict access to the data to those employees within the organization who need access to it to perform their job duties.
3. Personal information should be released outside the organization collecting the data only when the person has agreed to its disclosure.
4. When information is collected about an individual, the individual should know that the data is being collected and have the opportunity to determine the accuracy of the data.

Date	Law	Purpose
2003	CAN-SPAM Act	Gives law enforcement the right to impose penalties on people using the Internet to distribute spam.
2002	Sarbanes-Oxley Act	Requires corporate officers, auditors, and attorneys of publicly-traded companies follow strict financial reporting guidelines.
2001	Children's Internet Protection Act (CIPA)	Protects minors from inappropriate content when accessing the Internet in schools and libraries.
2001	Provide Appropriate Tools Required to Intercept and Obstruct Terrorism (PATRIOT) Act	Gives law enforcement the right to monitor people's activities, including Web and e-mail habits.
1999	Gramm-Leach-Bliley Act (GLBA) or Financial Modernization Act	Protects consumers from disclosure of their personal financial information and requires institutions to alert customers of information disclosure policies.
1998	Children's Online Privacy Protection Act (COPPA)	Requires Web sites protect personal information of children under 13 years of age.
1998	Digital Millennium Copyright Act (DMCA)	Makes it illegal to circumvent antipiracy schemes in commercial software; outlaws sale of devices that copy software illegally.
1997	No Electronic Theft (NET) Act	Closes a narrow loophole in the law that allowed people to give away copyrighted material (such as software) on the Internet without legal repercussions.
1996	Health Insurance Portability and Accountability Act (HIPAA)	Protects individuals against the wrongful disclosure of their health information.
1996	National Information Infrastructure Protection Act	Penalizes theft of information across state lines, threats against networks, and computer system trespassing.
1994	Computer Abuse Amendments Act	Amends 1984 act to outlaw transmission of harmful computer code such as viruses.
1992	Cable Act	Extends the privacy of the Cable Communications Policy Act of 1984 to include cellular and other wireless services.
1991	Telephone Consumer Protection Act	Restricts activities of telemarketers.
1988	Computer Matching and Privacy Protection Act	Regulates the use of government data to determine the eligibility of individuals for federal benefits.
1988	Video Privacy Protection Act	Forbids retailers from releasing or selling video-rental records without customer consent or a court order.
1986	Electronic Communications Privacy Act (ECPA)	Provides the same right of privacy protection for the postal delivery service and telephone companies to the new forms of electronic communications, such as voice mail, e-mail, and cell phones.
1984	Cable Communications Policy Act	Regulates disclosure of cable television subscriber records.
1984	Computer Fraud and Abuse Act	Outlaws unauthorized access of federal government computers.
1978	Right to Financial Privacy Act	Strictly outlines procedures federal agencies must follow when looking at customer records in banks.
1974	Privacy Act	Forbids federal agencies from allowing information to be used for a reason other than that for which it was collected.
1974	Family Educational Rights and Privacy Act	Gives students and parents access to school records and limits disclosure of records to unauthorized parties.
1970	Fair Credit Reporting Act	Prohibits credit reporting agencies from releasing credit information to unauthorized people and allows consumers to review their own credit records.

FIGURE 10-20 Summary of the major U.S. government laws concerning privacy.

Social Engineering

As related to the use of computers, **social engineering** is defined as gaining unauthorized access or obtaining confidential information by taking advantage of the trusting human nature of some victims and the naivety of others. Some social engineers trick their victims into revealing confidential information such as user names and passwords on the telephone, in person, or on the Internet. Techniques they use include pretending to be an administrator or other authoritative figure, feigning an emergency situation, or impersonating an acquaintance. Social engineers also obtain information from users who do not destroy or conceal information properly. These perpetrators sift through company dumpsters, watch or film people dialing telephone numbers or using ATMs, and snoop around computers looking for openly displayed confidential information.

Employee Monitoring

Employee monitoring involves the use of computers to observe, record, and review an employee's use of a computer, including communications such as e-mail messages, keyboard activity (used to measure productivity), and Web sites visited. Many programs exist that easily allow employers to monitor employees. Further, it is legal for employers to use these programs.

A frequently debated issue is whether an employer has the right to read employee e-mail messages. Actual policies vary widely. Some companies declare that they will review e-mail messages regularly, and others state that e-mail is private. In some states, if a company does not have a formal e-mail policy, it can read e-mail messages without employee notification. Several lawsuits have been filed against employers because many believe that such internal communications should be private.

Another controversial issue relates to the use of cameras to monitor employees, customers, and the public. Many people feel that this use of video cameras is a violation of privacy.

Content Filtering

One of the more controversial issues that surround the Internet is its widespread availability of objectionable material, such as racist literature, violence, and obscene pictures. Some believe that such materials should be banned. Others believe that the materials should be filtered, that is, restricted. **Content filtering** is the process of restricting access to certain material on the Web. Content filtering opponents argue that banning any materials violates constitutional guarantees of free speech and personal rights.

Many businesses use content filtering to limit employees' Web access. These businesses argue that employees are unproductive when visiting inappropriate or objectionable Web sites. Some schools, libraries, and parents use content filtering to restrict access to minors.

Web filtering software is a program that restricts access to specified Web sites. Some also filter sites that use specific words. Others allow you to filter e-mail messages, chat rooms, and programs. Many Internet security programs include a firewall, antivirus program, and filtering capabilities combined (Figure 10-21).

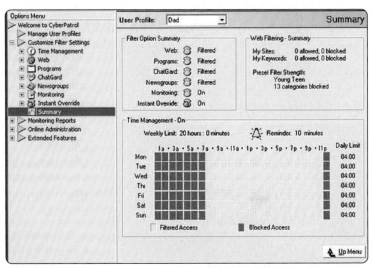

FIGURE 10-21   Many Internet security programs include content filtering capabilities, where users can block specified Web sites and applications.

Computer Forensics

Computer forensics, also called digital forensics, network forensics, or cyberforensics, is the discovery, collection, and analysis of evidence found on computers and networks. Forensic analysis involves the examination of computer media, programs, data and log files on computers, servers, and networks. Many areas use computer forensics, including law enforcement, criminal prosecutors, military intelligence, insurance agencies, and information security departments in the private sector.

A computer forensics analyst must have knowledge of the law, technical experience with many types of hardware and software products, superior communication skills, familiarity with corporate structures and policies, a willingness to learn and update skills, and a knack for problem solving. For a look at the next generation of forensics, read Looking Ahead 10-2.

LOOKING AHEAD 10-2

Computer Knowledge Assessment Using Brain Fingerprinting

A powerful forensic tool may one day replace the traditional lie detector test. Brain fingerprinting examines a subset of brain waves generated involuntarily when an individual recognizes familiar information.

To conduct the test, researchers place a strap equipped with sensors on an individual's head and then present a variety of relevant and irrelevant words, pictures, and sounds. If the stimulus is familiar, the brain generates unique brain waves 300 to 800 milliseconds after receiving the stimulus.

Computers store and then analyze the series of unique brain waves to determine if the person's brain has stored critical details of a situation, such as a fraudulent or criminal act. Researchers also have determined that brain fingerprinting could help identify the onset of Alzheimer's disease. For more information, visit scsite.com/dcf5e/ch10/looking and then click Brain Fingerprinting.

HEALTH CONCERNS OF COMPUTER USE

Users are a key component in any information system. Thus, protecting users is just as important as protecting hardware, software, and data.

The widespread use of computers has led to some important health concerns. The following sections discuss health risks and preventions, along with measures users can take to keep the environment healthy.

Computers and Health Risks

A **repetitive strain injury** (**RSI**) is an injury or disorder of the muscles, nerves, tendons, ligaments, and joints. Computer-related RSIs include tendonitis and carpal tunnel syndrome. RSIs are the largest job-related injury and illness problem in the United States today.

Tendonitis is inflammation of a tendon due to some repeated motion or stress on that tendon. Carpal tunnel syndrome (CTS) is inflammation of the nerve that connects the forearm to the palm of the wrist. Repeated or forceful bending of the wrist can cause CTS or tendonitis of the wrist. Symptoms of tendonitis of the wrist include extreme pain that extends from the forearm to the hand, along with tingling in the fingers. Symptoms of CTS include burning pain when the nerve is compressed, along with numbness and tingling in the thumb and first two fingers.

Long-term computer work can lead to tendonitis or CTS. Factors that cause these disorders include prolonged typing, prolonged mouse usage, or continual shifting between the mouse and the keyboard. If untreated, these disorders can lead to permanent damage to your body.

You can take many precautions to prevent these types of injuries. Take frequent breaks during the computer session to exercise your hands and arms (Figure 10-22). To prevent injury due to typing, place a wrist rest between the keyboard and the edge of your desk. To prevent injury while using a mouse, place the mouse at least six inches from the edge of the desk. In this position, your wrist is flat on the desk. Finally, minimize the number of times you switch between the mouse and the keyboard, and avoid using the heel of your hand as a pivot point while typing or using the mouse.

HAND EXERCISES

- Spread fingers apart for several seconds while keeping wrists straight.
- Gently push back fingers and then thumb.
- Dangle arms loosely at sides and then shake arms and hands.

FIGURE 10-22 To reduce the chance of developing tendonitis or carpal tunnel syndrome, take frequent breaks during computer sessions to exercise your hands and arms.

Another type of health-related condition due to computer usage is **computer vision syndrome** (CVS). You may have CVS if you have sore, tired, burning, itching, or dry eyes; blurred or double vision; distance blurred vision after prolonged staring at a display device; headache or sore neck; difficulty shifting focus between a display device and documents; difficulty focusing on the screen image; color fringes or after-images when you look away from the display device; and increased sensitivity to light. Eyestrain associated with CVS is not thought to have serious or long-term consequences. Figure 10-23 outlines some techniques you can follow to ease eyestrain.

People who spend their workday using the computer sometimes complain of lower back pain, muscle fatigue, and emotional fatigue. Lower back pain sometimes is caused from poor posture. Always sit properly in the chair while you work. Take a break every 30 to 60 minutes — stand up, walk around, or stretch. Another way to help prevent these injuries is to be sure your workplace is designed ergonomically.

Ergonomics and Workplace Design

Ergonomics is an applied science devoted to incorporating comfort, efficiency, and safety into the design of items in the workplace. Ergonomic studies have shown that using the correct type and configuration of chair, keyboard, display device, and work surface helps users work comfortably and efficiently and helps protect their health. For the computer work space, experts recommend an area of at least two feet by four feet. Figure 10-24 illustrates additional guidelines for setting up the work area.

TECHNIQUES TO EASE EYESTRAIN

- Every 10 to 15 minutes, take an eye break.
  - Look into the distance and focus on an object for 20 to 30 seconds.
  - Roll your eyes in a complete circle.
  - Close your eyes and rest them for at least one minute.
- Blink your eyes every five seconds.
- Place your display device about an arm's length away from your eyes with the top of the screen at eye level or below.
- Use large fonts.
- If you wear glasses, ask your doctor about computer glasses.
- Adjust the lighting.

FIGURE 10-23   Following these tips may help reduce eyestrain while working on a computer.

viewing angle: 20° to center of screen
viewing distance: 18 to 28 inches

arms: elbows at about 90° and arms and hands approximately parallel to floor

keyboard height: 23 to 28 inches depending on height of user

adjustable height chair with 4 or 5 legs for stability

feet flat on floor

FIGURE 10-24
A well-designed work area should be flexible to allow adjustments to the height and build of different individuals. Good lighting and air quality also are important considerations.

Computer Addiction

Computers can provide entertainment and enjoyment. Some computer users, however, become obsessed with the computer and the Internet. **Computer addiction** occurs when the computer consumes someone's entire social life. Computer addiction is a growing health problem. Symptoms of a user with computer addiction include the following:

- Craves computer time
- Overjoyed when at the computer
- Unable to stop computer activity
- Irritable when not at the computer
- Neglects family and friends
- Problems at work or school

Computer addiction is a treatable illness through therapy and support groups.

Green Computing

Green computing involves reducing the electricity and environmental waste while using a computer. People use, and often waste, resources such as electricity and paper while using a computer.

Experts estimate that more than 700 million personal computers are obsolete. Because of the huge volumes of electronic waste, the U.S. federal government has proposed a bill that would require computer recycling across the country. Local governments are working on methods to make it easy for consumers to recycle this type of equipment.

To reduce the environmental impact of computing further, users simply can alter a few habits. Figure 10-25 lists the ways you can contribute to green computing.

WEB LINK 10-9

Green Computing

For more information, visit scsite.com/dcf5e/ch10/weblink and then click Green Computing.

GREEN COMPUTING SUGGESTIONS

1. **Use computers and devices that comply with the ENERGY STAR program.**
2. **Do not leave the computer running overnight.**
3. **Turn off the monitor, printer, and other devices when not in use.**
4. **Use paperless methods to communicate.**
5. **Recycle paper.**
6. **Buy recycled paper.**
7. **Recycle toner cartridges.**
8. **Recycle old computers and printers.**
9. **Telecommute (saves gas).**

FIGURE 10-25
A list of suggestions to make computing healthy for the environment.

Test your knowledge of pages 376 through 387 in Quiz Yourself 10-3.

QUIZ YOURSELF 10-3

Instructions: Find the true statement below. Then, rewrite the remaining false statements so they are true.

1. Factors that cause CVS include prolonged typing, prolonged mouse usage, or continual shifting between the mouse and the keyboard.
2. Phishing is the discovery, collection, and analysis of evidence found on computers and networks.
3. Spam is Internet junk mail.
4. Web sites use electronic profiles to track user preferences, store users' passwords, keep track of items in a user's shopping cart, and track Web site browsing habits.
5. You can assume that information on the Web is correct.

Quiz Yourself Online: To further check your knowledge of information privacy and computer-related health disorders and preventions, visit scsite.com/dcf5e/ch10/quiz and then click Objectives 7 – 8.

CHAPTER SUMMARY

This chapter identified some potential computer risks and the safeguards that schools, businesses, and individuals can implement to minimize these risks. Wireless security risks and safeguards also were discussed. Read Ethics & Issues 10-3 for a related discussion.

The chapter presented ethical issues surrounding information accuracy, intellectual property rights, and information privacy. The chapter ended with a discussion of computer-related health issues, their preventions, and ways to keep the environment healthy.

 ETHICS & ISSUES 10-3

What Can Be Done to Stop the Growing Threat of Cybercrime?

By some estimates, cybercrime has become a worldwide criminal industry that involves more than $100 billion in illegal trade, which surpasses the illicit drug trade. Cybercrime includes online or Internet-based illegal acts. Some believe that the total cost of cybercrime to individuals and organizations may exceed a half trillion dollars. Furthermore, perhaps only five percent of those committing cybercrimes are caught. Legendary fraudster Frank Abagnale, whose criminal exploits 40 years ago involved forgery and impersonation, claims that, due to advances in technology, it is now 4,000 times easier to do what he did back then. Some people feel that cybercrime simply represents an evolution in criminal techniques and that any attempt to fight it only will result in the techniques evolving into more sophisticated methods. While no government agency has declared a war on cybercrime, many feel that it is time to raise awareness of this troubling issue. How can the cybercrime problem best be handled? Why? Why do you think that cybercrime might not be taken as seriously as other criminal problems? What might be the effects on society and the Internet if cybercrime is left largely unchecked? How would you know if you are a victim of cybercrime, and if you were, what could you do about it?

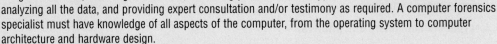

CAREER CORNER — Computer Forensics Specialist

Computer forensics is a rapidly growing field that involves gathering and analyzing evidence from computers and networks. It is the responsibility of the **computer forensics specialist** to take several careful steps to identify and retrieve possible evidence that may exist on a suspect's computer. These steps include protecting the suspect's computer, discovering all files, recovering deleted files, revealing hidden files, accessing protected or encrypted files, analyzing all the data, and providing expert consultation and/or testimony as required. A computer forensics specialist must have knowledge of all aspects of the computer, from the operating system to computer architecture and hardware design.

In the past, many computer forensics specialists were self-taught computer users who may have attended computer forensics seminars, or they may have been trained in the use of one or more computer forensics tools by software vendors. The computer forensics specialist of today needs extensive training, usually from several different sources. A degree in Computer Science should be supplemented with graduate courses and university level professional development certificates. The most widely recognized certifications available to computer forensics professionals are the Certified Information Systems Security Professional (CISSP) and the Certified Computer Examiner (CCE). The CCE is offered by the International Society for Computer Examiners (ISFCE), an organization created to maintain high standards for computer examiners.

Entry level salaries for computer forensics specialists range from $90,000 to $125,000. With experience and certifications, salaries can exceed $170,000. For more information, visit scsite.com/dcf5e/ch10/careers and then click Computer Forensics Specialist.

McAfee
Intrusion Prevention Products Developer

Researchers in 17 cities in 12 countries are hard at work at McAfee laboratories trying to prevent computer intrusions. The Anti-Virus Emergency Response Team (Avert) protects desktop computers, servers, networks, and wireless devices by collecting and then disassembling malware. The researchers also monitor online bulletin board systems for suspicious messages and expect to find more than 18,000 new threats each year.

More than 120 million consumers, small- and medium-sized businesses, governmental agencies, and large corporations rely on McAfee's intrusion prevention products to shield them from viruses, worms, Trojan horses, spyware and adware, and phishing schemes. In 2007, the Computing Technology Industry Association named McAfee VirusScan as one of the most influential technology products of the past 25 years. For more information, visit scsite.com/dcf5e/ch10/companies and then click McAfee.

Symantec
Computer Security Solutions Leader

Ninety percent of computer users have installed a virus protection program on their computers, but only 20 percent have a firewall to protect against malicious hackers, according to a survey conducted by Applied Marketing Research. Symantec's line of Norton products, including AntiVirus, Internet Security, and AntiSpam, can provide these users with peace of mind knowing that their computers are as secure as possible.

Gordon Eubank founded Symantec in 1982. Since then, more than 120 million users worldwide have used that company's products, helping it grow to one of the world's premier Internet security technology companies with operations in more than 40 countries. Symantec launched its nationwide Connected and Protected Child Safety Initiative in partnership with Miss America 2007 Lauren Nelson, whose personal platform is protecting children online. For more information, visit scsite.com/dcf5e/ch10/companies and then click Symantec.

TECHNOLOGY TRAILBLAZERS

Donn Parker
Cybercrime Authority

Computer criminals are troubled people, according to Donn Parker, so they violate the law in an attempt to solve their problems. In an attempt to fight cybercrime, Parker founded the International Information Integrity Institute (I-4), then interviewed hundreds of computer criminals and analyzed thousands of security crime cases during the past 30 years.

Security systems within corporations are critical, he says, but they should evolve constantly to defend against attackers. He created the International Information Integrity Institute (I-4) for industry leaders to meet regularly to share their strategies, ideas, experiences, and expertise on managing information-related business risks.

Parker has conducted security reviews for more than 250 companies and has written 6 computer security books. For more information, visit scsite.com/dcf5e/ch10/people and then click Donn Parker.

Clifford Stoll
Computer Philosopher

Computers have become integrated in practically every phase of our lives, but Clifford Stoll wants us to think about their effect on our quality of life. He questions the benefits technology presumably provides and the role computers play in schools.

In his books, *Silicon Snake Oil — Second Thoughts on the Information Highway* and *High Tech Heretic: Why Computers Don't Belong in the Classroom*, Stoll maintains that "life in the real world is far more interesting, far more important, far richer, than anything you'll ever find on a computer screen."

He first gained fame by writing the book, *The Cuckoo's Egg: Tracking a Spy through the Maze of Computer Espionage*, which describes his efforts tracking a hacker who was part of a spy ring selling computer secrets to the Soviet Union's KGB for money and drugs. For more information, visit scsite.com/dcf5e/ch10/people and then click Clifford Stoll.

Chapter Review

The Chapter Review section summarizes the concepts presented in this chapter. To obtain help from other students regarding any subject in this chapter, visit scsite.com/dcf5e/ch10/forum and post your thoughts or questions.

(1) How Can Users Safeguard against Computer Viruses, Worms, Trojan Horses, Botnets, Denial of Service Attacks, Back Doors, and Spoofing?

A computer **virus** is a potentially damaging program that infects a computer and negatively affects the way the computer works. A **worm** is a program that copies itself repeatedly, using up resources and possibly shutting down the computer or network. A **Trojan horse** is a program that hides within or looks like a legitimate program. Users can take precautions to guard against this **malware**, short for malicious software. Do not start a computer with removable media in the drives or ports unless the media are uninfected. Never open an e-mail attachment unless it is from a trusted source. Disable macros in documents that are not from a trusted source. Install an **antivirus program** and a personal firewall program. Stay informed about any new virus alert or **virus hoax**. To defend against a **botnet,** a **denial of service attack,** improper use of a **back door,** and **spoofing**, users can install a **firewall** and install **intrusion detection software**.

(2) What Are Techniques to Prevent Unauthorized Access and Use?

Unauthorized access is the use of a computer or network without permission. **Unauthorized use** is the use of a computer or its data for unapproved or illegal activities. A written acceptable use policy (AUP) outlines the activities for which the computer and network may and may not be used. Other measures include firewalls and intrusion detection software. An **access control** defines who can access a computer, when they can access it, and what actions they can take. An **audit trail** records in a file both successful and unsuccessful access attempts. Access controls include a **user name** and **password**, a possessed object, and a **biometric device**.

 Visit scsite.com/dcf5e/ch10/quiz or click the Quiz Yourself button. Click Objectives 1 – 2.

(3) What Are Safeguards against Hardware Theft and Vandalism?

Hardware theft is the act of stealing computer equipment. **Hardware vandalism** is the act of defacing or destroying computer equipment. Physical devices and practical security measures, passwords, possessed objects, and biometrics can reduce the risk of theft or render a computer useless if it is stolen.

(4) How Do Software Manufacturers Protect against Software Theft and Information Theft?

Software theft occurs when someone steals software, intentionally erases programs, or illegally copies programs. Software **piracy** is the unauthorized and illegal duplication of copyrighted software. To protect themselves from software piracy, manufacturers issue a **license agreement** that provides specific conditions for use of the software. During **product activation**, users provide the product's identification number to receive an installation identification number unique to their computer. Companies attempt to prevent **information theft** through user identification and authentication controls, **encryption**, a **digital signature**, a **digital certificate**, or a **certificate authority**.

(5) What Types of Devices Are Available to Protect Computers against System Failure?

A **system failure** is the prolonged malfunction of a computer. A common cause of system failure is an electrical power variation. A **surge protector** uses special electrical components to provide a stable current flow to the computer. An **uninterruptible power supply** (**UPS**) contains surge protection circuits and one or more batteries that can provide power during a power loss.

(6) What Are Risks and Safeguards Associated with Wireless Communications?

Wireless access poses additional security risks. Intruders connect to other wireless networks to gain free Internet access or to access a company's confidential data. Some individuals intercept and monitor communications as they are transmitted. Others connect to a network through an unsecured wireless access point (WAP). Some safeguards include firewalls, reconfiguring the WAP, and ensuring equipment uses a wireless security standard, such as **Wi-Fi Protected Access** and **802.11i.**

Visit scsite.com/dcf5e/ch10/quiz or click the Quiz Yourself button. Click Objectives 3 – 6.

 (7) What Are Issues Surrounding Information Privacy?

Information privacy is the right of individuals and companies to restrict the collection and use of information about them. Issues surrounding information privacy include electronic profiles, cookies, spyware and adware, phishing, spam, social engineering, employee monitoring, and computer forensics. An electronic profile combines data about an individual's Web use with data from public sources. A **cookie** is a file that a Web server stores on a computer to collect data about the user. **Spyware** is a program placed on a computer that secretly collects information about the user. **Adware** is a program that displays an online advertisement in a banner or pop-up window. **Phishing** is a scam in which a perpetrator sends an official looking e-mail message that attempts to obtain a user's personal and financial information. **Pharming** is a scam where a perpetrator attempts to obtain your personal and financial information, except they do so via spoofing. **Spam** is an unsolicited e-mail message or newsgroup posting sent to many recipients. As related to the use of computers, **social engineering** is defined as gaining unauthorized access or obtaining confidential information by taking advantage of the trusting human nature of some victims and the naivety of others. **Employee monitoring** uses computers to observe, record, and review an employee's computer use. **Computer forensics** is the discovery, collection, and analysis of evidence found on computers and networks.

(8) How Can Health-Related Disorders and Injuries Due to Computer Use Be Prevented?

A **repetitive strain injury** (RSI) is an injury or disorder of the muscles, nerves, tendons, ligaments, and joints. Computer-related RSIs include tendonitis and carpal tunnel syndrome (CTS). Another health-related condition is eyestrain associated with **computer vision syndrome** (CVS). To prevent health-related disorders, take frequent breaks, use precautionary exercises and techniques, and incorporate ergonomics when planning the workplace. **Computer addiction** occurs when the computer consumes someone's entire social life. Computer addiction is a treatable illness through therapy and support groups.

Visit scsite.com/dcf5e/ch10/quiz or click the Quiz Yourself button. Click Objectives 7 – 8.

Key Terms

You should know each key term. Use the list below to help focus your study. To further enhance your understanding of the Key Terms in this chapter, visit scsite.com/dcf5e/ch10/terms. See an example of and a definition for each term, and access current and additional information about the term from the Web.

802.11i (376)	cookie (380)	intrusion detection software (368)	social engineering (384)
access control (368)	copyright (378)	license agreement (372)	software theft (372)
adware (381)	cracker (362)	malware (364)	spam (382)
anti-spam program (382)	cybercrime (362)	online backup service (375)	spoofing (367)
antivirus program (365)	cyberextortionist (363)	password (369)	spyware (381)
audit trail (368)	cyberterrorist (363)	payload (364)	surge protector (374)
back door (367)	decrypt (373)	personal firewall (368)	system failure (374)
back up (375)	denial of service attack (367)	personal identification number	Trojan horse (364)
backup (375)	digital certificate (374)	(PIN) (370)	unauthorized access (368)
biometric device (370)	digital rights management (378)	pharming (382)	unauthorized use (368)
biometric payment (370)	digital signature (374)	phishing (381)	uninterruptible power
botnet (367)	DoS attack (367)	phishing filter (382)	supply (UPS) (375)
CAPTCHA (369)	e-mail filtering (382)	piracy (372)	user name (369)
certificate authority (374)	employee monitoring (384)	Pretty Good Privacy (PGP) (374)	virus (364)
computer addiction (387)	encryption (373)	product activation (372)	virus definition (366)
computer crime (362)	firewall (367)	quarantine (366)	virus hoax (366)
computer ethics (376)	green computing (387)	real time location system (RTLS)	virus signature (366)
computer forensics (385)	hacker (362)	(371)	war driving (376)
computer forensics specialist	hardware theft (371)	repetitive strain injury (RSI)	Web filtering software (384)
(388)	hardware vandalism (371)	(385)	Wi-Fi Protected Access (376)
computer security risk (362)	information privacy (379)	restore (375)	worm (364)
computer vision syndrome (386)	information theft (373)	script kiddie (362)	zombie (367)
content filtering (384)	intellectual property rights (378)	secure site (374)	

Checkpoint

Use the Checkpoint exercises to check your knowledge level of the chapter. To complete the Checkpoint exercises interactively, visit scsite.com/dcf5e/ch10/check.

True/False

Mark T for True and F for False. (See page numbers in parentheses.)

_____ 1. Script kiddies often are professional hackers that write complex programs used to break into computers. (362)

_____ 2. A firewall is hardware and/or software that allows users to bypass security controls when accessing a program, computer, or network. (367)

_____ 3. In order to safeguard against unauthorized access and use of its computers, a company should have a digital certificate. (368)

_____ 4. Biometric payment involves a customer's fingerprint being read by a fingerprint reader that is linked to a payment method such as a checking account or credit card. (370)

_____ 5. Some businesses use a real time location system (RTLS) to track and identify the location of high-risk or high-value items. (371)

_____ 6. Digital signatures often are used to ensure that an impostor is not participating in an Internet transaction. (374)

_____ 7. A digital certificate warns a user that software has been pirated. (374)

_____ 8. Digital rights management (DRM) is a strategy designed to prevent illegal distribution of computer viruses, worms, and Trojan horses. (378)

_____ 9. A phishing filter is a program that attempts to remove spam before it reaches your inbox. (382)

_____ 10. Green computing involves reducing the electricity while using a computer, but the practice increases environmental waste. (387)

Multiple Choice

Select the best answer. (See page numbers in parentheses.)

1. Malware is a term that can be used to describe _____. (364)
   a. viruses
   b. worms
   c. Trojan horses
   d. all of the above

2. The _____ is the destructive event or prank that malware is intended to deliver. (364)
   a. hash
   b. spam
   c. cookie
   d. payload

3. A _____ is an assault whose purpose is to disrupt computer access to an Internet service such as the Web or e-mail. (367)
   a. zombie
   b. denial of service attack
   c. Trojan horse
   d. virus hoax

4. Physical access controls, such as locked doors and windows, usually are adequate to protect against _____. (371)
   a. software piracy
   b. unauthorized access
   c. hardware theft
   d. all of the above

5. Unencrypted, readable data is called _____. (373)
   a. hypertext
   b. ciphertext
   c. subtext
   d. plaintext

6. _____ is a scam in which a perpetrator sends an official looking e-mail message that attempts to obtain your personal and financial information. (381)
   a. Pharming
   b. Phishing
   c. Spoofing
   d. E-mail filtering

7. As related to the use of computers, _____ is defined as gaining unauthorized access or obtaining confidential information by taking advantage of the trusting human nature of some victims and the naivety of others. (384)
   a. phishing
   b. a virus hoax
   c. social engineering
   d. pharming

8. _____ involves the examination of computer media, programs, data and log files on computers, servers, and networks. (385)
   a. Computer forensics
   b. E-mail filtering
   c. Encryption key
   d. Trusted source

Matching

Match the terms with their definitions. (See page numbers in parentheses.)

_____ 1. virus (364)

_____ 2. Trojan horse (364)

_____ 3. spoofing (367)

_____ 4. surge protector (374)

_____ 5. spyware (381)

a. technique intruders use to make their network or Internet transmission appear legitimate to a victim computer or network

b. service that blocks e-mail messages from designated sources

c. potentially damaging computer program that affects, or infects, a computer negatively by altering the way the computer works without the user's knowledge or permission

d. program that hides within or looks like a legitimate program

e. uses special electrical components to provide a stable current flow to the computer and other electronic equipment

f. program placed on a computer without the user's knowledge that secretly collects information about the user

Checkpoint

Short Answer

Write a brief answer to each of the following questions.

1. How do antivirus programs detect and identify a virus? _____ What is a virus hoax? _____

2. What is CAPTCHA, and how does it work? _____ Describe two other types of personal information that a system may ask a user to enter in addition to a user name and password. _____

3. What is information privacy? _____ List five ways to protect your personal information. _____

4. How does a pharming scam work? _____ What are three methods used to reduce spam? _____

5. What is content filtering, and who uses it? _____ Why is content filtering controversial? _____

Working Together

Working in a group of your classmates, complete the following team exercise.

1. Some schools have begun repetitive strain injury (RSI) prevention programs, but too many students still pay too little attention to ergonomic issues. How safe is your workplace? Each member of your team should compare the characteristics of his or her workplace to the ergonomic guidelines presented in this chapter. Make a sketch of the workplace indicating where it does, and does not, conform to the guidelines. Meet with the members of your team to discuss how each workplace could be improved. Create a group presentation and share your findings with the class.

Web Research

Use the Internet-based Web Research exercises to broaden your understanding of the concepts presented in this chapter. To discuss any of the Web Research exercises in this chapter with other students, visit scsite.com/dcf5e/ch10/forum and post your thoughts or questions.

 Blogs

More than 80,000 blogs are created daily according to Umbria Communications, a service that tracks new Internet media. Many information technology (IT) professionals maintain these blogs to tout companies' products and express personal observations. IT bloggers include Robert Scoble on Microsoft (scobleizer.com); Jeff Jaffe, Novell's chief technical officer (novell.com/ctoblog); Ed Brill on IBM (edbrill.com/ebrill/edbrill.nsf); and Tom Kyte on Oracle (tkyte.blogspot.com). Visit these blogs and read some of the posts. What new products are mentioned? What are the bloggers' backgrounds? What controversial topics are discussed? What personal views do the bloggers express?

 Scavenger Hunt

Use one of the search engines listed in Figure 2-8 in Chapter 2 on page 58 or your own favorite search engine to find the answers to the following questions. Copy and paste the Web address from the Web page where you found the answer. Some questions may have more than one answer. If required, submit your answers to your instructor. (1) Which Usenet newsgroup first mentioned the term, phishing, in 1996? (2) What term is John Scoch credited with creating at the Xerox Palo Alto Research Center in the late 1970s? When this term was coined, what was its intended meaning? (3) At what university is the Computer Emergency Response Team Coordination Center (CERT/CC) located? What is one of the latest advisories or incident notes reported by this organization?

 Search Sleuth

Internet subject directories are used to find information on specialized topics. One of the oldest and more popular subject directories is the WWW Virtual Library (VL) (vlib.org). This Web site is administered by a group of volunteers who are experts in particular topics. Visit this Web site and then use your word processing program to answer the following questions. Then, if required, submit your answers to your instructor. (1) Click the Donors link at the bottom of the page. Who has donated at least 1,000 Swiss francs for this library? (2) Click your browser's Back button or press the BACKSPACE key to return to the home page. Click the Computing and Computer Science link and then click the Safety-Critical Systems link. Review at least two articles that have new information or that are recommended and then write a 50-word summary that may be submitted to your instructor.

Learn How To

Use the Learn How To activities to learn fundamental skills when using a computer and accompanying technology. Complete the exercises and submit them to your instructor. Premium Activity: The icon indicates you can see a visual demonstration of the associated Learn How To activity by visiting scsite.com/dcf5e/ch10/howto.

 LEARN HOW TO 1: Back Up Files on an Offsite Internet Server

Note: The service described in this exercise allows 15 days of free access. After that time, you may be billed automatically for service unless you cancel your service in the given time frame.

Backing up files stored on your computer on another disk or computer located in a different geographical location is the ultimate safeguard for data on your computer. A good way to back up data is to use one of the services available on the Web. A leading service is found at www.IBackup.com. To subscribe to the IBackup service, complete the following steps:

1. Start a Web browser, type the Web address www.IBackup.com in the Address bar, and then press the ENTER key.
2. When the IBackup Web page is displayed, click Sign Up on the top horizontal toolbar.
3. Enter your e-mail address in the E-mail Address text box, and then click the Continue with Registration button to display a form (Figure 10-26).
4. Fill in the form. Select the plan you want in the Select a Storage Plan list. If you want to try the service for a short period of time before subscribing, select 5 GB free Trial for 15 Days.
5. To continue to the next pages, you must enter credit card information. If you select the 15-day trial, your credit card will not be charged, and an automatic billing at the end of 15 days will occur. After entering the required information, click the Continue button at the bottom of the page.
6. A message is displayed that confirms that you have signed up with IBackup, and also provides a link for you to download the IBackup for Windows program.
7. Click the DOWNLOAD button to download the IBackup for Windows program, and then follow the instructions to install the program on your computer.

FIGURE 10-26

After establishing an account, you can use it for the time for which you subscribed. Complete the following steps to use the service:

1. Start the IBackup for Windows program.
2. Enter your user name and password, and then click the Login button to display a window containing your files, as well as the contents of your My IBackup folder (Figure 10-27).
3. To upload a file, locate the file in the left pane of the IBackup window, and drag it to the right pane. The Backup Progress dialog box will be displayed while the file is uploading. The file will be placed in the My IBackup folder.
4. For further activities you can accomplish in this program for backing up your files, click the buttons on the top horizontal toolbar and experiment.

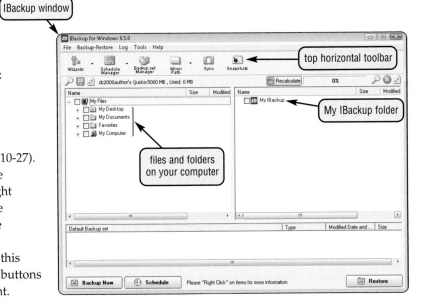

FIGURE 10-27

Exercise

1. Visit the IBackup Web site. Click View Demo and then follow the screen prompts to view all the services offered by IBackup. Which service is most appropriate for your home computer? Which service is most useful for the server that is used in the computer lab at your school? If you had critical data you needed to back up, would you use a service like this? Why or why not? Submit your answers to your instructor.

2. **Optional: Perform this exercise only for your own computer. Do not perform this exercise on a school computer.** Establish an account on IBackup.com. Upload two or more files from your computer. Download the files you uploaded back to your computer. Is this an efficient way to back up your files? Do you think the IBackup service would be useful for businesses? Submit your answers to your instructor.

LEARN HOW TO 2: Use the Windows Vista Firewall

When you use the Internet, data is sent both from your computer to the Internet and from computers on the Internet to your computer. A firewall is a barrier that checks information coming from the Internet and either turns it away or allows it to pass through to your computer, based on your firewall settings. It also checks data being sent from your computer to the Internet to ensure your computer is not sending unsolicited messages to other computers on the Internet. A firewall can be implemented using hardware or software.

Windows Vista contains a software firewall that starts automatically when you boot your computer. To control the firewall usage on your computer, complete the following steps:

1. Click the Start button on the Windows taskbar, and then click Control Panel on the Start menu.

2. In the Classic View of the Control Panel, double-click Security Center, and then click Windows Firewall in the Windows Security Center window to open the Windows Firewall window (Figure 10-28).

3. In the Windows Firewall window, click the Turn Windows Firewall on or off link to turn on or off the Windows firewall. The firewall automatically is on when you start your computer. You should NOT turn off the firewall unless you have a compelling reason to do so.

4. Click the 'Allow a program through Windows Firewall' link to display the Exceptions sheet in the Windows Firewall Settings dialog box (Figure 10-29). The exceptions that are checked can communicate with the Internet without your clicking a link.

5. You may want to allow programs that routinely communicate with the Internet, such as sports programs that display updated game scores, to have full access to your computer. To add a program to the Exceptions list, click the Add program button in the Exceptions sheet. The Add a Program dialog box is displayed. Select a program and then click the OK button.

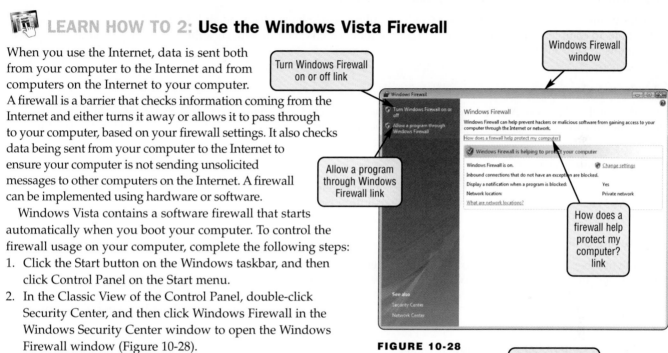

FIGURE 10-28

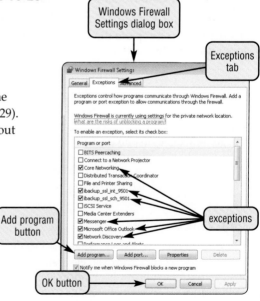

FIGURE 10-29

Exercise

1. Open the Windows Firewall window. Click the 'How does a firewall help protect my computer?' link. Read the information about Windows Firewall. What did you learn that you did not know? What is malicious software? What are some examples of malicious software? Submit your answers to your instructor.

Learn It Online

Use the Learn It Online exercises to reinforce your understanding of the chapter concepts. To access the Learn It Online exercises, visit scsite.com/dcf5e/ch10/learn.

(1) At the Movies — Attack of the Mobile Viruses

To view the Attack of the Mobile Viruses movie, click the number 1 button. Locate your video and click the corresponding High-Speed or Dial-Up link, depending on your Internet connection. Watch the movie to learn about the recent wave of viruses plaguing mobile phone users. Then, complete the exercise by answering the question that follows. How does a mobile device get a virus, and how can you protect your mobile device?

(2) Student Edition Labs — Protecting Your Privacy Online

Click the number 2 button. A new browser window will open, displaying the Student Edition Labs. Follow the on-screen instructions to complete the Protecting Your Privacy Online Lab. When finished, click the Exit button. If required, submit your results to your instructor.

(3) Practice Test

Click the number 3 button. Answer each question. When completed, enter your name and click the Grade Test button to submit the quiz for grading. Make a note of any missed questions. If required, submit your results to your instructor.

(4) Who Wants To Be a Computer Genius²?

Click the number 4 button to find out if you are a computer genius. Directions about how to play the game will be displayed. When you are ready to play, click the Play button. Submit your score to your instructor.

(5) Buying Online

Click the number 5 button to learn how to use the Internet to purchase merchandise. Follow the instructions to use Amazon.com and Barnes & Noble's Web site to compare prices and reviews of Joseph J. Ellis' *American Creation*. How did the prices of the book compare? Which site had more favorable reviews for the book? Which site would you recommend to a friend? Write a report summarizing your findings. Print the report and then submit it to your instructor.

(6) Student Edition Labs — Computer Ethics

Click the number 6 button. A new browser window will open, displaying the Student Edition Labs. Follow the on-screen instructions to complete the Computer Ethics Lab. When finished, click the Exit button. If required, submit your results to your instructor.

(7) Crossword Puzzle Challenge

Click the number 7 button, then click the Crossword Puzzle Challenge link. Directions about how to play the game will be displayed. Complete the puzzle to reinforce skills you learned in this chapter. When you are ready to play, click the Continue button. Submit the completed puzzle to your instructor.

(8) Vista Exercises

Click the number 8 button. When the Vista Exercises menu appears, click the exercise assigned by your instructor. A new browser window will open. Follow the on-screen instructions to complete the exercise. When finished, click the Exit button. If required, submit your results to your instructor.

Special Feature
Digital Entertainment
The Revolution Is Underway

Massachusetts Institute of Technology Professor Nicholas Negroponte coined the phrase, digital convergence, in his book, *Being Digital.* While some technology experts believe this term focuses on software, others believe it refers to hardware and networking, while still others see it as a service. The one commonality of all these views is the core of bits and bytes of data, music, video, graphics, text, and voice. Today, we are closer than ever in being able to share all these modes of entertainment seamlessly. Personal mobile devices allow us to record and listen to music; view favorite television programs or movies; keep in touch with the office, family, and friends; present ideas to others using real data and images; and entertain at home.

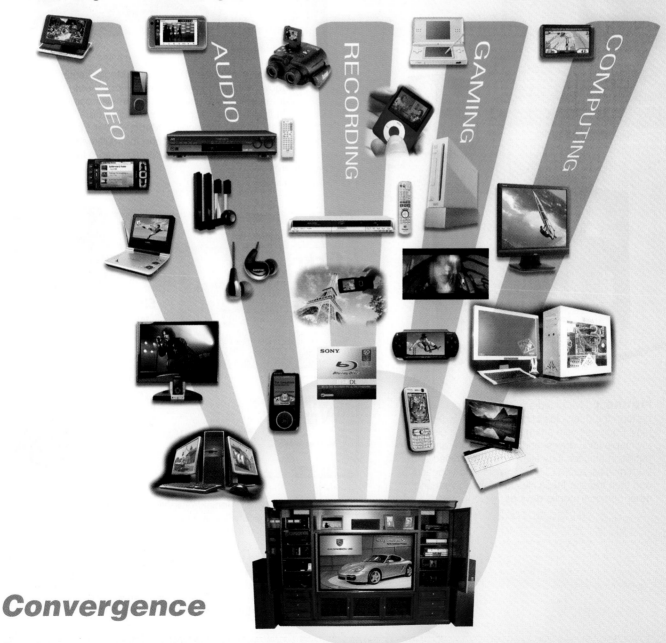

VIDEO   AUDIO   RECORDING   GAMING   COMPUTING

Convergence

The Personal Computer and Television

Falling prices for big-screen televisions and monitors have enticed consumers to update their media rooms and home offices. Flat panel and projection televisions have become the focal points of home entertainment systems. Their dramatic high-resolution pictures coupled with surround-sound systems and proper furniture provide the ultimate viewing experience.

FIGURE 2 Microsoft's Windows Media Center in Windows Vista allows you to experience viewing all your favorite digital entertainment on your computer, including live and recorded television programs, movies, music, and photos. Media Center Extenders, including the Xbox 360, expand the multimedia experience throughout your home on up to five televisions.

FIGURE 1 Multimedia personal computers can perform the dual roles of being used for work and play. Equipped with a large-capacity hard disk, rewritable DVD drives, and a wide-screen and high-definition monitor, they allow you to download and burn movies, audio CDs, podcasts, and vodcasts, and then transfer these files to smart phones and other personal mobile devices.

FIGURE 3 Social networking Web sites such as Facebook, MySpace, YouTube, TagWorld, and Bebo are popular forms of self-expression and pervasive ways to stay in touch and share experiences with friends and family. YouTube visitors watch more than 100 million video clips every day, with some individual videos viewed more than 5 million times. Some of these video Web sites pay users as much as $2,000 for uploading their videos.

Recording Audio and Video

Whether you are in the mood for an action-packed movie or some soothing new-age music, digital entertainment products can fulfill your needs. Download your favorite songs to a portable media player and play them in your car or while you work out at the gym, use your digital video recorder and record directly to a DVD to take to Grandma's house, or record movies and television programs on your digital video recorder when you are not at home and then play them at your convenience. Many smart phones, portable media players such as the iPod and Zune, and other personal mobile devices, are video capable, so that you can watch full-length movies or popular television programs. Video and music downloads are expected to generate more than $2.6 billion in sales this year.

FIGURE 5 Millions of music and movie fans use dedicated networks to download files legally. They then store their tunes and movies on their portable media players and smart phones and also burn these files to CDs and high-definition video discs that support the HD DVD and Blu-ray recording formats.

FIGURE 4 DVD burners are considered essential peripherals and can be mounted internally in your computer or connected externally using USB or FireWire cables. Dual-format, dual-layer drives allow you to purchase and download files onto the DVDs without recompression, which preserves the original image quality. Many people are using DVD burners to transfer and consequently preserve their photos and home videos.

FIGURE 6 Storing and sharing digital content is easy with advances in convergence technologies. You can use your smart phone or other personal mobile device to record and then play videos and also to listen to songs and podcasts stored on your computers. High-definition digital video recorders let you record hundreds of hours of current and off-air digital broadcasts, pause and rewind live television programs for up to 90 minutes, and create your own instant replays with slow motion.

Bring Music to Your Ears

A computer now can be considered an essential component of a home entertainment system. A multimedia computer should have at least 2 GB of RAM, a video card with 256 MB of memory, 500 GB of hard disk storage space to save thousands of CDs or digital audio files, a dual DVD/CD burner, and several USB 2.0 ports to connect peripherals.

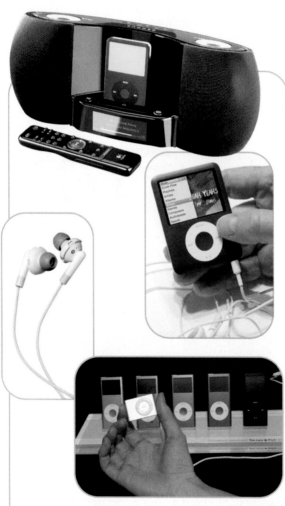

FIGURE 8 Music downloading services allow you to purchase individual tracks or entire albums, download the music to your computer, and then transfer the files to a portable media player or burn them to a CD. Top downloading services are Apple iTunes, Amazonmp3, and Rhapsody. Retailers, including Best Buy and Wal-Mart, also offer music downloads.

FIGURE 9 Apple TV takes control of your living room by streaming movies wirelessly to your computer. Apple's iTunes store offers movies from several studios, including Disney, Pixar, Touchstone, and Miramax, for downloading to your computer and transferring to your iPod. You can purchase movies the day they are released on DVD, preorder movies, and view trailers before making a purchase.

FIGURE 7 Apple has sold more than 110 million iPods. The iPod accessory market has grown to a multimillion-dollar industry, with inventors developing such products as earphones, clothing, calendars, cases, FM transmitters, and docking stations.

FIGURE 10 Marathon runners as well as daily joggers can keep in shape with the help of Nike and Apple. The Nike + iPod Sport Kit contains a small wireless device that fits in specially designed Nike shoes and works with an iPod Nano to provide a coach's advice, information about the run, and a set of tunes designed to motivate and keep a steady rhythm. Voice feedback gives progress reports and congratulates you upon reaching a personal best.

FIGURE 11 The abundance of wireless home networks makes it easy to stream digital music stored on your computer to your stereo or other devices throughout the home using devices such as Apple's AirPort Express and Apple's AirTunes. Your iTunes automatically detects the existence of the AirPort Express and allows you to choose your remote speakers from a list of devices. You also can play music through an Xbox 360 game console that is connected to your computer.

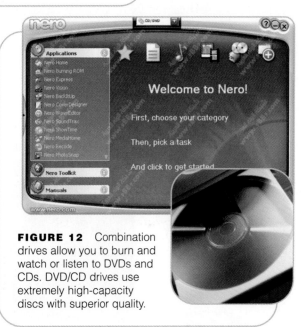

FIGURE 12 Combination drives allow you to burn and watch or listen to DVDs and CDs. DVD/CD drives use extremely high-capacity discs with superior quality.

FIGURE 13 Apple's creativity software, GarageBand, uses a Macintosh computer to transform any room of the house into a recording studio. GarageBand is the tool to use for creating your creative podcast, and with one click you can store it on iWeb. The program allows you to play on a virtual stage with a hand-picked band. Jam Packs add professional backup musicians and singers in multiple genres and styles.

All the World Is a Game

Computer and video game software is an $18 billion industry, according to the NPD Group. From one-player games to serious competition with fellow gamers, it is easy to find sports, strategy, and action games to suit everyone's interests. Gaming hardware can be sorted into three categories: personal computer, console, and handheld. With a broadband connection and home network, you can compete online and tie together multiple personal computer and game consoles.

FIGURE 15 Nintendo's Wii gives gamers new experiences with motion control. The Wii includes different types of input devices; the Wii Remote and the Nunchuk use a device called an accelerometer, which measures acceleration forces electromechanically. The accelerometers sense motion and transmit a signal using Bluetooth technology to a sensor bar, which can be up to 30 feet away. Up to four Wii Remotes can be connected simultaneously for multiplayer interaction.

FIGURE 14 The three gaming consoles — Nintendo Wii, Sony PlayStation 3, and Microsoft Xbox 360 — offer a variety of game titles.

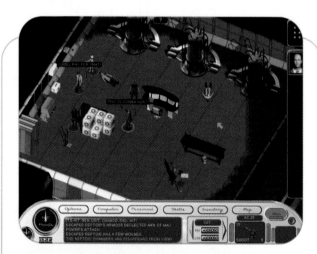

FIGURE 16 In a computer role-playing game (CRPG), players interact with each other and generally attempt to accomplish a quest. They navigate through complex landscapes and often must decide which path to travel by using maps and logic. Their decisions affect subsequent paths, and a game can have multiple endings based on the actions taken. Some gaming enthusiasts modify the original games by adding venues and stories.

FIGURE 17 Handheld multimedia devices weigh less than one pound and have large, high-resolution screens and incredible sound to play audio, video, and photos. Bluetooth technology allows networked gaming and syncing with other handheld units or a personal computer.

FIGURE 19 You can have your own virtual personal trainer or coach with the help of gaming technology. Devices equipped with radar can measure the velocity of a swing from a baseball bat or golf club. Baseballs can record the pitch speed on an LCD panel on the ball at the moment of impact when caught. The wireless Nintendo Wii Balance Board shown in the above figure synchronizes with on-screen Wii activities, such as yoga. Users can play solo or with up to four players simultaneously.

FIGURE 18 Millions of gamers worldwide are competing with friends living across the street or across the globe with massively multiplayer online games (MMOGs). Ultra-fast processors, enormous amounts of memory, a high-end video card, large monitor, superb speakers, and case fans are necessary components.

Convergence: Tying the Loose Ends Together

With wired and wireless home networking and broadband Internet connections, all components are linked together to provide entertainment in innovative ways. A central media hub, digital video recorder, and other devices can stream music and video files, Internet radio, and slide shows of photos seamlessly throughout your house.

FIGURE 20   The ultimate home network requires a variety of hardware to store, share, and stream audio and video files.

The entertainment revolution has worked its way into virtually every facet of our lives. From the largest media rooms to the smallest portable media players, we can watch our favorite television programs and movies any place at anytime. We can browse the Web, play games with partners on the other side of the world, listen to personalized music, and have fun wherever life takes us. No matter where we are, we always can have the best seat in the house for digital entertainment.

Information System Development and Programming Languages

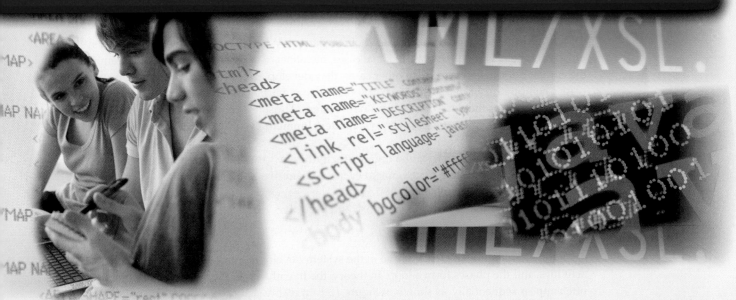

OBJECTIVES

After completing this chapter, you will be able to:

1. Discuss the importance of project management, feasibility assessment, documentation, data and information gathering techniques, and information system security during system development

2. Discuss the purpose of each phase in the system development cycle

3. Differentiate between low-level languages and procedural languages

4. Identify the benefits of object-oriented programming languages and program development tools

5. List other programming languages and other program development tools

6. Describe various ways to develop Web pages

7. List the six steps in the program development cycle

8. Explain the basic control structures used in designing solutions to programming problems

CONTENTS

THE SYSTEM DEVELOPMENT CYCLE

A system is a set of components that interact to achieve a common goal. Businesses use many types of systems. A billing system allows a company to send invoices and receive payments from customers. Through a payroll system, employees receive paychecks. A manufacturing system produces the goods that customers order. An inventory system keeps track of the items in a warehouse. Very often, these systems also are information systems.

An **information system** (**IS**) is a collection of hardware, software, data, people, and procedures that work together to produce quality information. An information system supports daily, short-term, and long-range activities of users. Some examples of users include store clerks, sales representatives, accountants, supervisors, managers, executives, and customers.

The type of information that users need often changes. When this occurs, the information system must meet the new requirements. In some cases, members of the system development team modify the current information system. In other cases, they develop an entirely new information system.

As a computer user in a business, you someday may participate in the modification of an existing system or the development of a new system. Thus, it is important that you understand the system development process. The **system development cycle** is a set of activities used to build an information system.

System development cycles often organize activities by grouping them into larger categories called **phases**. Most system development cycles contain five phases:

1. Planning
2. Analysis
3. Design
4. Implementation
5. Operation, Support, and Security

As shown in Figure 11-1, each phase in the system development cycle consists of a series of activities, and the phases form a loop. In theory, the five phases in the system development cycle often appear sequentially, as shown in Figure 11-1. In reality, activities within adjacent phases often interact with one another — making the system development cycle a dynamic iterative process.

System Development Cycle

1. Planning
- Review project requests
- Prioritize project requests
- Allocate resources
- Form project development team

2. Analysis
- Conduct preliminary investigation
- Perform detailed analysis activities:
  - Study current system
  - Determine user requirements
  - Recommend solution

3. Design
- Acquire hardware and software, if necessary
- Develop details of system

4. Implementation
- Develop programs, if necessary
- Install and test new system
- Train users
- Convert to new system

5. Operation, Support, and Security
- Perform maintenance activities
- Monitor system performance
- Assess system security

Ongoing Activities
- Project management
- Feasibility assessment
- Documentation
- Data/information gathering

FIGURE 11-1 The system development cycle consists of five phases that form a loop. Several ongoing activities also take place throughout the entire system development cycle.

System development should follow three general guidelines: arrange activities into phases, involve the users, and develop standards.

1. The system development cycle should group activities into phases. Many system development cycles contain the five major phases shown in Figure 11-1. Others have more or fewer phases. Regardless, all system development cycles have similar activities and tasks.

2. Users must be involved throughout the entire system development cycle. **Users** include anyone for whom the system is being built. Customers, employees, students, data entry clerks, accountants, sales managers, and owners all are examples of users. Users are more apt to accept a new system if they contribute to its design.

3. The system development cycle should have standards clearly defined. **Standards** are sets of rules and procedures a company expects employees to accept and follow. Having standards helps people working on the same project produce consistent results.

Who Participates in the System Development Cycle?

System development should involve representatives from each department in which the proposed system will be used. This includes both nontechnical users and IT professionals. During the system development cycle, the systems analyst meets and works with a variety of people (Figure 11-2). A **systems analyst** is responsible for designing and developing an information system. The systems analyst is the users' primary contact person.

FIGURE 11-2
A systems analyst meets with a variety of people during a system development project.

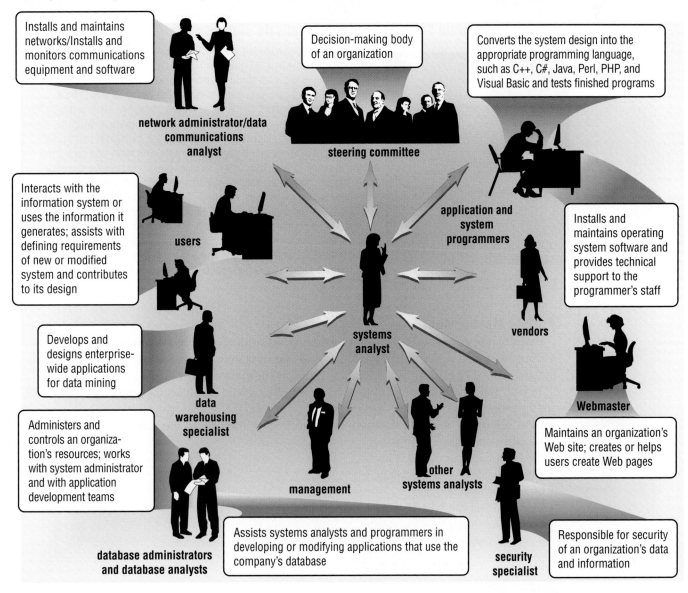

Installs and maintains networks/Installs and monitors communications equipment and software

network administrator/data communications analyst

Decision-making body of an organization

steering committee

Converts the system design into the appropriate programming language, such as C++, C#, Java, Perl, PHP, and Visual Basic and tests finished programs

application and system programmers

Installs and maintains operating system software and provides technical support to the programmer's staff

vendors

Interacts with the information system or uses the information it generates; assists with defining requirements of new or modified system and contributes to its design

users

Develops and designs enterprise-wide applications for data mining

data warehousing specialist

Administers and controls an organization's resources; works with system administrator and with application development teams

systems analyst

Webmaster

Maintains an organization's Web site; creates or helps users create Web pages

management

other systems analysts

database administrators and database analysts

Assists systems analysts and programmers in developing or modifying applications that use the company's database

security specialist

Responsible for security of an organization's data and information

Small companies may have one systems analyst or even one person who assumes the roles of both systems analyst and programmer. Larger companies often have multiple systems analysts. Some companies refer to a systems analyst as a **system developer**. Read Looking Ahead 11-1 for a look at the future skills for systems analysts.

Systems analysts are the liaison between the users and the IT professionals. They convert user requests into technical specifications. They must be familiar with business operations, be able to solve problems, have the ability to introduce and support change, and possess excellent communications and interpersonal skills. Systems analysts prepare many reports, drawings, and diagrams. They discuss various aspects of the development project with users, management, other analysts, database analysts, database administrators, network administrators, the Webmaster, programmers, vendors, and the steering committee. The **steering committee** is a decision-making body in a company.

For each system development project, a company usually forms a **project team** to work on the project from beginning to end. The project team consists of users, the systems analyst, and other IT professionals. One member of the team is the **project leader**, who manages and controls the budget and schedule of the project. The systems analyst may or may not be selected as the project leader of the project.

LOOKING AHEAD 11-1

Right-Brain Skills Essential for Analysts' Success

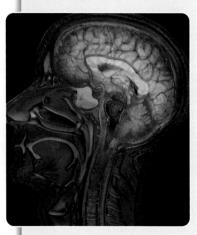

Systems analysts use the left side of their brains to think in a logical, analytical manner when designing and developing information systems. What will matter most for these people, however, is how they use the right side of their brain, according to researchers such as Daniel Pink. Right-brain abilities affect creativity, self-expression, and artistry, and these skills will be essential for survival in our technological world.

According to Pink, automation has replaced the hard labor that helped build much of America in the twentieth century, and today computers are replacing many routine tasks, such as balancing checkbooks and preparing wills. The right-brain abilities systems analysts and other developers will need for success include empathy, meaning, and play. These aptitudes will create professional success and personal fulfillment.

Pink says everyone has these right-brain attributes, but they must develop their minds to master their imaginative and emotional abilities through exercises and critical thinking. For more information, visit scsite.com/dcf5e/ch11/looking and then click Future Systems Analysts.

Project Management

Project management is the process of planning, scheduling, and then controlling the activities during the system development cycle. The goal of project management is to deliver an acceptable system to the user in an agreed-upon time frame, while maintaining costs.

To plan and schedule a project effectively, the project leader identifies the following elements for the project:

- Goal, objectives, and expectations of the project, collectively called the scope
- Required activities
- Time estimates for each activity
- Cost estimates for each activity
- Order of activities
- Activities that can take place at the same time

When these items are identified, the project leader usually records them in a project plan. A popular tool used to plan and schedule the time relationships among project activities is a Gantt chart (Figure 11-3). A Gantt chart, developed by Henry L. Gantt, is a bar chart that uses horizontal bars to show project phases or activities. The left side, or vertical axis, displays the list of required activities. A horizontal axis across the top or bottom of the chart represents time. A tool used for planning and scheduling large, complex projects is the PERT chart. A PERT chart, short for Program Evaluations and Review Technique chart, analyzes the time required to complete a task and identifies the minimum time required for an entire project.

WEB LINK 11-1

PERT Charts

For more information, visit scsite.com/dcf5e/ch11/weblink and then click PERT Charts.

When the project features and deadlines have been determined, the project leader monitors and controls the project. Some activities take less time than originally planned. Others take longer. Project leaders should have good **change management** skills so that they can recognize when a change in the project has occurred and take actions to react to the change. It is crucial that everyone is aware of and agrees on any changes made to the project plan.

ID	Task Name	Duration	Jan	Feb	Mar	Apr	May	Jun	Jul	Aug
1	**Planning**	2w	1/20	2/1						
2	**Analysis**	12w		2/8			5/10			
3	**Design**	12w			3/20			6/15		
4	**Implementation**	7w						6/16		8/9

FIGURE 11-3 A Gantt chart is an effective way to show the time relationships of a project's activities.

Feasibility Assessment

Feasibility is a measure of how suitable the development of a system will be to the company. A project that is feasible at one point of the system development cycle might become infeasible at a later point. Thus, systems analysts frequently reevaluate feasibility during the system development cycle.

Four tests to evaluate feasibility are:

- Operational feasibility: Measures how well the proposed information system will work. Will the users like the new system? Will they use it? Will it meet their requirements?
- Schedule feasibility: Measures whether the established deadlines for the project are reasonable. If a deadline is not reasonable, the project leader might make a new schedule. If a deadline cannot be extended, then the scope of the project might be reduced to meet a mandatory deadline.
- Technical feasibility: Measures whether the company has or can obtain the hardware, software, and people needed to deliver and then support the proposed information system.
- Economic feasibility, also called cost/benefit feasibility: Measures whether the lifetime benefits of the proposed information system will be greater than its lifetime costs.

Documentation

During the entire system development cycle, project members produce much documentation. **Documentation** is the collection and summarization of data and information. It includes reports, diagrams, programs, or any other information generated during the system development cycle.

It is important that all documentation be well written, thorough, consistent, and understandable. The final information system should be reflected accurately and completely in documentation developed throughout the development cycle. Maintaining up-to-date documentation should be an ongoing part of system development.

Data and Information Gathering Techniques

Systems analysts and other IT professionals use several techniques to gather data and information. They review documentation, observe, survey, interview, conduct joint-application design sessions, and do research.

- Review Documentation — By reviewing documentation such as a company's organization chart, memos, and meeting minutes, systems analysts learn about the history of a project. Documentation also provides information about the company such as its operations, weaknesses, and strengths.
- Observe — Observing people helps systems analysts understand exactly how they perform a task. Likewise, observing a machine allows you to see how it works. Read Ethics & Issues 11-1 for a related discussion.
- Survey — To obtain data and information from a large number of people, systems analysts distribute surveys.

FIGURE 11-4 During a JAD session, the systems analyst is the moderator, or leader, of the discussion. Another member, called the scribe, records facts and action items assigned during the session.

- Interview — The interview is the most important data and information gathering technique for the systems analyst. It allows the systems analyst to clarify responses and probe for face-to-face feedback.
- JAD Sessions — Instead of a single one-on-one interview, analysts often use joint-application design sessions to gather data and information. **Joint-application design (JAD)** sessions are a series of lengthy, structured, group meetings in which users and IT professionals work together to design or develop an application (Figure 11-4).
- Research — Newspapers, computer magazines, reference books, trade shows, the Web, vendors, and consultants are excellent sources of information. These sources can provide the systems analyst with information such as the latest hardware and software products and explanations of new processes and procedures.

ETHICS & ISSUES 11-1

Do You Work Harder When Someone Is Watching?

During the data and information gathering stage of the system development cycle, employees are involved actively in the process. They complete surveys, participate in interviews, and are observed while performing their jobs. Many researchers suggest that during observation, employees may not exhibit everyday behavior and may perform above and beyond their normal workday activities. They base this premise on the Hawthorne Effect, which is the result of a study performed in the 1920s in the Western Electric Company plant in Hawthorne, Illinois. The study discovered that productivity improved during observation, whether the conditions were made better or worse. Researchers concluded that productivity seemed to improve whenever the workers knew they were being observed. What is your opinion of the Hawthorne Effect? Do you agree with the research? If someone is observing you at work or if you are receiving increased attention, does this cause you to alter your behavior? Why or why not? Is such observation ethical, and can it have other psychological effects on employees? If productivity increases during observation, is observation a good data gathering technique in a system study? Why or why not?

What Initiates the System Development Cycle?

A user may request a new or modified information system for a variety of reasons. The most obvious reason is to correct a problem. Another reason is to improve the information system. Organizations may want to improve hardware, software, or other technology to enhance an information system. If an unauthorized user gains access to the information system, then changes must be made to the security of the system.

Sometimes situations outside the control of a company require a modification to an information system. Corporate management or some other governing body may mandate a change. Competition also can lead to change. In recent years, another source of change has resulted from one company merging with or acquiring another company.

A user may request a new or modified information system verbally in a telephone conversation or written as an e-mail message (Figure 11-5a). In larger companies, users write a formal request for a new or modified information system, which is called a request for system services or **project request** (Figure 11-5b). The project request becomes the first item of documentation for the project (read Ethics & Issues 11-2 for a related discussion). It also triggers the first phase of the system development cycle: planning.

FIGURE 11-5a   (informal project request)

FIGURE 11-5b
(formal project request)

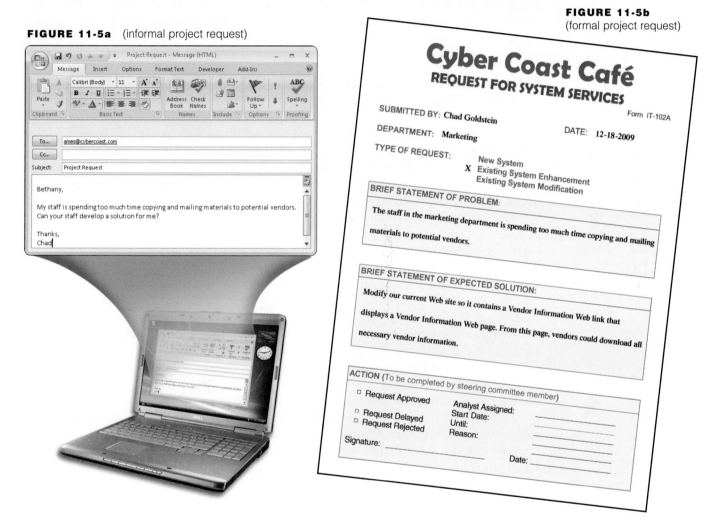

FIGURE 11-5   Sometimes users informally communicate a project request verbally or as an e-mail message. In larger companies, requests often are documented on a form such as this Request for System Services.

ETHICS & ISSUES 11-2

How Can Workers Overcome Writer's Block When Preparing Documentation?

Proper documentation is one of the most important tasks for workers during the development cycle. Many people, however, find that writing documentation is a tedious and anxiety-inducing endeavor. The term, writer s block, describes a range of reasons why some people cannot start or finish the writing process. Too often, writer's block simply leads to a lack of documentation or a poorly documented project. Experts, including psychologists and authors, have determined a number of reasons why writer's block occurs, including fear, self-consciousness, and lack of structure. They also have determined a number of strategies for dealing with writer's block, including adding structure to the process, rewarding oneself after writing a certain number of sentences or paragraphs, and talking through ideas with inanimate objects.

Other experts claim the notion of writer's block does not really exist, but rather is a simple, socially accepted excuse for not completing a job. Some blame the educational system, including colleges, for turning out generations of professionals who have not been taught to write. What strategies should employers encourage to overcome writer's block related to documenting a project? Is writer's block a convenient excuse for not completing a job? Why or why not? Should the educational system demand more from students with respect to their ability to write? Why or why not?

FAQ 11-1

How can systems analysts build relationships with users?

Systems analysts have much more credibility with users if the analysts understand user concerns and have empathy for how the workers are feeling. If users are involved, they are more likely to accept and use the new system — called user buy-in. One reason systems fail is because some systems analysts create or modify systems with little or no user participation. For more information, visit scsite.com/dcf5e/ch11/faq and then click Systems Analyst.

Cyber Coast Café — A Case Study

This chapter includes a case study to help you understand real-world system development applications. The case study appears shaded in purple immediately after the discussion of each phase in the system development cycle. The case is based on Cyber Coast Café, a fictitious cybercafé. The following paragraphs present a background about Cyber Coast Café.

Cyber Coast Café is a worldwide chain of cybercafés. With locations in 45 cities around the world, Cyber Coast Café is one of the more technologically advanced cybercafés on the planet. At these cafés, you can connect to the Web while drinking your favorite specialty beverage; chat with others online or send e-mail messages; and play online games or read an online book.

Through high-speed T3 lines, customers have fast Internet access. LCD monitors are 20 inches. Each café has a minimum of 30 computers, along with two color laser printers, a digital camera, and a scanner. All computers have popular software such as Microsoft Office 2007 and Adobe Photoshop. The café also is a hot spot, which means customers can use their own mobile computer or mobile device to connect wirelessly to the Internet. For each beverage purchased, customers receive 30 minutes of free computer use and/or Web access. For additional time, the fee is $3.00 per hour.

Since Cyber Coast Café started operations in 1997, business has been thriving. The cafés serve thousands of customers around the world. Allison Popovich, chief information officer (CIO) for Cyber Coast Café, offers one suggestion for the company's financial success. "We do not pay for the computers and equipment in our cafés. Instead, we allow computer vendors to use our café as a storefront for their products. This provides customers with the opportunity to try out the hardware and software before making a purchase. When customers are ready to purchase computers, we direct them to the vendor's online storefront for discount pricing."

To showcase their hardware and software in the cafés, computer vendors request information from Chad Goldstein, the marketing manager. The number of these requests is rising quickly. The cost of copying and mailing this material is becoming excessive. For this reason, Chad would like this vendor information made available on the Web. Vendors could download information sheets, press releases, photos, and other information from the Web site. Placing this information on the Web would save Chad and his staff a great deal of time and money.

Chad realizes this task will require substantial company resources. He believes a systems study is necessary. He sends an e-mail message to the vice president of information systems (Figure 11-5a on the previous page). She agrees and tells him to fill out a Request for System Services form (Figure 11-5b on the previous page) and submit it to Juanita Mendez, chair of the steering committee at Cyber Coast Café.

Planning Phase

The **planning phase** for a project begins when the steering committee receives a project request. This committee usually consists of five to nine people. It typically includes a mix of vice presidents, managers, nonmanagement users, and IT personnel.

During the planning phase, four major activities are performed: (1) review and approve the project requests; (2) prioritize the project requests; (3) allocate resources such as money, people, and equipment to approved projects; and (4) form a project development team for each approved project.

The projects that receive the highest priority are those mandated by management or some other governing body. These requests are given immediate attention. The steering committee evaluates the remaining project requests based on their value to the company. The steering committee approves some projects and rejects others. Of the approved projects, it is likely that only a few will begin their system development cycle immediately. Others will have to wait for additional funds or resources to become available.

Planning at Cyber Coast Café

After receiving the project request (Figure 11-5b on page 411) from Chad, Juanita Mendez distributes it to all members of the steering committee. They will discuss the request at their next meeting. The steering committee members of Cyber Coast Café are Juanita Mendez, controller and chair of the steering committee; Milan Sciranka, vice president of operations; Suzy Zhao, Webmaster; Donnell Carter, training specialist; Karl Schmidt, systems analyst; and Bethany Ames, vice president of information systems. Juanita also invites Chad Goldstein to the next steering committee meeting. Because he originated the project request, Chad will have the knowledge to answer questions.

During the meeting, the committee decides the project request identifies an improvement to the system, instead of a problem. They feel the nature of the improvement (to make vendor information available on the Web) could lead to considerable savings for the company. It also will provide quicker service to potential vendors.

The steering committee approves the request. Juanita points out that the company has enough funds in its budget to begin the project immediately. Thus, Bethany assembles a system development project team. She assigns Karl Schmidt, systems analyst, as the project leader. Karl and his team immediately begin the next phase: analysis.

Analysis Phase

The **analysis phase** consists of two major activities: (1) conduct a preliminary investigation and (2) perform detailed analysis. The following sections discuss these activities.

THE PRELIMINARY INVESTIGATION The main purpose of the **preliminary investigation**, sometimes called the feasibility study, is to determine the exact nature of the problem or improvement and decide whether it is worth pursuing. Should the company continue to assign resources to this project? To answer this question, the systems analyst conducts a general study of the project.

The first activity in the preliminary investigation is to interview the user who submitted the project request. Depending on the nature of the request, project team members may interview other users, too.

In addition to interviewing, members of the project team may use other data gathering techniques, such as reviewing existing documentation. Often, the preliminary investigation is completed in just a few days.

Upon completion of the preliminary investigation, the systems analyst writes the feasibility report. This report presents the team's findings to the steering committee. The feasibility report contains these major sections: introduction, existing system, benefits of a new or modified system, feasibility of a new or modified system, and the recommendation (Figure 11-6).

In some cases, the project team may recommend not to continue the project. If the steering committee agrees, the project ends at this point. If the project team recommends continuing and the steering committee approves this recommendation, then detailed analysis begins.

Cyber Coast Café
MEMORANDUM

To: **Steering Committee**
From: **Karl Schmidt, Project Leader**
Date: **December 29, 2009**
Subject: **Feasibility Study of Vendor Web System**

Following is the feasibility study in response to the request for a modification to our Web site. Your approval is necessary before the next phase of the project will begin.

Introduction

The purpose of this feasibility report is to determine whether it is beneficial for Cyber Coast Café to continue studying the Vendor Web System. The marketing manager has indicated his staff spends a considerable amount of time duplicating and distributing materials to potential vendors. This project would affect the marketing department and customer service. Also, any person that uses the Web site would notice a change.

Existing System

Background

One of the reasons for our financial success at Cyber Coast Café is we do not pay for the computers and equipment in our cafés. Instead, we allow computer vendors to use our cafés as a storefront for their products. This provides customers with the opportunity to try the hardware and software before making a purchase. When customers want to purchase computers, we direct them to the vendor's online storefront for discount pricing.

To showcase their hardware and software in the cafés, computer vendors request information from our marketing manager. The number of these requests is rising quickly. The cost of copying and mailing this material is becoming excessive.

Problems

The following problems have been identified with the current information system at Cyber Coast Café:

■ Employees spend too much time copying and duplicating vendor materials

■ Potential vendors do not receive material as quickly as in the past, which possibly could cause poor relations

■ Resources are wasted including employee time, equipment usage, and supplies

FEASIBILITY STUDY
Page 2

Benefits of a New or Modified System

Following is a list of benefits that could be realized if the Web site at Cyber Coast Café were modified:

■ Potential vendors would be more satisfied, leading to possible long-term relations

■ Cost of supplies would be reduced by 30 percent

■ Through a more efficient use of employees' time, the company could achieve a 20 percent reduction in temporary clerks in the marketing department

■ Laser printers and copy machines would last 50 percent longer, due to a much lower usage rate

Feasibility of a New or Modified System

Operational

A modified system will decrease the amount of equipment use and paperwork. Vendor information will be available in an easily accessible form to any vendor. Employees will have time to complete meaningful job duties, alleviating the need to hire some temporary clerks.

Schedule

The established deadline for the Cyber Coast Café project is reasonable.

Technical

Cyber Coast Café already has a functional Web site. To handle the increased volume of data, however, it will need to purchase a database server.

Economic

A detailed summary of the costs and benefits, including all assumptions, is available on our FTP server. The potential costs of the proposed solution could range from $15,000 to $20,000. The estimated savings in supplies and postage alone will exceed $20,000.

If you have any questions about the detailed cost/benefit summary or require further information, please contact me.

Recommendation

Based on the findings presented in this report, we recommend a continued study of the Vendor Web System.

FIGURE 11-6   A feasibility report presents the results of the preliminary investigation. The report must be prepared professionally and be well organized to be effective.

Preliminary Investigation at Cyber Coast Café

Karl Schmidt, systems analyst and project leader, meets with Chad Goldstein to discuss the project request. During the interview, Karl looks at the material that Chad's staff sends to a potential vendor. He asks Chad how many vendor requests he receives in a month. Then Karl interviews the controller, Juanita Mendez, to obtain some general cost and benefit figures for the feasibility report. He also calls a vendor. He wants to know if the material Chad's department sends is helpful.

Next, Karl prepares the feasibility report (Figure 11-6). After the project team members review it, Karl submits it to the steering committee. The report recommends proceeding to the detailed analysis phase for this project. The steering committee agrees. Karl and his team begin detailed analysis.

DETAILED ANALYSIS   Detailed analysis involves three major activities: (1) study how the current system works; (2) determine the users' wants, needs, and requirements; and (3) recommend a solution. Detailed analysis sometimes is called logical design because the systems analysts develop the proposed solution without regard to any specific hardware or software. That is, they make no attempt to identify the procedures that should be automated and those that should be manual.

During these activities, systems analysts use all of the data and information-gathering techniques. They review documentation, observe employees and machines, distribute surveys, interview employees, conduct JAD sessions, and do research.

While studying the current system and identifying user requirements, the systems analyst collects a great deal of data and information. A major task for the systems analyst is to document these findings in a way that can be understood by everyone. Systems analysts use diagrams to describe the processes that transform inputs into outputs and diagrams that graphically show the flow of data in the system. Both users and IT professionals refer to this documentation.

THE SYSTEM PROPOSAL   After the systems analyst has studied the current system and determined all user requirements, the next step is to communicate possible solutions for the project in a system proposal. The purpose of the **system proposal** is to assess the feasibility of each alternative solution and then recommend the most feasible solution for the project, which often involves modifying or building on the current system. The systems analyst presents the system proposal to the steering committee. If the steering committee approves a solution, the project enters the design phase.

When the steering committee discusses the system proposal and decides which alternative to pursue, it often is deciding whether to buy packaged software from an outside source, build its own custom software, or outsource some or all of its IT needs to an outside firm.

- **Packaged software** is mass-produced, copyrighted, prewritten software available for purchase. Packaged software is available for different types of computers. Chapter 3 presented many types of application software available for personal computers. These include word processing, spreadsheet, database, document management, note taking, desktop publishing, paint/image editing, Web page authoring, personal finance, legal, tax preparation, educational/reference, e-mail, and Web browser software.

    Vendors offer two types of packaged software: horizontal and vertical. Horizontal market software meets the needs of many different types of companies. The programs discussed in Chapter 3 were horizontal. If a company has a unique way of accomplishing activities, then it also may require vertical market software. Vertical market software specifically is designed for a particular business or industry. Examples of companies that use vertical market software include banks, schools, hospitals, real estate offices, libraries, and insurance companies. Each of these industries has unique information processing requirements.

- Instead of buying packaged software, some companies write their own applications using programming languages such as Java, C++, C#, and Visual Basic. Application software developed by the user or at the user's request is called **custom software**.

    The main advantage of custom software is that it matches the company's requirements exactly. The disadvantages usually are that it is more expensive and takes longer to design and implement than packaged software.

- Companies can develop custom software in-house using their own IT personnel or **outsource** it, which means having an outside source develop it for them. Some companies outsource just the software development aspect of their IT operation. Others outsource more or all of their IT operation. Depending on a company's needs, outside firms can handle as much or as little of the IT requirements as desired. A trend that has caused much controversy relates to companies that outsource to firms located outside their homeland.

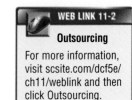

WEB LINK 11-2

Outsourcing

For more information, visit scsite.com/dcf5e/ ch11/weblink and then click Outsourcing.

Detailed Analysis at Cyber Coast Café

Karl and his team begin performing the activities in the detailed analysis phase of the Vendor Web System. As part of the study and requirements activities, they use several of the data and information gathering techniques available to them. They interview employees throughout the company and meet with some vendors. They observe the marketing staff copy and mail vendor information. They prepare documents that become part of the project documentation. Members of the project team refer to these documents during the remainder of the system development cycle.

After two months of studying the existing system and obtaining user requirements, Karl discusses his findings with his supervisor, Bethany Ames. Karl recommends that a link to Vendor Information be added to their current Web site. When a vendor clicks this link, a Vendor Information page will be displayed. This Web page should contain all information that the marketing department usually sends to a vendor.

Based on Karl's findings, Bethany writes a system proposal for the steering committee to review. Suzy Zhao, Webmaster at Cyber Coast Café, developed the current Web site. Thus, Bethany recommends that Suzy's staff modify the Web site in-house. Bethany also recommends that Cyber Coast Café invest in a larger database server to handle the additional vendor information.

The steering committee agrees with Bethany's proposal. Karl and his team begin the design phase of the project.

Design Phase

The **design phase** consists of two major activities: (1) if necessary, acquire hardware and software and (2) develop all of the details of the new or modified information system. The systems analyst often performs these two activities at the same time instead of sequentially.

ACQUIRING NECESSARY HARDWARE AND SOFTWARE   When the steering committee approves a solution, the systems analyst begins the activity of obtaining additional hardware or software. The systems analyst may skip this activity if the approved solution does not require new hardware or software. If this activity is required, it consists of four major tasks: (1) identify technical specifications, (2) solicit vendor proposals, (3) test and evaluate vendor proposals, and (4) make a decision.

Identifying Technical Specifications   The first step in acquiring necessary hardware and software is to identify all the hardware and software requirements of the new or modified system. To do this, systems analysts use a variety of research techniques. They talk with other systems analysts, visit vendors' stores, and search the Web. Many trade journals, newspapers, and magazines provide some or all of their printed content as e-zines. An **e-zine** (pronounced ee-zeen), or electronic magazine, is a publication available on the Web.

After the systems analyst defines the technical requirements, the next step is to summarize these requirements for potential vendors. The systems analyst can use three basic types of documents for this purpose: an RFQ, an RFP, or an RFI. A request for quotation (RFQ) identifies the required product(s). With an RFQ, the vendor quotes a price for the listed product(s). With a request for proposal (RFP), the vendor selects the product(s) that meets specified requirements and then quotes the price(s). A request for information (RFI) is a less formal method that uses a standard form to request information about a product or service.

Soliciting Vendor Proposals   Systems analysts send the RFQ, RFP, or RFI to potential hardware and software vendors. Another source for hardware and software products is a value-added reseller. A **value-added reseller** (**VAR**) is a company that purchases products from manufacturers and then resells these products to the public — offering additional services with the product (Figure 11-7).

Instead of using vendors, some companies hire an IT consultant or a group of IT consultants. An **IT consultant** is a professional who is hired based on computer expertise, including service and advice. IT consultants often specialize in configuring hardware and software for businesses of all sizes.

WEB LINK 11-3

Value-Added Reseller

For more information, visit scsite.com/dcf5e/ch11/weblink and then click Value-Added Reseller.

FIGURE 11-7   Many VARs provide complete systems, often called turnkey solutions.

Testing and Evaluating Vendor Proposals   After sending RFQs and RFPs to potential vendors, the systems analyst will receive completed quotations and proposals. Evaluating the proposals and then selecting the best one often is a difficult task. It is important to be as objective as possible while evaluating each proposal.

Systems analysts use many techniques to test the various software products from vendors. They obtain a list of user references from the software vendors. They also talk to current users of the software to solicit their opinions. Some vendors will give a demonstration of the product(s) specified. Other vendors provide demonstration copies or trial versions, allowing the companies to test the software themselves.

Sometimes it is important to know whether the software can process a certain volume of transactions efficiently. In this case, the systems analyst conducts a benchmark test. A **benchmark test** measures the performance of hardware or software. For example, a benchmark test could measure the time it takes a payroll program to print 50 paychecks. Comparing the time it takes various accounting programs to print the same 50 paychecks is one way of measuring each program's performance.

Making a Decision Having rated the proposals, the systems analyst presents a recommendation to the steering committee. The recommendation could be to award a contract to a vendor or to not make any purchases at this time.

Hardware Acquisition at Cyber Coast Café

Karl and his team compile a requirements list for the database server. They prepare an RFP and submit it to twelve vendors: eight through the Web and four local computer stores. Ten vendors reply within the three-week deadline.

Of the ten replies, the development team selects two to evaluate. They eliminate the other eight because these vendors did not offer adequate warranties for the database server. The project team members ask for benchmark test results for each server. In addition, they contact two current users of this database server for their opinions about its performance. After evaluating these two servers, the team selects the best one.

Karl summarizes his team's findings in a report to the steering committee. The committee gives Karl authorization to award a contract to the proposed vendor. As a courtesy and to maintain good working relationships, Karl sends a letter to all twelve vendors informing them of the commitee's decision.

DETAILED DESIGN The next step is to develop detailed design specifications for the components in the proposed solution. The activities to be performed include developing designs for the databases, inputs, outputs, and programs.

- During database design, the systems analyst works closely with the database analysts and database administrators to identify those data elements that currently exist within the company and those that are new.

The systems analyst also addresses user access privileges. This means that the systems analyst defines which data elements each user can access, when they can access the data elements, what actions they can perform on the data elements, and under what circumstances they can access the elements.

- During detailed design of inputs and outputs, the systems analyst carefully designs every menu, screen, and report specified in the requirements. The outputs often are designed first because they help define the requirements for the inputs. Thus, it is very important that outputs are identified correctly and that users agree to them.

The systems analyst typically develops two types of designs for each input and output: a mockup and a layout chart. A mockup is a sample of the input or output that contains actual data (Figure 11-8). The systems analyst shows mockups to users for their approval. Because users will work with the inputs and outputs of the system, it is crucial to involve users during input and output design.

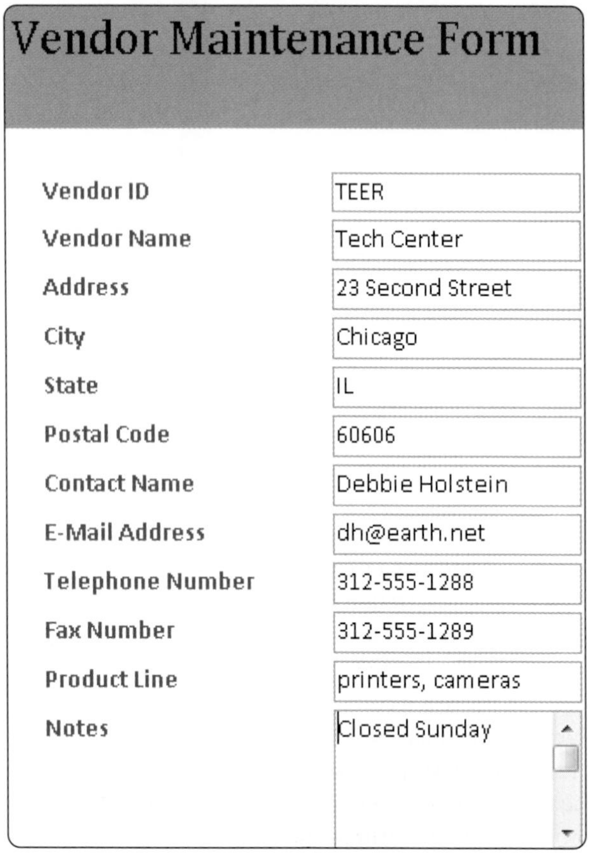

Vendor Maintenance Form

Vendor ID	TEER
Vendor Name	Tech Center
Address	23 Second Street
City	Chicago
State	IL
Postal Code	60606
Contact Name	Debbie Holstein
E-Mail Address	dh@earth.net
Telephone Number	312-555-1288
Fax Number	312-555-1289
Product Line	printers, cameras
Notes	Closed Sunday

FIGURE 11-8 Users must give their approval on all inputs and outputs. This input screen is a mockup (containing actual sample data) for users to review.

After users approve the mockup, the systems analyst develops a layout chart for the programmer. A layout chart is more technical and contains programming-like notations. Many database programs provide tools for technical design (Figure 11-9).

Other issues that must be addressed during input and output design include the types of media to use (paper, video, audio); formats (graphical or narrative); and data entry validation techniques, which include making sure the inputted data is correct (for example, a state code has to be one of the fifty valid two-letter state abbreviations).

• During program design, the systems analyst prepares the program specification package, which identifies required programs and the relationship among each program, as well as the input, output, and database specifications.

PROTOTYPING   Many systems analysts today use prototypes during detailed design. A **prototype** is a working model of the proposed system. The systems analyst actually builds a functional form of the solution during design. The main advantage of a prototype is users can work with the system before it is completed — to make sure it meets their needs. As soon as users approve a prototype, system analysts can implement a solution more quickly than without a prototype.

CASE TOOLS   Many systems analysts use computer software to assist in system development. **Computer-aided software engineering (CASE)** software tools are designed to support one or more activities of the system development cycle (Figure 11-10).

Form Header
Vendor Maintenance Form

Detail	
Vendor ID:	Vendor ID
Vendor Name:	Vendor Name
Address:	Address
City:	City
State:	State
Postal Code:	Postal Code
Contact Name:	Contact Name
E-Mail Address:	E-Mail Address
Telephone Number:	Telephone Number
Fax Number:	Fax Number
Product Line:	Product Line
Notes:	Notes

FIGURE 11-9   Shown here is a technical view in Access 2007 of the mockup in Figure 11-8.

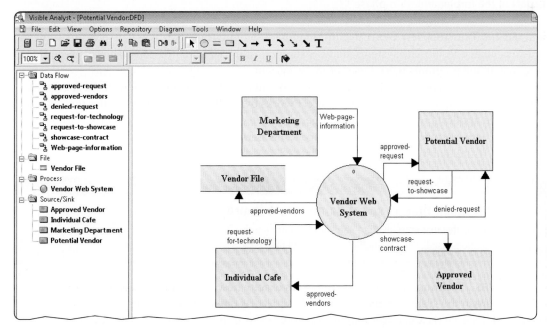

FIGURE 11-10
Computer-aided software engineering (CASE) programs assist analysts in the development of an information system. Visible Analyst by Visible Systems Corporation enables analysts to create diagrams, as well as to build the project dictionary.

QUALITY REVIEW TECHNIQUES   Many people should review the detailed design specifications before they are given to the programming team. Reviewers should include users, systems analysts, managers, IT staff, and members of the system development team. If the steering committee decides the project still is feasible, which usually is the case, the project enters the implementation phase.

Detailed Design at Cyber Coast Café

As approved by the steering committee, Karl and his team begin designing the Vendor Web System. After studying current vendor information and interviewing more users and vendors, the team designs changes to the company's database, Web site, and the associated programs. They prepare several documents including a mockup (Figure 11-8 on page 418) and a technical view in Access 2007 (Figure 11-9 on the previous page).

After completing the detailed design, Karl meets with several users and IT personnel to walk through the design. They locate two errors. He corrects the errors and then presents the design to the steering committee. The committee agrees with the design solution and consents to implement it.

Implementation Phase

The purpose of the **implementation phase** is to construct, or build, the new or modified system and then deliver it to the users. Members of the system development team perform four major activities in this phase: (1) develop programs, (2) install and test the new system, (3) train users, and (4) convert to the new system.

DEVELOP PROGRAMS   If the company purchases packaged software and no modifications to the software are required, the development team may skip this activity. For custom software or packaged software that requires modification, however, programs are developed or modified either by an outside firm or in-house. Programmers write or modify programs from the program specification package created during the analysis phase. Just as the system development cycle follows an organized set of activities, so does program development. These program development activities are known as the program development cycle.

The last sections of this chapter identify various programming languages and explain the program development cycle. The important concept to understand now is that program development is part of the implementation phase.

INSTALL AND TEST THE NEW SYSTEM   If the company acquires new hardware or software, someone must install and test it. The systems analysts should test individual programs. They also should be sure that all the programs work together in the system.

Systems analysts and users develop test data so that they can perform various tests. A unit test verifies that each individual program or object works by itself. A systems test verifies that all programs in an application work together properly. An integration test verifies that an application works with other applications. An acceptance test is performed by end-users and checks the new system to ensure that it works with actual data.

FAQ 11-2

How much time is spent fixing errors in programs?

One study estimates that more than 34 percent of a programmer's time is devoted to fixing program bugs. For more information, visit scsite.com/dcf5e/ch11/faq and then click Software Errors.

TRAIN USERS   Training involves showing users exactly how they will use the new hardware and software in the system. Some training takes place as one-on-one sessions or classroom-style lectures (Figure 11-11). Other companies use Web-based training, which is a self-directed, self-paced online instruction method. Whichever technique is used, it should include hands-on sessions with realistic sample data. Users should practice on the actual system during training. Users also should receive user manuals for reference. It is the systems analyst's responsibility to create user manuals, both printed and electronic. Read Looking Ahead 11-2 for a look at the next generation of training.

FIGURE 11-11 Organizations must ensure that users are trained properly on the new system. One training method uses hands-on classes to learn the new system.

LOOKING AHEAD 11-2

Training Delivery Becomes Flexible

More than 100 million employees will attend a training session this year. Many of these workers will be technology users learning to use new software and hardware. Information technology trainers face the challenge of simplifying complex, technical material in a diverse worldwide corporate culture.

Employees will be experiencing more individualized, self-paced classes in the office or at home. These Internet-, intranet- or video-based training packages allow students to learn at their own pace when they need to master new skills. The programs give immediate feedback and stop when an employee has mastered the particular skill being taught.

Corporations will be offering just-in-time training, giving employees the opportunity to apply their new skills soon after the class has ended. An effective training session pays for itself within weeks and increases employee performance by nearly 20 percent, according to a *PC Computing* survey. For more information, visit scsite.com/dcf5e/ch11/ looking and then click Training.

CONVERT TO THE NEW SYSTEM The final implementation activity is to change from the old system to the new system. This change can take place using one or more of the following conversion strategies: direct, parallel, phased, or pilot.

With **direct conversion**, the user stops using the old system and begins using the new system on a certain date. The advantage of this strategy is that it requires no transition costs and is a quick implementation technique. The disadvantage is that it is extremely risky and can disrupt operations seriously if the new system does not work correctly the first time.

Parallel conversion consists of running the old system alongside the new system for a specified time. Results from both systems are compared. The advantage of this strategy is that you can fix any problems in the new system before you terminate the old system. The disadvantage is that it is costly to operate two systems at the same time.

Larger systems with multiple sites may use a phased conversion. In a **phased conversion**, each location converts at a separate time. For example, an accounting system might convert its accounts receivable, accounts payable, general ledger, and payroll sites in separate phases. Each site can use a direct or parallel conversion.

With a **pilot conversion**, only one location in the company uses the new system — so that it can be tested. After the pilot site approves the new system, other sites convert using one of the other conversion strategies.

Implementation at Cyber Coast Café

Upon receiving the program specification package, Karl forms an implementation team of Suzy Zhao, Webmaster; Adam Rosen, programmer; and Stephan Davis, data modeler. The team works together to implement the Vendor Web System.

Karl works closely with the team to answer questions about the design and to check the progress of their work. When the team completes its work, they ask Karl to test it. He does and it works great!

Karl arranges a training class for the employees of the marketing and customer service departments. During the training session, he shows them how to use the new Vendor Information page on the company's Web site. Karl gives each attendee a printed user guide and indicates that he will e-mail them the electronic file. He wants to prepare everyone thoroughly for the new Web pages once they are posted. Karl also sends a letter to all existing vendors informing them when this new service will be available and how to use it.

Operation, Support, and Security Phase

The purpose of the **operation, support, and security phase** is to provide ongoing assistance for an information system and its users after the system is implemented. The support phase consists of three major activities: (1) perform maintenance activities, (2) monitor system performance, and (3) assess system security.

Information system maintenance activities include fixing errors in, as well as improving on, a system's operations. To determine initial maintenance needs, the systems analyst should meet with users. The purpose of this meeting, called the post-implementation system review, is to discover whether the information system is performing according to the users' expectations. In some cases, users would like the system to do more. Maybe they have enhancements or additional requirements that involve modifying or expanding an existing information system.

During this phase, the systems analyst monitors performance of the new or modified information system. The purpose of performance monitoring is to determine whether the system is inefficient at any point. If so, is the inefficiency causing a problem? Is the time it takes to download vendor information reasonable? If not, the systems analyst must investigate solutions to make the information system more efficient and reliable — back to the planning phase.

Most organizations must deal with complex computer security issues. All elements of an information system — hardware, software, data, people, and procedures — must be secure from threats both inside and outside the enterprise.

Companies today often have a **chief security officer** (CSO) who is responsible for the physical security of a company's property and people and also is in charge of securing its computing resources. It is critical that the CSO is included in all system development projects to ensure that all projects adequately address information security. The CSO uses many of the techniques discussed in Chapter 10 to maintain confidentiality or limited access to information, ensure integrity and reliability of systems, ensure uninterrupted availability of systems, ensure compliance with laws, and cooperate with law enforcement agencies.

An important responsibility of the CSO is to develop a computer security plan. A **computer security plan** summarizes in writing all of the safeguards that are in place to protect a company's information assets. The CSO should evaluate the computer security plan annually or more frequently for major changes in information assets, such as the addition of a new computer or the implementation of a new application. In developing the plan, the CSO should recognize that some degree of risk is unavoidable; further, the more secure a system is, the more difficult it is for everyone to use. The goal of a computer security plan is to match an appropriate level of safeguards against the identified risks. Fortunately, most organizations never will experience a major information system disaster.

Operation, Support, and Security at Cyber Coast Café

During the post-implementation system review, Karl learns that the new Web page is receiving many hits. Vendors are using it and they like it. Customer service regularly receives e-mail messages from vendors that appreciate the new service. Chad says his staff is working efficiently on their primary tasks without the interruption and additional workload of making copies and sending out vendor data, now that the system has been automated. Data in the system has been accessed only by authorized users, leading him to conclude security measures work as planned.

Six months after the Vendor Web System has been in operation, Chad would like to add more information to the Vendor Information page. He sends an e-mail message to Karl requesting the change. Karl asks him to fill out a Request for System Services and puts him on the agenda of the next steering committee meeting. Back to the planning phase again!

Test your knowledge of pages 406 through 422 in Quiz Yourself 11-1.

QUIZ YOURSELF 11-1

Instructions: Find the true statement below. Then, rewrite the remaining false statements so they are true.

1. A computer security plan summarizes in writing all of the safeguards that are in place to protect a company's information assets.

2. Feasibility is the process of planning, scheduling, and then controlling the activities during the system development cycle.

3. The five phases in most system development cycles are programming, analysis, design, sampling, and recording.

4. The purpose of the design phase is to provide ongoing assistance for an information system and its users after the system is implemented.

5. Upon completion of the preliminary investigation, the systems analyst writes the system proposal.

6. Users should not be involved throughout the system development process.

Quiz Yourself Online: To further check your knowledge of the system development cycle, visit scsite.com/dcf5e/ch11/quiz and then click Objectives 1 – 2.

PROGRAMMING LANGUAGES AND PROGRAM DEVELOPMENT TOOLS

The previous sections discussed the phases in the system development cycle. One activity during the implementation phase is to develop programs. Although you may never write a computer program, information you request may require a programmer to create or modify a program. Thus, you should understand how programmers develop programs to meet information requirements. A **computer program** is a series of instructions that directs a computer to perform tasks. A computer **programmer**, sometimes called a **developer**, creates and modifies computer programs.

To create a program, programmers sometimes write, or code, a program's instructions using a programming language. A **programming language** is a set of words, abbreviations, and symbols that enables a programmer to communicate instructions to a computer. Other times, programmers use a program development tool to create a program. A program that provides a user-friendly environment for building programs often is called a **program development tool**. Programmers use a variety of programming languages and tools to create programs (Figure 11-12).

Several hundred programming languages exist today. Each language has its own rules for writing the instructions. Languages often are designed for specific purposes, such as scientific applications, business solutions, or Web page development.

FIGURE 11-12 Programmers must decide which programming languages and program development tools to use when they create programs.

Two types of languages are low-level and high-level. A low-level language is a programming language that is machine dependent. A machine-dependent language runs on only one particular type of computer. Each instruction in a low-level language usually equates to a single machine instruction, discussed further in the next section. With a high-level language, by contrast, each instruction typically equates to multiple machine instructions. High-level languages often are machine independent. A machine-independent language can run on many different types of computers and operating systems.

The following pages discuss low-level languages, as well as several types of high-level languages.

Low-Level Languages

Two types of low-level languages are machine languages and assembly languages. **Machine language**, known as the first generation of programming languages, is the only language the computer directly recognizes (Figure 11-13). Machine language instructions use a series of binary digits (1s and 0s) or a combination of numbers and letters that represents binary digits. The binary digits correspond to the on and off electrical states. As you might imagine, coding in machine language is tedious and time-consuming.

With an **assembly language**, the second generation of programming languages, a programmer writes instructions using symbolic instruction codes (Figure 11-14). Examples of these codes include A for addition, C for compare, L for load, and M for multiply.

```
                                    00090
000090   50E0   30B2              010B4
000094   1B44
000096   1B77
000098   1B55
00009A   F273   30D6  2C81  010D8  00C83
0000A0   4F50   30D6              010D8
0000A4   F275   30D6  2C7B  010D8  00C7D
0000AA   4F70   30D6              010D8
0000AE   5070   304A              0104C
0000B2   1C47
0000B4   5050   304E              01050
0000B8   58E0   30B2              010B4
0000BC   07FE
                                    000BE
0000BE   50E0   30B6              010B8
0000C2   95F1   2C85              00C87
0000C6   4770   20D2              000D4
0000CA   1B55
0000CC   5A50   35A6              015A8
0000D0   47F0   2100              00102
0000D4   95F2   2C85              00C87
0000D8   4770   20E4              000E6
0000DC   1B55
0000DE   5A50   35AA              015AC
0000E2   47F0   2100              00102
000102   1B77
000104   5870   304E              01050
000108   1C47
00010A   4E50   30D6              010D8
00010E   F075   30D6  003E  010D8  0003E
000114   4F50   30D6              010D8
000118   5050   3052              01054
00011C   58E0   30B6              010B8
000120   07FE
                                    00122
000122   50E0   30BA              010BC
000126   1B55
000128   5A50   304E              01050
00012C   5B50   3052              01054
000130   5050   305A              0105C
000134   58E0   30BA              010BC
000138   07FE
```

FIGURE 11-13 A sample machine language program, coded using the hexadecimal number system. A hexadecimal number system can be used to represent binary numbers using letters of the alphabet and decimal numbers.

```
*              THIS MODULE CALCULATES THE REGULAR TIME PAY
CALCSTPY  EQU    *
          ST     14,SAVERTPY
          SR     4,4
          SR     7,7
          SR     5,5
          PACK   DOUBLE,RTHRSIN
          CVB    4,DOUBLE
          PACK   DOUBLE,RATEIN
          CVB    7,DOUBLE
          ST     7,RATE
          MR     4,7
          ST     5,RTPAY
          L      14,SAVERTPY
          BR     14
*              THIS MODULE CALCULATES THE OVERTIME PAY
CALCOTPY  EQU    *
          ST     14,SAVEOTPY
TEST1     CLI    CODEIN,C'O'
          BH     TEST2
          SR     5,5
          A      5,=F'0'
          ST     5,OTPAY
          B      AROUND
TEST2     SR     4,4
          SR     7,7
          SR     5,5
          PACK   DOUBLE,OTHRSIN
          CVB    4,DOUBLE
          PACK   DOUBLE,RATEIN
          CVB    7,RATE
          MR     4,7
          MR     4,=F'1.5'
          ST     5,OTPAY
AROUND    L      14,SAVEOTPY
          BR     14
*              THIS MODULE CALCULATES THE GROSS PAY
CALCGPAY  EQU    *
          ST     14,SAVEGPAY
          SR     5,5
          A      5,RTPAY
          A      5,OTPAY
          ST     5,GRPAY
          L      14,SAVEGPAY
          BR     14
```

FIGURE 11-14 An excerpt from an assembly language payroll program. The code shows the computations for regular time pay, overtime pay, and gross pay and the decision to evaluate the overtime hours.

Assembly languages also use symbolic addresses. A symbolic address is a meaningful name that identifies a storage location. For example, a programmer can use the name RATE to refer to the storage location that contains a pay rate.

Despite these advantages, assembly languages can be difficult to learn. In addition, programmers must convert an assembly language program into machine language before the computer can execute, or run, the program. That is, the computer cannot execute the assembly source program. A **source program** is the program that contains the language instructions, or code, to be converted to machine language. To convert the assembly language source program into machine language, programmers use a program called an assembler.

Procedural Languages

The disadvantages of machine and assembly (low-level) languages led to the development of procedural languages in the late 1950s and 1960s. In a **procedural language**, the programmer writes instructions that tell the computer what to accomplish and how to do it.

With a procedural language, often called a **third-generation language** (**3GL**), a programmer uses a series of English-like words to write instructions. For example, ADD stands for addition or PRINT means to print. Many 3GLs also use arithmetic operators such as * for multiplication and + for addition. These English-like words and arithmetic symbols simplify the program development process for the programmer.

As with an assembly language program, the 3GL code (instructions) is called the source program. Programmers must convert this source program into machine language before the computer can execute the program. This translation process often is very complex, because one 3GL source program instruction translates into many machine language instructions. For 3GLs, programmers typically use either a compiler or an interpreter to perform the translation.

A **compiler** is a separate program that converts the entire source program into machine language before executing it. The machine language version that results from compiling the 3GL is called the object code or object program. The compiler stores the object code on storage media for execution later.

While it is compiling the source program into object code, the compiler checks the source program for errors. The compiler then produces a program listing that contains the source code and a list of any errors. This listing helps the programmer make necessary changes to the source code and correct errors in the program. Figure 11-15 shows the process of compiling a source program.

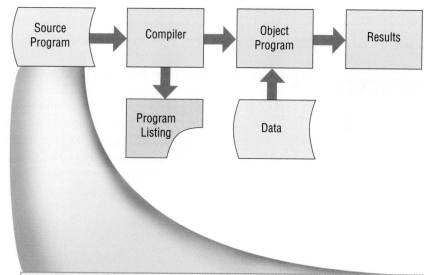

FIGURE 11-15   A compiler converts the entire source program into a machine language object program. If the compiler encounters any errors, it records them in a program-listing file, which the programmer may print when the entire compilation is complete. When a user wants to run the program, the object program is loaded into the memory of the computer and the program instructions begin executing.

```
*     COMPUTE REGULAR TIME PAY
      MULTIPLY REGULAR-TIME-HOURS BY HOURLY-PAY-RATE
          GIVING REGULAR-TIME-PAY.

*     COMPUTE OVERTIME PAY
      IF OVERTIME-HOURS > 0
          COMPUTE OVERTIME-PAY = OVERTIME-HOURS * 1.5 * HOURLY-PAY-RATE
      ELSE
          MOVE 0 TO OVERTIME-PAY.

*     COMPUTE GROSS PAY
      ADD REGULAR-TIME-PAY TO OVERTIME-PAY
          GIVING GROSS-PAY.

*     PRINT GROSS PAY
      MOVE GROSS-PAY TO GROSS-PAY-OUT.
      WRITE REPORT-LINE-OUT FROM DETAIL-LINE
          AFTER ADVANCING 2 LINES.
```

A compiler translates an entire program before executing it. An interpreter, by contrast, translates and executes one statement at a time. An **interpreter** reads a code statement, converts it to one or more machine language instructions, and then executes those machine language instructions. It does this all before moving to the next code statement in the program. Each time the source program runs, the interpreter translates and executes it, statement by statement. An interpreter does not produce an object program. Figure 11-16 shows the process of interpreting a program.

One advantage of an interpreter is that when it finds errors, it displays feedback immediately. The programmer can correct any errors before the interpreter translates the next line of code. The disadvantage is that interpreted programs do not run as fast as compiled programs.

Hundreds of procedural languages exist. Only a few, however, are used widely enough for the industry to recognize them as standards. These include COBOL and C. To illustrate the similarities and differences among these programming languages, the figures on the following pages show program code in these languages. The code solves a simple payroll problem — computing the gross pay for an employee.

The process used to compute gross pay can vary from one system to another. The examples on the following pages use a simple algorithm, or set of steps, to help you easily compare one programming language with another.

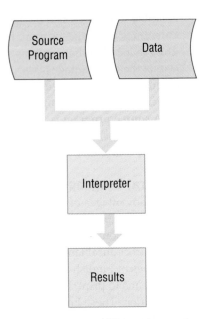

FIGURE 11-16   With an interpreter, one line of the source program at a time is converted into machine language and then immediately executed by the computer. If the interpreter encounters an error while converting a line of code, an error message immediately is displayed on the screen and the program stops.

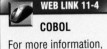
COBOL   COBOL (COmmon Business-Oriented Language) evolved out of a joint effort between the United States government, businesses, and major universities in the early 1960s. Naval officer Grace Hopper, a pioneer in computer programming, was a prime developer of COBOL.

COBOL is a programming language designed for business applications. Although COBOL programs often are lengthy, their English-like statements make the code easy to read, write, and maintain (Figure 11-17). COBOL especially is useful for processing transactions, such as payroll and billing, on mainframe computers.

```
*      COMPUTE REGULAR TIME PAY
       MULTIPLY REGULAR-TIME-HOURS BY HOURLY-PAY-RATE
            GIVING REGULAR-TIME-PAY.

*      COMPUTE OVERTIME PAY
       IF OVERTIME-HOURS > 0
            COMPUTE OVERTIME-PAY = OVERTIME-HOURS * 1.5 * HOURLY-PAY-RATE
       ELSE
            MOVE 0 TO OVERTIME-PAY.

*      COMPUTE GROSS PAY
       ADD REGULAR-TIME-PAY TO OVERTIME-PAY
            GIVING GROSS-PAY.

*      PRINT GROSS PAY
       MOVE GROSS-PAY TO GROSS-PAY-OUT.
       WRITE REPORT-LINE-OUT FROM DETAIL-LINE
            AFTER ADVANCING 2 LINES.
```

FIGURE 11-17   An excerpt from a COBOL payroll program. The code shows the computations for regular time pay, overtime pay, and gross pay; the decision to evaluate the overtime hours; and the output of the gross pay.

C The **C** programming language, developed in the early 1970s by Dennis Ritchie at Bell Laboratories, originally was designed for writing system software. Today, many programs are written in C (Figure 11-18). C runs on almost any type of computer with any operating system, but it is used most often with the UNIX operating system.

```
/* Compute Regular Time Pay                          */
rt_pay = rt_hrs * pay_rate;

/* Compute Overtime Pay                              */
if (ot_hrs > 0)
    ot_pay = ot_hrs * 1.5 * pay_rate;
else
    ot_pay = 0;

/* Compute Gross Pay                                 */
gross = rt_pay + ot_pay;

/* Print Gross Pay                                   */
printf("The gross pay is %d\n", gross);
```

FIGURE 11-18 An excerpt from a C payroll program. The code shows the computations for regular time pay, overtime pay, and gross pay; the decision to evaluate the overtime hours; and the output of the gross pay.

Object-Oriented Programming Languages and Program Development Tools

Programmers use an **object-oriented programming (OOP) language** or object-oriented program development tool to implement objects in a program. An object is an item that can contain both data and the procedures that read or manipulate that data. An object represents a real person, place, event, or transaction.

A major benefit of OOP is the ability to reuse and modify existing objects. For example, once a programmer creates an Employee object, it is available for use by any other existing or future program. Thus, programmers repeatedly reuse existing objects. Programs developed using the object-oriented approach have several advantages. The objects can be reused in many systems, are designed for repeated use, and become stable over time. In addition, programmers create applications faster because they design programs using existing objects. Programming languages, such as Java, C++, and C#, are complete object-oriented languages.

Object-oriented programming languages and program development tools work well in a RAD environment. **RAD** (rapid application development) is a method of developing software, in which the programmer writes and implements a program in segments instead of waiting until the entire program is completed. An important concept in RAD is the use of prebuilt components. For example, programmers do not have to write code for buttons and text boxes on Windows forms because they already exist in the programming language or tools provided with the language.

JAVA Java is an object-oriented programming language developed by Sun Microsystems. Figure 11-19 shows a portion of a Java program and the window that the program displays.

```
public class BodyMassApplet extends Applet implements ActionListener
{
        //declare variables
        Image logo; //declare an Image object
        int inches, pounds;
        double meters, kilograms, index;

        //construct components
        Label companyLabel = new Label("THE SUN FITNESS CENTER BODY MASS INDEX CALCULATOR");
        Label heightLabel = new Label("Enter your height to the nearest inch  ");
            TextField heightField = new TextField(10);
        Label weightLabel = new Label ("Enter your weight to the nearest pound  ");
            TextField weightField = new TextField(10);
        Button calcButton = new Button("Calculate");
        Label outputLabel = new Label(
        "Click the Calculate button to see your Body Mass Index.");

        inches = Integer.parseInt(heightField.getText());
        pounds = Integer.parseInt(weightField.getText());
        meters = inches / 39.36;
        kilograms = pounds / 2.2;
        index = kilograms / Math.pow(meters,2);
        outputLabel.setText("YOUR BODY MASS INDEX IS " + Math.round(index) + ".");
    }

    public void paint(Graphics g)
    {
        g.drawImage(logo,125,160,this);
    }
}
```

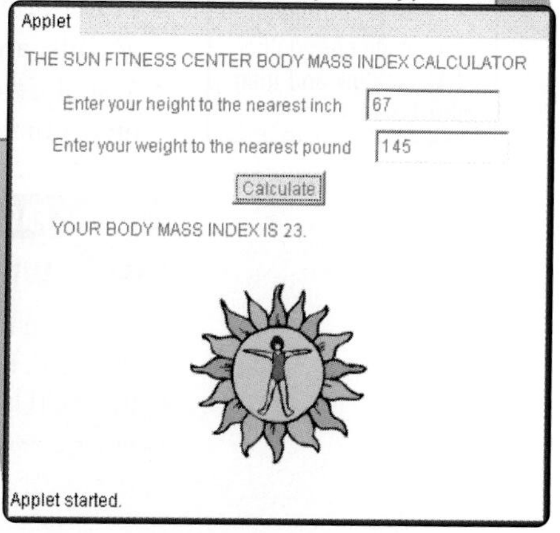

Applet

THE SUN FITNESS CENTER BODY MASS INDEX CALCULATOR

Enter your height to the nearest inch   67

Enter your weight to the nearest pound   145

Calculate

YOUR BODY MASS INDEX IS 23.

Applet started.

FIGURE 11-19 A portion of a Java program and the window the program displays.

WEB LINK 11-5

Java Platforms

For more information, visit scsite.com/dcf5e/ ch11/weblink and then click Java Platforms.

WEB LINK 11-6

C++

For more information, visit scsite.com/dcf5e/ ch11/weblink and then click C++.

When programmers compile a Java program, the resulting object code is machine independent. Java uses a just-in-time (JIT) compiler to convert the machine-independent code into machine-dependent code that is executed immediately. Programmers use various Java Platform implementations, developed by Sun Microsystems, which provide development tools for creating programs for all sizes of computers.

C++   Developed in the 1980s by Bjarne Sroustrup at Bell Laboratories, **C++** (pronounced SEE-plus-plus) is an object-oriented programming language that is an extension of the C programming language. C++ includes all the elements of the C language (shown in Figure 11-18 on the previous page), plus it has additional features for working with objects. Programmers commonly use C++ to develop database and Web applications.

C#   Based on C++, **C#** (pronounced SEE-sharp) is an object-oriented programming language that was developed primarily by Anders Hejlsberg, Microsoft chief architect and distinguished engineer. C# has been accepted as a standard for Web applications and XML-based Web services. Many experts see C# as Java's main competition.

VISUAL STUDIO   **Visual Studio** is Microsoft's suite of program development tools that assists programmers in building programs for Windows, Windows Mobile, or any operating system that supports Microsoft's .NET Framework. The Microsoft .NET Framework, or **.NET** (pronounced dot net), is a set of technologies that allows almost any type of program to run on the Internet or an internal business network, as well as stand-alone computers and mobile devices.

This latest version of Visual Studio is an integrated development environment. An **integrated development environment** (**IDE**) includes program development tools for building graphical interfaces, an editor for entering program code, a compiler and/or interpreter, and a debugger (to remove errors, which is discussed later in the chapter). Visual Studio also includes enhanced support for building security and reliability into applications through its programming languages, RAD tools, a specialized query language, and other resources that reduce development time. For example, Visual Studio includes **code snippets**, which are prewritten code and templates associated with common programming tasks. Visual Studio also includes a set of tools for developing programs that work with Microsoft's Office suite. The following paragraphs discuss these programming languages in the Visual Studio suite: Visual Basic, Visual C++, and Visual C#.

- **Visual Basic** is based on the Visual Basic programming language, which was developed by Microsoft Corporation in the early 1990s. This language is easy to learn and use. Thus, Visual Basic is ideal for beginning programmers.

  The first step in building a Visual Basic program often is to design the graphical user interface using Visual Basic objects (Steps 1 and 2 in Figure 11-20). Visual Basic objects include items such as buttons, text boxes, and labels. Next, the programmer writes instructions (code) to define any actions that should occur in response to specific events (Step 3 in Figure 11-20). Finally, the programmer generates and tests the final program (Step 4 in Figure 11-20).

- **Visual C++** is a programming language based on C++. Not only is Visual C++ a powerful object-oriented programming language, it enables programmers to write Windows, Windows Mobile, and .NET applications quickly and efficiently.

- **Visual C#** combines the programming elements of C++ with an easier visual programming environment. The purpose of Visual C# is to take the complexity out of Visual C++.

WEB LINK 11-7

Visual C#

For more information, visit scsite.com/dcf5e/ ch11/weblink and then click Visual C#.

FAQ 11-3

What are the more popular programming languages?

According to a recent study, Java, C, and Visual Basic are the top programming languages, with C++, PHP, Perl, Python, C#, Ruby, and JavaScript not far behind. For more information, visit scsite.com/ dcf5e/ch11/faq and then click Popular Programming Languages.

FIGURE 11-20 CREATING A VISUAL BASIC PROGRAM

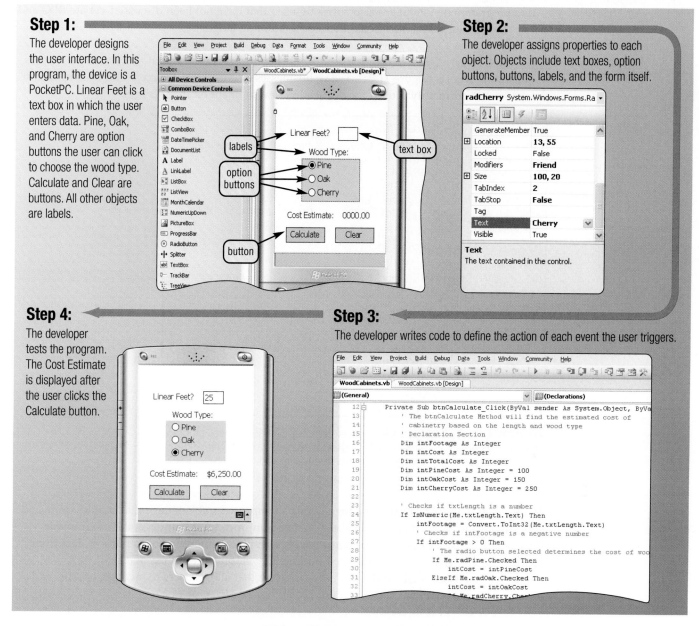

Step 1:

The developer designs the user interface. In this program, the device is a PocketPC. Linear Feet is a text box in which the user enters data. Pine, Oak, and Cherry are option buttons the user can click to choose the wood type. Calculate and Clear are buttons. All other objects are labels.

Step 2:

The developer assigns properties to each object. Objects include text boxes, option buttons, buttons, labels, and the form itself.

Step 4:

The developer tests the program. The Cost Estimate is displayed after the user clicks the Calculate button.

Step 3:

The developer writes code to define the action of each event the user triggers.

DELPHI Borland's **Delphi** is a powerful program development tool that is ideal for building large-scale enterprise and Web applications in a RAD environment. Programmers use Delphi to develop programs quickly for Windows, Linux, and .NET platforms.

POWERBUILDER **PowerBuilder**, developed by Sybase, is another powerful program development RAD tool best suited for Web-based and large-scale enterprise object-oriented applications. Programmers also use PowerBuilder to develop small- and medium-scale client/server applications.

VISUAL PROGRAMMING LANGUAGES A **visual programming language** is a language that uses a visual or graphical interface for creating all source code. The graphical interface, called a visual programming environment (VPE), allows programmers to drag and drop objects to build programs. Examples of visual programming languages include Alice, Mindscript, and Prograph.

Other Programming Languages

Two programming languages also currently used that have not been discussed yet are RPG and 4GLs. The following sections discuss these programming languages.

RPG In the early 1960s, IBM introduced **RPG** (Report Program Generator) to assist businesses in generating reports (Figure 11-21). Today, businesses also use RPG to access and update data in databases. RPG primarily is used for application development on IBM servers.

```
C* COMPUTE REGULAR TIME PAY
C            RTHRS     MULT RATE              RTPAY      72
C*
C* COMPUTE OVERTIME PAY
C            OTHRS     IFGT 0
C            RATE      MULT 1.5               OTRATE     72
C            OTRATE    MULT OTHRS             OTPAY      72
                       ELSE
C                      INZ                    OTPAY      72
C
C* COMPUTE GROSS PAY
C            RTPAY     ADD  OTPAY             GRPAY      72
C
C* PRINT GROSS PAY
C                      EXCPTDETAIL
C
C*
O* OUTPUT SPECIFICATIONS
OQPRINT  E             DETAIL
O                                    23 'THE GROSS PAY IS $'
O                      GRPAY  J      34
```

FIGURE 11-21 This figure shows an excerpt from an RPG payroll program. The code shows the computations for regular time pay, overtime pay, and gross pay; the decision to evaluate the overtime hours; and the output of the gross pay.

4GLs A **4GL** (fourth-generation language) is a nonprocedural language that enables users and programmers to access data in a database. With a **nonprocedural language**, the programmer writes English-like instructions or interacts with a graphical environment to retrieve data from files or a database. Many object-oriented program development tools use 4GLs.

One popular 4GL is SQL. **SQL** is a query language that allows users to manage, update, and retrieve data in a relational DBMS (Figure 11-22).

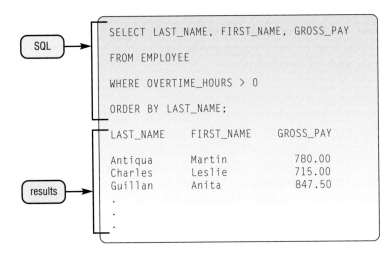

```
SQL →   SELECT LAST_NAME, FIRST_NAME, GROSS_PAY

        FROM EMPLOYEE

        WHERE OVERTIME_HOURS > 0

        ORDER BY LAST_NAME;

        LAST_NAME    FIRST_NAME    GROSS_PAY

        Antiqua      Martin          780.00
results →Charles      Leslie          715.00
        Guillan      Anita           847.50
        .
        .
        .
```

FIGURE 11-22 SQL is a fourth-generation language that can be used to query database tables. This query produces an alphabetical list of those employees who receive overtime pay; that is, their overtime hours are greater than 0.

Classic Programming Languages

In addition to the programming languages discussed on the previous pages, programmers sometimes use other languages (Figure 11-23). Some of the languages listed in Figure 11-23, although once popular, find little use today.

Ada	Derived from Pascal, developed by the U.S. Department of Defense, named after Augusta Ada Lovelace Byron, who is thought to be the first female computer programmer
ALGOL	ALGOrithmic Language, the first structured procedural language
APL	A Programming Language, a scientific language designed to manipulate tables of numbers
BASIC	Beginners All-purpose Symbolic Instruction Code, developed by John Kemeny and Thomas Kurtz as a simple, interactive problem-solving language
Forth	Similar to C, used for small computerized devices
FORTRAN	FORmula TRANslator, one of the first high-level programming languages used for scientific applications
HyperTalk	An object-oriented programming language developed by Apple to manipulate cards that can contain text, graphics, and sound
LISP	LISt Processing, a language used for artificial intelligence applications
Logo	An educational tool used to teach programming and problem-solving to children
Modula-2	A successor to Pascal used for developing systems software
Pascal	Developed to teach students structured programming concepts, named in honor of Blaise Pascal, a French mathematician who developed one of the earliest calculating machines
PILOT	Programmed Inquiry Learning Or Teaching, used to write computer-aided instruction programs
PL/1	Programming Language One, a business and scientific language that combines many features of FORTRAN and COBOL
Prolog	PROgramming LOGic, used for development of artificial intelligence applications
Smalltalk	Object-oriented programming language

FIGURE 11-23 Other programming languages.

Other Program Development Tools

As mentioned earlier, program development tools are user-friendly programs designed to assist both programmers and users in creating programs. In many cases, the program automatically generates the procedural instructions necessary to communicate with the computer. The following sections discuss application generators and macros.

APPLICATION GENERATORS An **application generator** is a program that creates source code or machine code from a specification of the required functionality. When using an application generator, a programmer or user works with menu-driven tools and graphical user interfaces to define the desired specifications. Application generators most often are bundled with or are included as part of a DBMS.

An application generator typically consists of a report writer, form, and menu generator. A report writer allows you to design a report on the screen, retrieve data into the report design, and then display or print the report. Figure 11-24 shows a sample form design and the resulting form it generates showing sample data a user may enter in the form. A menu generator enables you to create a menu for the application options.

FIGURE 11-24a (form design)

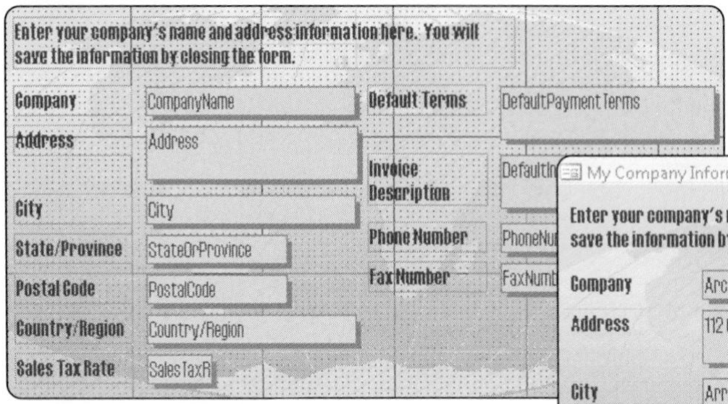

FIGURE 11-24b (resulting filled-in form)

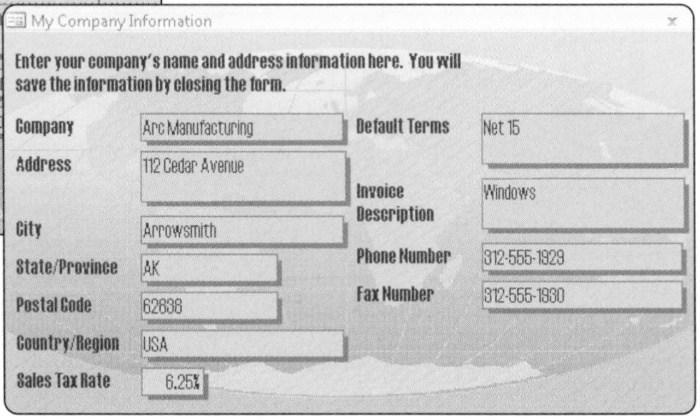

FIGURE 11-24 A form design and the resulting filled-in form created with Microsoft Access.

MACROS A **macro** is a series of statements that instructs a program how to complete a task. Macros allow users to automate routine, repetitive, or difficult tasks in application software such as word processing, spreadsheet, or database programs. That is, users can create simple programs within the software by writing macros. You usually create a macro in one of two ways: (1) record the macro or (2) write the macro.

If you want to automate a routine or repetitive task such as formatting or editing, you would record a macro. A macro recorder is similar to a movie camera because both record all actions until turned off. To record a macro, start the macro recorder in the software. Then, perform the steps to be part of the macro, such as clicks of the mouse or keystrokes. Once the macro is recorded, you can run it anytime you want to perform that same sequence of actions. For example, if you always print three copies of certain documents, you could record the actions required to print three copies. To print three copies, you would run the macro called PrintThreeCopies.

When you become familiar with programming techniques, you can write your own macros instead of recording them. Read Ethics & Issues 11-3 for a related discussion.

ETHICS & ISSUES 11-3

Who Should Be Held Accountable for Macro Security Threats?

In 1999, an individual downloaded and opened a small document from an Internet newsgroup. Upon opening the document, a macro was executed that sent the same document to the first 50 e-mail addresses in the person s e-mail contact list. The simple action of opening the document started a chain reaction that resulted in more than 100,000 infected computers, more than $80 million in damage, Internet e-mail usage being clogged for days around the world, and 20 months in prison for the creator of the document. The document contained a macro virus known as the Melissa worm. Thousands of such macro viruses have circulated around the Internet. Malware authors find that one of the easiest ways to spread viruses and worms is through the use of infected macros. The convenience and simplicity of macros are both their greatest strengths and weaknesses. These are weaknesses because hackers find it easy to exploit technologies with such traits.

As a result of damaging macro viruses such as Melissa, antivirus companies and software companies have strengthened their efforts against macro viruses. Companies often prohibit employees from running macros on their computers. Both responses have made the use of macros more difficult and confusing for users, who prefer the convenience and simplicity of the earlier days. Many claim that software companies that include the capability to use macros should be responsible for making it impossible for malware authors to take advantage of security problems in the software. Software companies and others blame users who open documents from unknown sources. Should users or software companies be held accountable for macro security threats? Why? Should a macro in a word processing document have the capability to access a person's e-mail contact list? Why or why not? How can users best be educated regarding handling documents from unknown sources?

Web Page Development

The designers of Web pages, known as **Web developers**, use a variety of techniques to create Web pages. The following sections discuss these techniques.

HTML   HTML (Hypertext Markup Language) is a special formatting language that programmers use to format documents for display on the Web. You view a Web page written with HTML in a Web browser such as Internet Explorer, Mozilla, Safari, Firefox, or Opera. Figure 11-25a shows part of the HTML code used to create the Web page shown in Figure 11-25b.

HTML is not actually a programming language. It is, however, a language that has specific rules for defining the placement and format of text, graphics, video, and audio on a Web page. HTML uses tags, which are words, abbreviations, and symbols that specify links to other documents and indicate how a Web page is displayed when viewed on the Web.

FIGURE 11-25a   (portion of HTML program)

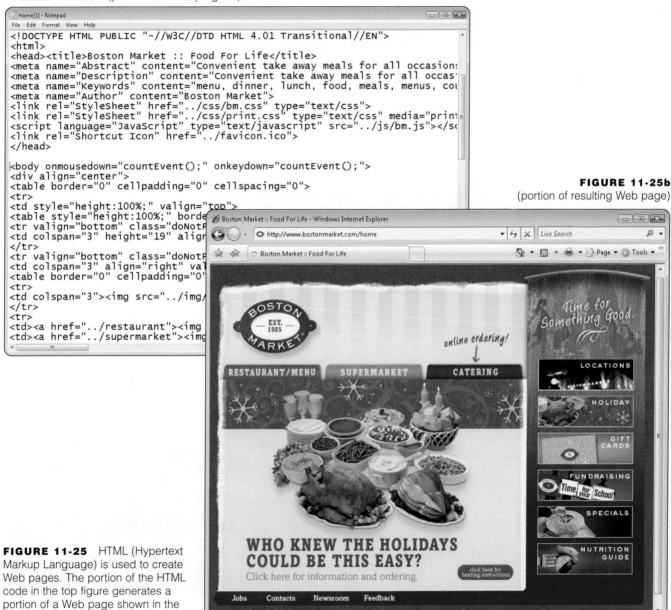

FIGURE 11-25b
(portion of resulting Web page)

FIGURE 11-25   HTML (Hypertext Markup Language) is used to create Web pages. The portion of the HTML code in the top figure generates a portion of a Web page shown in the bottom figure.

SCRIPTS, APPLETS, SERVLETS, AND ACTIVEX CONTROLS HTML tells a browser how to display text and images, set up lists and option buttons, and establish links on a Web page. By adding dynamic content and interactive elements such as scrolling messages, animated graphics, forms, pop-up windows, and interaction, Web pages become much more interesting. To add these elements, Web developers write small programs called scripts, applets, servlets, and ActiveX controls. These programs run inside of another program. This is different from programs discussed thus far, which are executed by the operating system. In this case, the Web browser executes these short programs.

One reason for using scripts, applets, servlets, and ActiveX controls is to add special multimedia effects to Web pages. Examples include animated graphics, scrolling messages, calendars, and advertisements. Another reason to use these programs is to include interactive capabilities on Web pages.

SCRIPTING LANGUAGES Programmers write scripts, applets, servlets, or ActiveX controls using a variety of languages. These include some of the languages previously discussed, such as Java, C++, C#, and Visual Basic. Some programmers use scripting languages. A scripting language is an interpreted language that typically is easy to learn and use. Popular scripting languages include JavaScript, Perl, PHP, Rexx, Tcl, and VBScript.

- **JavaScript** is an interpreted language that allows a programmer to add dynamic content and interactive elements to a Web page (Figure 11-26). These elements include alert messages, scrolling text, animations, drop-down menus, data input forms, pop-up windows, and interactive quizzes.

FIGURE 11-26a (JavaScript code)

FIGURE 11-26b (Web page)

FIGURE 11-26 Shown here is a Web page and a portion of its associated JavaScript code.

- **Perl** (Practical Extraction and Report Language) originally was developed by Larry Wall at NASA's Jet Propulsion Laboratory as a procedural language similar to C and C++. The latest release of Perl, however, is an interpreted scripting language. Because Perl has powerful text processing capabilities, it has become a popular language for writing scripts.
- **PHP**, which stands for PHP: Hypertext Preprocessor, is a free, open source scripting language. PHP is similar to C, Java, and Perl.
- **Rexx** (REstructured eXtended eXecutor) was developed by Mike Cowlishaw at IBM as a procedural interpreted scripting language for both the professional programmer and the nontechnical user.
- **Tcl** (Tool Command Language) is an interpreted scripting language created by Dr. John Ousterhout and maintained by Sun Microsystems Laboratories.
- **VBScript** (Visual Basic, Scripting Edition) is a subset of the Visual Basic language that allows programmers to add intelligence and interactivity to Web pages. As with JavaScript, Web developers embed VBScript code directly into an HTML document.

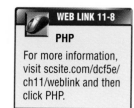

WEB LINK 11-8

PHP

For more information, visit scsite.com/dcf5e/ch11/weblink and then click PHP.

DYNAMIC HTML   Dynamic HTML (**DHTML**) is a newer type of HTML that allows Web developers to include more graphical interest and interactivity in a Web page. Typically, Web pages created with DHTML are more animated and responsive to user interaction. Colors change, font sizes grow, objects appear and disappear as a user moves the mouse (Figure 11-27), and animations dance around the screen.

FIGURE 11-27   Web pages at the PBS Kids Web site use DHTML. As you move the mouse around the window, a message is displayed that relates to the image to which you are pointing. As you move the mouse through images, the message changes based on the location of the mouse pointer.

XHTML, XML, AND WML   XHTML (eXtensible HTML) is a markup language that enables Web sites to be displayed more easily on microbrowsers in smart phones and other personal mobile devices. XHTML includes features of HTML and XML. **XML** (eXtensible Markup Language) is an increasingly popular format for sharing data that allows Web developers to create customized tags, as well as use predefined tags. With XML, a server sends an entire record to the client, enabling the client to do much of the processing without going back to the server.

XML separates the Web page content from its format, allowing the Web browser to display the contents of a Web page in a form appropriate for the display device. For example, a smart phone, a notebook computer, and a desktop computer all could display the same XML page.

Two applications of XML are the RSS 2.0 and ATOM specifications. **RSS 2.0**, which stands for Really Simple Syndication, and **ATOM** are specifications that content aggregators use to distribute content to subscribers. The online publisher creates an RSS or ATOM document, called a **Web feed**, that is made available to Web sites for publication. News Web sites, blogs, and podcasts often use Web feeds to publish headlines and stories. Most Web browsers can read Web feeds, meaning they automatically download updated content from Web pages identified in the feed.

Wireless devices use a subset of XML called WML. **WML** (wireless markup language) allows Web developers to design pages specifically for microbrowsers. Many Internet-enabled smart phones and PDAs use WML as their markup language.

AJAX   **Ajax**, which stands for Asynchronous JavaScript and XML, is a method of creating interactive Web applications designed to provide immediate response to user requests. Instead of refreshing entire Web pages, Ajax works with the Web browser to update only changes to the Web page. This technique saves time because the Web application does not spend time repeatedly sending unchanged information across the network.

Ajax combines several programming tools: JavaScript, HTML or XHTML, and XML. Web 2.0 sites, which allow users to modify and share content and have application software built into the site, often use Ajax. Examples of Web sites that use Ajax are Google Maps and Flickr.

RUBY ON RAILS   **Ruby on Rails** is an open source framework that provides technologies for developing object-oriented, database-driven Web sites. Ruby on Rails is designed to make Web developers more productive by providing them an easy-to-use environment and eliminating time-consuming steps in the Web development process.

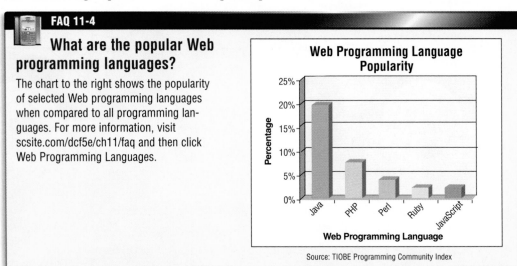

FAQ 11-4

What are the popular Web programming languages?

The chart to the right shows the popularity of selected Web programming languages when compared to all programming languages. For more information, visit scsite.com/dcf5e/ch11/faq and then click Web Programming Languages.

Web Programming Language Popularity

Source: TIOBE Programming Community Index

WEB PAGE AUTHORING SOFTWARE   As discussed in Chapter 3, you do not need to learn HTML to develop a Web page. You can use **Web page authoring software** to create sophisticated Web pages that include graphical images, video, audio, animation, and other special effects. Web page authoring software generates HTML tags from your Web page design.

Four popular Web page authoring programs are Dreamweaver, Expression Web, Flash, and Silverlight.

- **Dreamweaver**, by Adobe Systems, is a Web page authoring program that allows Web developers to create, maintain, and manage professional Web sites.
- **Expression Web** is Microsoft's Web page authoring program that enables Web developers to create professional, dynamic, interactive Web sites. Expression Web integrates with Visual Studio.
- **Flash**, by Adobe Systems, is a Web page authoring program that enables Web developers to combine interactive content with text, graphics, audio, and video.
- **Silverlight**, by Microsoft, is a Web page authoring program that also enables Web developers to combine interactive content with text, graphics, audio, and video.

WEB LINK 11-9

Silverlight

For more information, visit scsite.com/dcf5e/ch11/weblink and then click Silverlight.

Multimedia Program Development

Multimedia authoring software allows programmers to combine text, graphics, animation, audio, and video into an interactive presentation. Many developers use multimedia authoring software for computer-based training (CBT) and Web-based training (WBT). Popular multimedia authoring software includes ToolBook and Director. Many businesses and colleges use ToolBook to create content for distance learning courses (Figure 11-28).

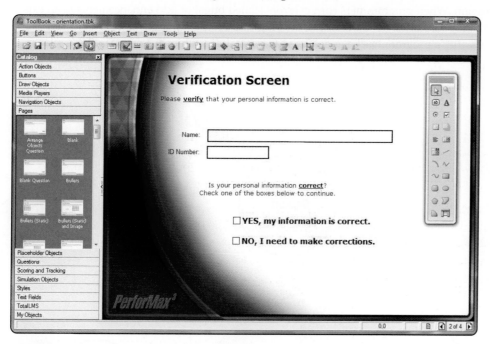

FIGURE 11-28 A sample ToolBook application.

Test your knowledge of pages 423 through 437 in Quiz Yourself 11-2.

THE PROGRAM DEVELOPMENT CYCLE

The **program development cycle** is a series of steps programmers use to build computer programs. As discussed, the system development cycle guides information technology (IT) professionals through the development of an information system. Likewise, the program development cycle guides computer programmers through the development of a program. The program development cycle consists of six steps (Figure 11-29):

1. Analyze Requirements
2. Design Solution
3. Validate Design
4. Implement Design
5. Test Solution
6. Document Solution

As shown in Figure 11-29, the steps in the program development cycle form a loop. Program development is an ongoing process within system development. Each time someone identifies errors in or improvements to a program and requests program modifications, the Analyze Requirements step begins again. When programmers correct errors (called bugs) or add enhancements to an existing program, they are said to be **maintaining** the program. Program maintenance is a ongoing activity that occurs after a program has been delivered to users. Read Ethics & Issues 11-4 for a related discussion.

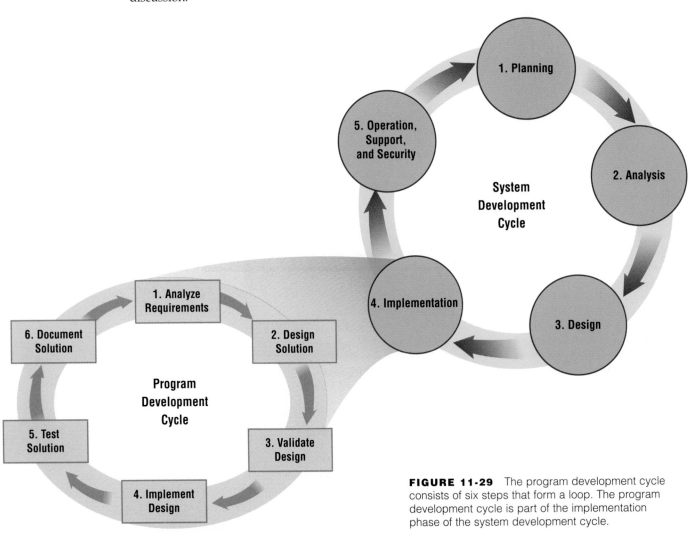

FIGURE 11-29 The program development cycle consists of six steps that form a loop. The program development cycle is part of the implementation phase of the system development cycle.

ETHICS & ISSUES 11-4

Who Is Responsible for Bugs?

The consequences of bugs, or errors, in computer programs can be staggering. A software error in a missile defense system resulted in the deaths of 29 U.S. soldiers. An error in the code controlling a Canadian nuclear facility caused more than 3,000 gallons of radioactive water to be spilled. A bug in long-distance switching software cost AT&T more than $60 million. Some sources say that the Microsoft Windows Vista operating system was considered ready for release when Microsoft reduced the number of known bugs to under 500. Experts estimate that there are 20 to 30 bugs per 1,000 lines of code in an average program. Given that many programs contain hundreds of thousands, even millions, of code lines, bugs are not surprising. Most software licenses absolve the software creator of any responsibility for the end user getting the wrong information from a bug-riddled program. Who should be responsible for mistakes in software? Why? If users provide incomplete or inaccurate specifications, should they be held accountable for the resulting deficiencies? Why? Should those who design a system or write programs for a system be legally responsible if their product results in errors or damages? Why?

What Initiates the Program Development Cycle?

As discussed, the system development cycle consists of five phases: planning; analysis; design; implementation; and operation, support, and security. During the analysis phase, the development team recommends how to handle software needs. Choices include purchasing packaged software, building custom software in-house, or outsourcing some or all of the IT operation.

If the company opts for in-house development, the design and implementation phases of the system development cycle become quite extensive. In the design phase, the analyst creates a detailed set of requirements for the programmers. Once the programmers receive the requirements, the implementation phase begins. At this time, the programmer analyzes the requirements of the problem to be solved. The program development cycle thus begins at the start of the implementation phase in the system development cycle.

The scope of the requirements largely determines how many programmers work on the program development. If the scope is large, a **programming team** that consists of a group of programmers may develop the programs. If the specifications are simple, a single programmer might complete all the development tasks. Whether a single programmer or a programming team, all the programmers involved must interact with users and members of the development team throughout the program development cycle.

By following the steps in the program development cycle, programmers create programs that are correct (produce accurate information) and maintainable (easy to modify). Read Looking Ahead 11-3 for a look at the future of software development.

LOOKING AHEAD 11-3

Software Factories Provide Low-Cost Programming Alternatives

As the need for new programs is increasing dramatically worldwide, the supply of highly trained software writers is decreasing. To combat this labor shortage, medium and large companies may rely on software factories to reduce costs and increase program reliability.

Programmers currently write programs manually for many specific applications. In contrast, software factories would rely on automation to generate lines of code. In much the same fashion as a chef follows a recipe using ingredients, the factories would assemble prewritten models in a specific order to build, compile, test, and debug programs. Programmers then would modify the computer-generated program to meet a specific organization's needs.

Widgets, such as menus, check boxes, and buttons, that are packaged in widget toolkits are becoming increasingly useful to help programmers build graphical user interfaces. For more information, visit scsite.com/dcf5e/ch11/looking and then click Software Factories.

Control Structures

When programmers are required to design the logic of a program, they typically use control structures to describe the tasks a program is to perform. A **control structure**, also known as a construct, depicts the logical order of program instructions. Three basic control structures are sequence, selection, and repetition.

SEQUENCE CONTROL STRUCTURE A **sequence control structure** shows one or more actions following each other in order (Figure 11-30). Actions include inputs, processes, and outputs. All actions must be executed; that is, none can be skipped. Examples of actions are reading a record, calculating averages or totals, and printing totals.

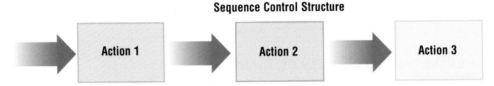

Sequence Control Structure

| Action 1 | Action 2 | Action 3 |

FIGURE 11-30 The sequence control structure shows one or more actions followed by another.

SELECTION CONTROL STRUCTURE A **selection control structure** tells the program which action to take, based on a certain condition. Two common types of selection control structures are the if-then-else and the case.

When a program evaluates the condition in an if-then-else control structure, it yields one of two possibilities: true or false. Figure 11-31 shows the condition as a diamond symbol. If the result of the condition is true, then the program performs one action. If the result is false, the program performs a different action. For example, the if-then-else control structure can determine if an employee should receive overtime pay. A possible condition might be the following: Is Hours Worked greater than 40? If the response is yes (true), then the action would calculate overtime pay. If the response is no (false), then the action would set overtime pay equal to 0.

In some cases, a program should perform no action if the result of a condition is false. This variation of the if-then-else is called the if-then control structure because the program performs an action only if the result of the condition is true.

With the case control structure, a condition can yield one of three or more possibilities (Figure 11-32). The size of a beverage, for example, might be one of these options: small, medium, large, or extra large. A case control structure would determine the price of the beverage based on the size purchased.

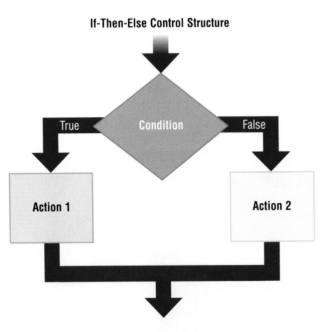

If-Then-Else Control Structure

True — Condition — False

Action 1   Action 2

FIGURE 11-31 The if-then-else control structure directs the program toward one course of action or another based on the evaluation of a condition.

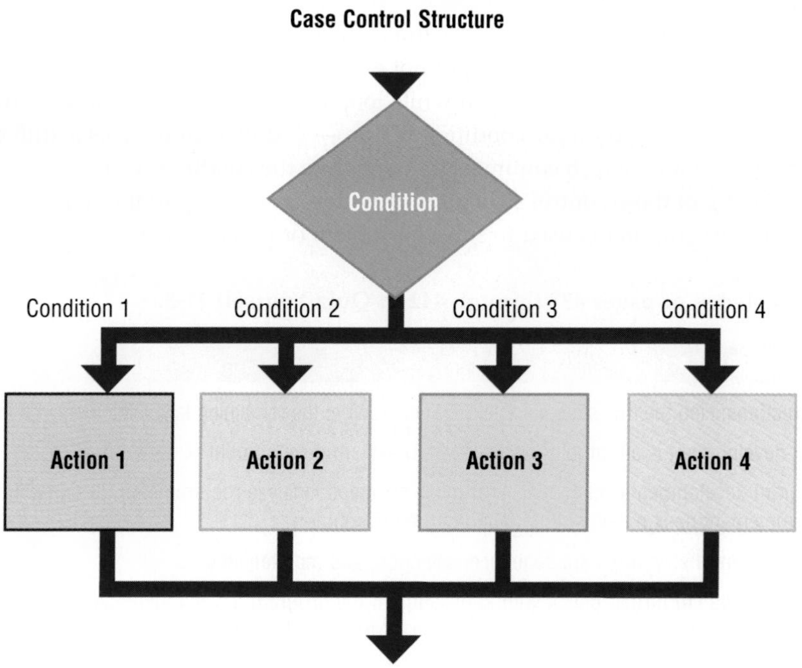

Case Control Structure

FIGURE 11-32   The case control structure allows for more than two alternatives when a condition is evaluated.

REPETITION CONTROL STRUCTURE   The **repetition control structure** enables a program to perform one or more actions repeatedly as long as a certain condition is met. Many programmers refer to this construct as a loop. Two forms of the repetition control structure are the do-while and do-until.

A do-while control structure repeats one or more times as long as a specified condition is true (Figure 11-33). This control structure tests a condition at the beginning of the loop. If the result of the condition is true, the program executes the action(s) inside the loop. Then, the program loops back and tests the condition again. If the result of the condition still is true, the program executes the action(s) inside the loop again. This looping process continues until the condition being tested becomes false. At that time, the program stops looping and moves to another set of actions.

The do-while control structure normally is used when the occurrence of an event is not quantifiable or predictable. For example, programmers frequently use the do-while control structure to process all records in a file. A payroll program using a do-while control structure loops once for each employee. This program stops looping after it processes the last employee's record.

The do-until control structure is similar to the do-while but has two major differences: where it tests the condition and when it stops looping. First, the do-until control structure tests the condition at the end of the loop (Figure 11-34).

Do-While Control Structure

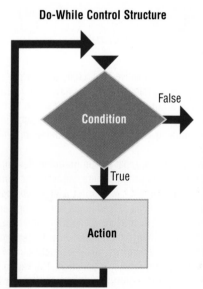

Do-Until Control Structure

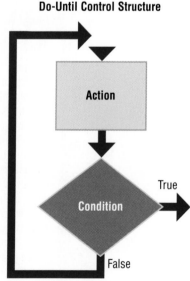

FIGURE 11-33   The do-while control structure tests the condition at the beginning of the loop. It exits the loop when the result of the condition is false.

FIGURE 11-34   The do-until control structure tests the condition at the end of the loop. It exits the loop when the result of the condition is true.

The action(s) in a do-until control structure thus always will execute at least once. The loop in a do-while control structure, by contrast, might not execute at all. That is, if the condition immediately is false, the action or actions in the do-while loop never execute. Second, a do-until control structure continues looping until the condition is true — and then stops. This is different from the do-while control structure, which continues to loop while the condition is true.

An understanding of these control structures provides an insight into the steps performed by a computer when the computer is used to solve a problem or process data.

Test your knowledge of pages 438 through 442 in Quiz Yourself 11-3.

 QUIZ YOURSELF 11-3

Instructions: Find the true statement below. Then, rewrite the remaining false statements so they are true.

1. Program development is an ongoing activity within system development.

2. The program development cycle consists of these six steps: analyze requirements, design solution, validate design, implement design, test solution, and hardcode solution.

3. Three basic control structures are sequence, selection, and maintenance.

Quiz Yourself Online: To further check your knowledge of the program development cycle and basic control structures and design tools, visit scsite.com/dcf5e/ch11/quiz and then click Objectives 7 – 8.

CHAPTER SUMMARY

This chapter discussed the phases in the system development cycle. The guidelines for system development also were presented. Activities that occur during the entire system development cycle, including project management, feasibility assessment, documentation, data and information gathering, also were addressed.

This chapter also discussed various programming languages and program development tools used to create and modify computer programs. It described a variety of Web development and multimedia development tools. Finally, the chapter presented the program development cycle and the tools used in this process.

CAREER CORNER   Programmer

If you are the curious, creative type, enjoy solving puzzles, and gain satisfaction in making things work, you may want to consider a career in programming. A programmer designs, writes, and tests the code that tells computers what to do. Most programmers specialize in one of three fields: system programming, application programming, or Web development programming.

Some jobs may require that the programmer develop an entire program, while other jobs require program maintenance. Likewise, programmers can work for a small company in which they are responsible for the entire system development cycle, or for a larger company in which they are part of a team and individual duties are specialized. Projects can range from computer games to essential business applications. Programmers enjoy the achievements of working with computers to accomplish objectives as well as developing efficient instructions that tell computers how to perform specific tasks.

Academic credentials are essential for success in this career. A bachelor's degree in Computer Science or Information Technology usually is required. The key to success is familiarity with programming languages and a good foundation in programming logic. Surveys indicate that average salaries for entry level programmers are about $60,000 and can exceed $100,000 for senior programmers. For more information, visit scsite.com/dcf5e/ch11/careers and then click Programmer.

Computer Sciences Corporation (CSC)
Global IT Services Company

Every airplane that takes off and lands is guided by the work of Computer Sciences Corporation (CSC)'s employees; they developed the 1.2 million lines of code running the nation's air traffic control system.

The 87,000 CSC workers' efforts extend far beyond the aerospace industry, however. Their global projects have stopped security breaches, simplified the patent application process used by the U.S. Patent and Trademark Office, and helped the California Department of Forestry fight wildfires. The company's Best Total Solutions approach helps their clients use technology to solve business problems.

The California-based company has grown from a two-person operation in 1959 to an international corporation focusing on front-end consulting and planning to systems integration and outsourcing. It ranked number two on the FORTUNE 500 list of Information Technology Services in 2007 and has been recognized as one of the world's technology leaders in the health-care, financial, and defense industries. For more information, visit scsite.com/dcf5e/ch11/companies and then click CSC.

Electronic Arts (EA)
Entertainment Software Developer

Harry Potter, James Bond, John Madden, and The Sims have been found in millions of homes worldwide thanks to Electronic Arts (EA), the world's leading independent developer and publisher of interactive entertainment software. EA's yearly revenues of more than $3 billion are generated from its games for the PlayStation, Xbox, GameCube, Wii, and Game Boy systems.

Since the company's beginnings in 1982, EA's software has had a strong market presence in video game systems, personal computers, the Internet, and cell phones. The more popular titles are Madden NFL Football, the Need for Speed, NBA Live, and The Sims. More than 5,500 developers work at EA's studios in the United States, Canada, the United Kingdom, and Japan. In 2007, twenty-four EA games sold more than one million units, and seven titles earned triple-platinum status. For more information, visit scsite.com/dcf5e/ch11/companies and then click Electronic Arts.

TECHNOLOGY TRAILBLAZERS

Grace Hopper
COBOL Developer

Women's participation in the computer programming world was shaped by the achievements of Grace Hopper. She was one of the first software engineers, and in 1953 she perfected her best-known invention: the compiler.

After earning her Ph.D. degree from Yale University, she began teaching mathematics at Vassar College. She resigned that position in 1943 to join the Navy WAVES (Women Accepted for Voluntary Emergency Service). Her work developing compilers ultimately led to the creation of the COBOL programming language.

Although her achievements are the foundation of today's computers, she said during her lifetime that she was most proud of her service to her country. Each year the Grace Hopper Celebration of Women in Computing is held to focus on women's research and career interests in the technology fields. For more information, visit scsite.com/dcf5e/ch11/people and then click Grace Hopper.

James Gosling
Java Engineer and Architect

Known as the "father of Java," James Gosling serves as Sun Microsystems Developer Products group's chief technology officer. He is the mastermind behind Java, the network programming language running across all platforms, from servers to cell phones.

Gosling grew up near Calgary, Alberta, and spent much of his spare time turning spare machine parts into games. At the age of 15, he wrote software for the University of Calgary's physics department. When he was hired at Sun Microsystems, he built a multiprocessor version of UNIX, developed compilers to convert program code into machine language, engineered a window manager, and wrote a UNIX text editor.

He received the Award of Distinction in Computer Science in 2007 for his contributions to the advancement of the profession and society as a whole. He also became an officer of the Order of Canada for demonstrating an outstanding level of talent and service to Canadians. For more information, visit scsite.com/dcf5e/ch11/people and then click James Gosling.

Chapter Review

The Chapter Review section summarizes the concepts presented in this chapter. To obtain help from other students regarding any subject in this chapter, visit scsite.com/dcf5e/ch11/forum and post your thoughts or questions.

(1) Why Are Project Management, Feasibility Assessment, Documentation, Data and Information Gathering Techniques, and Information System Security Important during System Development?

Project management is the process of planning, scheduling, and then controlling the activities during the system development cycle. **Feasibility** is a measure of how suitable the development of a system will be to the company. **Documentaton** is the collection and summarization of data and information. To gather data and information, IT professionals can review documentation, observe, distribute surveys, interview, participate in a **joint-application design** (**JAD**) session, and perform research. All elements of an information system must be secure from threats both inside and outside the enterprise.

(2) What Is the Purpose of Each Phase in the System Development Cycle?

Most system development cycles contain five **phases**. During the **planning phase**, a **project request** is reviewed and approved, project requests are prioritized, resources are allocated, and a project development team is formed for each approved project. During the **analysis phase**, a **preliminary investigation** is conducted to determine the exact nature of the problem or improvement, and detailed analysis is performed to study how the current system works, determine users' requirements, and recommend a solution. During the **design phase**, any necessary hardware and software are acquired, and the details of the new or modified information system are developed. In the **implementation phase**, the new or modified system is constructed and delivered to the users. During the **operation, support, and security phase**, ongoing assistance is provided for the information system and its users after the system is implemented.

 Visit scsite.com/dcf5e/ch11/quiz or click the Quiz Yourself button. Click Objectives 1 – 2.

(3) How Are Low-Level Languages Different from Procedural Languages?

A low-level language is a programming language that runs on only one type of computer. Each instruction in a low-level language usually equates to a single machine instruction. Procedural languages are high-level languages that can run on many different types of computers and operating systems. In a **procedural language**, a programmer writes instructions that tell the computer what to accomplish and how to do it.

(4) What Are the Benefits of Object-Oriented Programming Languages and Program Development Tools?

Programmers use an **object-oriented programming** (**OOP**) **language** or object-oriented program development tool to implement object-oriented design. A major benefit of OOP is the ability to reuse and modify existing objects, allowing programmers to create applications faster. OOP languages include **Java**, **C++**, and **C#**. Often used in conjunction with OOP, **RAD** (rapid application development) is a method of developing software, in which a programmer writes and implements a program in segments instead of waiting until the entire program is completed. **Visual Studio** is Microsoft's suite of program development tools and includes Visual Basic, Visual C++, and Visual C#.

(5) What Are Other Programming Languages and Other Program Development Tools?

Businesses use **RPG** to generate reports and access and update data in databases. A **4GL** (fourth generation language) is a **nonprocedural language** that users and programmers use to access the data in a database. Other program development tools include an **application generator,** which creates source code or machine code from a specification of the required functionality, and a **macro**, which is a series of instructions that instructs an application how to complete a task.

(6) How Are Web Pages Developed?

Web developers use a variety of techniques to develop Web pages. **HTML** (Hypertext Markup Language) is a special formatting language used to format documents for display on the Web. To add interactivity to Web pages, some programmers use a scripting language or **dynamic HTML** (**DHTML**). Other popular languages and tools include **XHTML**, **XML**, **WML**, **Ajax**, and **Ruby on Rails**. Web developers also use **Web page authoring software** to create sophisticated Web pages, including **Dreamweaver**, **Expression Web**, **Flash**, and **Silverlight**.

 Visit scsite.com/dcf5e/ch11/quiz or click the Quiz Yourself button. Click Objectives 3 – 6.

Chapter Review

(7) What Are the Six Steps in the Program Development Cycle?

The **program development cycle** is a series of steps programmers use to build computer programs. The program development cycle consists of six steps: (1) analyze requirements, (2) design solution, (3) validate design, (4) implement design, (5) test solution, and (6) document solution.

(8) What Are the Basic Control Structures Used in Designing Solutions to Programming Problems?

A **control structure** depicts the logical order of program instructions. Three basic control structures are the **sequence control structure, selection control structure,** and **repetition control structure.**

Visit scsite.com/dcf5e/ch11/quiz or click the Quiz Yourself button. Click Objectives 7 – 8.

Key Terms

You should know each key term. Use the list below to help focus your study. To further enhance your understanding of the Key Terms in this chapter, visit scsite.com/dcf5e/ch11/terms. See an example of and a definition for each term, and access current and additional information about the term from the Web.

4GL (430)
Ajax (436)
analysis phase (413)
application generator (431)
assembly language (424)
ATOM (436)
benchmark test (417)
C (427)
C# (428)
C++ (428)
change management (409)
chief security officer (422)
COBOL (426)
code snippets (428)
compiler (425)
computer program (423)
computer security plan (422)
computer-aided software engineering (CASE) (419)
control structure (440)
custom software (415)
Delphi (429)
design phase (416)
developer (423)
direct conversion (421)
documentation (409)
Dreamweaver (437)
dynamic HTML (DHTML) (435)
Expression Web (437)
e-zine (416)

feasibility (409)
Flash (437)
HTML (433)
implementation phase (420)
information system (IS) (406)
integrated development environment (IDE) (428)
interpreter (426)
IT consultant (417)
Java (427)
JavaScript (434)
joint-application design (JAD) (410)
machine language (424)
macro (432)
maintaining (438)
multimedia authoring software (437)
nonprocedural language (430)
object-oriented programming (OOP) language (427)
operation, support, and security phase (422)
outsource (415)
packaged software (415)
parallel conversion (421)
Perl (435)

phased conversion (421)
phases (406)
PHP (435)
pilot conversion (421)
planning phase (413)
PowerBuilder (429)
preliminary investigation (413)
procedural language (425)
program development cycle (438)
program development tool (423)
programmer (423)
programming language (423)
programming team (439)
project leader (408)
project management (408)
project request (411)
project team (408)
prototype (419)
RAD (427)
repetition control structure (441)
Rexx (435)
RPG (430)
RSS 2.0 (436)
Ruby on Rails (436)
selection control structure (440)

sequence control structure (440)
Silverlight (437)
source program (425)
SQL (430)
standards (407)
steering committee (408)
system (406)
system developer (408)
system development cycle (406)
system proposal (415)
systems analyst (407)
Tcl (435)
third-generation language (3GL) (425)
training (420)
users (407)
value-added reseller (VAR) (417)
VBScript (435)
visual programming language (429)
Visual Studio (428)
Web developers (433)
Web feed (436)
Web page authoring software (436)
WML (436)
XHTML (436)
XML (436)

Checkpoint

Use the Checkpoint exercises to check your knowledge level of the chapter. To complete the Checkpoint exercises interactively, visit scsite.com/dcf5e/ch11/check.

_____ 1. A Gantt chart is a bar chart that uses horizontal bars to show project phases or activities. (409)

_____ 2. The planning phase for a project begins when the steering committee receives a project request. (413)

_____ 3. The only major activity of the design phase is the development of all of the details of the new or modified information system. (416)

_____ 4. An advantage of the object-oriented approach is that objects are designed for repeated use and become stable over time. (427)

_____ 5. With a procedural language, the programmer writes English-like instructions or interacts with a graphical environment. (430)

_____ 6. An application generator typically consists of a report writer, form, and menu generator. (432)

_____ 7. ATOM allows Web developers to design pages specifically for microbrowsers. (436)

_____ 8. News Web sites, blogs, and podcasts often use Web feeds to publish headlines and stories. (436)

_____ 9. Expression Web, originally developed by Adobe, is a Web page authoring program that enables Web developers to combine interactive content with text, graphics, audio, and video. (437)

_____ 10. The if-then-else control structure is a type of selection control structure that can yield one of two possibilities. (440)

1. The _____ manages and controls the budget and schedule of the project. (408)
   a. project team
   b. system developer
   c. project leader
   d. steering committee

2. _____ measures whether the lifetime benefits of the proposed information system will be greater than its lifetime costs. (409)
   a. Operational feasibility
   b. Technical feasibility
   c. Economic feasibility
   d. Schedule feasibility

3. During the planning phase, the projects that receive the highest priority are those _____. (413)
   a. mandated by management or some other governing body
   b. suggested by the greatest number of users
   c. thought to be of highest value to the company
   d. proposed by the information technology (IT) department

4. The purpose of the _____ is to assess the feasibility of each alternative solution and then recommend the most feasible solution for the project. (415)
   a. project plan
   b. system proposal
   c. project request
   d. system review

5. A(n) _____ translates and executes one statement at a time. (426)
   a. compiler
   b. nonprocedural language
   c. source program
   d. interpreter

6. _____ is a subset of the Visual Basic language that allows programmers to add intelligence and interactivity to Web pages. (435)
   a. VBScript
   b. Flash
   c. Ajax
   d. Rexx

7. _____ is an open source framework that provides technologies for developing object-oriented, database-driven Web sites. (436)
   a. PHP
   b. Ruby on Rails
   c. Flash
   d. Ajax

8. _____, by Microsoft, is a Web page authoring program that also enables Web developers to combine interactive content with text, graphics, audio, and video. (437)
   a. PHP
   b. Ajax
   c. Flash
   d. Silverlight

_____ 1. system developer (408)

_____ 2. benchmark test (417)

_____ 3. source program (425)

_____ 4. macro (432)

_____ 5. Flash (437)

a. responsible for designing and developing an information system

b. the language instructions, or code, to be converted to machine language

c. series of statements that instructs an application how to complete a task

d. Web page authoring program that enables Web developers to combine interactive content with text, graphics, audio, and video

e. set of rules and procedures a company expects employees to follow

f. measures the performance of hardware or software

Short Answer

Write a brief answer to each of the following questions.

1. Why is feasibility evaluated during the system development cycle? _____ How are operational feasibility, schedule feasibility, technical feasibility, and economic feasibility different? _____

2. What are the four major activities of the implementation phase? _____ What are four types of conversions, and how do they differ? _____

3. What activities take place during the operations, support, and security phase? _____ How do the roles of the systems analyst and chief security officer differ in this phase? _____

4. How is a compiler different from an interpreter? _____ What is the advantage, and disadvantage, of an interpreter? _____

5. What is included in an integrated development environment? _____ Describe the programming languages in the Visual Studio suite. _____

Working Together

Working in a group of your classmates, complete the following team exercise.

1. Choosing a programming language is an important decision. A poor choice can result in a program that is difficult, incompatible, or unproductive. Each member of your team should interview someone in the IT department of a local organization about recently developed software. What application was developed? What programming language was used? Why? What factors were important in selecting the programming language? Were other factors considered (such as the expertise of available programmers)? In hindsight, was the best language chosen? Why or why not? Meet with your team to discuss the results of your interviews. Then, create a presentation to share your findings with the class.

Web Research

Use the Internet-based Web Research exercises to broaden your understanding of the concepts presented in this chapter. To discuss any of the Web Research exercises in this chapter with other students, post your thoughts or questions at scsite.com/dcf5e/ch11/forum.

① Blogs

Blogging can be an out-of-this-world experience when the topic involves space and astronomy. Space exploration, comets, telescopes, the International Space Station, and astrophotography are popular subjects. Enthusiasts ranging from NASA astronauts (blogs.nasa.gov) to backyard astronomers (tomsastroblog.com) share their discoveries and experiences on a variety of topics. Visit these blogs along with Jonathan's Space Report (planet4589.org/jsr.html), NASA Watch (nasawatch.com), Russian Space Web (russianspaceweb.com), Space Daily (spacedaily.com), and The Write Stuff (blogs.orlandosentinel.com/news_space_thewritestuff) and then read some of the features provided. What are three of the more recent topics? What images of the moon, Mars, or stars or from the Hubble Space Telescope are featured? What new discoveries have been made? When is the next launch at the Kennedy Space Center? How does the content on the Russian Space Web blog differ from that on the NASA blogs?

② Scavenger Hunt

Use one of the search engines listed in Figure 2-8 in Chapter 2 on page 58 or your own favorite search engine to find the answers to the following questions. Copy and paste the Web address from the Web page where you found the answer. Some questions may have more than one answer. If required, submit your answers to your instructor. (1) Who developed BASIC, the basis of the Visual Basic programming language? (2) What programming language has been called "the duct tape of the Internet"? (3) What is the purpose of the W3C Markup Validation Service? (4) What is quirks mode?

③ Search Sleuth

An international network of knowledgeable people provides the content for About.com, one of the top search Web sites. More than 37 million people view this resource every month to find practical advice and solutions written by more than 600 industry professionals who are called guides. Visit this Web site and then use your word processing program to answer the following questions. Then, if required, submit your answers to your instructor. (1) Click the Computing & Technology link in the Channels section. Locate the Programming section and then click the C / C++ / C# link. What are the two most recent posts the guide has written? (2) Click your browser's Back button or press the BACKSPACE key to return to the Computing & Technology page. Type "Visual Studio" in the Search box and then click the Search button. Click a link that discusses Visual Studio basics and then write a 50-word summary of your findings.

Learn How To

Use the Learn How To activities to learn fundamental skills when using a computer and accompanying technology. Complete the exercises and submit them to your instructor.

LEARN HOW TO 1: Conduct an Effective Interview

As you learned in this chapter, gathering information is a critical element in the system development cycle, because without accurate facts, it is unlikely that the finished system will perform in the desired manner. An important means of gathering information is the personal interview. Interviews are used in several stages throughout the system development cycle, and they must be thorough and comprehensive.

Prior to conducting an interview, you must determine that an interview is the best means for obtaining the information you seek. You have learned a variety of ways to obtain information, and you should use each of them appropriately. Because an interview interrupts a person's work and takes time, you must be sure the information gained in the interview justifies this interruption. Once you have determined you should conduct an interview to gather information required for system development, a variety of factors become relevant.

Goal: The most important element of a successful interview is for you to determine exactly what knowledge you hope to gain as a result of the interview. If you do not have a goal, you are unlikely to emerge from the interview with much useful information.

Do Your Homework: You should complete a variety of preparatory steps that will help ensure a successful interview. These steps include the following:

1. Gather as much information as you can from the fact-gathering processes that do not require an interview. Because an interview takes a person's time and interrupts work, you must be sure the information you are seeking is not available from other sources. Additionally, if you ask someone questions to obtain information they know is available elsewhere, you will lose credibility with them during the interview process.
2. Be sure you plan to interview the best person to obtain the information you need. To do this, you must research every person you plan to interview and understand their job, their position within the department in which they work, the knowledge they should possess relative to the information you need, the culture of their work environment, how the system being developed relates to them, and an estimate of the cooperation you can expect from them. If someone is the most knowledgeable person regarding a certain subject but is unwilling to share information other than with trusted coworkers, you likely will be better served by talking to someone else.
3. Prepare the questions you want to ask prior to setting up the interview. In this way, you can have a good estimate of the time required for the interview. While other questions will occur to you as the interview proceeds, you should have a good idea of the questions you need answered to reach your goal.
4. Prior to setting an appointment for an interview, be sure the management personnel of the people you will interview have approved. Because you will be disrupting employees' work days, you must obtain management approval before even asking for an appointment.

Make an Appointment: An appointment almost always is required. By making an appointment, you ensure the person to be interviewed will be available. Normally you should request an appointment in writing, often through the use of e-mail. In this written request, you should set a time and place for the interview, inform the interviewee what you need to know, and establish an agenda with an estimated time. You must recognize that most people do not like to be interviewed, so often you will not be seen as friendly. In addition, it might be possible that the system being developed could eliminate or change the person's job, and clearly this can establish an adversarial relationship. Your task when making an appointment, then, is to establish credibility with the interviewee and set the stage for a successful interview.

Conducting the Interview: When conducting an interview, remember that you are the "intruder." Therefore, you should be polite, prompt, and attentive in the interview. Always understand the perspective of the person being interviewed and understand his or her fears, doubts, and potential hostilities. Sometimes, the interviewee might feel he or she is in conflict with you, so by listening closely and being aware of the body language, you should be able to discern the amount of truth and the amount of hedging that is occurring. Some of the details of the interview of which you should be aware are as follows:

1. If possible, the interview should be conducted in a quiet environment with a minimum of interruptions.
2. The demeanor should be open and friendly, but as noted you should not expect to be welcomed with open arms.
3. Your questions should directly address the goals of the interview. Do not expect the person being interviewed to provide a tutorial. Your questions must generate answers that supply your information.
4. Your questions should be thought-provoking. Do not ask questions requiring a yes or no answer. Your questions should not lead the interviewee to an answer — rather, the questions should be open-ended and allow the person to develop the answer. As an interviewer, you never should argue with the person being interviewed, you should not suggest answers or give opinions, you should ask straight-forward questions rather than compound questions, you never should assign blame for any circumstance that might come up in the interview, and you must never interrupt while the person is talking. Finally, you, as the interviewer, should not talk much. Remember, you are conducting the interview to gain information and it is the person you are interviewing who has that information. Let him or her talk.
5. Listen carefully, with both your ears and your eyes. What you hear normally is most important, but body language and other movements often convey information as well. Concentrate on the interviewee — expect that you will make much more eye contact with the person than he or she will with you. Allow silences to linger — the normal impulse in a conversation is to fill the silence quickly; in an interview, however, if you are quiet, the person being interviewed might think of additional information.
6. As you listen, concentrate on the interviewee — when points are being made, do not take notes because that will distract from what the person is saying — stay focused. When the information has been conveyed, then jot down something so that you will remember.
7. Throughout the interview, offer reinforcing comments, such as, "The way I understand what you just said is …" Make sure when you leave the interview there are no misunderstandings between you and the person you interviewed.
8. Before you conclude the interview, be sure all your goals have been met. You likely will not have another opportunity to interview the person, so ensure you have nothing further to learn from the person.

Follow-Up: After the interview, it is recommended you send a follow-up letter or e-mail message to the person you interviewed to review the information you learned. This document should invite the interviewee to correct any errors you made in summing up your findings. In addition, for all the people you interview, keep a log of the time and place of the interview. In this way, if any questions arise regarding the interview, you will have a log.

Exercise

1. Using the techniques in this activity, conduct interviews with three students on your campus. Your interview goal is to find out about both the most successful class and the least successful class the student has completed. Why was the class successful or unsuccessful? Discuss the instructor, textbook, subject matter, and other relevant items. After the interviews, write a one-page paper summarizing your findings and identify common elements found in successful classes and in unsuccessful classes. Submit this paper to your instructor.

2. **Optional: Conduct this exercise only with permission of your instructor.** Using the techniques you learned in this activity, conduct interviews with three instructors on your campus. The goal of your interview should be to determine the manner in which these instructors conduct and grade examinations. Find out if the instructors are happy with the process or feel improvements can be made. After the interviews, write a one-page paper summarizing your findings and identify any common complaints among the instructors. Submit this paper to your instructor.

Learn It Online

Use the Learn It Online exercises to reinforce your understanding of the chapter concepts. To access the Learn It Online exercises, visit scsite.com/dcf5e/ch11/learn.

(1) At the Movies — Electronic Arts Going Mobile

To view the Electronic Arts Going Mobile movie, click the number 1 button. Locate your video and click the corresponding High-Speed or Dial-Up link, depending on your Internet connection. Watch the movie to hear EA Mobile's Travis Boatman discuss how the company is tackling the mobile video game market. Then, complete the exercise by answering the questions that follow. What are some of the issues that mobile game designers must consider when creating a new game? Can mobile players interact with other mobile game players?

(2) Student Edition Labs — Project Management

Click the number 2 button. A new browser window will open, displaying the Student Edition Labs. Follow the on-screen instructions to complete the Project Management Lab. When finished, click the Exit button. If required, submit your results to your instructor.

(3) Practice Test

Click the number 3 button. Answer each question. When completed, enter your name and click the Grade Test button to submit the quiz for grading. Make a note of any missed questions. If required, submit your results to your instructor.

(4) Who Wants To Be a Computer Genius^2?

Click the number 4 button to find out if you are a computer genius. Directions about how to play the game will be displayed. When you are ready to play, click the Play button. Submit your score to your instructor.

(5) eMedicine

Click the number 5 button to learn how to use the Internet to research medical information. Follow the instructions to use eMedicine.com to research an illness or disease. What are the initial symptoms of the illness or disease you selected? What kinds of treatments are available? What preventive measures are available for the selected illness or disease? Write a report summarizing your findings. Submit the report to your instructor.

(6) Student Edition Labs — Visual Programming

Click the number 6 button. A new browser window will open, displaying the Student Edition Labs. Follow the on-screen instructions to complete the Visual Programming Lab. When finished, click the Exit button. If required, submit your results to your instructor.

(7) Crossword Puzzle Challenge

Click the number 7 button, then click the Crossword Puzzle Challenge link. Directions about how to play the game will be displayed. Complete the puzzle to reinforce skills you learned in this chapter. When you are ready to play, click the Continue button. Submit the completed puzzle to your instructor.

(8) Vista Exercises

Click the number 8 button. When the Vista Exercises menu appears, click the exercise assigned by your instructor. A new browser window will open. Follow the on-screen instructions to complete the exercise. When finished, click the Exit button. If required, submit your results to your instructor.

OBJECTIVES

After completing this chapter, you will be able to:

1. Discuss the special information requirements of an enterprise-sized corporation
2. Identify information systems used in the functional units of an enterprise
3. List general purpose and integrated information systems used throughout an enterprise
4. List types of technologies used throughout an enterprise
5. Describe the major types of e-commerce
6. Discuss the computer hardware needs and solutions for an enterprise
7. Determine why computer backup is important and how it is accomplished
8. Discuss the steps in a disaster recovery plan

CONTENTS

WHAT IS ENTERPRISE COMPUTING?

The term, enterprise, commonly describes a business or venture of any size. In this chapter, the term enterprise refers to large multinational corporations, universities, hospitals, research laboratories, and government organizations. **Enterprise computing** involves the use of computers in networks that encompass a variety of different operating systems, protocols, and network architectures. A typical enterprise consists of corporate headquarters, remote offices, international offices, and hundreds of individual operating entities, called functional units. The types of functional units within a typical manufacturing enterprise are accounting and finance, human resources, engineering, manufacturing, marketing, sales, distribution, customer service,

FIGURE 12-1   Enterprise computing involves the management of large amounts of information over an extensive geographic area and disparate groups of people.

and information technology. Each type of functional unit has specialized requirements for its information systems. These functional units are summarized later in this chapter.

Enterprises produce and gather enormous volumes of information regarding customer, supplier, and employee activity. The information flows among an assortment of entities both inside and outside of the enterprise, and users consume the information during a variety of activities (Figure 12-1). Customers, suppliers, and employees interact with the enterprise in a number of ways, and computers track each interaction. Each sale of a product, purchase of a piece of equipment, or paycheck generates activity involving information systems.

Large computers connected by vast networks allow the enterprise to manage and distribute information quickly and efficiently.

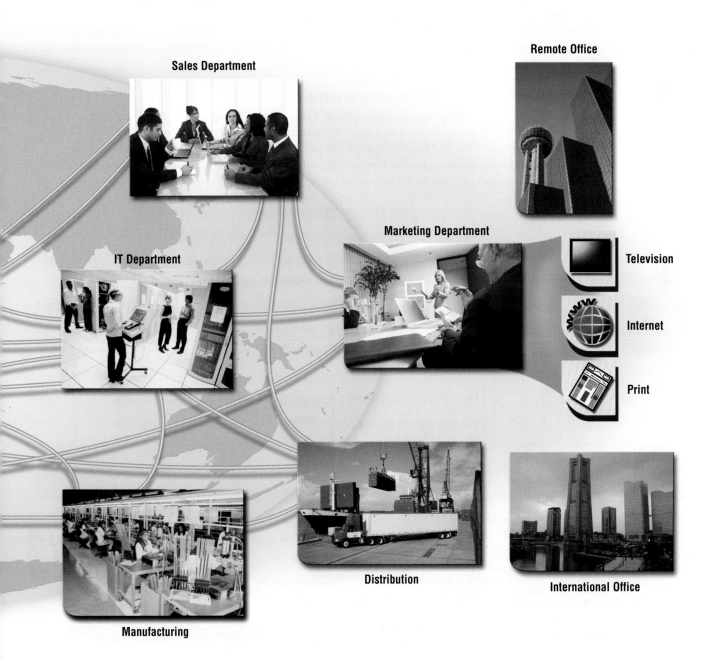

Sales Department

Remote Office

IT Department

Marketing Department

Television

Internet

Print

Manufacturing

Distribution

International Office

Types of Enterprises

Figure 12-1 on pages 452 and 453 shows an example of an enterprise whose main focus is in the manufacturing sector. Examples of some other types of enterprises are listed below.

- Retail enterprises own a large number of stores in a wide geographical area and use their size to obtain discounts on the goods they purchase; they then seek to sell the goods at a lower price than smaller retailers.
- Manufacturing enterprises create goods on a large scale and then distribute and sell the goods to consumers or other organizations.
- Service enterprises typically do not create or sell goods, but provide services for consumers or other organizations. Examples include companies in the insurance, restaurant, and financial industries.
- Wholesale enterprises seek to purchase and then sell large quantities of goods to other organizations, usually at a lower cost than retail.
- Government enterprises include large city governments, state governments, and the departments and agencies of the federal government.
- Educational enterprises include large universities or school systems that include executives, instructors, and other service personnel and whose reach extends throughout a county, a state, or the entire country.

Organizational Structure of an Enterprise

Most traditional enterprises are organized in a hierarchical manner. Figure 12-2 shows an example of an organization chart of a large manufacturing company. Managers at the first two levels at the top of the chart, including the chief executive officer (CEO), mainly concern themselves with strategic decisions and long-term planning. Read Looking Ahead 12-1 for a look at the changing roles of the next generation of CIOs.

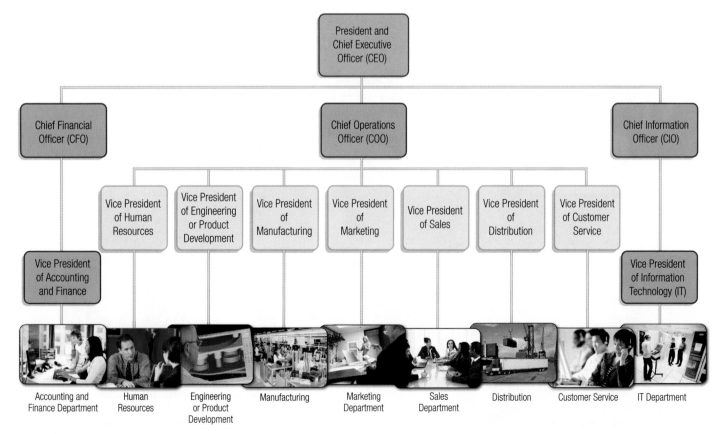

FIGURE 12-2   Example of an organization chart for a manufacturing enterprise illustrates the hierarchy within an enterprise.

In Figure 12-2, the chief operations officer (COO) manages the core activities. The supporting activities include financial departments and information technology (IT) departments. The chief financial officer (CFO) and the chief information officer (CIO) lead these supporting roles.

Each enterprise includes its own special needs and the organizational structure of every enterprise varies. Organizations may include all or some of the managers and departments shown in Figure 12-2.

Levels of Users in the Enterprise

In an enterprise, users of information typically fall into one of four categories: executive management, middle management, operational management, and nonmanagement employees (Figure 12-3). The types of information that users require often depend on their employee level in the organization.

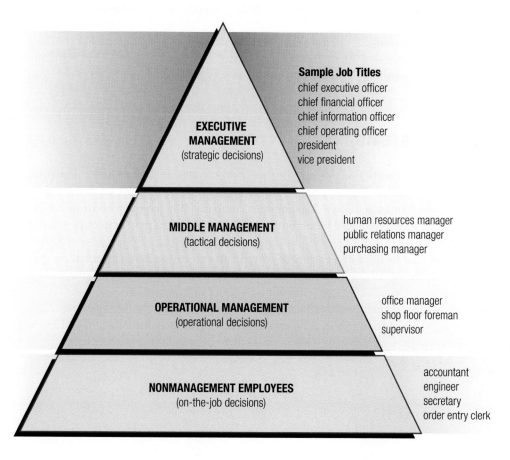

Sample Job Titles

EXECUTIVE MANAGEMENT (strategic decisions)
- chief executive officer
- chief financial officer
- chief information officer
- chief operating officer
- president
- vice president

MIDDLE MANAGEMENT (tactical decisions)
- human resources manager
- public relations manager
- purchasing manager

OPERATIONAL MANAGEMENT (operational decisions)
- office manager
- shop floor foreman
- supervisor

NONMANAGEMENT EMPLOYEES (on-the-job decisions)
- accountant
- engineer
- secretary
- order entry clerk

FIGURE 12-3 This pyramid illustrates the levels of users, sample job titles of each level of user, and the types of decisions these users make.

How Managers Use Information

Enterprise information is the information gathered in the ongoing operations of an enterprise-sized organization. Enterprise information begins with the day-to-day transactions that occur within a company, such as sales receipts or time cards. The company gathers and stores the information. Over time, employees collect, combine, and analyze the information. Ultimately, the role of information gathered in this way is to allow managers to make better decisions.

All employees, including managers, in a company need accurate information to perform their jobs effectively. **Managers** are responsible for coordinating and controlling an organization's resources. Resources include people, money, materials, and information. Managers coordinate these resources by performing four activities: planning, organizing, leading, and controlling.

- Planning involves establishing goals and objectives.
- Organizing includes identifying and combining resources, such as money and people, so that the company can reach its goals and objectives.
- Leading, sometimes referred to as directing, involves communicating instructions and authorizing others to perform the necessary work.
- Controlling involves measuring performance and, if necessary, taking corrective action.

Managers utilize a variety of tools and techniques to focus on information that is important to the decision-making process. These tools and techniques include business intelligence, business process management, and business process automation.

Business intelligence (BI) includes several types of applications and technologies for acquiring, storing, analyzing, and providing access to information to help users make more sound business decisions. BI applications include decision support systems, query and reporting, online analytical processing (OLAP), statistical analysis, and data mining. These activities are described later in this chapter.

Business process management (BPM) includes a set of activities that enterprises perform to optimize their business processes, such as accounting and finance, hiring employees, and purchasing goods and services. BPM almost always is aided by specialized software designed to assist in these activities.

Business process automation (BPA) provides easy exchange of information among business applications, reduces the need for human intervention in processes, and utilizes software to automate processes wherever possible. BPA offers greater efficiency and reduces risks by making processes more predictable.

WEB LINK 12-1

Business Process Management

For more information, visit scsite.com/dcf5e/ch12/weblink and then click Business Process Management.

INFORMATION SYSTEMS IN THE ENTERPRISE

An **information system** is a set of hardware, software, data, people, and procedures that work together to produce information (Figure 12-4). A procedure is an instruction, or set of instructions, a user follows to accomplish an activity. For example, a company may have a procedure for its payroll system that includes a manager filling out certain forms before a new employee is added to the payroll system.

Information systems can be used in a variety of ways in an enterprise. Some information systems are used exclusively by only one type of department, or functional unit, within the enterprise. General purpose information systems include categories of information systems that can be used by almost any department within the enterprise. Integrated information systems are used by multiple departments and facilitate information sharing and communication within the enterprise. The following sections discuss each of these three uses of information systems.

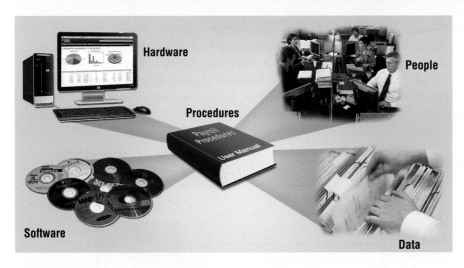

FIGURE 12-4 An information system typically contains five components: hardware, software, data, people, and procedures.

Information Systems within Functional Units

Figure 12-5 lists typical functional units, and their purpose within an enterprise, and examples of programs that each might use. The sections that follow discuss the types of information systems and software used within these units.

FUNCTIONAL UNITS WITHIN AN ENTERPRISE

Functional Unit	Description	Program Name
Accounting and Finance	Responsible for managing the business's money. Accounting department tracks every financial transaction that occurs within the company, including billing customers. Finance department manages the business' money as efficiently as possible.	Microsoft Dynamics GP Oracle Financials NetSuite
Human Resources (HR)	Responsible for recruiting and promoting employees, maintaining employee records, evaluating employees, training employees, and managing employee benefits and compensation.	Lawson Human Capital Management Oracle Peoplesoft Enterprise Human Capital Management Sage ABRA HRMS
Engineering or Product Development	Responsible for developing ideas into a product that can be used by customers. Ensures that the product can be manufactured effectively and designs the methods for manufacturing the product.	AutoCAD MicroStation ProductVision
Manufacturing	Responsible for converting raw materials into physical products.	CA-Plus MISys Manufacturing System Horizon Software MRP Plus Plexus Online
Marketing	Responsible for researching the market in which a business operates to determine the products and features that the business should develop. Determines the demographics to target with sales efforts and informs the target market about the company's products through advertising and education.	Aprimo Enterprise MarketingCentral MarketingPilot
Sales	Responsible for selling the company's products and services.	OpenBOX Sales Force Automation Prophet Professional SalesForce SFA
Distribution	Responsible for delivery of products to customers.	Activant Prophet 21 IBS's Advanced Inventory and Distribution Software John Galt Atlas Planning Suite
Customer Service	Responsible for maintaining a relationship with a customer both before and after a sale has been made.	SAP CRM Siebel CRM On Demand Apropos Interaction Management Suite
Information Technology	Responsible for designing, purchasing, implementing, testing, securing, and maintaining information systems for the rest of the organization. Sometimes called the information services (IS) department.	Microsoft System Center Configuration Manager VMWare InfraStructure 3 WebSense

FIGURE 12-5 An enterprise is composed of several functional units, each of which may use different programs to fulfill their needs.

ACCOUNTING AND FINANCE   Figure 12-6 illustrates the separate functions of accounting and financial systems used by accounting and finance departments. Accounting software manages everyday transactions, such as sales and payments to suppliers. Billing software helps the company reconcile purchases with customer payments. Financial software helps managers budget, forecast, and analyze. These types of software include comprehensive and flexible reporting tools to assist managers in making decisions, provide historical documentation, and meet regulatory requirements.

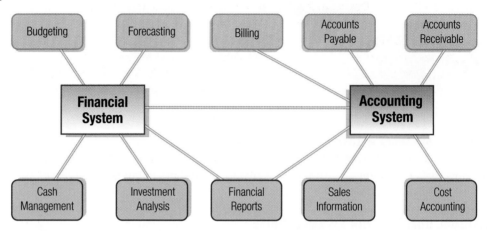

FIGURE 12-6   Accounting and financial systems perform different tasks, but share information and produce financial reports that help management make decisions.

HUMAN RESOURCES   A **human resources information system (HRIS)** manages one or more human resources functions (Figure 12-7). A human resources information system and its associated software help a company such as Wal-Mart maintain records on its more than 1.8 million employees. For example, when many retail employees arrive at work, they check in using an electronic clock that automatically allows managers to know who is late, early, or on time. The payroll department then can use this information when determining employee pay.

FIGURE 12-7
A human resources information system (HRIS) allows human resources personnel to manage employee information, such as benefits, personal information, performance evaluations, training, and vacation time.

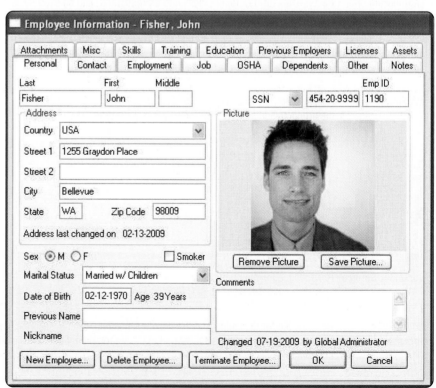

An employee relationship management (ERM) system automates and manages much of the communications between employees and the business. For example, an employee may interact with employee relationship management software to gather information regarding the employee's retirement account. Most employee relationship management software includes a Web interface for the employees and the human resources personnel, allowing both to interact with the system when they are in the office or at home.

ENGINEERING OR PRODUCT DEVELOPMENT   Professional workers, such as engineers, require specialized software and systems to perform their tasks. **Computer-aided design** (**CAD**) uses a computer and special software to aid in product design.

Computer-aided engineering (**CAE**) uses computers to test product designs. Using CAE, engineers can test the design of a car or bridge before it is built. These sophisticated programs simulate the effects of wind, temperature, weight, and stress on product shapes and materials. Engineers sometimes use 3-D visualization, which allows them to interact with a product without the need to build a prototype.

MANUFACTURING   Manufacturing information systems and software not only assist in the actual assembly process, but also assist in scheduling and managing the inventory of parts and products. **Computer-aided manufacturing** (**CAM**) is the use of computers to control production equipment. CAM production equipment includes software-controlled drilling, lathe, welding, and milling machines.

Computer-integrated manufacturing (**CIM**) uses computers to integrate the many different operations of the manufacturing process, using such technologies as CAD, CAE, and CAM (Figure 12-8).

Material Requirements Planning (**MRP**) is an approach to information management in a manufacturing environment that uses software to help monitor and control processes related to production. MRP focuses on issues related to inventory of parts and forecasting future demand so that materials needed for manufacturing can be on hand when they are needed.

FIGURE 12-8 Computer-integrated manufacturing (CIM) speeds the manufacturing process and reduces product defects.

QUALITY CONTROL   A quality control system helps an organization maintain or improve the quality of its products or services. A quality control system usually includes quality control software. Quality control software typically requires a great deal of continuous data gathering from the organization's ongoing processes. Using statistical analysis, the software can find and predict product defects and problems with the company's processes. While quality control systems often are costly and disruptive to the organization, the organization typically saves more money by producing a higher quality product or service.

MARKETING A **marketing information system** serves as a central repository for the tasks of the marketing functional unit. One type of marketing information system is a market research system, which stores and analyzes data gathered from demographics and surveys. Market research software assists in target marketing by allowing marketing personnel to query databases based on criteria such as income, gender, previous purchases, and favorite recreational activities.

SALES **Sales force automation (SFA)** software equips traveling salespeople with the electronic tools they need to be more productive. Sales force automation software helps salespeople manage customer contacts, schedule customer meetings, log customer interactions, manage product information, and take orders from customers.

Sales force automation software (Figure 12-9) often runs on notebook computers or other personal mobile devices. The notebook computer or other personal mobile device may connect wirelessly to the central office, allowing the salesperson to access up-to-date corporate information in real time no matter where he or she is located.

Some sales force automation programs allow the salesperson to upload information to the central office at the end of the day or end of the week. The programs also allow salespeople to download updated product and pricing information.

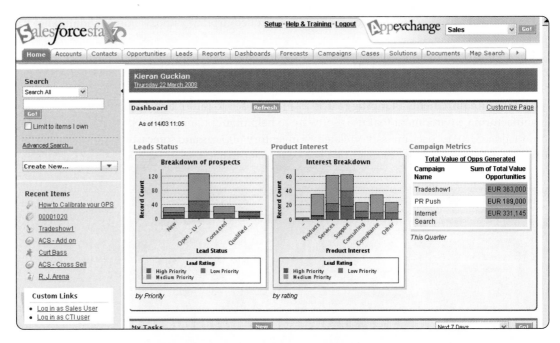

FIGURE 12-9
Sales force automation (SFA) software allows the sales force to manage customer and prospective customer relationships more effectively.

DISTRIBUTION **Distribution systems** provide forecasting for inventory control, manage and track shipping of products, and provide information and analysis on inventory in warehouses. Some distribution systems rely on GPS and other navigation technologies to track shipping in real time. Many companies now employ RFID to track inventory and shipping. Because of the complexity of the tasks of inventory management and shipping, distribution systems often integrate with quality control systems.

CUSTOMER SERVICE **Customer interaction management (CIM)** software manages the day-to-day interactions with customers, such as telephone calls, e-mail interactions, Web interactions, and instant messaging sessions. These interactions are logged so that a historical record of interactions with the customer can be viewed or analyzed at any time. A customer interaction management program routes customer telephone calls and support queries from the company's customer support Web site to the most appropriate support person depending on the identity of the customer or responses the customer gives to prompts. Customer interaction management software also assists support personnel in providing the best solutions for customers.

FAQ 12-1

When should I supply personal information to a company?

Companies gather personal information about consumers for a variety of reasons. Companies can gather information when you make a purchase, complete a survey, or enter a sweepstakes. Unless you are sure you want the company to communicate with you in some way, few reasons exist to supply personal information to a company. Ask the company why it needs the information and use your judgment. Most companies can supply you with a privacy policy upon request. For more information, visit scsite.com/dcf5e/ch12/faq and then click Sharing Personal Information.

INFORMATION TECHNOLOGY   The information technology department makes technology decisions for the enterprise, such as a decision whether to build or buy new customer interaction management information systems or when a computer or information system has outlived its useful life. Many organizations elevate the importance of information technology by including a **chief information officer (CIO)** executive position that reports to the CEO.

General Purpose Information Systems

Some information systems in an enterprise cross the boundaries of functional units. These general purpose, or enterprise-wide, systems become necessary in an enterprise for two reasons. First, functional units within an enterprise have a significant need to share data among the units. Second, enterprise-wide systems can collect and combine data more quickly and provide executive management access to a more up-to-date and accurate view of what is happening in the organization. Advances in computing speed, storage capacity, security, and networking have made enterprise-wide systems more attractive to organizations in recent years.

General purpose information systems generally fall into one of five categories: office information systems, transaction processing systems, management information systems, decision support systems, and expert systems. The following sections present each type of these general purpose information systems.

OFFICE INFORMATION SYSTEMS   An **office information system (OIS)** is an information system that enables employees to perform tasks using computers and other electronic devices, instead of manually. An office information system increases employee productivity and assists with communications among employees. Some people describe an office information system as office automation.

An office information system supports many administrative activities. With this type of system, users create and distribute graphics and documents, send messages, schedule appointments, browse the Web, and publish Web pages. All levels of users utilize and benefit from the features of an office information system.

An office information system uses many common software products to support its activities. Typical software in an office information system includes word processing, spreadsheet, database, presentation graphics, e-mail, Web browser, Web page authoring, personal information management, and groupware. To send text, graphics, audio, and video to others, an office information system uses communications technology such as voice mail, fax, and video conferencing.

TRANSACTION PROCESSING SYSTEMS   A **transaction processing system (TPS)** is an information system that captures and processes data from day-to-day business activities.

Transaction processing systems were among the first computerized systems that processed business data. Many people initially referred to the functions of a transaction processing system as data processing. The first transaction processing systems computerized an existing manual system. The intent of these transaction processing systems was to process faster, reduce clerical costs, and improve customer service.

Early TPSs mostly used batch processing. With batch processing, the computer collects data over time and processes all transactions later, as a group. As computers became more powerful, system developers created online transaction processing information systems. With online transaction processing (OLTP), the computer processes each transaction as it is entered. Today, most transaction processing systems use online transaction processing.

FIGURE 12-10
When you register for classes, you probably are using online transaction processing.

For example, when you register for classes at school or from home using the school's Web site (Figure 12-10), your school probably uses online transaction processing. You use the school's Web site to enter your desired schedule. The Web site immediately displays your statement of classes and sends you a schedule.

When you make a purchase with a credit card at a store, you are interacting with a transaction processing system. A transaction is an individual business activity. Examples of transactions are deposits, payments, orders, and reservations. Transactions take place in real time, meaning that as soon as you make a purchase with a credit card, you can visit your credit card company's Web site and view the transaction. In an organization, clerical staff typically uses computers and special software to perform activities associated with a transaction processing system.

MANAGEMENT INFORMATION SYSTEMS   A **management information system** (**MIS**) is an information system that generates accurate, timely, and organized information, so that managers and other users can make decisions, solve problems, supervise activities, and track progress.

Management information systems often are integrated with transaction processing systems. To process a sales order, the transaction processing system records the sale, updates the customer's account balance, and reduces the inventory count. Using this information, the related management information system produces reports that recap daily sales activities, summarize weekly and monthly sales activities, list customers with past due account balances, chart slow- or fast-selling products, and highlight inventory items that need reordering.

A management information system creates three basic types of reports: detailed, summary, and exception (Figure 12-11). A detailed report usually lists just transactions. For example, a Detailed Course Report lists courses available during a given period. A summary report consolidates data usually with totals, tables, or graphs, so that managers can review it quickly and easily.

FIGURE 12-11a (detailed report)

DETAILED COURSE REPORT for Spring 2009

Course Number	Course Description	Section — Instructor	Number Enrolled
CIS 101	Introduction to Computers	A – Berghoff B – Pankros	17 20
CIS 102	Microsoft Office Introduction	A – Washington B – Ramachadran C – Kensington	5 12 18
CIS 201	Advanced Microsoft Office	A – Berghoff B – Seifert	19 18
CIS 203	Introduction to Programming	A – Pankros B – Li	8 21

FIGURE 12-11b (summary report)

SUMMARY COURSE REPORT for Spring 2009

Course Number	Course Description	Number Enrolled	Location
CIS 101	Introduction to Computers	37	Brook Hall – Rm 217
CIS 102	Microsoft Office Introduction	35	Cary West – Rm 438
CIS 201	Advanced Microsoft Office	37	Tyrnbury – Rm 108
CIS 203	Introduction to Programming	29	Computer Science – Rm 204

FIGURE 12-11c (exception report)

LACK OF ENROLLMENT EXCEPTION REPORT for Spring 2009

Course Number	Section	Course Description	Number Enrolled	Enrollment Minimum
CIS 102	A	Microsoft Office Introduction	5	14
CIS 203	A	Introduction to Programming	8	12

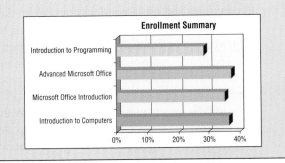

FIGURE 12-11   Three basic types of information generated in an MIS are detailed, summary, and exception.

An exception report identifies data outside of a normal condition. These out-of-the-ordinary conditions, called the exception criteria, define the normal activity or status range. For example, a Lack of Enrollment Exception Report notifies the registrar's office that some courses have not met minimum enrollment requirements.

Exception reports save managers time. Instead of searching through a detailed report, managers simply review the exception report. These reports help managers focus on situations that require immediate decisions or actions. Most information systems support all three types of reports shown in Figure 12-11.

DECISION SUPPORT SYSTEMS   A **decision support system (DSS)** helps users analyze data and make decisions. Often, a transaction processing system or management information system does not generate the type of report a manager needs to make a decision.

Programs that analyze data, such as those in a decision support system, sometimes are called online analytical processing (OLAP) programs. A decision support system uses data from internal and external sources. Internal sources of data might include sales orders, Material Requirements Planning results, inventory records, or financial data from accounting and financial analyses. Data from external sources could include interest rates, population trends, costs of new housing construction, or raw material pricing.

Some decision support systems include their own query languages, statistical analyses, spreadsheets, and graphics that help users retrieve data and analyze the results. Some also allow managers to create a model of the factors affecting a decision. A product manager might need to decide on a price for a new product. A simple model for finding the best price would include factors for the expected sales volume at various price levels. The model allows the user to ask what-if questions and view the expected results.

A special type of decision support system, called an executive information system (EIS), supports the strategic information needs of executive management. An executive information system presents information as charts and tables that show trends, ratios, and statistics (Figure 12-12).

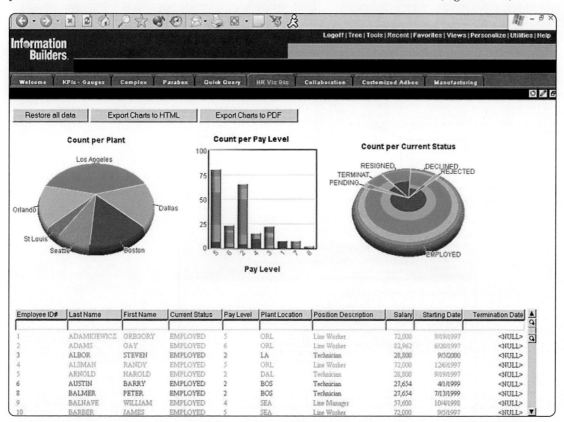

FIGURE 12-12   This executive information system (EIS) presents information to senior management in the form of graphics and reports.

EXPERT SYSTEMS   An **expert system** is an information system that captures and stores the knowledge of human experts and then imitates human reasoning and decision making. Figure 12-13 shows how one expert system assists with diagnosing a computer problem in Windows Vista.

Expert systems consist of two main components: a knowledge base and inference rules. A knowledge base is the combined subject knowledge and experiences of the human experts. The inference rules are a set of logical judgments that are applied to the knowledge base each time a user describes a situation to the expert system.

FIGURE 12-13 A SAMPLE EXPERT SYSTEM IN WINDOWS VISTA HELP AND SUPPORT

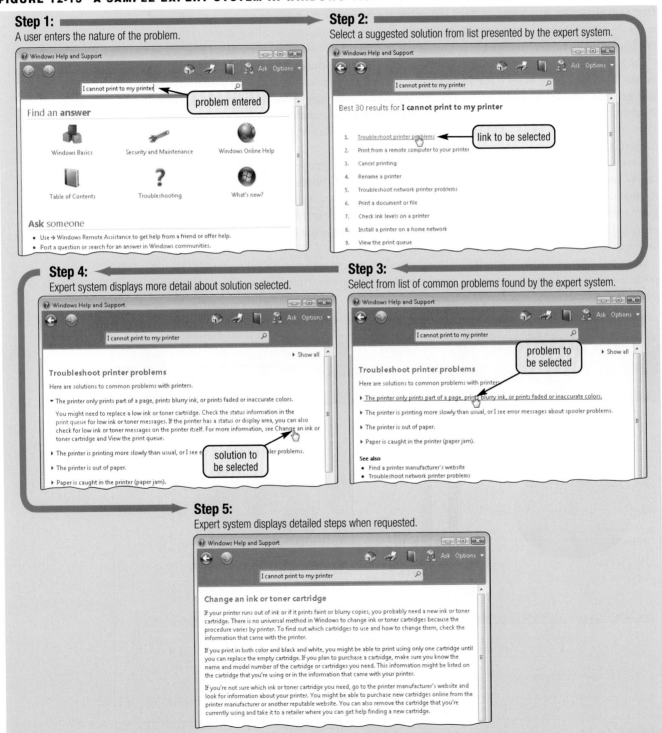

Expert systems are one aspect of an exciting branch of computer science called artificial intelligence. **Artificial intelligence (AI)** is the application of human intelligence to computers. Artificial intelligence technology senses a person's actions and, based on logical assumptions and prior experience, takes the appropriate action to complete the task. Artificial intelligence has a variety of capabilities, including speech recognition, logical reasoning, and creative responses. New research in the field of artificial intelligence tries to mimic the way that human memory works in order to expedite searches for information. Artificial intelligence has been used to play world-class chess, as well as in robots that manufacture complex goods, such as computers and automobiles.

Enterprises employ expert systems in a variety of roles, such as answering customer questions, training new employees, and analyzing data.

Integrated Information Systems

It often is difficult to classify an information system as belonging to only one of the five general types of information systems. Much of today's application software supports transaction processing and creates management information system reports. Other applications provide transaction processing, management information, and decision support.

ENTERPRISE RESOURCE PLANNING   **Enterprise resource planning (ERP)** provides centralized, integrated software applications to help manage and coordinate the ongoing activities of the enterprise, including manufacturing and distribution, accounting, finance, sales, product planning, and human resources. Figure 12-14 shows how ERP fits into the operations of an enterprise.

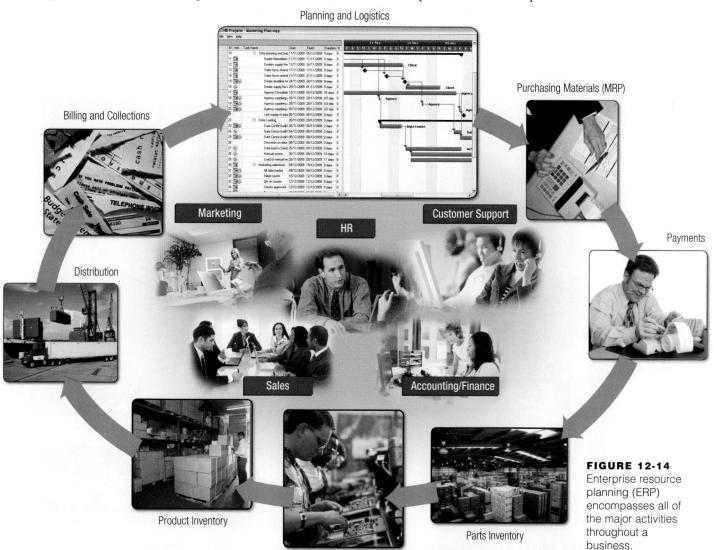

FIGURE 12-14
Enterprise resource planning (ERP) encompasses all of the major activities throughout a business.

The enterprise resource planning system installed at each organization must be customized to match the business requirements of the enterprise. At a large company, an enterprise resource planning system may take four to six years to implement and cost hundreds of millions of dollars. The organization hopes to regain the investment through the advantages offered by enterprise resource planning.

Advantages of enterprise resource planning include complete integration of information systems across departments, better project management, and better customer service. Better and faster reporting of the state of the enterprise leads managers to better decisions. Enterprise resource planning also helps to better manage the global nature of many enterprises. The reliance on one information system, rather than up to several hundred systems, allows the information technology department to focus on one type of technology and simplifies relationships with information technology vendors.

WEB LINK 12-3

Enterprise Resource Planning

For more information, visit scsite.com/dcf5e/ch12/weblink and then click Enterprise Resource Planning.

CUSTOMER RELATIONSHIP MANAGEMENT   A **customer relationship management (CRM)** system manages information about customers, interactions with customers, past purchases, and interests. Customer relationship management mainly is used across sales, marketing, and customer service departments. Customer relationship management software tracks leads and inquiries from customers, stores a history of all correspondence and sales to a customer, and allows for tracking of outstanding issues with customers.

CONTENT MANAGEMENT SYSTEMS   A **content management system (CMS)** is an information system that is a combination of databases, software, and procedures that organizes and allows access to various forms of documents and other files, including images and multimedia content. The content management system also provides security controls for the content, such as who is allowed to add, view, and modify content and on which content the user is allowed to perform those operations (Figure 12-15). Publishing entities, such as news services, use content management systems to keep Web sites up-to-date.

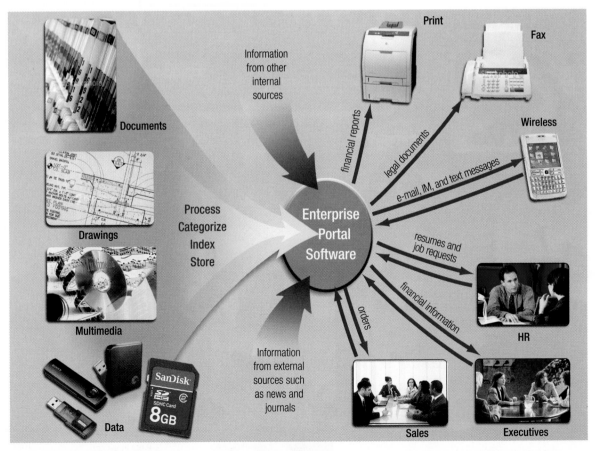

FIGURE 12-15   A content management system (CMS) helps a company classify and manage volumes of documents and media for future retrieval and use.

Test your knowledge of pages 452 through 466 in Quiz Yourself 12-1.

 QUIZ YOURSELF 12-1

Instructions: Find the true statement below. Then, rewrite the remaining false statements so they are true.

1. The main task of executive managers is to make tactical decisions.
2. An information system is a set of hardware, software, and people that work together to produce information.
3. A human resources information system serves as a central repository for the tasks of the marketing functional unit.
4. Customer interaction management software manages the day-to-day interactions with customers.
5. Decision support systems capture and store the knowledge of human experts and then imitate human reasoning and decision making.
6. Enterprise resource planning is a combination of databases, software, and procedures that organizes and allows access to various forms of documents and files.

Quiz Yourself Online: To further check your knowledge of enterprise information requirements and information systems used throughout the enterprise, visit scsite.com/dcf5e/ch12/quiz and then click Objectives 1 – 3.

ENTERPRISE-WIDE TECHNOLOGIES AND METHODOLOGIES

Several technologies adopted by enterprises allow them the flexibility and the ability to move swiftly in a business environment. Some of the common technologies used in enterprises include portals, electronic data interchange, data warehouses, extranets, Web services, workflow, and virtual private networks. Most of the hardware and software that contains these technologies is located in a **data center**, which is a centralized location for managing and housing those items. The following sections discuss each of these technologies.

WEB LINK 12-4

Data Centers

For more information, visit scsite.com/dcf5e/ch12/weblink and then click Data Centers.

Portals

A **portal** is a collection of links, content, and services presented on a Web page and designed to guide users to information they likely are to find interesting for their particular job function. A portal often includes searching capabilities or a link to a search engine, such as Google. Organizations often deploy **enterprise search** technology that allows users to perform searches across many enterprise-wide information systems and databases. Users typically can customize the portal Web site to meet their needs.

Information from external sources included on a portal Web page can include weather, news, reference tools, and instant messaging (Figure 12-16).

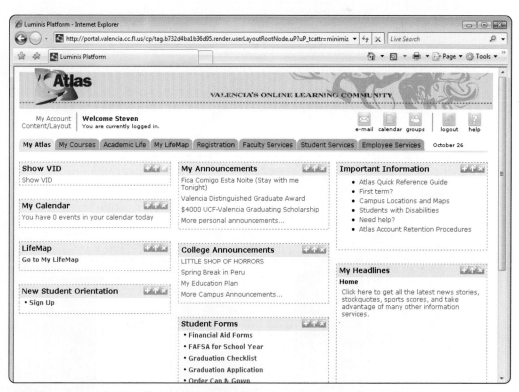

FIGURE 12-16 Portals allow users quick access to a multitude of information sources that they access on a regular basis.

Communications

The IT department, headed by the CIO, builds and maintains the electronic communications infrastructure of the enterprise. The communications infrastructure consists of hardware, software, and procedures. Examples of hardware include wired network connections, wireless network devices, routers, firewalls, servers, and a variety of long distance communications connections. Software can include e-mail, instant messaging, VoIP, and software applications to remotely manage servers and end users' computers. Procedures include the methods for using and managing the hardware and software.

In addition to the communications software used by end users in the enterprise, the IT department manages the software on servers to support the end users' programs. For example, the IT department manages e-mail servers that are used by the end users' e-mail programs.

For e-commerce, specialized software often is used to communicate with other computers. **EDI (electronic data interchange)** is a set of standards that controls the transfer of business data and information among computers both within and among enterprises. Today, businesses use these standards to communicate with industry partners over the Internet and telephone lines.

Data Warehouses

A **data warehouse** is a huge database that stores and manages the data required to analyze historical and current transactions. Software applications such as enterprise resource planning programs store and access data in a data warehouse.

Most data warehouses include one or more databases and one or more information systems storing data in the data warehouse. The data in the databases consists of transaction data required for decision making. This data may come from internal or external sources (Figure 12-17). Some data warehouses use Web farming for their external data. Web farming is the process of collecting data from the Internet as a source for the data warehouse.

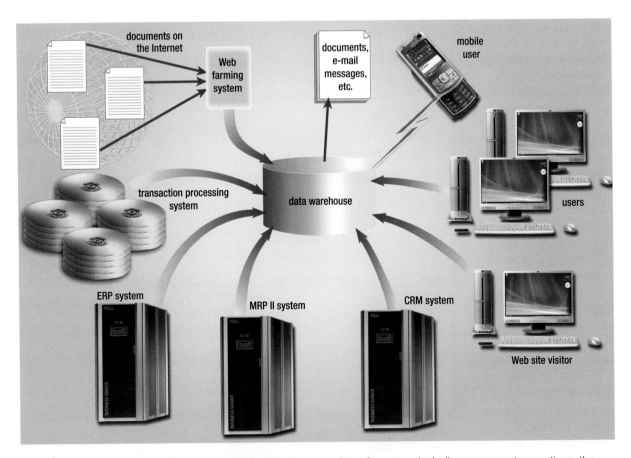

FIGURE 12-17 A data warehouse can receive data from a variety of sources, including company transactions, the Internet, and Web site visitor click streams.

Another growing external source of information is a click stream. A click stream is a collection of every action that users make as they move through a Web site. By analyzing visitors' click streams, companies identify consumer preferences and determine which Web pages are most attractive to visitors.

Extranets

An **extranet** is the portion of a company's network that allows customers or suppliers of a company to access parts of an enterprise's intranet. An extranet provides a secure, physical connection to the company's network. Customers may use the extranet to place and monitor orders electronically or to make payments. Suppliers may check inventory levels of the parts they supply to the company and receive orders and payments from the company. Extranets improve efficiency by replacing the postal service, faxes, or telephone calls as the communications medium of choice.

Web Services

Web services include a relatively new set of software technologies that allows businesses to create products and B2B (business-to-business) interactions over the Internet. Web services do not include traditional user interfaces, such as a Web page. Rather, users build their own interfaces to the Web services when necessary. Two popular platforms for building and running Web services are the Sun Microsystems Java EE platform and the Microsoft .NET Framework.

For example, an airline company may provide up-to-the-minute flight status information as a Web service (Figure 12-18). Travel Web sites, such as Expedia or Orbitz, can query the Web service and then display the information on their own Web pages for their customers. The travel Web site may ask for the status of a particular flight and receive back a scheduled departure or arrival time from the Web service. How the travel Web site then uses that information is of no concern to the Web service. The travel Web site may display the information to a customer who requested the information or it may send an e-mail notification with the information to the customer. Typically, the customer or consumer of the Web service — the travel Web site in this example — must write a program to use the Web service.

WEB LINK 12-5

Web Services

For more information, visit scsite.com/dcf5e/ch12/weblink and then click Web Services.

Workflow

A **workflow** is a defined process that identifies the specific set of steps involved in completing a particular project or business process. A workflow may be a written set of rules or a set of rules that exists in an information system.

A **workflow application** is a program that assists in the management and tracking of all the activities in a business process from start to finish. Enterprises use workflow applications to assist in defining complex workflows.

FIGURE 12-18 HOW A WEB SERVICE MIGHT WORK

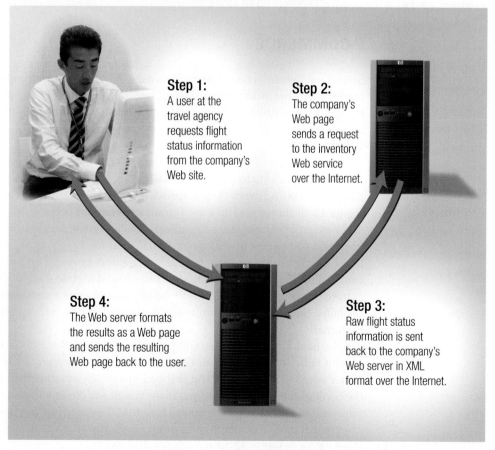

Step 1: A user at the travel agency requests flight status information from the company's Web site.

Step 2: The company's Web page sends a request to the inventory Web service over the Internet.

Step 3: Raw flight status information is sent back to the company's Web server in XML format over the Internet.

Step 4: The Web server formats the results as a Web page and sends the resulting Web page back to the user.

Virtual Private Network

Many companies today allow access to their company networks through a virtual private network. When a mobile user, remote office, vendor, or customer connects to a company's network using the Internet, a **virtual private network** (**VPN**) provides them with a secure connection to the company network server, as if they had a private line. Virtual private networks help to ensure that transmitted data is safe from being intercepted by unauthorized people (Figure 12-19). VPNs securely extend the company's internal network beyond the physical boundaries of the company. The secure connection created over the Internet between the user's computer and the company's network is called a VPN tunnel. Many companies allow external access to their internal networks only via a VPN connection.

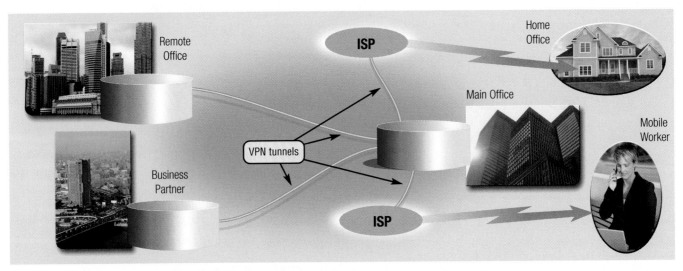

FIGURE 12-19   A virtual private network (VPN) allows a company to extend its internal network securely.

E-COMMERCE

Several market sectors have taken advantage of business opportunities on the Web. The more popular market segments include retail, finance, health, entertainment and media, and travel. The following paragraphs describe how the general public interacts with each of these types of enterprises on the Web.

E-Retailing

Retailing is one of the more visible market sectors of e-commerce. In retail, merchants sell products and services directly to a buyer. **E-retail**, also called e-tail, occurs when retailers use the Web to sell their products and services. Enterprises have adopted e-retail as a new way to reach customers. Figure 12-20 shows how an e-retail transaction might occur.

For example, a customer (consumer) visits an online business at the company's electronic store-front and adds items to a shopping cart. When ready to complete the sale, the customer proceeds to the checkout. At this time, the customer enters personal and financial data through a secure Web connection from his or her computer or personal mobile device. The transaction and financial data automatically are verified by the company's bank over a secure connection from the company to the bank. Several methods are available through which a company can accept payments from a customer.

If the bank or merchant account provider approves the transaction, the customer receives a confirmation notice of the purchase. Then, the e-retailer processes the order and sends it to the fulfillment center where it is packaged and shipped. Inventory systems then are updated. The e-retailer notifies the bank of the shipment, and payment is sent via electronic channels to the e-retailer. Shipping information is posted on the Internet, so that the customer can track the order from their computer or personal mobile device. The customer typically receives the order a few days after the purchase. Read Ethics & Issues 12-1 for a related discussion.

ETHICS & ISSUES 12-1

Who Can You Trust When Making Purchases Online?

When you walk into a store, at some point in your shopping experience you almost always interact with a person directly. The online shopping experience, however, distances you from a seller who may be five hundred or five thousand miles away. For many consumers, this type of nonhuman transaction can be a source of stress and concern about the trustworthiness of the merchant. For some merchants, the distance and anonymity of the Internet is an ideal climate for finding unknowing victims for unscrupulous activity, such as fraud. Consumer advocates and government agencies recommend many ways to avoid a bad online shopping experience. When you provide personal information, make sure that you are dealing with a secure Web site whose address begins with https:// rather than http://. Check the site's credentials, which may include seals from Truste, the Better Business Bureau (BBB), or other certifying organizations. Make sure that the price you pay matches the price listed on the site and that you are not paying too much for shipping your order. When available, check reviews of the merchant offered by other consumers, but be aware that many merchants try to offer phony, positive reviews of themselves. Finally, make it a habit to rate merchants as often as possible so that others can learn from your experience. When you shop online, how do you go about determining which online merchants are trustworthy? How do the methods that you use differ from merchants you visit when you walk into a store for the first time? Are consumer advocacy groups or the government the better choice for regulating online transactions? Why?

FIGURE 12-20 HOW AN E-COMMERCE TRANSACTION TAKES PLACE

Step 1:
The customer displays the e-retailer's electronic storefront.

Step 2:
The customer collects purchases in an electronic shopping cart.

Step 3:
The customer enters payment information in a secure Web site. The e-retailer sends financial information to a bank.

Step 4:
The bank performs security checks and sends authorization back to the e-retailer.

Step 7:
While the order travels to the customer, shipping information is posted on the Web.

Step 6:
The fulfillment center packages the order, prepares it for shipment, and then sends a report to the server where records are updated.

Step 5:
The e-retailer's Web server sends confirmation to the customer, processes the order, and then sends it to the fulfillment center.

Step 8:
The order is delivered to the customer.

Finance

Financial institutions include any business that manages the circulation of money, grants credit, makes investments, or meets banking needs. These include banks, mortgage companies, brokerage firms, and insurance companies. In the past, financial institutions were strictly traditional bricks-and-mortar institutions. Today, many also conduct business on the Internet.

Online banking allows users to pay bills from their computer or personal mobile device, that is, transfer money electronically from their account to a payee's account such as the electric company or telephone company. At anytime, online banking users also can download or view trans-actions such as cleared checks, ATM withdrawals, and deposits, which allows them to have an up-to-date bank statement.

With **online trading**, users invest in stocks, options, bonds, treasuries, certificates of deposit, money markets, annuities, mutual funds, and so on — without using a broker. Many investors prefer online stock trading because the transaction fee for each trade usually is substantially less than when trading through a broker.

Health

Many Web sites provide up-to-date medical, fitness, nutrition, or exercise information. As with any other information on the Web, users should verify the legitimacy of the Web site before relying on its information.

Some of these health-related Web sites maintain databases of doctors and dentists to help individuals find the one who suits their needs. They also may have chat rooms, so that people can talk to others diagnosed with similar conditions.

Many health-care providers offer online services for patients, such as online diagnosis, prescriptions, appointment booking, and the capability to view their health history. Physicians often communicate with patients through e-mail in order to speed up communications and minimize office visits. Read Looking Ahead 12-2 for a look at the next generation of smart health devices.

Many bricks-and-mortar pharmacies have an online counterpart that exists on the Web, allowing customers to refill prescriptions and ask pharmacists questions using customer interaction management software. Some Web sites even allow consumers to order prescriptions online and have them delivered directly to their door.

Entertainment and Media

The technology behind the Web has enabled entertainment and media to take many forms. Music, videos, news, sporting events, and 3-D multiplayer games are a growing part of the Web's future. Newsprint on the Web is not replacing the newspaper, but enhancing it and reaching different populations. Read Ethics & Issues 12-2 for a related discussion. Streaming technology currently supports live radio broadcasting, live videos, and live concerts. Users can purchase music online and download the music files directly to a computer hard disk, allowing them to listen to the purchased music immediately from a computer or any portable media player.

Not only do entertainment companies benefit from the ease of distributing electronic content, other industries use electronic media in a variety of ways. Companies provide interactive online tutorials regarding the use and care of their products. Consumers can find and download lost manuals for products. Interactive online advertising and seminars allow companies to pitch their products to a wider audience of consumers who show an interest in the companies' products.

ETHICS & ISSUES 12-2

Does Availability of News on the Web Threaten the Daily Newspaper?

For more than a decade, pundits have predicted the demise of the daily newspaper, claiming that people could get more news for free on the Web, and that most people would opt for the convenience of the Web over a printed newspaper. Large media companies have been merging and trimming down their staff. Furthermore, few have devised a formula to make publishing news on the Web as profitable a venture as selling printed newspapers. In fact, many media companies lose money when it comes to making their news available on the Web. Many large newspapers now employ half the number of reporters that they did before news became popular on the Web. During that time frame, total newspaper circulation decreased, but only by approximately 10 percent.

Many in the industry blame news consolidation Web sites, such as Google News, for misappropriating their news stories. Others blame bloggers, who typically are not trained journalists, for driving consumers away from newspapers by sensationalizing news, adding editorial content, and engaging in poor reporting practices that simply entice readers rather than educate them. Some industry analysts believe that the decline in newspaper circulation is due to natural industry consolidation. The phenomenon also may be a result of the rise of 24-hour news television channels in conjunction with the Web. How does the availability of news on the Web affect your news reading habits? Does blogging and the drop in the number of reporters cause a decline in the quality of the news that people may be reading? Why or why not?

Travel

The Web provides many travel-related services. If you need directions, you simply can enter a starting point and destination, and many Web sites provide detailed directions along with a map. Users can make airline reservations and reserve a hotel or car.

Some of these Web sites are shopping bots that save users time by doing all the investigative cost-comparison work. A **shopping bot** is a Web site that searches the Internet for the best price on a product or service in which you are interested (Figure 12-21).

Other Business Services

Enterprises use the Web to provide services to consumers and other businesses. Public relations, online advertising, direct mail, recruiting, credit, sales, market research, technical support, training, software consulting, and Internet access represent a few of the areas of service.

FIGURE 12-21   At Priceline.com, you name the price you are willing to pay, and Priceline.com finds available commodities such as flights, hotel rooms, and car rentals that meet your budget.

Test your knowledge of pages 467 through 473 in Quiz Yourself 12-2.

ENTERPRISE HARDWARE

Enterprise hardware allows large organizations to manage and store information and data using devices geared for heavy use, maximum availability, and maximum efficiency.

One of the goals of an enterprise's hardware is to maintain a high level of availability to end users. The availability of hardware to users is a measure of how often it is online. Highly available hardware is accessible 24 hours a day, 365 days a year.

The following sections discuss a variety of enterprise hardware solutions.

RAID

For applications that depend on reliable data access, users must have the data available when they attempt to access it. Some manufacturers provide a type of hard disk system that connects several smaller disks into a single unit that acts like a single large hard disk. As you learned in Chapter 6, a group of two or more integrated hard disks is called a **RAID (redundant array of independent disks)**. Although quite expensive for large computers, RAID is more reliable than traditional hard disks (Figure 12-22). Networks and Internet servers often use RAID.

A RAID system duplicates data, instructions, and information to improve data reliability. The simplest RAID storage design, called mirroring, writes data on two disks at the same time to duplicate the data. This configuration enhances storage reliability because, if a disk should fail, a duplicate of the requested item is available elsewhere within the array of disks. Some personal computers now include RAID storage.

FIGURE 12-22　A group of two or more integrated hard disks, called a RAID (redundant array of independent disks), often is used with network servers. Shown here is a rack-mounted RAID chassis including the hard disks.

Network Attached Storage and Storage Area Networks

Network attached storage (**NAS**) is a server that is placed on a network with the sole purpose of providing storage to users and information systems attached to the network (Figure 12-23a). A network attached storage server often is called a storage appliance because it is a piece of equipment with only one function — to provide additional storage. Administrators quickly add storage to an existing network simply by attaching a new network attached storage server to the network.

A **storage area network** (**SAN**) is a high-speed network with the sole purpose of providing storage to other servers to which it is attached (Figure 12-23b). A storage area network is a network that includes only storage devices. High-speed fiber-optic cable connects other networks and servers to the storage area network, so the networks and servers have fast access to large storage capacities.

WEB LINK 12-6

NAS and SAN
For more information, visit scsite.com/dcf5e/ ch12/weblink and then click NAS and SAN.

FIGURE 12-23a (network attached storage on a LAN)

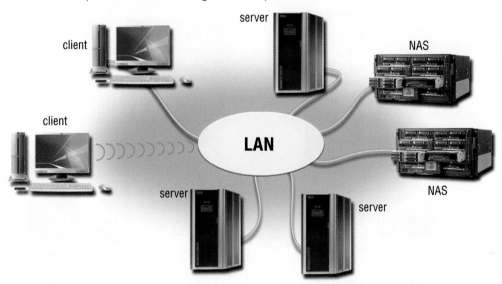

FIGURE 12-23b (a SAN provides centralized storage for servers and networks)

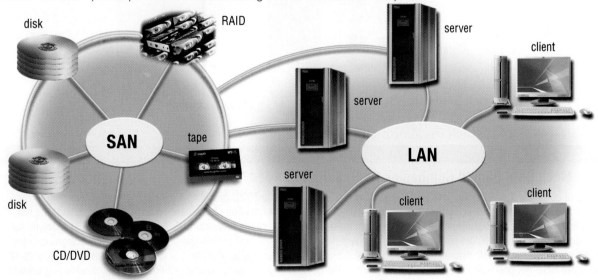

FIGURE 12-23 Network attached storage (NAS) and a storage area network (SAN) connect to existing servers and networks in different ways.

Enterprise Storage Systems

Many organizations use networks. Data, information, and instructions stored on the network must be easily accessible to all authorized users. The data, information, and instructions also must be secure, so that unauthorized users cannot access the network. An **enterprise storage system** is a strategy that focuses on the availability, protection, organization, and backup of storage in a company.

The goal of an enterprise storage system is to consolidate storage so that operations run as efficiently as possible. Most enterprise storage systems manage extraordinary amounts of data. For example, one large retailer manages a several-hundred TB storage system to store sales data. Read Ethics & Issues 12-3 for a related discussion.

To implement an enterprise storage system, an organization uses a combination of techniques. As shown in Figure 12-24, an enterprise storage system may use servers, RAID, a tape library, CD and DVD jukeboxes, Internet backup, network attached storage devices, and/or a storage area network. Enterprises often use **Fibre Channel** technology to connect to storage systems at data rates up to 4 Gbps.

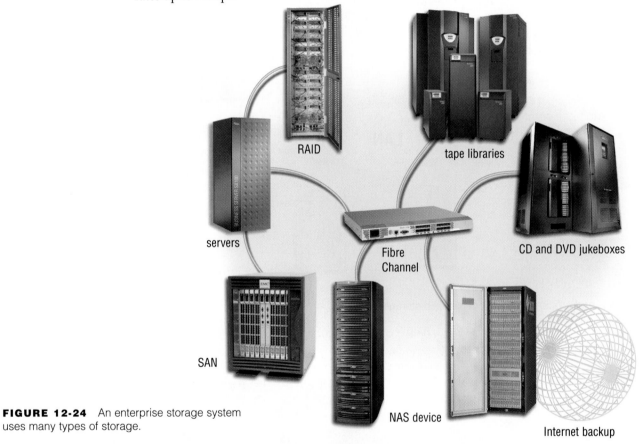

RAID

tape libraries

servers

Fibre
Channel

CD and DVD jukeboxes

SAN

NAS device

Internet backup

FIGURE 12-24 An enterprise storage system uses many types of storage.

ETHICS & ISSUES 12-3

How Much Data Should Companies Be Required to Keep?

After a string of corporate scandals, the Sarbanes-Oxley Act was signed into law in 2002, providing a myriad of financial reporting requirements and guidelines for public companies. A main focus of the law is the retention of business records. As provisions of the law slowly have come into effect, companies have been faced with massive new data storage requirements for these records. For example, all e-mail messages within a company are considered to be business records and must be retained. Deleting stored e-mail messages constitutes a destruction of evidence infraction. Penalties include 20 years in prison for any employee who alters or destroys records or documents. IT departments are faced not only with understanding this complex law, but also with ensuring accuracy of financial data, determining policies for record retention, and building storage capacity to hold all of the data. Supporters of the law cite its need due to the recent wave of corporate scandals. Opponents say that the law is overreaching and costs too much for the added benefits. Is the Sarbanes-Oxley Act an unfair burden on companies? Why or why not? Should companies be able to engage in internal communications without the fear that those communications could be used as evidence against them later? Why or why not? How should companies go about reacting to the law? Are such laws necessary in order to protect the public? Why or why not?

Some organizations manage an enterprise storage system in-house. Other enterprises elect to offload all (or at least the backup) storage management to an outside organization or online Web service. This practice is known as outsourcing. Some vendors focus on providing enterprise storage systems to clients. A data warehouse might seek this type of outside service.

Blade Servers

Blade servers, sometimes called ultradense servers, pack a complete computer server, such as a Web server or network server, on a single card, or blade, rather than a system unit. Each blade server includes a processor, memory, hard disk, network card, and ports on the card. The individual blades insert in a blade server chassis that can hold many blades. Using blade servers allows an organization to fit 16 or more blades in the physical space occupied by a single server. Figure 12-25 shows a blade and a chassis that holds many blades.

Besides the savings in space offered by blade servers, blade servers require less maintenance, use less energy, generate less heat, and easily are replaced or upgraded.

FIGURE 12-25
A blade server contains several very small servers, each on its own blade within the server.

High-Availability Systems

High-availability systems continue running and performing tasks for at least 99 percent of the time. Some users demand that high-availability systems be available for 99.99 percent of the time. A system that has uptime of 99.99 percent is nonfunctional for less than one hour per year. That one hour, called downtime, includes any time that the computer crashes, needs repairs, or requires installation of replacement or upgrade parts. A system with 99.9 percent availability is said to have three nines of availability, and a system with 99.99 percent availability is said to have four nines of availability.

Telecommunications companies, such as local telephone companies, rely on high-availability systems to deliver telephone service. Emergency 911 communications centers require almost 100 percent uptime for their hardware and software applications as mandated by law. Centralized accounting or financial systems must be available to gather sales and other accounting information from locations scattered around the globe.

High-availability systems often include a feature called hot-swapping. Hot-swapping allows components, such as a RAID hard disk or power supplies, to be replaced while the rest of the system continues to perform its tasks. A high-availability system also may include redundant components. **Redundant components**, such as redundant power supplies, allow for a functioning component to take over automatically the tasks of a similar component that fails. When a component fails, the system administrator is notified, but the computer continues to perform its tasks because a redundant component has taken its place automatically in the system.

WEB LINK 12-7

Blade Servers
For more information, visit scsite.com/dcf5e/ch12/weblink and then click Blade Servers.

Scalability

As an enterprise grows, its information systems either must grow with it or must be replaced. **Scalability** is a measure of how well a computer hardware system, software application, or information system can grow to meet increasing performance demands. A system that is designed, built, or purchased when the company is small may be inadequate when the company doubles in size. When making decisions for computing solutions, managers must be careful to consider the growth plans of the company.

A company may find that its Web site is becoming overwhelmed by customers and prospective customers. If the Web site is scalable, then the Web administrator can add more Web servers to handle the additional visitors to the Web site. Similarly, an enterprise's storage needs usually grow daily, meaning that storage systems should be scalable to store the ever-growing data generated by users.

Adding more hardware often is the easiest method to grow, or scale, an information system. Often, at some point, a system no longer scales and must be replaced with a new system.

Utility and Grid Computing

As the need for scalability increases, companies often find that using outside computing resources is more economical than building new computing capacity internally. Utility and grid computing are two new technologies that provide flexible and massive online computing power. **Utility computing**, or on demand computing, allows companies to use the processing power sitting idle in a network located somewhere else in the world. When the company uses the computing resources, they pay a fee based on the amount of computing time and other resources that they consume.

Grid computing combines many servers and/or personal computers on a network, such as the Internet, to act as one large computer. As with utility computing, a company may pay for the use of a grid based on the amount of processing time that it needs. Grid computing often is used in research environments, such as climate research and life science problems. For example, the SETI@home project uses a grid of millions of personal computers around the world to search radio signals for signs of extraterrestrial life.

Virtualization

Due to the often dynamic nature of enterprise computing needs, IT administrators often use virtualization to adapt quickly to the change. Virtualization is the practice of sharing or pooling computing resources, such as servers and storage devices. Server virtualization provides the capability to logically divide a physical server into many virtual servers. From the end user's point of view, a virtual server behaves just like a physical server. The advantages of server virtualization are that a virtual server can be created and configured quickly, does not require a new physical server, and is easier to manage.

Storage virtualization provides the capability to create a single logical storage device from many physical storage devices. For example, hard disks from many different servers located in geographically disparate areas can be combined to appear as a single hard disk to the users of the storage. The advantages of storage virtualization are that the storage can be configured quickly, may not require the purchase of additional storage devices because the necessary capacity already may exist, and is easier to manage than traditional storage.

Interoperability

Enterprises typically build and buy a diverse set of information systems. An information system often must share information, or have **interoperability**, with other information systems within the enterprise. Information systems that more easily share information with other information systems are said to be open. Information systems that are more difficult to interoperate with other information systems are said to be closed, or proprietary. Recent open systems employ XML and Web services to allow a greater level of interoperability.

BACKUP PROCEDURES

Business and home users can perform four types of backup: full, differential, incremental, or selective. A fifth type, continuous data protection, is used by large enterprises. A full backup, sometimes called an archival backup, copies all of the files in the computer. A full backup provides the best protection against data loss because it copies all program and data files. Performing a full backup can be time-consuming. A differential backup copies only the files that have changed since the last full backup. An incremental backup copies only the files that have changed since the last full or last incremental backup. A selective backup, sometimes called a partial backup, allows the user to choose specific files to back up, regardless of whether or not the files have changed since the last incremental backup. Continuous data protection (CDP), or continuous backup, is a system in which all data is backed up whenever a change is made. A continuous data protection plan keeps a journal of every transaction — reads, writes, and deletes — made to a server or servers.

Whatever backup procedures a company adopts, they should be stated clearly, documented in writing, and followed consistently.

Disaster Recovery Plan

A **disaster recovery plan** is a written plan describing the steps a company would take to restore computer operations in the event of a disaster. A disaster recovery plan contains four major components: the emergency plan, the backup plan, the recovery plan, and the test plan.

THE EMERGENCY PLAN   An emergency plan specifies the steps to be taken immediately after a disaster strikes. All emergency plans should contain the following information:

1. Names and telephone numbers of people and organizations to notify (e.g., management, fire department, police department)
2. Procedures to follow with the computer equipment (e.g., equipment shutdown, power shutoff, file removal)
3. Employee evacuation procedures
4. Return procedures; that is, who can reenter the facility and what actions they are to perform

THE BACKUP PLAN   Once the procedures in the emergency plan have been executed, the next step is to follow the backup plan. The backup plan specifies how an organization uses backup files and equipment to resume information processing. The backup plan should specify the location of an alternate computer facility in the event the an organization's normal location is destroyed or unusable.

When operations are so important that an organization cannot afford to lose the operations to a disaster, the organization often maintains a hot site, which is a separate facility that mirrors the systems and operations of the critical site. The hot site always operates concurrently with the main site, so that if either site becomes unavailable, the other site continues to meet the organization's needs. The process of one system automatically taking the place of a failed system is called **failover**.

The backup plan identifies these items:

1. The location of backup data, supplies, and equipment
2. The personnel responsible for gathering backup resources and transporting them to the alternate computer facility
3. A schedule indicating the order in which, and approximate time by which, each application should be up and running

For a backup plan to be successful, the organization must back up all critical resources. Also, additional people, including possibly nonemployees, must be trained in the backup and recovery procedures because the organization's personnel could be injured in a disaster.

FAQ 12-4

Should I have a backup plan?

Yes! Even home computers need a backup plan. You probably know someone who lost valuable personal information due to a hard disk crash or other problem. Most modern operating systems include backup software. You should familiarize yourself with the software, develop a plan, and test both backing up and recovering data. For more information, visit scsite.com/dcf5e/ch12/faq and then click Backup Software.

THE RECOVERY PLAN   The recovery plan specifies the actions to be taken to restore full information processing operations. To prepare for disaster recovery, an organization should establish planning committees, with each one responsible for different forms of recovery. For example, one committee is in charge of hardware replacement. Another is responsible for software replacement.

THE TEST PLAN   To provide assurance that the disaster plan is complete, it should be tested. A disaster recovery test plan contains information for simulating various levels of disasters and recording an organization's ability to recover. In a simulation, all personnel follow the steps in the disaster recovery plan.

Test your knowledge of pages 474 through 479 in Quiz Yourself 12-3.

QUIZ YOURSELF 12-3

Instructions: Find the true statement below. Then, rewrite the remaining false statements so they are true.

1. Network attached storage is a high-speed network with the sole purpose of providing storage to other servers to which it is attached.

2. Scalability refers to the ability of an information system to share information with other information systems.

3. A differential backup copies only the files that have changed since the last full or last incremental backup.

4. An emergency plan specifies how a company uses backup files and equipment to resume information processing.

5. The recovery plan specifies the actions to be taken to restore full information processing operations.

Quiz Yourself Online: To further check your knowledge of enterprise hardware, backup procedures, and a disaster recovery plan, visit scsite.com/dcf5e/ch12/quiz and then click Objectives 6 – 8.

CHAPTER SUMMARY

This chapter reviewed the special computing requirements present in an enterprise-sized organization. Various types of users within an organization require different types of information systems. Large information systems become more valuable when they communicate with each other and offer users a great deal of flexibility in interacting with the information system and other users. The chapter discussed e-retailing and the types of businesses that use e-commerce.

Enterprises manage complex hardware, including storage area networks, RAID, and blade servers. Requirements for this enterprise hardware often include high-availability, scalability, and interoperability which they meet with technologies such as grid and utility computing. The chapter also discussed the backup procedures present in a large organization.

CAREER CORNER　　　　**CIO**

CIO (chief information officer) is the highest-ranking position in an information technology (IT) department. The CIO manages all of an organizations's information systems and computer resources. In large organizations, the CIO typically is a vice president and reports directly to the organization's CEO.

Depending on the organization, a CIO can be called an MIS (management information systems) manager, an IS (information systems) manager, or an IT (information technology) manager. Regardless of the title, the CIO determines an organization's information needs and provides the systems to meet those needs. The CIO sets an IT department's goals, policies, and procedures. In addition, the CIO evaluates technology, hires and supervises staff, oversees the network, directs user services, develops backup and disaster recovery plans, and manages the department budget. Perhaps most important, the CIO provides leadership, creating a vision for an IT department and helping the department deliver that vision.

Some CIOs work as consultants, providing corporate IT departments with short-term or long-term guidance. Most CIOs rise through the ranks of an organization's IT department. Generally, CIOs have a bachelor's degree or higher in computer science and at least ten years' experience in an IT department. Today, many CIOs also have an MBA. Pay reflects the importance of the CIO, with salaries ranging from $150,000 for smaller companies to $350,000 for large companies. For more information, visit scsite.com/dcf5e/ch12/careers and then click CIO.

EMC
Information Management and Storage Provider

Information lives at EMC Corporation, a world leader in information management and storage products, services, and solutions. The company helps organizations manage their increasing volumes of data. Customers include health-care organizations, airlines and transportation companies, educational institutions, and financial services firms, including Harvard University, Discover Financial Services, and MasterCard International.

EMC has become the leader in the external storage systems and storage management software markets. Its RAID systems, networked storage systems, and storage management software are ranked at the top of the industry revenue shares. The largest commercial database ever identified is stored on an EMC system: a 100.4 TB Oracle database.

The Massachusetts-based business was established in 1979 and employs 26,000 people worldwide. In 2007, the company sold 10 percent of its assets of VMWare; it also forecast that 988 billion GB of digital information will be created worldwide in 2010, which represents a six-fold annual information growth from 2006. For more information, visit scsite.com/dcf5e/ch12/companies and then click EMC.

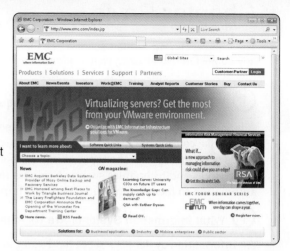

IBM
World's Largest Information Technology Company

Nearly one-half of the world's supercomputer total processing power is supplied by IBM systems, but the company's products reach more than power users; IBM is the world's largest information technology corporation and works with consumers of all sizes.

IBM has a reputation for pioneering products. In 1911, three companies merged to sell a variety of business-related gadgets, including a machine that used punched cards to catalog data. Nine years later, the company changed its name to International Business Machines (IBM). In its history of computer innovation, the company has developed the first family of computers with interchangeable software and peripherals, the personal computer with 16 KB of memory and a floppy disk drive, and the ThinkPad notebook computer. For more information, visit scsite.com/dcf5e/ch12/companies and then click IBM.

TECHNOLOGY TRAILBLAZERS

John Chambers
Cisco Chairman and CEO

Investors and employees give John Chambers standing ovations at business meetings for his enthusiasm, excellent listening skills, and quick decisions. But the Cisco chairman and CEO did not always enjoy such sweet success. As a youth, he struggled from dyslexia. During the dotcom crash of 2001, Cisco's growth dropped from 70 percent to negative 30 percent in 45 days as inventories rose. But Chambers overcame these obstacles and has turned his life and his company into success stories.

He is active in philanthropic activities worldwide and has received the Woodrow Wilson Award for Corporate Citizenship from the Woodrow Wilson International Center for Scholars of the Smithsonian Institution and the Excellence in Corporate Philanthropy Award from the Committee to Encourage Corporate Philanthropy, an international forum of CEOs focused on corporate philanthropy.

Chambers earned a law degree from West Virginia University and an MBA degree from Indiana University. He worked at IBM and Wang Laboratories for 14 years before joining Cisco in 1991 as head of sales and operations. For more information, visit scsite.com/dcf5e/ch12/people and then click John Chambers.

Jim Clark
Technology Innovator

When Jim Clark has an idea, people listen. As a professor at Stanford University, he developed a computer chip that processed 3-D images in real time. The high-powered chip formed the basis of Clark's first company, Silicon Graphics, and was used to create everything from suspension bridges to scenes in Hollywood movies.

Seeking more innovation opportunities, Clark contacted Marc Andreessen, creator of the Web browser, Mosaic. Together, they launched Netscape Communications Corporation, the source of one of the world's more successful Web browsers, Netscape Navigator.

Since then, Clark has started other computer-related companies: Healtheon, which links doctors, patients, and health insurance providers; MyCFO, a Web-based financial advisory firm; and Shutterfly, an online digital photo printing service. For more information, visit scsite.com/dcf5e/ch12/people and then click Jim Clark.

Chapter Review

The Chapter Review section summarizes the concepts presented in this chapter. To obtain help from other students regarding any subject in this chapter, visit scsite.com/dcf5e/ch12/forum and post your thoughts or questions.

(1) What Are the Special Information Requirements of an Enterprise-Sized Corporation?

A large organization, or enterprise, requires special computing solutions because of its size and geographical extent. **Enterprise computing** uses computers in networks or a series of interconnected networks to satisfy the information needs of an enterprise. The types of information employees require depend on their level in the company. **Managers** utilize tools and techniques such as **business intelligence**, **business process management**, and **business process automation** to focus on information that is important to the decision-making process.

(2) What Information Systems Are Used in the Functional Units of an Enterprise?

An **information system** is a set of hardware, software, data, people, and procedures that work together to produce information. In an enterprise, each type of functional unit has specialized requirements for their information systems. Accounting and financial systems manage everyday transactions and help budget, forecast, and analyze. A **human resources information system (HRIS)** manages one or more human resources functions. Engineers use **computer-aided design (CAD)** and **computer-aided engineering (CAE)**. **Computer-aided manufacturing (CAM)** and **computer-integrated manufacturing (CIM)** speed manufacturing. A **marketing information system** serves as a central repository for marketing tasks. **Sales force automation (SFA)** software equips salespeople with the tools they need. **Distribution systems** control inventory and manage shipping. **Customer interaction management (CIM)** software manages interactions with customers. The information technology (IT) department makes technology decisions for an enterprise.

(3) What Information Systems Are Used throughout an Enterprise?

Some general purpose information systems, or enterprise-wide systems, are used throughout an enterprise. A **transaction processing system (TPS)** captures and processes data from day-to-day business activities. A **management information system (MIS)** generates accurate, timely, and organized information, so users can make decisions, solve problems, and track progress. A **decision support system (DSS)** helps users analyze data and make decisions. **Enterprise resource planning (ERP)** provides applications to help manage and coordinate ongoing activities. **Customer relationship management (CRM)** systems manage information about customers. A **content management system (CMS)** organizes and allows access to various forms of documents and files.

 Visit scsite.com/dcf5e/ch12/quiz or click the Quiz Yourself button. Click Objectives 1 – 3.

(4) What Are Types of Technologies Used throughout an Enterprise?

Technologies used throughout an enterprise include portals, electronic data interchange, data warehouses, extranets, Web services, workflow, and virtual private networks. A **portal** is a collection of links, content, and services on a Web page designed to guide users to information related to their jobs. **EDI (electronic data interchange)** controls the transfer of data and information among computers. A **data warehouse** stores and manages the data required to analyze transactions. An **extranet** allows customers or suppliers to access part of an enterprise's intranet. **Web services** allow businesses to create products and B2B interactions. A **workflow application** assists in the management and tracking of the activities in a business process. A **virtual private network (VPN)** provides users with a secure connection to a company's network server.

(5) What Are the Major Types of E-Commerce?

E-retail occurs when retailers use the Web to sell their products or services. **Online banking** allows users to pay bills from their computers or personal mobile devices, and **online trading** lets users invest without using a broker. Entertainment and media on the Web include music, videos, news, sporting events, and 3-D multiplayer games. Travel-related services on the Web include directions; airline, hotel, or car reservations; and a **shopping bot** that searches for the best price on a product or service.

 Visit scsite.com/dcf5e/ch12/quiz or click the Quiz Yourself button. Click Objectives 4 – 5.

Chapter Review

6 **What Are the Computer Hardware Needs and Solutions for an Enterprise?**

Enterprise hardware allows large organizations to manage and share information and data using devices geared for maximum availability and efficiency. A **RAID (redundant array of independent disks)** is a group of integrated disks that duplicates data, instructions, and information to improve data reliability. **Network attached storage (NAS)** is a server that provides storage for users and information systems. A **storage area network (SAN)** provides storage to other servers. An **enterprise storage system** consolidates storage so that operations run efficiently. **Blade servers** pack a complete computer server on a single card. **High-availability systems** continue running and performing tasks for at least 99 percent of the time. **Utility computing** allows companies to use the processing power sitting idle in a network located elsewhere. **Grid computing** combines many servers and/or personal computers to act as one large computer.

7 **Why Is Computer Backup Important, and How Is It Accomplished?**

A backup duplicates a file or program to protect an enterprise if the original is lost or damaged. A full backup copies all of the files in a computer. A differential backup copies only files that have changed since the last full backup. An incremental backup copies only files that have changed since the last full or incremental backup. A selective backup allows users to back up specific files. With continuous data protection (CDP), all data is backed up whenever a change is made.

8 **What Are the Steps in a Disaster Recovery Plan?**

A **disaster recovery plan** describes the steps a company would take to restore computer operations in the event of a disaster. A disaster recovery plan contains four components. The emergency plan specifies the steps to be taken immediately after a disaster strikes. The backup plan stipulates how a company uses backup files and equipment to resume information processing. The recovery plan identifies the actions to be taken to restore full information processing operations. The test plan contains information for simulating disasters and recording an organization's ability to recover.

Visit scsite.com/dcf5e/ch12/quiz or click the Quiz Yourself button. Click Objectives 6 – 8.

Key Terms

You should know the Key Terms. Use the list below to help focus your study. To further enhance your understanding of the Key Terms in this chapter, visit scsite.com/dcf5e/ch12/terms. See an example of and a definition for each term, and access current and additional information about the term from the Web.

artificial intelligence (AI) (465)
blade servers (477)
business intelligence (BI) (456)
business process automation (BPA) (456)
business process management (BPM) (456)
chief information officer (CIO) (461)
computer-aided design (CAD) (459)
computer-aided engineering (CAE) (459)
computer-aided manufacturing (CAM) (459)
computer-integrated manufacturing (CIM) (459)
content management system (CMS) (466)
customer interaction management (CIM) (460)

customer relationship management (CRM) (466)
data center (467)
data warehouse (468)
decision support system (DSS) (463)
disaster recovery plan (479)
distribution systems (460)
EDI (electronic data interchange) (468)
enterprise computing (452)
enterprise hardware (474)
enterprise information (456)
enterprise resource planning (ERP) (465)
enterprise search (467)
enterprise storage system (476)
e-retail (470)
expert system (464)
extranet (469)

failover (479)
Fibre Channel (476)
grid computing (478)
high-availability systems (477)
human resources information system (HRIS) (458)
information system (456)
interoperability (478)
management information system (MIS) (462)
managers (456)
marketing information system (460)
Material Requirements Planning (MRP) (459)
network attached storage (NAS) (475)
office information system (OIS) (461)

online banking (472)
online trading (472)
portal (467)
RAID (redundant array of independent disks) (474)
redundant components (477)
sales force automation (SFA) (460)
scalability (477)
shopping bot (473)
storage area network (SAN) (475)
transaction processing system (TPS) (461)
utility computing (478)
virtual private network (VPN) (470)
Web services (469)
workflow (469)
workflow application (469)

Checkpoint

Use the Checkpoint exercises to check your knowledge level of the chapter. To complete the Checkpoint exercises interactively, visit scsite.com/dcf5e/ch12/check.

True/False

Mark T for True and F for False. (See page numbers in parentheses.)

_____ 1. The term, enterprise, commonly describes a business or venture of any size. (452)

_____ 2. The Chief Operations Officer (COO) manages core activities. (455)

_____ 3. Business process management rarely is aided by specialized software designed to assist in these activities. (456)

_____ 4. An information system is a set of hardware, software, data, people, and procedures that work together to produce information. (456)

_____ 5. Computer-aided design uses computers to integrate the many different operations of the manufacturing process. (459)

_____ 6. Customer relationship management software tracks leads and inquiries from customers, stores a history of all correspondence and sales to a customer, and allows for tracking of outstanding issues with customers. (466)

_____ 7. A data center is a collection of links, content, and services presented on a Web page and designed to guide users to information they likely are to find interesting for their particular job function. (467)

_____ 8. VPNs secure the company's internal network within the physical boundaries of the company. (470)

_____ 9. Blade servers pack a complete computer server on a single card rather than a system unit. (477)

_____ 10. Utility computing, or on demand computing, allows companies to use the processing power sitting idle in a network located somewhere else in the world. (478)

Multiple Choice

Select the best answer. (See page numbers in parentheses.)

1. _____ includes several types of applications and technologies for acquiring, storing, analyzing, and providing access to information to help users make more sound business decisions. (456)
   a. Business process management
   b. Business intelligence
   c. Business process automation
   d. None of the above

2. Many companies elevate the importance of information technology by including a _____ executive position that reports to the CEO. (461)
   a. chief operations officer (COO)
   b. chief information officer (CIO)
   c. chief security officer (CSO)
   d. chief financial officer (CFO)

3. An advantage of ERP is _____. (466)
   a. complete integration of information systems across departments
   b. better project management
   c. better customer service
   d. all of the above

4. _____ allows users to pay bills from their computer, that is, transfer money electronically from their account to a

payee's account such as the electric company or telephone company. (472)
   a. Online trading   b. Online banking
   c. E-retail   d. A shopping bot

5. _____ is a Web site that searches the Internet for the best price on a product or service in which you are interested. (473)
   a. A shopping bot
   b. E-retail
   c. EDI (electronic data interchange)
   d. Business process automation

6. The _____ of hardware to users is a measure of how often it is online. (474)
   a. redundancy   b. scalability
   c. availability   d. interoperability

7. _____ continue running and performing tasks for at least 99 percent of the time. (477)
   a. Distribution systems b. High-availability systems
   c. Blade servers   d. Virtual private networks

8. A(n) _____ can be time-consuming but provides the best protection against data loss. (478)
   a. differential backup   b. incremental backup
   c. full backup   d. selective backup

Matching

Match the terms with their definitions. (See page numbers in parentheses.)

_____ 1. computer-aided engineering (459)

_____ 2. expert system (464)

_____ 3. portal (467)

_____ 4. EDI (electronic data interchange) (468)

_____ 5. RAID (474)

a. set of standards that controls the transfer of business data and information among computers both within and among enterprises

b. captures and stores the knowledge of human experts and then imitates human reasoning and decision making

c. allows a business to create products and B2B interactions

d. a group of two or more integrated hard disks

e. uses computers to test product designs

f. collection of links, content, and services presented on a Web page and designed to guide users to information they likely are to find interesting for their particular job function

Checkpoint

Short Answer   Write a brief answer to each of the following questions.

1.   What are managers? _____ What four activities do managers perform to coordinate resources? _____

2.   What is a decision support system (DSS)? _____ Describe some of the features of a decision support system. _____

3.   What is a content management system (CMS)? _____ What type of content may be processed by a content management system? _____

4.   What is an extranet, and how might users use an extranet? _____ What are two platforms for building and running Web services? _____

5.   What does a backup plan identify? _____ What factors contribute to the success of a backup plan? _____

Working Together   Working in a group of your classmates, complete the following team exercise.

1.   The type of information system employed and the purpose for which it is used depend on an individual's place in an organization. Each member of your team should interview a manager and a nonmanagement employee at a local company. What type of information systems do they use? Why? How do the information systems influence their work? How were their jobs different before the information systems were introduced? Meet with the members of your team to discuss your findings. Then, create a presentation and share with the class how different managers and nonmanagement employees use information systems.

Web Research

Use the Internet-based Web Research exercises to broaden your understanding of the concepts presented in this chapter. To discuss any of the Web Research exercises in this chapter with other students, post your thoughts or questions at scsite.com/dcf5e/ch12/forum.

(1) Blogs

The brain's 100 billion cells help us function throughout the day. The left half, often called the judicial mind, controls logical and reasoning tasks, and the right half, referred to as the creative mind, interprets and gives meaning to stimuli. The brain works best when both halves work together, but building right-brain skills is the key to achieving professional and personal success. Many blogs contain exercises and research on developing the right brain. They include The Thinking Blog (thethinkingblog.com), Creative Generalist (creativegeneralist.blogspot.com), Creative Think (blog.creativethink.com), and InnovationTools (innovationtools.com). What creativity tools and strategies are suggested on these blogs? How are enterprises incorporating creative thinking? Are mind mapping and brainstorming resources listed? What creativity software and books are promoted?

(2) Scavenger Hunt

Use one of the search engines listed in Figure 2-8 in Chapter 2 on page 58 or your own favorite search engine to find the answers to the following questions. Copy and paste the Web address from the Web page where you found the answer. Some questions may have more than one answer. If required, submit your answers to your instructor. (1) How does a company obtain a VeriSign Secured Seal for its Web site? (2) What are the names of two e-commerce enterprises where you can obtain free investing information? What services do these organizations provide? (3) Compare the services offered by two online news and entertainment services such as Google News and USA Today. Which of the two would you prefer to use? Why?

(3) Search Sleuth

One of the newer online academic research tools is Google Scholar (scholar.google.com). Visit this Web site and then use your word processing program to answer the following questions. Then, if required, submit your answers to your instructor. (1) Type "online banking" in the Search box and then click the Search button. How many results were found? (2) Choose one of the recently published articles and note the number of times it has been cited by other authors. Click the link to the article. What is the article's title, and who is the author? What journal published the article? When? How many works cite this article? (3) Click your browser's Back button or press the BACKSPACE key twice to return to the Google Scholar home page. Delete the text in the Search box, type "shopping bot" in the Search box, and then click the Search button. Click the Recent Articles link and then find two articles published within the past three years that have been cited by at least 10 other works. Write a 50-word summary of these two articles.

Learn How To

Use the Learn How To activities to learn fundamental skills when using a computer and accompanying technology. Complete the exercises and submit them to your instructor. Premium Activity: The icon indicates you can see a visual demonstration of the associated Learn How To activity by visiting scsite.com/dcf5e/ch12/howto.

LEARN HOW TO 1: Use VoIP (Voice over Internet Protocol)

Every enterprise organization depends on reliable communications. An important means of communication is voice, or telephone, communications. In most organizations today, a telephone company is the primary vendor for providing telephone communications. In the near future, however, the Internet might be the largest provider of telephone communications.

You learned in a previous chapter about VoIP, which provides for voice communications using the Internet instead of standard telephone connections. Two advantages claimed for VoIP are improved reliability and much lower costs. Both of these advantages are attractive to businesses, and VoIP is forecasted to become the standard voice communications method within the next 5 – 10 years.

VoIP also is available to individual users. One primary means to use VoIP is through the service offered by Skype, a company that offers free, unlimited calls through an Internet connection. The Skype software also is free. Using Skype, you can talk to another Skype user via the Internet anywhere in the world for no cost whatsoever. If the person you call is not a Skype user, you can use Skype to call their ordinary landline or mobile telephone quite inexpensively. For example, to call someone on a landline telephone in the United Kingdom from anywhere in the world, the cost is approximately 2 cents per minute.

The following quote indicates the potential future of VoIP and services like Skype:

"I knew it was over when I downloaded Skype," Michael Powell, chairman of the Federal Communications Commission, explained. "When the inventors of KaZaA are distributing for free a little program that you can use to talk to anybody else, and the quality is fantastic, and it's free — it's over. The world will change now inevitably."
Fortune Magazine, February 16, 2004

To download Skype, complete the following steps:

1. Start your Internet browser, type www.skype.com in the Address bar, and then press the ENTER key.
2. When the Skype home page is displayed, explore the Web site for information about using Skype. When you are ready, click the Download Skype link.
3. When the File Download — Security Warning dialog box is displayed, click the Save button.
4. In the Save As dialog box, select the Desktop for the location of the saved file. Then, click the Save button. The Skype Setup file will download. This may take a few minutes, depending on the speed of your Internet connection, because of the large file size.
5. When the Download complete window is displayed, click the Close button. The SkypeSetup icon is displayed on the desktop.
6. Double-click the SkypeSetup icon on the desktop. If any warning dialog boxes appear, click the Run button. If the User Account Control dialog box appears, click the Continue button.
7. In the Skype Install window, select the language you would like to use, click the check box to agree to the Skype End User License Agreement and the Skype Privacy Statement, and then click the Install button.
8. Remove the check mark from the check box prompting you to install the free Google Toolbar, and then click the Next button.
9. When the installation is completed, click the Finish button.

Skype now is installed on your computer. The Skype icon should appear on your desktop. To start and use Skype, complete the following steps:

1. Double-click the Skype icon on your desktop. The first time you start Skype, the Create a new Skype Account dialog box is displayed (Figure 12-26). In this dialog box, you enter your full name, Skype name, and password. The Skype name is the name you will use to start Skype each time, together with the password. You can use any name and password that has not already been used on Skype. Also, be sure to check the Skype End User License Agreement check box, and then click the Next button to display the next dialog box requesting your E-mail address, Country/Region, and City (Figure 12-27).

2. Enter your E-mail address, Country/Region, and City, and then click the Sign In button.

3. If your Skype name and password have not been used, Skype automatically will sign into your account and open the Skype window (Figure 12-28). If your Skype name or password already have been used by another user, you must select another Skype name or password.

4. Once you are logged into Skype, if the Skype - Getting Started dialog box is displayed, click the Close button.

5. After installing Skype, you can make calls to other Skype users anywhere in the world for no cost.

6. To learn the techniques for calling another Skype user, click Help on the menu bar in the Skype window, click Help on the Help menu, and then select the subject about which you want to learn.

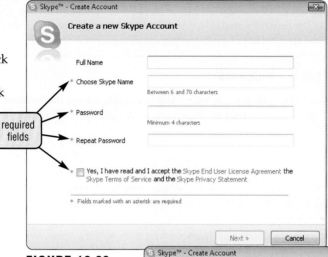

FIGURE 12-26

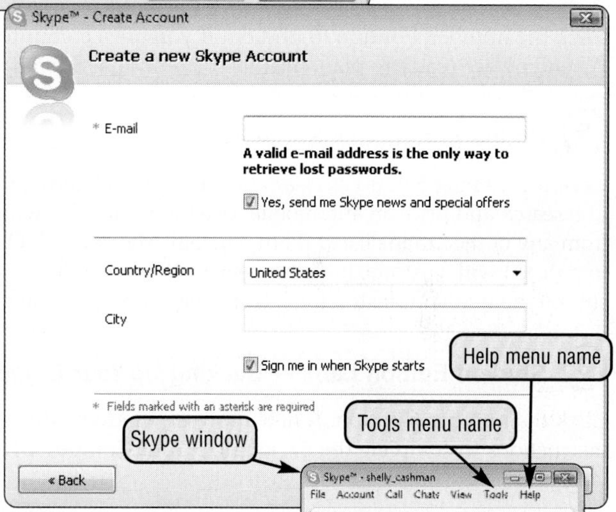

FIGURE 12-27

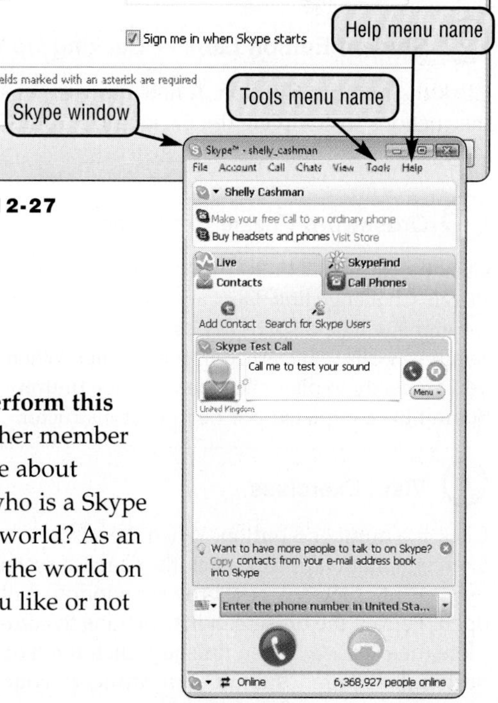

FIGURE 12-28

Exercise

1. Visit the Skype Web site. Examine the various screens and examples shown on the Web site. Do you think this type of service can be useful to you? Why? What are the advantages and disadvantages of using Skype? If you were calling a friend in Australia on a regular telephone, how much per minute would you have to pay? Submit your answers to your instructor.

2. **Optional: Perform this exercise only on your own computer. Do not perform this exercise on a school computer.** Establish an account on Skype. Call another member of your class who also has established a Skype account. What do you like about Skype? What do you not like? If you know someone in Europe or Asia who is a Skype user, call him or her. Do you like the fact the call is free anywhere in the world? As an option, subscribe to SkypeOut and then call someone somewhere else in the world on his or her regular telephone. Is the quality of the call good? What did you like or not like about the call? Submit your answers to your instructor.

Learn It Online

Use the Learn It Online exercises to reinforce your understanding of the chapter concepts. To access the Learn It Online exercises, visit scsite.com/dcf5e/ch12/learn.

 At the Movies — New Edge 2.0: Virtually Face to Face

To view the New Edge 2.0: Virtually Face to Face movie, click the number 1 button. Locate your video and click the corresponding High-Speed or Dial-Up link, depending on your Internet connection. Watch the movie to explore HP HALO, the virtual work world that helped bring all the creators of the animated movie *Shrek the Third* together. Then, complete the exercise by answering the questions that follow. Why did DreamWorks studio turn to HP HALO for collaboration software and video conferencing in making the movie *Shrek the Third*? What are HP HALO's two top priorities?

 Student Edition Labs — E-Commerce

Click the number 2 button. A new browser window will open, displaying the Student Edition Labs. Follow the on-screen instructions to complete the E-Commerce Lab. When finished, click the Exit button. If required, print a copy of your results to submit to your instructor.

 Practice Test

Click the number 3 button. Answer each question. When completed, enter your name and click the Grade Test button to submit the quiz for grading. Make a note of any missed questions. If required, submit your results to your instructor.

 Who Wants To Be a Computer Genius²?

Click the number 4 button to find out if you are a computer genius. Directions about how to play the game will be displayed. When you are ready to play, click the Play button. Submit your score to your instructor.

 Online Automobile Shopping

Click the number 5 button to learn how to use the Internet to price an automobile online. Follow the instructions to use Ford.com to research and price an automobile. Use the Vehicle Showroom Tool to select an SUV in the $30,000 to $51,000 price range. Choose from any of the brands listed (Ford, Lincoln, Mazda, etc.). Once you have selected your vehicle, click the More Information button to proceed with customizing your vehicle. When you have completed pricing your vehicle, print the specifications and price and submit them to your instructor. If available, use the payment calculator to calculate your monthly payments.

 Student Edition Labs — Backing Up Your Computer

Click the number 6 button. A new browser window will open, displaying the Student Edition Labs. Follow the on-screen instructions to complete the Backing Up Your Computer Lab. When finished, click the Exit button. If required, print a copy of your results to submit to your instructor.

 Crossword Puzzle Challenge

Click the number 7 button, then click the Crossword Puzzle Challenge link. Directions about how to play the game will be displayed. Complete the puzzle to reinforce skills you learned in this chapter. When you are ready to play, click the Continue button. Submit the completed puzzle to your instructor.

 Vista Exercises

Click the number 8 button. When the Vista Exercises menu appears, click the exercise assigned by your instructor. A new browser window will open. Follow the on-screen instructions to complete the exercise. When finished, click the Exit button. If required, submit your results to your instructor.

APPENDIX A
Quiz Yourself Answers

Following are possible answers to the Quiz Yourself boxes throughout the book.

Quiz Yourself 1-1

1. A computer is ~~a motorized~~an electronic device that processes ~~output~~input into ~~input~~output.
2. A storage device records (~~reads~~writes) and/or retrieves (~~writes~~reads) items to and from storage media.
3. An ~~output~~input device is any hardware component that allows you to enter data and instructions in a computer.
4. True Statement
5. Four commonly used ~~input~~output devices are a printer, a monitor, speakers, and a portable media player.

Quiz Yourself 1-2

1. A ~~resource~~network is a collection of computers and devices connected together via communications devices and transmission media.
2. True Statement
3. Popular ~~system~~application software includes Web browsers, word processing software, spreadsheet software, database software, and presentation graphics software.
4. The ~~Internet~~Web is one of the more popular services on the ~~Web~~Internet.
5. Two types of ~~application~~system software are the operating system and utility programs.

Quiz Yourself 1-3

1. A ~~desktop computer~~notebook computer (or laptop computer) is a portable, personal computer designed to fit on your lap.
2. True Statement
3. Each ~~large business~~home user spends time on the computer for different reasons that include budgeting and personal financial management, Web access, communications, and entertainment.
4. A ~~home~~power user requires the capabilities of a workstation or other powerful computer.
5. ~~Mainframes~~Supercomputers are the fastest, most powerful computers — and the most expensive.
6. With ~~embedded computers~~online banking, users access account balances, pay bills, and copy monthly transactions from the bank's computer right into their personal computers.

Quiz Yourself 2-1

1. True Statement
2. ~~A WISP~~An IP address (or Internet Protocol address) is a number that uniquely identifies each computer or device connected to the Internet.
3. ~~An IP address~~A domain name, such as www.google.com, is the text version of ~~a domain name~~an IP address.
4. A satellite modem allows access to high-speed Internet services through ~~the cable television network~~a satellite.

Quiz Yourself 2-2

1. True Statement
2. A ~~Web browser~~subject directory classifies Web pages in an organized set of categories and related subcategories.
3. ~~Business~~Consumer-to-consumer e-commerce occurs when one consumer sells directly to another, such as in an online auction.
4. The more widely used ~~search engines~~Web browsers for personal computers are Internet Explorer, Firefox, Opera, and Safari.
5. To develop a Web page, you do not have to be a computer programmer.

Quiz Yourself 2-3

1. True Statement
2. An e-mail address is a combination of a user name and ~~an e-mail program~~a domain name that identifies a user so that he or she can receive Internet e-mail.
3. ~~FTP~~Internet telephony uses the Internet (instead of the public switched telephone network) to connect a calling party to one or more called parties.
4. Netiquette is the code of ~~unacceptable~~ behaviors while on the Internet.
5. VoIP enables users to ~~subscribe~~speak to other users over the Internet.

Quiz Yourself 3-1

1. True Statement
2. ~~Public domain~~Packaged software is mass produced, copyrighted retail software that meets the needs of a wide variety of users, not just a single user or company.
3. To use ~~system~~application software, your computer must be running ~~application~~system software.
4. When a program is started, its instructions load from ~~memory~~a storage medium into ~~a storage medium~~memory.

Quiz Yourself 3-2

1. ~~Enterprise computing~~Image editing software provides the capabilities of paint software and also includes the ability to modify existing images.
2. Millions of people use ~~spreadsheet~~word processing software every day to develop documents such as letters, memos, reports, fax cover sheets, mailing labels, newsletters, and Web pages.
3. Professional ~~accounting~~DTP (or desktop publishing) software is ideal for the production of high-quality color documents such as textbooks, corporate newsletters, marketing literature, product catalogs, and annual reports.
4. ~~Spreadsheet~~Presentation graphics software is application software that allows users to create visual aids for presentations to communicate ideas, messages, and other information to a group.
5. Popular ~~CAD programs~~software suites include Microsoft Office 2007 and Apple iWork.
6. True Statement

Quiz Yourself 3-3

1. An ~~anti-spam~~antivirus program protects a computer against viruses by identifying and removing any computer viruses found in memory, on storage media, or in incoming files.
2. ~~Computer~~Web-based training is a type of ~~Web~~computer-based training that uses Internet technology and consists of application software on the Web.
3. True Statement
4. ~~Legal~~Personal finance software is a simplified accounting program that helps home users and small office/home office users balance their checkbooks, pay bills, track investments, and evaluate financial plans.
5. ~~Personal DTP~~Photo editing software is a popular type of image editing software that allows users to edit digital photos.

Quiz Yourself 4-1

1. True Statement
2. Four basic operations in a machine cycle are: (1) ~~comparing~~fetching, (2) decoding, (3) executing, and, if necessary, (4) ~~pipelining~~storing.
3. Processors contain a ~~motherboard~~control unit and an arithmetic logic unit (ALU).
4. The ~~central processing unit~~motherboard, sometimes called a system board, is the main circuit board of the system unit.
5. The leading processor chip manufacturers for personal computers are ~~Microsoft~~Intel, AMD, IBM, and Motorola.

6. The system unit is a case that contains ~~mechanical~~ electronic components of the computer used to process data.

Quiz Yourself 4-2

1. True Statement
2. A gigabyte (GB) equals approximately 1 ~~trillion~~ billion bytes.
3. Memory cache helps speed the processes of the computer because it stores ~~seldom~~ frequently used instructions and data.
4. Most computers are ~~analog~~ digital, which means they recognize only two discrete states: on and off.
5. Most RAM ~~retains~~ loses its contents when the power is removed from the computer.
6. Read-only memory (ROM) refers to memory chips storing ~~temporary~~ permanent data and instructions.

Quiz Yourself 4-3

1. A ~~bus~~ port is the point at which a peripheral attaches to or communicates with a system unit so that the peripheral can send data to or receive information from the computer.
2. An ~~AC adapter~~ expansion slot is a socket on the motherboard that can hold an adapter card.
3. ~~Serial~~ USB ports can connect up to 127 different peripherals together with a single connector type.
4. The higher the bus clock speed, the ~~slower~~ faster the transmission of data.
5. True Statement

Quiz Yourself 5-1

1. A keyboard is an ~~output~~ input device that contains keys users press to enter data into a computer.
2. A ~~trackball~~ touch pad is a small, flat, rectangular pointing device commonly found on notebook computers.
3. True Statement
4. An optical mouse has no moving mechanical parts inside.
5. ~~Many smart phones and other personal mobile devices~~ Tablet PCs use a pressure-sensitive digital pen and ~~Tablet PCs~~ many smart phones and other personal mobile devices use a stylus.

Quiz Yourself 5-2

1. True Statement
2. A fingerprint reader captures curves and indentations of a ~~signature~~ fingerprint.
3. After swiping a credit card through ~~an MICR~~ a magnetic stripe card reader, it reads the information stored on the magnetic stripe on the card.
4. ~~Instant messaging~~ Voice recognition (or speech recognition) is the computer's capability of distinguishing spoken words.
5. Many smart phones today have ~~POS~~ PDA capabilities.
6. RFID is a technology that uses ~~laser~~ radio signals to communicate with a tag placed in an object, an animal, or a person.

Quiz Yourself 5-3

1. A ~~lower~~ higher resolution uses a greater number of pixels and thus provides a smoother image.
2. An output device is any type of ~~software~~ hardware component that conveys information to one or more people.
3. LCD monitors have a ~~larger~~ smaller footprint than CRT monitors.
4. True Statement

Quiz Yourself 5-4

1. A ~~laser~~ thermal printer generates images by pushing electrically heated pins against heat-sensitive paper.
2. A ~~photo~~ laser printer creates images using a laser beam and powdered ink, called toner.
3. An ink-jet printer is a type of nonimpact printer that forms characters and graphics by spraying tiny drops of liquid ~~nitrogen~~ ink onto a piece of paper.
4. Many personal computer users add surround sound ~~printer systems~~ speakers to their computers to generate a higher-quality sound.
5. Multifunction peripherals require ~~more~~ less space than having a separate printer, scanner, copy machine, and fax machine.
6. True Statement

Quiz Yourself 6-1

1. True Statement
2. SATA is a hard disk interface that uses ~~parallel~~ serial signals to transfer data, instructions, and information.
3. ~~Storage media~~ A storage device is the computer hardware that records and/or retrieves items to and from ~~a~~ storage ~~device~~ media.
4. A widely used type of ~~manual~~ magnetic disk is a hard disk.

Quiz Yourself 6-2

1. A ~~CD-RW~~ CD-ROM is a type of optical disc on which users can read but not write (record) or erase.
2. A ~~DVD-RAM~~ Picture CD is a single-session disc that stores digital versions of film using a jpg file format.
3. DVDs have ~~the same~~ much greater storage capacities ~~as~~ than CDs.
4. Optical discs are written and read by ~~mirrors~~ laser light.
5. True Statement

Quiz Yourself 6-3

1. A USB flash drive is a flash memory storage device that plugs in a ~~parallel~~ USB port on a computer or mobile device.
2. True Statement
3. Microfilm and microfiche have the ~~shortest~~ longest life of any storage media.
4. Tape storage requires ~~direct~~ sequential access, which refers to reading or writing data consecutively.

Quiz Yourself 7-1

1. A ~~buffer~~ driver is a small program that tells the operating system how to communicate with a specific device.
2. True Statement
3. A password is a ~~public~~ private combination of characters associated with the user name that allows access to certain computer resources.
4. The program you currently are using is in the ~~background~~ foreground, and the other programs running but not in use are in the ~~foreground~~ background.
5. Two types of system software are operating systems and ~~application~~ utility programs.

Quiz Yourself 7-2

1. A ~~file manager~~ personal firewall is a utility that detects and protects a personal computer from unauthorized intrusions.
2. ~~Fragmenting~~ Defragmenting a disk is the process of reorganizing it so that the files are stored in contiguous sectors.
3. Windows Vista Home Basic uses Windows ~~Aero~~ Vista Basic.

4. True Statement

5. ~~Flip 3D~~Linux is a UNIX-type operating system that is open source software.

Quiz Yourself 7-3

1. A ~~pop-up blocker~~file compression utility shrinks the size of a file(s).

2. An ~~anti-spam~~antivirus program protects a computer against viruses.

3. True Statement

4. Pocket PCs use ~~Palm OS~~Windows Mobile as their operating system.

5. ~~Web filtering~~CD/DVD burning software writes text, graphics, audio, and video files to a recordable or rewritable CD or DVD.

Quiz Yourself 8-1

1. A ~~cybercafé~~hot spot is a wireless network that provides Internet connections to mobile computers and devices.

2. True Statement

3. ~~Receiving~~Sending devices initiate an instruction to transmit data, instructions, or information.

4. Users can send pictures, and sound files, as well as short text messages, with ~~text~~picture messaging.

Quiz Yourself 8-2

1. A wireless LAN is a LAN that uses no physical wires.

2. An intranet is an internal network that uses ~~video conferencing~~Internet technologies.

3. Five types of digital ~~dial-up~~dedicated lines are ISDN lines, DSL, FTTP, T-carrier lines, and ATM.

4. In a client/server network, ~~servers~~clients on the network access resources on the ~~client~~server.

5. True Statement

Quiz Yourself 8-3

1. A ~~cable~~dial-up modem converts a computer's digital signals to analog signals before they are transmitted over standard telephone lines.

2. True Statement

3. ~~Analog~~Digital signals consist of individual electrical pulses that represent bits grouped together into bytes.

4. ~~Physical~~Wireless transmission media send communications signals through the air or space using radio, microwave, and infrared signals.

5. Most wireless home networks use ~~powerline cables~~Wi-Fi.

Quiz Yourself 9-1

1. A ~~database~~field is a combination of one or more related characters or bytes and is the smallest unit of data a user accesses.

2. A ~~record~~database is a collection of data organized in a manner that allows access, retrieval, and use of that data.

3. ~~Data~~Information is processed ~~information~~data.

4. ~~Hierarchy of data~~File maintenance procedures include adding records to, changing records in, and deleting records from a file.

5. True Statement

Quiz Yourself 9-2

1. A DBMS is ~~hardware~~software that allows you to create, access, and manage ~~an operating system~~a database.

2. A ~~query~~data dictionary contains data about each file in the database and each field in those files.

3. True Statement

4. Strengths of the database approach include ~~increased~~reduced data redundancy, ~~reduced~~ improved data integrity, shared data, easier access, and ~~increased~~reduced development time.

Quiz Yourself 9-3

1. ~~Object-oriented~~Relational databases store data in tables.
2. True Statement
3. SQL is a ~~data modeling~~query language that allows users to manage, update, and retrieve data.
4. The database ~~analyst~~administrator requires a more technical inside view of the data than does the ~~database administrator~~data analyst.

Quiz Yourself 10-1

1. A ~~back door~~denial of service attack is an assault whose purpose is to disrupt computer access to an Internet service such as the Web or e-mail.
2. True Statement
3. Computer viruses, worms, and Trojan horses are malware that acts with~~out~~ a user's knowledge.
4. ~~Shorter~~Longer passwords provide greater security than ~~longer~~shorter ones.
5. Updating an antivirus program's ~~quarantine~~signature file protects a computer against viruses written since the antivirus program was released.

Quiz Yourself 10-2

1. An end-user license agreement (EULA) ~~permits~~does not permit users to give copies to friends and colleagues, while continuing to use the software.
2. Encryption is a process of converting ~~ciphertext~~plaintext into ~~plaintext~~ciphertext to prevent authorized access.
3. Mobile users are ~~not~~susceptible to hardware theft.
4. True Statement
5. To prevent against data loss caused by a system failure, computer users should ~~restore~~back up files regularly.

Quiz Yourself 10-3

1. Factors that cause ~~CVS~~tendonitis and CTS (carpal tunnel syndrome) include prolonged typing, prolonged mouse usage, or continual shifting between the mouse and the keyboard.
2. ~~Phishing~~Computer forensics is the discovery, collection, and analysis of evidence found on computers and networks.
3. True Statement
4. Web sites use ~~electronic profiles~~cookies to track user preferences, store users' passwords, keep track of items in a user's shopping cart, and track Web site browsing habits.
5. You can~~not~~ assume that information on the Web is correct.

Quiz Yourself 11-1

1. True Statement
2. ~~Feasibility~~Project management is the process of planning, scheduling, and then controlling the activities during the system development cycle.
3. The five phases in most system development cycles are ~~programming~~planning; analysis; design; ~~sampling~~implementation; and ~~recording~~operation, support, and security.
4. The purpose of the ~~design~~operation, support, and security phase is to provide ongoing assistance for an information system and its users after the system is implemented.
5. Upon completion of the preliminary investigation, the systems analyst writes the ~~system proposal~~feasibility report.
6. Users should ~~not~~be involved throughout the system development process.

Quiz Yourself 11-2

1. COBOL and C are examples of ~~assembly~~procedural languages.
2. ~~Delphi~~Java is an object-oriented programming language developed by Sun Microsystems.
3. Popular ~~first generation~~scripting languages include JavaScript, Perl, PHP, Rexx, Tcl, and VBScript.

4. Four popular ~~markup languages~~Web page authoring programs are Dreamweaver, Expression Web, Flash, and Silverlight.
5. Two types of low-level languages are machine languages and ~~source~~ assembly languages.
6. True Statement

Quiz Yourself 11-3

1. True Statement
2. The program development cycle consists of these six steps: analyze requirements, design solution, validate design, implement design, test solution, and ~~hardcode~~document solution.
3. Three basic control structures are sequence, selection, and ~~maintenance~~repetition.

Quiz Yourself 12-1

1. The main task of executive managers is to make ~~short~~long-term, ~~tactical~~strategic decisions.
2. An information system is a set of hardware, software, data, procedures, and people that work together to produce information.
3. A ~~human resources~~marketing information system serves as a central repository for the tasks of the marketing functional unit.
4. True Statement
5. Decision support systems ~~capture and store the knowledge of human experts and then imitate human reasoning and decision making~~help users analyze data and make decisions.
6. Enterprise resource planning provides centralized integrated software to help manage and coordinate the ongoing activities of the functional units of an enterprise, including manufacturing and distribution, accounting, finance, sales, product planning, and human resources~~is a combination of databases, software, and procedures that organizes and allows access to various forms of documents and files~~.

Quiz Yourself 12-2

1. ~~A portal~~An extranet is the portion of a company's network that allows customers or suppliers of a company to access parts of an enterprise's intranet.
2. True Statement
3. A VPN provides mobile users, remote offices, vendors, or customers a secure connection to the company network server, as if they had a private line~~is a server that is placed on a network with the sole purpose of providing storage to users and information systems attached to the network~~.
4. A workflow application is a program that assists in the management and tracking of all the activities in a business process from start to finish~~helps an enterprise collect, archive, index, and retrieve its resources~~.

Quiz Yourself 12-3

1. ~~Network attached storage~~A storage area network is a high-speed network with the sole purpose of providing storage to other servers to which it is attached.
2. Scalability is a measure of how well computer hardware, software, or an information system can grow to meet increasing performance demands~~refers to the ability of an information system to share information with other information systems~~.
3. A differential backup copies only the files that have changed since the last full ~~or last incremental~~ backup.
4. ~~A full~~An incremental backup is the fastest backup method, requiring only minimal storage.
5. ~~An emergency~~A backup plan specifies how a company's users back up files and equipment to resume information processing.
6. True Statement

INDEX

Garbage in, garbage out (GIGO): Computing phrase that points out the accuracy of a computer's output depends on the accuracy of the input. **333**

Gates, Bill, 27, 38, 48

GIF files, 64

Gigabyte (GB): Approximately 1 billion bytes. **142, 222**

Gigahertz (GHz): One billion ticks of the system clock per second. **139**

Global positioning system (GPS): Navigation system that consists of one or more earth-based receivers that accept and analyze signals sent by satellites in order to determine the receiver's geographic location. **301**

Google, 46, 75

Gosling, James, 443

government
  computer usage for, 23
  Web sites, 91

GPS. *See* Global positioning system

Graphic: Digital representation of nontext information such as a drawing, chart, or photo. **64**
  clip art, 105
  and multimedia software, 112–115
  types of, 100

Graphic designers: Employee who creates visual impressions of products and advertisements in the fields of graphics, theater, and fashion. **198**

Graphic illustrators: Employee who creates visual impressions of products and advertisements in the fields of graphics, theater, and fashion. **198**

Graphical user interface (GUI): Type of user interface that allows a user to interact with software using text, graphics, and visual images, such as icons. **10, 253**

Graphics card: Adapter card that converts computer output into a video signal that travels through a cable to the monitor, which displays an image on the screen. **147, 158.** *See also* **Video card**

Graphics tablet: Flat, rectangular, electronic, plastic board that is used to create drawings and sketches. **171**

Green computing: Computer usage that reduces the electricity and environmental waste involved in using a computer. **387**

Grid computing: Technology that combines many servers and/or personal computers on a network to act as one large computer. **478**

Groupware: Software that helps groups of people work together on projects and share information over a network. **302**

GUI. *See* Graphical user interface

H

Hacker: Someone who accesses a computer or network illegally. **362**

Handheld computer: Computer small enough to fit in one hand. **15.** *See also* **Handhelds** and **Ultra-Mobile PC (UMPC)**

Handhelds: Computer small enough to fit in one hand. **16.** *See also* **Handheld computer** and **Ultra-Mobile PC (UMPC)**

Hard disk: Type of storage device that contains one or more inflexible, circular platters that store data, instructions, and information. Also called a hard disk drive. 7, **223**
  buying, 282
  defragmenting, 261

maintaining, 246–247
  types, controllers, 223–227

Hardware: Electric, electronic, and mechanical components contained in a computer. **6**
  enterprise, 474–478
  guidelines for buying, 282–283
  See also specific component

Hardware theft: The act of stealing computer equipment. **371**

Hardware vandalism: The act of defacing or destroying computer equipment. **371**

Hawkins, Jeff, 199

HD DVD disc: High-density-DVD. Optical storage disc with storage capacities up to 60 GB with future projections of 90 GB capacities. **233**

HD DVD-RW: High-capacity rewritable DVD format. **234**

HD VMD: Versatile Multilayer Disc; high-density format that potentially will contain up to 20 layers, each with a capacity of 5 GB. 48, **233**

Headphones: Audio output device that covers or is placed outside the ear. **194**

health
  automated patient care, 472
  care, computer usage for, 23–24
  concerns of computer use, 385–387
  and enterprise computing, 472
  Web sites, 96
  See also medical

Help Desk specialist: Employee who answers hardware, software, or networking questions in person, over the telephone, and/or in a chat room. **124**

Help, online, 123

Hewlett-Packard (HP) company profile, 199

hierarchy of data, 335–336

High-availability systems: Systems that continue running and performing tasks for at least 99 percent of the time. **477**

Home design/landscaping software: Application software that assists users with the design, remodeling, or improvement of a home, deck, or landscape. **119**

Home network: Network consisting of multiple devices and computers connected together in a home. **316–317**
  installing Wi-Fi, 328–329

Home page: First page that a Web site displays. **55**
  changing Web browser's, 80

home/personal/educational software, 100, 115–120

home software, 100

Home user: User who spends time on a computer at home. **18–19**

Hopper, Grace, 36, 443

Host: Any computer that provides services and connections to other computers on a network. **50.** *See also* **Server**

Hot spot: Wireless network that provides Internet connections to mobile computers and other devices. **300**

Hot spots: Public locations, such as airports, hotels, schools, and coffee shops, that provide Wi-Fi Internet connections to users with mobile computers or devices. **52**

HTML: Hypertext Markup Language. Special formatting language that programmers use to format documents for display on the Web. **433**

hub, USB, 149

Human resources information system (HRIS): Information system that manages one or more human resources function(s). **458**

English-like statements that allows users to specify the data to display, print, or store. **344**

Queue: Lineup of multiple print jobs within a buffer. **256**

R

RAD: Rapid application development; method of developing software in which a programmer writes and implements a program in segments instead of waiting until an entire program is completed. **427**

radiation, and cell phones, 309

radio, broadcast and cellular, 321

RAID (redundant array of independent disks): Redundant array of independent disks. A group of two or more integrated disks that acts like a single large hard disk. **226, 474, 481**

RAM: Random access memory. Type of memory that can be read from and written to by the processor and other devices. Programs and data are loaded into RAM from storage devices such as a hard disk and remain in RAM as long as the computer has continuous power. **143**

adding to your computer, 145

buying, 283

overview of, 143–144, 158

Range check: Validity check that determines whether a number is within a specified range. **340**

RAW camera format: 211

Reading: Process of transferring data, instructions, and information from a storage medium into memory. **222**

Read-only memory (ROM): Type of non-volatile memory that is used to store permanent data and instructions. **145**

Real time: Describes users and the people with whom they are conversing being online at the same time. **71**

Real time location system (RTLS): Safeguard used by some businesses to track and identify the location of high-risk or high-value items. **371**

recalculation with spreadsheets, 108

Receiving device: Device that accepts the transmission of data, instructions, or information. **296**

Record: Group of related fields in a database. **336**

recording videos, 214

records, adding, changing, deleting database, 336–339

Recovery utility: DBMS feature that uses logs and/or backups to restore a database when it becomes damaged or destroyed. **346**

Red Hat open source software distributor, 271

Redundant components: Components used so that a functioning computer can take over automatically the tasks of a similar component that fails. **477**

redundant data, and databases, **342**

Reference software: Application software that provides valuable and thorough information for all individuals. **119**

Relation: Term used by developers of relational databases for file. **347**

in relational databases, 348–349

Relational database: Database that stores data in tables that consist of rows and columns, with each row having a primary key and each column having a unique name. **347**

types and capabilities of, 347–349

Relationship: Connection within data in a database. **348**

Removable hard disk: Hard disk that can be inserted and removed from a drive. **226–227**

Repetition control structure: Type of control structure that enables a program to perform one or more actions repeatedly as long as a certain condition is met. Also called a loop. **441–442**

Repetitive strain injuries, avoiding, 168

Repetitive strain injury (RSI): Injury or disorder of the muscles, nerves, tendons, ligaments, and joints. **385**

Report generator: DBMS feature that allows users to design a report on the screen, retrieve data into the report design, and then display or print the report. Also called a report writer. **346**

Research In Motion (RIM), 271

research
trusting wikis for, 63
Web sites, 85

Resolution: The number of horizontal and vertical pixels in a display device. **176**

on LCD monitors, 185

Restore: To copy backed up files by copying them to their original location on the computer. **375**

Restore program: Program that reverses the backup process and returns backed up files to their original form. **261**

resumes, publishing on the Web, 67

Rexx: Restructured Extended Executor. Procedural interpreted scripting language for both professional programmers and nontechnical users. **435**

RFID: Short for radio frequency identification; standard, specifically a protocol, that defines how a network uses radio signals to communicate with a tag placed in or attached to an object, an animal, or a person. 45, **178–179, 309**

RFID reader: Reading device that reads information on an RFID tag via radio waves. **178–179**

Ring network: Type of network topology in which a cable forms a closed loop (ring) with all computers and devices arranged along the ring. **307**

Ripping: Process of copying audio and/or video data from a purchased disc and saving it on digital media. **233**

robots, 22

Router: Communications device that connects multiple computers or other routers together and transmits data to its correct destination on a network. **315**

Row: Term used by users of relational databases for record. **347**

RPG: Report Program Generator. Developed by IBM in the early 1960s to assist businesses in generating reports. **430**

RSS 2.0: Really Simple Syndication; specification that content aggregators use to distribute content to subscribers. **63, 436**

RSS aggregator application software, 120

RSS specification, 298

Ruby on Rails: Ruby on Rails. Open source framework that

PHOTO CREDITS

Chapter 1: Opener Courtesy of Microsoft Corporation; Courtesy of Microsoft Corporation; istockphoto.com; © Apple Handout/epa/Corbis; © Getty Images; Courtesy of Microsoft Corporation; Figures 1-1a, © Patrick Olear / PhotoEdit;1-1b, Courtesy of Agilix Labs, Inc; 1-1c, © Jens Koenig /Getty Images; 1-1d, Courtesy of Nokia; 1-1e, © Patrick Lin/AFP/Getty Images; 1-1g, © SuperStock / Alamy; 1-1h, © Michael Turek / Getty Images; 1-1i, Courtesy of Nokia; 1-1j, © Masterfile Royalty-Free; 1-1m, Courtesy of Microsoft Corporation; 1-3a, Courtesy of Hewlett-Packard Company; 1-3b, Courtesy of SanDisk Corporation;1-3c, iStockphoto; 1-3d, Courtesy of SanDisk Corporation; 1-3e, Courtesy of Kingston Technology Company; 1-3f, Courtesy of Seagate Technology LLC; 1-3g, Courtesy of Logitech; 1-3h, Courtesy of Hewlett-Packard Company; 1-3i, Courtesy of Hewlett-Packard Company; 1-3j, Courtesy of Motorola; 1-4, Courtesy of Seagate Technology LLC; 1-5, © Wm. Baker / GhostWorx Images / Alamy; 1-6a, AP Photo/PR Newswire; 1-6b, AP Photo/ PRNewsFoto/Sound Solutions Americas; 1-6c, Courtesy of Hewlett-Packard Company; 1-6d, Courtesy of Hewlett-Packard Company; 1-6e, Courtesy of Hewlett-Packard Company; 1-6f, Courtesy of Hewlett-Packard Company; 1-6g, Courtesy of Microsoft Corporation; 1-6i, Courtesy of Microsoft Corporation; 1-6n, Courtesy of Nokia; 1-6o, Courtesy of Acer America, Inc; 1-6p, Courtesy of Palm, Inc; 1-6q, Courtesy of Acer America, Inc; 1-6r, Courtesy of Nokia; 1-6s, Courtesy of Acer America, Inc; 1-6t, Courtesy of Acer America, Inc; 1-9, © Tony Freeman/PhotoEdit; 1-10a, Courtesy of Fujitsu-Siemens Computers; 1-10b, Courtesy of Fujitsu-Siemens Computers; 1-10c, Courtesy of Fujitsu-Siemens Computers; 1-10d, Courtesy of Kingston Technology Company; 1-13a, Courtesy of Hewlett-Packard Company; 1-13b, Courtesy of Microsoft Corporation; 1-14, Courtesy of Apple; 1-15, Dmitry Bomshtein / iStockphoto; 1-16, Courtesy of MotionPC; 1-17, Jaimie D. Travis /iStockphoto; 1-18, Courtesy of Apple; 1-19a, Courtesy of Nintendo Corporation; 1-19b, Courtesy of Nintendo Corporation 1-19c, AP Photo/Richard Drew; 1-20, Courtesy of Sun Microsystems, Inc; 1-21, AP Image; 1-22, JAMSTEC/ESC; 1-23, Courtesy of Toyota; 1-23, Courtesy of Toyota; 1-23, Courtesy of Daimler Mercedes-Benz; 1-23, Courtesy of Toyota; 1-23, © Jupiter Images; 1-23, Courtesy of Toyota; 1-24, © Image Source Black /Getty Images; 1-24, Courtesy of Intuit; 1-24c, Courtesy of Skype; 1-29, © Pixland / Imagestate; 1-25c, Courtesy of Microsoft Corporation; 1-25b, Courtesy of Microsoft Corporation; 1-25a, © Dennis MacDonald / PhotoEdit; 1-26a, © Somos/Veer /Getty Images; 1-26c, © Michael Newman/PhotoEdit; 1-26d, Courtesy of Sony Ericsson Mobile Communications AB. All Rights Reserved; 1-26b, © kolvenbach / Alamy; 1-27, © Tom Stoddart/Getty Images; 1-28, RALF HIRSCHBERGER/ dpa /Landov; 1-30, © Thomas Barwick/Getty Images; 1-32, AP Photo/The Post-Tribune, Leslie Adkins; 1-33, © Jose Luis Pelaez /Getty Images; 1-34a, AP Photo; 1-34c, Reza Estakhrian/Getty Images; 1-36, Courtesy of Garmin Ltd; 1-37, AP Photo/ Lee Jin-man; LA 1-1, Yuriko Nakao/ Reuters/Landov; LA1-2, Pål Liljebäck, SINTEF IKT; Career Corner 1, Haruyoshi Yamaguchi/ Bloomberg News /Landov; Technology Trailblazer 1, © Justin Sullivan/Getty Images; Technology Trailblazer 2, Photo by Business Wire via Getty Images; Page 31, © SuperStock / Alamy; **Special Feature 1:** 1937 Courtesy of Iowa State University; 1937 Courtesy of Iowa State University; 1937 Courtesy of Iowa State University; 1943 Photo courtesy of The Computer History Museum; 1943 Photo courtesy of The Computer History Museum; 1945 Courtesy of the Archives of the Institute for Advanced Study; 1946 From the Collections of the University of Pennsylvania Archives; 1947 © IBM Corporate Archives; 1947 © IBM Corporate Archives; 1951 Courtesy Unisys Corporation; 1952 Courtesy of Hagley Museum and Library; 1953 © IBM Corporate Archives; 1957 © IBM Corporate Archives; 1957 © IBM Corporate Archives; 1957 Courtesy of the Department of the Navy; 1958 Courtesy of Texas Instruments; 1958 Courtesy of Texas Instruments; 1958 Courtesy of Texas Instruments; 1959 © IBM Corporate Archives; 1960 Courtesy of Hagley Museum and Library; 1964 © IBM Corporate Archives; 1964 © IBM Corporate Archives; 1964 © IBM Corporate Archives; 1965 Courtesy of Dartmouth College; 1965 Courtesy of Digital Equipment Corporation; 1969 Courtesy of IBM Corporation; 1970 © IBM Corporate Archives; 1971 Courtesy of Intel Corporation; 1971 Courtesy of Intel Corporation; 1975 Photo courtesy of Computer History Museum; 1975 Courtesy of InfoWorld; 1976 Courtesy of Apple; 1976 © Bettmann/CORBIS; 1979 Photo courtesy of Computer History Museum; 1980 Courtesy of Microsoft Corporation; 1981 © IBM Corporate Archives; 1982 Courtesy of Zoom Telephonics, Inc; 1983 © Time Life Pictures/ Getty Images; 1983 © IBM Corporate Archives; 1984 Courtesy of Apple; 1984 Courtesy of Hewlett-Packard Company; 1989 © 1997–1998W3C (MIT, INRIA, Keio); 1989 Courtesy of Intel Corporation; 1992 Courtesy of Microsoft Corporation; 1993 Courtesy of Intel Corporation; 1993 Courtesy of Microsoft Corporation; 1993 © Costa Cruise Lines/Getty Images; 1994 Courtesy of Netscape Communications Corporation; 1994 Courtesy of Larry Ewing and The Gimp; 1995 Courtesy of Sun Microsystems, Inc; 1995 Courtesy of Microsoft Corporation; 1996 Courtesy of Microsoft Corporation; 1996 Courtesy of Palm, Inc; 1997 Courtesy of Intel Corporation; 1998 Courtesy of Apple; 1998 Courtesy of Microsoft Corporation; 1999 Courtesy of Microsoft Corporation; 2000 AP Photo/PR Newswire; 2000 Courtesy of Microsoft Corporation; 2000 Courtesy of Microsoft Corporation; 2000 © B Busco/Getty Images; 2000 Courtesy of Intel Corporation; 2001 Courtesy of Microsoft Corporation; 2001 Courtesy of Microsoft Corporation; 2002 Courtesy of Sharp Electronics; 2002 Courtesy of Intel Corporation; 2003 Courtesy of ViewSonic Corporation; 2002 Courtesy of Intel Corporation; 2002 © Scott Goodwin Photography; 2002 Courtesy of Handspring, Inc; 2003 ©LWA-JDC/ CORBIS; 2003 © Royalty-Free/CORBIS; 2003 © Jim Cummins/CORBIS; 2003 © Ed Bock/CORBIS; 2003 © Koichi Kamoshida/Getty Images; 2003 Courtesy of Microsoft Corporation; 2003 © Getty Images; 2003 © REUTERS/Mannie Garcia; 2004 Courtesy of Sony Electronics Inc; 2004 Courtesy of SanDisk Corporation; 2004 Courtesy of Larry Ewing and The Gimp; 2004 Courtesy of Apple; 2004 Courtesy of Palm, Inc. 2005 Courtesy of Apple; 2005 Courtesy of Microsoft Corporation; 2005 © PRNewsFoto/Microsoft Corp; 2006 Microsoft Corporation; 2006 AP Images/Kevork Djanseqian; 2006 © Mitchell Funk/Getty Images; 2006 Courtesy of Facebook; 2006 Courtesy of Intel Corporation; 2006 Courtesy of Intel Corporation; 2006 Courtesy of Microsoft Corporation; 2007 Courtesy of Belkin International; 2007 Courtesy of Apple; 2007 iStockphoto; 2007 Courtesy of Microsoft Corporation; 2007 Courtesy of Memorex; 2008 Courtesy of Microsoft Corporation; 2008 Courtesy of New Medium Enterprises, Inc.;2008 Courtesy of Microsoft Corporation; 2008 Courtesy of Google, Inc.; 2008 Courtesy of Coby Electronics Corporation; 2008 iStockphoto; 2008 AP Topic Gallery Photo; 2008 Courtesy of Hewlett-Packard Company; **Chapter 2:** Opener © Andrew Manley/ istockphoto.com; istockphoto.com; © Steve Smith/ Getty Images; Figures 2-1e, Courtesy of Logitech; 2-2a, © Rob Lewine/CORBIS; 2-2b, © Royalty-Free/Corbis; 2-2c&d, ©LWA-Dann Tardif/CORBIS; 2-2e, © Paul C. Chauncey/CORBIS; 2-3 Step 1, Courtesy of Motorola, Inc.; 2-3 Step 2, Courtesy of Terayon Communication Systems, Inc.; 2-3 Step 3, © Stephen Chernin/Getty Images; 2-3 Step 4, © Stephen Chernin/ Getty Images Courtesy of Fujitsu Siemens Computers; 2-7, Courtesy of Nokia; 2-20 Step 2, Courtesy of Western Digital Corporation; 2-20 Step 3b, © Jeremy Woodhouse /Getty Images; 2-20 Step 3a,Courtesy of Hewlett-Packard Company; 2-24 Step 1, © MedioImages; 2-24 Step 2, © Inmagine / Alamy; 2-24 Step 2, © MedioImages; © Noel Hendrickson/Getty Images; 2-27, © Royalty-Free Corbis; 2-28 Step 1, Courtesy of Hewlett-Packard Company; 2-28 Step 2, Copyright 2005 Sun Microsystems, Inc. All Rights Reserved. Used by permission; 2-28 Step 3, Courtesy of Juniper Networks, Inc; 2-30 Step 2, Courtesy of Hewlett-Packard Company; 2-30 Step 4, Courtesy of Hewlett-Packard Company; 2-32a, Courtesy of Sony Electronics Inc; 2-32b, Courtesy of Hewlett-Packard Company; 2-32 center, © Blend Images / Alamy; Fig 2-34a, Courtesy of Hewlett-Packard Company; 2-34b, Courtesy of D-Link Systems; 2-34c, Courtesy of D-Link Systems; 2-34d, Courtesy of Siemens; Career Corner, © Manchan/Getty Images; Tech Trailblazer 1, © EPA / Landov; Tech Trailblazer 2, © LAURENT FIEVET/AFP/Getty Images; LA 2-1, Courtesy of Internet2; LA 2-2, © Darren McCollester/Getty Images; page 105a, Courtesy of Nokia; page 105b, ©LWA-Dann Tardif/ CORBIS; **Special Feature 2:** Opener A,© Howard Huang/ Getty Images; Opener B, Courtesy of OQO; Opener C, © Bruce Laurance /Getty Images; Opener D, © Bambu Productions /Getty Images; Opener E, © Amy Eckert /Getty Images; Opener F, © CAP /Getty Images; Opener G, iStockphoto; **Chapter 3:** Opener Courtesy of Hewlett-Packard Company; Courtesy of Intuit; Courtesy of Microsoft Corporation; Figures 3-2a, Courtesy of Hewlett-Packard Company; 3-2, Courtesy of Hewlett-Packard Company; 3-2, © Marcus Mok/Getty Images; 3-11, Courtesy of Microsoft Corporation; , © Kimberly White/Corbis; 3-12, Courtesy of CS Odessa LLC; 3-13, Courtesy of Intuit Inc; 3-16, Courtesy of AutoDesk;

3-17, Courtesy of Quark, Inc; 3-18, Screen shots are Copyright 2003 Corel Corporation and Corel Corporation Limited, reprinted by permission. Artwork © 2004 Cher Threinen-Pendarvis; 3-19, Courtesy of Adobe Systems, Incorporated; 3-20, Courtesy of SumTotal Systems, Inc; 3-22, Courtesy of Intuit Inc; 3-22, © Digital Vision/Getty Images; 3-23, Courtesy of COSMI Corporation; 3-24, Courtesy of Intuit Inc; 3-27, Courtesy of Nova Development Corporation; 3-28, Courtesy of Corel Corporation; 3-29, Courtesy of Punch! Software; 3-30, Courtesy of DeLorme; 3-31, Courtesy of Innovative Knowledge, a division of Fogware Publishing; 3-32, Courtesy of Microsoft Corporation; 3-37, Courtesy of Blackboard Inc; LA 3-1, Courtesy of IO2Technology; LA 3-2, © Steven Hunt/Getty Images; Page 124, © Royalty-Free/CORBIS; **Chapter 4:** Opener Courtesy of Hewlett-Packard Company; iStockphoto; Courtesy of Corsair; Courtesy of AMD; Courtesy of Intel Corporation; Figures 4-1a, Courtesy of Hewlett-Packard Company; 4-1b, Courtesy of Apple; 4-1c, Courtesy of Hewlett-Packard Company; 4-1d, © Getty Images; 4-1e, Courtesy of OQO; 4-1f, Courtesy of TabletKiosk; 4-1g, Courtesy of BlackBerry; 4-1i, AP Photo/Microsoft Corp; 4-1j, © Issei Kato/Reuters/Corbis; 4-2a, Courtesy of Hewlett-Packard Company; 4-2b, Courtesy of Hewlett-Packard Company; 4-2c, Courtesy of Creative Technology Ltd; 4-2d, Courtesy of Advanced Micro Devices; 4-2e, Courtesy of Intel Corporation; 4-2f, Courtesy of Corsair; 4-3, Courtesy of Intel Corporation; 4-5, © JUPITERIMAGES/ Thinkstock / Alamy; 4-9a, Courtesy of Microsoft Corporation; 4-9b, Courtesy of Hewlett-Packard Company; 4-9c, Courtesy of Hewlett-Packard Company; 4-10, © Wayne Eastep/Getty Images; 4-12a, Courtesy of Seagate Technologies LLC; 4-12b, Courtesy of Corsair; 4-13a, © Andrew Howe /iStockphoto; 4-13b, © Jaroslaw Wojcik/iStockphoto; 4-14b, Courtesy of MPIO America; 4-16, © WireImageStock/Masterfile; 4-16, © WireImageStock/Masterfile; 4-18, Andrew Howe/ iStockphoto; 4-19, Courtesy of SanDisk Corporation; 4-20, Courtesy of PCMCIA; 4-21a, Courtesy of Hewlett-Packard Company; 4-21b, © Tim Gilman Photography;4-24a, Courtesy of Intel Corporation; 4-24b, Courtesy of Kingston Technology; 4-25, Courtesy of Hewlett-Packard Company; 4-26a, Courtesy of Hewlett-Packard Company; 4-26b, Courtesy of Nokia; 4-26c, Courtesy of SanDisk Corporation; 4-26d, Yanik Chauvin/iStockphoto; 4-27a, Courtesy of Fujitsu Siemens Computers; 4-28, Courtesy of Acer America Corp; 4-29a, © Image Source Black /Getty Images; 4-29b, © Dennis MacDonald/PhotoEdit; 4-29c, © Somos/Veer /Getty Images; 4-29d, © Tom Stoddart/Getty Images; 4-29e, © Ralf Hirschberger/dpa /Landov; 4-30, Courtesy of Fellowes, Inc; 4-30a, Courtesy of First-Aid- Product.com, a division of American CPR; 4-30b, Courtesy of Belkin International; 4-30c, Courtesy of Fellowes, Inc; 4-30d, © Gary Herrington Photography; Career Corner, © Stephen Derr/Getty Images; Tech Trailblazer 1, © CORBIS SYGMA;Tech Trailblazer 2, © Andy Rain/Bloomberg News /Landov;LA 4-1, Courtesy of Intel Corporation; LA 4-2, AP Photo/ Shizuo Kambayashi; Page 158, Courtesy of Creative Technology Ltd;Page 161 , Ingvald kaldhussæter /iStockphoto; **Chapter 5:** Opener Courtesy of Nokia; iStockphoto; © Bloomimage/Corbis; Courtesy of Hewlett-Packard Company; Figures 5-1a, © Stockbye/Getty Images; 5-1b, © Joel Benard/Masterfile; 5-1c, AP Photo/Kevin Sanders; 5-1e, © Sebastian Widmann/dpa/Landov; 5-1f, Courtesy of Wacom; 5-1g, © picturesbyrob / Alamy; 5-1h, © ColorBlind Images/Getty Images; 5-1i, AP Photo/Paul Sakuma; 5-1j, © Yellow Dog Productions/Getty Images; 5-1k, © David Muir/Getty Images; 5-1m, © AFP/Getty Images; 5-1n, Courtesy of Hewlett-Packard Company; 5-1o, Stefan Klein /iStockphoto; 5-1q1, © David Young/Wolff-PhotoEdit; 5-1q2, Konstantin Voznikevich /iStockphoto; 5-1r, © Don Farrall/Getty Images; 5-1s1, dwphotos/iStockphoto; 5-1s2, Eugene Bochkarev /iStockphoto; 5-1t, © Myrleen Ferguson/PhotoEdit; 5-1u, © Bill Aron/PhotoEdit; 5-1v2, AP Photo/Michael Probst; 5-1v3, © Jon Feingersh/zefa/Corbis; 5-2, Courtesy of Microsoft Corporation; 5-3b, Courtesy of Logitech; 5-4, Courtesy of Logitech; 5-5, Suprijono Suharjoto /iStockphoto; 5-6, © Photodisc/Getty Images; 5-7, AP Photo/M. Spencer Green; 5-8, Courtesy of Microsoft Corporation; 5-9, Courtesy of Wacom; 5-10a, Courtesy of Microsoft Corporation; 5-10b, © ilian studio / Alamy; 5-10c, Courtesy of Nintendo Corporation; 5-10d, Courtesy of Logic3 plc; 5-10e, Courtesy of Nintendo; 5-10f, Courtesy of Logitech; 5-11, © Getty Images;5-12, © ICP / Alamy; 5-13, Courtesy of Nokia; 5-14, Courtesy of Palm, Inc.; 5-15, Courtesy of Motion Computing, Inc; 5-16, © Masterfile (Royalty-Free Div.); 5-17, © Jochen Tack / Alamy; 5-18, © Steve Chenn/CORBIS;5-19b, Courtesy of C-Technologies/Anoto Group AB; 5-19a, Courtesy of Hewlett-Packard Company; 5-19c, Courtesy of Visioneer, Inc;5-19d, Howtek HiResolve 8000 Drum Scanner, image courtesy of Howtek, Inc; 5-21b, © Phil Degginger/Getty Images; 5-21a, ©Colin Young-Wolff / Photo Edit 5-22, Courtesy of Tibbett & Britten Group; 5-23, ©Spencer Grant / Photo Edit; 5-25, © Robin Nelson / PhotoEdit; 5-26, © Bill Aron/PhotoEdit; 5-27, AP Photo/Matt Sayles; 5-28, AP Photo/ Nancy Palmieri; 5-29a, PRNewsFoto/SimulScribe; 5-29b, Courtesy of Hewlett-Packard Company; 5-29c, Courtesy of Hewlett-Packard Company; 5-29d, Courtesy of Logitech; 5-29e, Courtesy of Nokia; 5-29f, Courtesy of TabletKiosk; Courtesy of Microsoft Corporation; 5-29g, Courtesy of Creative Technology Ltd; 5-29h, Courtesy of Hewlett-Packard Company; 5-29i, Courtesy of Nokia; 5-29j, Courtesy of Hewlett-Packard Company; 5-30, Courtesy of ASUS Computer International; 5-31a, Courtesy of Acer America Inc; 5-31b, Courtesy of Acer America Inc; 5-31c, Courtesy of Microsoft Corporation; 5-31e, PRNewsFoto/Microsoft Corp; 5-31f, Courtesy of Nokia; 5-32, Courtesy of Panasonic; Courtesy of Microsoft Corporation; 5-33, Courtesy of Viewsonic Corporation; 5-35a1, Courtesy of Hewlett-Packard Company; 5-35a2, © Gari Wyn Williams/Alamy; 5-35b, Courtesy of Hewlett-Packard Company; 5-35c, Courtesy of Hewlett-Packard Company; 5-35d, © Michael Newman/PhotoEdit; 5-35e, Courtesy of Hewlett-Packard Company; 5-35f, Courtesy of Hewlett-Packard Company; 5-35g, Courtesy of Nokia; 5-35h, Courtesy of Sony Electronics Inc; 5-36a, Courtesy of Hewlett-Packard Company; 5-36b, Courtesy of Hewlett-Packard Company; 5-36c, Courtesy of Xerox Corporation; 5-37, Courtesy of Hewlett-Packard Company; 5-38a, Courtesy of Hewlett-Packard Company; 5-38b, Courtesy of Xerox Corporation; 5-40, Courtesy of Canon; 5-41, Courtesy of MacDermid ColorSpan Inc. 5-42a, Courtesy of Oki Data Amercas, Inc; 5-43, Courtesy of Creative Technology Ltd;5-45, Courtesy of Lexmark International; 5-46a, Courtesy of InFocus® Corporation; 5-46b, Courtesy of InFocus® Corporation; 5-47, Copyright 2001–2007 SMART Technologies Inc. All rights reserved; 5-48a, © Image Source Black /Getty Images; 5-48b, © Dennis MacDonald/PhotoEdit; 5-48c, © Somos/Veer /Getty Images; 5-48d, © Tom Stoddart/Getty Images; 5-48e, © Ralf Hirschberger/dpa / Landov; 5-49, Courtesy of NaturalPoint, Inc; 5-50a, Courtesy of Enabling Technologies; 5-50b, © Don Farrall/Getty Images; Page 198, © David Young-Wolff/PhotoEdit; Courtesy of Intel Corporation; Tech Trailblazer 1, AP Photo/Michael Schmelling;Tech Trailblazer 2, AP Photo/John Todd; LA 5-1, Courtesy of Legit Reviews; LA 5-2, Courtesy of Intermec Technologies;LA 5-3, Courtesy of Paper Four, Fiber Science and Communications Network/Mid Sweden University;Page 200, AP Photo/M. Spencer Green; Page 202, Courtesy of Canon; **Special Feature 5:** Page 208 opener, © Frans Lemmens/Getty Images; Page 208 opener, © Ryan McVay/Getty Images; Figures 1a, Courtesy of Hewlett-Packard Company; 1b, Courtesy of Sony Electronics, Inc;Fig 1c, Courtesy of Nokia; 1d, Courtesy of Hewlett-Packard Company; 1f, Courtesy of Hewlett-Packard Company; 1g, Courtesy of Pioneer Electronics; 2a, Courtesy of Hewlett-Packard Company; 2b, Toshiyuki Aizawa/Reuters / Landov; 2c, Courtesyof FUJIFILM U.S.A., Inc; 5a, Courtesy of SanDisk Corporation; 5b, Courtesy of Sony Electronics, Inc; 5c, Courtesy of SanDisk Corporation; 5d, Courtesy of SanDisk Corporation; 5e, Courtesy of SanDisk Corporation;6, Courtesy of Iogear Inc;8, © Stephen Hilger/Bloomberg News /Landov; 10a, Courtesy of JVC Company of America; 10b, Courtesy of JVC Company of America; 10c, © Royalty-Free/CORBIS; 11a, Courtesy of Hewlett-Packard Company; 11b, Courtesy of JVC Company of America; 11c, Courtesy of Panasonic; 12a, Courtesy of Hewlett-Packard Company; 12b, Courtesy of Panasonic; 12c, Courtesy of Panasonic; 12d, Courtesy of Pinnacle; 12e, © Image Source Pink/Getty Images; 13, Courtesy of Corel Corporation; 15, Courtesy of Corel Corporation; 16, Courtesy of Corel Corporation; 17, Courtesy of Sonic Solutions; **Chapter 6** Opener Courtesy of Seagate Technologies LLC; © Beaconstox / Alamy; Courtesy of SanDisk Corporation; Elena Koulik-Vargas /iStockphoto; Figures 6-1a, Courtesy of Seagate Technology LLC; 6-1b, Courtesy of Hitachi Global Storage Technologies; 6-1c, Courtesy of Western Digital Corporation; 6-1d, Courtesy of LaCie; 6-1e, Mark Goddard /iStockphoto; 6-1f, Courtesy of PCMCIA; 6-1g, Courtesy of Kyocera-Wireless; 6-1h, Courtesy of SanDisk Corporation; 6-1i, Courtesy of Hewlett-Packard Company; 6-1j, Courtesy of SanDisk Corporation; 6-1k1, Courtesy of Hewlett-Packard Company; 6-1k2, Courtesy of Hewlett-Packard Company; 6-1l, © Helene Rogers / Alamy; 6-1m, © Bill Aron/ PhotoEdit; 6-4a, Courtesy of Hewlett-Packard Company; 6-4b, Courtesy of Seagate Technology LLC; 6-6, Courtesy of Western Digital Corporation; 6-9, Courtesy of Hitachi Global Storage; 6-10, Courtesy of Western Digital Corporation; 6-11, Courtesy of Western Digital Corporation; 6-13, © Marcus Jones/iStockphoto; 6-14a, © Gary Herrington Photography; 6-16a, Courtesy of Merriam-Webster Inc; 6-16b, Courtesy of Memorex Products, Inc; 6-16c, Courtesy of Memorex Products, Inc; 6-16d, Cou`tesy of DeLorme; 6-16f,